An International Finance Reader

International finance has grown to be one of the most important areas of interest in economics and business. With the deregulation and liberalization of international capital over the last half-century, capital has flowed in and out of countries at amazing rates.

This collection, featuring such experts as Barry Eichengreen, Alan S. Blinder, Anne O. Krueger and Kenneth Rogoff, examines issues such as:

- financial globalization;
- multilateral financial institutions;
- exchange rate regimes in a globalizing financial world;
- capital flows to emerging economies.

The topical contributions are well written and accessible for those interested in international finance, while the comprehensive nature of the book along with its pedagogical features, such as exam-style questions and areas for further research, make the book ideal for students on an international finance course. The lessons that can be learned from the distinguished authors are equally useful for businessmen and policy-makers.

Dilip K. Das has been a professor at several prestigious institutions and has been associated with business schools around the globe, including the European Institute of Business Administration (INSEAD) in France, the Graduate School of Business at the University of Sydney, and the Australian National University. He has also worked as a consultant to USAID and the World Bank in Washington DC, USA. Another of his books, *Global Trading System at the Crossroads*, published in 2001, is also available from Routledge.

An International Finance Reader

Edited by
Dilip K. Das

Routledge
Taylor & Francis Group

LONDON AND NEW YORK

First published 2003
by Routledge
11 New Fetter Lane, London EC4P 4EE

Simultaneously published in the USA and Canada
by Routledge
29 West 35th Street, New York, NY 10001

Routledge is an imprint of the Taylor & Francis Group

Typeset in Baskerville by
Newgen Imaging Systems (P) Ltd, Chennai, India
Printed and bound in Great Britain by
The Cromwell Press, Trowbridge, Wiltshire

British Library Cataloguing in Publication Data
A catalogue record for this book is available from the British Library

Library of Congress Cataloging in Publication Data
Das, Dilip K., 1945–
    An international finance reader / Dilip K. Das.
        p. cm.
    Includes bibliographical references and index.
    1. International finance. I. Title.

  HG3881.D328 2003
  332′.042–dc21   2002037159

ISBN 0–415–31262–0 (hbk)
ISBN 0–415–31263–9 (pbk)

The Master in the art of living makes little distinction between his work and his play, his labor and his leisure, his mind and his body, his education and his recreation, his love and his religion. He hardly knows which is which. He simply pursues his vision of excellence in whatever he does, leaving others to decide whether he is working or playing. To him he is always doing both.

from *Tao Te Ching*

For Mish,
the newest and littlest member of my family,
whom I am yet to meet, or see.

Contents

List of illustrations

Figures

Tables

Boxes

About the editor

Professor Dilip K. Das has been associated with several prestigious business schools around the globe, including the European Institute of Business Administration (INSEAD), Fontainebleau, France; the ESSEC, Paris; the Graduate School of Business at the University of Sydney and Webster College, Geneva. The areas of his interest and expertise are international finance and banking, international trade and WTO-related issues, international business and strategy. His recent interest has been globalization. Professor Das has taught courses in all these areas and has acted as a mentor to doctoral students. He organized thirteen major international conferences during the last ten years.

The author has worked as a consultant to several international organizations such as USAID, the World Bank, and the World Commission on Development and Environment in Geneva. Based in Toronto, Canada he acts as a consultant to several international organizations and Canadian banks, and teaches in two local business schools.

Dilip K. Das has an immense appetite for research and writing. He has written extensively and published widely and is the author of numerous books. He has contributed a large number of articles to professional journals and his papers have appeared in many prestigious research paper and discussion paper series. They have also been posted on the web sites of many well-known business schools and universities. His last book, *Global Trading System at the Crossroads: A Post-Seattle Perspective*, was published by Routledge in 2001. His next book, *Financial Globalization and the Emerging Market Economies* is at an advanced stage of preparation.

Dilip K. Das was educated at St John's College, Agra, India, where he gained his BA and MA Degrees. He went on to study at the Institut Universitaire des Hautes Etudes Internationales, the University of Geneva, where he did his MPhil and PhD in international economics. He is fluent in French.

Contributors

Graham Bird
University of Surrey, Guildford, UK

Alan S. Blinder
Princeton University, Princeton, USA

Willem H. Buiter
European Bank for Reconstruction
 and Development
London, UK

Zhaohui Chen
Shanghai Jiao Tong University
Shanghai, China

Stijn Claessens
Universiteit van Amsterdam
Amsterdam, The Netherlands

Jonathan Coppel
Reserve Bank of Australia
Canberra, Australia

Andrew Crockett
Bank for International Settlement
Basle, Switzerland

Martine Durand
Organization for Economic
 Co-operation and Development
Paris, France

Barry Eichengreen
University of California
Berkeley, USA

Jeffrey A. Frankel
Harvard University, Cambridge, USA

Graciela L. Kaminsky
George Washington University
Washington DC, USA

Mohsin S. Khan
International Monetary Fund
Washington, DC, USA

Daniela Klingebiel
World Bank
Washington, DC, USA

Anne O. Krueger
International Monetary Fund
Washington DC, USA and Stanford
University, Stanford, USA

Luc Laeven
World Bank
Washington, DC, USA

Hans Peter Lankes
European Bank for Reconstruction
 and Development
London, UK

David A. Marshall
Federal Reserve Bank of Chicago
Chicago, USA

Allan H. Meltzer
Carnegie Mellon University
Pittsburgh, USA

Ramon Moreno
Federal Reserve Bank of
  San Francisco
San Francisco, USA

Florian Pelgrin
Bank of Canada, Ottawa, Canada

Carmen M. Reinhart
University of Maryland
College Park, USA

Kenneth Rogoff
Harvard University, Cambridge, USA

Dane Rowlands
Carleton University, Ottawa, Canada

Alain de Serres
Organization for Economic
  Co-operation and Development
Paris, France

Sebastian Schich
Organization for Economic
  Co-operation and Development
Paris, France

Ignazio Visco
Banca d'Italia, Rome, Italy

Peter G. Warr
Australian National University
Canberra, Australia

Prefatory and introductory comments

Although the twenty-first century did not begin on an upbeat note for the global economy and financial markets, the last decades of the twentieth century witnessed an enormous expansion in the global financial markets. They dwarfed global trade by a large margin. Conventional wisdom had considered trade a prime mover behind global financial flows. This relationship did not hold for a long time and the global financial markets picked up their own momentum. Financial globalization has progressed significantly over the last two decades and large volumes of capital flows are now generated by the large size of the financial market system. The major financial markets are closely integrated now, albeit global financial flows have yet to reach the level they did at the beginning of the twentieth century.

A whole new range of financial instruments is currently helping the integration of global financial markets. The decades of the 1980s and 1990s saw the evolution of a large number of instruments. Several that were in use in the past went out of vogue, while new more pragmatic ones were developed. Still others that were popular during an earlier era and then had gone out of use, returned. Syndicated loans come under this category. The other principal instruments in use are bank deposits denominated in all the SDR currencies plus the Swiss francs, Eurobonds in several currencies, interest rate swaps, futures contracts in foreign exchange, foreign exchange swaps, zero-coupon bonds and bonds with interest payable in one currency that are convertible into another currency. Deregulation and liberalization in the matured market economies as well as emerging market economies gave an immense impetus to global financial integration (refer to Chapters 2 and 3). To be sure, the pace, scope and direction of deregulation of individual markets varies, progress made on this count was substantial and so was its impact. Market liberalization affected interest rate ceilings, reserve requirements and barriers to geographical expansion, which in turn stimulated freer global movement of finances. Another development that gave a fillip to closer financial integration was "cross-penetration" of foreign ownership, which is visible in the sharp increase in the number of foreign banks, investment banking houses and securities firms in all the major financial centers around the globe.

As an academic sub-discipline, the significance of international finance has gone on increasing since the Bretton Woods period. The same trend continued over the 1980s. Severe financial crises struck during 1990s in different parts of the globe, and with them the interest and insights in this sub-discipline further deepened. This reader sets out to identify and analyze several germane issues in global finance that have attracted the attention of academics and policy mandarins around the turn of the century. Topicality is the principal strength of the volume. It includes issues that encompass some of the most germane, current and useful facets of global finance and centers around the following seven themes, namely (i) financial globalization, (ii) global financial architecture, (iii) multilateral financial institutions, (iv) exchange rate regimes and arrangements, (v) capital flows to emerging market economies, (vi) financial and currency crises, and (vii) financial and macroeconomic issues. Accordingly, The Reader has been divided into seven parts, each part containing chapters relevant to a common theme.

The Reader can be useful in global finance and international economics courses and modules on traditional lines. A carefully selected volume of this kind is essential at this point in time when the popularity of the study of global finance is on the rise among several streams of students. There are three good introductory textbooks, which are popular with instructors and students alike. They cover factual material and concepts. However, when a student tries to go beyond this set of books, she is a trifle flustered because she is generally referred to journal articles or books, which are either too formal and technical or over-specialized or both. There is hardly any book that covers global financial issues at a medium technical level. In addition, the standard textbooks incompletely cover several practical, topical and policy-related issues. The highly motivated students indeed make forays in the literature and sporadically locate what they need but this endeavor tends to be time-consuming and frustrating.

Covering the middle ground and covering issues not generally covered in standard textbooks, therefore, became the twin logic of selection of papers for this collection. In addition, the range of quantitative techniques employed in the readings is not very high and therefore this compendium would appeal to a wide range of readers. The *raison d'être* of this volume is to fill these gaps in the teaching of global finance. It is intended to offer a complementary role in terms of existing teaching and textbooks that are either overly formal in approach or completely lack analytical rigor.

For the reasons noted above, this volume avoids highly technical pieces where techniques overshadow the substance. It offers more accessible coverage of a range of key issues facing the global financial community. The chapters are analytical and necessarily pitched at medium level of technique. They are neither introductory in nature nor over-specialized. Therefore, readers would be expected to have a fair bit of background knowledge in this area. In my view, this would maximize the utility of The Reader to the target audiences. I have attempted to speak to the student audiences at masters' level in economics, finance, business administration and international relations. Senior level undergraduates, bankers, financial analysts and policy-makers at national, regional and international level are sure to find this collection useful. Thus viewed, the pedagogical structure is the principal advantage of this compendium.

I have taught global finance for a long time in several prestigious business schools and noted a gradual shift in modules toward financial markets. This volume reflects the same shift. It takes a global perspective, and includes developing-country, emerging-market-economy as well as industrial-economy view points. It would indeed be suboptimal to take one viewpoint and exclude the others. While selecting chapters, care has been taken to pick only the most recent contributions penned by top-of-the-line scholars so that the collection has the highest value to students and nonstudent readers.

Dilip K. Das
Toronto, Canada

Acknowledgments

While working on a volume of this kind one accumulates many debts. Besides, earlier versions of some of the contributions in this volume were published in prestigious academic journals or research paper series. In such cases, it is a legal obligation to acknowledge where the earlier version was published as well as seek copyright clearance from the first publisher. As the editor of the volume, I have not been remiss in these duties. An equally important legal obligation is to mention disclaimers of the scholars who, although work for a multilateral organization or Federal Reserve System in the United States, have contributed a chapter in their personal capacity. Missing out on their disclaimer can be a source of embarrassment to them. Their disclaimers are systematically noted below.

Chapter 5, *Strengthening the International Financial Architecture: Where do We Stand?* by Barry Eichengreen was first published in the *ASEAN Economic Bulletin*, 17, August 2000. It is being reproduced here with the kind permission of the publisher, Institute of Southeast Asian Studies, Singapore. Chapter 7, *A New Global Financial Order: The Art of the Possible* by Alan S. Blinder was first published in *Foreign Affairs*, 78(5), September/October 1999, under the title *Eight Steps to a New Financial Order*. It is being reproduced here with the kind permission of the publisher. Chapter 8, *Promoting International Financial Stability: Sovereign Debt Restructuring* by Anne O. Krueger was first published by the International Monetary Fund, Washington, DC, in April 2002, under the title *A New Approach to Sovereign Debt Restructuring*. It is being reproduced after copyright permission from the International Monetary Fund. Chapter 10, *International Institutions for Reducing Global Financial Stability* by Kenneth Rogoff was first published in *Journal of Economic Perspectives*, 13(4), Fall 1999. It is being reproduced here with the kind permission of the publisher. Chapter 11, *The Catalysing Role of Policy-Based Lending by the IMF and the World Bank: Fact or Fiction* by Graham Bird and Dane Rowlands was first published in the *Journal of International Development*, 12(5) in 2000. It is being reproduced here with the kind permission of the publisher. Chapter 13, *Solving the Currency Conundrum* by Barry Eichengreen was first published in *Economic Notes*, 29(3), November 2000. It is being reproduced here with the kind permission of the publisher. Chapter 14, *Pegging and Stabilization Policy in Developing Economies* by Ramon Moreno was first published in *Federal Reserve Bank of San Francisco Quarterly Review*, 2001. The opinions expressed in the chapter are those of the author and not necessarily of the Federal Reserve Bank of San Francisco or the Board of Governors of the Federal Reserve System. Chapter 15, *EMU, the Euro and the European Policy Mix: The Nascent Stage* by Jonathan Coppel, Martin Durand and Ignazio Visco was first published in the *Journal of Asian Economics*, 11(1), 2000, 31–63. It has been reprinted with permission from Elsevier Science. The opinions expressed in the chapter are those of the authors and not of the organizations they work for. Chapter 18, *Patterns of Capital Flows to Emerging Markets: A Theoretical Perspective* by Zhaohui Chen and Mohsin S. Khan has been contributed by the authors in their personal capacity. It does not represent the views of the *organizations* they work for. Chapter 19, *On Crisis, Contagion and Confusion* by Graciela L. Kaminsky and Carmen M. Reinhart was first published in the *Journal of International Economics*, 51(2), June 2000. It is being reprinted here with permission from Elsevier Science. Chapter 21, *The Crisis of 1998 and the Role of the Central Banks* by David A. Marshall was first published in *Economic Perspectives*, First Quarter 2001, a publication of the Federal Reserve Bank of Chicago. The views expressed in this chapter are those of the author and do not necessarily represent the views of the Federal Reserve Bank of Chicago or the Federal Reserve System. Chapter 22, *Financial Restructuring in Banking and Corporate Sector Crises – What Policies to Pursue* by Stijn Claessens, Daniela Klingebiel and Luc Laeven was first published in *Managing Currency Crises in Emerging Markets* edited by M. Dooley and J. Frankel, published by the University of Chicago Press, Chicago, in 2001. It is being reproduced here with the kind permission of the publisher. Chapter 23, *Buoyant Investment in OECD Economies: How Much Can the Fundamentals Explain?* by Florian Pelgrin, Sebastian Schich and Alain de Serres, was contributed by the authors in their personal capacity. The views expressed in this chapter are those of the author and do not necessarily represent the views of their respective organizations.

Dilip K. Das
Toronto, Canada

Part I
Financial globalization

1 Global financial markets

The twenty-first century

Dilip K. Das

Deceleration in the global economy

Although the twenty-first century began well for the global economy and financial markets, the transformation of the global scenario began in the middle of 2000.[1] The following period, so far, has been problematic and full of uncertainties.[2] Several economic factors and non-economic events caused macroeconomic volatility, and gyrations of serious order, in the global financial markets. By the middle of 2002, both the global economy and financial markets had suffered a serious loss of dynamism. At this point in time, the global economy was waiting for some signs of recovery, while the global financial markets were waiting to emerge from the trough they were in. Financial markets in matured industrial economies as well as emerging market economies were at their lowest levels in a long period and global financial flows were stagnating.

After a brisk GDP growth rate of 3.9 percent and trade volume expansion of 13.1 percent in 2000, global economic growth rate decelerated to 2.1 percent in 2001. World trade slumped to −0.8 in 2001.[3] Steady decline in the manufacturing sector output in several industrial economies was at the root of the economic downturn. This deceleration in the global economic growth rate was deep and sharp. In the last four decades it was sharper only in 1974, in the aftermath of the first oil crisis. In addition, the global slowdown was broad and affected both matured industrial economies and developing economies. The deceleration of 14 percent in global trade volume between 2000 and 2001 was unprecedented.

The slowdown in the global economy and deterioration in the financial environment came about in four stages. The first stage was marked by the deceleration in the growth rate of the US economy in the middle of 2000. Tightening of the monetary policy by the Federal Reserve Board (or Fed) was partly responsible for it. Fed took this measure to slow the economy down because the general perception was that it was growing well above its long-term capacity trend. The high-tech bubble burst in the first phase. The second phase began at the end of 2000 when the high-tech bubble burst further. The stock market declined sharply and so did the high-tech production. During this phase, Japanese output fell precipitously because it was highly dependent on high-tech exports. Falling exports and sharply declining equity prices exacerbated the bad loan problem of the Japanese banks. Growth rate in Europe had not exceeded its long-term capacity trend, therefore, its internal cyclical forces were weaker than those in the US. Furthermore, deceleration in global trade (noted in the preceding paragraph) affected European exports. The high-tech sector in Europe shared the fate of the global high-tech sector.

The events of September 11, 2001 ushered in the third phase in global economic and financial deceleration. As expected, this period was marked by a dramatic, albeit temporary, loss of consumer confidence and serious deterioration in business sentiment. The fourth phase began with the bankruptcy announcement by Enron in the US during the first quarter of 2002.

Genesis of deceleration

The genesis of the current global economic deceleration can be traced back to the sudden decline in the US financial markets in the middle of 2000. This was the end of the longest upswing in the US business cycle, which had begun after the recession of 1990–91. This was also the end of global equity value bubble in the US. Bubbles are known to create overcapacity. This one had created large overcapacity, particularly in the global high-tech sector. The downturn in the US business cycle and declining stock markets weakened investment demand as well as consumer confidence. Both of these characteristics spread to Europe soon and were first reflected in the stock markets in the Euro area, and then in the weakening of investor demand and consumer confidence. Import demand in Europe and the US contracted in combination with the reversal of incipient recovery in Japan. Global investors found that before 1994, many investment sectors showed negative results in several countries. Fairly well-synchronized contractions in the major economies heralded the unprecedented deceleration in global trade noted above, which in turn adversely affected the developing economies.

A sharp deceleration in the high-tech sector *vide ut supra* began in the middle of 2000. The so-called "tech-wreck" highlighted the fact that many technology companies were being valued on the basis of their potential earnings many years into the future. This trend and, therefore, investment perspective changed. The new investment perspective took quite a different tack. As markets became focused on the certainty of short-term earnings rather than on company's future growth potential, stock prices in the high-tech sector began falling globally and a large number of high-tech companies found it impossible to stay afloat.

Around half of the US investment during the equity bubble period of the 1990s was in computers, electronics, telecommunications and other high-tech products. The post-bubble contraction in the US high-tech demand had a telling effect on the IT-intensive exports of the East Asian economies. They contracted in tandem with the contractions in demand in Europe and the US. Economies in the Euro area were reaching the peak of their business cycle in 2001 and were in gear for a slowdown. Reacting to the US downturn, they began contracting more rapidly than they would have done on their own. Demand contractions, particularly that in the US, rippled through Latin America as well. It particularly affected the fellow North American Free Trade Area (NAFTA) partner, Mexico.

Further bursting of the high-tech bubble at the end of 2000 and rising oil prices led to sagging profits of the large European and US corporations. While monetary authorities in major economies had loosened their policies, the European Central Bank (ECB) held off slashing interest rates. The ECB was apprehensive of the possibility of inflation that could be ignited by the rising oil prices and the plunging value of the Euro. Weakness in global demand caused Japanese exports to slump, severing the tenuous string preventing the economy from slipping back into yet another recession. These economic forces coalesced with soft commodity prices and reduced GDP growth rates all over the developing world. Economies that were essentially dependent on the commodity exports suffered more because commodity prices had remained soft since the Asian crisis of 1997. Therefore, these developing economies were unable to build reserves to cushion for further losses in their terms-of-trade.

Two more causes of deceleration were mentioned above. Events of September 11, 2001, impacted upon the climate in the global financial markets in a pernicious manner. As discussed in the section on "Changing perceptions of recovery," toward the end of the third quarter of 2001, global economy was performing the precarious balancing act between recession and recovery. With the terrorist attack of September 11, the first signs of an incipient rebound in the US manufacturing production were snuffed out. Perceived risks in the global financial markets increased substantially, causing a decline in stock markets around the world as well as in global capital flows. Depressed as they were, global trade flows further suffered from rising security costs and more post-attack slackening of demand. Furthermore, the destructive impact of revelations of accounting irregularities by several major US corporations and their subsequent bankruptcies in early and mid-2002 was unprecedented. In all the large financial markets, several years of bull market gains were wiped off in a short period. Markets in Europe were the worst hit.

Changing perceptions of recovery

Markets had naturally recorded a sharp reaction to the events of September 11. Owing to heightened uncertainty, they became highly risk averse. In hindsight, global financial markets had overreacted in their perception of the potential impact of the events of September 11. But their impact did not linger for a long time. Apprehensions that the events of September 11 would trigger a deep and long recession in the US did not come true. Global financial markets also escaped a severe long-term impact of September 11. Prompt reaction by policy makers in the form of various measures including actions to ensure functioning of financial systems and reduced monetary interest rates were important factors that limited the severity of the impact. Lack of inflationary pressures during this period offered an opportunity to the monetary authorities to relax policies substantially. Many sectors of the economy recovered more quickly than expected and industrial production continued to recover steadily. Somewhat unexpectedly, spending by households held up despite uncertainties in the economic climate. Retail sales in the US picked up. Spurred by low and zero interest rates, people started buying cars in record numbers. Home sales grew strong because people started benefiting from low mortgage rates, the lowest in four decades. All this was indirectly supportive of capital markets.

By November, market perception was significantly revised, although disagreement regarding timing and strength of potential global recovery persisted. As a result of progress in operations in Afghanistan, political risk was seen as receding. Therefore, measures of risk aversion recorded a decline.[4] Expecting improvement in the global economy, global financial market began to rally to price in an imminent recovery.

As estimated by the International Monetary Fund (IMF) (see IMF, 2002a), at the end of 2001, global risk aversion level fell to below the pre-September 11 levels. Global investors in the US had stopped investing in stocks and bonds in September as global risk aversion had risen, however, by November, as risk aversion declined, they started participating in stock and bond market rallies. Weakening oil prices supported a low inflation outlook. Consequently, equity markets rallied in the US, which was followed by a sell-off in the bond markets. Spreads on high-yield or sub-investment grade bonds as well as emerging market bonds shrank. The only exception to this generalization was Argentina for which bond spreads remained wide because of the default and prevailing precarious situation.

Changes in perception regarding outlook for growth and financial market performance in the US led to steepening of the US yield curve. Some technical factors buttressed this trend. One of the important factors was the rebalancing by asset allocation funds. The rebalancing entailed moving funds from government bond portfolios toward equity portfolios. The former had turned in an impressive performance – in fact they had over-performed – in the aftermath of September 11. Second such factor was that the portfolios that had mortgage-based securities (MBS) faced a significant increase in the duration of their holdings as a result of decline in interest rates by as much as 40 percent. To bring the duration of their portfolios back, MBS holders sold longer maturity US Treasury bonds. This move contributed to a spike in US yields.[5]

Global and the US financial markets emitted more and clearer signals of recovery during the fourth quarter. Some of them were as follows: All Country World Index, which is an equity index, prepared by Morgan Stanley gained 9 percent points during this quarter. Technology stocks performed exceedingly well, with NASDAQ posting a record 30 percent quarterly return. Returns for this sector exceeded the average for other sectors by more than two standard deviations. This quarter also saw a pick up in syndicated lending, but this was concentrated in the matured economies (IMF, 2002a). Financial markets in the emerging market economies followed the broad trends set by the US and the matured economies. Notwithstanding the uncertainties regarding Argentina, both equity and bond markets in the emerging market economies turned in strong performances. During the final quarter of 2001, perceptions regarding the prospects of recovery of the global economy and financial markets kept on alternating between favorable and unfavorable.

Favorable prospects for recovery

A moderate recovery was on track in the US during the first quarter of 2002. It was being assumed – and logically so – that the US economy would prove to be a locomotive for the Euro area and the rest of the global economy. At the end of the first quarter of 2002, the *World Economic Outlook* was able to see "increasing signs that the global slowdown, which began in the middle of 2000, has bottomed out … leading indicators have turned up, consumer and business confidence have strengthened, and industrial production – including the information technology sector – is leveling off. This has been most apparent in the US and increasingly in the Euro area.…"[6] Prospects for global economic recovery improved financial market conditions in the first quarter.

According to the IMF (2002b), several negative features persisted during this quarter. The principal ones among them were the "level and quality of reported corporate profits" and high equity valuations. Matured industrial economies were particularly plagued by these two problems. Apprehensions regarding poor quality of reporting of profits had existed for a while and were soon to give a disastrous shock to the US financial markets and economy. Private debt levels were high both in the European economies and the US. The latter continued its reliance on capital inflows from abroad. The Japanese financial system remained under enormous stress. Concern about spillover of Japanese financial problems into Asia and other parts of the globe continued.

Global financial environment during the first quarter was generally regarded as benign. Financial flows to emerging market economies increased. This was essentially because of a rise in risk appetite and expectation of recovery in the global financial markets and economy.[7] Many sovereign governments were in the financial market for their 2002 financial needs. Consequently, substantial emerging market flows took place. Volume of bond issuance equaled that of the preceding quarter. Although Argentinean default and economic malaise continued to be an unresolved issue, most emerging market asset classes remained unaffected. Anticipating a global economic recovery, consumer cyclicals remained the best performing sectors in the matured economies, particularly in Europe and the US, although investment spendings continued to remain weak. The high-tech sectors performed poorly because of high leverage and considerable overcapacity, which was a legacy of the bubble period.

Post-Enron credit risk awareness led to reduced syndicated bank lending to the emerging market economies during the first quarter of 2002. One consequence of the Enron debacle was tightening in lending norms by financial institutions, which reduced loan volumes to emerging market economies to half of the preceding quarter. Bank credit quality became a crucial issue in the matured economies, causing all relatively high-risk lending to decline. Emerging economies from Latin America suffered the steepest decline in loan volumes. As opposed to them, emerging market economies from Asia expressed little demand for fresh capital, although refinancing of old loans continued.

Enronitis

The so-called Enronitis belied educated estimates and expectations of recovery during the first quarter of 2002. It struck the US financial markets in January and represented hidden accounting problems of large corporations. There was a question mark over the quality of reported corporate earnings. In the wake of unexpected Enron debacle, and high profile bankruptcies of Kmart and Global Crossing the stock prices of highly leveraged firms were adversely affected. Corporate malpractices and accounting fiddles had a devastating impact over the US equity markets. Revelations regarding wrongdoing and corporate excess continued, adversely affecting business confidence. Consequently, the equity markets continued its dive. From the beginning of May 2002, when the Dow Jones Industrial Average stood above 10,000, it slid to a low of 7,702 in July. The broader S&P 500 index and London's FTSE 100 followed similar routes south. Having been stamped on heavily after earlier slips, the Nasdaq Composite Index, with a heavy weighting of technology companies, had little strength to resist and so sank too. Its contagion effect soon spread to Europe and other global bourses.[8]

Global economic and financial environment was severely undermined by volatility in the bourses, which in turn created an extremely high degree of uncertainty in the investment climate. Probability of a continued global downturn and a delay in the global recovery increased sharply. Revised economic performance statistics were issued by the US government on July 31, 2002, which showed that the US economy grew much more slowly than expected in the second quarter of 2002 – by only 1.1 percent at an annualized rate. The revised statistics also indicated that the 2001 recession was significantly worse than previously estimated, and growth in the first quarter of 2002 a bit less impressive than earlier statistics had indicated. The backward changes implied a necessary downward revision to America's spectacular productivity figures and cast doubt on the "miracle" of the new economy. Recovery in the global financial markets is conditional upon the recovery in the global economy.[9]

Although toward the end of August 2002, equity markets regained their nerves, concerns about corporate misdeeds weighed on all the major indexes (*Business Week*, 2002). In addition, there were too many question marks like poor outlook for corporate profits in the Euro area and US, two quarters of steadily rising energy prices,[10] and little possibility of a fiscal stimulus in the US.[11] The future impact of changes in accounting rules and corporate governance was uncertain. Therefore, as at the end of the third quarter 2001, once again the prospects for a global and financial market recovery were mixed. Investment in the US economy continued to be weak, although consumer spending remained buoyant. The global economy was precariously balanced between recovery and recession.

After four consecutive quarters of decline, Japan's GDP rose faster than that of the US during the second quarter of 2002 – at 2.6 percent annualized rate. Yet, its recovery was fragile. Average wages and retail sales continued to decline and deflation continues. Europe's sluggish performance even during the boom years of the 1990s constantly fell short of expectations (*The Economist*, 2002). During the first half of 2002, the Euro area economies continued to disappoint. Not only GDP growth was weak but also that growth came from exports. Domestic demand in the Euro area was tepid. Prospects for the third quarter are that of contraction.

Uncertain economic outlook in the US economy is sure to retard global recovery. What happens to the US economy in the third and fourth quarters of 2002 is the key to prospective policy changes not just in the US but also around the globe. The IMF discounted the risk of a recession in the US but growth may not be strong enough to prevent the onset of deflation – falling prices – in several countries. The world's largest economy is the only potential engine of world economic growth. The US economy led the global economy and global financial markets into a deceleration over two years ago. It will also be responsible to lead them out of it. Recovery in the global financial markets is conditional upon the recovery in the global economy.

Conclusions and summing up

Although the twenty-first century began well for the global economy and the global financial markets, global financial climate began to change as early as the middle of 2000. Deceleration in the global economy and deterioration in the financial environment came about in four stages. The first stage was marked by the deceleration in the growth rate of the US economy in the middle of 2000. Fed took definitive measures to slow the economy down. The high-tech bubble burst during this phase. The second phase began at the end of 2000 when the high-tech bubble burst further. The stock market declined sharply and so did the high-tech production. The contagion effect of the slowdown in the US soon spread to the Euro area, Asia and Latin America.

Toward the end of the third quarter of 2001, global economy was performing the precarious balancing act between recession and recovery. Events of September 11, 2001, ushered in the third phase in global economic and financial deceleration. Global financial markets reacted sharply to the terrorist attack. As expected, this period was marked by a dramatic, albeit temporary, loss of consumer confidence and serious deterioration in business sentiment. Prompt reaction by policy makers in the form of various measures including actions to ensure functioning of financial systems and reduced monetary interest rates were important factors that limited the severity of the impact. The impact did not linger for a long time and market perception began to change by the end of the year.

A moderate recovery was on track in the US during the first quarter of 2002. There were several signs of global economy bottoming out. The logical assumption was that the US economy would prove to be a locomotive for the Euro area and the rest of the global economy. Prospects for global economic recovery improved financial market conditions in the first quarter. The market environment during this quarter was considered benign, although several negative features persisted during this quarter. The principal ones among them were the "level and quality of reported corporate profits" and high equity valuations.

The fourth phase began with the bankruptcy announcement by Enron in the US during the first quarter of 2002. Prospects for a global economic and financial market recovery evaporated. Global economic and financial environment was severely undermined by volatility in the bourses, which in turn created an extremely high degree of uncertainty in the investment climate. Probability of a continued global downturn and a delay in the global recovery increased sharply. Credit risk awareness led to reduced syndicated bank lending to the emerging market economies during the first quarter of 2002. One consequence of the Enron debacle was tightening in lending norms by financial institutions.

Toward the end of August 2002, equity markets regained their nerves, albeit the prospects for a global and financial market recovery were mixed. The global economy was precariously balanced between recovery and recession. What happens to the US economy in the third and fourth quarters of 2002 is the key to prospective policy changes not just in the US but also around the globe. The largest global economy can lead the global economy and financial markets out of their present travails. Recovery in the global financial markets is conditional upon the recovery in the global economy.

Notes

1 While I am aware of the unresolved controversy regarding the year 2000 being the last year of the twentieth century or the first year of the twenty-first, in this chapter I am assuming that the twenty-first century began in 2000.
2 This chapter was written in August 2002.
3 Statistics used in this section come from the World Bank, *Global Economic Prospects* 2002.
4 An important measure is JP Morgan's Liquidity and Credit Premia Index (LCPI), which is a broad measure of risk aversion.
5 Refer to IMF (2002a) for greater details.
6 Refer to chapter 1, *World Economic Outlook*, April 2002.
7 Risk appetite is measured by an index. The variables used are changes in various market indicators of credit risk and liquidity premia.
8 The silver lining behind the Enron cloud was that numerous weaknesses in accounting rules and their implementation as well as those in corporate governance were exposed. Consequently, some progress has been made in addressing these weaknesses. They are being studied in the international fora. To this end, three major endeavors have been launched by (1) the Financial Stability Forum, (2) the International Organization of Securities Commissions (IOSCO) and (3) the Basle Committee on Banking Supervision.
9 These are based on IMF 2002a,b.
10 Toward the end of August price of West Texas Intermediate, the benchmark for American crude oil, reached $30 a barrel. There were understandable fears of interruptions of energy supply if the US launched an attack on Iraq to depose Saddam Husain.
11 Fed chairman, Alan Greenspan, noted in his August 2002 testimony to the US Congress, that "the productivity of the US economy has continued to rise at a remarkably strong pace." However, since 1999 those gains in productivity have failed to feed through into companies' profits. Therefore, while profits had begun to rise again, "managers seem to remain skeptical of the evidence of an emerging upturn."

References

Business Week. 2002. "Stocks Finish with Steep Losses," August 23. p. 22.

The Economist. 2002. "Ripples from America," August 16. p. 17.

The International Monetary Fund (IMF). 2002. *World Economic Outlook*. Washington, DC. April.

The International Monetary Fund (IMF). 2002a. *Global Financial Stability Report*. Washington, DC. March.

The International Monetary Fund (IMF). 2002b. *Global Financial Stability Report*. Washington, DC. June.

The World Bank (WB). 2002. *Global Economic Prospects 2002*. Washington, DC.

2 Globalization in the world of finance

Dilip K. Das

Globalization

Although the contemporary wave of globalization is a quarter century old, during the last decade, the concept of globalization acquired a great deal of currency and emotive force. Many scholars have attempted to define globalization from their own respective perspectives. It can simply and functionally be defined as gradually evolving interaction and integration of economies and societies around the world. Keohane and Nye (2001) defined globalization as "a state of the world involving networks of interdependence at multicontinental distances." These networks need to be spatially extensive. They can interact through the flow of finance, goods, services, information, ideas and people.

As economies are progressively integrating globally, *pari passu* the financial structures of markets and the world of finance is changing. This applies to both domestic and international financial markets. A quarter century ago a business-man was restricted to borrowing from his domestic market. Several options are open to him in a globalized financial market. For instance, he can choose between issuing stocks and bonds in domestic or foreign financial markets. He can reduce his cost of capital if foreign currency loans are available at more attractive terms than the domestic loans. These loans can be hedged by using a variety of financial products. He can also consider selling equity at foreign bourses.

One of the many definitions of financial globalization is integration of domestic financial system of a country with the global financial markets and institutions. Enabling framework of financial globalization essentially includes liberalization and deregulation of the domestic financial sector as well as liberalization of the capital account. Integration between domestic and global financial markets occurs when trans-border capital flows take place. In a globalized financial environment domestic lenders and borrowers participate in the global markets, and utilize global financial intermediaries for borrowing and lending.

A caveat is necessary here. Financial globalization is not truly global. Initially, members of the Organization for Economic Co-operation and Development (OECD) used to be the most active participants in the financial globalization process. They also used to be the principal players in the global financial markets. Over the last quarter century, financial globalization has expanded to the emerging market economies. This set of economies are somewhat imprecisely defined as the newly industrialized economies[1] (NIEs) and middle-income developing countries in which governments and corporations "have access to private international capital markets, or can attract institutional portfolio investment, or both (WB, 2002)". Different international institutions include slightly different sets of countries in this category. For example, the Institute of International Finance (IIF) includes twenty-nine countries from Asia, Africa, Europe, Latin America and the Middle East. The International Monetary Fund (IMF) includes all the NIEs and the middle-income developing countries in its definition of the emerging market economies. *The Economist* classifies twenty-five developing and transitional economies as the emerging market economies.[2]

Novelty of financial globalization

Neither the concept nor the phenomenon of financial globalization can be considered novel. Trans-country capital movements are centuries old. One of the early eras of well-documented financial globalization was the 1870–1914 period. To be sure, this was not the first period of global integration. Using different measures and indicators, several analysts tried to establish that a greater degree of financial globalization existed in the previous epochs of globalization. Using the share of current account balance in national income as a proxy for the external capital flows, Obstfeld and Taylor (1998) established that larger external capital flows were recorded in the previous periods of financial globalization than during the contemporary period. Their study also presented evidence on nominal interest rate differential and real interest rate dispersion as proxies for the financial market integration during various periods. Relationship between domestic investment and savings has also been used as a proxy for financial mobility to reach the conclusion that greater financial globalization existed in earlier periods (Taylor, 1998). Several important empirical studies analyzed this issue. Baldwin and Martin (1999) have reviewed this literature at length.

One important distinction between the past and the present periods of financial globalization was that in the past a limited number of countries, and a small number of sectors in the participating economies, participated in financial globalization. Also, in general, capital followed the migration of population and it was *inter alia* utilized in supporting trade flows. Long-term bonds of varying maturity were the most popular financial instruments in the past. Financial activity was highly concentrated in the hands of a small number of large freestanding companies. Similarly, a small number of wealthy family groups and banks dominated financial intermediation. This was the era of gold standard, according to which gold and other precious metals backed the national currency. Therefore, currency value fluctuations were unknown. The gold standard facilitated cross-country capital movements.

This system functioned smoothly until the eve of the First World War. Its welfare implications for the global economy were obvious. The First World War not only ended this era of globalization but also led to serious instability. Consequently policy makers switched their stance and instead of recreating the globalized financial markets of the past after the war, they began making policy moves in the reverse direction by imposing capital controls to regain monetary policy autonomy. The textbook argument in this regard is that only two out of the following three can coexist: fixed exchange rates, autonomous monetary policy and free capital mobility. As most governments were concerned about their exchange rate and autonomy in monetary policy, free capital movement had to be abandoned as a priority policy option.[3] The Great Depression of the 1930s and the Second World War added to crises and instability in the global economy. Cross-country capital movements reached their historical low level in the 1950s and failed to pick up during the 1960s. The Bretton Woods era of fixed but adjustable exchange rates is known for limited capital mobility and for policy makers' preference for adopting autonomy in monetary policy (Das, 2002).

Driving forces behind financial globalization

According to Mundell (2000), the contemporary era of financial globalization began soon after the oil shock of 1973 and the collapse of the Bretton Woods system. Both these developments were momentous and were responsible for laying the foundation of the contemporary era of financial globalization. After the collapse of the Bretton Woods system, some middle-income developing economies began to liberalize and open up for greater capital mobility, while keeping an autonomous control over their monetary policy. Given the impossible trinity, fixed exchange rates could no longer be a popular policy option. Capital flows increased sharply during the 1970s and the early 1980s, leading to the debt crisis of 1982, which started with Mexico declaring a moratorium in July 1982 on its external liability. Brady Bonds were invented toward the late 1980s to resolve the debt crisis of the developing countries (Das, 1989). This development subsequently helped in the development of bond markets for the emerging market economies. Investors in the industrial countries found that deregulation, privatization, merger and acquisitions (M&As), and advances in the information technology (IT) was making foreign direct investment (FDI) and equity investment in the emerging market more attractive than before and easy. The result was an FDI and equity investment spike in the emerging market economies in the 1990s.

Advances in IT and computer technology are cited as one of the most important factors driving and supporting financial globalization. They have reduced the cost of communications, increased power of computers, shrunk the globe and made national boundaries less significant. New developments in IT facilitated collection and processing of information for the market participants as well as for monetary and banking authorities and banks. They made it possible to measure, monitor and manage financial risk for the market participants. Without computers pricing and trading of complex new financial instruments was not feasible. Managing of large and rapid transactions, and then managing books for these transactions, which are widely spread across continents, and countries, could not be accomplished without the support of IT and computers.

Transnational corporations (TNCs) have expanded their networks by merging with or acquiring other national and international firms. They managed to "slice the value chain" and created production and distribution networks spanning the globe. As noted above, many emerging market economies began liberalizing their domestic economies in a methodical manner, lowering barriers to trade and financial flows, consequently increasing both global trade in goods and services. These developments resulted in heightened demand for trans-border financial flows. Therefore, an internationally mobile pool of capital and liquidity was created, which allowed financial globalization to make further advances.

Liberalized domestic economic strategies, advances in IT and globalizing economies coalesced to catalyze financial innovation. Responding to the demand for trans-border financial flows, financial intermediation activity globalized. It was further buttressed by declining barriers to trade in financial services as well as deregulation and removal of entry restrictions on foreign financial institutions into domestic markets in a large number of emerging market economies. Consequently, trans-border flows increased at a rapid clip. Huang and Wajid (2002) estimated that between 1970 and 2000, they increased from less than 3 percent of GDP to 17 percent for the industrial economies and from virtually nothing to about 5 percent of GDP for the developing economies. Global gross capital flows in 2000 amounted to $7.5 trillion, a fourfold increase over 1990. The growth in cross-border capital movements also resulted in larger net capital flows, rising from $500 billion in 1990 to nearly $1.2 trillion in 2000 (Hausler, 2002).

The regulatory authorities in many countries, particularly the emerging market economies, modernized their structure and role. Their new set of regulations facilitated a broader range of institutions to provide financial services. Also, new categories of non-bank institutions and institutional investors were launched. Gradually, investment banks, securities firms, asset managers, mutual funds, insurance companies, specialty and trade finance companies, hedge funds, and even telecommunications, software and food companies began providing services similar to those traditionally provided by banks. Technological advances and financial innovation joined hands to increase competition among the institutions that provided intermediary services. These developments have supported the advance of financial globalization.

The flip side of the coin is that in spite of the progress in financial globalization, the global financial system is far from being perfectly integrated. Not all the forces are driving financial globalization onward. Several counter-globalization forces are still at work. Analysts have provided evidence of inadequate progress in financial integration, imperfections in the global capital markets, persistent capital market segmentation, continuing home country bias and correlation between domestic savings and investment.[4] Yet, a reversal of the recent trend is difficult to visualize, albeit it is not impossible. It is largely because of liberalization and deregulation of economies, and technological advances in the financial services sector. Also, the channels of financial globalization are so many and so diverse that a reversal of financial globalization will be difficult. This observation applies to both partially integrated and fully integrated economies. Having witnessed the recent benefits of financial globalization, policy makers and economic agents in the emerging market economies are likely to work toward a more financially integrated world in future and toward achieving a deeper degree of financial integration. The newest developments in the IT and ineffectiveness of public policy will further underpin cross-border financial flows.

Agents of financial globalization

The prime movers in financial globalization are governments, borrowers, investors and financial institutions. Each one of these market participants propelled economies toward financial integration in a proactive manner. Governments play an indispensable role in promoting financial globalization. By creating an enabling policy framework, they make financial globalization feasible. Two policy actions are considered a pre-condition of financial globalization. The first is liberalization and deregulation of the domestic financial sector, while the second is liberalization of the capital account of balance-of-payments. Strict regulation of domestic financial sector, with a vast array of difficult-to-comprehend restrictions, used to be a popular practice in the past. This applied to most developing economies where governments controlled credit allocation and kept surveillance over its disbursement through control on prices and quantities. Multiple bodies were created to enforce a complex body of regulations. Governments routinely controlled cross-country capital movements in a stringent manner, both inward and outward. A large number of instruments were devised in different policy areas to restrict capital account transactions. These areas were foreign exchange transactions, derivative transactions, lending and borrowing activities by banks and corporations, as well as entry and participation of foreign investors in the domestic financial system.

Policy structure in these areas gradually started changing in the 1970s and the traditional controls and restrictive regulations over the domestic financial sector and capital account noted above began to be relaxed in many industrial economies, NIEs and the emerging market economies. Lifting of restrictions was closely studies by Kaminsky and Schmukler (2001). They selected six restrictions on the capital account and five restrictions on the financial markets and made two indices: (i) financial restrictions on capital account and (ii) restrictions on the domestic financial sector. They concluded that over the 1973–2000 period these restrictions declined to the maximum extent in the industrial economies. In the Asian emerging market economies they declined significantly, although not as much as those in the industrial economies. Similarly, Latin American emerging market economies recorded a decline in these restrictions and controls but it was less than that in Asian economies. Industrial economies always used more liberal financial policies than the other economies. The NIEs and emerging market economies certainly liberalized the restrictions but they were not only slow to do that, but there also were periods of policy reversals.

There were several motivating factors behind liberalizing restrictions over the domestic financial sector and capital account. The World Bank (2001) argues that policy makers found the vast array of restrictions and controls increasingly costly and difficult to maintain effectively. Besides, they began to make distinction between government-led financial system – or a statist financial system – and the market-led one, and saw that the government-led, non-market system, failed to achieve the desired objectives. The experiences of the last two decades revealed that there were periods when external capital flows helped both governments and corporate sector. At the times of crises, external capital was needed to re-capitalize banks whose capital base had seriously eroded as well as for conducting corporate restructuring. During the crises of the 1980s and 1990s, many countries had to rely on external capital flows to tide them over their periods of crisis. During such periods, foreign investors provided capital for privatization of public sector enterprises in the emerging markets economies, which helped increase financial receipts from these enterprises. Myriad experiences of this nature changed the mindset of policy makers. At the beginning of the twenty-first century, policy makers seem more convinced than ever regarding a liberalized and deregulated financial system being more efficient for growth and stability of the economy.

Financial globalization is also proactively promoted by firms and households, which represent savers, investors and borrowers. By borrowing abroad households and firms can go beyond their immediate financial constraints and consume or invest according to their preferences. In particular, by raising capital abroad through bonds and equity issues firms can potentially reduce the cost of capital and expand their investor base. Benefits of external resources are not limited to lower cost. When external capital comes in the form of FDI, the recipient firms in the home country benefit by way of acquiring technology of more recent vintage, if not the latest. FDI is also known to usher in new management techniques and employee training.

Trans-border capital flows benefit international investors as well. In their endeavor to find new and more profitable investment opportunities they explore the global investment scenario. In addition, financial globalization benefits them by providing cross-country risk diversion possibilities. As the emerging market economies grow at a faster clip than the industrial ones, international investors can reasonably expect to have higher real returns on their investment in these economies. With the liberalization and deregulation of the financial markets, institutions and individuals in the industrial economies can easily find opportunities for profitable investment in the NIEs and the emerging markets only by buying shares of international mutual funds. There is a wide choice of mutual funds, which could be global, regional or country-specific. Other easy instruments are American Depository Receipts (ADRs) and Global Depository Receipts (GDRs), as well as international corporate and sovereign bonds. All these modes of global investment are currently in vogue (Schmukler and Zoido-Lobaton, 2001).

Financial institutions are important purveyors of financial globalization. They have helped in deepening financial globalization through the spread of financial services. In this endeavor the newest advances in IT assisted them. With the help of IT, large financial institutions can serve several markets from one location.

Advances in IT have promoted a more intensive use of international financial institutions. They also assisted in consolidating and restructuring the global financial services industry. IT was instrumental in the creation of global banks and conglomerates that provide a large mix of financial products and services in several markets and countries (Crockett, 2000; IMF, 2000). As financial liberalization and deregulation in the NIEs and emerging market economies progressed, international financial institutions began to participate in the domestic markets of these economies. Privatization of financial institutions provided them with opportunities to enter the local financial markets. Macroeconomic stabilization, improved economic and business environment, and in general, stronger fundamentals in these economies ensured healthier economic climate and encouraged greater integration of large financial institutions with the global financial markets.

Financial globalization and capital markets

Financial globalization has caused dramatic changes in the structure of national and international capital markets. The most significant change in the capital markets was in the banking system, which went through a process of disintermediation. This was a market transformation of fundamental nature. It has radically changed the operation of the financial markets.[5] Tradable securities increasingly replaced financial intermediation through banks. The role of bank loans and deposits progressively declined over the last quarter century. Markets participants – financial and non-financial institutions, and saving and investing households – were responsible for ushering in this metamorphosis. They played a crucial role in bringing it about because they benefited from it. Financial risks, particularly credit risks, are no longer borne by banks. They are increasingly moved off balance sheets. Assets are converted into tradable securities, which in turn eliminate credit risks. Derivative transactions like interest rate swaps also serve the same purpose. Risk elimination enables banks to improve their risk-adjusted returns on capital as well as be more competitive in the market. Reduced risk also tends to lower their capital requirements according to the regulatory norms. In the new globalized financial environment a diversified group of investors has emerged that is willing to own an array of credit and other financial risks. Improvements in IT have made these risks easier to monitor, analyze and manage (Hausler, 2002). This group of investors is growing fast.

Second, major financial markets, centers and institutions now serve borrowers and investors all over the globe, or those in economies that are now financially globalized. They also serve sovereign borrowers at various stages of economic development. TNCs and financial intermediaries not only tap financial resources and raise capital from the globalized financial centers, but they can also manage risk more flexibly by accessing larger pools of capital in these centers. Accordingly, the volume of cross-border financial flows has increased substantially. The importance of institutional investors has grown in the capital markets because they manage a large and growing share of global financial wealth. They have become adept at enhancing their risk-adjusted returns by diversifying their portfolios globally. This diversification is reflected in their investment in a wide range of economies, industries and currencies. Therefore, wholesale financial integration in the global economy is far greater than that at the retail end of the financial market.

Third, due to the changes in the structure of the capital markets, competition between banks and non-banking financial institutions has intensified. The two categories of institutions keenly compete for household savings and corporate finance mandates, forcing prices of financial instruments to decline. Non-banking financial institutions have succeeded in capturing a rising share of household savings. For instance, mutual funds provide higher return instruments to households, encouraging them to ignore the traditional banking saving channels. They are able to diversify risk better, and have grown enormously in size and sophistication. Competition between banks and non-banking financial institutions has slimmed down the profit margin of banks and forced them to find new sources of revenues and new methods of intermediating funds. They have also been driven toward fee-based businesses. This applies most to banks in the European Union, where there was little consolidation of financial institutions. However, in North America and the United Kingdom mergers of banks with other banks and non-banking financial institutions like securities firms enabled them to exploit economies of scale. It provided banks an opportunity to remain competitive.

Fourth, changing nature of capital markets, and their deepening and broadening, created new sources of business for banks. Underwriting of corporate bond and equity issues was one such business. To meet their liquidity needs for investment, banks turned to over-the-counter (OTC) derivatives markets. This is a decentralized market where derivatives, like currency and interest rate swaps, are privately traded between buyers and sellers.[6] Transformations in regulatory framework and norms enabled banks to venture beyond their traditional array of activities. They entered into other areas of profitable activities, like investment banking, asset management, insurance and the like, which allowed them to diversify their revenue sources and business risk.

Vulnerabilities associated with financial globalization

Contagion-related spillovers from national, regional and global crises are the downsides of financial globalization. Economic and financial crises of the 1990s portend to the fact that financial globalization is not a win–win game, and that it can potentially lead to serious disorder and high cost in terms of bank failures, corporate bankruptcies, stock market turbulence, depletion of foreign exchange reserves, currency depreciation and increased fiscal burden. Together they tell on the real economy and create an environment of depression and job losses, leading to social turbulence.

Statistics in the section on "Driving forces behind financial globalization" show that households, banks, corporations and sovereign borrowers utilized the globalizing financial markets well. However, a unique characteristic of globalized financial markets is the reversal of capital flows when market perception regarding the creditworthiness of the borrowing entity changes. When financial markets grow skeptical about the viability of domestic policies and financial institutions, or when they retrench in response to financial crisis in another part of the world, or when they eschew an economy having similarities in economic and financial indicators with one in crisis, national and international financial stability comes under serious threat. The crises of the 1990s sufficiently testify to these facts. Because of advances in IT, reverse flows of capital can now be really rapid. It implies that the probability of a contagion setting in, or an economy suffering from a financial crisis has increased with progress in financial globalization. Empirical research in this area suggests that the probability of a randomly selected country experiencing a crisis has doubled since 1973 (Eichengreen and Bordo, 2001). The Asian crises of 1997–98 and the Russian crisis of 1998 demonstrated that financial instability in one country could destabilize the entire global financial system. When Russia defaulted on its external liabilities and devalued the ruble, stock markets in emerging market economies as well as industrial economies tumbled and investors around the globe suffered large losses.

To avoid recurrences of such scenarios, policy makers must strive to make their financial systems deep, broad and resilient. They must address financial weaknesses that make financial structure weak and vulnerable to external shocks. This needs to be achieved both at national and global levels. To this end, the IMF and the World Bank have adopted a three-pronged approach, which includes comprehensive assessments of financial sector vulnerabilities for member countries, strengthening the monitoring and analysis of financial sectors and helping countries build strong institutions. They conceived and launched the Financial Sector Assessment Program (FSAP) in 1999 as a collaborative endeavor. It is a large program involving the two supranational bodies and national banking and non-bank financial institutions as well as the financial markets (securities, foreign exchange and money markets). The FSAP had to be country-specific and was carefully devised to identify strength and vulnerabilities of the financial system as well as identify measures to reduce the potential crisis in that country. Functioning and importance of various financial institutions and their sensitivity to external shocks are scrutinized under the FSAP. Various financial soundness indicators (like capital-adequacy ratios, extent of non-performing loans, earning trends in banks) are also examined. The acceptance of FSAP was encouraging and over a third of the 183 member countries of the IMF had begun participating in it by the end of 2001.[7]

For strengthening the monitoring and analysis of financial sector and making it more transparent, IMF is endeavoring to improve the intelligence and information systems in the member countries. The objective of this endeavor is to conduct a deeper and thorough analysis of the financial sector of the economy. Frequent monitoring of the financial sector should enable policy makers to refine their stress-testing methodologies. The Bretton Woods twins are also assisting those countries that lack the institutional capacity to supervise and regulate their financial sectors. They provide technical assistance for institutional building. The FSAP and its integrated approach was found to be helpful in identifying vulnerabilities of financial systems and devising stabilizing strategies (Huang and Wajid, 2002).

Dimension of net capital flows to emerging markets

Among the three sets of economies to financially globalize, the emerging market economies were the most recent. Cross-country financial flows to this country group were low, at a paltry $28 billion, during the mid-1970s. Net flows to the emerging market economies reached $306 billion in 1997 in real terms, at the eve of the Asian financial crisis (Schmukler and Zoido-Lobaton, 2001). This was their peak level. Net flows suffered a sharp decline after that because of the Asian and Russian financial and economic crises. The composition of external capital underwent a dramatic transformation during this period. Official flows or official development assistance (ODA) either stagnated or declined. As a result their relative significance in global capital flows dwindled. In their place, private capital flows became the major source of external finance for a good number of emerging market economies. FDI became an important and dependable source of finance for the emerging markets and other middle-income economies during the decade of the 1980s and 1990s. Its growth was particularly strong during the decade of 1990s. A large part of FDI to emerging market economies was utilized in M&As deals. Many large developing economies were privatizing their public sector enterprise during this period. Those that were rated as creditworthy by the financial markets succeeded in attracting FDI in the process (Lipsey, 1999).

While syndicated bank loans were a popular instrument during the 1970s, they gradually went out of use after the Latin American debt crisis of 1982. In the 1970s, developing countries hardly attracted portfolio investment in stocks and bond markets. They were as low as $100 million in 1970. Like the FDI, they began to increase in the 1980s and peaked at $103 billion in 1996 in real terms (Schmukler and Zoido-Lobaton, 2001). Global institutional investors found this channel of investment functional and profitable. Mutual funds, insurance companies and pension funds channeled large amounts through portfolio investment into the emerging market economies. The Asian and Russian crises had a strong adverse influence over them as well and they sharply declined after that.

The emerging market economies have been defined above as those where governments and corporations have access to private international capital markets, or can attract institutional portfolio investment, or both. However, not all the emerging market economies have an equal access to the international capital markets. Their access is directly related to their perceived creditworthiness in the global financial marketplace. Therefore, distribution of global capital among the recipient economies is highly uneven. Some economies like the People's Republic of China (hereinafter China), East Asian and Latin American ones have easy access and receive large amounts of global capital resources, while others like South Asian ones (India being an exception in this group) have limited access. Many like the African economies have not been able to attract any global capital.

Using *Global Development Finance* database, Schmukler and Zoido-Lobaton (2001) have shown that low-income developing economies receive very little amount of net global capital, while the middle-income developing economies do receive some amount. In accordance with the creditworthiness concept, lion's share of global capital is attracted by top twelve recipient countries.[8] All of these fall in the category of emerging market economies. These economies are relatively more globalized than the others. During the 1990s, global capital flows to these twelve emerging market economies accelerated at a steep rate, which affected the composition of the total global financial resources going to developing economies. The proportion of financial flows dedicated to the low- and middle-income developing economies decreased at the end of the 1990s. For all appearance, many economies in this group of rapidly financially globalizing economies are diverging from the rest of the developing economies.

Globalizing financial services

As alluded to earlier, when domestic savers (or lenders) and borrowers make use of the global financial markets, intermediaries and institutions, financial services are said to be globalizing. Over the 1990s, presence of international financial intermediaries has expanded considerably. This applies more to international commercial banks than to investment banks, insurance companies and mutual funds. It is incorrect to say that their global expansion has been uniform because this has occurred unevenly. Conversely, globalization of financial services also occurs when domestic savers (or lenders) and borrowers are able to make use of financial intermediaries located globally. For instance, financial services are said to be globalized when domestic stocks are traded on large international bourses abroad.

During the 1990s, presence of foreign banks increased in three regions, namely East Asia, Eastern Europe and Latin America. Foreign bank ownership of assets increased rapidly. Total assets held by them increased maximum in the emerging market economies in Latin America, particularly in Argentina, Brazil, Mexico, Peru and Venezuela. In the emerging market economies in Eastern European (Czech Republic, Hungary and Poland) share of total assets controlled by foreign banks crossed 50 percent of the total. As compared to these two regions, the activities of the foreign banks expanded less rapidly in the emerging markets of East Asia, like Korea (Republic of), Malaysia and Thailand (Schmukler and Zoido-Lobaton, 2001). However, it must be stated that to begin with foreign bank activity was greater in the emerging markets of East Asia than in the other emerging markets.

International bond issuance activity by emerging market economies recorded a sharp spurt in 1993, crossing $50 billion for the first time. It stabilized around this level until 1996, when it nearly doubled. Both 1993 and 1996 were the years of high global capital flows. In 1997, issuance activity by emerging market economies peaked at $120 billion. Due to Asian financial crisis and its contagion effects, international bond issuance dropped to around $75 billion over the next three years.[9]

Emerging market economies began using ADRs and GDRs for raising capital from the global capital markets, in 1990, in a small way. ADRs and GDRs are negotiable certificates representing ownership of shares in a corporation in another country. They are held by a depository, which in turn issues a certificate that can be traded in another country, for example, the United States. The middle-income developing countries began using them in 1992. Firms from both emerging market and middle-income developing economies increased their participation in the US equity markets using ADRs and GDRs. The top six emerging market economies that had the highest participation over the decade of the 1990s were: Argentina, Brazil, China, India, Korea (Republic of) and Mexico. They accounted for most of the activity by developing countries in the US equity markets. In terms of capital flows, this group of countries may be creating a divergence among the developing countries. This group benefited more from the global capital markets by way of lower cost of capital and longer maturity structure of its debt (Schmukler and Zoido-Lobaton, 2001).

Summary and conclusions

The contemporary wave of globalization is around a quarter century old. One of the many definitions of financial globalization is integration of domestic financial system of a country with the global financial markets and institutions. Enabling framework of financial globalization essentially includes liberalization and deregulation of the domestic financial sector as well as liberalization of the capital account. As economies progressively integrate globally, *pari passu* the financial structures of markets and the world of finance change. This applies to both domestic and international financial markets. Integration between domestic and global financial markets occurs when trans-border capital flows take place. It needs to be stressed that financial globalization is not truly global. During the contemporary period, only the industrial economies, the NIEs and the emerging market economies are financially globalizing.

Financial globalization cannot be considered a novel phenomenon. Trans-country capital movements are centuries old. Greater degree of financial globalization existed in the previous epochs of globalization. Larger external capital flows were recorded in the previous periods of financial globalization than during the contemporary period. One important distinction between the past and the present periods of financial globalization was that in the past a limited number of countries, and a small number of sectors in the participating economies, took part in financial globalization.

The oil shock of 1973 and the collapse of the Bretton Woods system, both of these developments were momentous and were responsible for laying the foundation of the contemporary era of financial globalization. After the collapse of the Bretton Woods system, some middle-income developing economies began to liberalize and open up for greater capital mobility, while keeping an autonomous control over their monetary policy. Advances in IT and computer technology are cited as one of the most important factors driving and supporting financial globalization. TNCs also helped in global financial integration. They expanded their networks by merging with or acquiring other national and international firms. Liberalized domestic economic strategies, advances in IT and globalizing economies coalesced to catalyze financial innovation. Responding to the demand for trans-border financial flows, financial intermediation activity globalized. It was further buttressed by declining barriers to trade in financial services as well as deregulation and removal of entry restrictions on foreign financial institutions into domestic markets in a large number of emerging market economies. The regulatory authorities in many countries, particularly the emerging market economies, modernized their structure and role.

The prime movers in financial globalization are governments, borrowers, investors and financial institutions. Each one of these market participants propelled economies toward financial integration in a proactive manner. Restrictive regulations, so popular in the past, were relaxed in many countries. There were several motivating factors behind liberalizing restrictions over the domestic financial sector and capital account. Policy makers found the vast array of restrictions and controls increasingly costly and difficult to maintain effectively. Besides, the experiences of the last two decades revealed that there were periods when external capital flows helped both governments and corporate sector. Financial globalization was also proactively promoted by firms and households. Trans-border capital flows tend to benefit international investors as well.

Financial globalization has caused dramatic changes in the structure of national and international capital markets. The most significant change in the capital markets was in the banking system, which went through a process of disintermediation. This was a market transformation of fundamental nature. Second, major financial markets, centers and institutions now serve borrowers and investors all over the globe, or those in economies that are now financially globalized. They also serve sovereign borrowers at various stages of economic development, TNCs and financial intermediaries. Accordingly, the volume of cross-border financial flows has increased substantially. The importance of institutional investors has grown in the capital markets because they manage a large and growing share of global financial wealth.

Contagions and crises are the downsides of financial globalization. Economic and financial crises of the 1990s portend to the fact that financial globalization is not a win–win game, and that it can potentially lead to serious disorder and high cost in terms of bank failures, corporate bankruptcies, stock market turbulence, depletion of foreign exchange reserves, currency depreciation and increased fiscal burden. A unique characteristic of globalized financial markets is reversal of capital flows when market perception regarding the creditworthiness of the borrowing entity changes. The probability of a randomly selected country experiencing a crisis has doubled since 1973. To avoid recurrences of such scenarios, policy makers must strive to make their financial systems deep, broad and resilient. They must address financial weaknesses that make financial structure weak and vulnerable to external shocks. This needs to be achieved both at national and global levels. To this end, the IMF and the World Bank have adopted a three-pronged approach, which includes comprehensive assessments of financial sector vulnerabilities for member countries, strengthening the monitoring and analysis of financial sectors, and helping countries build strong institutions. They conceived and launched the FSAP in 1999 as a collaborative endeavor.

Cross-country financial flows to the emerging market economies were low, during the mid-1970s. They increased at a healthy pace during the decades of 1980s and 1990s, peaking in 1997. They suffered a sharp decline after that because of the Asian and Russian financial and economic crises. The composition of external capital underwent a dramatic transformation during this period. Official flows either stagnated or declined. As a result their relative significance in global capital flows dwindled. In their place, private capital flows became the major source of external finance for a good number of emerging market economies. FDI became an important and dependable source of finance for the emerging markets and other middle-income economies during the decade of the 1980s and 1990s. Portfolio investment in stocks and bond markets also increased substantially. Global institutional investors found this channel of investment functional and profitable. Mutual funds, insurance companies and pension funds channeled large amounts through portfolio investment into the emerging market economies.

As financial globalization progressed, presence of international financial intermediaries has expanded considerably. This applies more to international commercial banks than to investment banks, insurance companies and mutual funds. It is incorrect to say that their global expansion has been uniform because this has occurred unevenly. International bond issuance activity by emerging market economies recorded a sharp spurt in 1993. Emerging market economies began using ADRs and GDRs for raising capital from the global capital markets, in 1990, in a small way.

Notes

1 Chile, Hong Kong SAR, Korea (Republic of), Singapore and Taiwan. Hong Kong is a special administrative region (SAR) of the People's Republic of China.
2 This held until the end of 2002.
3 This is referred to as the impossible trinity.
4 For evidence to this effect, refer to Frankel (2000), Obstfeld and Rogoff (2000), Tesar and Werner (1998) and Okina *et al.* (1999).
5 Please refer to Krueger (2002) where she discusses this issue in the first half of the paper.
6 Please refer to Hausler (2002) for greater details on these issues.
7 For more details on FSAP and its functioning readers are referred to Huang and Wajid (2002).
8 They are Argentina, Brazil, Chile, China, India, Indonesia, Korea (Republic of), Malaysia, Mexico, Russian Federation, Thailand and Turkey.
9 Statistics used here come from Schmukler and Zoido-Lobaton (2001).

References

Das, Dilip K. 1989. "Brady Plan and the International Banks: A Cautious Reception," *The Business Standard*, Bombay, August 24. p. 6.

Das, Dilip K. 2002. "Globalization: A guide for the Concerned Policy Maker," The University of Warwick. CSGR Working Paper No. 91/02.

Baldwin, R.E. and P. Martin. 1999. "Two Waves of Globalization: Superficial Similarities, Fundamental Differences," Cambridge. Mass. National Bureau of Economic Research. NBER Working Paper No. 6904.

Crockett, A. 2000. "How should Financial Market Regulators Respond to the New Challenges of Global Economic Integration?" *Global Economic Integration: Opportunities and Challenges*, Kansas City, USA. The Federal Reserve Bank of Kansas City.

Eichengreen, B. and M. Bordo. 2001. "Crisis Now and Then: What Lessons from the Last Era of Financial Globalization?" unpublished paper, University of California at Berkeley and Rutgers University.

Frankel, J. 2000. "Globalization of the Economy," Cambridge. Mass. National Bureau of Economic Research. NBER Working Paper No. 7858.

Hausler, G. 2002. "The Globalization of Finance," *Finance and Development*, 29(1) 14–17.

Huang, H. and S.K. Wajid. 2002. "Financial Stability in the World of Global Finance," *Finance and Development*, 29(1) 18–24.

International Monetary Fund (IMF). 2000. "International Capital Markets: Challenges, Prospects and Opportunities," Washington, DC.

Kaminsky, G. and S. Schmukler. 2001. "On Financial Booms and Crashes: Regional Patterns, Time Patterns, and Financial Liberalization," Washington, DC. The World Bank. (Processed.)

Keohane, R.O. and J.S. Nye. 2001. "Introduction," in Keohane and Nye (eds) *Governance in a Globalizing World*, Washington, DC. Brookings Institution Press. pp. 1–41.

Krueger, A.O. 2002. *A New Approach to Sovereign Debt Restructuring*. Washington, DC. International Monetary Fund. April.

Lipsey, R.E. 1999. "The Role of Foreign Direct Investment in International Capital Flows," Cambridge. Mass. National Bureau of Economic Research. NBER Working Paper No. 7094.

Mundell, R.A. 2000. "A Reconsideration of the Twentieth Century," *American Economic Review*, 90(3) 327–40.

Obstfeld, M. and K. Rogoff. 2000. "The Six Major Puzzles in International Macroeconomics: Is There a Common Cause?," in The NBER Macroeconomic Annual, Cambridge. National Bureau of Economic Research. pp. 124–48.

Obstfeld, M. and A.M. Taylor. 1998. "The Great Depression as a Watershed: International Capital Mobility Over the Long Run," in M.D. Bordo, C. Goldin and N. White (eds) *The Defining Moment: The Great Depression and the American Economy in the Twentieth Century*, Chicago. University of Chicago Press. pp. 353–402.

Okina, O., M. Shirakawa and S. Shiratsuka. 1999. "Financial Market Globalization: Present and Future," *Monetary and Economic Studies*, 17(3) 48–82. Bank of Japan. Institute for Monetary and Economic Studies.

Schmukler, S.L. and P. Zoido-Lobaton. 2001. "Financial Globalization: Opportunities and Challenges for Developing Countries," Washington, DC. The World Bank. (Processed.)

Taylor, A.M. 1998. "International Capital Mobility in History: The Saving–Investment Relationship," *Journal of Development Economics*, 57(1) 147–84.

Tesar, L. and I. Werner. 1998. "Internalization of Securities markets Since the 1987 Crash," in R.E. Litan and A. Santomero (eds) *Brookings-Wharton Papers on Financial Services*, Washington, DC. Brookings Institution Press. pp. 281–372.

The World Bank. 2001. *Finance for Growth: Policy Choices in a Volatile World*. Washington, DC. Policy Research Report.

World Bank, 2002. *Globalization, Growth and Poverty*, New York, Oxford University Press.

3 Managing globalization

Macroeconomic, financial sector and exchange rate volatility*

Dilip K. Das

Financial globalization and volatility

This chapter has reviewed the opportunities and threats for the emerging market economies posed by globalization. Its premise is that powerful economic and non-economic forces are likely to render the world economy even more globalized in the future than it is today. There is serendipity in globalization and several emerging market economies benefited immensely from it during the last quarter century. However, there is an imperious need for globalization to be handled in a pragmatic, clairvoyant and sagacious manner. Otherwise its negative effects can seriously destabilize an economy. The primary focus of the chapter is financial globalization, although it does encapsulate the other related aspects as well.

As set out in Chapter 2, initially, members of the Organization for Economic Co-operation and Development (OECD) used to be the most active participants in the financial globalization process. They also used to be the principal players in the global financial markets. Over the last quarter century, financial globalization has expanded to the emerging market economies. This set of economies are somewhat imprecisely defined as the newly industrialized economies[1] (NIEs) and middle-income developing countries in which governments and corporations "have access to private international capital markets, or can attract institutional portfolio investment, or both (WB, 2002)".

The World Bank distinguishes between "more globalized" and "less-globalized" developing economies (WB, 2002). To this end, trade to GDP ratio was used as an indicator. Developing countries were arranged in terms of increase in trade to GDP ratio between the 1970s and 1990s. The top one-third, or twenty-four countries of this list, were christened more globalized countries.[2] If the OECD economies and the NIEs are added to these countries, the larger group of financially globalized economies becomes comparable to the one proposed in the preceding paragraph.

* I would like to acknowledge that this chapter grew out of collaboration with Barry Eichengreen, University of California, Berkeley, which in turn evolved out of a background paper for the Asian Development Outlook 2001. This is a revised, rewritten and abridged version.

The globalizing developing economies have gradually removed, albeit not all, restrictions over their capital account transactions. In the aftermath of the financial crises of the 1990s, in some cases capital account liberalization was reverted. Global capital flows, including capital flows to emerging market economies, have recorded dramatic increases during the last quarter century, and particularly during the decade of the 1990s. The quantitative dimension of these trans-border flows has been discussed in Chapter 1. Greater supply of investible resources is one of the benefits of integrating with the global economy. As the neoclassical economics tells us, superior resource allocation is a more important benefit of financial globalization, which in turn improves global welfare. Thus, financial globalization can potentially bring benefits to all kinds of economies, small, large, developing, developed.

In the recent past, globalization has been associated with financial crisis carrying devastating economic and social costs. As economies integrate with the global economy, they inevitably become exposed to economic and financial disturbances from across the border.[3] There is a perception that financially open economies are more volatile and that financial market integration makes them susceptible to contagion-related spillovers from national, regional and global financial crises.[4]

Over the long haul, volatility tends to decline following liberalization and integration with the global economy. Stability results from diversification of asset portfolios and healthier development of the financial sector. However, the fact that liberalized, open and globally integrated economies are more stable and less volatile over the long haul provides little solace because the very process of liberalizing increases volatility and the risk of crisis. Therefore, World Bank (WB, 2002) emphasizes the distinction between *being open* on the one hand and *becoming open* on the other. While the former is associated with greater stability, the latter under certain circumstances can lead to financial and exchange rate crises, having high costs. This is not to imply that the cost of globalization necessarily swamps its benefits, but high costs do call for a pressing need to develop institutions and pursue policies aimed at limiting volatility and minimizing its consequences.[5]

Like trans-border financial flows, financial crises are not new. It has been debated whether the contemporary crises are more frequent and problematic than those in the past. A study of the duration, frequency and deleterious impact over output of financial crises was conducted by Bordo *et al.* (2001). To this end, they examined financial crises over a long period and concluded that the crises during the contemporary period of financial globalization are more frequent than those in the earlier eras. However, they found little evidence of crisis becoming longer in duration or output losses becoming larger than those in the past. In the contemporary period, the degree of integration with the global economy is greater than that in the past. Therefore, the impact crises on output losses should have been worse than in the past. Also, the crises should have been of longer duration. A likely possibility is that institutional innovations of the contemporary period – at both local and global levels – have prevented crises from having more severe impact over the affected economies.

Volatility and its impact

Large literature exists on the causal factors behind volatility and crises. Among other factors, it stresses the contribution of domestic factors to the crisis scenario. For instance, both poor and erroneous microeconomic and macroeconomic policies have contributed to banking crises in the past. It was also observed that financial crises were determined not only by ex post value of various macroeconomic indicators (like actual deficits) but other factors that generate large prospective deficits. Reported fiscal deficit of an economy may be reasonable but if the implicit policy is to bailout failing banks, the prospective deficit numbers may be much worse and lead to a perception of an impending crisis. During the Asian crises, economies either had fiscal surpluses or reasonable deficits, but financial markets perceived them as deteriorating economies because of their implicit liabilities related to guarantees to the banking system (Caprio and Klingebiel, 1999; Das, 2000; Burnside *et al.*, 2001).

During the initial phase of liberalization of the financial sector, or the *becoming open* phase as noted above, volatility is caused by vulnerable fundamentals and institutional weaknesses. Kaminsky and Schmukler (2001) have pointed out that the process of financial liberalization accentuates a financial market cycle. They found that in a typical emerging economy financial market, stock prices are doubled during the eighteen months before the price cycle reaches a peak. This is typically followed by a 20 percent decline over the first six months. This scenario changes during the first cycle after financial liberalization. Stock prices triple during the same period and having peaked, they decline by 50 percent over the first six months. This shows the extent of stock market volatility that follows financial liberalization. If the financial institutions are not robust enough to manage this volatility, a crisis can ensue.

Sound fundamentals and robust institutions do not always assure stability. Financial and other asset market bubbles can adversely affect and destabilize economies that otherwise have sound fundamentals and robust institutions.[6] Other comparable market aberrations are "irrational exuberance," herding behavior, speculative attacks and market crashes. For instance, if market participants perceive that exchange rate has stayed at an unrealistic level for sometime and is not supported by market and economic fundamentals *in their perception*, they decide that it is unsustainable. A speculative attack may be launched against the currency, leading to a self-fulfilling balance-of-payments crisis. Similarly, moral hazard can generate a crisis, notwithstanding sound fundamentals and robust institutions. In an environment of implicit government guarantee, overborrowing and overlending frequently takes place when economies are liberalizing. This creates a situation of volatility in a liberalizing economy making it vulnerable to a crisis (Obstfeld and Rogoff, 1996; McKinnon and Pill, 1997; Das, 2000). Thus, the *becoming open* period of an emerging market economy has serious pitfalls.

In a globalized financial market, external factors can also cause volatility. They are known to aggravate fragilities of domestic banking and the financial system. They can destabilize an economy with sound fundamentals, robust institutions and without market aberrations. Having globalized its domestic financial markets, when an economy becomes dependent on external finances, sudden shift in the financial flows can create serious financial difficulties and economic downturns. Such a shift has no relation with market or economic fundamentals in the country in question. Only external factors, like movements in world interest rates, are enough to cause it. This one factor was a principal motivator behind capital flows to Asian and Latin American emerging economies in the 1990s (Calvo *et al.*, 1996). Frankel and Rose (1996) have empirically demonstrated the role played by foreign interest rate movements in determining the financial crises of the 1990s.

Herding behavior of market participants caused serious volatility in the past. It forced a crisis situation to spread from one economy to another, sometimes making it a region-wide crisis. This was the so-called contagion effect. Normal economic linkages did not explain the magnitude of movements in exchange rates and stock prices across the countries. They affected countries that were neither closely linked nor that had any similarity in economic and financial indicators. The reason was that crisis in one country changed market expectations in others. Herding behavior caused panic among the investors, therefore capital exited from even unrelated economies. Contagion works as an irrational external shock. It can occur anytime when perception of investors changes.

The costs of macroeconomic volatility tend to be high. Easterly and Kraay (1999) found that an increase in standard deviation of GDP growth reduces the annual average rate of per capita growth by one-fifth of 1 percent per annum. Inter-American Development Bank (IDB) (1995) controlled for the other determinants of secular rate of growth that are standard in the empirical literature and found that growth rate is negatively corelated to volatility of terms-of-trade, volatility of real exchange rate, volatility of monetary policy and the volatility of fiscal policy. Of these, terms-of-trade volatility and exchange rate volatility were associated with the largest negative effect on GDP growth (Easterly and Kraay, 1999; Guillaumont *et al.*, 1999).

The negative association of volatility with growth reflects adverse impacts on both, productivity and investment. The former suffers when predictable changes in relative prices render one technology appropriate but volatility leads firms to invest in another. In the face of relative price uncertainty, firms may hedge their bets by investing in several alternative technologies, all of which may be less efficient and productive than the optimal technology. Economies with high volatility are also known to be economies with low investment rates. This reflects both the reluctance and inability of investors and entrepreneurs to commit to projects when relative prices and macroeconomic conditions change in unpredictable directions (IDB, 1995).

So far we have only focused on the impact of volatility on growth and ignored a major source of volatility, that is, financial and economic crises. Crises are incompatible with growth. They lead to *ad hoc* and stop–go policies, interfere with the operation of domestic financial system, cause distress in corporate sector and force governments to cut investment. Bordo *et al.* (2001) computed that a typical post-1972 crisis cost the country a cumulative of 8 percent GDP. This amounts to 1–2 years of growth endeavors for a rapidly growing economy. Different kinds of crises have different impact in terms of loss of output. The estimates made by Bordo *et al.* (2001) suggested that output costs ranged from 6 percent for currency and banking crises to 19 percent for the twin crises having banking and currency components.

Volatility adversely impacts social indicators like income distribution, poverty and educational attainment. The poor, unskilled and uneducated suffer disproportionately from volatility because they are unable to hedge their incomes and diversify their investments. Empirical studies of cross-sections of countries revealed that volatility of real GDP has a strong negative effect on income distribution. Also, countries with more volatile rates of inflation display greater income inequality and poor values of Gini coefficients.[7] Crisis and policy adjustments that follow, are much worse for income inequality than mere volatility. The same applies to poverty rates. Those living below or near the poverty line work in sectors that are affected by volatility and crises. Also, crisis-related reductions in social spending disproportionately affect this category. Those living near the poverty line have little savings, worst collateral and most tenuous access to credit or insurance. Most of all volatility and crises exacerbate poverty through their negative impact on growth.

Elasticity of poverty with respect to income rises sharply during the periods of crisis. Dollar and Kraay (2001) found that in Indonesia during the 1997–98 crisis, the rate of increase of poverty was ten times the rate of decline in income. Similarly, in Korea (Republic of) the poverty rate more than doubled during the same period.[8] Crises were found to affect educational attainment by forcing children out of schools so that they could contribute to household incomes – many never returned. This effect was found to be more pronounced in poor countries.[9]

Managing volatility

Financial globalization can be responsible for volatility and crisis, which in turn have painful economic and social costs. It is important to develop policies and institutions that contain the deleterious effects of globalization so that global welfare improvement is the principal, or only, outcome of globalization. Many economists have addressed the issue of limiting volatility in globalizing emerging markets and safeguarding against crisis. While there is no consensus among contributors, they do agree on several points.

That foreign direct investment (FDI) and portfolio investment augment investable capital stock and have a salutary effect on growth is well accepted, but the latter have some questionable traits. When capital account is liberalized, allowing portfolio investment into the domestic economy, theoretically it should relax financial growth constraints and deepen capital markets. It should also make FDI more attractive by providing opportunities to hedge exposures and to repatriate profits. However, in practice preexisting policy and market distortions interact with portfolio investment flows heightening volatility and risk of a crisis.

How distortion free is the domestic economic environment is of material importance. In the industrial economies where generally policy and market distortions are minimum, portfolio investment inflows are known to stimulate financial deepening and growth. However, they were found to have a perverse effect on the financial sector in many emerging market economies where there were enough distortions (Klein and Olivei, 1999).

As globalization progresses, it will become progressively difficult to continue statutory restrictions on capital account without disturbing and constraining other forms of economic activity. This would make it imperative to coordinate financial liberalization with the elimination of distortions. A lack of such a coordination is sure to heighten volatility and crisis risk. To this end, if the following policy measures are adopted they will go a long way in dampening volatility and minimizing the risk of a crisis.

Strengthening financial sector

Hindsight reveals that during the 1980s and 1990s capital account was prematurely liberalized in many emerging market economies. Economic and financial distortions should have been eliminated and financial sector should have been strengthened before taking such a measure. Policy reforms like removal of implicit guarantees, imposition of hard budget constraints on financial institutions, rationalization of prudential supervision on financial institutions and adequate capitalization of financial institutions, would have helped in reducing the probability of a crisis.[10] Capital account liberalization should follow, not precede, recapitalization of banks. The distortions enumerated above made the crises of this period more acute than those of the past. Conservative as it may appear, a safe and prudent strategy is to keep capital account restriction in place until prudential supervision is strengthened and implicit guarantees on loans are dismantled.

Liberalizing FDI

FDI is not only known to come in packaged with technological and managerial know-how, but it is also known to least likely aggravate fragilities of domestic banking and financial system. It is neither associated with capital flight nor with creditor panic. Therefore, liberalizing capital account for FDI should be the first priority. Although this seems intuitive, majority of governments did not heed this advice. Some of them were reluctant to do so even after a crisis.[11] Although there are skeptics, FDI is more stable than other kinds of capital flows.[12] It is obvious that an investor cannot unbolt and lift all the tangible components of his factory to join the herd of panicking creditors.

Internationalizing the banking system

Closely associated with liberalization of FDI at an early stage is the process of opening for external financial institutions. Entry of foreign banks is a low-cost way of upgrading the risk management capability of domestic banking sector through knowledge spillover from the foreign banks to the domestic ones. As the foreign banks are supervised by their home-country prudential supervisors, it raises the general quality of prudential supervision. Similarly, better-capitalized foreign banks are averse to excessive risk. Thus, they upgrade the domestic financial markets making further capital account liberalization possible. However, bank-to-bank lending needs to be discouraged because it is likely to lead to excessive capital inflows, not compatible with the objective of containing volatility.[13]

Using market-friendly instruments

In order to avoid excessive capital inflows from the international banking sector, market-friendly instruments should be used. Creating a large bureaucracy at the level of the finance ministry or the central bank would be cumbersome, expensive, inefficient and conducive to rent-seeking. Therefore, the Chilean approach to capital import tax won a lot of admirers. Chile required a non-interest-bearing deposit of one year from the investors seeking to borrow capital from the international capital markets. As the deposit had to be maintained for a year, the implicit tax fell more heavily on the investors who wanted a short-maturity loan compared to those who were in for the long period. The Chilean scheme was considered transparent, without any administrative discretion. Effectiveness of this measure generated enormous debate. Ulan (2000) provides a comprehensive review of this literature.

As the short-term inflows pose a greater risk of volatility and crisis, Chilean scheme of a holding-period can be justified as a form of prudential supervision. This measure can prove to be futile if the domestic non-financial corporations are free to borrow abroad and pass the proceeds on to the banks. Such a scheme should be regarded only as a transitional policy to be pursued until more conventional forms of prudential supervision and regulation have been devised. Chile treated this measure as a transitional measure and abandoned it in the late 1990s.

Liberalizing stock and bond markets

In simplistic terms, one can say that withdrawal of foreign deposits from banks destabilizes the system more than liquidating stocks and bonds. The latter is only reflected in the reduced prices of securities, which is relatively less destabilizing to the financial system.[14] When banks and firms fund themselves by both the means, that is, floating bonds and issuing short-term debt, interest rate variations destabilize their balance sheets much less. Likewise, when they fund themselves by issuing bonds denominated in foreign as well as domestic currencies, exchange rate variations destabilize their balance sheets to a much lesser extent. Thus, diversifying sources of corporate debt by developing bond markets, on the one hand, and developing stock market to diversify the sources of capital itself, on the other, are healthy developments for the balance sheets of domestic banks and firms. Well-developed stock and bond markets, by allowing opportunities to diversify sources of capital, contribute to reducing volatility of the financial system. However, foreign access to domestic stocks and bond markets should be liberalized before freeing domestic banks to fund themselves offshore.

The above scenario is somewhat idealized because in reality securities markets take time to develop. This applies to both stocks and bond markets alike. Historically, markets in corporate bonds are born before deep and liquid equity markets. The reason is that the informational requirements for corporate bonds markets are less. However, even these markets grow after deep and reliable equity markets develop in benchmark assets, like treasury bonds. Transactions in the benchmark assets provide liquidity and minimum efficient scale as well as an important reference point for other issues (Baskin and Miranti, 1997). Requirement for development of deep and liquid markets in treasury bonds is a government with a record of sound and stable macroeconomic and financial policies. When such a record is absent, banks become the captive customers of the government bond placements. This status of captive customers is not good for the balance sheets of the banks, therefore, in return they receive favors like implicit bank guarantees from the governments. It has been noted above that these guarantees are an invitation to volatility.

Creating active stock and bond markets is a difficult, demanding and time consuming task. In industrial economies it took decades. The development process entails putting in place a regulatory framework mandating the disclosure of accurate and up-to-date financial information, the use of recognized auditing and accounting standards, penalties for insider trading and statutes protecting the rights of minority shareholders. East Asian economies had the advantage of latecomers and they developed their stock and bond markets in a relatively shorter period. The emerging market economies that are now trying to develop them can telescope the process by importing proven regulatory, accounting and auditing techniques.

Accumulating reserves

They provide a cushion against volatility. Some economies were able to ward off crisis by accumulating large reserves.[15] Academics and policy mandarins alike have supported the strategy of having such a cushion because it works as an insurance against disruptive domestic financial effects as well as abrupt capital outflows.[16] One suggestion was that emerging market should hold reserves equal to total short-term liability, which is going to fall due, for repayment over the next twelve months (Greenspan, 1999). An International Monetary Fund (IMF) study recommended holding of even larger reserves, as much as twice that suggested by Greenspan (Bussiere and Mulder, 1999). For economies that run chronic current account deficits, even this level is inadequate.

However, this advice has been questioned for several reasons. First, large reserves are small compared to the liquidity of the markets. Second, they can provide dangerous encouragement to carry trade and may end up making a crisis larger in terms of financial volume. Third, holding reserves against short-term liabilities tends to be expensive as US treasury bonds bear lower interest rates than Korean, Mexican or Thai bank deposits.

Arranging commercial credits

Another method of ensuring liquidity at a short notice is to negotiate commercial credit lines. These credit lines could be tapped in times when investors' sentiment plummets and capital withdrawal starts. When international banks and investors refuse to roll over their loans, the authorities can use these credit lines as the lender-of-last-resort. Again, for a fee, these lines of credit can be rolled over and made into a stand-by arrangement.

These credit facilities do not have the "no adverse material change clause," which allows banks to back out at the time of a veritable crisis. When problem of asymmetric information creates volatility in the financial, stock or currency market, these lines of credit can partially overcome the burden. They can help make the economy flash signals of its creditworthiness to the global investors. These credit facilities are not available to all the emerging markets. Evidence of institutional reforms as well as sound macroeconomic and financial policies are essential to qualify for them. For commercial banks credit quality matters.

For a commitment fee, Argentina, Mexico and Indonesia negotiated credit lines with international banks and drew credits when there was a pressing need of hard currency.[17] Of the three, first two economies took strong measures to strengthen their financial institutions before they began negotiations with the commercial banks.

Strengthening fiscal and monetary institutions

Building credible policy-making institutions are necessary, although not sufficient, for limiting volatility in a financially globalizing world. Risk of a crisis is inversely proportional to the credibility of fiscal and monetary institutions. Over the years, if these institutions have accumulated sufficient credibility and goodwill of the market, it would do much of the stabilizing work for them. This applies to both, fiscal and monetary institutions. Sometimes able policy makers of high credibility help in imparting their reputation to the institutions. Alternatively, institutions can be so designed as to follow the predetermined mandates, no matter who runs them. In the monetary area, an autonomous central bank can be given a mandate, that of maintaining price stability, and left to run its show. Likewise, for fiscal policy an independent fiscal authority can be created and made responsible for setting a ceiling of fiscal deficit as well as a set of rules for cutting expenditure in the event when the limit is crossed.

Managing exchange rates

In a financially integrating world managing national currency is a daunting challenge. It encapsulates some of the most difficult issues posed by financial globalization. In the next section we focus on country policies chosen unilaterally at the national level.

Vanishing middle ground

Experiences of the 1990s have led to a general consensus that intermediate arrangements turn out to be problematic in a financially integrating world. These intermediate arrangements include soft pegs, pegged-but-adjustable rates, crawling bands and the like. Why is it so? If financial markets are globalized, it becomes difficult for the monetary authorities to support an untenable currency peg. This is because the resources of a globalized market far outstrip the reserves of any central bank. Defending a shaky peg under these circumstances will require raising interest rates and restricting domestic credit, both of which are costly to the economy.[18] However, if there are any weaknesses in the economic indicators, which are likely to make it difficult to raise interest rates – high unemployment rates, heavy burden of short-term debt repayment, or an undercapitalized banking system – the market will be quick to notice that and a speculative attack will follow.

In a democratic country, top priority cannot be assigned to defending a currency peg. If a government does decide to bear (or inflict) the combined of pain of high interest rates and austerity policies in the interest of the long-term benefits to the economy, it does earn the reputation for following policies of exchange rate and prices stability. But when the economy comes under market attack, the government may find that the game is not worth the candle. The cost of adopting the twin policies would be austerity in the form of high unemployment, more financial and corporate failures and a weaker economy in general. When this is the outcome, the authorities are forced to abandon the currency peg. Markets know that the authorities attach importance to other aspects of economic performance in addition to exchange rate stability. Therefore, they have an incentive to force the issue.[19]

Prior to the spread of democratization, governments could use their policy instruments to minimize unemployment and foster long-term economic growth. They could assign top priority of maintaining the currency peg. This is no longer possible. Changes making for exchange rate flexibility are not only financial and technological but also social and political. They render currency pegs an inappropriate policy as they rob the governments the capacity to defend them. In globalized financial markets the currency pegs give the markets incentives and ammunition with which to attack them.

A typical emerging market economy is likely to find it hard to maintain an exchange rate peg or band in the face of open capital markets. Many of them are still trying to find a strong export niche in the global markets, rendering them vulnerable to terms-of-trade shocks. Their financial systems are small relative to the global markets, or even to the assets of a handful of hedge funds, mutual funds or investment banks. Their banking systems are not capable of withstanding sharp hikes in interest rates. Finally, their political systems are incapable of delivering a broad-based, stable consensus in favor of exchange rate stabilization over other economic and social goals.

It is argued that depreciation of a pegged currency can enhance competitiveness and stimulate growth.[20] In emerging market economies, this may not be the case. The Mexican and Asian crisis point to the contradictory effect of depreciation. As the emerging market economies borrow in foreign currency, depreciation increases the debt service and worsens the financial condition of domestic banks and firms. As the banks and firms do not hedge their foreign exchange exposures, they collapse with the currency band.

Why the twin issues of abandoning the peg on time and hedging of foreign exposure are left unattended? As for the first, authorities are tempted to put off exiting from the peg for another day because they build their entire monetary policy around the maintenance of the band. It is believed that the peg anchors the monetary policy. Abandoning it may mean a shock to the confidence they are trying to build. Also, authorities cannot announce anything in this context. If they announce abandoning the peg, it will ignite the beginning of currency traders' betting process against the currency.

When the authorities are committed to a band or peg, banks and firms do not hedge their foreign exchange exposure. Their commitment prevents exchange rates to bounce around too much beyond certain limits. To defend the peg, governments are forced to assert that prospects of change are nonexistent. Given such an assurance, how many finance managers will be rewarded for purchasing costly exchange rate insurance? A pegged rate is a logical and irresistible inventive to accumulate unhedged foreign exchange debts. An unhedged foreign debt implies a crisis if the band or hedge collapses.

Indonesia provides an excellent illustration of authorities' commitment encouraging unhedged foreign exchange exposure (Goelthom, 1999). Prior to the Asian crisis it was operating on a crawling band allowing for fluctuations of ± 4 percent against a basket of currencies. It had high interest rates, so typical of an emerging market economy. High rates make emerging markets attractive for foreign investors. The large capital inflows that followed in Indonesia pushed the rupiah toward the strong end of the band. The commitment of the authorities to limit exchange rate fluctuations was obvious. The strength of the currency lent credibility to the commitment. Therefore, domestic banks and corporations accumulated large unhedged foreign exchange exposures. When Thailand devalued the bath, contagion affected Indonesia also and capital flows reversed. In mid-October,[21] the rupiah went from the strong edge of the band to the weak edge in one day – while the band was widened to 6 percent. The 12 percent depreciation in one day was a sharp shock to Indonesian corporations with unhedged exposure. Their solvency was cast in doubt. The stability of the economy came under question. Furthermore, interest rate increases to defend the currency were not an option because of the financial distress in the corporate sector and banking system. Subsequently the band was abandoned and exchange rate plummeted further. Given the damage to the economy, it fell like a stone, as much as 10 percent a day. This stylized scenario shows how fragile currency bands can be as well as how high the cost of their collapse is.

A valid theoretical query is, why the prerequisite for the smooth operation of floating rates and inflexible pegs are also not the prerequisites for the smooth operation of intermediate regimes. For a well functioning – one with limited volatility and providing a framework conducive to economic growth – floating exchange rate regime fiscal policy must be strengthened, debt management and prudential regulation must be upgraded, and a coherent and credible monetary policy must be installed. Without these prerequisites, the floating exchange rate is likely to fluctuate erratically. On the other end of the spectrum, for a currency board or dollarization to be conducive to stability and growth, the same set of prerequisites must be in place. Otherwise the rigid peg will bequeath unemployment and inflation, which in turn will undermine public support for and therefore the credibility of the monetary policy. This will heighten the risk of a banking crisis.

Why the same set of prerequisites cannot support an intermediate regime like a crawling peg, a narrow band or a target zone? Is it not sufficient for the maintenance of an intermediate regime to have fiscal, financial and monetary policies to be consistent with the exchange rate target? One sees no reason why. Countries that failed to successfully operate intermediate regimes did so because their monetary and fiscal policies were too expensive. This is incompatible with an adjustable peg. They failed because poor debt management, inadequate prudential regulation and lax supervision rendered their financial systems too fragile to survive the requisite levels of interest rates. Thus, intermediate regimes did not work, not because of the lack of viability of the model, but because the implementation was inadequate.

If a country commits either to abandoning or adopting a currency peg, there will be a strong incentive for policy makers and market participants to bring their affairs into conformance with the new regime. It is not so with the intermediate regime. Incentives for adaptation for the policy makers or market participants will be less. To take one example, banks will have limited incentives to raise their capital standards or risk management practices because they would think that any exchange rate related limits on the capacity of the authorities to act as lenders of last resort are temporary. Likewise, debt managers and fiscal policy makers will also have mixed incentives for adjusting to the imperatives of the policy regime. Lack of adaptation will make it harder for the authorities to defend the exchange rate when it comes under attack. Thus, the failure of markets and policies to conform to the imperatives of an intermediate regime is more than a manifestation of sub-optimal policy. It is an essential feature of a hybrid regime.

Choosing between the options

The clear choice is between a free float and a currency peg, which are taken to mean an option between credibility and flexibility. When a hard peg is adopted, the domestic currency is anchored to a particular currency. The central bank of the country whose currency provides the external anchor comes to have a great deal of influence over the domestic monetary policy. It comes to acquire all the credibility accumulated by the anchor-currency issuer. The commitment to the peg receives political acquiescence by way of a constitutional amendment of some nature. A mandate is issued to the central bank to defend the rate, which works as a barrier to exit. Its salutary effect is greater credibility of the currency and its exchange rate, minimizing the speculative pressure. External stability enhances access to foreign capital. The rigidity of a currency peg can be harmful to an economy. Fixed exchange rate regimes are vulnerable to asymmetric shocks. There are severe costs associated with hanging on to a pegged, overvalued exchange rate. The currency peg between the peso and the dollar caused Argentina's 2001–02 crisis (*The Economist*, 2002).

As the name indicates, floating rates maximize flexibility with which authorities can use monetary policy for stabilization purposes. If the need be, the central banks can work as a lender of last resort to financial market. However, there is little agreement over the value of these benefits of floating exchange rates. There are few stabilizing effects of floating exchange rate when shocks are real rather than monetary and a country's external obligations are denominated in foreign currencies. By the same token, when domestic banks and firms incur foreign currency denominated debts the capacity of the central bank to act as a lender of last resort is questionable.[22]

Which of the two options would be apt for most countries? The diversity of economic structure and different stages of economic and financial development make any generalization impossible. For an illustration, let us take Asian economies. As most emerging market economies in Asia are quite open, standard optimum currency area arguments favor adoption of hard pegs. But the diversification of Asian exports across markets – and their tendency of selling into the Japanese and the US markets simultaneously – make hard peg to any one of the two currencies (the yen or the dollar) illogical. As these economies have relatively underdeveloped domestic bond markets, they borrow long term mainly in foreign currency. Sharp exchange rate changes can wreck havoc with the domestic currency cost of external debt services. Therefore, a flexible exchange rate will make external borrowing difficult and therefore it is not quite the optimal currency regime for these countries either. But this argument is somewhat weak because savings rates in most of these economies are high and there is no pressing need for foreign capital. Banks and firms seeking foreign exchange resources can obtain it at home from the banking system or utilize supplier credit. Thus, the argument that hard pegs are needed by Asian economies to enhance access to foreign credits is not compelling. A balanced view in this regard is that the real side of many emerging market economies in Asia is relatively flexible, the value of monetary autonomy for them is less. By international standards policies and policy-making institutions in these countries are relatively credible, therefore their capacity to exploit the advantages of policy credibility is greater. Insofar as there are so many crosscutting considerations, not all of these economies would find it suitable to have the same kind of exchange rate regime. As stated earlier, possibility of a continued diversity in the region in currency regimes is the greatest.

Catalyzing institutional changes

Compared to the analysis of the nature of the institutions required for stability and growth in the globalized world, less attention has been paid to the *process* by which those institutions are developed. The literature on this issue distinguished three levels at which institution building can take place: local, regional and global. In this section we review the arguments for fostering institutional change at these three levels.

Economists tend to assume the existence of appropriate institutions. Davis and North (1971) posited that if certain set of institutions is considered efficient, they would develop in response to the latent demand. The demand will cause the birth of these institutions and their growth. In concrete terms, the assumption is that if new technologies generated by start-up firms are the motor of growth, and if supporting their development requires financial markets capable of providing venture capital and bidding for initial public offerings, then a market-based financial system will spring up in response to the profit incentives perceived by the aspiring venture capitalists. If to attract FDI, countries must adopt demand corporate disclosure standards and legal systems providing strong protection to creditor rights, then they will do so in order to prevent FDI from being diverted to regions that are quicker to respond.

However, this is only an assumption and may not work in reality. In fact, it may not be so at all. Under most conditions, demand need not elicit a corresponding supply. Institutions are coordinating mechanisms, coordinating the actions of different economic and social agents. They do so by providing standards of socially constructive behavior. As they work as standards, they are a source of network externalities. Like any technology that throws off network externalities, once established they tend to become locked in. Therefore, institutional change needs to be catalyzed by the "regime leaders" (Campos and Root, 1996).

Constructive role of crises

Inertia is a part of the institutional character. Radical institutional change is an exception, not the rule. Large transformations require that the political and economic system be displaced from its equilibrium. It follows that radical change often times occurs in response to major shocks – crises, for example.[23] By definition, crises disrupt the operation of existing institutions. That disruption creates a vacuum in which new arrangements can develop.[24] More generally, the suboptimal performance of existing institutions made clear by a crisis can foster the consensus needed for agreement on changes in prevailing arrangements. Thus, the political and economic crises of the 1940s and 1950s are commonly credited with creating a hothouse environment conducive to the growth of the institutions that served Asia so well in its period of rapid economic growth. Countries like Korea and Taiwan emerged from the Second World War and from the Asian conflicts that erupted in its wake in a parlous economic state.

In the wake of the financial crises of 1997–98, it is again clear that crisis can catalyze reforms.[25] This is evident in the steps taken by Asian emerging market economies to update and strengthen their financial institutions, with the aim of restoring investor confidence and also the long-run goal of equipping themselves with the institutional prerequisites for navigating a world of global finance.

Prudential supervision and regulation have been strengthened, and new rules have been adopted to encourage arms-length dealing between financial institutions and their customers. Governments have encouraged the development of bond markets long suppressed in favor of bank-based intermediation. Foreign investment has been liberalized in all countries in the region. Thailand replaced its Alien Business Law with new provisions allowing foreign firms to hold up to 100 percent equity in Thai banks, and thirty-nine sectors have been opened to increased foreign participation. Korea, meanwhile, opened real estate, securities dealing and other financing business to foreign investors and granted foreigners the right to purchase 100 percent of equity in domestic firms.

East Asian countries have taken comprehensive action to facilitate mergers and acquisitions (M&A), both domestic and international.[26] Indonesia and Thailand have adopted significant legislative changes to their bankruptcy systems. In the second half of 1998, Indonesia created a specialized commercial court with jurisdiction over bankruptcy-related matters and adopted an automatic stay provision similar to that provided for under the US bankruptcy code. In Thailand, new bankruptcy legislation pushed through over political opposition had a decidedly positive impact on the equity valuation of financial and non-financial companies (Foley, 1999). Such reforms can be seen as prerequisites for growth and stability in a financially globalized world. While financial reform has long been on Asia's agenda, it is hard to imagine such rapid progress in the absence of the crisis. To be sure, while crisis can breed reform, reform without crisis is to be preferred. The question is how it is best achieved.

Conclusions and summary

This chapter has reviewed the opportunities and threats for the emerging market economies posed by globalization. Its premise is that powerful economic and non-economic forces are likely to render the world economy even more globalized in the future than it is today. Globalization has been rolled back before but only under extraordinary circumstances. And the costs today for the world economy were a sizeable number of countries to turn their back on global markets could exceed even those incurred in the 1930s, given the decline in the cost of international transportation and communication, the spread of global production networks, and the progress made in drawing countries and regions once only marginally integrated into the world economy, more deeply into the global system. Countries, their governments and their citizens have substantial investments in globalization. Significant costs have been sunk, making it less likely that the clock will be turned back. Contingency planning is always prudent, but extensive planning for the disintegration of international markets makes little sense if this is in fact an extremely remote possibility.

The challenge for national economies is therefore how to capitalize on the opportunities for growth and development afforded by globalization while at the same time minimizing the risks. In an obvious sense this means following appropriate policies: stable macroeconomic policies, prudent financial policies and sound regulatory policies. But the appropriate policies are easier to describe than to implement. And their specifics are likely to vary over time. The more fundamental problem is thus how to develop institutions with the capacity to determine appropriate policies, implement them and stick to them until circumstances change.

Institutions with this capacity are likely to have the following characteristics. They combine insulation from capture with accountability to their principals. They facilitate the development of a social consensus on goals and instruments and an equitable sharing of the benefits from their implementation. They allow governments to make credible commitments but also provide escape clauses designed to allow those commitments to be modified or revoked in the event of fundamental changes in circumstance.

Globalization also has a dark side, as observed from the crises of the 1990s and that of 2001.[27] Capitalizing on globalization means preventing its risks from disrupting growth and development and from engendering a backlash against open markets. This means tailoring policies to contain the heightened risk of crisis and the volatility created by the integration and liberalization of financial markets. It means creating a social safety net to support those who are left behind. In a succinct manner, this chapter provides several strategic guidelines for successfully integrating with the global economy and earn welfare gains from it. There is serendipity in globalization, albeit it needs to be handled in a pragmatic, clairvoyant and sagacious manner.

Notes

1 Chile, Hong Kong SAR, Korea (Republic of), Singapore, and Taiwan. Hong Kong is a special administrative region (SAR) of the People's Republic of China.
2 These twenty-four developing countries were Argentina, Bangladesh, Brazil, China, Colombia, Costa Rica, Cote d'Ivoire, the Dominican Republic, Haiti, Hungary, India, Jamaica, Jordan, Malaysia, Mali, Mexico, Nepal, Nicaragua, Paraguay, the Philippines, Rwanda, Thailand, Uruguay and Zimbabwe.
3 A recent example is the global semiconductor price slump, which was responsible for the adverse terms-of-trade shocks to Korean economy in the run up of its 1997–98 crisis.
4 The 1997–98 Asian financial crisis passed China and South Asian economies by. One of the reasons was that these economies did not liberalize their capital account, or did not liberalize it completely. They were not deeply integrated into the global financial markets. Eichengreen *et al.* (1995) show that economies that are not fully integrated into the global financial markets are able to contain speculative pressure better.
5 That openness causes volatility is a commonplace view held by policy makers. It strikes as something intuitive. However, empirical evidence supporting this view is mixed. Kraay (1998) analyzed the link between financial openness and the volatility in capital flows. He failed to detect a consistent effect.
6 The most recent financial and asset market bubbles were generated in Japan during the 1980s. Both stock and real estate prices tripled in a short span of time. The economy, particularly the financial sector, is yet to come out of the after effects of these bubbles.
7 Please refer to Gavin and Hausmann (1995) and Guitan 1995 for these results.
8 Cutler *et al.* (2000) studied several Mexican crises and concluded that crisis-related volatility worsened health indicators. The Tequila crisis of 1995–96 sent mortality rate among the elderly soaring. It increased by 7 percent.

9 In the aftermath of the Asian crisis of 1997–98, Frankenberg *et al.* (1999) found that while school enrollment fell sharply in Indonesia, the declines in Korea and Thailand were moderate.

10 Thailand had liberalized its capital account to portfolio investment without strengthening its financial system and rationalizing prudential supervision and paid the high cost of having to deal with a crisis.

11 During the Korean crisis of 1997–98, the government was not willing to allow FDI, but was willing to open other components of the capital account.

12 See Kraay (1998) for disagreements on this count.

13 This mistake was made in Thailand where banks gave incentives to borrow offshore and on-lend the proceeds in foreign currency so that Bangkok International Banking Facility could be created. The consequence was heightened volatility and crisis.

14 In reality, life is not as simple as this. A steep decline in stock- or bond-markets damages the balance-sheet positions of banks that themselves own stocks and bonds. However, in the copious literature on the leading indicators of currency crisis the single most reliable predictor is the term structure of portfolio capital flows. Radelet and Sachs (1998) and Rodrik and Velasco (1999) have discussed these issues at length.

15 China and Taiwan both had large reserves during the period of Asian crisis, which helped them in keeping the contagion at bay.

16 See writings of Feldstein (1999), Guidotti (1999) and Greenspan (1999).

17 Argentina made an agreement with thirteen commercial banks in 1996 for providing a $6.1 billion line of credit. Mexico negotiated a pure, uncollateralized, credit line of $2.5 billion in 1998. Similarly, Indonesia negotiated a credit line of $3 billion in 1998.

18 Reserves allow the monetary authorities to engage in sterilized intervention, that is, they support the exchange rate by selling foreign exchange without simultaneously altering the domestic money supply. When speculative sales of the currency are large, this strategy is no longer feasible. A credible defense will then require the authorities to buy the domestic currency that market participants are selling, reining in domestic credit, raising interest rates and forcing weak banks and corporations to clean up their act.

19 This is a simplistic illustration of how problem of multiple equilibria can arise in foreign exchange markets. In this case, the currency peg would collapse under speculative attack. However, if there is no attack this situation can persist indefinitely. Thus, there are two equilibria, one in which the currency peg collapses and the other in which it does not.

20 Gordon (1999) shows that this was the case for Italy and the UK at the time of the ERM break up in 1992.

21 This happened on October, 13 1997.

22 Hausmann (1999) and Buiter (1999) question the capability of central banks to be a stabilizer or the lender of last resort.

23 A model of the linkage is provided by Drazen and Grilli (1993).

24 This is the story famously told by Mancur Olson of institutional change in the wake of war and crisis (Olson, 1982).

25 A similar argument has been made about the debt crisis and the "lost decade" of the 1980s breeding reform in Latin America by, *inter alia,* Edwards (1995).

26 Indonesia and Malaysia appear to be exceptions: the Indonesian system does not favor M&As, while Malaysia's appears to favor domestic but not international M&A activity.

27 The latest crisis in Argentina began in 2001.

References

Baskin, J. and P. Miranti. 1997. *A History of Corporate Finance*. Cambridge. Cambridge University Press.

Bordo, M., B. Eichengreen, D. Kiligebiel and M.S. Martinez-Peria. 2001. "Is the Crisis Problem Growing More Severe?" *Economic Policy*, 32(2) 34–80.

Buiter, W. 1999. "Optimum Currency Areas: Why Does Exchange Rate Regime Matter," London. UK. Bank of England (unpublished manuscript).

Burnside, C., M. Eichembaum and S. Rebelo. 2001. "Prospective Deficits and the Asian Currency Crises," *Journal of Political Economy*, 53(4) 63–90.

Bussiere, M. and C. Mulder. 1999. "External Vulnerability in Emerging Market Economies," Washington, DC. International Monetary Fund. IMF Working Paper No. WP/99/98. July.

Calvo, S., L. Leiderman and C. Reinhart. 1996. "Inflows of Capital to Developing Countries in the 1990s," *Journal of Economic Perspective*, 10(2) 123–36.

Campos, J.E. and H. Root. 1996. *The Key to the Asian Miracle: Making Shared Growth Credible.* Washington, DC. The Brookings Institution.

Caprio, G. and D. Klingebiel, 1999. "Episodes of Systematic and Borderline Financial Crises," Washington, DC. The World Bank. Available on the Internet at http://www1.worldbank.org/finance/assets/images/crisistableproduct1.doc.

Cutler, D., F. Knaul, R. Lozano, O. Mendez and B. Zurita. 2000. "Financial Crisis, Health Outcomes, and Aging: Mexico in the 1980s and 1990s," Cambridge, Mass., USA. National Bureau of Economic Research. NBER Working Paper No. 7746. June.

Das, Dilip K. 2000. "Asian Crisis: Distilling Critical Lessons," Geneva, United Nations Conference on Trade and Development (UNCTAD). Discussion Paper No. 152. December.

Davis, L. and D. North. 1971. *Institutional Change and American Economic Growth.* Cambridge. Cambridge University Press.

Dollar, D. and A. Kraay. 2001. "Growth is Good for the Poor," Policy Research Working Paper No. 2199. Washington, DC. The World Bank.

Drazen, A. and V. Grilli. 1993. "The Benefits of Crisis of Economic Reforms," *American Economic Review*, 83(3) 598–607.

Easterly, W. and A. Kraay. 1999. "Small States, Small Problems," Washington, DC. The World Bank. Policy Research Working Paper No. 2139.

Edwards, S. 1995. *Crisis and Reforms in Latin America.* New York. Oxford University Press.

Eichengreen, B., A. Rose and C. Wyplosz.1995. "Exchange Market Mayhem: The Antecedents and Aftermath of Speculative Attacks," *Economic Policy*, 21(2) 249–312.

Feldstein, M. 1999. "Self Portrait for Emerging Market Economies," Cambridge, Mass., USA. National Bureau of Economic Research. NBER Working Paper No. 6907. January.

Foley, C.F. 1999. "Going Bust in Bangkok: Lessons from Bankruptcy Reform in Thailand," Cambridge. Mass. Harvard University (unpublished manuscript).

Frankel, J. and A. Rose. 1996. "Currency Crashes in Emerging Markets: An Empirical Treatment," *Journal of International Economics*, 41(3–4) 351–66.

Frankenberg, E., D. Thomas and K. Beegle. 1999. "The Real Cost of Indonesia's Economic Crisis," Santa Monica. California. USA. The Rand Corporation. Labor and Population Program Working Paper No. 99-04.

Gavin, M. and R. Hausmann. 1995. "Overcoming Volatility in Latin America," Washington, DC. International Monetary Fund. IMF Seminar Paper No. 95/34. August.

Goelthom, M. 1999. "Remarks," in *Rethinking the International Monetary System*, Boston, Mass., USA. The Federal Reserve Bank of Boston.

Gordon, R. 1999. "The Aftermath of the 1992 ERM Breakup: Was There a Macroeconomic Free Lunch," Cambridge, Mass., USA. National Bureau of Economic Research. NBER Working Paper No. 6964. February.

Greenspan, A. 1999. Remarks by the Chairman of the Board of Governors of the Federal Reserve System before the World Bank Conference on Recent Trends in Reserve Management, Washington, DC. 29 April.

Guidotti, P. 1999. "Currency Reserves and Debt," Paper presented at the World Bank Conference on Recent Trends in Reserve Management, Washington, DC. 29 April.

Guillaumont, P., S.G. Jeanneney and J.F. Bern. 1999. "How Instability Lowers African Growth," *Journal of African Economics*, 8(1) 87–107.

Guitan, M. 1995. "Monetary Policy: Equity Issues in IMF Policy Advice," Washington, DC. International Monetary (unpublished manuscript).

Hausmann, R. 1999. "Financial Turmoil and the Choice of Exchange Rate Regime," Washington, DC. Inter-American Development Bank (unpublished manuscript).

Inter-American Development Bank (IDB). 1995. *Overcoming Volatility: Economic and Social Progress in Latin America*. Washington, DC. Inter-American Development Bank.

Kaminsky, G. and S. Schmukler. 2001. "On Financial Booms and Crashes: Regional Patterns, Time Patterns, and Financial Liberalizations," Washington, DC. The World Bank. Processed.

Klein, M. and G. Olivei. 1999. "Capital Account Liberalization, Financial Depth and Economic Growth," Cambridge, Mass., USA. National Bureau of Economic Research. NBER Working Paper No. 7384. October.

Kraay, A. 1998. "In Search of Macroeconomic Effects of Capital Account Liberalization," Washington, DC. The World Bank. Processed.

McKinnon, R.I. and H. Pill. 1997. "Credible Economic Liberalization and Overborrowing," *The American Economic Review*, 87(2) 179–93.

Obstfeld, M. and K. Rogoff. 1996. *Foundations of International Macroeconomics*. Cambridge, Mass. The MIT Press.

Olson, M. 1982. *The Rise and Decline of Nations*. New Haven. Yale University Press.

Radelet, S. and J.D. Sachs. 1998. "The Onset of the Asian Financial Crisis," Cambridge, Mass., USA. National Bureau of Economic Research. NBER Working Paper No. 6680. August.

Rodrik, D. and A. Velasco. 1999. "Short-Term Capital Flows," Cambridge, Mass. Harvard University (unpublished manuscript).

The Economist. 2002. "International Financial Crisis," July 9. pp. 19–20.

Ulan, M.K. 2000. "Is A Chilean-Style Tax on Short-Term Capital Inflows Stabilizing?" *Open Economies Review*, 11(1) 149–77.

World Bank, The (WB). 2002. *Globalization, Growth and Poverty*. New York. Oxford University Press.

4 Challenges regarding euro area financial market integration*

Sebastian Schich

Introduction

European markets for financial services are apparently outpacing a global trend towards financial integration. Over the last two decades, capital accounts liberalisation, financial deregulation and advances in information and telecommunications technology have contributed to making financial markets more integrated worldwide. In the case of the European Union, these developments were further compounded by policy action. For instance, as part of the EU Internal Market Programme, considerable progress was made in creating a common regulatory framework for the provision of financial services. More recently, the introduction of the euro has taken the European financial markets closer towards full integration by eliminating currency risk between those EU countries that have adopted the currency. That said, important legal, regulatory, tax and other impediments to full integration still remain.

Regarding the future, encouraging further financial market integration is a high priority on the EU agenda.[1] The Lisbon 2000 meeting of the European Council of Minister set a deadline of 2005 for completing the Single Market for financial services. Moreover, the Stockholm 2001 meeting of the Council recommended that an acceleration of the full integration of securities markets be brought forward to 2003. Arguably just as important is the fact that policy makers and members of civil society have become more alert to the costs of financial market fragmentation and to the benefits that could be reaped from a more speedy integration. Finally, market participants appear to be stepping up pressure on policy makers to address the remaining sources of fragmentation.

This chapter discusses current issues regarding the state of the integration of EU financial markets, highlighting three elements of the financial sector,[2] namely: (i) government bond markets, (ii) stock exchanges and (iii) banking sectors. As regards the first of these elements, government bond markets are, as was

* The author is grateful to Hans Christiansen, Carl Gjersem, Ayumi Kikuchi and Stephen Lumpkin for comments. The views expressed in this chapter are those of the author and not necessarily shared by the OECD.

widely expected by market participants before the introduction of the euro, one of the fastest integrating components of the EU financial markets – second only to money markets. Convergence is almost achieved in this market, nevertheless, some barriers to complete integration persist. At the same time, the emergence of an equity culture across Europe, partly due to an increasing reliance on private savings for retirement income, has highlighted the issues of efficiency and consolidation of European stock markets. Changes in the composition of the portfolios of institutional investors, such as investment and pension funds and insurance companies seem to suggest a reduction in the 'home bias'. To accelerate these developments, it has been argued, that the remaining inefficiencies in the European stock market infrastructure would need to be substantially reduced. Concerning the banking sectors, the introduction of the euro has further intensified competition in what was already a competitive environment. European countries were generally regarded as 'over-banked' in the early 1990s, but since then some consolidation has taken place, though mostly at the national level. Cross-border merger and acquisition activity and cross-border provision of banking services remain relatively limited and there appears to be considerable room for further integration. Indicators of integration based on bank charges show weak evidence of convergence across the euro area and indicators of foreign bank penetration, as will be discussed below, yield similar patterns. These sectoral issues are addressed in more detail in the section on 'Integration of selected elements of the financial service sectors'. Before that, the next section discusses the macroeconomic rationale for financial market integration. The final section concludes this chapter.

Why financial market integration?

Financial market integration is expected to produce significant welfare gains, but the exact quantitative importance of financial market integration and the contributions of the different transmission channels through which financial integration affects economic performance are uncertain. In assessing the macroeconomic consequences of financial market integration one approach is to focus on consumption patterns and the greater scope for the smoothing of consumption over time. Investors hold too many domestic assets in relation to international assets as compared with an 'optimal portfolio', reflecting a lack of risk-sharing across different countries and often referred to as the 'home bias' in asset portfolios. Holding an optimal international portfolio of assets would provide the opportunity to eliminate the impact of domestic shocks on domestic consumption, so that the latter only reacts to uninsurable global shocks. Assuming that market integration tends to reduce the 'home bias', financial market integration has the scope to improve international risk-sharing.

To what extent greater risk-sharing has been achieved can be approximated by the extent to which domestic consumption is correlated with either domestic output or alternatively international consumption (Lewis, 1999). Figure 4.1 illustrates that the thus measured extent of risk-sharing in the European Union is indeed far from complete, with changes in domestic consumption in most countries being

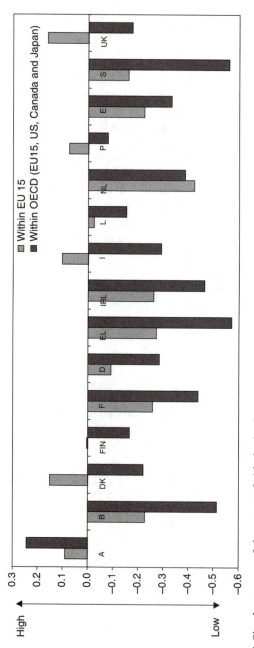

Figure 4.1 Simple measure of the extent of risk-sharing.*

Source: OECD.

Note

* Difference between two correlation coefficients, that is (1) correlation between private consumption growth in country j and international private consumption growth (either EU aggregate or OECD aggregate, both excluding country j) and (2) correlation between private consumption growth in country j and output growth in country j. A value of +1 suggests perfect risk-sharing and a value of −1 absence of risk-sharing.

more closely linked with domestic output changes than with changes in international consumption, as evidenced by the negative values shown there. The figure also shows that, according to this simple measure, risk-sharing within EU countries is greater than within OECD countries. Nevertheless, risk-sharing across European national borders appears to be substantially lower than across regions in the case of Canadian provinces, US states and Japanese prefectures (Crucini and Hess, 2000). This points to the scope for improved risk-sharing across countries within the European Union. Provided that greater financial integration facilitates more complete risk-sharing by reducing the 'home bias' in portfolios, accelerating financial market integration will help making consumption patterns smoother over time.

In assessing the economic consequences of financial market integration, some recent studies have focused on the link between finance and growth (e.g. European Commission (EC), 2001). This approach has the advantage that it could draw on the results from the many recent studies of the empirical relationship between financial development and growth. Specifically, to the extent that the relationship between financial development and growth is positive and that financial integration contributes to financial development, it could be concluded that financial integration enhances growth.

Financial systems play a role in the growth process because they are integral to the provision of funding for capital accumulation and for the diffusion of new technologies. The microeconomic rationale for financial systems is based largely on the existence of frictions in the trading system. In a world in which writing, issuing and enforcing contracts consume resources and in which information is not symmetric and its acquisition costly, properly functioning financial systems can reduce these information and transactions costs. In the process, savers and investors are brought together more efficiently and, ultimately, economic growth is affected. In this context, financial systems perform several functions that serve to ameliorate these frictional costs and thus bear on capital accumulation and technological progress. They include the (i) mobilising of savings, (ii) diversifying risk, (iii) allocating savings and (iv) monitoring managers. (a) A well-developed financial system attracts and collects the small-denomination savings of individuals, so that profitable large-scale investments can be funded, thus potentially raising the overall level and possibly the efficiency of investment. (b) Financial systems provide insurance to individual savers against the idiosyncratic risk that a single investment pays no return and the liquidity risk that savers may need to withdraw investments before returns are available. As a result, high-return projects with long gestation periods or high but diversifiable risk are more likely to be funded. (c) While for individual savers, the costs of acquiring and evaluating information on prospective projects can be high, financial intermediaries that specialise in acquiring and evaluating information on prospective investment projects enable small investors, for a nominal fee, to locate high return investments. (d) The establishment of financial intermediaries that can monitor investments for groups of savers/investors reduces the duplication of monitoring costs that would be incurred if the savers conducted their own monitoring individually. Performing these various functions, broad and deep financial systems are expected to imply faster capital accumulation as well as increasing the productivity of capital, thus enhancing growth. As regards the empirical relationship between finance and growth, recent work in the framework of the OECD project on economic growth points to a significant contribution of financial development to enhancing growth. In particular, there are significant relationships in OECD countries between investment and financial development, as measured by indicators of the scale of financial activity (Hahn, 2002; Schich and Pelgrin, 2002). Evidence is also found of significant relationships between financial development and growth – over and above the links via investment – indicating impacts via overall economic efficiency (Bassanini *et al.*, 2001; Leahy *et al.*, 2001). While questions remain regarding the direction of causation in these relationships – as with most studies of this nature – the balance of evidence provided in recent work seems to support the view that finance leads economic growth (World Bank, 2001).

Moving from segmented to integrated financial markets could enhance financial development through the exploitation of the scale effects inherent in financial activity and by intensifying competition. Scale effects could emerge through an increase in the number of actual and potential counterparts for financial transactions. In banking, the average costs for the administration of savings as well as for the evaluation, selection and monitoring of investment projects should become smaller, the larger is the number of depositors and borrowers. Survey-based evidence suggests that financial integration is perceived by managers as an opportunity to exploit economies of scale in terms of cost and revenue and economies of scope through consolidation (EC, 2001). As well, consolidation has the potential to reduce *x*-inefficiencies in management and rationalise the use of labour; however, the scope for the latter may be limited in Europe because of tight labour protection laws. Possibly even more important, financial integration is likely to improve efficiency of intermediation by intensifying the competition among financial intermediaries. Competition among intermediaries eliminates quasi-rents to intermediaries and provides greater incentive and scope for financial innovation. The availability of new financial products will offer the possibility of more efficient financing of investment and risk management especially to small and medium-sized enterprises by expanding the range of financing opportunities at their disposal. It is likely that integration will also enhance the competition for funds among borrowers, with spillover effects on management efficiency, innovative capacity, accountability and transparency towards shareholders and stakeholders. In this way, integration can be expected to spur best governance practices and contribute to a business environment that is more conducive to growth.

Unfortunately, empirical research on the link between financial integration and growth seems to provide relatively little guidance so far. Growth is affected by a large variety of different factors, which makes it difficult to isolate the effect of financial integration, and the results of empirical studies of the integration–growth link appear to depend on the control variables used (Arteta *et al.*, 2001). As well, measuring integration is complicated by the complex interaction of various barriers and controls affecting prices or quantities and the choice of measure affects the results

(Edison *et al.*, 2002). Taking the various studies together, it appears that the evidence for a positive relationship between measures of financial integration and growth is stronger for countries with relatively well-developed financial systems – such as the euro area countries – as compared to countries with weak financial systems.

Integration of selected elements of the financial service sectors

Government bond markets

The most apparent effect of the introduction of the euro has been on the size of the euro area government bond market, as had been expected by financial market participants before the introduction of the euro. Indeed, the market can be considered fairly large in comparison with two different benchmarks. First, despite the recent dynamic growth of issuance in the non-sovereign segments and a declining issuance of sovereign debt over the past few years reflecting mainly budgetary consolidation in the euro area, government bond issuance is the dominant source of supply in the euro-denominated bond market. Looking forward, the trend of declining issuance is expected to be reversed, reflecting the deterioration of the fiscal situation in many euro area countries. As well, going forward, issuance of non-sovereign bonds will likely be less dynamic, given currently high default rates. Second, the market is large by international comparison. Already the combined outstanding volume of the three major sovereign bond issuers in the euro area is broadly on par with US Treasury marketable government debt (which includes bills and notes). The combined outstanding volume of all euro area government bonds comes even close to that of Japan. However, even though the re-denomination into a common currency of all individual euro area government debt has meant that an important distinguishing feature of government securities – their currency denomination – has ceased to exist, the market seems to differ from its corresponding counterparts in the United States or Japan. Specifically, market participants still differentiate between issues of different governments in terms of credit risk and other factors. Indeed, ratings on long-term debt denominated in euro according to the rating agencies differ considerably across sovereigns.

As government debt managers compete for funds in the euro area market with instruments in a common currency, competition has increased. Driven in part by attempts to achieve the cheapest funding under increasingly competitive conditions and as part of an OECD-wide trend towards standardisation of government debt policies (OECD, 2002b), EU debt management policies have converged. This has been reflected in convergence of the composition of debt by type of instrument and maturity, the coordination of issuing procedures and the harmonisation of market conventions. For example, to improve liquidity in their instruments, smaller euro area countries have used buy-back and switching operations to concentrate debt in fewer and larger series. They have stopped issuing instruments covering the entire maturity spectrum and, instead, focus on a limited number of benchmark maturities. Nevertheless, liquidity appears to be mostly concentrated in the debt instruments of the three largest issuers (Germany, France and Italy), which together account for almost three quarters of all euro-denominated public debt, with favourable implications for their funding costs. Standardisation of debt instruments has also encouraged the introduction of electronic trading platforms on which government bonds of several EU countries are traded side-by-side (OECD, 2002b).

Management of euro area government debt remains decentralised. And the same competition among public debt managers that has lead to convergence in their management policies, thus fostering integration, has also been mentioned as a source for fragmentation in euro area government debt markets (IMF, 2001). It has been questioned whether there is a potential for coordination failure with respect to issuance strategies among public debt managers acting independently, which may turn out to deter bond market integration (Mylonas *et al.*, 2000). A suggestion has been made by de Silguy (1999) to create a single body responsible for issuing some part of euro-zone government bonds. However, the scheme has met with considerable scepticism, as it would imply some form of collective responsibility for national debts, a notion that runs contrary to the principles of the Treaty of Maastricht. The Giovanni Group (2001) has concluded that reforms required to allow more coordinated issuance currently appear too costly and time-consuming compared to the possible gains. Less formal forms of cooperation, whereby governments would coordinate the calendar and structure of their issues so as to maximise issue volumes, have so far only existed as unilateral measures. For example, Austria has issued ten-year bonds with conditions identical to those of the German Bunds of the same maturity (Galati and Tsatsaronis, 2001). But without further efforts of increased coordination, it is sometimes argued, there may be incentives for individual debt managers to abandon the passive issuance strategies adopted by many countries over recent years. Instead, they may choose to pursue more active strategies, competing against other governments, as well as trying to take advantage of what are perceived as market anomalies. In recognition of some of these potential problems, progress has been made in the form of an exchange of information among European debt managers (e.g. within the European Economic and Financial Committee on EU Government Bonds and Bills). This has helped transparency and is expected to limit the effect of these potential problems.

As a result of all these issues, a truly pan-European government benchmark yield curve does not exist. Typically, a government debt yield curve has been the focal point for the operation and development of financial markets. Over the past few decades, yield curves based on government securities were widely recognised as the pre-eminent benchmark for pricing the cost of funds at differing borrowing horizons. In Europe, at one time the German Bund served this function. More recently, some observers have suggested that the swaps market seems to have become the benchmark market in providing the yield curve that is used as the single reference for pricing instruments of different maturities (Barth *et al.*, 2002).[3] Others have suggested that this role may be split among different issuers. In particular, it is argued that the ten-year Bund has firmly established itself as the long-term benchmark bond for the euro area, while French government bonds have become the medium-term reference and Italian government securities are used to trade cross-country interest rate spreads. In large part, the differences in assessments reflect differences in the concepts used to define benchmark securities. While there is widespread agreement that the benchmark is a security, which is used as a reference to price other securities, there are different views regarding the *empirical* definition and identification of this role. Some have concluded that it is simply the security with the lowest yield, which takes that role. Indeed, the most common view associates the benchmark bond with the lowest yield at a given maturity. If this definition were to be adopted, then the German Bunds would provide the benchmark at almost all maturities. An alternative is to interpret benchmark to mean the most liquid bond. If this definition were used, then the Italian market would be the benchmark for short-term maturity bonds and the French market for medium-term maturity bonds. Dunne *et al.* (2002) suggest defining the benchmark bond as the instrument to which the prices of other bonds react. If this view were taken, defining benchmark status would require empirical estimation and cannot simply be read from the observed data. Using two different estimation methods (Granger causality and cointegration test), the authors failed to confirm the unambiguous benchmark status for German securities that would come from a simple focus on the securities with the lowest yield. Their estimation results suggest the existence of a benchmark portfolio rather than a single benchmark security.

Stock exchanges

Consolidation of stock markets is not an 'EU-phenomenon', but reflects a world-wide trend towards a single global market for certain instruments.[4] Nevertheless, there have been a few high-profile consolidation efforts in Europe. They include the creation in 1998 of a common Nordic equity market, NOREX, by Stockholmsbörsen and the Copenhagen Stock Exchange, later in 2000 joined by the Iceland Stock Exchange and the Oslo Exchange. Even though the exchanges remain independent, they allow cross-membership, use a single buy-and-sell order book for each security, common trading rules and a common trading platform. In another high-profile consolidation, Euronext was formed by a merger of the Amsterdam, Brussels and Paris exchanges in mid-2000 and was floated as a public company in mid-2001. The Lisbon Exchange joined in 2001. Shares continue to be listed at national levels, but a uniform trading platform is used at Euronext. There has also been evidence of consolidation within Member States, such as in Spain. The process of integration also goes beyond traditional exchanges, as illustrated by the Virt-X merger that combined the Swiss Exchange and the UK-based electronic exchange Tradepoint. Not all consolidation efforts have been successful, however, with the failed merger of Deutsche Börse and the London Stock Exchange a notable example.

Consolidation of stock exchanges is likely to be beneficial, as stock exchanges have been shown to display economies of scale both in operations and in trading

(Pagano, 1989; Steil, 2001). Operational economies of scale can arise from the establishment of compatible or shared trading platforms, eliminating the need for redundant investment in different trading systems. In addition, common or shared trading platforms could benefit banks or brokers that engage in cross-border transactions and currently face significant access costs to maintain connections with a variety of trading systems. Trading economies of scale can be realised from the attainment of heightened market liquidity. Establishing common or shared trading platforms across Europe could reduce the cost of cross-border transactions, attracting new investors to the equity markets and generating higher trading volumes. These benefits are likely associated with increased liquidity, which in turn reduces price volatility. When buyers and sellers are few in number and arrive sporadically at the market, they may not find each other immediately. This type of inefficiency could translate into significant price fluctuations (Pagano, 1989). Recent empirical research points indeed to the scope for efficiency gains. While recent progress regarding integration has indeed been reflected in increased efficiency of European stock exchanges, inefficiencies still remain on a considerably high level (Schmiedel, 2001).

Despite the potential benefits of consolidation, there are several barriers that tend to prevent fast consolidation. These include cross-country legal and regulatory differences and the widespread fragmentation of Europe's clearing and settlement systems. There is no single body that regulates equity markets euro-area wide and each country has its own set of rules. Important differences include listing requirements and trading practices. In this context, differences in the national requirements on the structure and content of equity prospectuses make it difficult for small firms to distribute information in order to raise equity on a pan-European basis. Harmonisation is more advanced in the case of large firms, which, in any case, are also already followed more closely by analysts and the financial press. There are also substantial differences in national accounting standards and practices, making it sometimes difficult to evaluate the health, in particular of smaller companies across borders. And tax treatment is uneven across Europe and in some countries, favourable tax treatment is granted to domestic equity investment. Diversity of accounting and corporate governance standards poses another obstacle. National accounting and disclosure norms vary widely across Europe. Only from 2005 are all listed companies in the European Union required to file at least their consolidated financial statements using International Accounting Standards (IAS) according to a new regulation adopted by the EC. Corporate governance codes in EU countries differ and the EC currently studies whether the European Union should adopt a common one. All EU member countries except Luxembourg and Austria have such codes of conduct, which offer guidelines to, for example, ensure that boards objectively supervise management's work and that financial statements accurately reflect a company's health. The importance of the latter issue has been highlighted by the recent bankruptcies of large US corporations and the circumstances surrounding them. Finally, differences in language, business culture or habit persistence have also been cited as further obstacles. Removing the latter, if considered beneficial, will necessary be a slower process.

Another obstacle is the number of clearing and settlement systems, which are currently sharply divided along national lines. This tends to increase the number of redundant clearing and settlement processes as well as increase the costs of cross-border transactions. For example, it has been estimated that cross-border transactions in Europe can cost ten times as much as domestic trades in Europe (Skorecki, 2002) and almost fifty times as much as trades in the United States (McAndrews and Stefanidis, 2002). Although there are a lot of uncertainties associated with such estimates, several other studies confirm that settlement costs are significantly higher in Europe than in the United States. As a general rule, clearing and settlement functions can be arranged in a variety of institutional settings and current practices at the major European exchanges differ. Unlike trade execution, which occurs at exchanges, clearing and settlement can be completed at agencies that are either independent or controlled by an exchange. The two functions, clearing and settlement,[5] can be handled by separate organisations, as they are in London by the London Clearing House and Crest, or combined, as they are at Clearstream, which handles trades in Germany. Looking at the three different functions together, a 'horizontal' model as in London, with separate exchange, clearing house and settler has been contrasted to Deutsche Börse's 'vertical' silo where all functions are combined under one single business. The different settings have implications for cost effectiveness and competition, as well as for the models being proposed for Europe. Three different models proposed for Europe could be distinguished. According to one proposal, there will be a single European clearing house, acting as a central counter-party, which would process trades from many exchanges and then sending them on to many settlers. An alternative is a model whereby clearers and settlers are merged, as in the United States. A third proposal, instead of advocating mergers, suggests a network of links to achieve 'inter-operability' by putting in place technologies that would allow connections between Central Securities Depositories (CSD), the organisations that record share holdings and provide the mechanisms for their transfer. It has been argued that the latter may be particularly desirable to withstand shocks such as that of the September 11 attacks, because 'inter-operability' would enable CSDs to pass backlogs of work to one another.

Banking sectors

The introduction of the euro has further intensified competition in an already highly competitive environment for banks, by enhancing price transparency, reducing foreign exchange revenues and eliminating the competitive advantage for domestic players associated with the existence of national currencies. Already existing competitive pressures in the financial services industry reflect among other things technological change, which tends to lower the costs of both information and transactions and facilitates securitisation. Technological change facilitates competition from non-banks for corporate and retail banking business and also challenges the basis of traditional relationship banking by encouraging securitisation. Going forward, the trend towards increasing securitisation is likely to benefit further from the increasing reform pressure towards fully funded pension systems. Most pension systems in the European Union are still based on the pay-as-you-go principle. But with an ageing population, the reform pressure towards a fully funded pension system has increased considerably. Last year, Germany took a step towards partial funding with the so-called Riester reform; other major European countries such as France and Italy will follow. It is often argued that these changes are likely to further promote the development of broader and more liquid securities markets. But the promotion of long-term bank deposits is also envisaged in the pension reform concepts in some countries (see, e.g. Deutsche Bundesbank, 2002), so that the implications for the structure of the financial sector may depend on the specific policy measures taken. Current competitive pressures in the banking sector also reflect the fact that the process of financial deregulation in Europe has been under way for several decades. Some of the associated legislation, for example, the Second Banking Coordination Directive (1993), was aimed explicitly at encouraging a heightened level of international competition in the member countries of the European Union in the area of banking services. This appeared to have indeed been successful, especially in the corporate lending market, while consumer-lending markets are still more fragmented (Kleimeier and Sander, 2002).

One response of banks to these competitive pressures has been consolidation either through mergers and acquisitions or through cross-shareholdings, involving banks as well as other financial institutions. So far, most of the consolidation in the European Union has taken place mainly within national boundaries. This has implied a significant increase in industry concentration at the national level in some smaller Member States. Going forward, further mergers and acquisitions between big institutions in these countries are seen as unlikely given the already high concentration in their financial sectors, in particular, in the area of retail banking.

Cross-border activity has been relatively more limited and much of it has occurred within relatively homogeneous regions such as the Benelux region or Scandinavia and has failed to produce any truly European bank. The limited cross-border activity is reflected in a relatively low share of foreign banks in most euro area countries, except Luxembourg, Ireland and Belgium. As well, cross-border provision of financial services has been limited, particularly in the area of retail banking services (Heinemann and Schüler, 2002). While wholesale markets appear to be overall more closely integrated than retail markets, a distinct lack of integration in some areas of the former have, nevertheless, been identified, such as in the short-term corporate loan market (Adam *et al.*, 2002). Some efforts have been made by European banks to provide services on the internet beyond national borders. However, this type of cross-border provision of financial services has been quite limited so far and concentrated in a small number of start-up banks operating in a range of countries (Christiansen, 2002).

To explain the limited cross-border activity, persistent cross-country tax and regulatory and legal differences, in areas such as bankruptcy proceedings, efficiency of court proceedings, investor and consumer protection, have been regularly cited as the most obvious barriers to fuller integration. It has also been argued that international mergers and acquisitions may be more costly than domestic ones, as different cultures and languages have to be blended and as cultural differences have sometimes already been an issue in the case of domestic mergers. As well, the prospect of significantly increasing market power through mergers may be more limited in the case of the cross-border as compared with the domestic mergers and acquisitions. As well, European countries may be sufficiently heterogeneous – compared for instance to US states – to provide ample opportunity for asset risk diversification (Danthine *et al.*, 1999). Moreover, as the significant differences in national legal and regulatory environments (e.g. consumer and competition laws) make a pan-European product range impractical at this time, the scale and scope economies from cross-border mergers would seem to be less than those from domestic mergers (EC, 2001). In this context, the lack of harmonisation of consumer protection rules and the related issue of transparency have been cited as important reasons for a more limited consolidation in retail as opposed to wholesale banking. But limited integration in the former area may also reflect the existence of non-regulatory barriers, for example, cultural differences in consumer behaviour such as preferences for types of credit. Also, retail products may be less exposed to international competitive pressures as proximity to customers remains important, despite advances in modern information and distribution technologies.

Increases in competitive pressures are likely to have implications not just for efficiency, but also for financial stability. In this context, questions have been raised about the decentralised setting of banking supervision and lender of last resort functions. It might be argued that these functions ought to be bundled with the centralised mandate for monetary and exchange rate policy to prevent duplication of information gathering and create a level-playing field (OECD, 2002a). Currently, responsibility for supervision is decentralised and national authorities retain their responsibilities in the area of supervision, even though there exists an extensive committee to promote cooperation between the competent authorities for supervisory matters. At the national level, the organisation of supervision is related to the legal and regulatory tradition of that Member State (Lumpkin, 2002). The dominant forms of supervision in the Union are through separate entities for bank, insurance and securities supervision or one integrated supervisor for all industries. Some Member States integrate some, but not all of these functions. Efficiency gains may be reaped by moving away from supervision focused on objectives or sectors (banks, insurance companies, securities markets) towards supervision focused on functions (trading, issuance, back-office work, retail activities, etc.). It is still a matter for discussion whether the need for group-wide oversight necessarily requires the establishment of a consolidated supervisory authority, but a growing number of countries world-wide have moved to some form of consolidated supervision.

Concluding remarks

The introduction of the euro has taken financial market integration in the area a step further. As discussed, integration has been different across various components of the euro area financial markets. This reflects the different impact of the remaining barriers to integration and the differences in challenges currently facing each of those components. Full integration is almost achieved in the euro area government debt markets and current challenges in this sector include issues such as developments in electronic trading systems and government debt benchmark yield curves. The main issue facing stock exchanges seems to be the need for consolidation. In this respect, issues include the integration or consolidation of the fragmented clearing and settlement systems. As regards banking sectors, cross-border consolidation and integration has been limited. This seems to reflect the existence of various barriers, including tax, legal and regulatory differences. Removing remaining barriers to integration in all sectors will allow markets to fully reap the potential benefits from the introduction of the euro.

Notes

1 Since the early 1970s the EC has pushed for the creation of a European financial area. Rather than establishing uniform regulation and supervision for a single financial market, the principles of home country control, harmonisation of essential principles and mutual recognition were applied. Accompanied by the global trend of financial market liberalisation, this sparked competition between financial centres in the area, changing their structure over time to become more integrated. Nevertheless, several barriers to full integration of the markets for financial services in the European Union continue to exist, as discussed in OECD (2002a).
2 For more comprehensive recent studies see EC (2001), Galati and Tsatsaronis (2001) and OECD (2002a), on which the section on 'Integration of selected elements of the financial service sectors' draws in parts. As regards the evaluation of the degree of integration, the present chapter draws on the empirical analysis presented by Adam *et al.* (2002).
3 The introduction of the euro has collapsed several distinct, albeit closely linked, markets into a single swap market. Even if swap yields are not necessarily the lowest yields reflecting banking sector credit risk, such risks are standard across markets (McCauley and White, 1997). Moreover, to construct a yield curve equally spaced observations are available from one to ten years and liquidity is relatively even across the curve, as compared to term structures from government bonds, where time-varying spreads exist between on-the-run and off-the-run and between deliverable and non-deliverable bonds. These aspects facilitate the use of the swap curve as a yardstick for valuation. However, there are also other functions typically performed by government securities, including their role as collateral. Clearly, swaps cannot be used to replace government securities in this function. But other securities, such as asset- and mortagage-backed securities, for example, the German Pfandbriefe, may be an alternative in this respect (Blanco, 2001).
4 Gaa *et al.* (2001) suggest that the consolidation process will result in a single global market in the most liquid securities, while less liquid products may continue to be traded on national-level markets.
5 Clearing and settlement are the two functions performed after a trade has been agreed. Clearing takes place when the buyer and seller confirm the terms of their trade and the clearing agency calculates the counterparties' obligations. Settlement entails the actual transfer of funds and asset ownership between buyer and seller.

References

Adam, K., T. Jappelli, A. Menichini, M. Padula, M. Pagano (2002), 'Analyse, Compare, and Apply Alternative Indicators and Monitoring Methodologies to Measure the

Evolution of Capital Market Integration in the European Union', (unpublished; Centre for Studies in Economics and Finance, University of Salerno, January).

Arteta, C., B. Eichengreen and C. Wyplosz (2001), 'On the Growth Effects of Capital Account Liberalization', (unpublished; Berkeley: University of California).

Barth, Ill, M.J., E.M. Remolona and P.D. Woodridge (2002), 'Changes in Market Functioning and Central Bank Policy: An overview of the Issues', BIS Working Paper No. 120, October.

Bassanini, A., S. Scarpetta and P. Hemmings (2001), 'Economic Growth: The Role of Policies and Institutions – Panel data Evidence from OECD Countries', *OECD Economics Department Working Paper* No. 283.

Blanco, R. (2001), 'The Euro-area Government Securities Markets – Recent Developments and Implications for Market Functioning', Paper prepared for the BIS Autumn Central Bank Economist's Meeting, October 2001.

Christiansen, H. (2002), 'Electronic Finance: Economics and Institutional factors', *Financial Market Trends* 81, OECD, April 2002.

Crucini, M. and G. Hess (2000), 'International and Intranational Risk Sharing', In: G. Hess and E. van Wincoop (eds), *Intranational Macroeconomics*, Cambridge, UK: Cambridge University Press.

Danthine, J., F. Giavazzi, X. Vives and E. von Thadden (1999), 'The future of European banking', *Monitoring European Integration* No. 9, CEPR, London.

de Silguy, Y.-T. (1999), 'The Euro: The Key to Europe's Lasting Success in the Global Economy', speech given at the Corporation of London, 26 July.

Deutsche Bundesbank (2002), 'Funded Old-age Provision and the Financial Markets', Monthly Report July, pp. 25–39.

Dunne, P.J., M.J. Moore and R. Portes (2002), 'Defining Benchmark Status: An Application Using Euro-area Bonds', NBER Working Paper No. 9087, August.

Edison, H.J., R. Levine, L. Ricci and T. Sløk (2002), 'International Financial Integration and Economic Growth', *NBER Working Paper* No. 9164, September.

European Commission (EC) (2001), Chapter 4 'Financial Market Integration in the EU' in the 'EU Economy: 2001 Review', *European Economy* 73, European Commission (available at http://europa.eu.int/comm/economy_finance/publications/european_economy/2001/ee73adv4en.pdf).

Gaa, C., S. Lumpkin, R. Ogrodnick and P. Thurlow (2001), 'Future Prospects for National Financial Markets and Trading Centres', *Financial Market Trends* No. 78, OECD, March.

Galati, G. and K. Tsatsaronis (2001), 'The Impact of the Euro on Europe's Financial Markets', *BIS Working Paper* No. 100, July.

Giovanni Group (2001), 'Report on EU Cross Border Clearing and Settlement Arrangements' (available at http://europa.eu.int/comm/economy_finance/giovannini/clearing_settlement_en.htm).

Hahn, F.R. (2002), 'The Finance–Growth Nexus Revisited: New Evidence from OECD Countries', Österreichisches Institut für Wirtschaftsforschung (WIFO) Working Paper No. 176, April.

Heinemann, F. and M. Schüler (2002), 'Integration Benefits on EU Retail Credit Markets – Evidence from Interest Rate Pass-through', ZEW (Zentrum für Europäische Wirtschaftsforschung) *Discussion Paper* 02-26, Mannheim, January.

IMF (2001), Chapter IV 'The Changing Structure of the Major Government Securities Markets' in *International Capital Markets*, IMF, Washington (available at http://www.imf.org/external/pubs/ft/icm/2001/01/eng/index.htm).

Kleimeier, S. and H. Sander (2002), 'European Financial Market Integration: Evidence on the Emergence of a Single Eurozone Retail Banking Market', Paper presented at the 29th Annual Meeting of the European Finance Association, Berlin, August.

Leahy, M., S. Schich, G. Wehinger, F. Pelgrin and T. Thorgeirsson (2001), 'Contributions of Financial Systems to Growth in OECD Countries', *OECD Economics Department Working Paper* No. 280.

Lewis, K.K. (1999), 'Trying to Explain Home Bias in Equities and Consumption', *Journal of Economic Literature* Vol. XXXVII, June, pp. 571–608.

Lumpkin, S.A. (2002), 'Supervision of Financial Services in the OECD Area', *OECD Financial Market Trends* 81, April.

McAndrews, J. and C. Stefanidis (2002), 'The Consolidation of European Stock Exchanges', Federal Reserve Bank of New York, *Current Issues in Economics and Finance*, 8(6) June.

McCauley, R.N. and W.R. White (1997), 'The Euro and European Financial Markets', BIS Working Paper No. 41 May.

Mylonas, P., S. Schich, T. Thorgeirsson and G. Wehinger (2000), 'Challenges for Public Debt Management in the Major OECD Economies', *Financial Market Trends* 75, OECD, March.

OECD (2002a), *OECD Economic Surveys: The Euro Area*, Paris, July.

OECD (2002b), Chapter V, 'Overview of Trends and Policies in European Bond Markets' in *OECD Public Debt Markets – Trends and Recent Challenges*, Paris.

Pagano, M. (1989), 'Trading Volume and Asset Liquidity', *Quarterly Journal of Economics* 104(2) 255–74.

Schich, S. and Pelgrin, F. (2002), 'Financial Development and Investment: Panel Data Evidence for OECD Countries from 1970 to 1997', *Applied Economics Letters*, 9 1–7.

Schmiedel, H. (2001), 'Technological Development and Concentration of Stock Exchanges in Europe', Bank of Finland *Discussion Paper* No. 21, October.

Skorecki, A. (2002), 'T + 1 pipedream is close to reality', *Financial Times*, 19 August.

Steil, B. (2001), 'Borderless Trading and Developing Securities Markets', Paper presented at the World Bank, International Monetary Fund, and Brookings Institution Third Annual Financial Markets and Development Conference, April.

World Bank (2001), *Finance for Growth – Policy Choices in a Volatile World*, Oxford University Press, New York.

Questions for Part I

1   For the global financial markets the decade of the 1990s and the early 2000s seems markedly different. Enumerate the causes.
2   Compare and contrast the earlier waves of globalization. Was the global economy more integrated during the earlier waves of globalization than during the contemporary period?
3   After a complete reversal during the inter-war period, the global economy returned to financial globalization. Why? How? Who are the principal agents of globalization during the contemporary period?
4   Why is *being open* associated with stability and *becoming open* with the possibilities of financial and economic crises?
5   Are the European Union economies moving towards the Lisbon 2000 target of financial market globalization? How do you rate the current progress in that direction?

Areas for further research

1   Is the American economy the only locomotive for the global financial markets? What are the principal pull factors?
2   Explore the various definitions of financial globalization in the literature. Which one do you think is the most expressive and correct?
3   Explore the economic role of transnational corporations in financial globalization.
4   What is the role of capital account liberalization in financial globalization?
5   What were the causes behind the 'contagion effect' during the 1990s? Why did we not see it during the early 2000s?
6   What is the evidence, if any, of the euro integrating the European Union economies?

Part II

Global financial architecture

5 Strengthening the international financial architecture

Where do we stand?*

Barry Eichengreen

Novel vision of financial architecture

It is now nearly five years since former US Treasury Secretary Robert Rubin (1998) made his famous speech calling for steps to strengthen the international financial architecture. Unfortunately, this choice of words conjured up visions of an architect's blueprint and a floor-to-ceiling renovation, where this is not in fact how the international financial system evolves. It evolves incrementally, changing on the margin in response to pressures from markets and governments, not discontinuously in response to the radical visions of some economic Frank Lloyd Wright. The existing system is made up of a dense network of social, economic and financial institutions. As with any network (think telecommunications), its components are lent inertia by their interaction, while evolving incrementally in response to technological and other stimuli. So it is, I would argue, with the international financial system.

History supports this interpretation, and the associated prediction. The international monetary and financial system has evolved incrementally from the gold standard to the gold-exchange standard, to the Bretton Woods gold–dollar standard and now to the post-Bretton Woods system of managed floating. Only in 1944 can it be said that it was radically remade on the basis of an architectural blueprint. And the circumstances then were unique. The prewar system had been discredited. George Soros (1998) may have recently published a book entitled *The Crisis of Global Capitalism*, in which he argues that the global financial system is "coming apart at the seams," but his conclusion that the current system should be consigned to the dustbin of history is not widely shared. The prevailing view, as I have put it elsewhere, is that financial markets are a worst way of organizing the allocation of resources except for the available alternatives. And even among those who agree on the need for change, there is a striking lack of consensus on the nature of the reforms to be undertaken. Achieving a consensus is immensely

* Financial support for this research was provided by the Ford Foundation through the Berkeley Program on International Financial Architecture. Earlier versions were presented at meetings at the East-West Center in Honolulu, the Social Science Research Council in Palo Alto, and the University of California in Washington, DC; the comments of participants are acknowledged with thanks.

more complicated than in 1944 by virtue of the sheer numbers involved. Where in 1944 there were basically one-and-a-half countries at the table, the world today is a more multi-polar place.[1] This undeniable fact of modern political and financial life greatly complicates the process of reaching an agreement.

Finally, it should be acknowledged that proposals to create new international institutions to deal with the crisis problem are politically unrealistic. Ours may be the age of global markets, but it is not an age of global government. There is no appetite for powerful supranational bodies with the power to usurp the traditional prerogatives of sovereign nation states. Proposals like Lord Eatwell and Professor Taylor's for the creation of a World Financial Authority must be dismissed as quixotic.[2] The existing multilaterals – the Fund and the Bank – will continue to possess limited powers.

Given these obstacles to radical reform, those of skeptical temperament will be inclined to ask whether real progress is possible. In this chapter I argue that the answer is yes. Initiatives are already underway to strengthen the international financial architecture within the constraints described above. The new international financial architecture is designed to be organized around four pillars: international standards, Chilean-style taxes on short-term foreign borrowing, greater exchange-rate flexibility and collective-action clauses in loan contracts to create an alternative to ever-bigger International Monetary Fund (IMF) bailouts. These four elements are designed to strengthen crisis prevention, moderate the severity of crises when they take place, speed the process of recovery and contain moral hazard in international financial markets. This, in a nutshell, is what the official community means when it talks about strengthening the international financial architecture (Camdessus, 1999). My own assessment is that, if these initiatives are pursued to their conclusion, they will succeed in making the world a safer financial place.

The danger is that the process is losing steam. This in turn reflects two developments, which are themselves unavoidable aspects of the process of reform. First, these particular reform efforts were identified through efficient agenda setting by the US Treasury, the G-7 and the IMF. As additional voices are now added to the chorus, the consensus built by the early agenda setters has come under strain. Asian participants and emerging-market participants more generally, having come late to the table, complain that existing blueprints do too little to address the special problems of small nations in large markets. In particular, they fail to adequately address the hedge-fund problem. Latin American participants complain that the addition of renegotiation-friendly provisions to loan contracts will raise borrowing costs, making it more difficult for them to access the foreign funds needed to deepen their financial markets, reduce their financial fragility and stimulate their growth. Financial-market participants similarly warn against the disruptive effects of any change.

Second, as time passes, the sense of urgency recedes and second thoughts inevitably develop. Early enthusiasm for greater exchange-rate flexibility has become tempered by awareness that more exchange-rate volatility can mean less capital-market access. Enthusiasm for Chilean-style holding period taxes to discourage excessive dependence on short-term capital flows is tempered by questions about the scope for evasion and increases in the cost of trade credit.

The push for collective-action clauses has been slowed by worries that they can be a source of moral hazard. Enthusiasm for international standards has been weakened by doubts about their effectiveness.

New voices and second thoughts can help to invigorate a stagnant debate, but disputes need to be settled in order to prevent the momentum for reform from being lost. In the social sciences we think that resolution results when there accumulates an overwhelming body of evidence on the effects of alternatives. This may be where academics and the staff of the multilaterals have fallen down. The other message of this chapter, then, is the need for more systematic empirical work, and quickly, on the key issues in the architecture debate.

Standards

The IMF has been criticized for expanding its surveillance and conditionality from the monetary, fiscal and exchange-rate policies that are its bread and butter to prudential supervision, auditing and accounting, bankruptcy procedures, corporate governance and competition policy, among other issues. Its intrusion into everything from the Suharto family's clove monopoly to Indonesia's national car program is attacked as invasive, unnecessary and counterproductive (Feldstein, 1998; Rodrik, 1999). It is invasive because it interferes with the traditional prerogatives of sovereign states. It is unnecessary because microeconomic and structural conditions are inappropriate for dealing with currency and financial crises that are essentially macroeconomic in nature. And it is counterproductive because different institutional arrangements are appropriate for different economic, legal and cultural settings and because ignoring this runs the risk of provoking a populist backlash.

The counter-argument is that high capital mobility makes it impossible to fix the international financial system without also fixing the domestic financial systems of countries active on international markets. International financial stability requires domestic financial stability, given the propensity for financial problems to spill across borders. And domestic financial stability can only be attained through institutional reform. This is the problem with Feldstein's conclusion that the IMF should stick to giving advice on monetary and fiscal policies and not meddle in the other internal arrangements of countries. Stabilizing a country's financial system requires institutional reforms extending well beyond policies toward external trade and payments. Few would question that creating a stable financial environment presupposes disclosure requirements for banks and corporations to make available the information required for market discipline to work, and prudential supervision to compensate for the shortcomings of banks' and firms' own risk-management practices. In a world where financial crises can spread contagiously, the international community has a common interest in seeing that all countries active on international markets adopt minimally acceptable domestic arrangements in these areas.

Some will argue that this is as far as the IMF and the international community should go in intruding into countries' internal affairs. I find it impossible to resist concluding that they must go further – that the need for domestic institutional reforms with implications for the stability of international financial markets extends beyond this point. It extends to the use of internationally recognized auditing and accounting practices, in whose absence lenders will be unable to accurately assess the financial condition of the banks and corporations to which they lend. It extends to effective creditor rights, in whose absence claimants will be unable to monitor and control the economic and financial decisions of managers. It extends to investor-protection laws to prevent insider trading, market cornering and related practices, in whose absence securities markets will not develop. It extends to fair and expeditious corporate bankruptcy procedures, without which debt problems can cascade from borrower to borrower. Countries can satisfy these desiderata in different ways, but in a world of capital market integration there is no avoiding the need to satisfy them.

The fear is that international pressure for reform will force all emerging markets to don what Friedman (1999) has dubbed the "golden straitjacket," denying them all opportunity to design regulatory institutions responsive to their distinctive economic, cultural and legal traditions. This is where standards come in. Standards, which define criteria to be met by all countries but permit them to satisfy them in different ways, offer a way of reconciling the common imperatives created by participation in international markets with the diversity of economic systems and structures. The complaint that the IMF's structural interventions are arbitrary and capricious at least partly explains the backlash they have provoked; with the promulgation of standards there will exist an objective set of criteria to which the Fund can refer when it demands structural reforms.

Designing international financial standards is a complex and multi-faceted process. It must proceed on many fronts, reflecting the extent to which the international financial system itself is multi-faceted. The IMF has taken the lead in this process, issuing a series of Experimental Studies on Transparency and attempting to coordinate its own standards-related initiatives with those of the World Bank, the Basle Committee and various private-sector bodies.[3] As a result it has become evident that neither the IMF nor the official community as a whole possesses the human resources necessary to design and monitor compliance with detailed international standards in all the relevant areas. In its experimental studies, the Fund has been forced to rely on self-evaluations by the subject countries, a practice, which compromises the objectivity of the process. For the Fund to carry out this function in a satisfactory way would require a very significant increase in its staff and a radical change in expertise, which are unlikely for the foreseeable future.[4]

This means relying as heavily as possible on the private sector: on the International Accounting Standards Committee, the International Federation of Accountants, the International Organization of Supreme Audit Institutions, Committee J of the International Bar Association and the International Corporate Governance Network, among others. Most of these self-organizing bodies have emerging-market members; some have subcommittees expressly concerned with issues of concern to emerging markets. The multilaterals should of course participate in the deliberations of these bodies as a way of taking "ownership" of the standards they set. But the private sector must take the lead. While the IMF and the other multilaterals can take on some standard-setting responsibilities themselves – witness the Fund's Special Data Dissemination Standard and Codes for Monetary and Fiscal Policies – the bulk of the work will have to take place elsewhere. This may already be the case for standard setting, but it is not yet true of compliance evaluation. My own idea (Eichengreen, 1999a) is that each self-organizing body should be encouraged to rate countries' compliance with their standards and to establish an electronic bulletin board on which to post this information. Hyperlinks should be provided to the Fund's own electronic bulletin board (as they already are, to a limited degree, for macroeconomic and financial data). Where the self-organizing committee is comprised of national regulators, the rating function could still be privatized; it could be spun off to commercial concerns like Fitch-IBCA, Moody's and Standard & Poor's.

Do the self-organizing bodies, or for that matter the rating agencies, have adequate incentive to stay on top of the task? Given the checkered record of the latter, there are real questions about the adequacy of their evaluations. In the end it may be necessary for the IMF to take on the compliance-evaluation function itself. The best way of doing so would be by publishing an annual report in which it rated each of its members' compliance in each of the relevant subareas (perhaps in conjunction with its annual or biannual Article IV consultations, and with help from the World Bank and the BIS). This is what the Fund's aforementioned Experimental Studies in Transparency are designed to do. But these studies do not include the kind of blunt ratings that effective evaluation requires. There are no bullet points akin to those for capital-account liberalization that appear in the Fund's *Exchange and Trade Restrictions* Annual. If the Fund is to reserve compliance evaluation for itself, then it will have to take the hard decision to move in this direction.

Lenders having a limited attention span, the IMF will in any case have to reinforce market discipline by offering the carrot of concessionary interest rates on its loans to countries that comply and by conditioning its programs on steps to bring national practice into conformance. It has taken a first step in this direction by specifying compliance with a range of transparency-related standards as a prerequisite for qualifying for its newly established Contingent Credit Facility. Unfortunately, at the time of writing no country has deemed it worthwhile to apply for a Contingent Credit Line. Moreover, the Articles of Agreement do not appear to permit differential interest rates for countries meeting different standards. Fixing this problem would require some fast footwork on the part of the Legal Department, or amending the Articles of Agreement.[5]

Notwithstanding wide international backing, reservations have been expressed about how much can be accomplished through the promulgation of international standards. There is widespread disagreement about the definition of acceptable standards – observe the dispute between the United States and Europe over accounting standards or the wide variation among the advanced-industrial countries in the provisions of bankruptcy and insolvency codes. There is the danger that an international standard broad enough to encompass these variations will tend toward a lowest common denominator. Moreover, standards, by defining the minimum acceptable threshold, may weaken the incentive for countries to do better. What will prevent governments from taking steps to meet the letter of the requirement without in fact satisfying its spirit?

Such qualms are reinforced by the experience with the most important experiment in standard setting to date, the Basle Capital Standards. The 1988 Capital Accord established an 8 percent minimum (weighted) capital adequacy standard for international banks. It deserves some credit for steps taken subsequently, by countries represented on the Basle Committee of Banking Supervisors and others, to bring capital adequacy up to this minimum. Reassuringly, the existence of the Basle Accord has not prevented countries like Argentina from doing better. But, at the same time, the Basle Standard has been subject to evasion. The gap between the reported and actual capital of Japan's international banks is notorious, and the Basle Accord did nothing to head off or resolve the Japanese banking crisis. Banks have discovered ways of shifting assets subject to high capital charges off balance sheet through securitization and the use of complex derivatives without modifying the underlying risks. This should serve as a warning of the danger that the standard setters will always be one step behind the markets. Finally, experience with the 1988 Capital Accord points up the fact that poorly designed standards, or standards that lag behind circumstances, can create perverse incentives. One need only recall the incentive in the 1988 Accord to engage in short-term lending to non-OECD countries.[6] Observers of the Asian crisis will be aware of the consequences.

Perhaps the most fundamental critique of this push for standards is that it is based on the dubious notion that stabilizing markets requires additional regulation. Many of the aforementioned standards (for prudential supervision, bank capitalization, etc.) are meant as guides for regulation. They are designed to identify minimally acceptable levels of regulation for all countries active on international financial markets. Yet, experience with the Basle Capital Standard creates real reasons to think that the regulators will always be one step behind the markets. This is why alternative approaches to prudential supervision, like requiring banks to issue uninsured subordinated debt, are gaining ground in the United States. The solution to the financial-instability problem, it is argued, lies in strengthening the market discipline – in the present context by creating a constituency of subordinated debt holders who stand to gain nothing from additional risk taking and are likely to be especially averse to exceptional losses – not in adding additional regulation. This has led some to dismiss the entire standard-setting enterprise as misguided.

This critique is too strong. Many of the standards on which the international policy community is focusing are designed precisely to strengthen market discipline. This is the case for auditing, accounting, public disclosure of corporate and financial balance sheets and corporate governance generally; their purpose is to strengthen the information provision and creditor rights without which market discipline cannot be effective. Whether one believes that the emphasis should be placed on government regulation or market discipline, standards are the way to proceed.

Exchange rates and the capital account

The single most reliable leading indicator of crisis risk in emerging markets (maybe the only reliable leading indicator) is short-term external debt, the short-term external debt of the banking system in particular.[7] Short-term debt is liquid, and if investors choose to liquidate it, serious financial problems can arise. When the debt in question is debt of the banking system, whose assets are relatively illiquid (by definition, since banks are in the business of providing liquidity-transformation services to information-impacted segments of the economy), the result can be bank runs and banking crises. The consequences are especially disruptive in late-developing countries, where the informational prerequisites for securitized markets are missing and banks dominate the market in intermediation services.

Capital requirements can apply appropriate incentives on both the borrowing and lending sides, although there are reasons to worry about their effectiveness in politicized environments where capital is all too rarely written down, and given the scope for regulatory arbitrage.

Holding-period taxes *a la* Chile can also be used to lengthen the maturity structure of the debt. There is an enormous debate over the effectiveness of these taxes. Some critics insist that evasion remains a problem. Others observe the lack of evidence that Chile's taxes limited the overall level of foreign borrowing. The second objection can be dismissed on the grounds that the goal was never to limit the overall level of foreign borrowing but to alter its average maturity, and on the maturity front the evidence is compelling. As for the first objection, it is important to recall that such a measure, in order to lengthen the maturity structure of the debt, need not be evasion free. For the time being, the last word on this issue goes to Chile's finance minister, who has asked (I paraphrase), "If these capital-import taxes are so easily evaded, then why do we have so many non-interest-bearing foreign deposits at the central bank?" But better pinning down the effects of these policies should be a high priority for empirical work.[8]

The other way of discouraging banks and corporates from developing excessive dependence on short term, unhedged foreign debt is by pursuing policies of greater exchange-rate flexibility. Allowing the exchange rate to fluctuate is the only credible way of encouraging agents to hedge their exposures. A pegged rate provides an incentive for the private sector to accumulate unhedged foreign debts. To defend the peg, the government is forced to insist that there is no prospect that it will change. How many chief financial officers will then be rewarded before the fact for purchasing costly exchange-rate insurance on currency forward and futures markets? If the currency is allowed to fluctuate on a day-to-day basis, banks and firms will learn the importance of purchasing insurance against currency swings. Then, when the exchange rate does move by an unexpectedly large amount, they will not be thrust into bankruptcy by the increase in the cost of servicing short-term foreign debts. A currency crash will not automatically mean a financial crash, as it did, for example, in Indonesia in 1997–98, and the greater stability of the domestic financial system will in turn stabilize the exchange rate.

While this was the consensus of first-generation contributions to the architecture debate, opinion has been swinging back in the other direction. Skeptics argue that greater exchange-rate variability means less access to foreign capital, which in turn means shallower financial markets, greater financial fragility and slower growth.[9] A fluctuating currency makes it less attractive for foreign lenders to lend, especially in the currency of the borrowing country. Capital flows, especially short-term portfolio capital flows, are less. This is apparent in the strikingly low correlation of savings and investment in particular regions of larger countries, in contrast to the much higher correlations for countries as a whole. Another way of making the point is that a fluctuating (or potentially fluctuating) currency, which discourages foreign investors from lending in the currency of the borrowing country, also limits the ability of banks and firms to hedge their foreign-currency exposures in the aggregate. They can reshuffle those exposures so as to avoid dangerous concentrations, but the overall level of foreign-currency exposure is given. Greater exchange-rate flexibility, which creates an incentive to hedge these risks shows up in a lower level of foreign borrowing.

Indeed, if the costs as well as the benefits of hedging rise with exchange-rate volatility, more volatility will not necessarily mean more hedging. In currency forward and futures markets, where there is uncertainty about whether the counterparty will be able to deliver on the contract, costs can be sharply rising. Markets in currency hedges are insurance markets, and, as in any insurance market, adverse selection can interfere with the tendency for the quantity of insurance to rise with the underlying risk. As the risks go up, it may pay to buy and sell less. Combining the greater risks due to currency volatility with the increased cost of purchasing insurance cover suggests that the reduction in unhedged exposures will be achieved through a fall in the level of borrowing and lending.

Thus, greater exchange-rate variability may reduce crisis risk, but it may also slow economic growth in countries whose development strategies depend on capital imports. Some may therefore want to go all the way in the other direction, to dollarization, to obtain freer access to capital flows. But making dollarization work requires putting in place supportive conditions. The banking system must be strengthened to compensate for the absence of a lender of last resort. The budget must be balanced to compensate for the reduced scope for the central bank to backstop the market in public debt. Otherwise, dollarization may only convert currency crises into financial crises.

The interesting question, familiar to observers of European monetary unification, is whether such reforms must be put in place prior to abandoning the domestic currency, which implies that this solution to the currency conundrum will not occur anytime soon, or whether they can be induced by an early shift to dollarization. The proponents of early dollarization would argue as follows. Abandoning a national currency for the dollar will bring down interest rates by eliminating currency risk, thereby strengthening the fiscal position (as in countries like Ireland, Portugal, Spain and Italy in Stage II of the Maastricht convergence process). Moreover, to the extent that the weakness of banking systems in emerging markets reflects currency and maturity mismatches that inevitably arise when a country has a weak national currency, the definition of a weak currency being an inability to borrow abroad in domestic-currency terms (hence the currency mismatches), and to borrow at home long-term (hence the maturity mismatches) dollarization, by eliminating these constraints, will strengthen the banking system. Dollarization need not wait on prior reform, in this view, because it delivers that reform.

Even if this is the case, the number of emerging markets that are willing to pursue this alternative is likely to remain few. The story would be different were it possible for Mexico or Argentina to obtain a seat on the Federal Reserve Board and influence the stance of their common monetary policy. But the day when the United States is prepared to grant Mexico or Argentina a seat on the Open Market Committee, or even extend US bank regulation and limited lender-of-last-resort services to the country, is still very away. Monetary unification may be the vision of the future, but more flexible rates are the reality for today.

Bailing in the private sector

Ensuring greater private-sector burden sharing has proven to be immensely complicated, making it one of the sticking points in efforts to strengthen the architecture. Initiatives along these lines are motivated by the perception that IMF programs starting with Mexico have let private investors off the hook and are therefore a source of moral hazard. In addition, because the Fund is almost always paid back, these payoffs to investors are effectively transfers from the taxpayers of the crisis country to the international financial community.

In thinking about the problem, it is important to emphasize two points. First, what has worked before is unlikely to work again, due to changes in market structure and circumstances. Second, we should be cautious of rules-based approaches to bailing in the private sector. The problem is that this may only precipitate additional crises, as the markets anticipate the authorities' response and scramble out the day before.

The most widely cited instance of bailing in the private sector was at the end of 1997, when bankers and officials canceled their Christmas and New Year holidays in order to negotiate a debt rollover for Korea. The country's maturing bank loans were renewed (typically for an additional ninety days) and subsequently converted into bonds, averting a full-fledged financial meltdown. There is the question, of course, of whether this was actually an instance of private-sector burden sharing, since the banks did not "take a hit" (in fact they were compensated generously for their forbearance). Equally important, however, is whether this approach can be used again in the future. There are reasons for thinking not. For one, future debt will not be bank debt to the same extent. The securitization of claims is ongoing: bond debt has risen from about 20 percent of total non-official credit to emerging markets in 1990 to 70 percent in 1997. There will be more holders of these securities (hedge funds, pension funds, insurance companies and individual investors), making it harder to bring the players to the table. Moreover, not all other countries will have the recently elected democratic governments with a reformist mandate, which in Korea encouraged the banks to stay in. Not all other countries will have fundamentally strong economies affected mainly by liquidity problems and well positioned to bounce back subsequently. Finally, the sovereign guarantee the Korean Government provided first to the domestic banks and then to the bonds into which the bank credits were converted, which also reassured investors, was viable only by virtue of the sovereign's light debt load, an advantage that not all governments will enjoy.

Efforts to arrange private-sector burden sharing for Ukraine and Pakistan in late 1998 and early 1999 are more informative insofar as these cases involved mainly securitized debts. In Ukraine the securities in question were a 375 million hryvnia ($90 million) tranche of treasury bills falling due on September 22, 1998, which the country found impossible to roll over due to the Russian crisis. The IMF then arranged a $2.2 billion credit, of which $257 million was made available immediately. But to prevent its disbursement from being used to pay off private creditors, the Fund set a target for exchange reserves, conformance with which effectively prevented the Ukrainian Government from paying back these bills in hard currency. The government pressured the creditors to restructure (to exchange their treasury bills for longer term zero-coupon eurobonds) and payed investors who resisted in local currency, which could be used to purchase goods and services domestically but could not be repatriated.

While this is a straightforward way of bailing in the bondholders, it is not without risk. When a country is declared to be in default, the bondholders can sue, triggering cross-default clauses in the country's other debt instruments and requiring immediate repayment. In Ukraine's case, reassuringly, the creditors did not sue. But before concluding that the Fund should employ this approach more widely, it is worth noting the aspects in which Ukraine's situation was special. The debts in question were domestic-currency-denominated securities, not eurobonds, which are effectively regarded as senior by the markets. And the bonds in question were governed by Ukrainian law, rendering legal recourse unattractive.

Pakistan's case involved eurobonds. The country was driven to consider renegotiating them, along with its much larger debts to official creditors, by a combination of domestic economic problems and the disruption to its market access following its tests of nuclear devices in May 1998, and did so through the Paris Club. In the context of the negotiations a country undertakes in the Paris Club for debt relief from its official creditors, it is normal practice for the government to be required to seek comparable treatment from its private creditors. Typically, the private creditors of Paris Club supplicants have been banks (whose credits are renegotiated through the London Club), not bondholders, since low-income countries with an overhang of official debts have found it understandably difficult to borrow on the bond market. Thus, the inclusion of bonds in the comparability provision of Pakistan's Paris Club Minute is precedent setting.

However, this case is again not representative of the situation in which many other countries will find themselves. Pakistan's eurobonds are British-style instruments, which can be restructured subject to the approval of only a majority of the holders, not unanimous consent as is the case with American-style bonds. This limits the likelihood that a restructuring agreement will precipitate legal action.

This brings us to the case for amending loan contracts to include sharing clauses, majority voting clauses and minimum legal threshold clauses. It is worth restating how this idea fits into the architecture debate. A credible commitment by the IMF not to automatically run to the rescue of a country that would otherwise find it impossible to keep current on its obligations presupposes the existence of a viable mechanism for dealing with problem debts. It is easy to *say* that the Fund should not automatically bail out governments and their creditors, but it is hard for it not to *do* so as long as there do not exist other ways of reasonably addressing financial problems when they arise. The shortcoming of existing arrangements is that they make workouts excessively difficult. Since many international bonds include provisions requiring the unanimous consent of bondholders to the terms of a restructuring agreement, there is an incentive for "vultures" to buy up the outstanding debt and threaten legal action. Unlike syndicated bank loans, most such bonds lack sharing clauses requiring individual creditors to share with other bondholders any amounts recovered from the borrower and thereby discouraging recourse to lawsuits.

Those who believe that countries may have to take occasional recourse to suspensions and restructurings argue that these provisions in bond covenants should be modified. Majority voting and sharing clauses would discourage maverick investors from resorting to lawsuits and other ways of obstructing settlements beneficial to the debtor and the majority of creditors alike. Collective-representation clauses, which specify who represents the bondholders and make provision for a bondholders committee or meeting, would allow orderly solutions to be reached. This was suggested in 1996 by the G-10 in its post-Mexico report and echoed in a series of recent G-22 and G-7 reports and declarations. The G-7 then placed the issue on its work program for reforming the international financial system with the goal of reaching a consensus by the Cologne Summit in June of 1999.

The objection to this idea is that it would raise the cost of borrowing by making it too easy for countries to walk away from their debts. Collective-action clauses would weaken the bonding role of debt. They would create moral hazard. They would disrupt credit-market access.

The counter-argument is that provision for orderly restructurings would make emerging-market issues more attractive by minimizing acrimonious disputes, unproductive negotiations and extended periods when no service is paid and growth is depressed by a suffocating debt overhang. As *The Economist* put it in a leader, "the prospect of an orderly renegotiation rather than a messy default might actually make some bonds more attractive" (*Economist*, 1999, p. 21).

The analogy with domestic bankruptcy procedures supports this more optimistic interpretation. Presumably, few of the critics would argue that countries should abolish their bankruptcy laws and reinstitute debtor's prison to discourage borrowers from walking away from their debts. Rather, they acknowledge the need in the domestic context for balancing measures designed to strengthen the ex ante bonding role against the efficiency advantages of ex post procedures to efficiently restructure problem debts. They may still object that recent proposals move too far from the first end of the spectrum to the second: it could be that, given the legal immunity sovereign borrowers enjoy and the special legal difficulties of seizing the assets of foreign borrowers in general, collective-action clauses would seriously weaken the bonding role of debt. But this is an empirical question.

Unfortunately, it is one that has been informed by little empirical analysis. This is disappointing insofar as there already exists a market in London on which "British-style bonds" incorporating collective-action clauses are issued. Comparisons of the spreads on these bonds with spreads on otherwise equivalent "American-style" bonds are an obvious way of evaluating the afore-mentioned arguments.

Upon reflection it becomes apparent that the comparison is not straight-forward. Not only does one have to control for observable borrower characteristics and market conditions affecting emerging-market spreads, but the choice of governing law is likely to be endogenous and depends on the issuer's characteristics. Borrowers who anticipate the need to restructure may be attracted to instruments that anticipate this eventuality, as will lenders who value quick resolution. Alternatively, borrowers thought likely to default on their obligations may incur the greatest surcharge if they issue a loan with collective-action provisions, encouraging them to opt for bonds that exclude these clauses. Thus, while the possibility of bias due to the endogeneity of the choice of governing law cannot be ignored, not even its direction is clear.

Indeed, not just the costs of funding but also the very ability of developing-country borrowers to access the market may be affected by collective-action clauses. High-risk borrowers, far from just being charged more for contracts including these provisions, may not be able to obtain loans at any price. Alternatively, if collective-action clauses increase borrowing costs, they might cause high-quality borrowers to quit the market. Either way, the implication is that even estimates of the effect of choice of governing law on spreads that control for the endogeneity of the choice of governing law will still be contaminated by selectivity bias. Any attempt to infer the impact of collective-action clauses on borrowing costs from the existing pool of borrowers would still be biased insofar as the composition of that pool could change with the introduction of those provisions.

This does not mean that it is impossible to analyze the impact of collective-action clauses on emerging-market spreads, only that this must be done using a framework that takes these problems into account. Eichengreen and Mody (2000) attempt to do just that. Looking at all international bonds issued in the 1990s for which the relevant information is available (approximately 2,000 bonds), we find that the choice of governing law (United Kingdom, which generally includes collective-action clauses, versus New York, which does not) has a negligible impact on borrowing costs, as if the advantages of orderly resolution and the disadvantages of moral hazard offset. But when we disaggregate by creditworthiness, sharper results emerge. Issuers from countries with high credit ratings pay significantly lower spreads on bonds issued under UK law. In contrast, issuers from countries with low credit ratings feel the opposite effect. These findings are intuitive. The most creditworthy borrowers will go to the wall to avoid having to suspend service on their debts. (Think of South Korea and the implications of its geopolitical alliance with the United States for its attitude toward the maintenance of debt service.) For creditworthy countries, the moral-hazard effect is negligible. The advantages of orderly restructuring in the event of truly extraordinary events beyond the control of the country are attractive to investors, who take up the bonds in question at lower spreads. For countries with less sterling credit, in contrast, moral hazard remains a concern, perhaps the dominant one. For them, collective-action provisions that weaken the bonding role of debt result in higher spreads.

So while mandating collective action clauses in bond contracts might make life more difficult for less creditworthy borrowers, it should make life easier for the more creditworthy. This is a reminder of the dangers of lumping together all emerging markets whether the issue is architecture or another topic. But if one of the goals of architectural reform is to encourage the markets to better differentiate among borrowers and more generously reward efforts to improve creditworthiness, then mandating the inclusion of collective-action clauses in loan contracts becomes more attractive. And for those concerned with distribution and with the welfare of the least creditworthy countries, it suggests the need to marry this kind of architectural reform to other initiatives (like debt relief) expressly tailored for their problems.

More generally, the backward-looking, case-by-case approach relied upon so far by the IMF and the US Treasury to bail in the private sector fails to meet minimally acceptable standards for clarity, transparency and equity. The international policy community is experimenting on small countries whose default is unlikely to threaten systemic stability, which may be prudent from a systemic point of view but is hardly equitable. Insofar as these countries are special, bailing in the private sector hardly constitutes the kind of useful precedent the "bailers" wish to set. It would be better to devote less of the international community's scarce political capital to backward-looking efforts to deal with these special cases and more to forward-looking efforts to amend loan contracts.

The hedge-fund problem

The hedge-fund problem has attracted considerable attention in Asia and elsewhere. It is important to recognize that this is not just a bee in Mr Mahathir's bonnet. Official reports from countries other than Malaysia (namely Reserve Bank of Australia, 1999) have argued that hedge-fund operations in their markets have considerably aggravated volatility. While such allegations can be disputed, given how little public information is available about hedge-fund trades and positions, they deserve to be taken seriously.

The most important point about hedge funds is how little is special about them. Hedge funds are highly leveraged, but so are investment banks and other financial institutions. They take short positions in assets markets, but so do other investors. They utilize exotic and "plain-vanilla" derivative securities, but so do other market participants. They move in and out of emerging markets, but so do mutual funds, commercial banks, investment banks and a variety of other financial entities. One can argue that hedge funds are more flexible, more aggressive or more predatory, but given the extent to which their capital is swamped by, say, the proprietary trading desks of investment banks, their impact on market outcomes is easily swamped as well.

Consider, for example, the issue of leverage. George Soros has testified to the US Congress that the Quantum Funds are leveraged by a factor of 2 to 3. This is typical of the macro funds surveyed by Hennessee Associates, MAR/Hedge and other consulting firms. According to MarHedge, a third of hedge funds do not use leverage at all, and fewer than one in six lever their assets more than twice. Such simple measures of leverage are highest for market neutral-arbitrage funds, since the volatility of an unlevered market-portfolio would normally be low.[10] Macro funds use moderate leverage on an average: nearly 70 percent claim to lever their capital less than two times. To be sure, one can question the accuracy of such generalizations. The survey data on which they are based are provided voluntarily and not verified independently. However, US Government (1999) reports, on the basis of mandatory Commodity Pool Operator (CPO) filings with the CFTC, that as of September 1998 it was aware of only ten hedge funds with on-balance-sheet leverage of more than 10 to 1, and one hedge fund with leverage of more than 30 to 1.[11] The omission of off-balance sheet items, which may be particularly important for certain classes of hedge funds, may lead their leverage to be understated. That said, banks would still appear to be even more leveraged than hedge funds as a group. The typical gearing ratio for commercial banks is on the order of 10 to 1, while the ratio of total assets to equity, or gross leverage, for the top investment banks ranges from 25 to 35 (the ratio of gross assets excluding matched-book financing to equity, or net leverage, ranges from 10 to 25).[12] Admittedly, investment banks and other institutional investors have more diversified portfolios; they are unlikely to concentrate their positions in particular markets.[13] But their capital is orders of magnitude larger, so even a small portfolio share can swamp the entire hedge-fund industry.

Hence, changing the way hedge funds are regulated or forcing them to disclose information about their operations would change nothing from the emerging-market point of view. To be sure, hedge funds have played a prominent role in a certain emerging-market crises; the IMF's hedge fund study pointed to Thailand as an example.[14] But given the growing international activities of other institutional investors including not just investment banks but also commercial banks, mutual funds and pension funds, the instances where hedge funds dominate conditions in individual emerging markets are likely to be even less common in the future than the past. Tighter regulation of hedge funds would change little in terms of aggregate market outcomes.[15]

This has not stemmed the flood of reports on the industry from, *inter alia*, the BIS, the US Treasury, the Fed, the Securities and Exchange Commission, the Commodity Futures Trading Commission, and the Financial Stability Forum. Some of their suggestions are uncontroversial. To whit: supervisors should better monitor the exposure of their banks and nonbank intermediaries to hedge-fund counterparties, since the failure of a major hedge-fund counterparty like Long-Term Capital can threaten systemic stability; and the Basle Capital Standards should be amended to require capital surcharges for lending to counterparties (including hedge funds) that do not disclose information on their balance sheets and positions. In addition, the US–German proposal for a "credit registry" to assemble in one place national regulators' data on their banks' exposures to highly leveraged institutions could be usefully revived. One of the major problems uncovered in the course of the LTCM crisis was that US regulators knew the exposure of US banks to LTCM, while Swiss regulators knew the exposure of Swiss banks to LTCM, but they did not know the exposure of one another's banks or the overall degree of leverage acquired by the firm, and hence the risk it posed to systemic stability. Creating mechanisms for effective information sharing is the obvious solution.[16]

The most radical report on the hedge-fund issue to date is that of the Joint Task Force of the US President. It recommends that hedge funds registered as CPOs, and which therefore are obliged to report to the CFTC, should be made to file more comprehensive reports on a quarterly (rather than an annual basis), and that this information should be made public. Funds that are not registered as CPOs should be required to disclose similar financial information, presumably also on a quarterly basis. Financial institutions, for their part, should be required to disclose a summary of their exposure to hedge-fund counterparties.

While this push for disclosure is understandable, serious doubts can be raised about its efficacy. First, will quarterly reports be a significant improvement over annual reports, given the speed with which hedge funds put on and take off positions? Would a report for the second quarter of 1998 made available to the public in the third quarter have provided significant advance warning of the difficulties of LTCM to the regulators or have headed off subsequent difficulties through the operation of market discipline? This seems unlikely.

In addition, requiring additional disclosure may simply lead hedge funds to relocate offshore. The task force therefore recommends that offshore financial centers adopt and comply with internationally agreed upon standards for disclosure and prudential supervision. Recommend it can, but offshore financial centers and tax havens are a long-standing problem.[17] From this point of view, the recommendation that regulators (and the Basle Committee) apply tougher capital standards on counterparty transactions for banks doing business with financial entities offshore that do not comply with the Basle Core Principles is useful, but there is again the danger that any such initiative would be neutralized by regulatory arbitrage.

Then there is the question of whether there is justification for additional *public* disclosure. The Task Force appears to believe that public disclosure will strengthen market discipline on hedge-fund counterparties (as opposed to hedge funds themselves, on which few members of the public hold claims). This proposition is as dubious as the mechanism is indirect. The case for additional disclosure to regulators is strong, but that for additional disclosure to the public is weak.

How then should the hedge-fund problem be addressed? For regulators concerned with systemic stability, there is no alternative to tightening up oversight of hedge-fund counterparties. Regulators responsible for seeing that banks and other credit providers stay on top of the operations of their hedge-fund customers should continue to scrutinize these functions in the course of the normal supervision process. In addition, regulators should more systematically share information on the exposure of the intermediaries for which they are responsible. For developing countries concerned with the potential for large hedge funds to destabilize small markets, the available options are entry and exit taxes to discourage the kind of short round-trips in which hedge-funds engage, and more flexible exchange rates to avoid offering the one-way bets hedge-fund managers find so appealing. Neither policy offers foolproof protection against threats to market integrity, but these are the only instruments whose costs do not exceed their benefits.

Regional funds

The idea of an Asia Fund to supplement the IMF was advanced by the Japanese Government following the outbreak of the Asian crisis and has been developed further by various academics and officials.[18] Three rationales for the approach can be usefully distinguished. While I discuss them here in the Asian context, the implications are more general.

First, peer pressure may work better at the regional level. Europe, where mutual surveillance has a long history and a procedure by that name has been enshrined in the Maastricht Treaty, is frequently cited a case in point. But in contrast with Europe, Asia (and other regions) lacks institutions with track records comparable to those of the EU's Monetary Committee and Ecofin Council. Nor do Asian countries appear ready to negotiate an international treaty that makes provision for serious sanctions and fines like those of the Maastricht Treaty for countries that fail to adjust their domestic policies. More fundamentally, Asia lacks the tradition of integrationist thought and the web of interlocking agreements that encourage monetary and financial cooperation in Europe. There is no counterpart to the social and political "pillars" of the Maastricht Treaty to support the application of peer pressure. There is no wider web of political and diplomatic agreements to be placed at risk by a failure to cooperate on monetary and financial matters.

Second, because economic structures and conditions vary by region, neighboring countries have a comparative advantage in diagnosing their distinctive economic problems and crafting appropriate solutions. All Asian economies have bank-based financial systems and highly geared corporate sectors, which the IMF overlooked, the argument goes, when prescribing interest-rate hikes to deal with the crisis; an Asian Monetary Fund would not have committed such an egregious error. This seems to me to exaggerate structural similarities within the region. It is hard to think of three more structurally different economies than Japan, Indonesia and China, for example.

Third, and related to the preceding, it is argued that the creation of regional monetary funds will intensify competition in the market for ideas. If countries in crisis could appeal to both the IMF and a regional monetary fund, whose assistance was conditioned on different policy actions, then a genuine market in ideas would develop, and only institutions giving sound advice would be able to retain a customer base. If it has a poorer understanding of the roots of the Asian crisis and what measures should be taken to address it than experts employed by the Asia Fund, the IMF will lose business to its regional competitor.

Unfortunately, the analogy with market competition is questionable. In a competitive economy, the firm with the best ideas produces the best product, makes the most profits and ends up dominating its market. It is not clear that the same is true of the market in policy advice and official financial assistance. Intergovernmental organizations do not behave like profit-maximizing firms. A multilateral that offers inferior advice does not necessarily end up losing market share and "filing for bankruptcy." The IMF is paid before other creditors whether its advice is good or bad. It does not follow that a regional fund that lent to governments at unrealistically low interest rates would be driven out of business, since it would more likely than not have its coffers replenished by the high-income countries that were its principal shareholders.

Thus, while the idea of regional funds to supplement the crisis-prevention and crisis-management functions of the IMF has intuitive appeal, closer scrutiny raises serious questions about the approach.

Changing the governance of the IMF

My book on architecture (Eichengreen 1999a) is subtitled "A *Practical* Post Asia Agenda." Given that focus, I have been criticized for not offering more ambitious, far-reaching proposals. While officials need to be practical, the critique goes, academics should be provocative and ambitious. This chapter therefore closes with an ambitious scheme.[19]

A problem with IMF decision-making, in the view of many critics (emerging-market critics in particular), is that it is excessively politicized. Excessive weight tends to be attached to national interests, interfering with the IMF's ability to pursue its global mandate. It has been argued, for example, that several of the Fund's recent programs, like those for Mexico, serve the interests of creditor countries by providing financial assistance that allowed foreign portfolio investors to be repaid at the expense of the taxpayers of the crisis country. Here the implication is that IMF policies were used to advance creditor interests, at the expense of creating moral hazard and at considerable cost to the Mexican taxpayer. It is similarly argued that the US Government arm-twisted the Fund into agreeing to continued disbursements for Russia in 1997–98, despite evidence that economic and financial reform there was off track, in an effort to prop up what it perceived as a reform-minded government and out of concern that failure would bring to power extremists who could not be trusted with the country's nuclear capability. Again, the implication is that IMF policies were used to further US security objectives rather than in the pursuit of financial stability, aggravating moral hazard rather than furthering reform. It is argued that the conditionality the Fund attached to its Asian programs, requiring the crisis countries to open their financial markets and distribution systems to foreign competition, served the interests of advanced-industrial countries seeking market access more than the crisis countries themselves.

If the problem is that the Fund's decisions are distorted by the parochial concerns of national governments, then greater independence from those governments is the logical solution. The obvious way of achieving this is by amending the Articles of Agreement to enhance the independence of the Executive Board. Executive Directors could still be appointed by national governments or groups of governments, just as central bank governors in some federal systems are appointed by state or regional governments. But if Directors are too inclined to take advice from those governments, then the Articles should be amended to discourage them from doing so. If the Statute of the European System of Central Banks prohibits members of the ECB Board from taking advice from their governments, in other words, why should not the IMF's Articles of the Agreement impose the same prohibition on Executive Directors?

Effective independence may require amending the Articles to appoint Directors to multi-year terms of office and to create high hurdles to their dismissal. Their independence will be strengthened if they receive adequate compensation.[20] It may be desirable to include a provision barring them from moving laterally into government or finance for a specified period following their term on the Board. True independence may in addition require budgetary independence. All large international rescue packages in the 1990s have been cobbled together out of contributions from the IMF, other multilaterals and national governments. Given the rapid expansion of international liquidity, IMF resources alone have not been enough. The Fund's dependence on financial supplementation from national governments would be another check on the institution's independent Directors. It may be desirable therefore to amend the Articles of Agreement to give the Fund the option of borrowing on the market, subject to the concurrence of a supermajority of the Board (see also Lerrick, 1999).

The danger with such reforms is that they would vest too much power in an all-powerful board of monetary technocrats. This could be addressed by amending the Articles to give Directors an explicit mandate and by insisting on greater transparency, notably by requiring more decisions to be taken on the basis of up-or-down votes and releasing the results. In addition, Directors should be required to explain their decisions, and the substance of Board discussions should be made public. If Directors have idiosyncratic objectives, greater transparency of decision-making will reveal their hidden agendas, which will in turn strengthen their incentives to pursue the Fund's mandate. Directors' ultimate constituencies will then be able to judge whether their representatives supported or resisted a particular Fund policy, and Directors, rather than going along to get along, will have an incentive to register their dissents.

Ultimately, a specific body must have the power to hold the Executive Board accountable. The obvious candidate is the Interim Committee (recently transformed into the International Monetary and Financial Committee, by a decision of the IMF Executive Board). Individual Directors or even the entire Board could be dismissed by a supermajority vote of the Interim Committee. The French Government among others has suggested vesting additional power with the Interim Committee as a way of reinvigorating the Fund.[21] Making provision for the Interim Committee to hold Directors accountable is a way of achieving this without politicizing the activities of the Fund.

More than a few readers will be inclined to dismiss this proposal as unrealistic. Perhaps. But who could have imagined a few years ago how many countries would have moved to establish independent central banks? In an age when some observers call for abolishing the IMF and others recommend creating a "true international lender of last resort," enhancing the independence of its Board is a limited reform. For those who recognize that financial markets are imperfect and acknowledge that those imperfections create the need for an institution to back-stop the markets, but who at the same time worry that national agendas too often distort IMF decision-making, this is a logical way to proceed.

Where we stand

Official efforts to strengthen the international financial architecture are organized around four pillars: international standards for financial management and regulation, Chilean-style taxes on short-term foreign borrowing as a form of prudential regulation to be imposed until countries have brought other forms of banking-sector supervision up to world-class levels, greater exchange-rate flexibility for the majority of emerging-market economies, and collective-action clauses to create an alternative to ever-bigger IMF bailouts. All four elements would have to be adopted to make the world a safer financial place. The good news is that all four elements are on the agenda. Each of them has been embraced by either the United States or other countries. The bad news is that not all four elements have been embraced by *both* the United States and other countries.

International standards are one element on which everyone agrees, although much remains to be done to ensure effective monitoring and adequate incentives to comply. The United States has endorsed greater exchange-rate flexibility for emerging markets and the use of Chilean-style capital-inflow taxes. But it is still reluctant to do more than utter some encouraging words to bring about the introduction of collective action clauses into loan agreements. Unfortunately, without the addition of renegotiation-friendly provisions to loan contracts, the IMF cannot credibly promise to stand aside when a country is pushed to the brink. And if the IMF cannot credibly refuse to organize a financial rescue, then the incentives for emerging markets to adopt greater exchange-rate flexibility and taxes on short-term capital inflows will remain weak.

European policy makers, for their part, are even more concerned about private sector burden sharing. They are less reluctant to require the introduction of new provisions in loan contracts. But given their own experience, they are less understanding of the need for exchange-rate flexibility. And the same is true of Asia, where there continues to be talk of a yen bloc based on basket pegs with common weights for the countries of the region, the disastrous experience with pegs in the first half of the 1990s, to the contrary, notwithstanding. Without greater exchange-rate flexibility, the temptation to engage in excessive short-term foreign borrowing will remain, and the adverse financial consequences of large exchange-rate changes, when they come, will be all the more devastating. Again, asserting that the IMF could simply stand aside and let events play themselves out is not credible.

Thus, while constructive steps have already been taken to strengthen the international financial architecture, the new table on which the system will rest remains rickety. It has at best three legs, not four. And without all four legs, stability will be lacking.

Notes

1 This is to say that historians debate the extent to which the United Kingdom provided an effective counterweight to the United States at Bretton Woods.
2 See Eatwell and Taylor (1999). There are cross currents, to be sure – think of the European Union's institutions of transnational economic governance, or NATO in the Balkans – which raise profound questions about the nature of national sovereignty in the twenty-first century. Still, the reality for the foreseeable future will be one of global markets but national governments.
3 These documents would more accurately be labeled "Experimental Studies of Standards." That "transparency" instead appears in the title reflects the fact that British officials, who were first to push the idea of annual IMF reports in this area, used the transparency moniker.
4 See the discussion of resource implications in IMF (1999).
5 Another potential step in this direction, to be adopted not by the Fund but by national regulators, has been suggested by the Basle Committee, whose proposal for revising the 1988 Capital Accord would key the risk weights on international lending to the compliance of the capital-importing countries with a range of financial standards (Basle Committee, 1999). It is yet to be seen whether this idea features in any ultimate revision of the Accord.
6 While lending to OECD banks was given a risk weight of 20 percent irrespective of the term of the loan, lending to non-OECD banks carried this reduced weight only for loans of less than a year, whereas loans of longer maturity carried the full 100 percent risk weight.
7 To be sure, saying that short-term debt is a useful leading or concurrent indicator is different from saying that it plays a causal role in financial instability. The accumulation of short-term debt may simply be a manifestation of other economic and financial problems in whose presence countries will find it impossible to roll over their maturing long-term loans and find it impossible to avoid accumulating short-term external liabilities (Eichengreen and Hausmann, 1999). Thus, in economic analysis – as opposed to forecasting – it is important to distinguish alternative sources of the accumulation of short-term debt.
8 A start has been made by Calvo and Reinhart (1999), who find in a fifteen-country panel, including Chile, that the presence of capital controls is significantly associated with a lower share of portfolio plus short-term capital flows as a percentage of total flows. That they do not find the same when they look at portfolio flows alone suggests that the impact on short-term flows is doing most of the work.
9 See Hausmann *et al.* (1999).
10 This is, of course, the category in which LTCM is traditionally placed. This suggests that some hedge funds with exceptionally high investment to capital ratios may be

lurking in the survey returns referred. LTCM normally leveraged its capital 20–30 times; the much higher ratios *c*. September 1998 that were reported in the press reflected the extraordinary losses of capital following Russia's default.

11 No extra credit for guessing the one hedge fund with an exceptionally high leverage ratio. Unpublished data from Hennessee Associates suggests that 12 percent of all hedge funds had leverage ratios greater than 8 to 1 at the end of 1998, including 8 percent of macro funds, 33 percent of emerging market funds, 25 percent of technology funds and 71 percent of distressed securities funds. I thank Lee Hennessee for this information.

12 As reported in International Monetary Fund (1999). The five largest commercial bank holding companies had average leverage ratios of 14 to 1 at the end of 1998 according to US Government (1999).

13 As argued by Reserve Bank of Australia (1999), p. 5.

14 Eichengreen and Mathieson *et al.* (1998). Yam (1999) and Grenville (1999) similarly conclude that they moved markets in Hong Kong and Australia in 1998.

15 A recent piece on hedge funds in the *New Yorker Magazine*, of all places, by the financial journalist John Cassidy makes exactly this point. As Cassidy puts it, hedge funds are not the problem, investment banks are.

16 To be sure, there is danger that information pooling will remain partial, and that information pooling not accompanied by adequate information analysis will create a dangerous sense of complacency. But these are useful cautions, not reasons to reject the credit-registry idea.

17 At the time of writing, it is being studied by another working group of the Financial Stability Forum.

18 See, for example, Ito *et al.* (1999).

19 Due to De Gregorio *et al.* (2000).

20 History suggests that this should not be a problem.

21 Related proposals were included in the G-7 Finance Ministers' Cologne Summit Report on Strengthening the International Financial Architecture.

References

Basle Committee on Banking Supervision (1999), "A New Capital Adequacy Framework," Basel (3 June), http://www.bis.org/press/index/htm

Calvo, Guillermo A. and Carmen M. Reinhart (1999), "When Capital Inflows Come to a Sudden Stop: Consequences and Policy Options," unpublished manuscript, University of Maryland at College Park.

Camdessus, Michel (1999), "Address by Michel Camdessus to the Board of Governors of the Fund," Washington, DC (28 September), http://www.imf.org/external/np/speeches/1999/092899/HTM

De Gregorio, Jose, Barry Eichengreen, Takatoshi Ito and Charles Wyplosz (2000), *An Independent and Accountable IMF*, Geneva Report on the World Economy 1, London: CEPR.

Eatwell, John and Lance Taylor (1999), "Capital Flows and the International Financial Architecture," unpublished manuscript, New School for Social Research.

Economist (1999), "Sovereign Policy," (13 February), p. 21.

Eichengreen, Barry (1999a), *Toward a New International Financial Architecture: A Practical Post-Asia Agenda*, Washington, DC: Institute for International Economics.

Eichengreen, Barry (1999b), "Policy-Making in an Integrated World: From Surveillance to ... ?" in Federal Reserve Bank of Boston, *Policy-Making in an Integrated World*, Boston: Federal Reserve Bank of Boston.

Eichengreen, Barry and Ashoka Mody (2000), "Would Collective Action Clauses Raise Borrowing Costs," *NBER Working Paper No.* 7452 (January).

Eichengreen, Barry and Donald Mathieson *et al.* (1998), *Hedge Funds and Financial Market Dynamics*, Washington, DC: International Monetary Fund.

Eichengreen, Barry and Ricardo Hausmann (1999), "Exchange Rates and Financial Fragility," in Federal Reserve Bank of Kansas City, *Issues in Monetary Policy*, Kansas City: Federal Reserve Bank of Kansas City (forthcoming).

Feldstein, Martin (1998), "Refocusing the IMF," *Foreign Affairs* 77, 20–33.

Friedman, Thomas (1999), *The Lexus and the Olive Tree*, New York, Farrar, Straus, Giroux.

Grenville, Stephen (1999), "Financial Crises and Globalisation," unpublished manuscript, Reserve Bank of Australia, http://www.rba.gov.au/speech/sp_dg_150799.html

Hausmann, Ricardo, M. Gavin, C. Pages-Serra and E. Stein (1999), "Financial Turmoil and the Choice of Exchange Rate Regime," unpublished manuscript, Inter-American Development Bank.

International Monetary Fund (1999), "International Standards and Fund Surveillance – Progress and Issues," Washington, DC (16 August), http:/www.imf.org/external/np/rosc/stand.htm

Ito, Takatoshi, Eiji Ogawa and Yuri Nagataki Sasaki (1999), "Establishment of the East Asian Fund," Chapter 3 of Institute for International Monetary Affairs (ed.), *Stabilization of Currency and Financial Systems in East Asia and International Financial Coordination*, Tokyo: Institute for International Monetary Affairs.

Lerrick, Adam (1999), *Private Sector Financing for the IMF: Now Part of an Optimal Funding Mix*, Washington, DC: The Bretton Woods Committee.

Reserve Bank of Australia (1999), "Hedge Funds, Financial Stability and Market Integrity," paper submitted to House of Representatives' Standing Committee on Economics, Finance and Public Administration's Inquiry into the International Financial Markets' Effects on Government Policy (June).

Rodrik, Dani and Andres Velasco (1999), "Short-Term Capital Flows," unpublished manuscript, Harvard University and New York University (April).

Rubin, Robert (1998), "Remarks on Reform of the International Financial Architecture to the School of Advanced International Studies," *Treasury News* (21 April), RR-3093.

Soros, George (1998), *The Crisis of Global Capitalism*, New York: Public Affairs Press.

Yam, Joseph (1999), "Capital Flows, Hedge Funds, and Market Failure: A Hong Kong Perspective," paper presented to the Reserve Bank of Australia Conference on Capital Flows and the International Financial System, Sydney, 9–10 August.

6 Strengthening the international financial architecture

Making markets work better

Andrew Crockett

The need for reforms

The East Asian crisis of 1997–98 gave rise to sustained efforts to strengthen the global financial architecture. These efforts focused on crisis prevention, on the one hand, and crisis resolution, on the other. The former included improving macroeconomic policies and strengthening banking systems and corporate governance, while the later entailed finding better ways to manage systemic difficulties when they arose.

This chapter will try to place the current international financial arrangements (or the 'architecture', to use the now popular jargon) in a historical and institutional context. Its aim will be to show how the international monetary system has evolved from the Bretton Woods system of the post-war period, and what are now its principal characteristics. The basic thesis will be that monetary arrangements have gradually changed from an administered or *government-led* system, to a decentralised or *market-led* system.[1] This has been an inevitable and in many ways desirable evolution. For all their flaws, markets are a more efficient mechanism for resource allocation than any conceivable alternative.

The broad architecture of the system (market based), is therefore with some exceptions, appropriate to the needs of the world economy. However, any system based on markets is vulnerable to market failures. Markets have at times shown alarming disequilibrium tendencies. Private institutions have got into difficulties with potential spillover or systemic consequences. Weaknesses in national banking systems have caused or exacerbated broader economic difficulties. Prices in financial markets have at times been excessively volatile.

The causes lie in specific aspects of market functioning that must be corrected if support for open markets and the benefits they can bring is to be preserved. Thus, the central focus of attempts to strengthen the international monetary system must lie in identifying and addressing sources of market failure in private financial markets. The first two sections of the chapter analyse the main features, as well as the strengths and weaknesses of, respectively, the Bretton Woods system, and the current, more market-based system. The next two sections discuss the question of how to deal with market failure, both as an economic issue and from the viewpoint of political process. The final section concludes.

The Bretton Woods system

Main features

It is convenient to begin by considering the main characteristics of the monetary arrangements established after the Second World War, and the factors that led to their downfall. At Bretton Woods, the founders of the post-war international monetary system sought to impose an order on international financial arrangements that had been conspicuously lacking in the 1930s. They did this by designing clear rules, based upon the Treaty establishing the International Monetary Fund (IMF) and the World Bank, defining the operating characteristics of the monetary system.[2] These covered: (i) the exchange rate regime; (ii) trade and payments arrangements; (iii) the balance of payments adjustment process; (iv) international liquidity and (v) financial market arrangements.

(i)   *Exchange rates.* Stable exchange rates were assumed to provide the best environment for a balanced growth of international trade, which in turn was seen as crucial to secure economic growth and increased living standards. Exchange rate stability was to be achieved by each country establishing a par value for its currency and using domestic policies as the primary tool of maintaining a sustainable balance of payments. Proposed changes in par values, which were envisaged in cases of fundamental disequilibrium, were subject to a process of international review and approval through the IMF. Potentially destabilising capital flows could be dealt with through exchange controls.

(ii) *Trade and payments arrangements.* The payments arrangements of the Bretton Woods system were based on the gradual removal of restrictions on payments for current transactions, but permitted controls on capital account. The basic thinking was that free trade in goods and services promoted economic welfare, but that short-term capital flows could be a source of disturbance to exchange rate stability, thus undermining conditions for stable growth. Long-term capital flows, say for direct investment, occupied an intermediate position. Their contribution to welfare was acknowledged and it was expected (but not required) that countries would gradually remove restrictions on them.

(iii) *The balance of payments adjustment process.* The balance of payments adjustment process refers to the mechanism through which a country's external payments are brought back into equilibrium after any development that creates excess demand or supply for its currency. The adjustment process of the Bretton Woods system resembled that of the Gold Standard in that countries were expected to use domestic monetary and fiscal policies to manage domestic demand relative to output and thus secure a sustainable balance between exports and imports. However, certain features were introduced to temper the harshness with which adjustment had occurred under the Gold Standard. First, during the period in which adjustment was taking place, a payments gap could be covered by the use of reserves, or through borrowing from the IMF. Second, capital controls could deal with problems that might otherwise be created by short-term speculative flows. And, third, if a payments problem was judged a 'fundamental disequilibrium' an exchange rate adjustment could be used as part of the adjustment mechanism.

(iv) *International liquidity.* The availability of international liquidity was viewed as playing an important role in the efficient working of the adjustment process. If there were too much liquidity, countries would be tempted to delay adjustment to emerging balance of payments disequilibrium. Inflationary pressures might then be allowed to get out of hand, leading to a 'fundamental disequilibrium'. On the other hand, if there was too little liquidity, countries might be forced to cut domestic demand by an excessive amount to deal with an incipient loss of reserves. And if such a response was judged politically unacceptable, they might respond by imposing damaging restrictions on international trade. For these reasons, the mechanism for the supply of liquidity was seen as an important feature of the Bretton Woods system. In addition to primary liquidity (gold), secondary liquidity was available in the form of borrowing rights at the IMF, which could be periodically adjusted through changes in quotas.

(v) *Financial market arrangements.* Financial markets were not an explicit focus of the Bretton Woods system, but were heavily affected by the existence of capital controls. In the early post-war period, they were largely domestic in scope and heavily regulated. Interest ceilings, credit controls and entry restrictions were among the measures that protected domestic financial institutions from competition, reducing the incentive for risk taking. Capital controls segregated national financial markets, reducing the scope for contagion in the event of a financial crisis.

This 'administered' international monetary system was logically coherent and, indeed, highly successful in facilitating the rehabilitation of war-damaged economies and the post-war growth of trade. The industrial economies recorded high rates of economic growth and liberalised their trade and payment systems. By the end of the 1950s, most countries had reintroduced de facto convertibility for current account payments. World trade grew rapidly, and exchange rates were stable.

Note that in this 'administered' architecture, the capacity of financial market inefficiencies to do damage was limited. There were no integrated capital markets, so that spillover effects from financial problems in one country were minor. The competitive climate for financial institutions was benign, so they had no incentive to run risks with their solvency. And sophisticated financial instruments with complex payoff characteristics hardly existed.

Weaknesses in the Bretton Woods system

There were, of course, a number of problems with this managed system. For example, it was apparent that there was no mechanism to ensure that primary liquidity in the system (gold) could increase in line with the growth of the world economy. As a result, holdings of dollars came to play a growing role. This provoked criticism that the United States benefited from an arrangement that enabled it to absorb resources from the rest of the world, while paying only in IOUs. In a different vein, economists inside and outside the IMF feared that the accumulation of dollar balances would eventually become unsustainable (the 'Triffin dilemma').[3] If the holdings of dollars by countries other than the United States became too large relative to the US gold stock, confidence in the convertibility of dollars into gold at a fixed price would come into question. The solution that was eventually found to this problem at the end of the 1960s was to create an internationally controlled supply of liquidity in the form of issues of Special Drawing Rights. (Few noticed at the time that market developments were beginning to make the concept of international liquidity itself obsolete.)

Another perceived problem was the working of the international adjustment process. With the growth of world trade and the liberalisation of trade and payments regimes, the size of current account disequilibria was tending to increase. This was viewed as a problem for two reasons. First, it exacerbated protectionist pressures, and second, the eventual correction of imbalances might not be possible without exchange rate tensions, or disruptive shifts in output and employment.

Given the multilateral nature of the balance of payments adjustment process, it was felt that its working should be managed internationally. The idea was that the impact of demand restraint in countries seeking to adjust to a balance of payments deficit should be roughly balanced by demand expansion in countries with payments surpluses. Various mechanisms to this end were put in place, of which perhaps the most noteworthy was the establishment of a high-level committee of the Group of Ten industrial countries (Working Party 3 (WP3) of the OECD). WP3's objective was to promote the harmonisation of domestic macroeconomic policies so as to make them consistent with continued stability in the pattern of international exchange rates.

In the end, however, it was the growth of international financial markets that undermined the administered international monetary system, and spelt the end of the Bretton Woods system of fixed exchange rates. Fixed exchange rates would anyway have been hard to sustain with divergent policies and cyclical positions among the key countries in the system. These divergences were beginning to grow as inflationary tendencies picked up in the late 1960s.

But an even more important influence was the growing freedom of capital movements. Countries were gradually relaxing restrictions on domestic banking and financial systems, recognising the costs of the 'financial repression' created by oppressive regulation. This was permitting the development of new financial instruments and creating a demand for ways to hedge against cross-border risks. At the same time, capital controls were becoming less effective, either as a result of deliberate liberalisation, or as private agents found ways to get around them. In a word, financial markets were becoming more efficient.

Open capital markets make it possible for market participants to 'discount' into today's prices the expectations about the future evolution of all economic and financial variables. In the early 1970s, market participants could see the potential for unsustainable trends developing and used the financial markets to protect themselves against their consequences. With exchange rates fixed in a narrow band they had almost a one-way bet. The incentive structure virtually guaranteed the build-up of pressure on suspect currencies.

As just noted, capital controls were unable to provide a sufficient defence. For one thing, comprehensive capital controls did not enjoy widespread support in an environment in which businessmen, policymakers and the public at large were looking for increased freedoms to undertake cross-border transactions. For another, the growing sophistication of financial technology was offering alternative opportunities to take market positions.

It was recognised, moreover, that the function of capital flows was not simply to provide finance to 'accommodate' (in the then popular jargon) autonomously generated imbalances in the current account. Capital flows made an important contribution to welfare in their own right. They were a reflection of divergences in savings/investment preferences among countries, they were a vehicle for the transfer of technological and managerial know-how, and they were a useful source of external discipline on unsustainable official policies.

The market-led system

Main features

The fixed exchange system eventually collapsed in 1971–73, and the attempt to recreate it was abandoned following the first oil shock. With this, the international monetary system passed a critical stage in its evolution from a 'government-led' system to a decentralised or 'market-led' system. Subsequently, the central features of international financial arrangements – the exchange rate mechanism, trade and payments arrangements, the adjustment process, liquidity provision and financial market arrangements – have progressively become more subject to market forces. Let us again consider each of these key features in turn.

(i) *Exchange rates.* There are now no formal rules concerning which exchange rate regime countries should follow. Major currencies float against one another, with relatively little intervention. As for the currencies of smaller countries, a variety of recent experiences have exposed the difficulty of maintaining 'fixed but adjustable' exchange rates. Many countries thus either allow continuous flexibility in their exchange rate, or else credibly renounce an independent monetary policy, either through the creation of a currency board or by joining a monetary union. It is widely accepted that exchange rates cannot be sustained if they are inconsistent with market forces.

(ii) *Trade and payments arrangements.* There has been no change from the Bretton Woods system as far as the presumption in favour of an open and liberal regime for trade is concerned. The vast majority of countries have by now removed all controls on payments for current transactions. What has changed, however, is the attitude towards the capital account. It is now recognised that capital flows serve a valuable purpose in distributing global savings, facilitating technology transfer and imposing discipline on unsustainable policies. Moreover, the development of new financial instruments has made controls difficult and costly to maintain. The presumption now, therefore, is that market forces should be allowed to be the main determinant of capital account, as well as current account, flows.

(iii) *The adjustment process.* The adjustment process has likewise been increasingly left to market forces. Governments have largely abandoned the attempt to formulate balance of payments objectives and to use domestic macroeconomic policies to pursue them. Rather, the balance of payments and the associated exchange rate are seen as being jointly determined by underlying saving and investment propensities. Market forces are accepted as the best available way of allowing these propensities to be reflected in relative prices and resource flows, even if they do sometimes exhibit undesirable instability.

(iv) *International liquidity.* Liquidity provision also takes place through the operation of market forces. If we think of liquidity as being the ability to realise value, creditworthy economic agents (governments, companies and financial institutions) can, *at a price*, obtain the liquidity they believe they need through financial operations in international capital markets. It is therefore hard to conceive of international liquidity being too great or too scarce, independently of a judgement about the appropriateness of domestic monetary policies in the principal national centres. Moreover, the purposes for which liquidity is held are somewhat different than under the Bretton Woods system. With floating exchange rates, it is less necessary to use reserves to cover a balance of payments deficit on current account. It is, therefore, difficult to relate the need for reserve holding to conventional measures, such as months of import cover. Today, reserves are generally held as longer term investments, and as a means of maintaining the confidence of international investors.

(v) *Financial market arrangements.* Finally, and in some ways most important for the purpose of the present discussion, domestic financial systems have become more open, competitive and internationally integrated. Internally, countries have abandoned restrictions on competition and portfolio allocation constraints. This has not meant the end of regulation. But the *focus* of regulation has shifted. Domestic regulations no longer control activities and prices of financial instruments; rather they seek to ensure that risks are prudently managed, and adequately capitalised. In other words, they seek to reinforce market disciplines, rather than to impede them. Externally, geographical barriers in the provision of financial services have come down. Evolving financial technology and the ascendancy of the philosophy of deregulation have interacted to create what is increasingly a single global capital market. This has required, relative to the Bretton Woods system, a greater degree of international cooperation in prudential regulation.

It is apparent from the analysis so far that the shift from governmental- to market-influence in international monetary arrangements has covered virtually all aspects of the functioning of the financial system. Some have labelled the result a non-system. But in fact there is nothing unsystematic about international monetary arrangements based on decentralised market forces. Indeed, most theory teaches us that such a framework will, in general, be superior to the alternative, *provided* (and it is an important proviso) that the necessary preconditions for markets to operate efficiently are in place. In other words, the key questions are less to do with the architecture of the system than with the associated mechanisms needed to make this market-based architecture work effectively.

Weaknesses of a market-led system

It is sometimes supposed (by 'market fundamentalists') that reliance on unregulated market forces results in an optimal allocation of resources. This of course is only the case if markets are complete and efficient. Markets are 'complete' if market participants are able to trade all conceivable claims, actual or contingent. And they are 'efficient' if market prices contain all knowable information. In these terms, it is clear that markets can never be fully complete or efficient. Markets for contingent claims in all future states-of-the-world do not exist. And there are numerous cases of lack of information, or its asymmetric availability.

Financial markets have made an important contribution to completeness through the developments of an increasingly wide range of derivative instruments. These allow market participants to make contingent contracts on future outcomes of financial and economic variables. Yet, financial markets are particularly prone to market failure, in part because the assets traded in them yield services over a prolonged period and because fundamental value is difficult to assess. Returns depend on future states of the world and are therefore subject to uncertainties and information asymmetries. Herd behaviour and externalities are endemic, since individual asset values depend on collective expectations of future outcomes. Moreover, the public good of financial stability is likely to be undersupplied in the absence of conscious intervention by the authorities.

Recent advances in game theory have helped us understand better some of the reasons why financial markets are so prone to disequilibrium tendencies. And actual experience, not least in the East Asian crisis, has provided forceful empirical confirmation of the potential strength of such tendencies. It is worth spending a few moments to consider in more depth some of these sources of market failure.

(i) *Information asymmetries.* Market efficiency depends on all market participants having access to available information on the characteristics of the goods, services or assets being traded. In practice, however, certain markets are characterised by asymmetric information. This is a particular problem in financial markets, which are by their nature information-based. Information asymmetries give rise to two specific types of problem.

    One is *adverse selection*. This occurs when the seller of a product or service, say, an agent trying to obtain external funding (the insider) has private information about some exogenous key characteristic of what he is selling. The issue here is how the insider can credibly transmit that information to the 'outsider' (i.e. the purchaser of the good or the provider of finance). Where this is not possible (or is costly), suboptimal outcomes will result. The classic article on this subject is Akerlof's 'The Market for Lemons'.[4] Sellers of good used cars cannot easily and credibly convey quality information to buyers. Buyers therefore offer a lower price, which induces only sellers of low-quality cars to enter the market. A similar phenomenon can affect the market for loans, unless some quality assessment mechanism can be put in place.

A second consequence of information asymmetries is *moral hazard*. In this case, the information insider (the 'agent') can affect economic outcomes, but the outsider (the 'principal') is unable to observe or infer correctly the actions taken by the insider. The inability of the insider costlessly and credibly to commit to particular courses of action creates 'time inconsistency', which typically results in suboptimal outcomes, relative to the full information equilibrium.

(ii) *Aggregation effects and externalities.* In financial markets, more so than in most other markets, decisions by individual agents are conditioned by expectations of what others will do. (Hence the natural application of 'game' theory.) Uncertainties about how others will act introduce costs that, in principle, might be alleviated by contracting, but in practice often cannot be.

In the financial system, the inability to enter binding conditional contracts on future states-of-the-world means that individual agents have to protect themselves against the consequences of potential actions by others. But individually rational behaviour, if followed by a large number of agents simultaneously, can produce suboptimal social results. A familiar example of this phenomenon is provided by the literature on bank runs. Once confidence in a bank is called in question, it becomes rational for each depositor to withdraw her funds, whatever her subjective view of the bank's soundness. But of course, this rational reaction precipitates the very consequences against which it is designed to guard. A similar sequence of events can occur in currency markets or indeed in any market where price is fixed and the ability of the supplier to meet demand at the fixed price is not infinite.

Other examples of aggregation effects are to be found in credit-granting behaviour and rules. When an economic downturn is in prospect, it is natural that lenders seek to cut back lending or exercise greater caution in credit extension. Supervisory rules often work in the same direction. But reduced credit availability can itself create or intensify a recession. Yet another example is the tendency of lenders (and supervisors) to treat short-term credits as less risky than longer term lending. For a single lender in isolation, this may be true. But for borrowers, short-term finance is more vulnerable than long-term. If all lending is short term, the liquidity of the loans is an illusion, and lenders have less security, not more.

Aggregation effects lie behind the now familiar phenomena of overshooting and multiple equilibria. Once a market movement away from an initial equilibrium is initiated it may gather pace. A new equilibrium may not be quickly or easily established, nor is there any guarantee that it will be socially superior to the previous equilibrium.

(iii) *Inadequate supply of public goods.* A final potential source of market failure lies in arrangements for the provision of public goods. Because public goods benefit everyone but cannot easily be charged for, there is a danger that they will be undersupplied. Information has itself elements of a public good, since it is costly to produce and its use cannot always be restricted to its producer. But in addition, the infrastructure of financial markets is dependent on public goods such as the structure of contact law and law enforcement, sound accounting and valuation conventions, appropriate information disclosure requirements, effective regulatory and supervisory systems, safety net arrangements and so on. In the absence of this infrastructure, uncertainties will be greater and financial contracting will be more costly. Markets will be smaller in size and more prone to disruptions.

The combined effect of these phenomena is that markets cannot be counted on to smoothly move to socially optimal equilibria, even with rational private behaviour and in the absence of mistakes of government policy. In practice, of course, bad policies and imprudent private behaviour often compound the problem. Unsustainable macroeconomic policies (excessive fiscal deficits, inflationary monetary policies, overvalued fixed exchange rates) have been behind many financial crises. And weak banking and financial systems, often traceable to an underdeveloped 'credit culture' have often contributed to make the problem worse.

The manifestation of these phenomena has been the frequency and intensity of financial crises in the period since financial markets have been liberalised. Beginning with the debt crisis of the 1980s, the financial system has witnessed an increasing number of national and international financial crises. In a disturbingly large number of cases, the direct fiscal costs of banking crises have exceeded 10 per cent of GDP.[5] Losses in terms of output forgone have been even larger.

Sometimes, the problems have had their root in weaknesses of macroeconomic policy (high inflation, excessive fiscal deficits). But in others, the problems were caused, or at least substantially compounded, by imprudent behaviour by private market participants.

Dealing with market failure

So far, this chapter has argued that there is no satisfactory alternative to a market-based international financial system, but that such a system is prone to costly market failures. It follows that attempts to strengthen the international financial architecture have to focus heavily on how to deal with these sources of market failure. Market failures have in fact provoked a variety of institutional and regulatory responses. Some may occur spontaneously in private markets, and some may be undertaken by the authorities. Some responses have been at the national level, and some have dealt with international interactions.

Market failures at the national level

(i) *Asymmetric information.* The asymmetric information problem is one of the principal reasons explaining the establishment and subsequent evolution of financial intermediaries. Specialised credit institutions such as banks can alleviate both the adverse selection and moral hazard problems. They perform the function of assessing the *ex ante* creditworthiness of borrowers and monitoring their *ex post* performance better than could any individual lender. Similarly, investment banks help the issuers of securities provide standardised information to potential purchasers that improves the marketability of the securities concerned.

These institutional responses to the asymmetric information problem have been largely spontaneous. Banks evolved without official intervention, and market places developed their own rules to make themselves a more attractive location for trading financial claims. But there has also been official encouragement. Rules protecting investors and providing for information disclosure have been enshrined in legislation and contracts.

(ii) *Aggregation effects and externalities.* If financial intermediation helps deal with certain types of market failure, it can create others, through aggregation effects and externalities. Because they are highly leveraged, financial institutions, and particularly banks, can be subject to a loss of confidence that can threaten the effective functioning of financial intermediation. Bank runs can develop. As a result, most economists and policymakers accept that there is a need for some form of safety net for the financial system. Two forms of safety net are the lender of last resort functions of the central bank, and deposit insurance schemes.

Once again, however, the institutional response to one kind of market failure creates the soil for another to grow. The existence of an effective safety net tends to exacerbate the problem of moral hazard. The obvious danger is that banks, or their depositors, will become less careful in managing risks and monitoring counterparties. The direct loser is the deposit insurance authority, which has to underwrite the losses that arise from imprudent lending. More generally, of course, society at large loses from the resource misallocation that flows from the mispricing of risk.

The official response to the moral hazard problem and other forms of perverse incentive has been through the refinement of regulation and supervision. Initially, regulation focused rather crudely on limiting risk taking, or adding to capital cushions. Gradually, more sophisticated approaches have gained ground. Supervisors now aim to see that risk is not simply reduced, but that it is appropriately monitored and priced, and covered by a commensurate cushion of capital. Conceptually, the goal is to replicate the incentives to prudent behaviour that would exist in a perfectly competitive environment without the distortions of a safety net.

(iii) *Public goods.* Finally, the supply of public goods. Because banks can control and monitor the quality of their portfolios, and because they can pool credit and repayment risk, they are able to add liquidity to the financial system. Since market liquidity has public good aspects, this contributes to alleviating another potential source of market failure. The same can be said for the broking and dealing activities of investment banks. It is in the nature of public goods, however, that private incentives are insufficient for their optimal provision. So governments have typically accepted a responsibility to intervene: to mandate information disclosure; to collect and disseminate needed economic and financial data; to provide rules for payment and settlement systems; to provide a secure and predictable legal environment for contracts, including insolvency arrangement in the event of the failure of commercial institutions; and to underwrite, through the financial safety net, the overall stability of the system.

Market failures in the international financial system

At the level of the international financial system, the institutional mechanisms developed to deal with financial market failure do not always work in quite the same way as at the national level. Moreover, contagion can be more difficult to deal with.

(i)   *Asymmetric information* is probably more acute in cross-border lending than in national lending. Lenders tend to know less about borrowers, and there are added uncertainties related to exchange and transfer risk. Sovereign borrowers, who are virtually risk-free when they borrow from local sources in their own currency, are very far from risk-free when they borrow in foreign currencies. Moreover, sovereign immunity and the absence of international insolvency procedures further complicate matters.

   All these factors were evident in lending to the East Asian economies. Lenders were often only partially informed about the uses to which their funds were put. They failed to properly understand the nature of the security offered by sovereign guarantees. And they did not appreciate the underlying fragility of banking systems. Rating agencies' assessments also reflected these misapprehensions. In some cases, official misrepresentation of key reserve data encouraged them further.

(ii) *Externalities and aggregation effects* also loom larger at the international level. Bank runs are more likely to occur and spread when the nature of deposit protection is uncertain, and when banks have net exposure in foreign currencies, which the authorities cannot underwrite. Currency attacks can develop, because market participants know that the resources are lacking to defend the exchange rate.

   This can lead to a vicious circle with added potential for multiple equilibria. Kaminsky and Reinhardt[6] have shown how a domestic banking crisis can contribute to a currency crisis, which then intensifies the banking crisis and adds to its real economic costs. In the case of Indonesia, for example, even if the pre-crisis exchange rate was somewhat overvalued, it is hard to justify the loss of five-sixths of its external value (as in fact happened initially) on grounds of fundamentals. Korea and Thailand similarly experienced exchange rate overshooting, as indeed, in somewhat different circumstances, did the United Kingdom following sterling's exit from the European exchange rate mechanism.

Domestically, the threat of financial instability due to overshooting, vicious circles and multiple equilibria is answered by the provision of a safety net, or the existence of a lender of last resort. Such a mechanism does not exist internationally, nor could it easily be created without a global political authority. The IMF performs some of the functions of a lender of last resort, making its resources available, on conditions, to limit adjustment costs and help prevent excessive exchange rate movements. But the IMF does not have the resources or the authority to provide a fully credible protection against financial disturbances.

Despite the absence of a fully credible lender of last resort, international lending has still been subject to moral hazard and other forms of perverse incentive. It is hard to explain the enthusiasm of lenders to Russia unless they expected some kind of official or unofficial support from the international community. And lenders to Thailand, Indonesia and Korea obviously attached value to the authorities' commitment to maintain fixed exchange rates or to underwrite claims on the domestic banking system.

Other forms of perverse incentive also appear to have played a role in international financial crises. Countries have an incentive to engage in time inconsistent policies, for example, committing to exchange rate regimes in one set of circumstances that would prove impossible to adhere to in others. And there is a principal/agent problem reflected in the fact that lending officers are sometimes rewarded for the volume of loans made, without sharing equivalently in the risks incurred.

As noted earlier, regulation and supervision are the mechanisms by which perverse incentives are dealt with within national economies. This becomes harder to do when the activity to be regulated is global, but the regulatory authority is national. In the case of the financial sector, additional complications are presented by the fact that many countries supervise different categories of financial institution separately and according to differentiated rules. Moreover, the development of financial technology – new products that can unbundle and repackage complex risks – further adds to the difficulties of effective supervision.

The East Asian crisis revealed that supervisory guidelines were not only different in different countries, but were implemented with varying degrees of stringency. Countries like Indonesia, Korea and Thailand had risk management guidelines in place, but lacked the supervisory infrastructure to enforce the rules in spirit. The banking systems in these countries were prone to loan concentration, insider lending, currency and maturity mismatches and other lapses from prudent standards. Moreover, they were often inadequately capitalised, since despite meeting formal minimum capital ratios, accounting rules allowed bad loans to go unrecognised until they had deteriorated to uncollectible status.

(iii) *Public goods.* It is generally accepted that national governments have a responsibility to ensure that public goods are adequately supplied at the national level. This is much more complicated at the international level. Examples of relevant public goods are internationally consistent, high quality supervisory guidelines (without which there may be competition in supervisory laxity); the provision of comparable and timely information on economic and financial variables; accounting and disclosure standards; secure and transparent legal environments and a safety net to underwrite financial stability.

To help promote the supply of international public goods, intergovernmental organisations and groupings have been established. These have done a useful job of developing harmonised standards for national application, of promoting sustainable macroeconomic policies, of disseminating comparable statistical information, and of providing facilities for the management of financial stress. By their nature, however, international agreements are more limited than the power of national governments within their respective jurisdiction. Many international bodies do not have enforcement powers; the doctrine of sovereign immunity introduces added uncertainty into debt contracts, and the IMF does not have lender of last resort powers comparable to those of national central banks.

Beyond market failures due to the inherent characteristics of markets, instability can also arise from bad or imprudent policies on the part of governments or other economic agents. Here the answer has been seen as lying in a greater role for market discipline, backed up by strengthened prudential oversight. Market disciplines can be strengthened by improved transparency (more, and better, information) and better incentives (less moral hazard, more congruence between rewards and the quality of decisions). Where market discipline alone is inadequate, supervisory rules (or peer-pressure, in the case of governments) can push decisions in the desired direction.

Strengthening the international architecture

The strategy

Let us recall the argument so far. The international financial architecture has evolved from an administered, government-led system to a decentralised market-based system. The current architecture offers the opportunity for greater efficiency and resilience but can only reach its potential if the associated sources of market failure are effectively dealt with. Potential sources of market failure are particularly significant in the financial sector, and the global nature of financial activity only adds to the difficulty of addressing these problems.

Against this background, how can the operation of a market-based financial system be made more secure? Three components of a well-functioning financial system can be distinguished: the intermediary institutions that channel funds from ultimate savers to ultimate investors, the markets in which financial claims are traded and priced; and the infrastructure of law and market practices within which transactions take place.

The three components are intimately related. Financial markets will not be stable or function efficiently unless the institutions that are active in them are sound and prudently managed. In turn, financial institutions cannot be efficiently managed in a volatile financial environment, or where there is uncertainty about the underlying financial infrastructure. So while it is important to deal with each of these three pillars of the financial systems, it must be remembered that parallel and consistent progress needs to be made on all three fronts.

(i) *Prudential regulation of financial institutions.* The natural place to start is with the soundness of the institutions that are the key players in financial markets: mainly banks, but also securities issuers, insurance companies, fund managers and other types of intermediary. This is primarily a national responsibility. But it is given an international dimension by the global reach of many key players, and by the fact that so many of the crises of recent years have been created or aggravated by imprudent cross-border lending. What is needed is improved standards of risk management, consistently applied, together with appropriate levels of capital adequacy.

Realising the shortcomings of previous supervisory arrangements, financial supervisors have now put in place internationally agreed 'core principles' for financial sector supervision.[7] However, much work remains to be done to ensure that the principles are implemented in a consistent fashion across countries and in different industry segments. When this is achieved, it will go a long way in ensuring that financial sector weaknesses do not exacerbate economic disturbances in the way they did in the Asian crisis.

(ii) *Improving the functioning of financial markets.* Strong institutions, while necessary, are not a sufficient condition for financial stability. Large swings in market prices, or the drying up of market liquidity, can also have damaging consequences. For example, the dramatic falls in the exchange rates of East Asian currencies, and the disappearance of liquidity in the wake of the near failure of LTCM in September 1998, threatened financial stability more broadly.

To function more stably, markets need a stable economic environment and adequate information. To reinforce the incentives for information disclosure, standards of transparency need to be developed and enforced. Once again, three elements can be distinguished. *First*, information about the macroeconomic environment. This calls for timely release of meaningful data, including for financial variables such as reserve levels and indebtedness. *Second*, information is needed about the build-up of market positions. Only if markets fully understand the sources of volume and price trends in financial markets will destabilising extrapolative expectations be contained. *Third*, market participants need information about their counterparties, to enable them to make informed judgements about credit extension.

(iii) *Market infrastructure.* Finally, market infrastructures need to be strengthened. The importance of sound, internationally consistent accounting and valuation conventions has already been mentioned. Also important are principles of corporate governance; contract law provisions and enforcement procedures; insolvency arrangements, and payments and settlements infrastructures. Deficiencies in any of these areas can undermine institutions that seem otherwise sound.

Developing and implementing standards and codes

If it is accepted that the underpinning of the financial system requires a broad-based effort to improve standards in a number of different areas and across all national jurisdictions, how is this to be done? And just as important, what kind of machinery is needed to ensure that the functioning of financial systems remains robust in the face of continued rapid innovation?

One way would be to have a global super-regulator with powers to set and enforce standards throughout the industry on a worldwide basis. Whatever one thinks of this idea, it is clearly outside the realm of the practical for the foreseeable future. So it seems inevitable that if financial practice is to be upgraded, it will be through a process in which national authorities come together to develop common standards, which are then implemented internationally. Adherence to standards of best practice will be promoted by transparency-induced market pressures, as well as through monitoring by international organisations.

This is not the place to comment in detail on the substantive content of financial standards. However, it may be useful to make five general comments about their development.

First, standards are *inter-related* and need to be developed in a consistent way. Prudential microeconomic standards can have macroeconomic consequences. Regulatory arbitrage can push financial intermediation to the least regulated jurisdictions and market segments. A mechanism for coordinating the development of standards is therefore needed.

Second, the aim of standards is not to eliminate risk, but to reinforce a *credit culture*. The financial system is the 'brain' of the economy that directs resources to their end uses. Efficient resource use requires an appropriate understanding and pricing of risk. To achieve this involves qualitative improvement of risk management practice more than simply the quantitative application of balance sheet ratios.

Third, proper attention needs to be given to the role of a *capital cushion*. A principal function of capital is to allow economic activity to proceed normally in the face of adverse shocks to cash flow. This need is common to all economic agents; governments, individuals and non-financial corporations as well as financial institutions. Leverage needs to be limited to prudent levels for all economic agents.

Fourth, the process of standard setting requires *legitimacy*, if it is to be accepted. Representative groups of countries have to be involved, and all have to have the opportunity to be consulted. National experts need to be involved, since it is they rather than international organisations that have primary responsibility for monitoring and enforcing standards. At the same time standardsetting has to be done in bodies that are small enough for efficiency.

Fifth, and last, a process based on the decentralised development of standards, needs protection against the danger of *inertia*. Overlapping responsibilities generate issues of turf, which can divert participants from making progress on issues of substance. And dealing with difficult questions becomes harder when the pressure of an immediate crisis recedes. We need to make sure that mechanisms are in place to ensure the impetus to reform is sustained.

The recently established Financial Stability Forum represents an attempt to deal with some of these issues. It brings together representatives of central banks, finance ministries, supervisory agencies and the principal international organisations and standard-setting bodies. It therefore has the breadth to recognise the interconnectedness of financial stability issues. It is at a high political level (Deputy Finance Ministers, Deputy Governors and Heads of Supervision) so that it should have the authority to encourage needed compromises on difficult issues. Moreover, being constituted by the G-7 Finance Ministers, it can appeal to their influence to break deadlocks.

Of course, the establishment of a coordinating body is no more than a facilitating mechanism. Whether or not it succeeds depends on the collective will of those that participate in the broader process.

A concluding thought

This chapter has sketched a world in which financial instability can be mitigated by actions designed to improve the functioning of markets. This can go a considerable way towards reducing the incidence and severity of crises in the international financial system. If this is not done, the inherent tendency towards excesses of optimism and pessimism in financial markets are likely to perpetuate, and even intensify, the instability documented in studies such as those of Kindleberger[8] and Minsky.[9]

In such a case, the choice would be an unpalatable one between accepting damaging instability, and a far greater degree of administrative control over financial markets.

Accepting instability would, I suspect, be unsustainable. Public opinion would not accept such a price for a market system, whatever benefits it might have. Imposing wider ranging controls, while superficially attractive to some, would have just as damaging consequences. It would erode the efficiency of resource allocation, and condemn the international economy to a constant struggle between financial engineers trying to circumvent restrictions and regulators trying to plug loopholes.

Neither is a pretty prospect. That is why it is so important to strengthen the resilience of financial systems, in order to make the international financial architecture work in a more stable fashion.

Notes

1 The terminology is due to Padoa-Schioppa, Tommaso and Fabrizio Saccomanni, 'Managing a Market-Led Global Financial System', in Peter B. Kenen, ed., *Managing the World Economy*, Institute for International Economics, Washington, DC, September 1994, pp. 235–68.
2 See, for instance, Chapters III through VIII of the Articles of Agreement of the IMF (amended version, effective 28 July 1969).
3 Triffin, Robert, *Gold and the Dollar Crisis*, Yale 1958.
4 Akerlof, George, 'The Market for Lemons: Quality, Uncertainty and the Market Mechanism', *Quarterly Journal of Economics* 84 (August 1970) 488–500.
5 Goldstein, Morris, 'The Case for an International Banking Standard', Institute for International Economics, Policy Analysis in International Economics, No. 47, April 1997.
6 Kaminsky, G. and Reinhardt, C. 'The Twin Crises: The Causes of Banking and Balance of Payment Problems', *American Economic Review*, 89(3) (June 1999) 473–500.
7 These cover all aspects of the oversight of financial institutions, from initial licensing requirements through risk management of ongoing financial operations, to merger and closure procedures.
8 Kindleberger, Charles, *Manias, Panics and Crashes: A History of Financial Crises*, New York, Basic Books, 1978.
9 Minsky, Hyman, P., 'The Financial Instability Hypothesis, Capitalist Processes and the Behavior of the Economy', in Charles P. Kindleberger and Jean Pierre Laffargue, eds, *Financial Crises, Theory, History and Policy*, Cambridge and New York, Cambridge University Press, 1982, pp. 13–39.

7 A new global financial order

The art of the possible

Alan S. Blinder

Back to Bretton Woods

Financial crises once made most people's eyes glaze over; they were subjects of intense interest to only a limited clientele, many of whom wore green eyeshades. Not any longer. The topic has unfortunately acquired a mass audience since the mid-1990s. Stunning currency collapses in Mexico (1995), Southeast Asia (1997), Russia (1998), Brazil (1999), Argentina (2000) and Turkey in (2001) have pushed the subject to the front page. Financial conflagrations have become too frequent, too devastating and too contagious to be ignored.

As the World Bank's former Chief Economist Joseph Stiglitz has put it, when so many cars run on the road, you start wondering whether the road itself might be the problem. And indeed, many questions have been raised about the global financial architecture. Much of the discussion centers around the concept of "moral hazard," an awkward phrase that economists borrowed years ago from the world of insurance. In the financial context, it means that people (or banks, or governments) who are shielded from the consequences of their actions may take imprudent risks – hoping they will be bailed out if things go wrong.

But there is a vastly more important hazard of much greater moral urgency: the fact that financial crises afflict literally hundreds of millions of innocent bystanders who play no part in the speculative excesses but nonetheless suffer when the bubbles burst. The present global financial system manifestly fails to protect these poor people from extreme hazards. This failure is the chief reason to seek reform. Those who bet wrongly in financial markets should suffer losses. And borrowers should repay their debts, even when they are onerous. But citizens who take no part in the game should be shielded from the consequences of financial collapse to the maximum extent possible. This is plainly not happening now. How did we get into such an awful mess?

The story starts back in 1944, when the major Allied nations met at Bretton Woods, New Hampshire, to design a mechanism for restoring the shattered world economy to health. They created a new international financial architecture based on fixed exchange rates and the convertibility of the US dollar into gold. And they established a new multilateral institution, the International Monetary Fund (IMF), to police the system.

The demise of fixed exchange rates in the 1970s robbed the IMF of its principal *raison d'être*. But the fund morphed its mission several times and now has evolved into a global advice-and-rescue squad – one part wealthy benefactor, one part stern schoolmarm and one part global firefighter. It lectures countries on economic orthodoxy, proffers financing in return for approved behavior and rides dramatically to the rescue when countries fall prey to financial crises.

The fund has long had its critics, and their criticisms grew louder and more frequent in the 1990s. Since the Mexican crisis erupted at the close of 1994, the IMF's schoolmarmish advice and firefighting work have been attacked as wrongheaded. Some prominent voices – among them former Secretary of State and Treasury George P. Shultz's – have even called for the fund's abolition. That raises a key question: Have all the recent financial travails happened despite, or because of, the IMF? There now seems to be a widely shared consensus – even within the fund – that the current design is old and creaky and needs to be brought up-to-date. Unfortunately, the consensus ends right there.

How can we make the international financial architecture designed in 1944 work better in today's fast-paced, high-octane world? The eight-point plan below focuses on broad principles of design rather than on the detailed bricks and mortar – but not because the latter are unimportant. On the contrary, both God and the Devil (to merge the two clichés) will ultimately be found in the details. However, meaningful debates over numerous important issues must wait until we first agree on basic principles to govern the new financial system. The physics must precede the engineering.

The art of the possible

A logical way to begin is by setting forth the goals of international financial reform. What do we want to accomplish? We cannot expect to design an international financial system that totally eliminates risk. Manias, panics and speculative excesses are inherent in free-market capitalism. Speculative markets have always been subject to alternating waves of greed and fear; they go to extremes, exhibit herd-like behavior and probably always will. All this is part of the price we pay for our vibrant, highly productive capitalism – a necessary blemish on an economic system that has produced a dazzling record of achievement.

But we should recognize the blemish for what it is. The current system breeds too many crises that are too severe. Much of the non-Western world has suffered through one or another such malady in the past few years. What the global economy needs now is a way to minimize the frequency and intensity of crises. Moreover, the present system lets financial epidemics blossom into global pandemics. Our new financial architecture should have sturdier defenses against contagion. Perhaps most critical of all, but least mentioned, the world badly needs a system that protects innocents from the financial hurricanes that sometimes swirl around them.

But how? Grandiose schemes involving elaborate international institutions tend to get nowhere fast. Regardless of its merits, no world central bank will be created in my lifetime. Even establishing a global financial super-regulator, a far more modest step, would require an implausible surrender of national sovereignty. And an international bankruptcy court would require coordination among nations that have very different bankruptcy laws. Better to stick with more modest plans that require little or no institution building. The world's poor cannot wait for grand edifices to be built.

The plan outlined here can be accomplished through two channels: reform of the IMF, and changes in national practices that countries can implement on their own (indeed, some are already being implemented). The recommendations divide neatly into two categories, corresponding roughly to the IMF's roles as schoolmarm and firefighter.

Four ounces of prevention

The first four recommendations focus on policies designed to build a financial system with fewer vulnerabilities – including both policies that sovereign nations should adopt on their own, and the advice that the IMF should dispense to its client states. As will be seen, parts of the schoolmarm's catechism need to change.

Principle 1: Don't fix your exchange rate. This point seems the most fundamental, but was curiously de-emphasized until former Treasury Secretary Robert E. Rubin more or less endorsed it at an April 1999 IMF meeting. All the international financial crises of the 1990s, like most of the crises of the 1970s and 1980s, have shared a common element: a fixed exchange rate that crumbled under speculative attack. Indeed, in the cases of Mexico, Southeast Asia, Russia, Brazil and Argentina, the defense of an exchange rate pegged at an untenable level was at the very heart of the crises. The lesson seems painfully obvious: Fixed exchange rates, being hazardous to a country's economic health, should be avoided. This is not an ideological position founded on religious devotion to free markets. It is, rather, based on pragmatic observation of many painful experiences. Nor do I insist on purity – "dirty" or managed floats are just fine. Indeed, even some versions of exchange-rate fixity may make sense under the right circumstances. But floating rates ought to be considered the norm by the IMF of today, just as fixed rates were in 1944.

I do not believe in a "one size fits all" exchange-rate policy. Particular countries at particular times may have good reasons to peg their exchange rates to a hard currency. For example, Brazil's crawling peg and Argentina's currency board (which guaranteed the convertibility of pesos into dollars) helped rid those nations of hyperinflation in the 1990s. Hong Kong's currency board helped restore confidence that was badly shaken in the 1980s by the prospect of Chinese rule. Some small countries dominated by a big neighbor may deem it either foolhardy or hopeless to have an independent exchange rate. And fixed rates may be necessary for other reasons; remember the European Exchange Rate Mechanism, a stepping-stone to monetary union. But these should be viewed as exceptions to a general rule. As global financial markets grow bigger and more fluid, the viability of fixed exchange rates that are not literally locked in place forever (as in a monetary union) diminishes accordingly. Market forces are simply too powerful relative to the resources at central banks' command.

In this important respect, we need to recognize that today's world is quite different from the world of 1944. Just as fixed exchange rates were the linchpin of the financial architecture designed at Bretton Woods, floating rates should be the accepted norm in the new financial architecture.

Any nation that decides to peg its exchange rate will be well advised to have an exit strategy – and to use it at a propitious moment before speculators take aim. Forced devaluations can be disastrous. Think how much easier and smoother the necessary adjustments would have been if the Mexican peso, the Indonesian rupiah and the Argentine peso had floated down gradually over a period of months or years rather than dropping abruptly. As George Soros (among others) has observed, with no fixed exchange rate for a target, speculators have nothing to shoot at.

Principle 2: Borrow less in foreign currency. A second common element in the financial crises of the 1990s – with the possible exception of Brazil's – has been an excessive amount of borrowing in foreign currency, especially for the short term. This extremely risky practice should be actively discouraged by both the IMF and national governments.

When combined with an allegedly fixed exchange rate, such borrowing makes for an especially volatile – and sometimes toxic – brew that I call the "fixed exchange rate bubble." It works like this: banks and corporations in emerging markets, where local interest rates are comparatively high, find the lure of lower US (or German, or Japanese) rates irresistible. So they borrow in, say, dollars and then either lend in local currency or invest in local assets.

That is precisely what the Mexican government did in 1994, and what many Southeast Asian banks and businesses did throughout the 1990s. When the fixed exchange rate collapsed, they found themselves buried under an avalanche of unpayable debt. Worse yet, millions of innocent victims fell with them as the economies crumbled under the weight of all that debt.

Critics will object that borrowers in emerging markets cannot afford to pay expensive local-currency interest rates. They must borrow at lower rates in dollars, some claim, or else development will be retarded. I disagree – on at least three grounds.

First, in the case of Southeast Asia (though not Mexico or Russia) much of the foreign borrowing was not necessary for development. Each of the Asian "tigers" generated an enormous volume of domestic saving relative to the size of its economy. The influx of foreign capital seeking quick returns just "boomed the boom," leading to overcapacity and to speculative bubbles in equity and real estate markets.

Second, the risk premium for borrowing in home currency may not be all that onerous if a country's fundamentals are reasonable, a liquid market is created, and the exchange-rate regime does not present market participants with a one-way bet by signaling to speculators that the currency can only go down. For example, markets for years charged South Africa an average of only roughly three percentage points more to borrow in rand rather than in dollars – not an outlandish premium.

Third, and most fundamental, pretending that borrowing a US dollar was just another name for borrowing, say, 25 Thai baht or 2,500 Indonesian rupiah was a cruel hoax that led to excessive borrowing and inappropriate allocation of risk. By borrowing dollars and lending baht (or making loans collateralized by baht assets), Thai banks and finance companies took on much more risk than those bargain basement dollar interest rates indicated. The higher baht interest rates, which included a market-determined premium for exchange-rate risk, indicated risk more accurately. Had Thai companies been forced to pay those higher rates, they would likely have borrowed much less – which would have been a good thing. As it was, when the exchange rate finally tumbled, millions of innocent Thai citizens were left holding the bag. Similar scenarios played out in Indonesia, South Korea and Malaysia.

The point is that borrowing in dollars does not eliminate foreign exchange risk – it just forces the wrong people to bear it. Wouldn't it have been better if, say, hedge funds and international banks had lent the money to Thailand in baht, rather than in dollars, thereby assuming the exchange rate risk themselves? They would have charged a market-determined fee for doing so, of course. But that would have better reflected the actual risks rather than covering them up.

Of course, no one can force financial market participants to lend to emerging markets in local currencies. Thus, this principle constitutes a policy recommendation only in the sense that national and international supervisory agencies (like the IMF and the Bank for International Settlements) should cast a jaundiced eye on unhedged foreign-currency borrowing – and place handicaps, like lower supervisory ratings and higher capital charges, on banks that do so. National governments should also shift their sovereign borrowing toward home currency, rather than dollars.

Principle 3: Don't rush to open capital markets. Unfettered international capital mobility is not the best system for all countries. I do not recommend the cessation of global capital flows, or emulation of Malaysia's heavy-handed approach to restricting them. And I certainly do not favor protectionism in the financial service industries. Chile set a fine moderate example by being open to foreign banks while imposing prudential controls on capital inflows rather than outflows. Other countries may find different ways, tailored to their own unique circumstances, to slow down the flow of international hot money. But the former hard-core Washington consensus – which held that international capital mobility was always a blessing, full stop – needed to be tempered by a little common sense.

Fortunately, this seems to be happening now. But as late as 1997, the IMF was well on its way toward requiring full capital account convertibility of all its member states. During the Asian crises, the IMF saw open capital accounts as part of the solution, rather than part of the problem. I found that attitude badly misguided, and it pains me to admit that the US government was a primary pusher of this bad advice. The fund has now backed away from its former position.

The problem is one of proper sequencing. Too many emerging market countries rush to open up their capital markets too soon – before, for example, they have proper supervisory structures in place. Full openness to international capital flows is a fine long-range goal. But the IMF should not encourage, much less require, premature liberalization. Nations should not adopt America's bad financial habits until they are rich enough to afford them. Malaysia and Indonesia plainly were not.

Principle 4: Follow sound macroeconomic and financial policies. I have saved the platitudes for last – not because I disagree with them, but because they have been said so many times before. Most contemporary suggestions for international financial reform focus on urging countries to follow "sound" fiscal and monetary policies, to avoid large current account imbalances, to develop strong and competent financial regulatory and supervisory structures, and to adopt various codes of good conduct in such areas as transparency, accounting standards and bankruptcy law.

Most of the items on this list are uncontroversial in principle. Who, after all, favors unsound macroeconomic policies, opaqueness and incompetent regulation? But things become highly contentious once you get down to specifics. I will therefore simply endorse the general approach – noting only two things. First, I would assign top priority to two of the most boring topics on the standard list: bank supervision and accounting standards. Second, although transparency – which is the current rage – is all to the good, no one should expect it to accomplish very much in the way of crisis prevention. Bubbles form and burst even in extremely transparent markets like the New York Stock Exchange.

Redesigning the fire-and-rescue squad

No matter how sound the new policies, accidents will happen and financial crises will occur. When they do, the IMF must remain the world's designated fire-and-rescue squad. I see no need to reassign the task and certainly would not want the IMF abolished. If that were done, the world would soon reinvent a similar institution from scratch. But the IMF's modus operandi needs significant change.

Critics charge that the fund has sometimes aggravated crises rather than mitigating them. Although exaggerated, such criticisms contain important elements of truth. So what should IMF crisis-management teams do differently?

Principle 5: Austerity is not always the right medicine. One common criticism holds that no matter what the problem, austerity always seems to be part of the IMF's proposed solution. As a former central banker, I well understand that fiscal and monetary orthodoxies have their place. But that place is not every place. For example, tighter budgets and slower money growth helped much of Latin America in the

1980s, when irresponsibly large budget deficits financed by money creation had fueled inflation. But the fund was wrong to prescribe austerity in Southeast Asia in 1997, when neither budget deficits nor high inflation were part of the problem. Indeed, the IMF itself has all but acknowledged this error.

The standard rationale for imposing fiscal and monetary stringency is, of course, to defend a fixed exchange rate – just as was done under the old Bretton Woods system and the gold standard before that. The IMF regularly answers critics of its tight monetary policies by scoffing at the notion that lower interest rates will help defend a currency from speculative attack. They won't, of course, but that is precisely the point. If currencies were allowed to float, there would be no pegged rates to defend, and hence much less need for crushingly high interest rates. Furthermore, killing a nation's economy hardly seems the best way to bolster confidence in its currency. It didn't work very well in Asia.

The IMF was slow to recognize that the global macroeconomic situation in the late 1990s differed fundamentally from conditions in the 1970s and early 1980s. In particular, inflation – which was the bane of the 1970s and early 1980s, and the other rationale for austerity – was no longer a problem. Instead, a worldwide shortage of aggregate demand emerged as the world's premier macroeconomic malady. Programs that force austerity everywhere aggravate this problem rather than ameliorating it. In a world with floating exchange rates and low inflation, fiscal and monetary austerity ought to be prescribed far less. Not never, just less frequently than is the IMF's current habit.

Principle 6: Devote more resources to protecting innocent bystanders. As I stated at the outset, the new financial architecture needs to give greater weight to developing and strengthening the social safety nets that shield innocent bystanders from the fallout of financial crises. This idea is not alien to the IMF's way of thinking. But neither is it central. The fund pays inadequate attention to the protection of innocents – compared, say, to the protection of creditors who may have made ill-considered loans.

The IMF, we are assured, always strives to preserve social spending. But let's think realistically about what happens to a country in crisis. Mexico, Argentina or any of several Asian countries can serve as examples. The government sees its tax receipts falling due to a recession. The interest rates it must pay on its outstanding debt soar. In addition, it will probably have to shoulder the budgetary burden of a major banking bailout. Now the IMF team arrives, demanding that the overall budget deficit be cut. How, in these circumstances, can the country increase transfer payments to its poor and its unemployed? The answer is obvious: it probably cannot, and so the needy suffer from budget austerity.

A reformed IMF, working in conjunction with the World Bank and regional development banks, should ensure that foreign creditors are not bailed out while local populations drown.

Principle 7: Agree on some procedures for orderly debt settlement. Financial crises typically mean that some beleaguered entities – be they governments or private businesses – cannot pay all their debts. When this occurs, an obvious question arises: Who will get paid, and how much? In the aftermath of the 1994–95 Mexican crisis, the G-10 deputies issued a report that suggested, among other things, that some sort of orderly workout procedure for resolving conflicting claims might be preferable to the current system, in which each creditor grabs whatever he or she can get. The underlying idea was the same one that motivates domestic bankruptcy laws: assets lose value in a mad scramble, so a more orderly procedure for apportioning losses might leave both creditors (as a class) and debtors better off. Furthermore, the IMF does not have the financial means to ride to the rescue time and again.

Unfortunately, the private sector was singularly uninterested in any such proposal in 1996, and the idea died. But I was glad to see one of the 1998 reports by the G-22 (a committee of nations working to strengthen the international financial system) revive this suggestion – with a greater sense of urgency. By now, the world has experienced several additional financial crises, each with its own disorderly scramble for an inadequate pile of assets. One might hope that these unhappy experiences, plus the realization that the IMF has limited funds, would have convinced some private creditors that orderly workout arrangements are preferable to the status quo. But, alas, this does not appear to have happened. Nonetheless, the IMF and several national governments now seem eager to travel down this road.

There are many ways to solve this problem. Collective action clauses in bond contracts – which, for example, might allow bondholders' committees to make decisions about restructuring – are one. The clever proposal by Willem Buiter (a former member of Britain's Monetary Policy Committee) and Anne Sibert (an economist at Birkbeck College in London) for mandatory rollover of debt, but at a penalty rate, is another. The private sector must be intimately involved in designing this aspect of the new architecture. Debt workout provisions should not be dictated by governments against the wishes of private investors, lest credit markets dry up. But national governments and the IMF can and should push things along. For example, G-7 nations could lead the way by incorporating collective action clauses in their own sovereign bonds.

Principle 8: Prevention is better than cure. Recent economic history amply demonstrates that, once a country has been devastated by a financial crisis, there are no good options. The economic and social costs become enormous; it is devilishly difficult to restore growth. It is therefore imperative to find a way to deter speculative attacks on countries with sound fundamentals.

Under the traditional approach, rich countries and the IMF come to the rescue only after a poorer country has collapsed in financial ruin. Thus, much of the house burns down before the fire brigade arrives. But the financial world of today moves to a much faster beat than did the world of 1944, or even 1973. So the new global architecture should offer protection to countries that follow sound policies, before they collapse. One good way to do so would be to put enough international money on the table in foreign reserves to scare speculators away. If the idea worked flawlessly – which, of course, it will not – no money would ever be spent. That was the essential idea behind the IMF's experimental (and not entirely successful!) "contingent credit lines" (CCLs).

Unfortunately, implementing this idea effectively is extremely difficult. Among the thorny issues to resolve are, what criteria will be used to decide which countries prequalify for international assistance and which do not? What happens to the countries that fail to make the grade – are they just left to the financial wolves? And what happens when a country that was once prequalified slips and falls below the standards? Wouldn't defrocking it invite speculative attack?

Although many details need to be worked out, I offer the following two-part answer to these questions. First, the principles discussed earlier – including sound macroeconomic and financial policies, a flexible exchange rate (or very good reasons to fix it) and little borrowing in foreign currency – are a good place to start compiling a list of IMF "dos" and "don'ts." Indeed, the IMF's published guidelines for the CCLs embody such a list already.

Second, prequalification should not be treated as an either–or question, as the fund has been doing. Finer gradations need to be made. The most worrisome aspect of the prequalification idea is that markets might react violently when a country crosses the line from being prequalified for IMF assistance to being unqualified. But no such bright line exists in well-functioning credit markets. When they operate smoothly, financial markets gradually impose higher interest rates and stricter terms as a borrower's creditworthiness deteriorates. Only when panic sets in – which, unfortunately, seems to happen all too frequently in emerging markets – do markets resort to all-or-nothing evaluations. The IMF's prequalification plan should emulate orderly markets, not panicky ones.

How can this be done? As part of its regular surveillance procedures, the IMF could classify member nations into several categories – much as rating agencies do now. The ratings would be based on the sorts of criteria discussed earlier. In case of a contagious crisis, countries in the highest class would have unquestioned access to sizable amounts of IMF lending, with few if any conditions, at near-market interest rates. The next highest class would face less credit availability, more conditions and higher rates – and so on down to the lowest rated class, which would have no guarantee of support. They would have to apply to the IMF in duress, as at present.

Although there are difficulties with such a scheme, perfection is not required. Since a workable prequalification system might prevent some crises and mitigate others, the potential gains from getting one in operation are large enough that the details – difficult as they may be – should not be allowed to stand in the way. The billions of innocent victims of future crises, many of them desperately poor, should not be asked to wait until the perfect design is found.

Eight is enough

It would be a conceit to claim that all eight principles of my suggested financial architecture must be held together as a package. In truth, it is possible to mix and match them – and the first two (floating exchange rates and less foreign-currency borrowing) are far more important than the rest.

But the list has a certain internal integrity: one principle supports and reinforces another. For example, borrowing in foreign currency would be both less alluring and less dangerous if exchange rates were allowed to float. Less-open capital markets in developing nations and a workable IMF prequalification plan should reduce the incidence of crises. Floating rates and the IMF reforms suggested here would reduce the need for fiscal and monetary austerity – and that would, in turn, ease the plight of the poor and unemployed, reducing the strain on social safety nets. Orderly workout procedures and more social spending would limit the economic devastation when crises hit. And so on.

None of the eight principles is revolutionary; you have probably read all of them (or variants) before. But together they constitute an agenda that is ambitious yet eminently achievable. And if instituted, they will make the financial world a far safer place – helping not just market players, but the billions of people who unknowingly depend on them and suffer from their failures.

8 Promoting international financial stability

Sovereign debt restructuring

Anne O. Krueger

Need for a new approach

Greater integration of capital markets and the shift from syndicated bank loans to traded securities have had a profound impact on the way that emerging market sovereigns finance themselves. Sovereigns increasingly issue debt in a range of legal jurisdictions, using a variety of different instruments, to a diverse and diffuse group of creditors. Creditors often have different time horizons for their investment and will respond differently should the sovereign encounter a shock to its debt servicing capacity. This is a positive development: it expands sources of sovereign financing and diversifies risk.

But the greater diversity of claims and interests has also made it more difficult to secure collective action from creditors when a sovereign's debt service obligations exceed its payments capacity. This has reinforced the tendency for debtors to delay restructuring until the last possible moment, increasing the likelihood that the process will be associated with substantial uncertainty and loss of asset values, to the detriment of debtors and creditors alike.

During the past several years there has been extensive discussion inside and outside the International Monetary Fund (IMF) on the need to develop a new approach to sovereign debt restructuring. There is a growing consensus that the present process for restructuring the debts of a sovereign is more prolonged, more unpredictable and more damaging to the country and its creditors than would be desirable. Exploring ways to improve the sovereign debt restructuring process is a key part of the international community's efforts to strengthen the architecture of the global financial system.

The absence of a predictable, orderly and rapid process for restructuring the debts of sovereigns that are implementing appropriate policies has a number of costs. It can lead a sovereign with unsustainable debts to delay seeking a restructuring, draining its reserves and leaving the debtor and the majority of its creditors worse off. Perhaps most crucially, the absence of a mechanism for majority voting on restructuring terms can complicate the process of working out an equitable debt restructuring that returns the country to sustainability. The risk that some creditors will be able to hold out for full payment may prolong the restructuring process, and even inhibit agreement on a needed restructuring. The absence of a predictable process creates additional uncertainty about recovery value.

This chapter seeks to outline the broad features of an improved sovereign debt restructuring process that would address these shortcomings. A sovereign debt restructuring mechanism (SDRM) should aim to help preserve asset values and protect creditors' rights, while paving the way toward an agreement that helps the debtor return to viability and growth. It should strive to create incentives for a debtor with unsustainable debts to approach its creditors promptly – and preferably before it interrupts its payments. But it should also avoid creating incentives for countries with sustainable debts to suspend payments rather than make necessary adjustments to their economic policies. Debt restructuring should not become a measure of first resort. By the same token, however, when there is no feasible set of policy adjustments to resolve the crisis unless accompanied by a restructuring, it is in the interests of neither the debtor nor the majority of its creditors to delay the inevitable.

Of course, difficulty in securing collective action is only one of a number of factors that have made sovereigns extremely reluctant to restructure their debt. Even if mechanisms for debt restructuring are improved, concerns about economic dislocation, political upheaval and long-term loss of access to capital markets will make countries loath to default on their debt service obligations in all but the most extreme circumstances. As a result, it is very unlikely that alleviating the collective action problem somewhat would significantly weaken the credit culture or create moral hazard.

The chapter begins by establishing the case for improving the present framework for sovereign debt restructuring and then sets out the core features that any new approach would need to include. It then discusses the relative roles that the IMF and private creditors could play in an improved mechanism. Finally, before concluding, it discusses the circumstances when exchange controls may need to be relied upon in the context of the resolution of financial crises.

Sovereign debt restructuring mechanism

The objective

The objective of an SDRM is to facilitate the orderly, predictable and rapid restructuring of unsustainable sovereign debt, while protecting asset values and creditors' rights. If appropriately designed and implemented, such a mechanism could help to reduce the costs of a restructuring for sovereign debtors and their creditors, and contribute to the efficiency of international capital markets more generally.

Use of the mechanism would be for the debtor country to request; and not for the IMF or creditors to impose. If the debtor and creditors were able to agree a restructuring between themselves, they would of course be free to do so without having to invoke the mechanism. Indeed, the intention is that the existence of a predictable legal mechanism will in itself help debtors and creditors to reach an agreement without the need for formal activation.

It is envisaged that an SDRM would be invoked only in very limited circumstances. Specifically, when the debt burden is clearly unsustainable. In other words, the mechanism would be invoked where there is no feasible set of sustainable macroeconomic policies that would enable the debtor to resolve the immediate crisis and restore medium-term viability unless they were accompanied by a significant reduction in the net present value of the sovereign's debt. In such cases, the country concerned would probably already have been implementing corrective policies, but would have reached the point where financial viability could not be restored without a substantial adjustment in the debt burden. Countries that are judged to have sustainable sovereign debt burdens may on occasion need to approach their creditors for a reprofiling of scheduled obligations. But it is not intended that an SDRM should be used for such cases.

There are two key challenges to the successful design and implementation of an SDRM. The first is to create incentives for debtors with unsustainable debt burdens to address their problems promptly in a manner that preserves asset values and paves the way toward a restoration of sustainability and growth, while avoiding the creation of incentives for the misuse of the mechanism. The second is to design the mechanism so that, once activated, the relative roles assigned to the sovereign debtor and its creditors create incentives for all parties to reach rapid agreement on restructuring terms that are consistent with a return to sustainability and growth. The policies of the IMF regarding the availability of its resources before, during and after a member seeks a restructuring of its debt currently play a critical role in shaping these incentives. This would remain the case under an SDRM, whatever shape it were to take.

If an SDRM were designed and implemented in a manner that achieved an appropriate balance of incentives, it would provide a number of benefits. Debtors would benefit from addressing their unsustainable debt burdens at an early stage, thereby avoiding the exhaustion of official reserves and unnecessarily severe economic dislocation. They would also benefit from a greater capacity to resolve collective action problems that might otherwise thwart a rapid and orderly restructuring. Most creditors would also gain if the debtor acted before it had dissipated its reserves and would benefit from the resolution of collective action problems that would otherwise impede a sustainable restructuring. Moreover, creditors would benefit from the creation of a predictable restructuring framework that provides assurances that the debtor will avoid actions that reduce the value of creditor claims. Finally, if an SDRM is sufficiently predictable, it will help creditors make better judgments regarding how any restructuring will take place and the recovery value of the debt. This should make sovereign debt more attractive as an asset class, increase the efficiency of international capital markets and result in a better global allocation of capital.

The problem

Developments in the composition of international sovereign borrowing over the past decade – notably the shift away from syndicated bank loans toward traded securities as the principal vehicle for the extension of financial credits to sovereigns – have improved the efficiency of international capital markets. In particular, they have broadened the investor base for financing to emerging market sovereigns and have facilitated the diversification of risk. But the increasingly diverse and diffuse creditor community poses coordination and collective action problems in cases in which a sovereign's scheduled debt service exceeds its payments capacity. This leads to considerable uncertainty among all participants as to how the restructuring process will unfold, and contributes to reluctance by the sovereign, its creditors and the official sector to pursue a restructuring, other than in the most extreme circumstances. This, in turn, increases the likely magnitude of the loss of asset values, which is harmful to the interests of both debtors and creditors.

During the 1980s debt crisis, collective action problems were limited by the relatively small number of large creditors, the relative homogeneity of commercial bank creditors, the contractual provisions of syndicated loans[1] and, on occasion, moral suasion applied by supervisory authorities. Incentives for collective action were reinforced by banks' interest in maintaining good relations as a means of safeguarding future business. Discussions between the sovereign and its creditors generally took place within a collective framework, with the major creditors negotiating through a steering committee. During the negotiations, the committee performed a number of functions, including the resolution of intercreditor problems, the assessment of the acceptability of the offers made by the sovereign, and the preservation of confidentiality. Moreover, the provision of new financing was facilitated by an agreement between the committee and the debtor that any financing provided after a specified date would be excluded from any future restructuring. This provided a basis for banks both to extend medium-term credits and to provide normal trade financing.

The move away from commercial bank lending as a source of external finance for emerging market sovereigns has made the coordination of creditors much more difficult than it was in the 1980s. Many creditors have no ongoing business relationship with the debtor to protect and are not subject to suasion by the official sector. The number and diversity of creditors has increased, with an associated increase in the diversity of interests and appetite for risk. These changes have been accompanied by an increase in the complexity of creditor claims. These developments have made creditor organization more complicated. A sovereign restructuring may require coordination across many bond issues, as well as syndicated loans and trade financing. This organization problem has been exacerbated by the repackaging of creditor claims in ways that separate the interests between the primary lender (the lender of record) and the end investor (the beneficiaries that hold the economic interest).

Sovereigns with unsustainable debt burdens and a diffuse group of creditors can face substantial difficulties getting creditors collectively to agree to a restructuring agreement that brings the sovereign's debt down to a sustainable level. In particular, it may be difficult to secure high participation by creditors in a debt restructuring that would be in the interest of creditors as a group, as individual creditors may consider that their best interests would be served by trying to free ride in the hope of ultimately receiving payments in line with their original contracts. Both fears of free riding and other issues of intercreditor equity may inhibit creditors from accepting a proposed debt restructuring, prolonging the restructuring process and making it less likely that a deal will achieve the objective of restoring sustainability.

The absence of a mechanism that provides for majority action among a diverse set of creditors is a primary source of difficulties with collective action. Currently, a sovereign that obtained the support of a qualified majority of its creditors for a restructuring that could restore sustainability would lack the ability to bind in a minority that may hope to free ride and continue to receive their contracted payments.

Ideally, a country with an unsustainable debt would be able to reach agreement with its creditors on a needed restructuring prior to suspending payments and defaulting. But, in the current environment, it may be particularly difficult to secure high participation from creditors as a group, as individual creditors may consider that their best interests would be served by trying to free ride in the hope of ultimately receiving payments in line with their original contracts. If more than a small proportion of creditors attempt to free ride, a restructuring would not succeed in bringing debt to a sustainable level, and a default may be unavoidable. These difficulties may be amplified by the prevalence of complex financial instruments, such as credit derivatives, which in some cases may provide investors with incentives to hold out in the hope of forcing a default (thereby triggering a payment under the derivative contract), rather than participating in a restructuring. Difficulties in securing agreement on a needed restructuring prior to a payments suspension also may undermine confidence in the domestic financial system (to the extent that domestic banks have significant holdings of government securities) and may even trigger an unmanageable deposit run.

If a restructuring cannot be achieved prior to a default, collective action problems may still arise as creditors may decide to hold out in hope of a more favorable settlement, possibly through resort to litigation. To date litigation against a sovereign has been relatively limited and there is inadequate evidence to suggest that the prospect of such litigation will invariably undermine the sovereign's ability to reach an agreement with a majority of its creditors. Litigation is not an attractive option for many creditors. It is costly and may give rise to concerns relating to reputation damage. Potential holdouts face significant uncertainty regarding whether the debtor would be willing to make a more attractive offer to nonparticipating creditors. Nevertheless, the evolution of legal strategies has increased the uncertainties of post-default restructurings. For example, the recent legal action against Peru may make potentially cooperative creditors nervous about participating in a future restructuring agreement. They may be worried that a holdout will be able to extract full payment from a sovereign by, for example, threatening the interruption of payments on the restructured debt.

In addition to difficulties securing collective action, creditors have identified other factors that they consider hamper the prospects for rapid progress toward predictable and orderly restructuring agreements. In particular, concerns about intercreditor equity stemming from debtors' decisions to make payments to certain favored creditors after suspending payments on other creditors may introduce delays. Creditors have also pointed to the reluctance of debtors to participate in a collaborative dialogue to develop restructuring proposals. The design and implementation of more efficient mechanisms for resolving collective action could also catalyze the establishment of a more collaborative framework for debtor–creditor negotiations.

Core features of an SDRM

What features of a legal framework would need to be in place in order to establish adequate incentives for debtors and creditors to agree upon a prompt, orderly and predictable restructuring of unsustainable debt? As will be seen, although the features of existing domestic legislative models provide important guidance as to how to address collective action problems among creditors in the insolvency context, the applicability of these models is limited by the unique characteristics of a sovereign state.

Existing rehabilitation models and their limitations

When a financially distressed – but fundamentally viable – company finds that it can no longer service its debt, the company and its diverse creditors cannot generally turn to their domestic authorities for financing as a means of resolving the crisis. Instead, domestic insolvency legislation provides the necessary framework to overcome coordination problems as they work out restructuring terms. A court-administered reorganization chapter of an insolvency law provides the necessary incentives for a debt restructuring agreement (that often involves substantial debt reduction). To the extent that the insolvency system is well developed, most restructurings take place "in the shadow" of the law, that is, without the need – and expense – of actually commencing formal court administered proceedings. As is discussed in Box 8.1 most well-developed corporate rehabilitation laws include the following features:

(i)   a stay on creditor enforcement during the restructuring negotiations;
(ii) measures that protect creditor interests during the period of the stay;
(iii) mechanisms that facilitate the provision of new financing during the proceedings; and
(iv) a provision that binds all relevant creditors to an agreement that has been accepted by a qualified majority.

All of these features serve to maximize the value of creditor claims by preserving the going concern value of the firm. As will be discussed below, these features are relevant to a discussion of the design of a sovereign debt restructuring mechanism. It should be noted, however, that the applicability of the corporate model to the sovereign context is limited in a number of important respects.

- First, and perhaps most importantly, corporate reorganization provisions operate within the context of the potential liquidation of the debtor, which could not apply to a sovereign state. In the event that a reorganization plan does not attract adequate support from its creditors and the company continues to be in a state of illiquidity, most laws will provide for the automatic liquidation of the company. Moreover, the potential liquidation of the enterprise also limits the terms of any restructuring proposal. Most modern laws provide that creditors cannot be forced to accept terms under a reorganization plan that would result in their receiving less than what they would have received in a liquidation.

- Second, since one of the purposes of a reorganization law is to enable creditors to maximize the value of their claims through the going concern value of the enterprise, most modern laws allow for the creditors to commence proceedings unilaterally so as to acquire the company through a reorganization plan that includes a debt-for-equity conversion that, in some cases, may extinguish all ownership interests of the incumbent shareholders. Again, such a feature could not be applied to a sovereign state.
- Finally, it is difficult to envisage how the constraints that are applied to the activities of a corporate debtor to safeguard the interests of creditors during the proceedings could be made legally binding on a sovereign and enforced, particularly with respect to the exercise of its sovereign powers, including, for example, its fiscal powers. In the sovereign context, we must therefore rely on having the right incentives in place.

Box 8.1 Corporate reorganization model

Although corporate insolvency laws vary among countries, considerable work has been done to identify "best practices" in core areas.[a] The following features of well-developed insolvency laws provide the key incentives for corporate restructuring:

- *First, upon commencement of reorganization proceedings, a stay is imposed on all legal actions by creditors, thereby protecting the debtor from dismemberment.* This stay is designed not only to protect the debtor, but also addresses the intercreditor collective action problem. In the absence of a stay, creditors would probably rush to enforce their claims out of a fear that others would do so.
- *Second, during the proceedings, legal constraints are imposed upon the activities of the debtor and a reorganization plan must normally be prepared within a specified time frame.* As a means of ensuring that the interests of creditors are protected during the proceedings, the debtor is precluded from entering into transactions that would prejudice creditors generally (e.g. transferring assets to insiders or making payments to favored creditors). To ensure compliance, the laws of some countries also provide for a court-appointed administrator to oversee the activities of the debtor during this period.

- *Third, as a means of encouraging new financing, credit provided to the debtor after commencement of the proceeding must be given seniority over prior claims in any reorganization plan.* Normally, a creditor that provides financing during the proceedings would have the right to be repaid once the reorganization plan is approved.
- *Fourth, a debt-restructuring plan approved by the requisite majority of creditors will be binding on all creditors.* The law normally provides for the establishment of a committee of creditors that takes the lead in negotiating the terms of the debt-restructuring plan with the debtor. To ensure there is no fraud in the voting process, the court normally oversees the verification of creditors' claims.

A predictable insolvency system enables corporate restructuring to take place out-of-court but "in the shadow" of the formal insolvency system. Such an out-of-court process generally mimics certain features of the formal process. For example, creditors agree to a voluntary standstill in the knowledge that, if they refuse, the debtor can make a standstill mandatory by commencing formal proceedings. Similarly, potential holdout creditors realize that, if they are inflexible, the debtor and majority creditors can use the law to bind them to the terms of the restructuring agreement. In sum, each party negotiates with a clear understanding of the type of leverage it – and the others – would have if the formal system were to be activated.

Note

a Including by the IMF, World Bank and United Nations Commission on International Trade Law (UNCITRAL).

In many respects, Chapter 9 of the United States Bankruptcy Code, which applies to municipalities, is of greater relevance in the sovereign context because it applies to an entity that carries out governmental functions. Although it includes a number of the core features of a corporate reorganization law, it differs from the corporate model in a number of respects. For example, only the municipality (not its creditors) may commence proceedings and propose a reorganization plan. Moreover, the bankruptcy court may not interfere with any of the municipality's political or governmental powers, property or revenue or the municipality's use or enjoyment of any income-producing property. Finally, a Chapter 9 case cannot be converted into a liquidation case. All of these features could be appropriately integrated into a sovereign debt restructuring mechanism.

There are, however, important differences between a municipality and a sovereign state that would have implications on the design of any sovereign debt restructuring mechanisms. Unlike a sovereign state, a municipality is not independent. Chapter 9 legislation acknowledges – and does not impair – the power of the state within which the municipality exists to continue to control the exercise of the powers of the municipality, including expenditures. This lack of independence of municipalities is one of the reasons why many countries have not adopted insolvency legislation to address problems of financial distress confronted by local governments.

The sovereign context

Although the applicability of the above models to the sovereign context is necessarily limited, a number of their features – if appropriately adapted – provide useful guidance when contemplating the design of a sovereign debt restructuring mechanism. Bearing in mind the objective of the mechanism – to provide a framework for the orderly, predictable and rapid restructuring of debt problems in a manner that preserves value for the benefit of both the debtor and its creditors – the core features of the mechanism could include the following:

- *Majority restructuring.* The creation of a mechanism that would enable the affirmative vote of a qualified majority of creditors to bind a dissenting minority to the terms of a restructuring agreement would be the most important element of any new restructuring framework. From the perspective of creditors, such a mechanism would provide confidence that any forbearance exercised by the majority when agreeing to a restructuring would not be abused by free riders who could otherwise press for full payment after an agreement was reached. For the majority of creditors, the disruptive behavior of free riders not only raises intercreditor equity issues, but also reduces the ability of the debtor to service the newly restructured debt. From the perspective of the sovereign, the resolution of these collective action issues will make it more likely that it will be able to reach early agreement with creditors on a debt restructuring. Moreover, it eliminates the threat of disruptive litigation by dissenting creditors after the restructuring takes place.
- *Majority restructuring* provisions form the central element of the collective action clauses that are found in some international sovereign bonds. However, these provisions only bind bondholders within the same issue. They have no effect on bondholders of other issuances, which may in any event be governed by different legal jurisdictions. Moreover, they do not apply to other types of indebtedness, such as bank claims and domestic debt. To address the collective action problems that arise from the very diverse private creditor community that currently exists, such a mechanism would need to apply to all forms of private credit to sovereigns. This feature of a sovereign debt restructuring mechanism would be similar to the majority restructuring provisions of domestic insolvency laws, which aggregate the claims of all eligible creditors (irrespective of the nature of the instrument) when determining whether there is adequate support by a majority to make an agreement binding on all creditors. Aggregation, however, would not result in the equalization of all claims for debt restructuring purposes. For example, as in the case of the domestic insolvency law, safeguards would need to be in place to

ensure that the seniority of certain claims is protected. Ideally, the debtor and its creditors would activate the majority restructuring provision described above prior to a default on the original claims. As borne out by experience, avoiding a default would help minimize economic disruption in the debtor country and preserve asset values, including the secondary market value of creditors' claims.

- *Stay on creditor enforcement.* In the event that an agreement had not been reached prior to a default, a temporary stay on creditor litigation after a suspension of payments but before a restructuring agreement is reached would support the effective operation of the majority restructuring provision. In the context of corporate insolvency, a stay on litigation is intended to enforce collective action by preventing a rush to the courthouse and a "grab race" that could undermine the ability of a company to continue functioning, to the detriment of the debtor and its creditors (the value of whose claims is maximized when the company remains a going concern). The risk of widespread creditor litigation may be less pronounced in the sovereign than in the corporate context, largely on account of the relative scarcity of assets under the jurisdiction of foreign courts that could be seized to satisfy creditors' claims. Nevertheless, there is a risk that litigation could inhibit progress in the negotiations. This risk could increase if, as a result of the introduction of a majority restructuring provision, the only opportunity to use legal enforcement as a source of leverage is before rather than after the reaching of an agreement. This is one of the reasons why collective action clauses in international sovereign bonds also contain provisions that effectively enable a majority of bondholders to block legal action by a minority before an agreement is reached. But, as in the case of majority restructuring provisions, these provisions only apply to bondholders within the same issuance.

- *Protecting creditor interests.* An *SDRM* would need to include safeguards that give creditors adequate assurances that their interests were being protected during the period of the stay. These safeguards would have two complementary elements. First, the sovereign debtor would be required not to make payments to nonpriority creditors. This would avoid the dissipation of resources that could be used to service the claims of relevant creditors in general. Second, there would have to be assurances that the debtor would conduct policies in a fashion that preserves asset values. If, throughout the stay, the member was implementing an IMF-supported program or was working closely with the IMF to elaborate policies that could be supported with the use of IMF resources, this would provide many of these assurances. Beyond the fiscal, monetary and exchange rate policies that lay the basis for the resumption of debt service and a return to sustainability, creditors also have clear interests in other policies, including, for example, the nature and terms of any domestic bank restructuring, the continued operation of the domestic payments system, the country's bankruptcy regime and the nature of any exchange controls it imposes. Depending on the circumstances, the creditors of the sovereign may have a particular interest in the effective implementation of capital controls to prevent capital flight.

- *Priority financing.* A majority restructuring mechanism could also usefully be buttressed by a mechanism that would facilitate the provision of new money from private creditors during the period of the stay. It is in the collective interests of private creditors and the sovereign debtor that new money be provided in appropriate amounts. Such financing, when used in the context of good policies, can help limit the degree of economic dislocation and thereby help preserve the member's capacity to generate the resources for meeting debt-service obligations. In the sovereign context, new money could help cover the sovereign's need for trade credit and could also finance payments to priority creditors. Under the existing legal framework, however, individual creditors have no incentive to provide new money in such circumstances, as the resulting benefits of a return to debt servicing would be shared among creditors as a group, and there would be no assurance that the new financing would not also get caught up in the restructuring. An SDRM could induce new financing by providing an assurance that any financing in support of the member's program extended after the introduction of the stay would be senior to all preexisting private indebtedness. This assurance could be provided through a decision of a qualified majority of creditors.

As discussed further below, if this mechanism is to be both equitable and transparent for a broad range of creditors, it will have to be supported by independent arrangements for the verification of creditors' claims, the resolution of disputes and the supervision of voting. For example, such arrangements would protect against fraud that may arise through the creation of debt between related parties.

Among the many issues that will need to be addressed is the coverage of official creditors. Given the special role that the IMF and multilateral development banks play in providing finance during crises, their status as preferred creditors has generally been accepted by the international community. These claims would not be subject to the mechanism. However, this leaves the question of how to treat bilateral official debt; debt that is now routinely restructured in the context of the Paris Club. We will need to explore further whether it would be feasible to include bilateral official debt under an SDRM and, if so, how this would be done in a manner that pays due regard to the special features of these claims.

Another set of issues that needs careful consideration concerns the treatment of domestic debt in the context of an SDRM. Sovereigns typically have a wide range of debts to domestic residents. These may include marketable securities (issued under either domestic or foreign laws), loans from banks and suppliers' credits. With the growing integration of international capital markets, and the tendency for residents and nonresidents to hold similar instruments, the distinction between domestic and nondomestic debt has become increasingly blurred.

While the treatment of domestic debt will need to be considered on a case-by-case basis, in practice it may be necessary to include domestic debt within the scope of a restructuring that is intended to bring a sovereign's debt to a sustainable level. In particular, the magnitude of debt to nonresidents in relation to the scale of the required reduction in the overall debt burden may necessitate the inclusion of domestic debt. Moreover, nonresident investors may only be willing to agree to provide substantial debt reduction if they consider that adequate intercreditor equity has been achieved – they would be unlikely to be willing to provide such relief if it was seen as enabling other private creditors to exit whole.

Nevertheless, the treatment of domestic debt under a restructuring needs to weigh a number of factors that will have a bearing on the prospects for restoring sustainable growth. (These factors would need to be considered by both the debtor in the design of a restructuring proposal and by foreign creditors in their assessment of the adequacy of intercreditor equity.) First and foremost there is a need to ensure that the domestic banking system should remain solvent after a restructuring, in order that it can continue to serve as an intermediary for domestic savings and foreign financing, for example, trade credit. Second, it would be important to take account of the likely impact of a restructuring for the future operation of domestic capital markets, and, in particular, the possible tradeoff between the magnitude of debt reduction obtained through a restructuring, on the one hand, and the prospect that the sovereign will be able to mobilize savings from domestic capital markets in the aftermath of a restructuring – particularly in the period while access to international capital markets will likely remain closed.

In providing a legal basis for the treatment of domestic debt under an SDRM, a number of approaches could be considered. One would have the statutory framework cover a broad range of debt, including domestic debt. This would make the claims of all resident investors subject to the majority restructuring and other features of the mechanism. This need not preclude flexibility in the treatment of domestic debt under individual restructuring proposals, subject to the ability of the sovereign to attract the necessary degree of support from creditors for the overall package. An alternative approach would exclude domestic debt from the scope of the statutory approach and rely instead on the existing governing legal frameworks to facilitate any restructurings of these claims that may be required. Of course, this approach would not reduce the need to achieve an acceptable degree of intercreditor equity in order to garner the necessary support of nonresident creditors. It would also raise practical issues concerning the definition of domestic debt. Would this be based on the residency of investors, or the characteristics of the instruments, possibly the governing law, currency (or location) of debt service payments?

All of the above features, when taken together, would establish a framework within which an orderly and rapid restructuring could take place. Most importantly, the framework would address collective action problems that have, to date, made the cost of restructuring excessively high for debtors and creditors alike. This could help creditors and debtors reach an agreement on equitable restructuring terms more rapidly, and thus facilitate the country's recovery. As noted above, it may facilitate restructurings prior to defaults, thereby protecting asset values for the benefit of debtors and creditors alike. Moreover, if the framework were sufficiently predictable, it would create the incentive for debtors and creditors to reach an agreement without having to rely on its actual use.

For example, the voting provisions would encourage early creditor organization, and thus lay the basis for negotiations between the debtor and its creditors. In addition, potential holdouts would realize that, unless they are sufficiently flexible, the debtor and the majority of creditors could use the mechanism to bind them to the terms of an agreement.

More generally, to the extent that the establishment of a sovereign debt-restructuring framework serves to create a more structured negotiating framework between creditors and sovereign debtors, it may enhance the value of sovereign debt as an asset class. Over the past several years, a number of dedicated emerging market creditors have complained about the absence of a predictable and equitable process that guides sovereign debt restructuring negotiations. They have argued that this makes it more difficult to attract long-term capital to the emerging market asset class, thereby undermining the stability of the investor base. To provide greater structure to the negotiating process, consideration could be given to designing the mechanism in a manner that gives a creditors' committee an explicit role in the restructuring process, as is the case in most modern insolvency laws. Creditor committees played a major role during the sovereign debt restructuring process in the 1980s and further efforts could be made to facilitate their formation and operation, taking into consideration the profound changes that have taken place in capital markets over the past twenty years.

The role of the IMF

If appropriately designed and implemented, a sovereign debt restructuring framework would assist in achieving the IMF's purposes in a number of respects. First, if such a framework facilitates an early restructuring of unsustainable debt, balance of payments viability could more easily be attained in a manner that minimizes the resort to measures that are destructive to national or international prosperity. The achievement of this objective would in turn help the IMF safeguard its resources. Finally, to the extent that a predictable framework assists creditors in their assessment and pricing of risk, it will help to avert future crises, thereby enhancing the stability of the international financial system.

In light of the above, what role should the IMF play in the actual operation of the mechanism? The financial support that the IMF provides for an effective economic adjustment program already shapes incentives that surround the sovereign debt restructuring process and would continue to do so under an SDRM. This section addresses the critical question of whether, under an SDRM, the IMF's role could be limited to the exercise of its existing financial powers or whether it would need to exercise additional legal authority.

The role of IMF finance

In the present environment, decisions by the IMF regarding the availability of its resources already influence all stages of the sovereign debt restructuring process. Specifically:

- The judgment of the IMF about the scale of the financing it is willing to provide in the absence of a debt restructuring and the design of an economic program supported by the IMF both help determine the timing of a sovereign payment suspension. Before a member decides to seek a comprehensive debt restructuring, it typically approaches the IMF for financing (either in the context of an existing or future arrangement) with the aim of avoiding such a restructuring and the associated economic, social and political disruption. On being approached, the IMF is required to make a judgment whether the member's debt burden is or is not sustainable. This judgment determines the availability and the appropriate scale of IMF financing. Consequently, decisions about the availability of IMF resources strongly influence a member's decision as to whether to suspend payments in order to conserve its remaining international reserves.

- After a member has suspended payments, it is currently expected to work with the IMF on the development of an appropriate economic policy framework, and to negotiate a debt restructuring with its creditors. Approval of an IMF-supported program often, but not always, precedes final agreement on restructuring terms with creditors. In this context, the IMF currently makes judgments about the good faith of the member in its negotiations with its creditors in determining whether to lend into arrears on payments to private creditors. The IMF-supported program will specify a fiscal and external adjustment path, which will determine, in broad terms, the amount of resources available for debt service by the sovereign during the program period.

- When deciding whether to support a member that is about to conclude a restructuring of its obligations to private creditors, the IMF currently makes two important judgments. First, it assesses the consistency of the restructuring agreement with the adjustment path in the member's economic program. The payments stream that emerges from the private debt restructuring should be consistent with the member's program. Second, it assesses whether the resulting medium-term payments profile is consistent with the requirements for debt sustainability.

Under an SDRM, the nature of the financing decisions that the IMF would need to make before, during and after a debt restructuring would not change. Consistent with its mandate, the IMF would continue to ensure that its resources were being used to resolve the member's balance of payments problems without resorting to measures that were destructive of national and international prosperity. Moreover, the IMF would continue to need to ensure that there are adequate safeguards for the revolving character of its resources. Both of these imperatives would require it to continue to condition the availability of its resources on the adoption of appropriate policies and, where necessary, on a debt restructuring that laid the basis for a return to sustainability.

Operating the framework

In light of the central role that IMF financing plays, one could envisage a framework that empowered the IMF to make key decisions regarding its operation.

Bearing in mind the key features described in the previous section, these decisions would include the following:

- First, *activation of a stay on creditor action* would require a request by the sovereign debtor and IMF endorsement. Such endorsement would be based on the IMF's determination that the member's debt is unsustainable and that appropriate policies are being – or will soon be – implemented.
- Second, any *extension of the stay* would require a determination by the IMF not only that adequate policies continue to be implemented but also that the member is making progress in its negotiations with its creditors.
- Third, IMF *approval of a restructuring agreement* that had been accepted by the requisite majority of creditors would be a condition for its effectiveness. Such approval would be based on a determination that it provides for a sustainable debt profile.

While the IMF's involvement in the decision-making process, as described above, would help ensure that the framework was not abused, a number of concerns have been expressed regarding the above approach. As a creditor and as an institution whose members include debtors and bilateral official creditors, there are concerns that the IMF would not be perceived as being entirely impartial in exercising this authority. More generally, it is unclear whether the international community would be willing to confer additional powers on the IMF.

In light of these concerns, the remainder of this section discusses the benefits of an approach that would limit the role of the IMF in the operation of the mechanism itself. Under this alternative approach, decisions under the SDRM would be left to the debtor and the majority of the creditors. Accordingly, the IMF would have no power to limit the enforcement of creditor rights. Rather, the IMF would rely on its existing financial powers to create the incentives for the relevant parties to use the mechanism appropriately. How such an approach could be implemented is discussed below for each of the main features of the mechanism.

- *Approval of the restructuring agreement.* It would be possible to rely exclusively on the approval of the requisite majority of the creditors as a means of making the agreement binding on all creditors, that is, IMF endorsement of such an agreement would not be a condition for its effectiveness. Such an approach would make this element of the mechanism consistent with the majority restructuring provisions found in collective action clauses. The key difference would be that, while majority-restructuring provisions only apply to bondholders within the same issuance, an affirmative vote by the requisite creditors under the mechanism would bind the entire creditor body.

    This approach carries a risk that the debtor and creditors would conclude an agreement that did not achieve a sustainable debt profile. However, this risk could be addressed, as it is in the present context, if subsequent IMF financial support is conditioned on a judgment that the payments stream in the proposed restructuring was consistent with the adjustment path in the member's economic program and the requirements for medium-term debt sustainability. If it did not meet these conditions, the IMF would be effectively prevented from lending until the member had taken further steps to ensure debt sustainability, possibly involving a further restructuring.

- *Activation of the stay.* As an alternative to activating the stay upon the IMF's endorsement of a request, one could envisage a stay that would be activated only upon a request of the member that had been approved by the requisite majority of creditors. Such an approach would mimic, to an extent, certain provisions of collective action clauses found in many international sovereign bonds. These provisions effectively enable a qualified majority of holders of a single bond issuance to restrict a minority of holders of the same bond issuance from enforcing their claims against the sovereign during the negotiations of a debt restructuring agreement.[2] Under this approach, however, the decision would be made a qualified majority of all of the member's creditors, that is, creditor claims would be aggregated across instruments for voting purposes. Reliance on such an approach would serve to highlight the extent to which the problem being addressed by the mechanism is that of collective action.

A shortcoming of this approach is that, even if the requisite majority of the creditors were amenable to approving a stay that would be binding upon the entire creditor body, it could take considerable time to put one in place. In the context of a single bond issue where provisions exist that enable the majority of creditors to prevent enforcement by a minority, the process of ascertaining the will of the majority is relatively straightforward, although even that takes time. In contrast, a vote by all creditors (all bond issuances, bank debt, trade credit, certain official claims) as envisaged under the mechanism would need to be preceded by a verification of claims process that might take several months to complete.

There are several different ways in which the above shortcoming could be addressed.

- First, the mechanism could enable the sovereign to activate the stay unilaterally and enjoy the resulting legal protection for a limited ninety-day period. At the end of that period, claims would have been verified and creditors would vote as to whether the stay would be extended and, if so, for how long. Although the IMF would not have a legal veto, in most cases a member would likely only activate the mechanism in consultation with the IMF, that is, after the IMF had determined that the debt burden was unsustainable and that further financial assistance would not be forthcoming in the absence of a restructuring. But a key question would be whether the ability of the sovereign to activate the mechanism for a limited period unilaterally might be abused by members whose debt was not judged to be unsustainable.

- Second, IMF approval of the stay could be necessary for it to be effective for the initial ninety-day period. Any extension of the stay beyond this limited period would require the consent of the majority of the creditors. This approach would be designed to protect against the possibility of debtors' abuse of a purely unilateral stay prior to a creditors' vote. It would, however, entail IMF involvement in the decision-making process, albeit in a limited manner.
- Third, one could accept that a stay would not be in place until an affirmative vote of the creditors had taken place and focus instead on ways to limit the delay between a member's request and the creditors' vote. For example, as a means of accelerating the verification of claims and voting process, a standing organization could be established whose role would include registering claims against the sovereign and facilitating the organization of creditors in the context of a restructuring.

It should be noted that a brief delay between the member's suspension of payments and the activation of the stay would not leave a sovereign helpless in the event that the suspension gave rise to capital flight. Under certain circumstances, capital controls to stem outflows might be a necessary – but temporary – feature of an IMF-supported program. This is discussed further below.

- *Maintenance of the stay.* Just as a qualified majority of creditors might be given the authority to activate a stay, the majority of creditors might be given the authority to determine whether to extend the stay beyond the initial ninety-day period. By that time, the claims of creditors would have been verified, and creditors would be in a position to vote on the issue. If the member was already in a position to submit a restructuring plan for approval at the expiration of this initial period, the creditors would vote on the proposal, and an affirmative vote by the requisite majority would bind dissenting creditors. If, however, more time were needed for negotiation, creditors would decide (again by a vote of the requisite majority) whether the stay should be extended and, if so, for how long.

The IMF's decisions regarding the availability of its resources would have a major impact on whether an extension would be approved by creditors. Specifically, the requisite majority of creditors would normally only be willing to extend the stay beyond the initial period if they had some assurance that the member was adopting policies that were being supported by the IMF. When making a decision to extend the stay, the majority of creditors would be in a position to judge whether the member was negotiating with them in good faith and their interests were protected.

Would such an approach give creditors too much leverage in the process? The concept of a stay being imposed upon all creditors through a decision by a majority is roughly analogous to the majority enforcement provisions that are found in many international sovereign bonds. Such provisions limit the ability to initiate litigation without the support of a given percentage of the bond issue. But while such provisions bind the bondholders within the same issuance, an affirmative vote by the majority under the proposed statutory framework would bind the entire creditor body.

There may be a risk that creditors would withhold an extension of the stay in the hope that the IMF would provide more financing or call on the member to make additional adjustment efforts. For example, even in circumstances where the member is implementing good policies and negotiating in good faith, creditors may refuse to extend the period of the stay as a means of persuading the member to turn to the IMF for financing that could enhance the terms of any restructuring. The creditors could threaten to lift the stay to force the debtor to agree to more adjustment than contemplated under the IMF-supported program. Such risks could be reduced, however, by the resolute application of the IMF's policy of lending into arrears, under which it signals its willingness to continue to support a program, even if the member has interrupted payments to its creditors.

- *Priority financing.* As noted in the previous section, an SDRM could provide incentives for new financing by providing an assurance that any new financing in support of the members program extended after the introduction of the stay would be senior to preexisting private indebtedness. This could be achieved by giving a qualified majority of private creditors the power to subordinate the claims of all private creditors to claims arising from financing provided after the effectiveness of the stay.

The legal basis for an SDRM

As discussed above, there would be a number of benefits in designing a mechanism where the decision-making process resembles features of the collective action clauses found in international sovereign bonds. Decisions regarding both the terms of the restructuring and the activation and maintenance of the stay would be made by the requisite majority and would be binding on the dissenting minority. In light of the benefits of this approach, therefore, the question arises as to whether the essential objectives of the mechanism could be achieved through the progressive adoption of contractual provisions that address collective action problems. This section addresses this question and explains why, notwithstanding the benefits of collective action clauses, the most effective basis for the mechanism would be statutory. It also discusses a number of issues relating to the establishment of a statutory framework.

The benefits and limits of contract

The inclusion of collective action clauses in all international sovereign bonds would represent an important improvement in the international financial architecture. As has been discussed in earlier sections of this chapter, and has been demonstrated in recent cases, collective action clauses include two provisions that can facilitate an orderly restructuring of sovereign indebtedness: (i) a provision that enables a qualified majority of bondholders to bind all bondholders of the same issuance to the terms of a restructuring agreement and (ii) a provision that enables a qualified majority of bondholders to prevent all bondholders of the same issuance from enforcing their claims against the sovereign.

The insertion of collective action clauses in all future international sovereign bonds would not require wholesale statutory reform. For example, although such provisions are not typically found in international sovereign bonds governed by New York law, they could be introduced without any legislative changes.

Moreover, it should also be noted that, even if an SDRM was established through legislation, as discussed below, such clauses could still play an important role. For example, since a statutory mechanism would only apply in circumstances where the member's debt is unsustainable, collective action clauses could facilitate restructurings in circumstances where the problems faced by the member arise from illiquidity.

However, relying exclusively on contract as the legal basis for an SDRM would limit the effectiveness of such a mechanism.

First, it would be difficult to establish a purely contract-based framework.

There is, at the outset, the problem of incentives for the adoption of traditional collective action provisions in all new indebtedness. By definition, a contractual approach would require the sovereign and its creditors to agree to the inclusion of these provisions in all future international sovereign bonds, and also in other debt and debt-like instruments that the market developed. Recent experience demonstrates that sovereign debtors facing financial difficulties actually prefer to exclude such provisions as a way of demonstrating their firm intention to avoid a restructuring. Neither have creditors pressed for their inclusion, notwithstanding the fact that they may make an unavoidable restructuring more prompt and orderly. The advantage of giving the framework for sovereign debt restructuring a statutory basis is that the collective action provisions that it would contain would effectively override the restructuring and enforcement terms set forth in the underlying agreements, as is the case with the collective action provisions contained in domestic insolvency laws.

Another barrier to the establishment of such a framework is the transitional problem. Even if all new bonds make use of the needed contractual provisions, a large portion of outstanding bonds with long maturities, including bonds governed by New York law, do not contain such provisions.[3] While this problem could conceivably be addressed by a series of exchanges that retired existing bonds, it is not clear how debtors and creditors would be persuaded to take such action. It is also possible that use could be made of existing provisions that allow for amendment of terms not related to payment to facilitate debt restructurings in the interim. For example, Ecuador recently made use of "exit consents," to overcome the problem of holdout creditors generated by the absence of provisions allowing a majority to amend payment terms in outstanding bonds governed by New York law. Under this technique, bondholders who accepted the exchange voted to amend nonpayment terms in ways that made holding "old bonds" less attractive. However, this technique has been somewhat controversial and it may not be immune from legal challenge in the future.

Second, even if a contract-based framework could be established, it would not provide a comprehensive and durable solution to collective action problems.

Collective action clauses traditionally only bind bondholders of the same issue. In contrast, the collective action provisions of a statute would be designed to apply across a broad range of indebtedness (potentially including international and domestic debt, bank loans, trade credit and official claims, if applicable). This is one of the reasons why the collective action provisions of insolvency laws are so effective. To address issues arising from the relative seniority of certain indebtedness, insolvency laws often provide for the classification of debt for both voting and distribution purposes. As discussed earlier, similar safeguards would need to be established under the mechanism.

To address the above limitation, one could conceive of the introduction of contractual provisions that provide for the restructuring of the instrument in question on the basis of an affirmative vote of creditors holding a qualified majority of all private credit. While further study on the feasibility of developing such clauses should be encouraged, such an approach would raise its own set of issues.

- First, such a provision would exacerbate the incentive problem: if it is difficult to convince a sovereign and the purchasers of one bond issue to agree to the inclusion of a collective action clause in that issue, it would be even more difficult to persuade debtors and creditors to include such provisions in *all* forms of debt instruments in a uniform manner. Indeed, a sovereign facing financial difficulties would come under pressure from certain creditors to exclude such provisions as a means of giving such creditors effective seniority. Moreover, it can be expected that certain creditor groups would be particularly reluctant to agree voluntarily to an arrangement whereby, for voting purposes, their claims were aggregated with all other present or future creditors.

- Second, even if all debt instruments contained identical restructuring texts, which would be difficult to achieve, there would be no assurance of uniform interpretation and application unless they were governed by the same law and subject to the same jurisdiction. In the present environment, emerging market countries that have borrowed heavily often have a variety of bond issuances outstanding, which are governed by the laws of different jurisdictions.

- Third, it may not be feasible to establish a process by contract that would effectively guarantee the integrity of the voting procedure. Under the statutory framework that governs the domestic insolvency process, a court oversees this process, including the verification of claims, so as to guard against fraud. In the absence of an independent party to verify the true value of claims, a debtor could, for example, inflate its debt stock by establishing matching credit and debt positions with a related party. That entity – which could hold a qualified majority of all debt – could vote to reduce the value of all creditor claims.

- Fourth, it is not clear that such provisions would be consistent with the existing legislation of all members. The fact that traditional collective action clauses are not included in international sovereign bonds in some jurisdictions arises, in part, from the absence of a clear statutory basis that allows for the rights of a minority of creditors to be modified without their consent. This issue would be amplified if contractual provisions attempted to aggregate claims for voting purposes.
- Finally, and more generally, the financial markets have consistently demonstrated the ability to innovate. A statutory regime is therefore likely to provide a more stable background than contractual provisions even if it were feasible to overcome all of the other difficulties referred to above.

Implementing a statutory framework

If a statutory approach that creates the legal basis for majority action across all sovereign indebtedness offers the best method of achieving the objectives of an SDRM, the question arises as to how best to implement a change in the statutory regime.

There are a number of reasons why the statutory approach could be more effectively implemented through the establishment of universal treaty obligations rather than through the enactment of legislation in a limited number of jurisdictions.[4] First, it would prevent circumvention: if the statutory framework is only in place in a limited number of jurisdictions, creditors could ensure that future instruments enable them to enforce their claims in jurisdictions that have not adopted such jurisdictions but whose money judgments are recognized in key jurisdictions under treaties or local law.[5] Second, an international treaty would ensure both uniformity of text and (if there is an institution given interpretive authority) uniformity of interpretation. Third, it would address a potential "free rider" problem: without a treaty, countries would be reluctant to adopt a legislation until they were assured other countries had also done so. (A treaty could be designed that would enter into force at the same time for all signatory countries.) Finally, the establishment of a treaty facilitates the establishment of a single international judicial entity that would have exclusive jurisdiction over all disputes that would arise between the debtor and its domestic and international creditors and among such creditors. Moreover, such an entity would also have responsibility for the administration of a unified voting process, including the verification of all creditor claims. If one relied exclusively on domestic legislation in a variety of jurisdictions, the process for dispute resolution and claims verification would be a fragmented one, with different claims being subject to the jurisdiction of different courts, depending, *inter alia*, on the governing law of the instrument.

What would be the advantages of establishing the treaty framework through an amendment of the IMF's Articles? This would be a means of achieving universality in the absence of unanimity: an amendment of the Articles can be made binding upon the entire membership once it is accepted by three-fifths of the members, having 85 percent of the total voting power. Moreover, given the considerable benefits of IMF membership, it is very unlikely that a member would wish to opt out of IMF membership in order to avoid application of the SDRM. It should be emphasized that, if an amendment of the Articles were merely to provide the legal basis for the "majority action" decisions, as described in the previous section of the chapter, it would not give the Executive Board any additional legal authority. Rather, it would give a majority of creditors the legal authority to bind a dissenting minority.

Notwithstanding the above, relying on the IMF's Articles as a means of providing the statutory basis for majority action decisions to be taken by sovereign debtors and their creditors will require the resolution of an important institutional issue. As noted above, a treaty framework will require the establishment of a verification of claims and dispute resolutions process. However, the IMF's existing institutional infrastructure would not accommodate it playing such a role. Specifically, the IMF's Executive Board would not be perceived as impartial in this process since the IMF is a creditor and also represents the interest of the sovereign debtor and other bilateral creditors.

One way of addressing this institutional issue would be to rely on the same amendment of the Articles that would be used to establish the collective action framework, described above, as the basis for establishing a new judicial organ that would carry out these very limited functions. Clearly, a key question is whether there would be adequate safeguards to ensure that such an organ operated – and was perceived as operating – independently from the Executive Board and the Board of Governors.

As a legal matter, the independence of the organ could be established by the text of the amendment itself. The amendment would provide that decisions of the judicial organ would not be subject to review by any of the IMF's other organs and that, more generally, the judges appointed to this organ would not be subject to the interference or influence of the staff and management of the IMF, the Executive Board or any IMF member. The text of the amendment could also specify in some detail the qualifications of the judges to be selected and, to ensure security of tenure, the grounds for their dismissal. One way of ensuring that the judges serving on the organ maintain some distance from the staff and the Executive Board would be to appoint them for a limited, but possibly renewable period. Moreover, a procedure could be established whereby the judges appointed by the Managing Director (or the Board) would be derived from a list of candidates that would have been selected by a qualified and independent panel.

It should be emphasized that the role of this judicial organ – wherever it is located – would be a limited one. Specifically, the organ would have no authority to challenge decisions made by the Executive Board regarding, *inter alia*, the adequacy of a member's policies or the sustainability of the member's debt.

Exchange controls

In the context of financial crises, exchange controls may need to be relied upon in at least two circumstances. First, in circumstances where a sovereign defaults on its own indebtedness, it is likely that such a default will trigger capital flight, particularly where the restructuring will also embrace claims on the sovereign held by the domestic banking system and the member maintains an open capital account. Second, even where the external debt of the sovereign is not significant, a financial crisis can arise because of the overindebtedness of the banking and corporate sectors which, when coupled with a loss of creditor confidence, leads to a sudden depletion of foreign exchange reserves. In these circumstances, there may be a case for the authorities to impose exchange controls for a temporary period.

The possible resort to exchange controls raises a number of complex issues that would need to be addressed on a case-by-case basis. Inevitably, difficult judgments will need to be made against the background of considerable uncertainty regarding the ways in which events may unfold. Nevertheless, two broad sets of issues would need to be considered: first, the timing of the imposition of controls, and second, their coverage across different types of transactions.

As regards timing, there is a question of whether it would be appropriate to impose controls at an early stage of capital flight with a view to stanching the hemorrhage of reserves, thereby preserving the resources available to the economy, including for debt service. This would have the effect of reducing the difference in the ability of investors holding claims of various maturities to exit early, and from this perspective permitting a broader degree of equity in the treatment of various types of investors. It is worth noting, however, that differences in the ability of investors to exit early stemming from the relative maturity of claims is presumably reflected in the market pricing of the instruments concerned and compensates investors for the relative risks. Moreover, a shift toward a presumption that exchange controls would be imposed at an early stage of capital flight could reduce the ability of domestic banks to attract and intermediate domestic savings and foreign capital, as residents would be more likely to hold savings abroad and foreign creditors would raise the cost of short-term capital.

An alternative approach of waiting until resources are exhausted before resort to controls would lean in the direction of respecting the contractual rights of investors holding short-term claims. It would also keep open the possibility that if confidence stabilizes resort to exchange controls could be avoided. It has the drawback, however, that once controls are imposed the resources available to the economy have been depleted, which will have adverse effects on the pace of recovery and capacity to generate resources for debt service.

A second question relates to the scope of the controls. In cases where a member has the institutional capacity to implement exchange controls, it may be possible to arrest capital flight without an interruption in debt service and other contractual obligations. But this will depend on the severity of the crisis and the institutional capacity of the member. In circumstances where it is necessary to interrupt external debt service, it would be important for the authorities to put in place a framework for the eventual normalization of creditor relations by nonsovereign debtors, in order to minimize the long-term impact on corporations' market access. Such a framework could include two key features. First, the facilitation of an out-of-court workout mechanism operating in the shadow of domestic bankruptcy. Second, a specification of the minimum terms under which foreign exchange would be made available to service restructured debts.

The question arises, however, as to whether an SDRM should be designed to provide limited legal protection (in the form of a stay) during the period of renegotiation to domestic enterprises that might otherwise be subject to litigation as a result of the default arising from the imposition of controls.

It should be noted at the outset that, even if the decision were made to exclude nonsovereign debt from the coverage of an SDRM, exchange controls would still provide considerable legal protection in at least two respects. First, any restrictions imposed on the ability of residents or nonresidents to make transfers abroad would still be enforceable within the territory of the sovereign. Second, in the event that the controls give rise to payments arrears, foreign creditors would be precluded from enforcing their claims against a resident debtor in the territory of the sovereign. The legal protection that may *not* be provided by the controls would be protection against the enforcement of claims by nonresidents with respect to a resident debtor's assets that are located overseas. It is this latter category of protection that an SDRM could be designed to provide.[6]

Among the complex issues that would arise if an SDRM were to apply to exchange controls is the feasibility of making a distinction between those debtors that, except for exchange controls, would be able to service their debt, and other debtors that are not healthy and need to be restructured. While it would be reasonable for the former category to enjoy some temporary legal protection under an SDRM, it would be preferable to make the latter category subject to the local insolvency law. A second difficulty relates to the protection of creditor interests. During the period of the stay on litigation, what measures could be put in place that would give creditors the assurance that the debtor is not using the stay as a means of facilitating asset stripping?

A final question relates to the role of the IMF. As discussed above, in the context of sovereign indebtedness, it is possible to design a framework where the key decisions are made by the majority of creditors rather than the IMF. However, in the context of exchange controls that gives rise to the default of a multitude of debtors (each with their own group of creditors), such an approach would not be feasible. In these circumstances, the legal authority to approve a temporary stay, if that were deemed an eventual feature of a new statutory mechanism, would need to reside with the IMF.

Conclusion

The absence of a robust legal framework for sovereign debt restructuring generates important costs. Sovereigns with unsustainable debts often wait too long before they seek a restructuring, leaving both their citizens and their creditors worse off. And when sovereigns finally do opt for restructuring, the process is more protracted than it needs to be and less predictable than creditors would like.

The international financial system lacks an established framework for restructuring that is equitable across all of the sovereign's creditors. There are few effective tools to address potential collective action problems that threaten to undermine restructuring agreements acceptable to the debtor and most of its creditors. Holdout creditors may be able to use the threat of litigation to seek to avoid concessions that the majority have agreed to make.

All this explains why it is important for the official community, sovereign debtors and market participants to discuss how to improve the sovereign debt restructuring process.

This chapter has laid out a possible approach. An international legal framework could be created to allow a qualified majority of the sovereign's creditors to approve a restructuring agreement, and to make that decision of the majority binding on a minority. The vote would need to include all the relevant creditors of the sovereign, not just the holders of a single debt instrument. Broadening the majority voting process beyond a single debt instrument vastly simplifies the process of creditor coordination, and would facilitate the negotiation of a deal that treats all creditors fairly. This approach draws on the principles of well-designed corporate bankruptcy regimes, and is similar in concept to the decision-making procedures among holders of a single bond issue that contains a majority-restructuring clause.

Provisions for majority action would be most effective if supported by three other features, all of which protect the debtor's assets and capacity to pay while it works with its creditors to reach an agreement. The features are: a stay on creditor litigation after the suspension of payments; mechanisms that protect creditor interests during the stay; and the provision of seniority for fresh financing by private creditors. A single body would need to oversee the process of verifying claims and to resolve any disputes.

In such a framework, the decision whether to give legal protection for the sovereign and provide seniority for new private financing could be left to the debtor and a qualified majority of its creditors. Similarly, the sovereign and a qualified majority of creditors would agree on the terms of the ultimate restructuring. The primary purpose of an amendment of the IMF's Articles would be to provide the statutory legal basis to make an agreement between the debtor and the requisite majority of creditors binding on all relevant creditors.

There are a number of questions that would need to be fleshed out before such an approach could be made operational. Perhaps most crucial, and also most difficult, is the scope of the debt to be included in the voting process. It will also be important to explore with debtors and market participants how best to protect general creditor interests during the negotiating process, as well as how to structure the dispute resolution process.

These questions will not be easy to answer. But it is important not to shy away from the challenge. There is now widespread agreement that a new approach is necessary, and that a fairer, more efficient process for sovereign debt restructurings would represent a substantial strengthening of the international financial system. We should press ahead to achieve it.

Notes

1 Specifically, most syndicated loans contained sharing clauses that provided strong incentives for negotiated settlements rather than resort to litigation.

2 Upon an event of default, most international sovereign bonds provide that an acceleration (where the full amount owing becomes due and payable) may be blocked by a defined percentage of bondholders. In addition, international sovereign bonds issued under trust deeds (traditionally governed by English law) give the trustee the primary authority to initiate legal action, and the trustee is only permitted to do so if such action is supported by a threshold percentage of bondholders.

3 In contrast, if the mechanism relies upon a statutory basis, a transitional problem is less likely to arise. Most countries recognize that the establishment of a new legislative framework that is specifically directed at the suspension of creditor claims, such as insolvency laws, can apply to existing indebtedness. If the approach discussed in the previous section is followed, an SDRM would suspend the enforcement of the original claims by a minority of creditors (either prior to or after an agreement) in circumstances where the debtor and a qualified majority of creditors have agreed to such a suspension.

4 In many jurisdictions, an international treaty, once effective, automatically supercedes domestic legislation. In other jurisdictions, however, the domestic legislation must be modified to incorporate the terms of the treaty.

5 Overriding the recognition of such judgments could be achieved by uniform recourse to the "public policy" exception to these general rules.

6 As interpreted by the courts of some IMF members, Article VIII, Section 2(b) of the IMF's Articles may be invoked to stay creditor enforcement against debtors unable to service their external payments because of exchange controls that are consistent with the IMF's Articles.

Questions for Part II

1 How did the global financial architecture evolve since the beginning of the twentieth century?
2 Was the Bretton Woods system, when it was devised, a good enough system? If not, what in your view could have worked better?
3 What lessons have you drawn from the collapse of the Bretton Woods system for the future financial architecture?
4 It was believed that the Asian financial crises inspired concerted efforts to improve the global financial architecture. How?
5 What contributed to the demise of the fixed exchange rate system?
6 Do you agree with Alan Blinder's "art of the possible?" If you disagree, where? Suggest improvements.
7 Analyze the impact of recent shift from syndicated loans to traded securities. Was it a definitive improvement in terms of promoting stability of the financial system?

Areas for further research

1 Take a good look at the current global financial architecture. Analyze its strengths and weaknesses. Present your vision of the global financial architecture.
2 Focus on the institutional aspect of the global financial architecture. Where do we go from here?
3 Compare and contrast the fixed and floating exchange rate systems. Which of these is ideally suited for the twenty-first century? Perhaps you would find both unsuitable. If so, what alternative would you propose?
4 How would you restructure the debt of a crisis-ridden economy without jeopardizing the domestic and global economy?

Part III

Multilateral financial institutions

9 International financial institutions

Adapting to a world of private capital flows

Willem H. Buiter and Hans Peter Lankes

Transforming global scenario

Since the World Bank and the International Monetary Fund (IMF) were launched at Bretton Woods more than fifty-eight years ago, and the regional development banks in subsequent decades, the global economy has undergone transformation in several important respects.[1] Two fundamental transformations have taken place in the role of the international financial institutions (IFIs); both of which are of high significance for the global financial architecture. These changes are: First, globalisation has progressed a great deal over the preceding quarter century. This implies that foreign trade and private capital now play a far greater role in economic development than ever before. Second, the poor performance of statist models of development – so popular in the past – led to a re-examination of the role of the state, which in turn motivated a strong shift towards private, market-based approaches. As a result of these transformations, the private sector and private international finance have become prime agents of economic development.

In this chapter, we discuss how the IFIs can pursue their mandates by creating the conditions for the right kind of market-oriented growth and by forming partnerships with the private sector. We argue that partnership with the private sector calls for significant adjustments in the *modus operandi* of the IFIs as well as for clear principles of engagement. IFIs must complement and catalyse private finance, they must not displace it. A clearly defined approach to supporting private sector development will carry the IFIs well into the twenty-first century.

A world of private capital flows

World financial markets have witnessed profound changes over the last few decades. This has included the strong growth of private capital flows to developing countries. Net long-term private flows rose from $48 billion in 1980 (58 per cent of total long-term flows) to $239 billion in 1999 (82.6 per cent of total long-term flows). While 2001 was a turbulent year for the global economy and the global financial markets, long-term private capital flows to developing economies were $160 billion (81.5 per cent of the total long-term flows). The share of net official flows has correspondingly declined, both in absolute and relative terms. In 2001, they were measured at a paltry $36.5 billion.[2] If capital flight were taken into account net private flows would, however, be smaller. Private capital flows contribute not only to filling the savings–investment gap in developing countries but also to reducing dependencies by diversifying funding sources and, especially in the form of strategic investment, private capital flows have played a more direct role by transferring technologies, market-oriented behaviour, management skills and distribution channels. Gross flows are therefore as important as net flows in assessing the impact of private capital flows on recipient economies.

There have been negative experiences, such as collusion of foreign investors with bureaucracies in search of competition restraints and privileges, or the downgrading of value-added components in enterprises acquired by foreigners. Short-term capital flows have proved footloose. Nevertheless, there is a mounting body of evidence that foreign direct investment (FDI), in particular, has contributed positively to development and growth.[3] China has not only emerged as a major recipient of FDI but has also made profitable use of it. The double-digit real GDP growth during the decades of the 1980s and 1990s in China is partly attributed to FDI.

It is important to recognise that private capital flows remain focused on a relatively small number of developing countries. FDI flows to the top ten recipient developing countries never fell below 64 per cent during the 1990s, although these countries account for only about half of the total population of the developing world.[4] Market size appears to be a major explanation of FDI concentration. Of the top ten FDI recipients, six are also among the top ten developing countries in terms of GDP.[5] On the other hand, Africa stands out as one region that relies almost entirely on official flows for external finance. Many countries in the Commonwealth of Independent States (CIS) are in the same position.

The composition of these private flows has seen a marked change over the last two decades. While earlier flows were composed largely of commercial bank debt flowing to the public sector, recent years have witnessed a sharp increase in the level of private sector portfolio flows and direct investment, both of which had contributed little during the 1980s. For example, in 1980 debt flows constituted 89 per cent of private capital flows, whereas FDI constituted 9 per cent and portfolio equity was almost non-existent. In 1999, by far the largest share of net private flows into developing and transition economies was in the form of FDI (80 per cent of total private flows), followed by portfolio equity (12 per cent) and bonds (10 per cent). As a whole, the group experienced a small net outflow of commercial bank lending. The characteristics of these different types of financing vary on a number of important dimensions, including maturity, risk-sharing, managerial involvement, technology as well as volatility.

The flow of private capital to the transition economies of Eastern Europe and the former Soviet Union has reflected the same broad trends. In a distinct sequence, official funding, FDI, non-guaranteed public and private debt, dedicated equity funds and finally direct local stock and money market investments entered the market successively at 1–2 year intervals.[6] At the start of transition, official capital flows increased sharply, while private flows were negligible. Private flows began to exceed net official flows in 1993 and by 1997 they accounted for $58 billion in the seven largest recipient countries.[7] This represented 19 per cent of aggregate net private flows into developing countries, slightly more than their share in developing country GDP (a little under one-sixth) and almost twice their population share (about one-tenth).[8] These flows subsequently declined following the financial crisis in Russia.

The level and commitment of private capital flows depends crucially on perceptions of risks and returns. These, in turn, depend not only on basic endowments and opportunities but also on the ability to respond to opportunities in an effective, market-oriented fashion, or more generally the 'investment climate' in recipient countries. The investment climate includes macroeconomic stability, structural reforms and the institutional infrastructure, which underpin the market economy (financial institutions, reliable business practices, legal and regulatory framework, tax system etc.). It also includes political stability and consistent, transparent, responsible and 'market friendly' behaviour from the authorities. Equally important is the development of human capital and of physical infrastructure, both of which are vital ingredients for the success of enterprise investments.

One reflection of the importance of the investment climate is that the level, location and motive for FDI into the transition economies are all strongly associated with progress in transition. For instance, leaving out the three oil and gas economies of Central Asia (Azerbaijan, Kazakhstan and Turkmenistan), the rank correlation coefficient for twenty-three countries between the European Bank of Reconstruction and Development's (EBRD's) average indicator of transition in 2000 and cumulative FDI per capita over the period 1989–2000 is 0.92.[9] This provides strong support for the conclusion that it is the reform process which opens opportunities for profitable investment and which, through its impact on risks and returns, motivates investors to take advantage of them. It also suggests that direct equity investors have carefully evaluated the economic environment and made informed choices.[10]

The role of the IFIs in the changing market place[11]

In general terms the objectives of the IFIs have always been poverty alleviation, economic growth and protection of the environment.[12] Traditionally, the IFIs have promoted these objectives by working with governments and government agencies. This reflects the ideas and the capital structures which prevailed at the time of their creation. Broadly speaking, the IFIs have pursued these objectives with loans for public sector projects or programmes, technical assistance and policy-based lending. IFI loans have generally been made to, or guaranteed by, the borrowing states.

The EBRD is different from the other IFIs. Its later foundation and the special circumstances of this foundation pointed to a rather specific objective, namely to foster the transition of its countries of operations to open market economies.

The founders took it that the transition would indeed raise living standards over time as well as expanding basic choices and rights of the population.

In the new economic environment, the importance of IFIs and bilateral aid as sources of funds has decreased. While private flows are rising, official flows are constrained by tight budgets following fiscal laxity in the 1970s and 1980s. As budgets get squeezed, official aid, both bilateral and multilateral, has been a vulnerable target. Furthermore, the collapse of centrally planned economies and the poor performance of heavily distorted economies in Africa, Latin America and the Middle East have led to a re-examination of the role of the state in economic development. As a result, there is a growing understanding among developing countries that to achieve market-oriented economic growth, they must create the conditions in which a strong private sector can flourish.

Since the importance of the IFIs as a source of funds has decreased while the potential role of the private sector has increased, a central challenge for the IFIs is to find ways of fostering development through expanding opportunities for the private sector. They should view the private sector as a prime *vehicle* for the achievement of development goals. In so doing they must seek to ensure that the poor participate in the growth process and that growth is environmentally sustainable. There are two complementary ways in which the IFIs can pursue these objectives:

(i) they can help governments create the conditions for the right kind of market-oriented growth;

(ii) they can become participant investors, working with the private sector to expand and improve private capital flows.

The first of these embodies some of the more traditional IFI roles. This involves promoting macroeconomic stability and ensuring the provision of the necessary physical, institutional, legal and regulatory infrastructure. While these basics are crucial to investment and growth, participation in growth requires adequate provision for health and education, which in turn enhance growth itself. Poverty alleviation, however, calls for more than fostering participation. It also involves protecting those who are not in a position to provide for themselves by establishing a social safety net. In the past, the IMF, the World Bank and regional IFIs have played a major role in the establishment of macroeconomic stability, in the assistance with tax, legal and sectoral reform and in the creation of a social safety net through policy-based lending.[13] These are all areas that continue to be important for market-oriented growth.

The second approach represents territory that has been less well explored by the IFIs. The IFIs must ask how they can assist more directly in establishing the conditions for the expansion of the private sector. In doing so, they must recognise the increasing – and understandable – reluctance of governments to provide sovereign guarantees; a reluctance that stems from the pressures on public finances and the requirement for hard budget constraints if market-based incentives are to function effectively. While recognising that there will be important projects (particularly environmental and some infrastructure) for which sovereign guarantees will be necessary, the IFIs should support this resolve and avoid sovereign guarantees wherever possible. This means the IFIs must find new ways of operating; ways that harness private sector finance for broader development goals. The way to do this is for IFIs to work in *partnership with the private sector* and to become *participants in the investment process*.

The IFIs as participants in the process of private sector development

Partnership with the private sector implies that the IFIs must, in important respects, act and think like the private sector and subject themselves to the shifting opportunities and constraints of the market. The challenge, which we discuss in the next section, is to combine such an approach with the active pursuit of IFI public policy objectives. But it is clear that creativity and flexibility are of the essence in responding to market needs and IFIs will have to develop their expertise in a number of aspects of banking which have, so far, been less familiar to them.

There are also a host of other practical implications of partnerships between the IFIs and the private sector that will need to be considered. It is likely, for instance, that procedures of most IFIs would have to adapt to the flexibility and confidentiality required of private sector operations. This does not always sit easily with public sector accountability. A move away from sovereign guaranteed lending would also call for a new risk culture and the know-how required for the analysis of commercial risk.

Despite the constraints under which the IFIs inevitably operate, there are nevertheless good reasons why the private sector would often have an interest in teaming up with them. The IFIs bring a number of strengths to such partnerships. First, they are endowed with a capital structure that helps them to absorb many of the risks associated with taking a lead in high-risk environments.[14] Second is the relationship they have with governments in developing countries that enables them to reduce political risks for a project in a way which commercial banks cannot. This relationship also means that a government will often have more confidence in a project if an IFI – which has a duty to protect its members' interests – is acting with a private partner. A third strength which the IFIs have is their knowledge of, and experience in, these regions. Finally, this experience and their access to technical assistance mean they can mitigate the risks involved in project development. Without the project development support of the IFIs, many projects would never get off the ground.

Operational principles guiding partnerships with the private sector

Recognising their resource limitations the IFIs must be selective in their approach. They must build on their strengths to expand the frontiers of private sector

development and not simply displace the private sector in activities it is well prepared to undertake on its own. And they can be effective in this task only if they
themselves set an example of sound and well-run institutions. Thus they require
clear operational principles.

We see three principles which should govern the activities of the IFIs in this
area. At the EBRD we call them transition impact, sound banking and additionality. Any project we select must meet all three criteria. They ensure that our
activities make a broad contribution to the transition process. Closely related
to the transition criteria is the promotion of sound environmental practices,
a principle strongly grounded in the EBRD's mandate.

First and most importantly, IFI projects should have a wider development or transition impact.
This is in fact more than an operating principle, it is the basic purpose of the IFIs.
If the investment projects supported by the IFIs are to facilitate private sector
development, they should be appraised in relation to their influence both on the
investment climate – discussed earlier – and on the ability of enterprises and
financial institutions to respond to it.[15] Each IFI has to develop methods which
focus on its own mandate. For the EBRD, this is the promotion of the transition
process, but analogous methods can be developed for other objectives.

The public and private sector projects supported by the IFIs can have a
number of qualitative characteristics that serve to advance private sector development. The key foundations of a market economy are the markets themselves,
institutions and policies that support and promote markets, and market-based
conduct, skills and innovation. Project selection and design should embody an
assessment of project impact along these qualitative dimensions, in addition to
traditional economic rate-of-return criteria and an analysis of environmental
impacts. Box 9.1 provides a more detailed breakdown or 'checklist' of transition
impact.

Second, sound banking should be adopted and implemented with the highest integrity. The
financial return to the IFI should be commensurate with the risk. Sound market-
oriented development cannot be promoted by investments, which are commercially unsound. By ensuring their projects are financially sound and viable, the
IFIs set an example and establish important standards in accounting, disclosure
and corporate governance. The rigorous application of this principle also ensures
the financial health of the institution itself. This is crucial for credibility. The IFIs
must show their shareholders that they are running a tight ship and using
resources effectively if the continued support of shareholders is to be justified.

Additionality is the third key principle of IFI involvement. The privileges enjoyed by
the IFIs – including, above all, their capital base – would often allow them to displace private funding or provide an unfair competitive advantage to their private
partners. This cannot be the objective of IFI support. Instead they should stimulate the private sector into operating in areas or in manners in which it would not
otherwise be ready to operate. IFI additionality can arise in two ways: the IFI
contributes finance which is not available on reasonable terms elsewhere; and
its involvement exerts a profound influence on the generation, design and

Box 9.1   A checklist for transition impact

While in principle the impact of projects could be appraised with the help of sufficiently sophisticated cost–benefit analysis (CBA), in practice conventional CBA is ill-suited to capture the diffuse benefits of structural and institutional change and learning. However, the impacts embodied in these qualitative characteristics are intertwined with those captured in the analysis of economic rates of return and environmental benefits and the three analyses should be taken together in assessing projects (and in practice, it is fairly straightforward to avoid double-counting).

Contributions to competitive market structures

- A project or series of projects can *promote greater competition* in its sector of activity by creating a market or by altering the structure of an existing market. Increased competitive pressure is likely to improve the efficiency with which resources are used, demands are satisfied and innovations are stimulated.
- A project can also help to *increase competition in other markets*. There are two important ways in which markets can be extended and their functioning improved by projects: through interactions of the project entity with suppliers and clients and through project contributions to the integration of economic activities into the national or international economy, in particular by lowering the cost of transactions.
- To be effective, the contributions to the structure and extent of markets must be sustained. This can be achieved through projects which have a *strong demonstration effect* and, if necessary, through IFI support for more than one project in a particular sector of a country ('clustering' of projects).

Contributions to institutions and policies that support markets

- A project may result in *increased private ownership* through privatisation or new private provision of goods and services (including, importantly, the entry of new small businesses). This can generally be expected to strengthen market-oriented behaviour, innovation and entrepreneurship. Private ownership is also complementary to, and often a condition for, competitive markets.
- The process of investing in a project can contribute to the *reform of policies*, governmental institutions and practices that serve to enhance the investment climate though a project-related policy dialogue and the ability of the IFIs to mitigate certain types of political risks. Examples include: improvements in the functioning of regulatory institutions and

practices and contributions to laws and practices that protect or strengthen private ownership and the open economy. This is particularly relevant where not only the project entity benefits, but also other investors.

- The IFI can also take an active approach to the restructuring of problem projects in order to *establish and enforce standards of due legal process* with regard to creditor and shareholder rights and ensure that 'market exit' works. This may imply consciously galvanising creditor interests in restructuring situations, co-chairing or participating in debt negotiations and debt–equity swaps, calling on loan security, engaging in high-profile court cases, and seeking to state the IFI's position publicly.

Contributions to market-based conduct, skills and innovation

- A project can contribute directly to providing and *improving commercial skills* and technological know-how. Commercial skills can include accounting, banking and finance, management marketing and procurement. Skill transfers are often complementary to other project impacts such as institution building and expanding market competition.
- The transfer of skills and technology can have a particularly strong impact on development or transition by showing other enterprises what is both feasible and profitable and thereby *inviting replication*. Examples of demonstration effects relevant to development or transition are: (i) products and processes which are new to an economy, (ii) ways of successfully restructuring companies and institutions and (iii) new methods and instruments to finance activities.
- By *strengthening corporate governance*, a project can foster more effective private ownership of enterprises, and thereby enhance the legitimacy and functioning of the market economy and of private property. Demonstrating effective approaches to corporate governance can be particularly important in transition economies, where there is little recent experience with private ownership. Measures to strengthen private domestic financial institutions can be complementary to more effective corporate governance.

While the selection and design of projects with one or more of the above characteristics should be a fundamental principle guiding IFI support of investment projects, the potential impact does not end at this point. Rather, the experience of investing and operating investment projects can and should inform the policy dialogue with governments. A challenge for the IFIs is to strengthen the mechanisms through which this feedback from private sector experience to government policies, institutions and behaviour takes place.

implementation of a project. Good project design will help achieve both sound banking principles and development or transition impact.[16]

Meeting the three criteria does not necessarily imply seeking to maximise each in every project. What is important is that they are satisfied by the portfolio of activities as a whole. Sometimes the pursuit of particularly safe investment opportunities is warranted if it enables the IFI to take riskier positions elsewhere. Trade-offs may also exist between limiting the cost of developing projects and enhancing their transition or development impact. Again, the most sensible approach would be to consider the characteristics of the portfolio as a whole rather than individual projects.

Flexibility – both in terms of attitudes and instruments – is also needed in other respects. The activities of the IFIs must change as countries develop and finance becomes more widely available to different segments of the market. This process of constant change should be the key to IFI participation in the investment process. They must, in a sense, lead the way and open opportunities for private investment flows to follow and not prolong their involvement once sufficient private capital is available. We have seen this very clearly at the EBRD where we graduate our activities from one market segment to another as alternative sources of finance develop in some areas, and new, as yet unexplored opportunities, become practical possibilities.[17]

Forms of partnership and sectoral considerations

The IFI collaboration with the private sector can take a wide variety of forms. There is no obvious limitation on the financial structure of interventions, which can range from straight equity to quasi-equity instruments and debt, underwriting and guarantees. Intervention can also take the form of introducing financial instruments to capital markets, for instance through IFI treasury departments. We cannot discuss these different forms of intervention in detail here, but it is useful to consider particular sectoral challenges and possible IFI responses.

Development or transition impact can be achieved in most sectors of economic activity. In each case, the strength and value of impacts is determined by context. It is obvious, for instance, that a demonstration effect is particularly valuable where the technique, behaviour or product to be demonstrated is relatively new to the 'audience' and there is scope for replication. In many cases, it is immaterial whether the vehicle for IFI impact is a candy factory or the national power grid. In fact, the EBRD's experience has shown that cooperation with foreign and local investors in the general industrial and services sectors can have far-reaching benefits in terms of the functioning of markets, market-oriented behaviours and institutions. Nevertheless, because of the strategic role played in any economy by the financial system and the infrastructure these sectors can offer particularly interesting challenges for IFI involvement.

Partnerships in the financial sector

The IFIs can help build financial institutions by putting in place the funding needed to implement projects or strengthen their capital base by investing in them. This is a vital task in the transition but also in a broader development perspective. A market economy requires a well-functioning financial sector. It fulfils the crucial task of financial intermediation, that is, collecting savings and allocating them to fruitful investment. But it also takes steps to ensure that borrowers recognise the obligation to pay and will be in a position to repay, thus imposing hard budget constraints in the economy at large. Strengthening local financial institutions is therefore a priority in any developing country.

At the EBRD the collaboration with banks, which has taken the form of co-financing, credit lines, equity and mezzanine finance or syndications, has proved extremely fruitful. We are working directly with 188 local banks in our countries of operations (sixty-six of them on an equity basis), and we have worked with more than 100 international banks through our syndications programme in the past seven years. While we bring capital to all these investments, our involvement provides different benefits for different partners. To international banks we provide an umbrella of political comfort derived from our long-term relationships with governments and our preferred creditor status. To local banks we provide much needed medium-term capital and we can assist in their institutional development.

An area that is receiving increasing attention is the reform of social security systems, and in particular the involvement of the private sector in providing for old-age income security. Pension reforms that introduce privately managed individual retirement accounts will have a broad impact on how economies operate. Successful reform depends on the existence of a solid private pension fund management sector, on capital markets that fulfil some basic conditions (regarding liquidity, depth and diversity of instruments), and on reliable regulation. In working with the private sector (in addition to providing advice at the policy level) the IFIs can support such reforms by strengthening the institutional basis for their implementation and thus increasing public confidence in them. Both the EBRD and the International Finance Corporation (IFC) have invested in pension fund management companies to ensure that funds are professionally managed, prudent investment guidelines are followed, a level playing field is maintained, acceptable service levels are offered and accounts are transparent. A similar role can be played by the IFIs in other non-bank financial institutions, such as insurance and mutual funds.

A further area where the IFIs can play an important role is in promoting the availability of equity and especially venture capital. Equity is widely sought after in developing economies, particularly by small and medium-sized enterprises. The IFIs are well placed to participate in funds and help attract institutional investors, such as pension funds and mutual funds, into these countries. In this way they can also help to strengthen nascent capital markets. By being early in the game and showing good management and professionalism, they can provide a strong demonstration effect.[18]

Partnerships in the infrastructure sector

The financing of infrastructure has been a traditional focus of IFI activity. An efficient infrastructure is of crucial importance to private sector development.

However, the financing needs here are particularly large. Given that most countries are today facing severe budgetary constraints, this funding has become difficult to raise from traditional methods. Infrastructure is becoming more commercially oriented, an approach that can lead not only to the strengthening of operations, and improvements in efficiency, but also opens up access to private finance. Private funding with no recourse to the sovereign introduces important market disciplines which control costs, provide revenues and allocate risks. At the same time, private involvement calls for a strong and reliable regulatory framework, which remains a key challenge in many developing countries. While the potential for private involvement varies across sectors (being greater for example in telecommunications and power than in roads), there is significant scope for expansion in all sectors. Despite a rapid increase in recent years, private funding for infrastructure still represents only around 10 per cent of the total in developing countries.

When looking at private sector involvement in infrastructure, the starting point in most countries and sectors is a public monopoly which is either national or local in scope. Keeping this in mind, one can distinguish three levels at which infrastructure can become commercially oriented. At the very basic level authorities can begin to operate the public sector in a manner which reflects more closely the ways the private sector operates. This means paying close attention to revenues, costs and market demands. It also involves creating a governance structure which provides clear goals, makes management responsible for performance and allows them independence to carry out their tasks. This may involve bringing in a private sector partner on an advisory basis. Alternatively, governments can seek the limited entry of new private providers through various forms of public/private partnerships. This approach involves more active private sector participation, usually as an operator. Potential areas include independent power plants, cellular telephone networks, toll roads, municipal services, ports and airports. The basis for this involvement is usually some type of concession. The third alternative is for governments to opt for full privatisation of some public services.

Both the IFC's and the EBRD's experience show that the IFIs are well placed to develop financing structures which encourage such private sector participation: structures which are simple, cost-efficient and can be easily replicated. Careful design and innovative use of the wide variety of IFI instruments are the key to succeeding in this area. Risk allocation is also key. The IFIs should not only share the general project risk with private partners (through equity or non-recourse debt), they should also assume those risks that they are well placed to mitigate. These tend to include general economic and political risks and risks arising from shifts in regulatory regimes.

The difficulties involved in structuring and implementing such projects must not be underestimated. Not only do they require strong political backing from countries, they often require the enactment of specific legislation or the introduction of the necessary regulatory environment to support them. Furthermore, these are often complex projects to develop and certain costs tend to be front-loaded. Nevertheless, it is precisely this complexity, in which political, regulatory and commercial elements are interwoven, which creates the scope for valuable contributions by the IFIs.

Concluding remarks

The new focus on market-oriented economic development is here to stay. So too are the private capital flows. The task of the IFIs must be to facilitate these processes. The IFIs have the potential to further expand the frontiers of private sector development. To do this they must continue to adapt. They must build on their strengths. In this chapter we have tried to explain how. The IFIs must continue to work with governments, but they must also go beyond this and participate directly in the private investment process.

Private markets and private flows are powerful forces. The availability of a strong and dynamic partner in the development effort represents a great opportunity for the IFIs. The IFIs can help harness these forces. In so doing, it is crucial that they subject projects to clear principles of selection and design. It is also crucial that they work together. The tasks are immense and each IFI has its own strengths. They must exploit their comparative advantages to the benefit of the countries in which they work. While competition among IFIs can yield benefits (such as innovations in operations), it is important that this competition is constructive. Where competition does take place, it is important that all IFIs should work to achieve the same high standards in terms of project impacts on development or transition, additionality and conformity with sound banking principles. Competition by dropping standards not only results in departures from an IFI's mandate, but it also prevents other IFIs from fulfilling their role. Clearly, with their broadly similar shareholder bases the IFIs should not undermine or weaken each other's conditionality.

Ultimately, in the long term IFIs may not be needed. To some extent, their redundancy will be a sign of their success. In the meantime, the IFIs will continue to have significant goals and, if they successfully adjust to private sector led development, the capacity to achieve them.

Notes

1 For a comprehensive account of the launching of the Bretton Woods institutions and the regional development banks refer to Das (1986).
2 These statistics come from *Global Development Finance*, World Bank, 2000 and 2002. For simplicity, we adopt that publication's definition of developing countries here, which encompasses the transition economies of Eastern Europe and the former Soviet Union.
3 See successive issues of the *World Investment Reports*, UNCTAD, Geneva.
4 These ten countries are ranked in terms of volume of FDI flows during the decade of the 1990s: China, Brazil, Mexico, Argentina, Poland, Chile, Malaysia, Korea, Thailand and Venezuela.
5 Market size is not the only factor. The average ratio of FDI to GDP in the top ten recipients is a full percentage point higher than in developing countries as a group. While Brazil, China and Mexico alone account for almost half of the developing countries' FDI, they make up only a little more than one-third of developing countries' GDP. While FDI flows to India, the fourth largest developing country, have increased over the 1990s, it remains fourteenth on the list of developing countries FDI recipients.
6 See Hans Peter Lankes and Nicholas Stern, 'Capital flows to Eastern Europe and the former Soviet Union', EBRD Working Paper 27, February 1997.

7 Bulgaria, Czech Republic, Hungary, Poland, Romania, Russia and Slovak Republic. Data from the Institute for International Finance.

8 Source: *Global Development Finance: Analysis and Summary Tables*, World Bank, March 2000.

9 See *Transition Report 2000*, EBRD, London, for the EBRD's indicators of transition. The measure referred to here is the average of scores, on a scale from 1 to 4, along eight dimensions of transition, including large and small enterprise privatisation, enterprise restructuring, price liberalisation, trade and foreign exchange regime, competition policy, banking reform and development of securities markets and non-bank financial institutions. For an empirical analysis of the relation between motives for FDI and progress in transition see Lankes, H.P. and A. Venables, 'Foreign direct investment in economic transition: the changing pattern of investments', *Economics of Transition*, Volume 4(2), 1996, and EBRD, *Transition Report 1996*.

10 Causality also runs the opposite way, from FDI to progress in transition. FDI can have a variety of benefits for the transition process, in particular for successful restructuring and improvements in corporate governance, but also more broadly by educating officials, managers and workers in the recipient countries. At this stage in the transition process it seems reasonable to suppose that the dominant effect is from transition to FDI.

11 See also Jacques de Larosière's Per Jacobsson lecture entitled 'Financing development in a world of private capital flows: the challenge for MDBs in working with the private sector' which was given on 29 September 1996 at the Annual Meeting of the World Bank and the IMF.

12 See, for example, the Development Committee Report of the Task Force on Multilateral Development Bank (MDBs), 'Serving a changing world', Washington, DC, March 1996. It identified that the role of MDBs should involve reducing poverty, promoting effective government and a strong civil society, protecting the environment, investing in infrastructure and utilities and encouraging private sector development.

13 It should be remembered that, while the IMF has always been directly concerned with macroeconomic stability, the World Bank transformed itself from an infrastructure bank to a development bank in the years of the Presidency of Robert McNamara (1969–82), with structural adjustment loans appearing only at the end of that period.

14 This includes their preferred creditor status (which mitigates rescheduling or default risk), their conservative gearing ratio and their strong shareholder support in both industrialised and recipient countries.

15 The dividing line between the 'climate' in which private agents act and the ability to respond is not always clear cut (i.e. some issues could be placed on either side of the divide), but it is nevertheless a helpful distinction for some purposes. The analysis of the transition impact which follows focuses primarily on the ability to respond, but also covers some aspects of the investment climate.

16 The IFIs must have clear policies on how additionality is to be assessed. At the EBRD we have established a two-part 'additionality test' which is carefully applied in our project selection process. (i) EBRD *pricing* is pressed upwards relative to the 'market'. Relevant evidence on the market includes interaction with the client, knowledge of funding requests from commercial banks and reactions from competing funding sources. (ii) *Other terms* are pressed that influence a project's design or functioning in ways that are crucial for wider transition or development impact. Depending on circumstances, EBRD adopts a strong stance regarding issues which include governance, procurement, the environment and the regulatory framework. Clear negotiating positions along these lines help ensure that the IFIs do not compete with the private sector, but complement and catalyse it.

17 The importance of the IFIs operating at the frontiers of private activity is developed further in Jacques de Larosière (1996).

18 Capital markets development can also be supported by a variety of other means. At the EBRD, for example, we are working to improve the legal basis for share ownership; by

participating we help launch share privatisations; we are improving accounting and registry procedures, and we are ourselves issuing benchmark bonds in the local currencies of some of our countries.

References

European Bank of Reconstruction and Development (EBRD). *Transition Report 1996 and 2000*. London.

Das, Dilip K. 1986. *Migration of Financial Resources to Developing Countries*, The Macmillan Press Ltd, London and St Martin's Press, Inc., New York.

de Larosière, J. 1996. 'Financing development in a world of private capital flows: the challenge for MDBs in working with the private sector'. Per Jacobsson lecture, 29 September 1996 at the Annual Meeting of the World Bank and IMF.

Lankes, H.P. and N. Stern. 1997. 'Capital flows to Eastern Europe and the Former Soviet Union', European Bank Reconstruction Development. Working Paper 27, February.

Lankes, H.P. and T. Venables. 1996. 'Foreign direct investment in economic transition: the changing pattern of investment'. *The Economics of Transition*, vol. 4, no. 2. Oxford University Press, London.

United Nations Conference on Trade and Development (UNCTAD). *World Investment Report*. Geneva. Various issues.

The World Bank. 2000. *Global Development Finance*. Washington, DC.

The World Bank. 2002. *Global Development Finance*. Washington, DC.

10 International institutions for reducing global financial instability

Kenneth Rogoff

Introduction[1]

It is hard to open a business newspaper or magazine these days without confronting another sweeping proposal to reform the "international financial architecture." George Soros (1998) has called for the formation of an international deposit insurance corporation, while Jeffrey Sachs (1995) advocates the formation of an international bankruptcy court. Paul Krugman (1998a,b) suggests that economists need to rethink their traditional antipathy toward controls on capital controls *outflows*, whereas Barry Eichengreen (1999) is among many who advocate Chilean-style controls on capital *inflows*. Henry Kaufman (1998) recommends creating a single global super-regulator of financial markets and institutions, and Jeffrey Garten (1998) proposes a world central bank with responsibility for overseeing a new global currency. Fischer (1999) makes the case that, with a range of improvements in the system, an multilateral lender can effectively perform the main functions of a lender of last resort, even without being able to issue currency. Many of these ideas are not new, but they are being vented more forcefully, and taken more seriously, than at any time since Harry Dexter White and John Maynard Keynes masterminded the creation of the World Bank and the International Monetary Fund at the Bretton Woods conference at the end of the Second World War.

Is there a "crisis in global capitalism"? Is the current system actually in desperate need of repair? In this chapter, I will provide an overview of some of the main problems, and critically assess some illustrative alternative plans for dealing with them. The first part of this chapter gives an overview of the current system and a brief discussion of some of the conceptual issues. I then proceed to consider a range of plans that would purportedly improve things. My focus is more on ambitious grand schemes than on small marginal changes. Even though such schemes tend to be impractical, especially in the absence of a genuine world government, they throw the problems facing global leaders into sharp relief. I try throughout to highlight important research questions and show how they relate to the evaluating of the various plans. The section "Unilateral steps developing countries can take" reviews reforms that developing countries can implement unilaterally to reduce the costs of capital flow volatility. The final section highlights the importance of the bias in the current system towards debt financing and bank intermediation in sovereign lending.

The current system

Before turning to proposals for radical change of the international financial system, it is important to give a brief critical assessment of the main issues and motivations for change.

Alternative perspectives on the global financial system

Whether one views technology-driven innovation in the global financial system as an engine of growth, or as an agent of destruction, depends on where you sit. In the United States, where financial markets are the deepest and most sophisticated in the world, their benefits seem obvious. Despite having one of the lowest savings rates in the industrialized world, the US economy has enjoyed a remarkable period of sustained growth over the past seven years. The efficacy with which financial markets have helped lever a small pool of savings into a large effective increase in capital is remarkable, even when one takes into account the help of foreign capital inflows. Hyperefficient US financial markets can also be credited with helping to fuel the extensive corporate restructuring of the 1980s, thereby laying the foundations for the sustained rapid growth of the 1990s. Europe, with its introduction of the euro and its efforts at stimulating innovation and competition in financial services, clearly recognizes the importance of deep, sophisticated asset markets. True, the stunning volatility of stock and exchange rate markets is of genuine concern to policy-makers in industrialized countries. The August 1998 bankruptcy of Long-Term Capital Management (LTCM) underscored how the collapse of a single relatively small hedge fund could threaten to bring down a much wider circle of financial institutions. But in the United States, those voices seeking to quash capital markets are typically drowned out by those who argue that a better solution is for such markets to become broader and more deeply entrenched.

Matters look very different to citizens of the developing world, many of whom rue the day their governments started taking down barriers to international capital mobility. Starting with Mexico in 1994, and including a score of countries in Asia in 1997, one high-growth achiever after another has been leveled by sudden withdrawals of short-term capital. (This is not to say that low-growth achievers have been spared, but capital withdrawals from countries such as Russia are less difficult to explain.) Countries which had become accustomed to seeing GNP double every 10–15 years suddenly saw their currencies and stock markets collapse, and their economies go into deep recession. The financial crises of the 1990s have brought a sharp contraction of lending to the developing world, and there is serious concern that the fallout will continue to inhibit international capital markets for some time to come.

The exact timing and nature of speculative attacks on emerging market economies is a topic of great debate, as we shall see. But in the majority of cases, there is little question that the attacks were exacerbated by the way that many developing-country governments chose to radically open their capital markets to the rest of the world during the early 1990s. Critics of "excessive" capital market liberalization, whose numbers include such influential economists as Jagdish Bhagwati (1998) and Dani Rodrick (1997), can point to countries such as China and India whose capital controls, however repressive, did seem to make them relatively resistant to the Asian flu. Bhagwati (1998), in particular, has argued that the benefits to a high level of international capital market integration are grossly overrated, and that the parallels between the gains to trade in capital, and the gains to trade in goods, are quite thin. He criticizes the US Treasury and the International Monetary Fund (IMF) for rushing too many countries into bringing down their controls on international capital mobility, without sufficient consideration of whether domestic regulation was adequate to deal with the changes that rapidly ensued.

Are the benefits to international capital market integration overrated?

Perhaps a little, but they are important. From a theoretical perspective, there are strong analogies between gains from *inter*temporal trade in goods, and standard *intra*temporal trade (see, e.g. Svensson, 1988; Obstfeld and Rogoff, 1996, ch. 5). In theory, there are huge long-run efficiency gains to be reaped by allowing global investment to flow toward countries with low capital–labor ratios and high rates of return to capital though, as Ventura (1997) points out, trade in goods of differing capital intensity can achieve part of this gain. Global equity markets allow a small country that produces a relatively narrow range of goods to diversify its very risky income portfolio. In the case of foreign direct investment, there can also be benefits from an accelerated transfer of technology.

If there is a debate in the academic literature on the importance of gains from international capital market integration, it has mainly to do with whether, given trade in bonds, there is a substantial further gain to introducing complete equity markets. However, researchers have now come to believe that the marginal gains from trade in equity can be very large once one takes into account the ability to diversify production risk, which encourages small countries to specialize, and more generally to shift production toward higher-risk, higher-return projects (Obstfeld, 1994; Acemoglu and Zilibotti, 1997; Martin and Rey, 1998). The final section illustrates other political economy benefits to redirecting capital flows toward equity that are not captured in these models.

An unreconstructed real business cycle interpretation of the Asian flu

Rather than blame international capital markets for the severe recessions in Asia and elsewhere, a modern real business cycle economist (or an old-fashioned Schumpeterian) might just say "welcome to free market capitalism." How surprised should one be that economies racing along at 5–7 per cent growth rates for more than two decades should occasionally experience a significant downturn, albeit a severe one? Might not the sudden reversal of capital flows simply reflect underlying real shocks to say, patterns of global technology progress?

For example, if the US experiences an extraordinary period of growth, is it surprising that this leads to a temporary redirection of investment away from middle-income countries?[2] Besides, Japan had been mired in recession for several years prior to 1997, placing a major drag on the region.

This "unreconstructed real business cycle interpretation" of the developing country debt crisis clearly fails to capture the whole picture. There is a great deal of evidence suggesting that banking system collapses can play an important role in propagating and amplifying recessions, with Japan's recession of the 1990s being a prime case in point. Relatedly, many of the plans below aim to address either developing country bank runs, or runs on government debt. Imperfections in international capital markets, resulting especially from difficulties in enforcing contracts across borders, can sometimes lead to large misallocations in global savings.

But even if the real business cycle interpretation is incomplete, it probably does provide a very important part of the picture, a part that is all too often forgotten in policy discussions which tend to blame emerging economy recessions entirely on speculators. One should also bear in mind that the speculative attacks of the 1990s, even if they did cause or exacerbate recessions, may some day be viewed as mere hiccups, a small price to pay if capital market integration puts countries on a faster trajectory toward integration with the industrialized world.

Multiple equilibria as a rationale for a lender of an international last resort

Many have argued that there is a strong parallel between sudden massive withdrawals of capital from developing countries and bank runs; see, for example, Cole and Kehoe (1998) or Chang and Velasco (1998). Banks are vulnerable to runs because they issue highly liquid short-term liabilities (e.g. checking accounts) which their depositors can, if they choose, all withdraw simultaneously. At the same time, many of their assets are held in the form of highly illiquid long-term loans (e.g. to a local construction company) that can only be liquidated prematurely at great expense. One reason why the secondary market might be illiquid is that evaluating loans to local firms requires specialized expertise that banks build up only over a long period. Given the illiquidity of its assets, a bank may find itself in trouble if all its depositors suddenly decide to withdraw their money, even if it is fully solvent in an actuarial sense. Thus, as illustrated in the classic models of Bryant (1980) and Diamond and Dybvig (1983), bank panics can be self-fulfilling.

The parallel with country debt runs is twofold. First, many country debt runs are intimately linked to their banking sectors, as Chang and Velasco (1998) emphasize. In many developing economies, banks are implicitly insured by the government. A countrywide run on local banks will thus translate into a huge increase in government liabilities, and this in turn can lead to a flight from government securities. But the analogy runs much deeper. Fundamentally, many high-yield projects in developing countries (e.g. building a factory or a new highway) are highly illiquid and have only long-term payoff potential. At the same time, a considerable portion of lending to developing countries is in the form of relatively short-term debt. If creditors suddenly become unwilling to roll over short-term loans as they fall due, a country may find itself in a financial squeeze even if, absent a run, it would have had no problems servicing its debts. Devotees of the "multiple equilibrium" view believe that this is precisely what happened in the case of, say, Mexico in 1994, or Korea in 1997. For example, creditor panic at a relatively small devaluation of the peso in December 1994 suddenly made it impossible for Mexico to roll over its short-term debt, quickly precipitating a crisis. Instead of humming along in a "good" growth equilibrium as Mexico seemed to be doing prior to the crisis, it suddenly was bounced into a "bad" recessionary equilibrium. There was no adverse technology shock *a la* modern real business cycle theory – just good old-fashioned creditor panic.

If the multiple equilibrium view is correct (a conclusion the reader should not rush to accept), what is the solution? Bryant (1980) and Diamond and Dybvig (1983) show that in a domestic banking context, the problem can be eliminated, at virtually no cost, by having the government guarantee bank deposits, that is, serve as a lender of last resort. If depositors know they will always be paid even if their bank fails, bank runs will not be a problem and, in fact, the government will never (or at least seldom) have to honor its pledge. Thus their models provide a rationale for the Federal Deposit Insurance Corporation in the United States, and the broader set of implicit guarantees that the institution represents. Many of the proposals for reform of the international monetary system draw heavily on this analogy – if a lender of last resort can stop bank runs in a domestic context, why can't an analogous institution be created to stop country debt runs? What could be simpler?

Chinks in the theoretical case for a domestic lender of last resort

The case for having a *domestic* lender of last resort is far less coherent than many writers in the "save the global financial system" literature seem to realize. The Bryant–Diamond–Dybvig rationale for a lender of last resort relies on a number of assumptions that have been challenged in the literature (for a recent review, see Freixas and Rochet, 1997). The most obvious omission from the story we have told is that it neglects moral hazard: government deposit guarantees allow a bank to hold a risky portfolio while still borrowing at a risk-free interest rate. In principle, moral hazard problems can be mitigated through bank supervision, capital requirements and other devices, though in many countries these checks and balances are patently inadequate. As Caprio and Honohan (1999) discuss, in fifty-nine worldwide banking crashes in the twenty years prior to the Asian crises, the average cost of government bailouts was over 9 percent of GDP in developing countries and 4 percent of GDP in industrialized countries – hardly evidence in favor of the view that creating a lender of last resort is a free lunch. But even if the moral hazard problem could be substantially ameliorated, the case for having a lender of last resort is still somewhat shaky.

As Diamond and Dybvig (1983) themselves show, allowing banks to temporarily suspend deposits is a fully efficient mechanism for eliminating the multiple equilibrium problem, provided a bank knows when it is seeing the start of a run and not just an unusual surge in withdrawals. Wallace (1988) argues that the informational assumptions can be relaxed, once one allows for sophisticated partial suspension schemes. These involve having the bank start to place increasingly tight percentage caps on withdrawals during periods of abnormally high demand. Wallace shows that deposit insurance cannot improve on an optimal suspension policy, unless the lender of last resort has superior information. In a more general setting, one can imagine many other private sector responses to dealing with bank runs, such as the development of interbank credit agreements to deal with panics. Indeed, many of these have been seen in practice in earlier periods.

The reader should not conclude that theory shows decisively that we do not need a lender of last resort. One has a nagging feeling that the government is better positioned to make credible guarantees concerning its policy for dealing with bank runs than any private sector agent or network. But at the same time, it is important to be aware that theory does not provide an air-tight case for this assertion, despite many efforts to do so.

Finally, even the notion that country debt and currency runs might represent realizations of multiple equilibria can be challenged. In a closely related context, Morris and Shin (1998) argue that introducing a small amount of private information can eliminate the problem of multiple equilibria in models of currency attacks. In this class of models, government policies that affect transparency and the dissemination of information can be more useful than introducing insurance.

The G-7 as incumbent global lender of last resort

It would also be an overstatement to say that the world financial system has been living without any lender of last resort. There is one, just not an explicit one. Over the course of the 1990s, the so-called G-7 group of industrialized countries (United States, Japan, Germany, France, United Kingdom, Italy and Canada), acting in concert with the International Monetary Fund (IMF), the World Bank and other OECD countries, have found themselves cast in this role. In early 1995, they awarded Mexico an unprecedented $50 billion bailout package and, on paper, they subsequently offered similar sums to several Asian economies. Why would the G-7 act this way? I, for one, believe that some genuine (albeit modest) altruism is involved, but self-interest is clearly the main reason. Trade with the developing world provides OECD countries with a diverse range of benefits, which would be threatened by a sharp contraction of emerging market economies. More immediately, developing-country financial instability poses a potential threat to industrialized-country banks.[3] Concern over the precarious position of Japanese banks, especially, was a major factor motivating bailout packages to Thailand, Indonesia, Korea and other Asian countries. Last but not least, political instability in the developing world is also a serious concern. Thus, G-7 leaders have powerful incentives to help these nations when they are buffeted by the storms of international capital markets, even when the G-7 leaders recognize full well that whatever policies they attempt have costs and risks of their own attached.

So if the G-7 already provides a global lender of last resort, why would anyone want to think about a new institution? First and foremost, the resources the G-7 seems prepared to devote to developing country bailouts are far from sufficient to discourage country debt runs, at least if they occur on a large global scale; more on this shortly. Another criticism is that G-7 policy is not coherent, despite occasional high-level conferences aimed at developing a long-term strategy. Transparency and perceptions of equity are also important issues. For example, many Asian leaders feel that G-7 and IMF conditions on loans to their countries were far more stringent than those imposed on Mexico and Brazil. This, despite the fact that until the crisis, Asian countries had been seen as models of growth for the rest of the developing world. G-7 leaders might respond by saying that all modern lenders of last resort follow a practice of "constructive ambiguity" (Corrigan, 1990). If the terms of assistance are made too clear in advance, involved parties may come to rely on a bailout, and thus take exactly the sorts of excessive risks that make a bailout more necessary.

Having provided the background for the debate, we are now ready to examine some proposed reforms of the system. We first look at plans that would require multilateral implementation at a global level, and then look at plans that require mainly unilateral action on the part of developing countries.

The man (woman) who would be Keynes: grand plans to save the global financial system

There are no significant barriers to submitting an entry in the save-the-world-financial-system game, and as Eichengreen (1999) notes, most of the plans floating around are "politically unrealistic, technically infeasible, or unlikely to yield significant improvements in the way crises are prevented anticipated or managed."[4] Many readers who are familiar with this literature may think Eichengreen too kind. My own interpretation of the debate, however, is a bit more generous. It is easy to fall into the trap of thinking that big institutional changes are unrealistic or infeasible, especially in the United States where macroeconomic policy institutions have generally evolved only slowly for the past few decades. But not so long ago, the prospects for a single European currency seemed no more likely than those for the breakup of the Soviet empire or the reunification of Germany. Perhaps large institutional changes only seem impossible until they happen – at which point they seem foreordained. So, even if none of the plans is feasible in the present world political environment, after another crisis or two, the impossible may begin to seem realistic.

A "deep pockets" international lender of last resort

Many writers have proposed having an international institution serve as an international lender of last resort, including Mishkin (1994), Meltzer (1998), Garten

(1998), Calomaris (1998), Gionnini (1999) and Fischer (1999). The "Clinton proposal" offered at the October 1998 G-7 meetings is very much in this spirit. In proposals of this sort, the IMF would offer a new emergency line of credit, for which countries would have to prequalify by meeting certain macroeconomic and regulatory standards. The existence of this line of credit would stave off speculative attacks, just as deposit insurance in the United States reduces the incidence of bank runs, so that very few countries would actually ever have to draw on the facility.

The obstacles to having an international "deep pockets" style lender of last resort are formidable. The IMF today has lendable resources of roughly $200 billion. As a percent of world GNP, this amounts to less than a fifth of the resources the IMF had upon its creation at the end of the Second World War. All evidence suggests that the G-7 is simply not prepared to put up the kind of resources needed to preclude a broad-based attack on developing country debt. Moreover, a larger IMF fund would probably encourage more risk-taking by banks in industrialized countries. G-7 officials already have a hard time convincing their own banks that they will not bail them out in advent of default on developing-country debt – especially since, in the past, they have repeatedly done just that (Bulow *et al.*, 1992). Explicitly setting aside perhaps $1 trillion or more for a new multilateral lender of last resort would hardly make such protestations of toughness more convincing.[5]

Any plan for an international lending institution must confront the fact that most financial regulatory power will still lie in the hands of domestic authorities. The creation of a "deep pockets" international lender of last resort would almost certainly induce domestic authorities to be more lax in their oversight. They will know that if domestic banks do run into trouble, part of the cost will be passed on to other countries via the international guarantor. This problem could be mitigated by introducing a risk-based system for assessing country contributions to the international lending institution, but how effective this would be in practice is unclear.

An international financial crisis manager

Fischer (1999) and Gionnini (1999) argue that the main function of the lender of last resort in most modern industrialized economies is that of "crisis manager," a role that does not necessarily require vast amounts of capital. For example, in its August 1998 rescue of LTCM, the US Federal Reserve did not actually contribute any of its own resources. Rather, it jawboned LTCM's creditors into a "concerted lending operation" to keep the firm afloat. Indeed, organizing concerted lending is the most common bailout procedure for modern lenders of last resort, as Goodhart and Schoenmaker (1995) emphasize in their extensive empirical study of modern banking crises. When young Nick Leeson (portrayed in the recent B-movie "Rogue Trader") brought down Britain's venerable Barings Bank with his pyramid of losing futures market bets in the Far East, the Bank of England helped find a new owner who would protect depositors, but it did not bailout Barings with its own money. So by analogy, an international institution (say the IMF) does not necessarily need deep pockets to play what is perhaps the most essential role of a modern lender of last resort.

Purists like Meltzer (1998) would dispute this assertion, arguing that a true lender of last resort must employ the classic Bagehot (1873) rules: Lend freely, to temporarily illiquid but solvent banks, at penalty rates and using collateral that would be good under noncrisis circumstances. This is naïve. Most modern lenders of last resort do not scrupulously follow any of Bagehot's time-honored prescriptions (Gionnini, 1999). They are often gamed into rescuing institutions that are permanently insolvent, not just temporarily so. They seldom charge significant penalties, precisely because they are usually trying to strengthen the troubled bank's balance sheet. And whereas Bagehot would have lenders of last resort require collateral that would be good under ordinary circumstances, this advice is not always practical. It is often very hard to assess the value of highly specialized illiquid assets in times of crisis.

Consideration of a crisis manager has been included here because it follows naturally from any discussion of a lender of last resort. But having a crisis manager is not really a proposal for institutional innovation, it is just a characterization of what the IMF and G-7 do now. Absolutely none of the plans we will discuss would obviate the need for a crisis manager of some sort. But then the whole object of having a grand plan to improve the international financial system is precisely to find a way to rely less heavily on the crisis manager. (There is a residual question of whether the crisis manager needs to have *any* extensive lending funds of its own, a question I take up in the final section.)

An international bankruptcy court

Raffer (1990) and Sachs (1995), have proposed setting up an international bankruptcy court, with powers similar to a domestic bankruptcy court, as in chapters 9 and 11 of US bankruptcy law. Chari and Kehoe (1998) have also endorsed this approach. The basic idea is to give a debtor some breathing room in the event of default, and to prevent a grab race among creditors that would force the debtor country to liquidate or abandon potentially high-yield productive investment projects. Also, as Sachs (1995) especially emphasizes, the bankruptcy court would have the power to let the debtor issue new senior debt to provide essential working capital (e.g. trade credits).

A bankruptcy court can be seen as another way to try to deal with the "country debt runs" problem. Indeed, in terms of the bank run analogy we considered earlier, it is really just a way of allowing for orderly temporary suspension of payments, an approach which, in principle, can be just as effective as having a lender of last resort. An advantage of an international bankruptcy court is that it does not create the same sort of moral hazard problems that a trillion dollar country-loan insurance pool would. Bankruptcy courts have been found to be an extremely effective institutional device in a domestic setting – why shouldn't we have one for countries as well?

Unfortunately, the analogy between domestic and international bankruptcy is far from perfect. A domestic bankruptcy court can seize physical assets and fire a company's board of directors. However, it seems unlikely that an international court would have the right to enter a debtor country and seize physical assets, much less fire the "board of directors" – in this case the country's government. Advocates of an international bankruptcy proceeding point out that similar problems arise in the case of bankrupt states and local governments, and that the obstacles have not proved insurmountable. Chapter 9 of the US bankruptcy code, which governs municipalities, has proven relatively effective (Raffer, 1990).

The analogy to local government bankruptcies is certainly closer than to firm bankruptcies, but still far from perfect. During the New York City debt crisis of the 1970s, an outside board essentially ran the city's day-to-day finances. It is hard to think of any sovereign country submitting to a similar level of outside interference, absent the presence of an invading army.

Lack of enforcement clout in debtor countries is the main problem with international bankruptcy court. If the court has no teeth, and lenders can no longer fall back on national courts (whose jurisdiction would be superseded by the international court), there could be a sharp fall in bank lending.

Why do countries repay, anyway?

This brings us to a question which most researchers view as the crux of understanding international debt markets, but which many policy practitioners seem prepared to ignore. Why, exactly, are debtor countries willing to make repayments of any kind, partial or full? Are debtor nations primarily concerned about preserving their reputation for being a reliable debtor as in Eaton and Gersovitz's (1981) classic paper? (See also Grossman and Van Huyck, 1988; English, 1996.) Or is their main worry that foreign creditors will legally harass them when they try to borrow and trade abroad after a default? (See Bulow and Rogoff, 1989a,b) Or, are they concerned about their reputations, but in a more subtle indirect way, perhaps concerning their status as members in good standing of the international economic community? (See Bulow and Rogoff, 1989b; Cole and Kehoe, 1995, 1997.) I personally believe that it is some combination of the latter two motivations, but there is a lively debate in the literature, and the evidence is far from decisive.[6]

Whereas the debate over why countries repay may seem rather philosophical, it is quite dangerous to think about grand plans to restructure the world financial system without having a concrete view on it. If the Eaton and Gersovitz (1981) story is right – pure reputation for repayment is all that matters – then it is hard to see how introducing an international bankruptcy court could change matters, absent concomitant political integration. On the other hand, if creditors do have meaningful contractual rights, at least in their own countries, then introducing an international bankruptcy court certainly would have an effect. I speculated earlier that unless the court had at least equal clout to the domestic courts it supersedes, lending would probably drop. Now, it is just possible that an international bankruptcy court might help coordinate expectations about what constitutes being a "good international citizen" and have some effect on repayment incentives this way – this is the broader reputation channel I alluded to earlier. But this would seem a very speculative effect on which to hang such a major institutional change.

A global financial regulator

Henry Kaufman (1998) and others have suggested the creation of a world financial regulator, manned by investment professionals drawn from the private sector, that would oversee both banks and nonbank financial intermediaries. There is much to be said for harmonizing international banking standards in the global financial system. The 1988 Basle Capital Accord, and the more recent 1999 Basle II accord, are seen by most observers as very positive steps in this direction. Most famously, the Basle accords impose uniform capital adequacy standards across banks of the signatory countries. Basle I required that banks possess enough capital to cover 8 percent losses on most loans. Basle II allows for much richer and more sophisticated differentiation across loan classes, with capital reserve ratios reaching as high as 40 percent in some cases. The idea of requiring banks to have capital is simply so that bank managers will not be able to make one way bets: if risky loans pay off, the bank wins big, and if they do not, the taxpayer foots the bill for paying off depositors. Requiring higher capital ratios is thus a means of forcing financial institutions to internalize some of the costs of having a risky portfolio.

The Basle accords are useful but, as the case of Japan in the 1990s illustrates, enforcement of these standards by national authorities can be quite lax. In principle, a global financial regulator might be more distant from client banks, and better able to enforce regulations. But this is very hypothetical. Just as in the case of an international bankruptcy court, it is not at all obvious how a global financial regulator could be given any real bite, absent a far greater degree of world political integration than we currently observe.

There is another objection, well known from the literature on international policy coordination. Even if some day there did arise potent political mechanisms for creating a powerful international financial regulator, it would be important to think carefully about how much power to vest in it. Under a current decentralized regulatory structure, borrowers and lenders can shop around in offshore markets to circumvent domestic regulation. Regulators naturally see this as a problem, and one of the main arguments for harmonizing standards. But there is also a case to be made that global markets provide a safety valve against bad regulation in individual countries. During the early days of the offshore euro-market, which ultimately proved enormously innovative and successful, many participants used it to bypass stifling domestic banking regulations. Hedge funds, which have been responsible for some important innovations in global financial markets, initially thrived by making use of regulatory loopholes that exempted foreign investment firms from some US financial regulations. The idea that a certain degree of international governmental competition can be healthy for promoting investment and productivity is well known in the literature on international macroeconomic policy coordination; see, for example, Rogoff (1985) or Kehoe (1987).

An international FDIC

George Soros (1998) has proposed the creation of a new international authority to insure international investors against debt defaults. It would be a sort of Federal Deposit Insurance Corporation for country debt. Borrowing countries would pay for the insurance in advance when floating loans. The IMF would set limits on how much each country could borrow, and the G-7 would vigorously deny bailouts to uninsured loans.

This idea can be criticized on several counts. First, the G-7's promise not to bailout uninsured loans would hardly be credible, since the proposal does nothing to change the fundamental incentives that draw them into crises now.[7] After all, in most countries, the government's promise to guarantee the safety of bank deposits is implicit, not explicit. Second, it is not obvious how the IMF would determine limits on how much could be loaned, or what the appropriate insurance fee would be. Finally, it would be difficult to invest the insurer with any meaningful regulatory power, for much the same reasons as it is hard to create a powerful international bankruptcy court or global financial regulator.

The Soros proposal does, however, highlight an important issue. If private agents are engaged in risky activities that generate negative externalities – which include not only the costs of bailouts but the costs of greater vulnerability to financial crises – then, in an ideal theoretical world, the activities of such agents should be taxed. Modern approaches to domestic deposit insurance attempt to achieve this with variable capital requirements on different types of loans, and variable insurance charges. In practice, high levels of uncertainty, together with political pressure, make it very difficult to establish appropriate insurance charges, but the principle still holds. Again, the recent Basle II accord is an attempt to move in this direction.

A world monetary authority

The birth of the euro, not to mention despondency over exchange rate fluctuations, has led a number of observers to advocate forming a world central bank to oversee a global currency.[8] Needless to say, international political integration is hardly sufficient to support such a global central bank, or to maintain one should it come about.

Setting aside the political issues, there are theoretical objections as well. One objection is related to an issue already raised in the context of having a single financial regulator: having more than one competing global currency can be a good thing. Competition can enhance anti-inflation credibility, and this benefit can in principle outweigh any stabilization benefits from coordination of monetary policy (Rogoff, 1985). A second objection is that some regions may, at times, require a monetary policy that is sharply different from the one required by the rest of the world. In such cases, exchange rate adjustments may work better than movements of relative prices or migrations of labor in helping economies adjust. As Mundell (1961) and Kenen (1969) framed the question, is the entire world really an optimal currency area?

Some advocates of a world money argue that a global lender of last resort must have the ability to issue currency in order to address global liquidity crises, and in order to be sure of deep enough pockets for dealing with global runs (Capie, 1998). It is hard to agree with this rationale. The US Federal Reserve, the European Central Bank and the Bank of Japan are already large enough to supply liquidity to the market in a crisis; it is not necessary to have a global bank. And we have already shown that creating a "deep pockets" global lender of last resort can create severe moral hazard problems. Indeed, if a global monetary bank does ever emerge, a major question will be how to determine and constrain the scope of its lender of last resort functions.

Unilateral steps developing countries can take to reduce vulnerability to speculative capital flows

Are there any steps that countries can take unilaterally to help protect themselves? A number of alternatives have been advanced.

Controls on capital outflows

On September 28, 1998, Paul Krugman posted on the web a thoughtful and provocative article on the use of controls on capital outflows to combat a speculative attack.[9] The following day, Malaysia's Prime Minister Mahathir imposed such controls. And they say no one listens to economists! True, by February 1999, Malaysia had lifted most of its controls, and it is not obvious that the country has fared any better than other similar Asian countries in emerging from the region's crisis. But the episode raises the broader question of whether the simplest solution to speculative attacks is for countries to "put some sand in the wheels" of international capital markets, to borrow Tobin's (1978) famous analogy.

The crux of Krugman's (1998) argument is that emergency controls on outflows might be the least bad choice for a country whose currency and debt is under severe attack from domestic and foreign speculators. A nation that attempts to protect its currency through sharp rises in interest rates, a remedy the IMF has often prescribed in the past, puts tremendous pressure on its economy and especially on its banking system. On the other hand, allowing a sharp depreciation of the exchange rate, as advocated by Sachs (1998), also wreaks havoc with the domestic banking system. Developing-country banks often have heavy offshore borrowing in foreign currency, but loans in domestic currency, which means that depreciation renders them insolvent. So, Krugman argues, perhaps capital controls are sometimes the best alternative, however abhorrent they are to economists.

The first reaction of most academic economists is that policies that prevent international investors from repatriating their funds can't possibly be a good idea for any country that desires any future investment from abroad. Countries with a track record of imposing capital exit controls will surely drop to the bottom of most international investment "buy" lists.

This initial reaction may well be the right one, but economists should recognize that the issues are actually quite subtle and complex. I have already argued that, in theory, a temporary payments standstill may sometimes be the best response to a run, absent a lender of last resort. Moreover, in multi-period models of international borrowing, it is by no means the case that an efficient contract always calls for full debt repayment in every state of nature. Several authors have developed models in which the implicit contract between country debtors and international creditors calls for only partial repayment when growth is unexpectedly low (Grossman and Van Huyck, 1988; Bulow and Rogoff, 1989a; Obstfeld and Rogoff, 1996, ch. 6).

Of course, there are also a variety of powerful reasons why the international community might be concerned about seeing pervasive use of restrictions on capital outflows. Controls may scare off investors, who find them arbitrary and unpredictable, far more so than a bankruptcy court or a crisis manager. Controls are an open invitation to corruption, as investors with huge sums of money at stake will be tempted to try to bribe local officials. Thus, although it is a false reading of the theory literature to conclude that temporary outflow controls are absolutely never an optimal response to a run, it is quite possible that the problems far outweigh the benefits.

Controls on capital inflows

Another school of thought, less radical, holds that the international community (i.e. the G-7 and IMF) should allow and even encourage developing countries to place taxes on short-term capital inflows; Eichengreen (1999) is one recent advocate of this approach. Chile, which is generally held as the most successful economy in Latin America over the past two decades, is the poster country for capital inflow taxes. From May 1992 to May 1998, the Chileans required that all non-equity foreign capital inflows be accompanied by a noninterest bearing one-year deposit equal to the 30 percent of the initial value of the investment. Since the restricted account must be held for only a year, the effective tax rate imposed by this restriction is larger for a short-term investment and smaller for a long-term investment. The rationale for the Chilean tax is that it discourages locals from relying too heavily on short-term borrowing, and thereby mitigates the problem of maturity mismatch – that is, heavy short-term borrowing and long-term lending – that seems to underlie many episodes of speculative attack. Because the tax is completely transparent, it does not suffer from the arbitrariness that many investors associate with capital outflow taxes. Admittedly, Chilean-style controls must be very comprehensive to be effective. For example, domestic banks must be prevented from writing offshore derivative swap contracts with foreign holders of long-term Chilean debt. By including suitable margin and call conditions, such contracts can effectively make a Chilean bank the true holder of the long-term income stream, and the foreign bank the holder of a short-term loan.

There are various concerns with trying to apply the Chilean lesson too broadly. Chile has been relatively successful in avoiding speculative pressures, but as Edwards (1998) argues, this probably has had less to do with its system of capital controls than with a variety of other favorable conditions, especially the country's relatively well-developed system of prudential banking regulation. It may be the case that for Chile, lenders were willing to advance long-term loans at rates only slightly higher than for short-term loans. Many developing countries, however, may find that foreign investors demand a much higher premium. In this case, the borrower will have to choose between accepting short-term loans or not being able to borrow at all from abroad. Indeed, presently even Chile is not employing "Chile-style" controls on capital inflows: by September 1998, the tax had been reduced to zero in response to a persistent current account deficit. (When a country needs to borrow to pay for current consumption, it is less well positioned to impose taxes on foreign investors.)

In sum, if short-term capital inflow taxes can be enforced cleanly and transparently (a big qualification in countries where official corruption is a major problem), the objections to them are less, though they may only work for a small select number of countries.

Increasing transparency and improving financial regulation in developing countries

The G-22, which consists of a mixed group of developing and industrialized countries, has issued a series of reports recommending increased transparency and improved prudential regulation as positive steps that developing countries can take toward reducing the problem of financial crises.[10] This emphasis is partly based on the observation that countries such as New Zealand and Australia, which both have relatively strong financial regulation, seemed to suffer much less from the 1997–98 "Asian Flu" than countries without such safety provisions. Like motherhood and apple pie, it is hard to assess these recommendations as anything but positive.

Increased transparency would undoubtedly be useful in achieving more efficient global markets. But bank runs and country runs can still happen even in a totally transparent system. As long as banks have a maturity or currency mismatches, then the financial system is vulnerable to runs. Diamond and Dybvig's (1983) model of runs on banks and Cole and Kehoe's (1998) model of runs on country debt do not depend on asymmetric or poor information, but only on these sort of mismatches. Indeed, Morris and Shin (1998) take this argument one step further and claim that too much transparency can sometimes actually exacerbate the problem of multiple equilibria, helping speculators coordinate on the timing of a run.

Other measures

Two other measures countries can take are worth mentioning briefly. One is to build up a higher level of foreign reserves. Countries such as Taiwan and Hong Kong, with their massive foreign exchange reserves, were much better positioned to weather the storm. Perhaps this is a bit like saying that it is better to be rich than poor, but the point is also that countries should not underrate the gains from adding to reserves. A second change that has been widely recommended (e.g. Calomaris, 1998) is for countries to open themselves up much more to foreign banks. This would shrink the size of a country's own banking sector thereby reducing the costs of any bailout after a crisis. There are some potential credibility issues here about whether domestic authorities could still be gamed into bailing out foreign bank branches in the event of a run (after all, it is domestic depositors who stand to lose their money), but it nevertheless seems like an interesting option.

Another approach to addressing the legal and institutional bias in the composition of capital flows to developing countries

One problem with all the plans we have discussed so far is that they largely take the current make-up of international capital flows, which is heavily biased toward debt and away from equity, as given.

Equity finance must be put on a level playing field with debt finance

One widely recognized problem with the present system is that it contains strong biases toward debt finance, especially toward intermediation by banks. If flows to developing countries took the form of equity and direct investment, there would be an automatic device for risk sharing. Country runs could still lead to sharp drops in local stock markets, but there would be no liquidity effects, no need for a lender of last resort or a crisis manager. Indeed, the importance of redirecting capital flows toward equity and direct investment was one of the main lessons of the Latin debt crisis of the 1980s. Despite this consensus, banks lending and/or borrowing played a pivotal role, in all of the debt crises of the 1990s. On the borrowing side, developing-country banks built up large short-term liabilities in dollars, and were hammered when interest rates rose and their countries' currencies depreciated. On the lending side, sudden contractions in lending by industrialized-country banks played a major role in aggravating country debt runs in Asia.

Four sources of bias toward debt finance

Under the current system, there are four sources of bias toward debt contracts. The first is deposit insurance, in both creditor and debtor countries. Taxpayers subsidize bank intermediation, which expands the size of the banking system, which in turn makes it more difficult for authorities to credibly refuse to bailout these institutions. This is a difficult problem – it transcends the international context. The sums spent on bailouts of domestic banking systems over the past thirty years are at least comparable to expenditures on subsidies to international debt, and possibly larger depending on how one prices the portfolios of the international financial institutions.

Second, the current method of enforcing international lending contracts relies heavily on enforcement via creditor-country courts and G-7 institutions. Giving creditors legal rights in industrialized-country courts leads to a bias because it does far more to protect debt holders than providers of equity finance. If a country fails to repay its debt, this creates an obvious breach of contract that may be adjudicated by an outside arbiter. In the case of equity, there are many subtle ways for the debtor to chip away at the value of the equity holder's claim, without doing anything transparently egregious. Changes in tax and labor laws affect equity values, as do changes in local laws governing shareholder rights. The list is long.

Third, equity markets in developing countries are severely underdeveloped.

Fourth, aside from domestic deposit insurance, a strong case can be made that G-7 funds aimed at helping distressed country debtors often end up recycling to G-7 debt holders (both banks and bondholders) in the form of higher payments, providing a further subsidy to debt finance. (Bulow *et al.* (1992) argue that a careful analysis of the various complex web of side payments between industrialized and developing countries supports this viewpoint.)

Possible remedies

Eliminating subsidies to financial institutions is a thorny problem, not least because a large component of deposit insurance is implicit rather than explicit. A number of important steps have been taken, including the recent Basle II accords discussed earlier, and there are some creative suggestions floating around (e.g. Calomaris' (1998) idea for requiring banks to issue subordinated debt). For example, measures to reduce the contagion potential generated by the complex interbank clearing house systems might make it easier for governments to let individual financial institutions fail without incurring larger systemic costs. Of course, greater credibility not to bailout failed institutions translates into lower implicit subsidies.

One can also consider mitigating the bias in the curent legal system toward debt contracts in sovereign lending; see Bulow and Rogoff (1990). In particular, the evolution of legal doctrine in the United States and Britain – as codified in the 1976 US Sovereign Immunities Act and the 1978 UK State Immunity Act – appears to have contributed to an increased reliance by creditors on enforcing developing-country debt contracts in industrialized-country courts. Of course, if the legal underpinnings of the current debt finance system were changed, some countries might not be able to borrow very much at all from private markets, so there could be a significant transition period where capital flows were reduced. Lenders would avoid countries lacking (a) sound legal systems for enforcing commercial contracts, (b) transparent and fair regulatory systems and (c) favorable histories of treatment toward foreign investors. Countries wanting to draw on world capital markets would then have a strong incentive to develop institutions that would support foreign investor confidence.[11] By the same token, they will have an incentive to develop fair, transparent and well-regulated equity markets to help attract capital flows.

The implicit subsidy to bank and bond lending via international lending institutions is also affected by the capital structure of the IMF and the World Bank; see Bulow and Rogoff (1990).

Conclusions

In this chapter, we have tried to show how the academic literature on banking and sovereign lending can help one understand some of the ideas that are being vented for changing the international monetary system. True, the constraints of national sovereignty tend to make even the best of these grand schemes rather difficult to implement. Nevertheless, proposals for radical reform are very helpful in clarifying some of the problems facing the global financial system. Over the longer term, as global and regional political institutions become better developed, some of the plans may not seem so far-fetched. Indeed, a better understanding of the economic benefits of regional and global economic integration may in turn affect those processes.

Notes

1 The author has benefited from discussions with Peter Garber, Charles Goodhart and Mervyn King, and from detailed comments by Timothy Taylor and Brad DeLong on an earlier draft.
2 Bulow and Rogoff (1990) argue that the combination of adverse terms of trade shocks, rises in global real interest rates, and recessions in the industrialized world played a much larger role in the poor growth performance of Latin America during the first half of the 1980s than any debt overhang effects.
3 According to official statistics, western banks were somewhat less involved in developing-country loans in the 1990s than they were in the 1980s, but this is partly an illusion. Through offshore derivative contracts with developing-country banks, a great deal of foreign investment that nominally appears to be in the form of equity and long-term government bonds is actually better thought of as short-term hard-currency debt.
4 See also Goldstein (1998) for another excellent critical discussion of alternative reform plans.
5 Bulow and Rogoff (1988) develop a model showing how private debtors and country borrowers can sometimes game resources away from creditor-country taxpayers.
6 It is true that countries that have defaulted have generally been able to re-enter credit markets at reasonably favorable terms, but usually only after a long hiatus and after negotiating a settlement of outstanding claims (Ozler, 1993). The strongest weapon of disgruntled creditors, perhaps, is the ability to interfere with short-term trade credits that are the lifeblood of international trade. (If the reader finds these mechanisms somewhat

unconvincing as a device for enforcing large scale lending, bear in mind that international lending flows tend to be relatively small for precisely this reason.)

7 The same credibility problem applies to Calomaris's (1998) suggestion that the IMF require countries to impose a number of prudential restrictions on their banks in order to be eligible for assistance.

8 For a useful discussion that takes seriously the possibility of an international currency, see Cooper (1984).

9 See also Krugman's column in *Fortune*, September 7, 1998.

10 As of this writing, the text of the G-22 reports can be found on the home page of the Bank for International Settlements, at http://www.bis.org

11 In a related vein, Eichengreen and Portes (1995) propose that industrialized-country governments should take steps to change the standard terms on international lending contracts, so that it would only take a majority, and not unanimity, among debt holders to renegotiate terms in the event of a crisis. Their idea is similar to that of an international bankruptcy court – to make it easier for countries to reschedule payments in times of distress.

References

Acemoglu, Daron and Fabrizio Zilibotti, "Was Promotheus Unbound by Chance? Risk, Diversification and Growth," *Journal of Political Economy*, August 1997, *105*, 709–51.

Bagehot, Walter, *Lombard Street*, London: William Clowes and Sons, 1873.

Bhagwati, Jagdish, "The Capital Myth: The Difference Between Trade in Widgets and Trade in Dollars," *Foreign Affairs*, 1998, *77*, 7–12.

Bryant, John, "A Model of Bank Reserves, Bank Runs and Deposit Insurance," *Journal of Banking and Finance*, 1980, *4*, 335–44.

Bulow, Jeremy and Kenneth Rogoff, "Multilateral Negotiations for Rescheduling Developing Country Debt: A Bargaining-Theoretic Framework," *International Monetary Fund Staff Papers*, December 1988, *35*, 644–57.

Bulow, Jeremy and Kenneth Rogoff, "A Constant Recontracting Model of Sovereign Debt," *Journal of Political Economy*, February 1989a, *97*, 155–78.

Bulow, Jeremy and Kenneth Rogoff, "Sovereign Debt: Is to Forgive to Forget?" *American Economic Review*, March 1989b, *79*, 43–50.

Bulow, Jeremy and Kenneth Rogoff, "Cleaning Up Third-World Debt Without Getting Taken to the Cleaners," *Journal of Economic Perspectives*, Winter 1990, *4*, 31–42.

Bulow, Jeremy, Kenneth Rogoff and Afonso Bevilaqua, "Official Creditor Seniority and Burden Sharing in the Former Soviet Bloc," *Brookings Papers in Macroeconomic Activity*, Spring 1992, *1*, 195–222.

Calomaris, Charles W., "Blueprints for a New Global Financial Architecture," mimeo, Columbia Business School, 1998.

Capie, Forest, "Can There Be an International Lender of Last Resort?" *International Finance*, 1998, *1*, 311–25.

Caprio, Jerry and Patrick Honohan, "Beyond Capital Ideals: Restoring Banking Stability," *Journal of Economic Perspectives* 13 (Fall 1999).

Chang, Roberto and Andres Velasco, "Financial Crises in Emerging Markets: A Canonical Model," National Bureau of Economic Research, Working Paper No. 6606, June 1998.

Chari, V.V. and Patrick Kehoe, "Asking the Right Questions About the IMF," *Federal Reserve Bank of Minneapolis Annual Report, Special Issue*, 1998, *13*, 2–26.

Cole, Harold and Patrick Kehoe, "The Role of Institutions in Reputation Models of Sovereign Debt," *Journal of Monetary Economics*, 1995, *35*, 45–64.

Cole, Harold and Patrick Kehoe, "Reputation Spillover Across Relationships with Enduring and Transient Benefits: Reviving Reputation Models of Sovereign Debt," Minneapolis Federal Reserve, *Quarterly Review*, Winter 1997, *21*.

Cole, Harold and Timothy Kehoe, "A Self-Fulfilling Debt Crises," Federal Reserve of Minneapolis Staff Report 211, July 1998.

Cooper, Richard, "A Monetary System for the Future," *Foreign Affairs*, 1984, *63*, 166–84.

Corrigan, Gerald, *Testimony Before the Senate Committee on Banking, Housing and Urban Affairs*, Washington, DC, May 3, 1990.

Diamond, Douglas and Philip Dybvig, "Bank Runs, Deposit Insurance, and Liquidity," *Journal of Political Economy*, June 1983, *91*, 401–19.

Eaton, Jonathan and Mark Gersovitz, "Debt with Potential Repudiation: Theory and Estimation," *Review of Economic Studies*, April 1981, *48*, 289–309.

Edwards, Sebastion, "Capital Flows, Real Exchange Rates, and Capital Controls: Some Latin American Experiences," National Bureau of Economic Research, Working Paper No. 6800, November 1998.

Eichengreen, Barry, *Toward a New International Financial Architecture: A Practical Post-Asia Agenda*. Washington: The Institute for International Economics, 1999.

Eichengreen, Barry and Richard Portes, *Crisis, What Crisis? Orderly Workouts for Sovereign Debtors*. London: The Centre for Economic Policy Research, 1995.

English, William, "Understanding the Costs of Sovereign Default: American State Debts in the 1840s," *American Economic Review*, March 1996, *86*, 259–75.

Fischer, Stanley, "On the Need for an International Lender of Last Resort," *Journal of Economic Perspectives* 13 (Fall 1999).

Freixas, Xavier and Jean-Charles Rochet, *Microeconomics of Banking*. Cambridge: The MIT Press, 1997.

Garten, Jeffrey, "In This Economic Chaos, A Global Central Bank Can Help," *International Herald Tribune*, September 25, 1998, 8.

Gionnini, Curzio, "Enemy of None but Friend of All? An International Perspective on the Lender of Last Resort Function," *International Monetary Fund*, Working Paper WP/99/10, 1999.

Goldstein, Morris, *The Case for an International Banking Standard*. Washington: The Institute for International Economics, 1997.

Goldstein, Morris, *The Asian Financial Crisis: Causes, Cures, and Systemic Implications*. Washington: The Institute for International Economics, 1998.

Goodhart, Charles and Dirk Schoenmaker, "Should the Functions of Monetary Policy and Bank Supervision be Separated?" *Oxford Economic Papers*, October 1995, *47*, 539–60.

Grossman, Herschel and John Van Huyck, "Sovereign Debt as a Contingent Claim," *American Economic Review*, December 1988, *78*, 1088–97.

Group of 22, *Report of the Working Group on Transparency and Accountability*. Washington, Group of 22, 1998.

Kaufman, Henry, "Preventing the Next Global Financial Crisis," *Washington Post*, January 28, 1998, A17.

Kehoe, Patrick, "Coordination of Fiscal Policies in a World Economy," *Review of Economic Studies*, May 1987, *19*, 349–76.

Kenen, Peter, "The Theory of Optimal Currency Areas: An Eclectic View." In Mundell, Robert A. and Alexander K. Swoboda, eds, *Monetary Problems of the International Economy*. Chicago: University of Chicago Press, 1969, 41–60.

Krugman, Paul, "Saving Asia: It's Time to Get Radical," *Fortune*, September 7, 1998a, 74–80.

Krugman, Paul, "Heresy Time," http//web.mit.edu/krugman/www/heresy.html, September 28, 1998b.

Martin, Philippe and Helene Rey, "Financial Super-Markets: Size Matters for Asset Trade," " mimeo, London School of Economics, November 1998.

Meltzer, Allan, "Asian Problems and the IMF," Testimony Prepared for the Joint Economic Committee, US Congress, February 24, 1998.

Mishkin, Frederic S., "Preventing Financial Crises: An International Perspective," National Bureau of Economic Research, Working Paper No. 4636, February 1994.

Morris, Stephen and Hyun song Shin, "Unique Equilibrium in a Model of Self-fulfilling Currency Attacks," *American Economic Review*, June 1998, *88*, 587–97.

Mundell, Robert A., "A Theory of Optimum Currency Areas," *American Economic Review*, September 1961, *51*, 657–65.

Obstfeld, Maurice, "Risk-Taking, Global Diversification and Growth," *American Economic Review*, December 1994, *85*, 1310–29.

Obstfeld, Maurice and Kenneth Rogoff, "The Mirage of Fixed Exchange Rates," *Journal of Economic Perspectives*, Fall 1995, *9*, 73–96.

Obstfeld, Maurice and Kenneth Rogoff, *Foundations of International Macroeconomics.* Cambridge: MIT Press, 1996.

Ozler, Sule, "Have Commercial Banks Ignored History?" *American Economic Review*, June 1993, *83*, 608–20.

Raffer, Kunibert, "Applying Chapter 9 Insolvency to International Debts: An Economically Efficient Solution with a Human Face," *World Development*, 1990, *18*, 301–11.

Rodrick, Dani, *Has Globalization Gone too Far?* Washington: The Institute for International Economics, 1997.

Rogoff, Kenneth, "Can International Monetary Cooperation be Counterproductive?" *Journal of International Economics*, May 1985, *18*, 199–217.

Sachs, Jeffrey, "Do We Need an International Lender of Last Resort?" Princeton University, Frank Graham Memorial Lecture, 1995.

Sachs, Jeffrey, "Fixing the IMF Remedy," *The Banker*, February 1998, *148*, 16–18.

Soros, George, *The Crisis of Global Capitalism.* New York: Public Affairs Press, 1998.

Svensson, Lars E.O., "Trade in Risky Assets," *American Economic Review*, June 1988, *78*, 375–94.

Tobin, James, "A Proposal for International Monetary Reform," *Eastern Economic Journal*, 1978, *4*, 153–9.

Ventura, Jaume, "Growth and Interdependence," *Quarterly Journal of Economics*, 1997, *115*.

Wallace, Neil, "Another Attempt to Explain an Illiquid Banking System: The Diamond and Dybvig Model with Sequential Servicing Taken Seriously," Federal Reserve Bank of Minneapolis, *Quarterly Review*, Fall 1988, *12*, 3–16.

11 The catalysing role of policy-based lending by the IMF and the World Bank

Fact or fiction?

Graham Bird and Dane Rowlands

Introduction

Does the involvement of the IMF and the World Bank in developing countries and countries in transition (CITs) help them to attract capital from other sources, either in the form of private flows or bilateral aid? Do these multilateral institutions therefore exert a catalytic effect on other financial flows? There is a strong body of opinion that the basic answer to this question is 'yes'. Thus, in a recent UK Treasury Committee inquiry into the IMF (Treasury Committee, 1997), the minutes of evidence report one member as saying that, 'the drift of the evidence' received by the inquiry from 'people who claim to know' was 'a lot about catalytic effects and a lot about public leverage of private money … it is just a very commonly held view' (p. 30).

In a recent review of the World Bank and the IMF, Anne Krueger (1998) claims that an 'argument may be made that the presence of a Fund programme provides important signals for private creditors' (p. 2010), also suggesting that 'private creditors are often unwilling to extend credit lines unless the Bank and Fund have first signalled their acceptance of economic policies' (p. 2007). Dani Rodrik (1996) also claims that 'multilateral flows should act as a catalyst for private flows' (p. 182); an effect which he claims should work through the information and signals contained in conditionality.

The IMF itself has advocated a 'three pronged' approach to policy-based lending under which the third prong is 'the securing of external finance to support programmes' (Schadler *et al.*, 1995), and in the *IMF Survey* in March 1997 the Fund claims that by signalling policy credibility to markets IMF conditionality encourages additional private capital flows (see Dhonte, 1997).

At the same time, however, there are contraindications. Fund involvement in East Asian economies in 1997 was associated with accelerating capital outflows such that catalysis appeared to be negative. Here, Fund and Bank programmes seemed to be signalling severe economic distress. Moreover, a broad examination of aggregate data suggests that lending by the Fund tends to increase at times when private lending is falling, implying that lending by the multilaterals substitutes for private capital flows rather than complements them as the catalytic effect would predict.

But does it matter what the sign and strength of the catalytic effect is? There are a number of reasons why it does. First, in dealing with balance of payments deficits there will, in principle, be an optimal combination of adjustment and financing. Thus, a country experiencing a structural balance of payments problem may do better to phase adjustment over the medium to long term. This policy approach will imply a relatively strong demand for external financing in the short term. Can this demand be met? If not, the country will be forced to adopt an economic programme which aims to eliminate the payments deficit more rapidly, and this is likely to focus on compressing domestic aggregate demand. Such a strategy may have adverse supply-side consequences, with a negative impact on economic growth. Without adequate external financing developing countries and CITs will therefore be pushed towards suboptimal adjustment strategies, with the availability of external finance constraining economic development.[1]

A second implication is that if the supply of external finance constrains the design of adjustment programmes, it is also likely to limit their success. Suboptimal adjustment strategies will be less successful than optimal ones. At a time when the majority of Fund programmes remain uncompleted it is therefore relevant to ask whether this failure is connected with financial starvation.[2]

However the lending capacities of the IMF and the World Bank are themselves constrained by political factors, with the major shareholders often being reluctant to expand their resource base. In these circumstances the needs of developing countries for external finance will not be met by the multilateral institutions alone. There will therefore be a financing gap which either has to be filled by capital from other sources, or eliminated by policies which reduce economic growth. The catalytic effect is about the extent to which the multilateral institutions can entice others to lend and help close the external financing gap. The more effective the multilaterals are in catalysing other financial flows the less the need for them to lend themselves. By the same token a weak catalytic effect implies that the multilaterals will need to take on a larger share of the financing role or accept lower economic welfare in developing countries and CITs.

Third, therefore, the catalytic effect is important in the context of the debate about the international financial architecture and the roles and resource requirements of the multilateral agencies. Should the IMF and the World Bank concentrate on giving policy advice and rely on others to provide finance which they can catalyse via conditionality, or should they be lending institutions, and if so, how large should their lending role be? Catalysis is fundamental to answering these questions.

However, although widely discussed, catalysis by the multilaterals has also tended to be discussed rather loosely, and there have been relatively few studies that have set out to examine it in any depth. Perhaps the best known and frequently cited analysis of multilateral lending is that by Rodrik (1996), although other studies which have a bearing on the catalytic effect are reviewed in Bird and Rowlands (1997), which also provides additional new evidence. However, even Rodrik's research exhibits some shortcomings. First, it does not explore in any detail the theory of catalysis and simply assumes that, via signalling, IMF and

World Bank conditionality should have a positive catalytic effect. Second, the econometric results reported rely on grouping observations into six year periods for which there is only limited justification. Do other econometric methodologies and other time periods give different results? Third, Rodrik does not attempt to control the economic characteristics of each country. Finally, the econometrics is not augmented by case studies. Nor did Rodrik talk to fund managers, credit-rating agencies, and bilateral aid donors to gauge how important they perceive the multilaterals to be in influencing their investment and lending decisions.

The research reported in the chapter attempts to overcome some of these deficiencies. The chapter presents, in broad terms, the findings of a research project financed by the Department for International Development (DfID) in the United Kingdom. However, since in essence the chapter is a summary of the project, a considerable amount of significant detail has been omitted to ensure that its length does not become unmanageable. For those who want to pursue some of the issues raised here in more detail this chapter should therefore be read in conjunction with the other papers that have arisen from the project (Bird and Rowlands, 1997, 1999a,b; Bird, 1998, 1999; Bird *et al.*, 1999b).[3]

The layout of the chapter is as follows. The next section discusses the theory of catalysis by exploring the principal analytical issues to which it gives rise. The section 'Existing empirical evidence' briefly summarises the results of previous research that has a bearing on catalysis. The section 'Qualitative evidence' discusses the objective functions of the principal players and reports what private lenders and aid donors say about the importance of the Fund and the Bank in the context of catalysis. The section 'Quantitative evidence' presents a summary of our new econometric evidence incorporating various levels of disaggregation in terms of types of capital flow and multilateral lending. The section 'Case study evidence' provides a brief review of existing case study evidence and also reports some of our own case study findings. The penultimate section extracts the main policy implications from the foregoing discussion, and examines how the catalytic effect could be strengthened in future. The last section offers a few concluding remarks which, in particular, attempt to place our research on the catalytic effect in the context of the debate about the new international financial architecture.

Analytical issues

What theory lies behind the 'very commonly held view' that the multilaterals exert a catalytic effect on other financial flows? In principle, there are a number of modalities through which catalysis may occur. Route 1 is via conditionality. The idea here is that by agreeing to an IMF or World Bank programme, governments can signal to private capital markets or to aid donors that they are serious about and committed to economic reform. By involving the multilaterals, governments can overcome the time inconsistency problem and, effectively, import the superior reputation of the Fund or the Bank for economic management. The multilaterals will thus add value in terms of the *design* of the economic programmes and the *monitoring* and *enforcement* of implementation to make sure that they are carried through to completion.

According to this approach, private markets and bilateral aid donors lack the information and, individually, the clout to carry out these functions, and they are therefore content to delegate them to the multilaterals. In a sense the multilaterals then act as the agents of private lenders and bilateral aid donors. Route 1 has conditionality enhancing credibility which in turn generates catalysis.

Of these two links it is reasonable to assume that greater credibility will have a positive catalytic effect. However, the link between conditionality and credibility needs to be looked at more critically. Can it be safely assumed that the IMF and the World Bank will design appropriate policies, and furthermore does conditionality offer an effective means of ensuring that these policies will be implemented? This is not the place to get into a detailed discussion of the design of IMF and World Bank conditionality, since such discussions exist elsewhere.[4]

However, it can be noted that there are plenty of claims in the literature to suggest that the design of IMF and World Bank conditionality is inappropriate, or at least built on economic ideas about which there is legitimate debate.[5] Most recently, in the context of the East Asian crisis, the argument has been forcefully made by critics that the IMF endeavoured to deal with 'new' problems using 'old' policies which were misplaced and counterproductive (see, e.g. Feldstein, 1998). Meanwhile, the World Bank has been accused of showing over-zealous support for a market-based approach to economic development and economic growth, while in practice premature economic liberalisation often leads to difficulties (Fanelli *et al.*, 1994).

Stalwart components of conditionality in the form of raising interest rates and currency devaluation may, for example, have negative effects on capital flows just as easily as positive ones if they are believed to engender recession, domestic banking collapse, and the risk of further currency depreciation (Radelet and Sachs, 1998).

So doubts exist about the design of conditionality. On top of this, however, there are doubts about whether conditionality enhances implementation. Again some commentators have argued that there are built-in inconsistencies in conditionality in terms of the functions it is seeking to perform, and that implementation relies on government commitment which is, in many ways, at odds with conditionality.[6]

The acid test is to see whether conditionality as used by the multilaterals has been successful. But what are the criteria for success? Does conditionality ensure that agreed policy changes are made? Is conditionality fully implemented? Does conditionality lead to an improvement in ultimate indicators of economic performance? Again there is very large literature dealing with each of these questions, but in summary conditionality exhibits a less than spectacular track record. Thus the majority of Fund programmes remain uncompleted. Neither Fund programmes nor structural adjustment programmes supported by the World Bank have strongly significant positive results on subsequent economic performance, though this remains a controversial issue.[7] Moreover, recent evidence on World Bank conditionality suggests that even where specific policies do lead to beneficial outcomes, their enactment has little to do with conditionality (Dollar and Svensson, 1998).

Even the enforcement aspect of conditionality lacks teeth for as long as non-compliance is not heavily penalised by the multilaterals. Recidivism is a feature of both IMF and World Bank lending and, in this respect, a current programme with either multilateral may be seen as a lead indicator of future economic difficulties.[8]

Therefore, while private markets and aid donors will certainly be looking for governmental commitment to sound economic policies, there must be some doubt about whether the multilaterals will identify the best policies, and considerable doubt about whether conditionality will ensure that these policies are pursued. Indeed, conditionality may be inimicable to the commitment upon which implementation relies. If catalysis relies on conditionality it may be fundamentally flawed.

But conditionality may not be the only modality through which catalysis works. Route 2 is via liquidity. The multilaterals not only provide an adjustment input via conditionality but they also provide financial support. Financing by the multilaterals may fulfil a number of functions. First, it may improve the quality of their adjustment advice since they are now putting their money where their mouths are. Even if it does not improve the quality of conditionality, private markets may believe that it does and this will lead to positive catalysis. Second, where the problems encountered by countries turning to the multilaterals for assistance are of a liquidity type, the provision of finance may be seen as central in helping to resolve them. Thus private markets may be more prepared to lend to countries where they perceive the multilaterals as filling a large proportion of the financing gap. Of course the irony here is that the catalytic effect will then be stronger in precisely those cases where it is less needed.

Where the multilaterals provide large amounts of finance, it may also be the case that better designed adjustment strategies will be feasible which work more on the supply side of the economy and on the structural causes of balance of payments problems. To the extent that these allow adjustment with growth, private capital markets may be more attracted than they would be where adjustment relied on the compression of aggregate demand, which, especially where it hits investment, is likely to have a negative effect on economic growth at least in the short term.

How important this point is depends on what it is that private markets and bilateral aid donors are looking for. What are their objective functions, and how closely do these match those of the multilaterals? Analytically this raises a number of possibilities. If the IMF is more concerned about short-run stabilisation than about long-run economic growth, perhaps IMF conditionality will have a stronger impact on short-term capital flows than on long-term capital flows. If the World Bank is more growth and development oriented, its conditionality may be relatively more effective in catalysing long-term capital flows.

In the context of low-income countries, multilateral lending is likely a priori to have a stronger influence over bilateral aid flows than private capital flows because aid donors are not looking for a commercial rate of return and will have been involved in the design of the multilaterals' programmes. All this suggests that catalysis will only be properly understood at the appropriate level of disaggregation.

Finally, the moral hazard and bailout dimensions of multilateral lending call into question whether the theory of catalysis as conventionally presented has the correct sequencing. Instead of multilateral lending taking the lead, with private lending following it, the moral hazard hypothesis suggests that it is the perceived availability of multilateral lending, should the need arise, which encourages private markets to lend, and indeed overlend. Overlending by private capital markets then contributes to creating economic crises which in turn lead countries to turn to the IMF and World Bank. A catalytic effect is at work here, but it is an *ex ante* effect where private lending precedes and in a sense catalyses lending by the multilaterals.[9]

What emerges from this discussion of the analytics of catalysis? The basic message is that there is no clear a priori causal connection between multilateral lending in the context of IMF and World Bank programmes and financial flows from other sources. The catalytic effect is essentially an empirical issue. So it is to the empirical evidence that we now turn.

Existing empirical evidence

Although it is difficult to identify exactly when the catalytic effect was first described, its widespread currency was clearly facilitated by numerous anecdotal accounts of (primarily) IMF agreements being followed by fresh capital inflows, (de Vries, 1986; Kenen, 1986; McCauley, 1986; Buira, 1987; Pool and Stamos, 1987). The 'gatekeeper' role of the IMF was subsequently formalised in institutional settings such as the Paris Club (Milivojevic, 1985). The catalytic effect, however, cannot be proved definitively on the basis of these anecdotal observations since there was no way of testing the counterfactual. More systematic evidence is required.

Most of the existing systematic empirical evidence on the catalytic effect has been coincidental to work that has had a different focus. Attempts to estimate the demand function for IMF credit and to explain the economic characteristics of user and non-user countries have, for example, often included a variable designed to capture the significance of alternative (usually private) sources of finance (Bird and Orme, 1981; Cornelius, 1987; Joyce, 1992; Bird, 1994, 1995). The results of such studies have generally suggested the absence of any significant relationship, or at best only a weak relationship which is as likely to be negative as positive. A negative coefficient implies that IMF lending and private lending are substitutes, rather than the complements that the catalytic effect predicts.

With a focus on aspects of external debt, other research has also raised doubts about the complementarity hypothesis. Hajivassiliou (1987) examines the pattern of debt servicing problems in least developed countries (LDCs) between 1970 and 1982. His results reveal a significant negative relationship between IMF involvement and the supply of new loans, and with the level of arrears accepted by existing creditors. Unfortunately the model is not designed specifically to test the catalytic effect, and the results may be biased by the use of IMF agreements as part of a proxy for debt servicing problems. The absence of complementarily between IMF involvement and other forms of new lending, however, provides no support for the catalytic effect.

In a study of the impact of structural adjustment under the sponsorship of the IMF and the World Bank over the period 1982–86, Faini *et al.* (1991) also find a significant negative correlation between multilateral lending and net private credit. A similar result is discovered by Killick (1995), who finds that IMF agreements are generally associated with a net deterioration in the capital account of the balance of payments of the countries involved, with loans from the Fund in effect being used to pay off previous commercial loans rather than encourage new ones.[10]

The need to distinguish between the effects on private and public flows is highlighted by Rowlands (1994) who, on the basis of aggregate econometric investigation, discovers a catalytic effect of Fund lending on other public flows but not on private flows. Rowlands also shows that the catalytic effect, to the extent that it exists, is time variant.

Further evidence against the idea of a catalytic effect of IMF lending on private capital flows comes from Ozler (1993) who sets out to explain the determinants of interest rate spreads on commercial loans to developing countries over 1968 to 1981. He finds that countries that had had IMF standby agreements seem to have been charged higher interest rates than those that had not, suggesting that IMF involvement is taken to indicate higher risks and providing no support for a positive impact on credibility.

Most of the studies cited have concentrated on the IMF, where the claims for a catalytic effect have been strongest. Research that has examined the effects of World Bank structural adjustment lending has also discovered a generally neutral effect on private flows (Mosley *et al.*, 1991), or a negative correlation (Faini *et al.*, 1991). Thus the overall assessment must be that neither of the key multilaterals have been shown to have a particularly strong catalytic effect on lending.

As noted in the 'Introduction', the two most focused published studies on the catalytic effect to date are Rodrik (1996), and Bird and Rowlands (1997). Rodrik finds that multilateral lending is negatively but not significantly associated with future period private capital flows. He also notes a 'sharp dichotomy' between the IMF and other multilaterals. Thus, while other multilaterals have a negative effect on subsequent private flows, particularly bank lending, the IMF's catalytic effect appears to be positive. Bird and Rowlands (1997) search for a catalytic effect disaggregating the data in various ways. Although they find limited evidence for IMF catalysis on public flows, they conclude that their 'estimations do not generally support the notion of a positive catalytic effect'.

However, the limited scope of these studies counsels caution over their results. In what follows, a more rounded view of the empirical evidence is presented not only by running some new regressions but also by systematically examining the case study evidence and by seeking qualitatively the views of those involved in moving money around the world.

However there is another way in which existing empirical evidence may be used. With the surge of private capital flows to Latin America and Asia in the early part of the 1990s a number of studies were undertaken with a view to better understand why these capital movements occurred. Again this is not the place to offer a detailed review of this research, but one aspect of it is important in the context of the catalytic effect. The research conventionally distinguishes between pull and push factors. Pull factors include aspects of domestic economic policy and performance while push factors include changes in world interest rates and economic activity. Although the details of the results vary across studies a fairly consistent theme is the significance of push factors which lie outside the control of capital importing developing countries. In many cases changes in US interest rates were found to be the single most dominant factor in causing capital movements.[11]

Where does IMF and World Bank conditionality fit in? In principle, conditionality could influence pull factors. But in practice, and for reasons discussed in the previous section, conditionality is unlikely to have exerted a significant impact on them. The important factor here is the government's commitment to a programme of solid macroeconomic and microeconomic policies. Over the years the multilaterals have almost certainly had an impact over the choice of policy via their continuing dialogue with countries, but this is not captured by the conditionality contained in specific agreements. The conclusion follows that IMF and World Bank conditionality probably plays an insignificant role in influencing pull factors that in any case may be dominated by push factors that lie outside the influence of the multilaterals. The mere observation that there have been periods of feast and famine in terms of private capital flows to Latin America while the Fund's presence has been much more enduring suggests that capital flows are largely determined by other factors. This implies at best a *de minimus* role for the catalytic effect. But what about the qualitative evidence?

Qualitative evidence

What do money managers say about the relevance of the IMF and the World Bank to them in making their decisions? On the basis of a questionnaire we interviewed bankers, fund managers (including hedge funds, and pension and mutual funds), and credit-rating agencies and aid agencies.[12] First, and without exception, they claimed that their decisions are 'influenced' by the involvement of the IMF and the World Bank in individual countries. For the most part the influence is linked to adjustment programmes negotiated with the multilaterals, although other aspects of involvement in terms of policy dialogue or meeting standards of data dissemination may also be seen as relevant. Although some respondents claimed to distinguish between the nature of IMF and World Bank lending, this does not appear to involve discriminating between different IMF lending windows or even between the various arms of the World Bank. Closer investigation suggests that where a distinction is made, it relates to the sectors or projects in which the World Bank is involved.

With little exception, signing an agreement with the Fund or the Bank is claimed to make a country more attractive than it would otherwise have been, which provides some evidence against negative catalysis. IMF agreements are without exception seen as more important than World Bank structural adjustment lending. Interestingly, however, it is the level of financing involved that is seen as more significant than the precise nature of conditionality. This calls into question the often made assumption that catalysis works primarily through the modality of conditionality. However it did also come over in interviews that the importance of conditionality relative to liquidity depends on the nature of the loan or investment. For short-term financial flows the liquidity aspect of the agreement dominates more than it does in the case of longer-term capital movements. In no case, however, was the conditionality component seen as more important than the liquidity component. A strong message was that money managers form their own views about a country's policies, performance, and prospects, and that this might not always tally with that of the Fund or the Bank, in which case managers tend to back their own judgement.

At the same time, it was always maintained that the implementation of conditionality is monitored, albeit usually by press reports, and that the degree of implementation is interpreted as being important. If this is the case, the low completion rate of programmes serves to undermine the Fund's potential catalysing role.

There were mixed views as to whether Fund and Bank involvement had been perceived as increasingly important. Where the claim was made that it had, this was usually explained in the context of the incidence of specific crises rather than any systemic change. The involvement of the multilaterals is seen as more important in a bear market.

In no case, however, did the involvement of either the Fund or the Bank feature directly as one of the principal five determinants of lending and investment decisions. What factors are important depend on whether you talk to hedge fund managers or pension and mutual fund managers. But amongst the factors listed were, the prospects for economic growth, the degree of industrial diversification, the quality of infrastructure, the size and quality of domestic financial markets, and the degree of political stability. Credit-rating agencies appear to prioritise the short-run liquidity position and then move onto solvency indicators such as indebtedness before moving on to the quality of macroeconomic policy, the structural reform agenda, and political stability. A broad observation is that in undertaking country risk analysis the involvement of the Fund and the Bank is not generally taken into account in any formal way. Individual countries are treated *sui generis*, although the importance put on Fund and Bank involvement depends on whether a country is in a crisis phase. Certainly IMF and World Bank programmes do not confer an automatic seal of approval as the most extreme presentations of the catalytic effect claim.

But do things differ for bilateral aid donors? Fund agreements are seen as providing certain 'assurances' about macroeconomic policy and are claimed to be more important than Bank agreements in the context of short-term aid flows, although donors still make their own independent assessments. The crucial difference here is that donors will be involved in designing IMF and World Bank programmes both 'on the ground' and via their Executive Directors in Washington. The influence of individual aid donors in this respect has a regional dimension with, for example, the United Kingdom having a stronger influence over policy design in Africa than in Latin America or Asia. However, the general point is that bilateral aid and assistance from the multilaterals comes as a package, with IMF programmes only 'standing up' if accompanied by bilateral aid.

Aid donors claim to have received the 'big message' from recent research on aid effectiveness that aid works best when accompanied by the 'right' policy environment, and in this respect IMF endorsement is important, even though aid donors will look beyond this to issues of governance and social sector policies. There appears to be less recognition that the same research is rather ambiguous on the role of conditionality in bringing this environment about with some researchers claiming that it has fulfilled a more important function than others.[13] Aid donors do observe, however, that the Fund can provide assurances outside formal agreements and that these can influence their decisions. Moreover, bilateral aid does still go to countries with no current IMF agreement.

Neither the IMF nor the World Bank is taken as providing any guarantee on political stability and donors form their own views about this, although in some cases individual countries will be given the 'benefit of the doubt' on governance issues once a Fund agreement has been signed.

IMF agreements certainly appear to be seen as more significant than the World Bank's policy-based lending, which plays only a supporting role. Where the World Bank does become more important is in terms of its project lending, where it influences the sectoral composition of longer-term bilateral aid flows.

As in the case of private flows, there is no simple and universal model of catalysis which links IMF and World Bank policy-based lending to bilateral aid flows. On balance the multilaterals appear to be more important in the case of bilateral aid flows than in the case of private capital flows since the objective functions of bilateral aid donors may be closer to the objective functions of the multilaterals. However, the very fact that donor governments choose to direct some of their foreign aid through bilateral channels confirms that there will be other, probably country-specific, political factors influencing bilateral aid. Bilateral aid should not therefore be expected to perfectly match multilateral lending.

Nevertheless, a fundamental fact is that the modality through which catalysis occurs differs significantly as between public and private capital flows, since aid donors unlike private creditors will be directly involved in putting together IMF and World Bank programmes. Apart from anything else, this means that to the extent that IMF and World Bank lending is political, similar politics may also influence bilateral aid flows. It may be anticipated therefore that there will be a closer association between lending by the multilaterals and other public capital flows than there is with private capital flows.

Quantitative evidence

As noted earlier, much of the evidence on catalysis has emerged from anecdotal accounts of individual cases, as an indirect implication of studies designed for other purposes, or from larger sample studies that do not control for the economic circumstances of countries belonging to the Bretton Woods institutions. In order to address these deficiencies, our research has placed considerable emphasis on constructing a sufficiently extensive data set to allow for a large-sample analysis of the catalytic effect. While several models have been examined for both the IMF and the World Bank, the results reported here use an unbalanced panel of approximately ninety-six developing countries from the early 1980s to 1995. The sample size was restricted largely by the availability of data.

The activities of the Fund and the Bank were examined in terms of their effects on different types of capital flow. The different categories of flows included three private channels – foreign direct investment, portfolio flows, and government or government guaranteed debt (commercial bank, bond or other) – and bilateral official flows in the form of either grants or debt. These flows are presumably driven by different motivations, with private flows being assumed to be more concerned with commercial rates of return than bilateral flows. Furthermore, foreign direct investment may be expected to be more closely related to long-term economic performance than are, say, portfolio flows. By exploiting these differences, it was hoped that further insight into the catalytic effect could be gained.

The activities of the Fund and Bank were also differentiated to isolate the potential sources of catalysis. Thus lending instruments were differentiated on the basis of the degree of conditionality, and estimations were carried out using indicators of activity as well as levels of associated financing. In this way liquidity effects were separated from the influence of conditionality.

The estimation models performed quite well in terms of conforming to prior expectations about the effects of different economic characteristics.[14] On the one hand, commercially motivated capital flows did indeed seem to be affected positively by good economic events, and vice versa. The behaviour of official bilateral flows, on the other hand, was consistent with more altruistic motivations. While the details of these estimations are presented in Bird and Rowlands (1997, 1999a,b) the basic conclusion is that it is important to control for economic characteristics in any examination of the catalytic effect.

In terms of the catalytic effect itself, a nuanced story emerges. Specific results are provided for IMF programmes in Table 11.1, and for World Bank programmes in Tables 11.2 and 11.3. As a general conclusion, however, it seems that the empirical estimations cast considerable doubt on the proposition that IMF or World Bank conditionality transmits a positive signal to private capital markets. Private sources tend to react negatively, if at all, to these arrangements, and the negative reaction tends to be more pronounced for the higher conditionality agreements. Finally, there is no evidence to suggest that these private sources have begun to react more favourably in recent years, at least to IMF arrangements.

Table 11.1 Results of fixed-effects regressions using IMF programmes

Variable	Dependent variable = Portfolio flows/GDP	Dependent variable = Net FDI/GDP	Dependent variable = Net private debt/GDP	Dependent variable = Net official flows/GDP
Explanatory variables				
SBA_{t-1}	−0.00039 (−0.91)	−0.00032 (−0.28)	−0.00462*** (−3.27)	−0.01204 (−0.92)
EFF_{t-1}	0.00068 (0.42)	0.00029 (0.09)	−0.00714* (−1.87)	−0.01286 (−0.72)
$ESAF_{t-1}$	−0.00068 (−1.01)	0.0036 (1.21)	−0.00443* (−1.83)	0.00825 (0.17)
SAF_{t-1}	−0.00037 (−0.82)	0.00011 (0.02)	0.00051 (0.033)	0.01698 (0.74)
Observations	1,008	1,008	1,008	1,008
R^2	0.182	0.489	0.171	0.802
Adjusted R^2	0.079	0.425	0.068	0.777

SBA, EFF, ESAF and SAF refer respectively to dummy indicators for the presence of Stand-by arrangements, Extended Fund Facility, Enhanced Structural Adjustment Facility, and Structural Adjustment Facility, all lagged by one year. The t-statistics appear in parentheses. Coefficients identified with ***, **, and * are significant at the 1%, 5%, and 10% two-tailed test level of significance respectively. The equations are estimated using a fixed-effects model with heteroscedastic-consistent estimates and a simple correction for first-order autocorrelation. Only the results for the IMF variables are presented: the full estimating equation is similar to that provided in Bird and Rowlands (1999a).

Table 11.2 Results of fixed-effects regressions using World Bank indicators

Variable	Dependent variable = Portfolio flows/GDP	Dependent variable = Net FDI/GDP	Dependent variable = Net private debt/GDP	Dependent variable = Net official flows/GDP
Explanatory variables				
SAL_{t-1}	−1,120.0 (−1.26)	−917.8 (−0.84)	−2,427.7* (−1.82)	2,921.1 (0.14)
SAL_{t-2}	87.35 (0.18)	1,133.7 (0.93)	−1,326.0 (−1.04)	8,645.9 (0.46)
$SECAL_{t-1}$	−1,932.0 (−1.49)	3,965.7 (0.29)	1,831.1 (1.48)	15,648 (1.07)
$SECAL_{t-2}$	248.9 (0.51)	−3,314.6** (−2.32)	−2,017.2 (−1.53)	−4,322.6 (−0.35)
$WBPROJECT_{t-1}$	−290.1 (−0.66)	−1,497.1 (−0.66)	5,398.1** (2.28)	6,878.0 (0.18)
Observations	935	935	935	935
R^2	0.19	0.54	0.18	0.76
Adjusted R^2	0.09	0.48	0.07	0.73

SAL, SECAL and WBPROJECT refer respectively to dummy indicators for the presence of World Bank Structural Adjustment Loans, Sectoral Adjustment Loans, and IBRD or IDA project lending. Lags are indicated in the subscripts. The *t*-statistics appears in parentheses. Coefficients identified with ***, **, and * are significant at the 1%, 5%, and 10% two-tailed test level of significance respectively. The equations are estimated using a fixed-effects model with heteroscedastic-consistent estimates and a simple correction for first-order autocorrelation. Only the results for the Bank variables are presented: the full estimating equation is similar to that provided in Bird and Rowlands (1999b).

Table 11.3 Results of fixed-effects estimations using World Bank financing levels

Variable	Dependent variable = Portfolio flows / GDP	Dependent variable = Net FDI / GDP	Dependent variable = Net private debt / GDP	Dependent variable = Net official flows / GDP
Explanatory variables				
SAL_{t-1}	−0.0220 (−1.04)	−0.0273 (−0.46)	−0.0729* (−1.73)	0.499 (0.37)
SAL_{t-2}	−0.0142 (−1.02)	0.0125 (0.31)	−0.1038*** (−3.43)	0.708 (0.91)
$SECAL_{t-1}$	−0.0347 (−1.12)	0.0711 (0.72)	0.0181 (0.42)	−0.192 (−0.22)
$SECAL_{t-2}$	−0.00371 (−0.36)	−0.0214 (−1.56)	−0.0654 (−1.22)	−1.239 (−1.58)
$WBPROJECT_{t-1}$	0.0331 (1.09)	−0.0303 (−0.24)	0.00551 (0.09)	3.404*** (2.63)
Observations	935	935	935	935
R^2	0.19	0.54	0.17	0.80
Adjusted R^2	0.08	0.49	0.07	0.77

SAL and SECAL refer respectively to the amounts of financing agreed to in World Bank Structural Adjustment Loans, Sectoral Adjustment Loans, while WBPROJECT refers to the amount of disbursements of IBRD or IDA project lending. See Table 11.2 above for other relevant notes.

More specifically, while portfolio and FDI flows seem unaffected by any IMF activity, there is reasonably strong evidence to suggest that private debt flows react adversely to high conditionality IMF programmes. The reaction of private creditors to World Bank activity was also subdued. Conditional programmes have either no effect or a negative effect on these flows. The only positive reaction appears to accompany Bank project loans. Thus, viewed as a whole, the evidence from the large sample investigation casts considerable doubt on the proposition that conditionality is an important modality of positive catalysis. What emerges instead are reasonable grounds for presuming that Fund and Bank conditional programmes are not perceived by markets as enchancing the commercial prospects for recipient countries.

The only evidence of positive catalysis that emerges from these estimations is in the case of official bilateral sources of finance. Even in this case, however, the effect is generally weak and the significance of the results is not robust. In some formulations of the estimating equation official flows are associated positively with Fund agreements, especially Structural Adjustment Facility (SAF) programmes, but longer-term Extended Fund Facility (EFF) and Enhanced Structural Adjustment Facility (ESAF) arrangements as well. When corrected for cross-country heterogeneity and simple autocorrelation – both problems being evident from diagnostic tests – the statistical association becomes insignificant. A similar characterisation seems appropriate for World Bank catalysis, though in this case the positive association between project lending and official bilateral flows remains robust in the face of corrections to the estimating procedure.

In conclusion, the large sample empirical evidence suggests that the catalytic effect of the IMF and World Bank is generally insignificant or negative for commercial flows, and that conditionality does not have the expected positive role suggested by some of the earlier literature. If anything, high conditionality programmes have a more adverse effect on commercial finance than other Bank and Fund activity. Only Bank project financing appears to have any positive influence on commercial flows, though the effect is neither strong nor robust. The strongest evidence of positive catalysis is with official bilateral flows, though again this effect appears inversely related to the degree of conditionality.

Case study evidence

It may be that cross-country regression analysis obscures a catalytic effect that would be revealed by closer examination of individual case studies and episodes. To allow for this we selected eighteen countries to look at in some detail. These covered various regional locations and per capita income levels. Our approach was to build on and extend existing case study work which has focused more broadly on the effects of IMF and World Bank programmes (Killick, 1995, 1998). To do this we undertook an extensive and systematic electronic literature search in order to double check that the conclusions drawn in these earlier studies were sound and that important pieces of evidence had not been omitted. Initially we did this for the period covered by the studies themselves, but then updated our search as far as possible. We also collected our own data to see whether these were consistent with the conclusions that came out of the systematic review.[15]

In fact our case study evidence strongly confirms the findings of the qualitative and econometric research reported earlier. What general messages emerge from the case studies? These may be summarised in terms of the following working hypotheses:

(i)   involvement by the multilaterals will not guarantee an inflow of capital from other sources;

(ii) what really matters is the perceived commitment by a government to a policy agenda that is seen as sound and internally consistent;

(iii) catalysis associated with the multilaterals is likely to be stronger and more positive in the case of bilateral aid flows; and

(iv) the nature and extent of catalysis may differ as between the Fund and the Bank.

Experience drawn from almost every one of our case studies confirmed hypotheses (i) and (ii). It was only perhaps in Russia that an IMF-backed programme in 1996 seemed to induce positive catalysis in spite of a perceived lack of commitment by the government. Here the signal seemed to be that Russia would not be allowed to fail. In other countries the involvement of the multilaterals seemed to be largely irrelevant in determining capital flows. Argentina established a reputation for commitment to policy reform under its Convertibility Plan in conjunction with the IMF, while Chile and Malaysia (and for a time other countries in East Asia) achieved a strong reputation largely outside the auspices of the multilaterals, by in fact pursuing capital account policies of which the multilaterals did not approve. The apparent failure of the early IMF-backed programmes in the context of the East Asian crisis had much to do with the perceived lack of commitment by the governments in Thailand, South Korea, and Indonesia to the design of the programmes at that time. Similarly, the markets perceived the Fund's analysis of the Brazilian economy in the aftermath of the Real Crisis as being overoptimistic, with the government's failure to implement all the agreed fiscal measures calling into question the credibility of the adjustment programme. Previously it had been the government's perceived commitment to the Plan, and not involvement by the multilaterals that impressed capital markets. Similar examples may be drawn from Mexico, Turkey, Bulgaria, Ghana, Kenya, Zambia, and Tanzania.

Experience in Africa is particularly relevant in the context of hypothesis (iii), where the case study evidence lends some support. Bilateral and multilateral aid are frequently interconnected with aid donors also providing an input into the design of programmes. However, the relationship is not always straightforward and where it does exist it is more in the nature of coordination than catalysis. In Ghana bilateral aid seems to have reflected a desire by donors to provide support, and it continued to increase during times when support from the multilaterals was being interrupted. In Zambia there was the opposite scenario with bilateral donors reducing aid at the same time as the multilaterals continued to lend since Zambia was perceived to be meeting conditionality requirements. In Kenya the relationship between bilateral aid and multilateral lending was closer although it was not a catalytic one but one of mutuality. While Tanzania provides some support for a catalytic effect again what really seems to mater is the government's perceived commitment to reform.

The case study evidence is less clear with respect to hypothesis (iv), although it does appear that to the extent that there was a negative catalytic effect in the case of the East Asian crisis in 1997/98 this may be attributed to the design of the related IMF programmes.

It transpires that our case study evidence is, in large measure, consistent with both our qualitative and econometric evidence, as well as the case study research that has previously been undertaken, where, little, if any, evidence for a catalytic effect is discovered (Mosley *et al.*, 1991; Killick, 1995, 1998). In general, markets, and to a lesser extent bilateral aid donors, will want to form their own views about the quality of and commitment to economic policy reform. On its own IMF or World Bank conditionality is insufficient (or even unnecessary) to generate a positive catalytic effect.

Strengthening the catalysing role of the IMF and the World Bank

The first question is whether we should be seeking to strengthen the catalytic effect at all. Should the multilaterals always be encouraging private capital markets and aid donors to lend more? The East Asian crisis demonstrates how problems may be caused by excessive lending as well as by deficient lending. The multilaterals should therefore form a view at to the appropriate combination of economic adjustment and external financing and endeavour to ensure that this optimum quantity of financing is supplied (but not surpassed). How can they do this?

There are four channels through which the multilaterals may seek to exert a catalytic effect; leaving to one side the project-lending activities of the Bank which lie outside the scope of this chapter. The first channel is via the conditionality associated with policy-based lending. As noted earlier this has often been super-ficially taken to be the route through which catalysis already occurs. However deeper analysis combined with empirical evidence of various sorts suggests otherwise. But to say that conditionality has not had a catalytic effect in the past is not to say that it could not in the future. There is scope for catalysis via condi-tionality. The trick is to make conditionality more effective by working to improve both its design and its implementation. This implies taking a serious look at the range of proposals that there are for reforming conditionality rather than assum-ing that catalysis will be strengthened simply by more of the same sort of condi-tionality that there has been in the past. The key here seems to be in enhancing conditionality as a modality for encouraging economic reform by increasing the degree of ownership that governments feel. There is a good deal of evidence to support the idea that conditionality has worked better when it is combined with strong country ownership. If private markets and aid donors are able to sense the degree of government commitment to conditionality this also helps to explain why conditionality may appear to have an uneven catalytic effect. Implementation could also be strengthened by applying stricter penalties to non-completion via impaired access to future multilateral lending. In these circumstances private markets would have greater confidence in both the design of conditionality and its implementation and would be more prepared to interpret it as a lead indicator of future economic improvement.[16]

Yet it may also be appropriate that countries be allowed within the context of conditionality to manage capital inflows via various forms of taxation. In the long run the better management of capital inflows could enhance a country's creditworthiness and the durability of its access to private capital markets.[17]

The design and implementation of conditionality also depends on the amount of finance provided by the multilaterals; there is some evidence to suggest that the success of IMF programmes is an increasing function of the amount of finance that is provided (Killick, 1995). A message which comes strongly out of the qualitative research reported in this chapter is that liquidity is an important factor in catalysis, and it is liquidity that represents the second channel through which the multilaterals can have a catalytic effect.[18] While it is widely accepted that the multilaterals themselves need to lend in order to encourage others to do the same, it may be that in the past the lending capacity of the IMF and the Bank has been too low to inspire the confidence in country performance upon which catalysis relies. In this sense there may be a complementarity between lending by the multilaterals and lending by private markets. To some extent this has been recognised by the multilaterals since during the Asian crisis and its aftermath various devices were introduced, such as the Supplemental Reserve Facility, to allow countries to significantly exceed their conventional quota limits on borrowing from the IMF.

At the same time some early attempts to quantify the resource needs of the IMF suggested that even with ongoing quota reviews the Fund could often require substantial additional resources (Williamson, 1983; Bird, 1987). And although there have been periods when the Fund has had significant spare lending capacity there have also been times, particularly during the mid-1990s when its liquidity ratio has fallen to very low levels.

One way of providing these additional resources would be for the Fund to borrow directly from private capital markets in order to supplement the subscriptions it receives.[19] In this way the Fund would become more of a pure international financial intermediary. This could represent a more effective and efficient means of channeling private capital to developing countries. Certainly it would by-pass the need for catalysis. To the extent that the Fund believed that private markets would underlend in the aftermath of a Fund-backed agreement, and further believed that this would endanger the success of the related adjustment programme, direct borrowing from private capital markets would be a way of circumventing such problems. However this proposal is likely to be controversial.

The third channel of catalysis is less controversial. One problem associated with lending by private markets to developing countries and CITs relates to inadequacies of information. The multilaterals have a comparative advantage in data collection and dissemination. Superior information should, other things being equal, lead to superior lending decisions. In terms of private capital flows this may, of course, mean smaller capital flows in some cases where markets would otherwise have been excessively exuberant, as well as larger flows in other cases where markets would have been excessively pessimistic. Markets already take into account whether countries comply with the data dissemination standards of the IMF, and this has an impact on perceived country risk and therefore capital flows. Widening the range of relevant data disseminated, and understanding better what it means for future economic performance will have implications for catalysis.

Finally, co-ordination of creditors in conditions of crisis will have consequences for catalysis. Evidence suggests that the Fund's catalytic effect on private capital flows was perhaps at its strongest following the Third World debt crisis in 1982. This was because the Fund coerced commercial banks to lend and made its own involvement conditional on the banks continuing to lend. For various reasons, not least the wider array of creditors involved, coercion does not represent a long-term option. However in the immediate aftermath of currency crises the Fund could play a more significant role in coordinating creditors and in discouraging them from withdrawing capital simply in an attempt to get out ahead of the pack. The details of how such coordination might work (and the related problems) have been discussed in some detail by Eichengreen (1999). Via the coordination of creditors the Fund could seek to minimise the chances of its involvement having a negative catalytic effect in the context of currency crises.

Apart from these broad channels through which the multilaterals could strengthen their catalysing role, another feature of the research reported here is that catalysis needs to be analysed at a relatively high level of disaggregation. While, for example, IMF conditionality may be more important in catalysing short-term capital flows, the World Bank may have a more important catalysing role in the context of foreign direct investment. In order to maximise the effect of the multilaterals on other capital flows it is necessary to understand the details of their respective comparative advantages. However, to do this, it is also necessary to gain a better understanding of why capital moves in the way that it does. At present there is no clear cut theory of capital movements which allows us to see where the involvement of the Fund and the Bank fits in.

Concluding remarks

The catalytic effect of lending by the IMF and World Bank is important in the context of the debate surrounding the new international financial architecture. One model might envisage almost perfect catalysis. This would present the Fund as an exclusively adjustment-oriented agency not making its own loans. Here, the endorsement of the Fund would be sufficient to encourage private markets to lend. The Fund would be a genuine gatekeeper and the Fund's seal of approval would have a very high market value. Although this model is not so far removed from the 'commonly held view' reported in the introduction, it is a long way from the reality revealed by our research. The adjustment input of the Fund via the modality of conditionality just does not work in this way. Nor does World Bank conditionality perform any better.

At the other extreme a second model would have the multilaterals providing their own direct lending to fill the financing gaps encountered by developing countries and countries in transition. Here the multilaterals would not rely on there being any catalytic effect. Indeed if there were to be such an effect there would be a danger of overlending and of suboptimal adjustment which would make economic crises of one sort or another more likely. Two things are wrong with this model. First, both the quantitative and qualitative evidence shows that the IMF and the World Bank are – albeit to a limited extent – relevant in the decisions made by private markets and aid donors. Second, and more importantly political economy considerations rule out the expansion in IMF and World Bank resources via conventional means that would be necessary for them to take on this financing role.

A third model is the most relevant. This recognises the potential for the IMF and the World Bank to influence other capital flows. However, it also recognises that catalysis is complex and nuanced and that the potential for catalysis has remained largely untapped. At the very least a clear distinction needs to be made between private and bilateral public flows. In order to extract the full potential for catalysis the multilaterals will need to undergo fairly fundamental reform, covering the design and general *modus operandi* of their conditionality and the size of their resource base. The former needs to focus on improving the success rate of the multilaterals' conditionality, which in turn implies measures to strengthen ownership. With regards to the latter, there is scope for the Fund to take on a larger role as a financial intermediary, borrowing directly from private capital markets rather than relying on the vagaries of catalysis. There also needs to be closer co-ordination between the multilaterals and the private markets, particularly in the immediate aftermath of crises.

While only one part of the architecture debate, the issue of how best the multilaterals can mobilise other sources of external finance is important. The danger is that commonly held views that are in fact at odds with reality will result in inappropriate reform.

Acknowledgements

Financial support for the research upon which this chapter is based was provided by the UK Department for International Development. While gratefully acknowledging this support, the views and opinions expressed are those of the authors alone. Research assistance has been provided by Connie Tulus, Helgi Maki, and Antonella Mori.

Notes

1 This point is examined in more detail in Bird (1997).
2 Evidence on the completion rates of Fund programmes is presented in Killick (1995) with Bird and Rowlands (1999a) providing updated information. Killick finds evidence

to suggest that the 'success' of Fund programmes is positively linked to the amount of finance that is provided.

3 These papers also contain more extensive references, which have been kept to a minimum here, and are only used where directly relevant to a point that is being made in the text.

4 Indeed discussion of IMF and to a lesser extent World Bank conditionality has been something of a growth industry. Early contributions to the literature included Williamson (1983) and Killick *et al.* (1984). Other important and frequently cited papers include Edwards (1989) and Khan (1990). More recent studies include Conway (1994), Killick (1995) and ul Haque and Khan (1998). More generally IMF conditionality has often been linked to discussions of IMF lending (Bird, 1995). Mosley *et al.* (1991) still represents the most thorough investigation into the World Bank's policy-based lending.

5 Bird (1999) explores this issue in the context of discussing the meaning and relevance of 'sound' economic policy. Similar arguments are put forward by Rodrik (1999).

6 The incompatibilities between the various functions that conditionality is seeking to achieve are explored in detail in Collier *et al.* (1997). The question of implementation and its links with conditionality are explored in Killick (1998) and Bird (1998).

7 Reference can again be made to the works cited in endnote 5. ul Haque and Khan (1998) provide what is probably the most sanguine view of the effects of IMF programmes.

8 Many studies have identified these recidivist tendencies, e.g. Bird (1995), Killick (1995), and Conway (1994). There has, however, generally been little analysis of recidivism. For an attempt to provide just such an analysis, see Bird *et al.* (1999a).

9 At the same moment as the multilaterals are becoming involved private capital may be attempting to exit, implying negative contemporary catalysis. According to the moral hazard argument, however, it has been the expectation of future multilateral involvement that has positively catalysed previous period private flows. Rodrik (1996) reports some evidence to support this bail-out story.

10 Of course care needs to be exercised in interpreting these results. Conventional balance of payments accounting tells us that, with no changes in reserves, an 'improvement' in the current account of the balance of payments will be matched by an equivalent 'deterioration' in the capital account. Surely then IMF programmes that are successful in strengthening the current account must as a matter of accounting weaken the capital account? Of course in the midst of a current account balance of payments crisis, countries will almost certainly have experienced reserve losses which they will be anxious to make good, and in these circumstances current and capital account disequilibria will not sum to zero. Moreover governments will be anxious to make themselves more creditworthy as a consequence of agreeing to an IMF or World Bank programme, and in this context total capital inflows are not the relevant variable.

11 This research is summarised in Bird (1999). Illustrative examples include Calvo *et al.* (1993), Chuhan *et al.* (1993), Claessens *et al.* (1995), Fernandez-Arias (1996), Fernandez and Montiel (1996), and Taylor and Sarno (1997).

12 Copies of the questionnaire can be provided by the authors upon request. In total about fifteen interviews were conducted.

13 Thus while Burnside and Dollar (1997) attribute at best a very modest role to the conditionality of the multilaterals, Mosley and Hudson (1997) claim that increasing aid effectiveness is linked to improved dialogue with the World Bank as well as conditionality.

14 The results presented in Tables 11.1–11.3 are minor variants of the estimating equations in Bird and Rowlands (1999a,b). These papers have a more comprehensive discussion of the estimations, and report the complete results. It shoul be noted that while the results reported here are for equations using only lagged versions of the IMF or Bank variables, these are generally consistent with equations that used both lagged and unlagged variables. The latter are excluded to avoid contemporaneity and the resulting complications for interpreting causality.

15 The case study evidence upon which this section draws is much more fully reported and discussed in Bird *et al.* (1999b).
16 For a much fuller discussion of reform proposals along these lines see Killick (1995, 1998), Bird (1995, 1996), and Collier *et al.* (1997).
17 As the IMF has sought to extend conditionality to include the capital account of the balance of payments a great deal of interest has been shown in Chile which has set out to manage capital flows. For an essentially positive assessment of Chilean policies see, e.g. Eichengreen (1999). There is perhaps a growing consensus that developing countries should not rush to liberalise their capital accounts, certainly not in advance of domestic financial liberalisation and the introduction of an adequate prudential and regulatory framework.
18 The quantitative support for this qualitative view is, however, not strong.
19 This idea has been around for sometime but has received closer attention recently in the light of the Fund's liquidity shortage (Lerrick, 1999). The standard ripostes to this proposal are that first it is inconsistent with the basic nature of the Fund as a club of members, second, it is not something that central banks do, and third, it might crowd out other borrowers such as the World Bank and the developing countries themselves, (see IMF Survey, June, 21, 1999). Less often voiced is the argument that private borrowing could loosen the short leash by which the Fund's major shareholders may seek to constrain its activities. These criticisms are themselves open to criticism. Clubs borrow from time to time. The Fund is not a central bank and cannot easily create its own resources. There is little reason to believe that Fund borrowing would crowd out other borrowers. Indeed expanded Fund lending financed by borrowing from markets could crowd in additional flows if it resulted in superior programmes. Moreover if the Fund were only to borrow when the demand for its resources was high this would almost certainly be at a time when private capital markets were less prepared to lend to developing countries directly.

References

Bird, G. (1987), *International Financial Policy and Economic Development* (London, Macmillan).
Bird, G. (1994), 'The Myths and Realities of IMF Lending', *The World Economy*, 17, 759–78.
Bird, G. (1995), *IMF Lending to Developing Countries: Issues and Evidence* (London, Routledge).
Bird, G. (1996), 'The International Monetary Fund and Developing Countries: A Review of the Evidence and Policy Options', *International Organisation*, 50(3), Summer, 477–511.
Bird, G. (1997), 'External Financing and Balance of Payments Adjustment in Developing Countries: Getting a Better Policy Mix', *World Development*, 25(9), 1409–20.
Bird, G. (1998), 'IMF Conditionality and the Political Economy of Policy Reform: Is it Simply a Matter of Political Will?' *Journal of Policy Reform*, 1(1), 89–113.
Bird, G. (1999), 'How Important is Sound Domestic Macroeconomics in Attracting Capital Inflows to Developing Countries', *Journal of International Development*, 11(1), 1–26.
Bird, G. and T. Orme (1981), 'An Analysis of Drawings on the International Monetary Fund by Developing Countries', *World Development*, 9(6), 563–8.
Bird, G. and D. Rowlands (1997), 'The Catalytic Effect of Lending by the International Financial Institutions', *The World Economy*, 20(7), 967–91.
Bird, G. and D. Rowlands (1999a), 'Does IMF Conditionality Signal Policy Credibility to Markets', *Surrey Centre for International Economic Studies*, Working Paper Series 99/5.
Bird, G. and D. Rowlands (1999b), 'Does World Bank Policy Based Lending Catalyse Other Financial Flows?' *Surrey Centre for International Economic Studies*, Working Paper Series 99/4.

Bird, G., M. Hussain, and J. Joyce (1999a), 'Many Happy Returns: Recidivism and the IMF' (mimeograph).

Bird, G., A. Mori, and D. Rowlands (1999b), 'Do the Multilaterals Catalyse Other Capital Flows: What Does the Case Study Evidence Show?' *Surrey Centre for International Economic Studies*, Working Paper Series 99/2.

Buira, A. (1987), 'Adjustment with Growth and the Role of IMF in the 1980s', in S. Dell (ed.), *The International Monetary System and its Reform: Papers Prepared for the Group of Twenty-Four* (The Netherlands, Elsevier Science Publishers).

Burnside, C. and D.R. Dollar (1997), 'Aid, Policies and Growth', *World Bank Policy Research Working Paper*, No. 17777 (Washington, DC, World Bank).

Calvo, G.A., L. Leiderman, and C.M. Reinhart (1993), 'Capital Inflows and Real Exchange Rate Appreciation in Latin America: The Role of External Factors', *IMF Staff Papers*, 40(1), 108–51.

Chuhan, P., S. Claessens, and N. Mamingi (1993), 'Equity and Bond Flows to Asia and Latin America', *Policy Research Working Paper*, No. 1150 (Washington, DC, World Bank).

Claessens, S., M. Dooley, and A. Warner (1995), 'Portfolio Capital Flows: Hot or Cold'? *The World Bank Economic Review*, 9(1), 153–74.

Collier, P., P. Guillaumont, S. Guillaumont, and J.W. Gunning (1997), 'Redesigning Conditionality', *World Development*, 25(9), 1399–407.

Conway, P. (1994), 'IMF Lending Programs: Participation and Impact', *Journal of Development Economics*, 45(2), 365–91.

Cornelius, P. (1987), 'The Demand for IMF Credits by Sub-Saharan African Countries', *Economics Letters*, 23, 99–102.

de Vries, M. (1986), 'The Role of the International Monetary Fund in the World Debt Problem', in M. Claudon (ed.), *World Debt Crisis: International Lending on Trial* (Cambridge, MA, Ballinger Publishing Company), 111–22.

Dhonte, P. (1997), 'Conditionality as an Instrument of Borrower Credibility', IMF Paper on Policy Analysis and Assessment PPAA/97/2 (Washington, DC, IMF).

Dollar, D. and J. Svensson (1998), 'What Explains the Success or Failure of Structural Adjustment Programs?' *World Bank Policy Research Working Paper*, No. 1998 (Washington, DC, World Bank).

Edwards, S. (1989), 'The International Monetary Fund and the Developing Countries: A Critical Evaluation', *Carnegie Rochester Conference Series on Public Policy*, 31, 7–68.

Eichengreen, B. (1999), *Toward a New International Financial Architecture, Institute for International Economics*, Washington, DC.

Faini, R., J. deMelo, A. Senhadji-Semlali, and J. Stanton (1991), 'Macro Performance Under Adjustment Lending', in V. Thomas, A. Chhibber, M. Dailami, and J. deMelo, (eds), *Restructuring Economies in Distress. Policy Reform and the World Bank* (Washington, DC, World Bank), 222–42.

Fanelli, J.M., R. Frenkel, and L. Taylor (1994), 'Is the Market-Friendly Approach Friendly to Development: A Critical Review', in G. Bird and A. Helwege (eds), *Latin America's Economic Future* (London and San Diego, Academic Press).

Feldstein, M. (1998), 'Refocusing the IMF', *Foreign Affairs*, 77(2), 20–33.

Fernandez-Arias, E. (1996), 'The New Wave of Capital Inflows: Push or Pull?' *Journal of Development Economics*, 48(2), 389–418.

Fernandez-Arias, E. and P. Montiel (1996), 'The Surge of Capital Inflows to Developing Countries: An Analytical Overview', *The World Bank Economic Review*, 10(1), 51–77.

Hajivassiliou, V. (1987), 'The External Debt Repayment Problems of LDCs: An Econometric Model Based on Panel Data', *Journal of Econometrics*, 36(1/2) 205–30.

Joyce, J. (1992), 'The Economic Characteristics of IMF Program Countries', *Economics Letters*, 38(2), 237–42.

Kenen, P. (1986), *Financing, Adjustment and the International Monetary Fund* (Washington, DC, The Brookings Institution).

Khan, M.S. (1990), 'The Macroeconomic Effects of Fund-Supported Adjustment Programs', *IMF Staff Papers*, 37(2), 195–231.

Killick, T. (1995), *IMF Programmes in Developing Countries: Design and Impact* (London, Routledge/ODI).

Killick, T. (1998), *Aid and the Political Economy of Policy Change* (London, Routledge).

Killick, T., G. Bird, J. Sharpley, and M. Sutton (1984), *The Quest for Economic Stabilisation: The IMF and the Third World* (London: Overseas Development Institute).

Krueger, A. (1998), 'Whither the World Bank and the IMF?' *Journal of Economic Literature*, vol. XXXVI(4), 1983–2020.

Lerrick, A. (1999), *Private Sector Financing for the IMF: Now Part of an Optimal Funding Mix* (Washington, DC, Bretton Woods Committee, April).

McCauley, R. (1986), 'IMF: Managed Lending', in M. Claudon (ed.), *World Debt Crisis: International Lending on Trial* (Cambridge, MA, Ballinger Publishing Company), 123–46.

Milivojevic, M. (1985), *The Debt Rescheduling Process* (New York, St Martin's Press).

Mosley, P. and J. Hudson (1997), 'Has Aid Effectiveness Increased'? (mimeographed).

Mosley, P., J. Harrigan, and J. Toye (1991), *Aid and Power: The World Bank and Policy-Based Lending*, 2 Vols (London, Routledge).

Ozler, U. (1993), 'Have Commercial Banks Ignored History'? *American Economic Review*, 83(3), 608–20.

Pool, J.C. and S. Stamos (1987), *The ABCs of International Finance* (Lexington, MA, Lexington Books).

Radelet, S. and J. Sachs (1998), 'The East Asian Financial Crisis: Diagnosis, Remedies, Prospects', *Brookings Papers on Economic Activity*, 1, 1–75.

Rodrik, D. (1996), 'Why is There Multilateral Lending?', in Bruno M, Bleskovic B (eds), *Annual World Bank Conference on Development Economics* 1995, (Washington, DC, World Bank), 167–93.

Rodrik, D. (1999), 'Governing the Global Economy: Does One Architectural Style Fit All'? Paper prepared for the Brookings Institution Trade Policy Forum Conference on Governing in a Global Economy, April 15–16.

Rowlands, D. (1994), 'The Response of New Lending to the IMF', *The Norman Paterson School of International Affairs Development Studies Working Paper* 7, 1994.

Schadler, S., A. Bennett, M. Carkovic, L. Dicks-Mireaux, M. Mecagni, J.H.J. Morsink, and M.A. Savastano (1995), *IMF Conditionality: Experience Under Stand-By and Extended Arrangements: Part I: Key Issues and Findings, and Part II: Background Papers*, Occasional Papers, Nos 128 and 129 (Washington, IMF,).

Taylor, M.P. and L. Sarno (1997), 'Capital Flows to Developing Countries: Long and Short Term Determinants', *World Bank Economic Review*, 11(3), 451–70.

Treasury Committee (1997), *International Monetary Fund, Fourth Report* (together with Proceedings, Minutes of Evidence and Appendices), House of Commons, London Stationery Office.

ul Haque, N. and M. Khan (1998), " 'Do IMF-Supported Programs Work" A Survey of the Cross-Country Empirical Evidence', IMF Working Paper WP/98/169 (Washington, DC, IMF).

Williamson, J. (1983), *IMF Conditionality* (Washington, DC, Institute for International Economics).

12 International Financial Institution Advisory Commission*

Allan H. Meltzer

The Commission and its mandate

When the US Congress approved $18 billion of additional funding for the International Monetary Fund (IMF) in November 1998, it authorized a study of international financial institutions. Congressional concerns included the growing frequency, severity and cost of financial disturbances, the fragility of the international monetary system, the ineffectiveness of development banks, and corruption in Russia, Indonesia, Africa and elsewhere. But Congress also expressed concern about whether international financial institutions had adapted appropriately to the many changes since the Bretton Woods Agreement in 1944.

In July 1999, Congress completed appointment of the members of the International Financial Institution Advisory Commission (usually called the Meltzer Commission). Between September 9, 1999 and March 8, 2000, the Commission met twelve times and, in addition, held three days of public hearings. On March 8, 2000, it presented its Report to the Speaker and the Majority Leader of the House of Representatives. International Advisory Commission Report (2000) stimulated active discussion of issues that might have been addressed at the fiftieth anniversary of the Bretton Woods Conference, in 1994, but were not.

A dialogue was long overdue in both the academic and the policymaking worlds. As the US Congress recognized, the world economy and the international financial system are now very different from the world envisioned at Bretton Woods in 1944. The principal international financial institutions responded to many past changes and crises by expanding their mandate and adding new facilities and programs. New regional institutions opened to serve the needs of regional populations. Many of the activities of these agencies overlap with those of the World Bank.

The Commission had a very broad mandate and a very short life. The US Congress asked the Commission to evaluate seven major institutions and recommend changes in only six months. The Commission chose to concentrate on the IMF, the World Bank and the three regional development banks. It gave less attention to the Bank for International Settlements and the World Trade Organization.

* I am grateful to Adam Lerrick and Valeriano Garcia for many helpful suggestions. An earlier version of this chapter is included also as the introduction to the Spanish edition of the Report of the International Financial Institution Advisory Commission.

There were two broad sets of issues, organizational and functional. The former includes the structure of the institutions and the incentives that motivate individuals. Performance can be improved only by changing the incentives under which the staff works and member countries operate. A frequent criticism, discussed almost a decade ago in the Wapenhans Report, but still not fully addressed, is that the World Bank rewards lending, not poverty alleviation or successful economic and social development (World Bank 1992). A different set of incentives in a restructured organization would focus more attention on benefits to the citizens of client states.

The Commission started work with ten members, including six economists, so it seemed appropriate to focus attention on economic themes.[1] There was not enough time to treat all issues adequately. The Commission chose to emphasize the role of the multilateral institutions in supplying services that the private market would not provide and developing infrastructure that would permit market solutions where feasible and nonmarket solutions elsewhere. An economist's reflex response is to ask: What are the public goods that these institutions can supply effectively? What is their comparative advantage? Where do markets fail? Can an international financial institution effectively and efficiently supply the missing services?

A second set of issues soon became apparent. There is considerable overlap between the Bank and the IMF and between the Bank and the regional banks. The overlap might be justified as a type of competition to provide services to client states at lowest cost. Unfortunately, the overlap and duplication arise for reasons that have little to do with competition or efficiency. With the banks and the IMF involved in the two principal tasks – reducing risk and enhancing development – reform proposals must discuss the IMF and the development banks together.

The framework

In setting the Commission's charge, the US Congress recognized that two major changes in international financial arrangements required changes in the responsibilities of the international financial institutions (IFIs). First, the fixed but adjustable exchange rate system, agreed to at the Bretton Woods Conference, ended more than twenty-five years ago. Second, private financial institutions, corporations and individuals in the developed countries now supply the largest part of the capital flow to emerging market economies. The IFIs' share is now less than 5 percent of the total. The percentage varies across countries, however. Many of the poorest countries remain dependent on the IFIs.

Major problems of the system follow from these changes. Many developing countries rely excessively on short-term capital inflows to finance long-term development, a very risky approach that has caused crises throughout history. Financial systems in developing countries are, too often, used to subsidize favored industries or individuals, weakening the financial institutions and eroding their capital. This, too, increases the risk of crises and failures. Pegged exchange rates replaced the fixed exchange rate system in many developing countries, opening the countries to speculative attacks. With weak financial systems dependent on short-term capital, the system became subject to frequent, severe crises.

Further, the IFIs lend to governments and have very little influence over the use of funds. Often projects are not completed; funds are misappropriated, and promised reforms are not implemented. Instead of improving their performance as development agencies, the development banks have expanded their programs to overlap with the IMF. The reverse is also true. The IMF makes long-term loans for structural reform and poverty alleviation. Some countries remain permanently in debt to the IMF.

The majority report responds to these fundamental problems by proposing structural changes in the institutions. The Report recommends separate roles for the IMF and the development banks. It sees the proper role of the IMF as preventing financial crises and preventing the spread of crises that occur. This is a classic public responsibility – to reduce risk to the minimum inherent in nature and trading practices. It is very different from the role that the IMF has assumed. Crisis prevention does not mean, and in the Commission's majority view should not mean, that the IMF continues to "bailout" all lenders, or lend large amounts to maintain pegged exchange rates or dictate the policies followed in client countries. Financial stability does not require that all countries follow a "Washington consensus" or that the IMF lend for institutional reform. The IMF should give advice, but it should not tie the advice to assistance.[2]

Lending for institutional reform is one of the tasks of the development banks. The majority believes that their mission should have four parts: promoting economic and social development, improving the quality of life, reducing poverty and providing global and regional public goods. These institutions should not be banks. Their job should not be to increase the number and size of loans or to lend to creditworthy countries. To recognize that their mission is development, not lending, the Commission's majority recommended that the names of these institutions should be changed to development agencies from development banks.

The World Bank has started to create field offices in recipient countries. The majority believes that this is another waste of resources by an overly large and ineffective bureaucracy. The Inter-American (IDB), Asian (ADB) and African Development Banks have offices in all of the relevant countries. Many governments, and their constituents, have closer ties of language, culture and understanding to the regional agencies. The majority believes that effectiveness would be improved, and costly overlap reduced, if the regional banks assumed sole responsibility for many of the programs in their regions. The World Bank's direct role in transferring resources would be limited to regions without a development bank and to Africa, where poverty problems are most severe and difficult to solve, and where the regional bank has less experience. The World Bank would continue to supply technical assistance and promote knowledge transfer in all regions.

Critics contend that this proposal would "undermine the effectiveness of the overall development effort" (US Treasury 2000, p. 8), although they have not elaborated this argument.[3] This criticism avoids discussing the waste from duplication between the World Bank and the regional development banks, but this is not its main omission. The aim of the Commission recommendation is to force the World Bank to concentrate its financial resources on the region with the largest number of very poor countries. The Bank lends mostly to middle-income countries that have investment grade ratings and can, therefore, finance development in the market place. The Commission's majority believes that this change is overdue.

World Bank management argues that the proposed change would reduce its ability to learn from diverse experience in many parts of the world. This argument is puzzling. Often the most objective and useful examinations are made by those who are not directly involved in a project. They have less incentive to cover over failures and mistakes.

The more important reason, I believe, for opposing the transfer of program responsibilities from the World Bank to the ADB and IDB is very different. The United States has more direct influence over the World Bank. The US Treasury does not wish to see power and responsibility shift to the countries in the region. I believe a shift of this kind is likely in coming years, and it is best to make the transfer in an orderly way. Indeed, in Europe and Asia the movement toward greater regional control is well underway. South America seems likely to follow.

Organizational and structural changes are important, but they are not sufficient to increase operational or program effectiveness. Incentives to make programs work and to reduce waste and corruption must increase. The majority report gives considerable attention to these issues. The World Bank's current administration deserves credit for commenting publicly on corruption, but it has not developed effective programs to create the incentives to succeed. Public comment and exhortation are not enough to create lasting change. Incentives give people reasons to change their behavior. The majority report replaces exhortation and subsidies with strong incentives to improve performance and reform institutions.

The specific proposals in the majority report implement this framework. Our goal was to provide public goods efficiently, effectively and in ways that give countries and the IFIs incentives to increase economic stability, raise living standards, improve the quality of life for their citizens, and cooperate in providing regional and global public goods. The Bush administration adopted one of the Commission's principal recommendations by proposing to replace loans with grants to the poorest countries.

The IMF

The majority proposed that the IMF focus its efforts on four main tasks; crisis prevention, crisis management, improved quality and increased quantity of public information, and macroeconomic advice to developing countries. The Treasury's response endorsed these objectives. Our differences are limited to means, not ends.

Each of the serious crises since 1982 has its own special features and some common features. Before the crisis breaks out, investors begin to withdraw funds. The country often guarantees the foreign exchange value of the funds in an attempt to forestall the withdrawals. This postpones the crisis but does not prevent it. The IMF tries to help the country maintain its exchange rate by lending foreign currency to defend the exchange rate. The country may increase interest rates and promise reforms, but investors see increased risk. If the financial system depends on short-term capital inflow, it may collapse with the exchange rate. The most damaging crises are of this kind. Brazil in 1998 and Argentina in 2001, show the benefit of opening the financial system, as the Commission urged. Some depositors withdrew from local banks but deposited in branches of foreign banks. This reduced the drain to currency, and prevented a banking collapse.

The majority does not believe that all crises can be prevented. It does believe that the frequency and severity of crises can be reduced by reforming country and IMF practices to increase incentives for policies and behavior that enhance stability. The IMF should be a quasi lender of last resort, not first resort, providing liquidity when markets close.[4] It should work to prevent crises, act to mitigate them and leave structural reform and development to the capital markets and the development banks.

The majority proposed to establish preconditions for IMF assistance. Countries that met the conditions would not have to wait, as they presently do, while negotiators agree on a long list of structural, institutional and financial changes. Crises worsen during these delays, so we propose immediate assistance to qualifying countries.

The conditions must be straightforward, clear, easily monitored and enforced. The majority proposed four conditions, but the list could be altered or expanded slightly. Most important, I believe, are that the financial system is adequately capitalized, government financial policies are prudent, information on the maturity structure of foreign debt becomes available promptly and foreign banks are allowed to compete in local financial markets. Members of the World Trade Organization have agreed to phase-in this last condition, and several have done so. The majority would speed up implementation as Mexico, Brazil, Argentina, Hungary, Chile, Poland, Czech Republic, Venezuela, Peru and others have done, see *The Economist* (2000, p. 118). The majority recommended that the exchange rate system be either firmly fixed or floating, but it did not include that recommendation as a precondition. After further reflection, I would include that condition.

Countries would have strong incentives to meet and maintain the preconditions. Once a country qualifies, it would obtain more foreign capital on more favorable terms. IMF acceptance of the country as qualified for automatic assistance would serve as a seal of approval and reduce expected losses. The market would have a list of countries that qualified, and a list of those that did not. The latter would get fewer loans and would pay higher interest rates to compensate for the additional risk. Thus, preconditions redirect private sector flows away from high-risk borrowers toward those that pursue stabilizing policies. This reduces the risk in the entire system.

Preconditions are not a panacea. They will not increase incentives for stability or induce countries to reform, if the IMF bails out all countries and limits creditors' losses.[5] Countries that are crisis-prone because they follow profligate policies or use their financial system to finance politically favored projects must have an incentive to change their ways. If the IMF does not allow countries to fail, markets will not distinguish sufficiently between countries with proper and improper policies and standards except in time of crisis. Lenders will not have to bear the full risk of their decisions, so they will not charge enough to encourage governments to reform.

Argentina offers a recent example of how much a country can change if the IMF does not bailout the lenders. In March 2001, Mr Lopez Murphy became Economy Minister. His program called for expenditure reduction, a major change from the previous calls for tax rate increases under IMF programs. The government came close to collapse, so Minister Lopez Murphy resigned without enacting his program. The IMF gave no additional assistance at the time. In less than five months, the new Economy Minister, Domingo Cavallo, got agreement on a policy of zero deficits, computed monthly, and much greater reductions in public employee wages, transfers to the provinces, and other items than Minister Lopez Murphy had proposed. Charges that had been "unacceptable and unthinkable" became the law of the land.[6]

What about third countries, countries that are harmed by the collapse of a trading partner? The majority would assist such countries automatically, if they met the preconditions. In all other cases, it would help them only if there is a systemic crisis. We recognize that the IMF would have discretionary power. They could, and likely would, stretch the meaning of "systemic." The main risk is not, as several critics suggest, that the IMF would do too little. The more serious risk is they will continue to bailout most countries, thereby reducing the incentive to reform.

Some of the Report's critics claimed that the majority proposal was an effort to curtail the IMF's activities. Much too often, this claim attacks the members' motives and misrepresents the report. The IMF's activities would decline if crises declined, as the majority believes they would. The main reasons for reduced lending would be that there would be less need for lending, if there were fewer crises. And there would be fewer crises if preconditions were met.[7] Financial sectors would be solvent and open to competition from foreign banks, governments would be prudent and exchange rates would either float, even if not freely, or be firmly fixed and supported by adequate reserves and appropriate policies. Lenders to countries that did not adopt the preconditions would bear the losses they undertook. Hence, they would limit loans to nonqualifying countries increasing incentives for reform.

Treasury and other critics argue correctly that all crises are not liquidity or financial crises. They then claim that the majority report does nothing about other, nonliquidity crises (US Treasury 2000, p. 7). This is a misunderstanding. First, the majority required prudent fiscal policies to remove this source of disturbance.[8] Second, the majority did not neglect structural problems. It assigned these problems to the development banks and, as noted below, proposed to increase incentives for introducing and continuing structural reforms for ten or more years so that the reforms become institutionalized. Removing structural problems from the IMF's mandate is based on a well-known proposition: money can solve liquidity problems, not real structural problems. In developing countries, structural problems arise because of regulation, tariffs, inadequate financial supervision, absence of the rule of law and other impediments to investment (Burnside and Dollar

2000). As recent experience in Argentina and Asia, and earlier experience in Mexico, Argentina, Russia, Ukraine and elsewhere demonstrates, loans and liquid resources often allow countries to delay reform. More systematic research shows that foreign aid and liquidity do not produce development, and may retard development unless a country decides to implement structural reforms (ibid.).

Critics also made much of the elimination of (ex post) conditionality (Frankel and Roubini 2001, p. 73). There are three main reasons behind this decision. First, as the Report notes, there is no evidence that conditionality makes a difference on average. There are well-known problems in testing for the effects of conditionality, but the tests that have been reported, both within the IMF and outside, do not show economically important effects on output or economic growth. (Significant effects on the balance of trade or payments are found, but the "improvement" is certain to occur because the country cannot borrow when it has a crisis.) Second, the majority believes that local decisions should be encouraged in the interests of democratic accountability. Crises have become the occasion for IFIs to demand reforms that domestic majorities do not want and that governments will not enforce. Third, negotiating a long list of conditions delays action at times of crisis, deepening and spreading the crisis. Delay was very damaging to Mexico, Korea and others.

The Clinton Treasury claimed that the majority proposal "would preclude the IMF from being able to respond to financial emergencies in a potentially large number of its member countries" (US Treasury 2000, p. 7). This statement brings out clearly the principal difference in orientation between the Commission majority and many of its critics. The Treasury claims that countries would not respond to the incentives to reform despite the fact that private lenders and investors annually provide 50–100 times the amount of financial resources advanced by all the IFIs. They would not reform to meet the preconditions, so they would not qualify for assistance.

If it were true that most countries would not reform to gain access to financial markets and to enhance stability, what reason is there to believe that these countries will reform because the IFIs exhort them to do so and offer a tiny fraction of the resources they could acquire by reforming?

The majority report proposes to use market discipline in place of conditionality. Publication of timely, accurate information on economic, financial and political developments permits lenders and investors to make informed decisions. The IMF has a major role in improving the quality and increasing the quantity and timeliness of country data. Publication of reports of IMF missions and the IMF's recommendations is a welcome development. Improved information reduces uncertainty and improves lenders' decisions. Release of information encourages reform and permits investors to make continuous marginal adjustments instead of rushing to exit when anticipations change quickly. Further, improving information and opening the economy to foreign banks reduces reliance on renewable, short-term loans. Thus, it reduces one of the major problems of development finance, excessive reliance on short-term loans.

Many of the Commission's critics want to continue conditional lending after crises occur. Few, if any, defend the large number of conditions, often more than twenty but reaching 140 separate conditions on Indonesia's loan in the late 1990s. None show that the conditions are not in conflict, are enforced, are helpful to the country or are related to macroeconomic stability. It is gratifying to report that the IMF has decided to shorten the list of conditions that countries must meet to receive assistance. Like the majority, it proposes to shift its emphasis toward crisis prevention and reform of financial systems, and it will urge countries to avoid adjustable, pegged exchange rates. The IMF has greatly increased publicly available information about its decisions and actions, and it has encouraged member governments to do the same. The Clinton Treasury endorsed these changes.

Unfortunately, the IMF has not accepted the full logic of the Commission Report. Its members debate whether and how lenders can be "bailed-in" to force them to share the cost of a financial crisis. In practice, investors are "bailed-in" unless the IMF helps the country support a pegged exchange rate by lending enough to allow creditors to leave. A floating exchange rate raises the cost to the lenders who decide to bailout. In Argentina in 2001, the new IMF and US Treasury administrations allowed creditors to take their sizeable losses either by selling their bonds at a loss or renegotiating after default. No international crisis or contagion occurred. This suggests that markets distinguished more effectively between Argentina's problems and conditions in other countries than discussions of contagion presume. It remains to be seen whether recognition of risk will reduce capital flows to developing countries.

Under the majority proposal, countries that fail to satisfy preconditions for stability would not receive assistance until they implement reforms. Higher interest rates compensate lenders for taking the risk of lending to countries with weak financial systems or profligate policies. The lenders should bear the losses in a crisis so that they, and others, will know that the risk premiums they collect are payments that compensate for expected losses that they will bear. They would then price loans and assets correctly.

A related issue, known as "moral hazard," arises in international lending when governments or IFIs permit lenders to believe that they will be bailed out in a crisis. Most critics of the Report's discussion of moral hazard accept that moral hazard was encouraged by official policies in the 1994 Mexican crisis and contributed to the Russian debacle in 1998. Lenders received large payments for bearing risk, but they believed that the principal governments or the IFIs would prevent a Russian default.

Critics deny that moral hazard was present in Asia. They point to the lack of evidence in interest spreads and other market measures. Such data are not compelling, in part because they do not address whether the loans were correctly priced. These data are consistent with moral hazard. If lenders priced the risk correctly, spreads would not change significantly.

There is an additional problem. In Mexico, Thailand and Korea the government responded to the first large withdrawals by guaranteeing the dollar value of loans to foreign, private-sector lenders. The guarantee took different forms. What matters is that the local government could not honor the guarantee in the event of a run unless foreign governments or IFIs provided the dollars. The guarantee postpones or prevents capital from leaving only if the lenders believe that the guarantee will be honored by the IMF (or others). In most cases, this assumption has been at least partly correct. The finance minister knows that he must depend on assistance. The lenders act on the presumption that they will collect the risk premium but will not bear the full risk. This is moral hazard.

A related criticism is that the majority's approach requires the IMF to impose a "standstill," to prevent lenders from withdrawing from countries in crisis. This is false. The majority relies instead on a flexible exchange rate. The government would not borrow and pay out foreign exchange; the central bank would not support the currency. The exchange rate would fall until those who chose to exit were matched by private investors willing to lend or acquire assets at what they think are bargain prices. Settlement of the outstanding foreign currency claims of bondholders and lenders would be left to negotiation by the parties, as the Report notes. Recent experience in Ecuador suggests that agreements can be reached within a reasonably short time.

The majority does not believe that its proposals are painless. There are costs for the lenders and for the country. The answer does not lie in short-term solutions that force lenders to remain by imposing a "standstill." That policy would lead to an excessive reduction in the flow of loans and development finance. There are better policies.[9]

Part of the solution lies in letting financial institutions compete in the local market. They would hold both assets and liabilities denominated in local currency, so they would be less exposed to exchange rate risk. Opening the financial system would encourage entrants with a long-term commitment, thereby reducing the current excessive reliance on short-term capital. And, foreign banks would bring expertise in risk management and act as relatively safe havens if a crisis arises.

The IMF's Poverty Reduction and Growth Facility (PRGF) makes long-term loans at concessional interest rates to relatively poor countries. Development lending is the responsibility of the development banks. If these banks did a better job, there would be no need for the PRGF. The majority solution is to strengthen the development banks instead of adding another development institution within the IMF.

IMF staff is reluctant to criticize the development banks publicly, so they offer another rationale for the PRGF. The countries receiving long-term assistance do not require other types of IMF lending; PRGF makes membership attractive. The majority believes that duplication, without effective competition is costly. The IMF does not have the experience or expertise and should not develop it. The proper solution is to make the development banks more effective.

The regional development banks

The regional development banks' main problems are that their programs lack focus, are often loosely related, or unrelated, to their stated goals and, all too frequently fail to accomplish their objectives. After decades of programs and billions of dollars, many of the poorest nations have lower living standards than in the past. The World Bank's education program has failed dramatically. After years of educational assistance, Guatemala has a 33 percent illiteracy rate. Programs to improve health are not more successful. Overall, the World Bank's own assessments, though flawed, show very little achievement in the poorest countries. The entire fault does not lie with the development banks, but they have not found ways around the obstacles that some governments create. They continue to lend despite the obstacles and the resulting failures, and they give most of their loans to countries that can borrow in the capital markets many of which do not require subsidies.

Countries have made substantial progress where they have strengthened institutions and the role of markets and little if any progress in many of the poorest countries, where they have not reformed. Most of the very poor countries have large debts that cannot be serviced or repaid. The Commission voted unanimously to forgive the debts entirely, after countries institute reforms. The IFIs have more than enough accumulated reserves and provisions for loss to write off all debts of the poorest countries. I believe that reform of the IFIs and the recipient nations should be a precondition for donor country funding of debt forgiveness.

The majority favored major changes to focus efforts on three broad areas and improve incentives in the countries and the development banks. First, the development banks should work to improve the quality of life, even in countries where corruption or institutional arrangements prevent or hinder economic development. The majority proposed grants, instead of loans, to pay up to 90 percent of project costs approved by the development banks. To increase achievement and reduce waste, grants would be given after competitive bidding and would require independent monitoring and auditing of results. Payments would be made, after performance is certified, directly to providers or suppliers instead of governments. The suppliers would have an incentive to assure that inoculations are made, potable water is supplied, sanitation is improved, literacy rates increase, and that these and other programs produce measurable results. Before leaving office, Treasury Secretary Summers endorsed the use of grants in place of loans, and the Bush administration adopted this proposal. The Bank opposed it, perhaps because it called for monitoring results.

Second, long-term subsidized loans to develop effective institutions would assist countries that willingly adopt and sustain the necessary reforms. Here, too, independent auditors must certify that progress continues. This proposal replaces the command and control measures mandated by the development banks with incentives that encourage local support for development.

Third, many problems that prevent development or reduce the quality of life are common to many different countries. The development banks have maintained a country-specific focus. They have not tried to find solutions to common problems such as malaria, measles, tropical agriculture and many others. Research is costly, and individual market demand is too small to induce companies to do the research. By joining countries together and subsidizing research efforts, the development banks can close the gap between social and private rates of return.

The majority also recommended that scarce official financial resources be concentrated on poor countries without access to alternative funds and that countries graduate automatically and regularly from the programs. Graduation would release more money to help the poorest countries. The development banks should continue to offer technical assistance to countries that graduate, but these countries should borrow in the market and be subject to market discipline.

The World Bank and others responded to the majority proposals by claiming that ending loans to middle-income countries would harm the poorest countries by reducing the Bank's income (Gilbert *et al.*, 1999). This claim has no merit. The Bank lends at a rate very little above its own cost of funds; it adds a fractional fee to cover administrative expense. The only "profit" on the loan comes from the allocation of a portion of the Bank's costless equity capital. The same capital would be available to support grants. There would be no diminution of resources.

At times, some Bank officials claim that the Bank has unlimited borrowing capacity in the capital market. Hence, its loans could be increased indefinitely, and there is no reason to shift loans from middle-income countries toward the poorest countries. This is either a misstatement or an error. The Bank's borrowing limit is set by its industrialized member callable capital – the amount that countries have pledged to the Bank. Lender's risk increases once the Bank's loans approach the amount of its industrialized country callable capital, so lenders would demand higher interest rates to cover the increased risk. Given its history of rolling over uncollectable debts, the risk premium would rise rapidly. The Bank's borrowing capacity is unlimited only if the industrialized countries are willing to supply unlimited contributions to the Bank.

In his testimony before the Commission and in subsequent comments, the Bank's president claimed that replacing loans to poor countries with grants was a good idea in principle, but impractical.[10] He claimed it would require a large increase in support by donor countries. This claim is the very opposite of "unlimited borrowing capacity," but it too, is incorrect.

The Bank earns all of its net income by investing funds it has not disbursed and its own costless, paid-in capital in the securities market. These earnings would remain. As outstanding concessional loans are repaid, the volume of earning assets would increase. Would the available resources be large enough to support a large grants program?

After the Report was published, a senior staff member analyzed the amount of development programs that the Bank could support with current resources, if it replaced loans with grants, as the majority proposed. The calculation showed that the value of programs that could be financed with grants greatly exceeded the amount provided by traditional concessional loans now made. Lerrick (2000). Hence the amount of assistance would increase. Effectiveness would improve. Theft and misappropriation would be reduced. And there would be no debt burden for the poorest countries.

Several months after the Report appeared, a private foundation adopted the Commission's grants proposal, with monitoring, as part of a new health program for African nations. Former Treasury Secretary Summers also shifted the Clinton Treasury's position. His statements at the time of the Prague meeting of the IMF and the World Bank favor increased use of grants. In 2001, the Bush administration formally adopted the proposal to shift funding from loans to grants.

The Bank's president offered another defense of Bank loans to middle-income countries that can borrow in the capital markets. He claims that the Bank finances socially useful projects that do not earn monetary returns. Further, he claimed that the capital markets would not finance these projects.

This argument overlooks an important difference. The Bank receives a government guarantee of principal and interest. If private lenders received the same guarantee, they would not care how the country used the loan proceeds.

In fact, the Bank does not know what its loans to middle-income countries finance on the margin. Money is fungible. No outsider can know reliably which project or projects were financed by development aid. It is in the interest of the country and the Bank's officers to claim high marginal social returns. In most cases, projects with high returns could be financed without assistance from the IFIs, especially if the country guarantees repayment.

This problem arises in all but the poorest countries where there is true additionality. That's another reason why the development banks should focus on poor countries without access to financial markets.

Perspective: the IMF two years after the Commission's Report

Much has changed at the IMF in the nearly two years since the Commission Report appeared. Interest rates are higher; the number of lending programs has been reduced; there is greater transparency, more information, a less opaque accounting system and more information about member countries available for interested parties.

A new team is in charge. They appear to agree on some of the principles that the Commission highlighted, including the substitution of incentives for command and control in country programs. The Commission's majority believed that countries do not reform because they get loans from the international financial institutions. Lasting reform occurs when the country's parliament or government becomes convinced that reform is in their economic and political interest and that it benefits their constituents.

After giving Argentina substantial assistance in December 2000, the IMF changed course. In March 2001, a new Argentine Minister of Economy, Mr Lopez Murphy, announced his intention to reduce government spending. The Vice President resigned in protest; there was little political support, and Lopez Murphy resigned within two weeks of his appointment. By mid-summer, the government and parliament had accepted reductions in spending much larger and more encompassing than Lopez Murphy had proposed. The Congress voted, reluctantly, for a balanced budget. Adversity accomplished reforms that IMF lending did not achieve.

Although the IMF loaned $5 billion additional in August 2001, it insisted that Argentina meet the budget targets that it had promised to meet. Argentina defaulted on its debt, the largest nominal default ever recorded. Unlike Korea, Thailand, Indonesia and Mexico, the IMF did not rush in with a new program to "bailout" the creditors. It had discovered that the easiest way to "bail-in" a lender is to avoid bailing them out by providing additional loans to support an overvalued currency and excessive debt.

The IMF was not passive. During the summer, it agreed to lend money to Brazil to prevent the consequences of an Argentine default from spreading, as the Commission had proposed. And it advised Argentina that it had to adopt a comprehensive framework for its debt, exchange rate, monetary and fiscal policies. At the time this is written, Argentina's government has not developed a comprehensive, consistent plan to restore growth, and the IMF has not offered any money.

One case is not much evidence. In time, we will know whether there is a new set of rules that emphasize incentives to reform and the responsibility of the troubled country to adopt them. Nevertheless, the IMF's response to Argentina's problems is markedly different than its earlier responses to Argentina or its approach to many other countries. It allowed a default by a major country after permitting smaller defaults by Ecuador, Pakistan and Ukraine. Default and restructuring aligns risk and return. It is the single best means of reducing moral hazard in international lending.

Turkey is another change, but of lesser magnitude. Turkey's problems were mainly domestic problems. Turkey's debt was mainly internal, its banking problems overdue for reforms that Turkey's political system would not undertake.

The IMF's role in Turkey continued decades of support for an important US and G-7 ally. This time, however, the IMF insisted that the promised reforms be adopted, not just promised.

On the other hand, the IMF failed to create the incentives for reform that the Commission majority favored. The IMF's Contingent Credit Line (CCL) is the closest analogue to the Commission's recommendation of precommitment to support countries that meet and maintain a small number of reforms that are essential for stability. The problem is not that the IMF bureaucracy is unwilling to accept countries into the CCL. On the contrary, the Managing Director seems committed, and the Fund is officially eager. The problem is that the bureaucracy cannot produce a CCL program that attracts member governments. A main problem is that the IMF bureaucracy is reluctant to make assistance automatic.

Conclusion

The international economy has experienced several prolonged, deep financial crises in the past twenty years. At the same time, economic development has bypassed the poorest countries. Many of them are in Africa, but extreme poverty can also be found in Latin America, Asia, and southern and eastern Europe.

Reform of the international financial institutions is needed to increase economic stability, improve the flow of information, encourage economic development, support institutional reform, reduce moral hazard, reduce poverty and support provision of regional and global public goods. The Report of the International Financial Institution Advisory Commission offers an integrated approach to many of these problems.

This chapter develops the Commission majority's main recommendations and responds to criticisms by the US Treasury and others. It is useful to conclude by putting these criticisms into context in two ways. First, although the Treasury was critical of many of the majority's recommendations, they wrote: "[W]e share the Commission's desire to find new ways to encourage countries to reduce their vulnerability before crisis strikes. In this context, we agree with the report that it is critical for countries to strengthen the financial sector, improve the quality of disclosure, and reinforce the resilience of the exchange rate regime" (US Treasury 2000, p. 8).

Second, it is encouraging that, with the passage of time, and new Treasury officials, the Treasury has endorsed, and the IMF has adopted or considered, some of the majority's recommendations. The changes already adopted include reduction in the number of different lending arrangements, incentives for countries to repay more quickly, penalties in the form of higher interest rates for countries that remain in debt, and agreement that the IMF will emphasize short-term lending.

A recent interview with a senior IMF official suggests how much the IMF has changed. The IMF now aims for "a minimum amount of conditionality" instead of the lengthy list of reforms. Then, he added, "the IMF needs to be more flexible, not dictating to a country what policies are needed. The country should be allowed to present a program to the IMF ... And the IMF needs to be selective, patiently waiting for the country to be ready" (IMF Survey 2002, p. 14).

More remains to be done. The most difficult, but most important, changes are (1) to recognize that reform can only work if lenders to nonreformed countries are required to take the losses implied by the risk premiums they receive and (2) to replace command and control orders from Washington with incentives that encourage reform at the local level.

Finally, the Commission would welcome the opportunity to cite important reforms at the World Bank and the regional development banks. Regrettably, the regional development banks have moved more slowly, or not at all. One must hope that they will shift from a policy based on "bribe and exhort" to incentive-based policies before there is another crisis.

Notes

1 The members were: Professor Charles Calomaris, Congressman Tom Campbell, Dr Edwin Feulner, Jr, Dr Lee Hoskins, Mr Richard Huber, Dr Manuel Johnson, Professor Jerry Levinson, Professor Allan Meltzer, Professor Jeffrey Sachs and Congressman Esteban Torres. The eleventh member, Dr C. Fred Bergsten, also an economist, joined in January 2000, after most of the Commission's hearings had ended.

2 Private consultants charge for advice. The IFIs pay or subsidize countries. Many critics of the Commission report argue that countries would not accept advice if it were given without subsidized lending. See US Treasury (2000). This is a peculiar argument. Must countries be bribed to take the advice? Or, do they take the subsidized loan, ignore the advice, or give it lip service only? Russia is an extraordinarily bad example of a country that took the money but not the advice. There are many others.

3 There have been many criticisms and comments. Most of the principal criticisms are in the Treasury's mandated response. We refer to it wherever applicable.

4 A lender of last resort must have unlimited ability to create money. The IMF does not have that power, so its ability to act like a lender of last resort is limited. The Commission recommended that the IMF have commitments from principal central banks to lend to the IMF against collateral.

5 Several critics, including US Treasury (2000) either ignore or miss the role of incentives. The underlying theme of the majority report is that proper incentives are both more powerful than exhortation and, because they are adopted by the country through its own processes, more likely to be accepted. It is not the same to say, "we did this so we could get more investment on better terms" instead of "the IMF insisted that we do this."

6 Unfortunately the changes came late and were piecemeal. The government did not have a comprehensive program for growth and increased employment to accompany these changes. At the time of writing, the country is in default on its debt and has blocked foreign exchange transactions and frozen most bank accounts.

7 A frequent criticism is that, if the majority report had been adopted, the IMF would not have been able to assist countries in the Asian crisis. US Treasury (2000, p. 6). This criticism is not correct. The majority endorsed discretionary authority to act in a systemic crisis. Also, the critics do not say whether the reforms had been in place for the five-year phase-in that the majority report proposed. If the Asian countries met the preconditions for five years, they would have been much less vulnerable. The problem would have been smaller because countries would have had safer financial institutions and floating exchange rates.

8 It is easy to see how fiscal profligacy can waste resources and slow growth. Argentina provides the most recent example of a country that allowed an unbalanced budget to destroy a fixed exchange rate system. More difficult is how fiscal profligacy can continue in developing countries if it is not financed by domestic banks or foreign lenders.

9 The Treasury and other critics are right when they claim that limiting IMF loans to ninety days with one renewal, as the majority recommended, is too short. The Commission made this recommendation after testimony and discussion with lawyers who raised issues about subordination of other debt to IMF loans of longer maturity. They suggested ninety-day loans as a way around this problem. I accept this criticism. A year would have been a better choice.

10 US Treasury (2000, p. 8) opposes the proposed automatic graduation rule ($4,000 per capita income or investment grade rating). It does not make its own graduation proposal, but argues that most of the world's poor live in countries like China that would have graduated under the Commission's proposal. One of the Commission's minority endorsed the grants proposal in testimony after the report was published (Reform of the International Monetary Fund 2000, p. 38).

References

Burnside, C. and Dollar, D. (2000). "Aid Policies and Growth," *American Economic Review*, 90, 847–68.

Frankel, Jeffrey A. and Roubini, Nouriel (2001). "The Role of Industrial Country Policies in Emerging Market Crises." National Bureau of Economic Research, Working Paper 8634 (December), pp. 1–110.

Gilbert, C.L., Powell, A. and Vines, D. (1999). "Positioning the World Bank," *Economic Journal*, 109, F598–633.

International Advisory Commission (2000). *Report of the International Financial Institution Advisory Commission.* Washington: US Government Printing Office.

International Monetary Fund (2002). "IMF Conditionality." IMF Survey, 31, 1 (January 14), pp. 14–16.

Lerrick, Adam (2000). "Development Grant Financing: More Aid per Dollar." *Hearing before the Joint Economic Committee.* Washington: Government Printing Office (April 12).

Reform of the International Monetary Fund (2000). *Hearing before the Subcommittee on International Trade and Finance*, 106th Congress, 2nd session. Washington: Government Printing Office (April 27).

The Economist (2000). "Emerging Market Indicators" (November 4), p. 118.

US Treasury (2000). Response to the Report of the International Financial Institution Advisory Commission. Washington: Department of the Treasury (June 9).

World Bank (1992). "Effective Implementation: Key to Development Impact." Washington: The World Bank. Internal document (The Wapenhans Report).

Questions for Part III

1 How have the IFIs evolved since their inception? Have they responded to the changing needs of the different periods?
2 How can weaknesses of the present global financial system be ameliorated? Do we need a systematic change or would marginal improvements suffice?
3 Discuss the costs and benefits of global financial market integration.
4 Do IFIs help the developing and transitional economies in attracting capital from other sources?
5 Are the major IFIs worth their salt? Have they been able to live up to their mandate in a constantly changing global financial environment?

Areas for further research

1 IFIs as global public good.
2 The lender of last resort: from a domestic to a global concept. How far have we come from Bagehot?
3 Is the global financial system entering a turbulent phase?
4 The role of conditionality as a cache of good economic housekeeping.
5 Are the multilateral institutions providing adequate development infrastructure?

Part IV

Exchange rate regimes and arrangements

13 Solving the currency conundrum*

Barry Eichengreen

In recent months the debate over strengthening the international financial architecture has taken an unexpected turn. For more than a year that debate revolved around the causes of financial crises, the International Monetary Fund's (IMF's) response, and the need to involve the private sector in crisis resolution. Little was said about the exchange rate problem.

Now one cannot open a financial newspaper without encountering yet another article on how to "fix" the exchange rate system. What has changed? Well, Brazil changed once the real blew up in the face of the government and the IMF, providing one more illustration that fragile currency pegs are central to the problem of financial instability in emerging markets. Argentina changed as the government began exploring the possibility of replacing the peso with the dollar as a way of banishing exchange rate instability once and for all. The relationship between the world's leading currencies changed with the advent of the euro. And Asia changed as green shoots of recovery sprouted and the crisis countries used their respite to ponder a common basket peg as a way of containing exchange rate instability in the region.

For all these reasons, the question of what to do about the exchange rate has moved to center stage. Recent events have also highlighted the absence of a consensus answer. For Brazil it is a more flexible exchange rate backed by inflation targeting. For Argentina it is an immutably fixed currency peg leading to dollarization. For Europe it is a regional central bank and monetary union. For the United States, Japan and the euro area it is floating between their respective currencies.

This chapter reviews the debate over the exchange rate system and the choice of regime for countries in different economic, financial and political circumstances. It would be presumptuous to claim that it will bring to a close a debate that has driven the official and academic communities for the better part of

* This is a revision of a paper prepared for the Council on Foreign Relations Study Group on Development, Trade and International Finance and presented there in January 2000. For helpful comments I thank the members of this study group, and especially Alexander Swoboda. Support for this research was provided by the Ford Foundation through the Berkeley Project on New International Financial Architecture.

a century. Rather, it will attempt to provide a framework for thinking about the issues that should help readers and policy makers make up their own minds.

Going to extremes

If there is anything approaching a consensus on the exchange rate problem, it is that high capital mobility has rendered problematic the operation of arrangements between the extremes of floating and rigidly fixed rates.[1] The underlying premise is that rising capital mobility has undermined the viability of intermediate regimes. The presence of large and liquid international capital markets makes it more difficult for the authorities to support a shaky currency peg, since the resources of the markets far outstrip the reserves of even the best armed central banks and governments. Effective defense of the exchange rate requires raising interest rates and restricting domestic credit, something that will have significant costs unless the economy is strong.[2] If they detect a chink in the country's armor – be it high unemployment, a heavy load of short-term debt, or a weak banking system – that could render the authorities reluctant to raise interest rates in order to defend the currency, then the markets will pounce, exposing the authorities' weakness. For most governments, the choice between raising interest rates and further aggravating domestic economic difficulties on the one hand, and not raising rates and allowing the currency to collapse on the other, is no choice at all; collapse is almost always the result.

What is new and different about the current environment is the growth of international financial markets and transactions. Table 13.1 shows that net inflows of portfolio capital (the kind of capital flows that make exchange rate management particularly difficult) rose between the mid-1970s and mid-1990s, in absolute-value terms, by a factor of 10 in the industrial countries and a factor of 20 in emerging markets.

This growth of capital flows reflects the relaxation of statutory barriers to inward and outward financial transactions, which itself reflects the operation of deeper forces. Above all is the fact of domestic financial liberalization. So long as domestic financial markets and institutions were tightly regulated, it was straightforward to restrain international flows. Limitations on the types of business in which financial intermediaries could engage, together with strict oversight, limited the scope for evasion. But with the abandonment of domestic financial repression, it became harder to halt flows at the border. As it became easier for banks to channel international financial transactions through affiliates and subsidiaries and to disguise and repackage them as derivative securities, effective controls had to become increasingly draconian and distortionary and therefore less attractive to policy makers and their constituents. There is a logic, in other words, for why domestic and international financial liberalization have gone hand in hand.

Reinforcing this trend is the development of new information and communication technologies. Computerized trading, the Internet and cheap telephonic communications have made it increasingly difficult for governments to segment

Table 13.1 Portfolio and direct investment flows, 1973–96 (in billions of US dollars, annual averages)

	Gross outflows					Gross inflows					Net inflows				
	1973–78	1979–82	1983–88	1989–92	1993–96	1973–78	1979–82	1983–88	1989–92	1993–96	1973–78	1979–82	1983–88	1989–92	1993–96
Industrial countries															
Direct investment	28.6	46.9	–88.2	201.3	259.6	17.9	36.6	69.3	141.9	173.0	–10.7	–10.3	–18.9	–59.4	–86.6
Portfolio investment	11.8	35	126.5	274.6	436.4	24.4	51	139.1	343.0	549.9	12.2	15.9	12.8	68.4	113.5
Developing countries															
Direct investment	0.4	1.1	2.3	10.4	19.2	5	14.6	51.2	37.8	106.4	4.6	13.5	13.2	27.3	87.2
Portfolio investment	5.5	17.8	–5.1	10.3	19.2	1.3	3.1	53.9	27.5	95.9	–4.2	–14.7	9.1	17.2	76.7

Source: Eichengreen *et al.* (1998).

capital markets. Ensuring that controls are effective thus means clamping down on a wide range of economic activities and civil liberties. This is something that few governments are willing to contemplate in the age of democratization.

But the fundamental implication of democratization is that few governments can credibly attach priority to defending a currency peg above all other goals of policy. Consider a government just willing to bear the pain of high interest rates and other policies of austerity in return for enhancing its reputation for following policies of exchange rate and price stability, whose benefits accrue later. If the markets attack the currency, forcing the government to raise interest rates to defend it, the game may no longer be worth the candle. The costs of austerity now, in the form of higher unemployment, more financial and commercial failures and a weaker economy generally, having risen relative to the benefits accruing down the road, the authorities be may opt to let the currency peg collapse. And the markets, knowing that the authorities attach importance to other aspects of economic performance in addition to exchange rate stability, have an obvious incentive to force the issue.[3] Prior to democratization, governments enjoyed insulation from pressure to use their policy instruments to minimize unemployment and foster economic growth. They could credibly assign priority to the maintenance of exchange rate stability over and above all other economic goals. In our modern world this is no longer the case.

Thus, the changes making for greater exchange rate flexibility are not just financial and technological but also political. They render currency pegs increasingly fragile, since they rob governments of the capacity to defend them and at the same time give the markets more ammunition with which to attack them.

Maintaining an exchange rate peg or band in the face of open capital markets is especially difficult for developing and emerging market economies. Many developing countries depend on exports of a few primary commodities, rendering them vulnerable to terms-of-trade shocks. Their financial systems are small relative to world markets and even to the assets of a handful of hedge funds and investment banks. Their fragile banking systems are incapable of withstanding sharp hikes in interest rates. Their political systems are incapable of delivering a broad-based, stable consensus in favor of exchange rate stabilization over and above all other economic and social goals.

Moreover, while the devaluation of a previously pegged currency may enhance international competitiveness and even stimulate growth (or so the cases of the United Kingdom and Italy in 1992–93 suggest – see Gordon, 1999), the Mexican and Asian crises suggest that currency devaluations in developing countries can be strongly contractionary. Because developing countries borrow in foreign currency, depreciation increases the burden of debt service and worsens the financial condition of domestic banks and firms. Because those banks and firms don't hedge their foreign exposures, they get smashed when the currency band collapses.

The previous paragraph begs two questions: why don't banks and firms hedge if doing so is in their interest, and why don't the authorities abandon the peg before being forced to do so in a crisis? Taking the second question first, there is always an incentive to leave the exit problem for another day. If the government has built its entire monetary policy operating strategy around the maintenance of the band, abandoning it can be a sharp shock to confidence. To keep the exchange rate within its band, the authorities have to reiterate that this is their intention. Exiting means going back on that promise. If monetary credibility is anchored by the peg, then credibility is lost when the peg is abandoned. It is not possible (in the presence of open capital markets, anyway) to pre-announce that the peg will be abandoned tomorrow, or currency traders will start betting against it today.

This is why few banks and firms hedge their exposures when the authorities operate a band or peg. For that arrangement to be credible, the authorities have to commit to preventing the exchange rate from moving beyond certain limits. If they do not assert their willingness to do so, the exchange rate will not behave as desired. To defend the peg, the government is inevitably forced to insist that there is absolutely no prospect that it will change. How many Chief Financial Officers (CFOs) will then be rewarded for purchasing costly exchange rate insurance before the fact? A pegged rate thus provides an irresistible incentive for the private sector to accumulate unhedged foreign debts. And unhedged foreign debts imply a crisis if the band or peg collapses.

Indonesia illustrates the consequences.[4] For some time prior to the outbreak of the Asian crisis in 1997, the country had been operating a crawling band allowing for fluctuations of plus-or-minus 4 percent against a basket of currencies. As is typical of many emerging economies, it had relatively high interest rates, which made it attractive for international investors to place their money there. These large capital inflows worked to push the rupiah toward the strong end of its band. Because the authorities were committed to limiting exchange rate fluctuations (and because the strength of the currency lent credibility to that commitment), domestic banks and (especially) corporations accumulated unhedged foreign exposures.

When Thailand devalued the baht, capital flows reversed direction. On August 13 the rupiah went from the strong edge of the band (which had been widened to 6 percent) to the weak edge in one day. This 12 percent depreciation was a sharp shock to Indonesian corporations with unhedged exposures, whose solvency was cast into doubt. Now openly questioning the stability of the economy, investors scrambled out of the currency. Further interest rate increases to defend it were out of the question, given the financial distress in the corporate sector and banking system. Instead, the authorities abandoned the band, allowing the exchange rate to drop further. Given the damage already done to the economy, it dropped like a stone, falling by as much as 10 percent a day. This may be a stylized version of recent Indonesian history, but it makes an essential point about the fragility of currency bands and the high costs of their collapse.

Figure 13.1 summarizes the consequences. It shows that in developing countries, where these financial, technological and political changes have been particularly pronounced, the removal of exchange restrictions has been dramatic. Capital-account liberalization has been accompanied by the decline of pegged exchange rates in favor of greater flexibility. At the same time, some countries – most

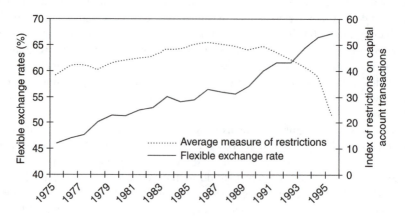

Figure 13.1 Capital controls and exchange rate regime in developing countries.

prominently in Western Europe but also in Argentina, Ecuador, Estonia, Bulgaria and Hong Kong – have moved in the other direction, seeking to eliminate the exchange rate problem by eliminating the exchange rate – by installing a currency board or going one step further and dollarizing the economy.

The backlash

The theory of the disappearing middle is not unanimously embraced. On the empirical front, Frankel (1999) observes that reports of the demise of the middle are greatly exaggerated. Of the 185 countries for which the IMF classifies the exchange rate regime by degree of flexibility, forty-seven were categorized at last count as independently floating and forty-five as having rigid pegs (currency boards or monetary unions, including the franc zone in Africa), leaving ninety-three still operating some kind of intermediate regime. Masson (2000) constructs transition matrices for exchange rates regimes for the past two-and-a-half decades and upon examining their properties finds little support for the hypothesis of disappearing middle. Calvo and Reinhart (1999) note that official IMF categorizations of member countries' regimes overstate the actual flexibility of their exchange rates, so that the conclusions of these previous authors are, if anything, rather conservative. Williamson (1996), in a tract written in reaction against the theory of the disappearing middle, observes that countries like Chile, Colombia and Israel long succeeded in operating crawling pegs, crawling bands and other hybrid systems.

Other evidence is not so obviously consistent with these claims. For one thing, the process of evacuating the unstable middle is still underway. The trend is clear in Figure 13.1, not to mention from recent events in countries like Brazil and Ecuador. Many countries that continue to inhabit the middle are able to do so because they still restrict capital inflows and outflows; there is nothing in the thesis of the disappearing middle that denies the ability of countries to occupy this space so long as they continue to limit capital movements, though there are reasons to believe that effectively controlling capital flows will become more difficult as market development proceeds. These pressures are evident in the tendency for countries operating crawling bands to widen the range of permissible fluctuations. And the point is directly applicable to Williamson's three counter cases. Chile widened its band from ±0.5 percent in 1984–85 to ±2.0 percent in 1985–87, ±3 percent in 1988–89, ±5 percent in 1989–91, ±10 percent in 1992–97 and ±12.5 percent since February 1997. In September 1999 a year after eliminating its last remaining taxes on capital inflows, it dropped the peso's fluctuation band entirely. Colombia widened its band from 14 percent from early 1994 through mid-1999 to 20 percent in the third quarter of 1999, before abandoning the band, also in September of 1999. Israel widened its band from ±0 in 1986–88 to ±3 percent in 1989–90, ±5 percent in 1990–95, ±7 percent in 1995–97 and to ±29 percent since June 1997.

Other examples could be cited. They all illustrate the growing difficulty of reconciling domestic priorities with narrow bands.

At the theoretical level, the question is why the prerequisites for the smooth operation of floating rates and rigid pegs are not also the prerequisites for the smooth operation of intermediate regimes. For a floating exchange rate to be well behaved – for it to display limited volatility and to provide a framework conducive to economic growth – fiscal policy must be strengthened, debt management and prudential regulation must be upgraded, and a coherent and credible monetary policy operating rule must be installed. In the absence of these prerequisites, the floating rate is likely to fluctuate erratically. Similarly, for a currency board or dollarization to be conducive to stability and growth, it is also the case that fiscal policy must be strengthened, financial policy must be upgraded, and a coherent and credible monetary policy rule must be adopted (this time by pegging to or adopting the currency of a country that itself follows a sound and stable monetary policy). Otherwise the rigid peg will only bequeath unemployment and inflation, undermining public support for and therefore the credibility of the monetary rule, while heightening the risk of debt and banking crises.

I elaborate on the importance of these prerequisites for a well-functioning float and a sustainable currency board in subsequent sections of the chapter. The question here is why these same prerequisites cannot also support a crawling peg, narrow band or target zone. To pose the question in traditional fashion, is it not sufficient for the indefinite maintenance of an intermediate regime for fiscal, financial and monetary policies to be consistent with the exchange rate target, and vice versa? Countries that have failed to successfully operate adjustable or crawling pegs and succumbed to crisis, in this view, have done so because their monetary and fiscal policies have been too expansionary – they have been incompatible with the currency peg. They have failed because poor debt management and lax supervision have rendered their financial systems too fragile to survive the requisite level of interest rates. The proper diagnosis is not that countries succumbing to crisis have done so because of the lack of viability of the model, but because implementation has been inadequate.

From this perspective, the key point would appear to be the following. If the country commits to either abandoning or hardening the currency peg, there will be strong incentives for policy makers and market participants to bring their affairs into conformance with the new regime. Consider, for example, the behavior of the banking system. If the exchange rate floats, banks will have an object lesson, on a daily basis, of the need to hedge their foreign currency exposures. If the exchange rate is pegged once and for all, they will appreciate the need to raise capital standards to compensate for the more limited lender-of-last-resort capacity of the monetary authorities. Adaptation may not be immediate, as explained in the next section, but there will be strong incentives for it to get underway.

Under an intermediate regime, in contrast, the incentives for adaptation are less. Neither markets nor policy makers have an irresistible incentive to adjust to the imperatives of the prevailing rate. Banks will have limited incentives to raise their capital standards or risk-management practices because they think that any exchange rate-related limits on the capacity of the authorities to act as lenders of last resort are only temporary. Debt managers will not shun short-term debt because they will be aware that the authorities retain the capacity to adjust the exchange rate and monetary policy to backstop the market. Fiscal policy makers will have mixed incentives to eliminate excessive deficits, because they will have reason to suspect that the revocation of the inflation tax is only temporary. For all these reasons, adaptation will be limited. And that will make it correspondingly harder for the authorities to defend the exchange rate when it comes under attack.

Thus, the failure of markets and policies to conform to the imperatives of a temporary peg – where the temporariness of the level of the exchange rate is the very definition of an intermediate regime – is more than a manifestation of suboptimal policy; it is an integral feature of this sort of hybrid system.

Which alternative?

For which extreme – freer floating or a hard peg – should countries opt? The choice is typically framed as a credibility/flexibility tradeoff. Floating rates maximize the flexibility with which the authorities can use monetary policy for stabilization policies. They leave the central bank free to intervene as a lender of last resort to financial markets. The value of these advantages is disputed. Some dispute the stabilizing value of exchange rate changes when shocks are real rather than monetary and a country's external obligations are denominated in foreign currency. They similarly question the capacity of the central bank to act as an effective lender of last resort when domestic banks and firms incur foreign-currency denominated debts.[5] The less the benefits of policy flexibility, the greater the appeal of the additional credibility imparted by the currency board/dollarization option. With domestic monetary policy now dictated by the United States, it immediately acquires all the credibility Alan Greenspan has accumulated over the last fifteen years. The commitment to the currency peg is enshrined in the adoption of a constitutional amendment (or by requiring a super-majority vote in the parliament) mandating that the central bank or the government defend the rate. These barriers to exit, by buttressing credibility, minimize the kind of speculative pressures described in the previous section. By ensuring greater exchange rate stability, they should in turn enhance the economy's access to foreign capital.[6]

These benefits do not come for free. In the case of dollarization, the immediate cost is seigniorage forgone. A currency-board country holds US treasury bills or equivalent foreign assets to back the domestic currency and earns interest on the backing. In Argentina this amounts to some $750 million a year, assuming an interest rate of 5 percent on the $15 billion of US treasury bills that back the $15 billion of pesos in circulation. This is not a insignificant cost for a government under budgetary strain.

The other cost, which is incurred with both dollarization and a currency board, is the loss of monetary policy flexibility. There may be no consensus regarding the value of this sacrifice, as noted above, but even if one believes that there are significant costs associated with the sacrifice of monetary autonomy, against which credibility gains must be weighed, those costs will be less if the economy adapts quickly to the absence of the monetary instrument. Given that there is essentially no prospect of a change in the exchange rate or of a domestically controlled monetary policy, there will be additional incentive to adapt to the newly inflexible monetary conditions. Labor markets will adapt to the absence of the exchange rate as an instrument of adjustment, as unions acknowledge the need for additional labor-market flexibility, wage flexibility in particular. Banks will adapt to the more limited lender-of-last-resort capacity of the authorities, raising their capital standards and strengthening their risk-management practices. Policy makers will adapt to the disappearance of the inflation tax by strengthening their fiscal self-discipline and eliminating excessive deficits. Financial managers, recognizing the absence of a domestic central bank to backstop short-term markets, will rely less on easily accessible short-term debt. Together, these adaptations will make it easier to live with the absence of exchange rate flexibility.

If one believes that such adaptations will occur quickly, then the currency board/dollarization option becomes more attractive, both because structural reform makes it easier to live with the absence of monetary-policy flexibility and because reform is desirable in its own right. Unfortunately, theory does tell us how quickly the requisite reforms are likely to take place. Consider, for example, labor-market reform. While there are assumptions under which labor-market reform will accelerate as a result of dollarization, there are also models in which dollarization will slow it down. In particular, insofar as labor-market reform no longer promises lower inflation in a dollarized economy, the incentive for labor-market reform is less.[7] Similar ambiguities arise in models of hard exchange rate constraints and fiscal consolidation (e.g. Tornell and Velasco, 1995). If exit from the currency peg is still an option, then there is no presumption that adoption of the peg will speed fiscal consolidation. While dollarizing (which, for present purposes, I take as analogous to eliminating all possibility of exit) will encourage fiscal consolidation by eliminating the inflation tax, it will not at the same time eliminate all possibility of debt default. So long as default remains an option, it is not clear at a theoretical level that progress toward fiscal consolidation will accelerate significantly.

What of the evidence? Observers of Argentine convertibility will be skeptical that a hard exchange rate constraint guarantees rapid labor-market reform.[8] Reform there has been, but it has been halting and partial. The same conclusion flows from the experience of Europe, where monetary union implies a similar reduction in monetary policy flexibility for the individual member states. Taking the OECD's quantitative measures of the extent of labor-market reform, it does not appear that countries that have been in the Exchange Rate Mechanism (ERM) for longest, or those which have been among the founding members of Europe's monetary union, have made the most progress in reforming labor markets.[9]

What about the argument that the adoption of a hard currency peg will lead banks to strengthen their risk-management practices? In Europe, there is little evidence that investors, bank managers and regulators have responded to the impending reduction in lender-of-last-resort services in the short run by raising capital standards and limiting risk taking. European banks were in the vanguard of lending to East Asia in the period that culminated in that region's financial crisis. Their exposure to the crisis countries was greater than that of US banks, prospects of a more limited safety net or not. The best way to understand this is as gambling for return in the effort to survive an increasingly brutal competitive environment. If dollarization leads to an intensification of competition in the financial sector and forces some scaling back of the financial safety net, Europe's experience suggests, it may lead to less rather than more risk taking in the short run.

What about pressure for fiscal consolidation? There is some evidence that removing the inflation tax from the hands of Europe's more inflation-prone governments intensified the pressure for consolidation. Budget deficits in the euro area fell from 4.8 percent of GDP in 1996 to 2.1 percent in 1998 and are projected to fall further. But Europe's experience also provides indirect support for the point that monetary union and dollarization do not rule out the possibility of default. The fear that fiscal profligacy could precipitate debt-servicing difficulties explains why the Maastricht Treaty features an extensive set of procedures designed to avert excessive debts and deficits along with penalties for countries failing to comply. Given the deep political links tying together the members of Europe's monetary union, there is reason to think that a debt crisis will be met with an inflationary debt bailout of the crisis country by the European Central Bank (ECB). The Maastricht Treaty and the Stability Pact negotiated subsequently are designed to limit this danger.

In summary, neither theory nor evidence suggests that eliminating all scope for an independent monetary policy will dramatically accelerate the pace of labor-market reform, financial-sector reform, and fiscal reform. Dollarizing will not automatically deliver the complementary reforms needed in order for the new regime to operate painlessly; those reforms will be completed only with the passage of time. Some countries with histories of erratic policy (one thinks of Argentina) may still opt for a currency board or dollarization on the grounds that the benefits associated with the additional credibility will outweigh the losses from the reduced flexibility. Others with particularly strong ties to a large partner (one thinks of Mexico) or extensive dependence on foreign capital (one thinks of Panama) may opt for a currency board or dollarization to solidify these links. Some countries with a desperate need for structural and policy reform (one thinks of Ecuador) may still opt for a currency board or dollarization on the grounds that, even if this new regime provides no guarantee of quick progress, it nevertheless ratchets up the pressure for reform. But for the foreseeable future at least, the majority of emerging markets are likely to continue to prefer the other alternative, namely greater exchange rate flexibility.[10]

Monetary union

A scenario in which all of Latin America goes over to the dollar is far-fetched. More plausible is that some countries will dollarize while others will not. This raises the specter of trade and exchange rate tensions within Mercosur, the Southern Cone's free trade area. Brazil absorbs more than 30 percent of Argentina's sales abroad. Thus, Brazil's depreciation of the real in early 1999 dealt a heavy blow to Argentina. Argentine producers demanded protection from cheap imports from Brazil, while exporters demanded compensation for their loss of competitiveness. Mercosur consequently came under threat. If Argentina dollarizes while Brazil continues to float, this volatility could become an everyday event. It is not clear that the free trade agreement would survive the resulting tensions.

For those who see free trade agreements in Latin America's Southern Cone and elsewhere as the wave of the future, this provides obvious motivation for monetary unification. In fact, the idea of a single currency for Mercosur has been under discussion for some time. Argentine President Menem raised the idea in December 1997 and again at a regional summit in June 1998. Argentina's former Finance Minister Domingo Cavallo mooted the idea in the spring of 1999.

Does monetary unification make sense as a corollary of regional commercial and economic integration? Europe's experience – and the Western Hemisphere's own – suggests that whether Mercosur needs a common currency depends on what kind of regional market its architects are building.[11] A free trade area like NAFTA in which integration is limited to the removal of barriers at the border and which therefore produces a limited rise in cross-border trade can be sustained in the presence of exchange rates that fluctuate against one another. A free trade area like Mercosur can survive exchange rate fluctuations because, while Brazil absorbs 30 percent of Argentine exports, exports account for only 8 percent of Argentine GNP. And integration in the Southern Cone is limited to trade integration; it has not yet extended far beyond the border. Deeper integration, extending to the harmonization of domestic regulations of all kinds, *a la* the European Union, implies more open domestic markets, more rapid growth of international transactions, and more intense cross-border competition, rendering exchange rate changes more disruptive. If South American policy makers are prepared to stop at the customs-union stage, then limited exchange rate fluctuations should be tolerable. But if they intend to push ahead to deeper integration, then they, like their European predecessors, will need to contemplate monetary integration.

Brazil would be the 400 pound gorilla of any South American monetary union. For Argentina, trading monetary stability for the uncertainties of monetary cohabitation with Brazil is unattractive. This has led Cavallo to suggest that the single Mercosur currency should be anchored to a fixed currency basket with positive weights on the dollar, euro and perhaps the yen (Bronstein, 1999). A common peg would deliver many of the benefits of monetary unification by eliminating exchange rate fluctuations within the economic and commercial zone; at the same time, relying on a basket rather than a single currency would better accommodate the diverse trading patterns of countries in the region. A common basket peg would relieve countries of dependence on the Federal Reserve, while the peg's currency-board structure would ensure monetary discipline. Such an arrangement would lack the transparency of a single-currency peg, however, which would lessen its credibility. In any case, this proposal assumes that Brazil is prepared to put in place the economic and financial prerequisites for the adoption of a currency board, something that it has not been willing to do to date.

This leaves the option of regional monetary union. This is a theoretically impeccable solution to the financial instabilities and economic and commercial strains created by distinct national currencies. And the European Union has shown that what works in theory can also work in practice. Unfortunately, a single Latin American currency that floats, *a la* the euro, against the US dollar is unlikely to be attractive to the potential issuers; the Southern Cone countries may trade with one another, but they import capital mainly the United States. Thus, even if a Mercosur currency is attractive on trade-related grounds, it is unlikely to be attractive on financial grounds. For a monetary union to be attractive to the Latins, it would have to include the United States.

Here enters another lesson of European experience: that monetary unification is likely to be feasible only as part of a larger political bargain. Monetary unification is a concession for the strong-currency country that dominates financial conditions throughout the region absent the creation of a single currency; it would want to obtain something in return, which implies an ability on the part of the partners to make binding political commitments. Thus, the German government sacrificed monetary autonomy and accepted additional inflation uncertainty by agreeing to European monetary unification, in return for a commitment by its partners to pursue political integration in whose context Germany hopes to obtain a greater foreign policy role in the context of an EU foreign policy.[12] This commitment to political as well as economic and monetary integration allowed Europe to build truly transnational institutions like a ECB to formulate the common monetary policy and a European Parliament to hold it accountable, however imperfectly. Not only does the euro, as part of this larger political bargain, insulate the members of Europe's monetary union from intra-European exchange rate fluctuations, but one can imagine that it will provide monetary and exchange rate stability over an even wider zone as the holdouts join and the countries to the east, already regarded as integral members of the European polity, become members first of the European Union and then of its monetary union.

This interpretation of Europe's monetary history underscores why this path will be difficult to trod in the Americas and East Asia. NAFTA is not seen in Canada, Mexico and United States as a platform for political integration. And there would be strong resistance in the United States to giving a sovereign Argentina, Mexico or Canada votes on the Open Market Committee of the Federal Reserve System. This would be regarded as an unacceptable compromise of US economic and monetary sovereignty. The same is true in Asia: given the history of tensions between Japan and Korea and between Japan and China, it is hard to conceive of them moving toward significantly deeper political integration any time soon. To be sure, circumstances can change. Europe emerged from the Second World War driven by equally deep divisions. But the fact that it took Europe fifty years of effort – and this in the context of an integrationist tradition stretching back over centuries – suggests that this transition takes many years to complete even under favorable circumstances. Europe is *sui generis*; its approach is unlikely to provide a solution to Asia and the Americas' currency conundrum any time soon.

Achieving greater flexibility in emerging markets

Saying that many emerging markets should adopt policies of greater exchange rate flexibility is easy; creating a framework and incentives that make it attractive is harder. Where the currency peg has been the cornerstone of the government's entire economic policy strategy, abandoning it will come as a sharp shock to confidence. If investors already harbor doubts about the government's commitment to the pursuit of sound and stable policies, jettisoning it will be seen as the equivalent of an obese man announcing that he has stopped going to Weight Watchers; the markets will fear that the government is about to revert to its bad old ways of monetary and fiscal excess. Capital will flee, undermining economic and financial stability. Fearing the consequences, the authorities have an obvious incentive to postpone the transition to greater exchange rate flexibility to another day.

Emerging markets therefore need to create a framework within which the transition to greater flexibility can occur smoothly. Specifically, this means that:

- Governments should initiate the transition to greater flexibility when global market conditions are favorable and not wait until sentiment begins to turn. Historically, emerging markets have been reluctant to move to greater flexibility when foreign capital is freely available; instead, they have held onto their currency pegs in order to maximize their access to cheap foreign finance. In fact, when the markets are flush is the best time to undertake the transition. Since investors have a favorable view of emerging markets and since the country is not being forced to abandon its peg under duress, the shock to confidence will be least. The fact that the exchange rate will begin its more flexible life by appreciating should reassure investors in domestic-currency-denominated assets that greater flexibility does not necessarily imply capital losses. Moreover, greater exchange rate flexibility is helpful for moderating the domestic-credit booms and asset-market bubbles that tend to cause small-open economies to overheat when large amounts of capital are flowing in.

- If the authorities substitute an alternative monetary policy operating strategy, investors will be reassured that abandoning the currency peg does not mean that the government has lost all monetary and fiscal discipline. The classic substitutes are monetary targeting and inflation targeting. Targeting the money stock is unlikely to be credible and effective in emerging markets, which are undergoing rapid structural change which disturbs the relationship between the monetary aggregates and inflation rates.[13] Inflation targeting, in which the authorities specify a target for inflation and explain how they plan to alter their policies if they miss it, is a more feasible and credible alternative.
- Domestic corporations can better cope with exchange rate flexibility when there exist currency forward and futures markets on which to hedge their exposures. Financial liberalization and deepening, including opening the financial sector to entry by international banks, is therefore important for fostering the growth of an interbank market in foreign currency forward contracts. Similarly, the adoption of transparent and effective securities-market regulations can encourage the growth of exchange-traded futures products.
- Even if greater flexibility is in the social interest, it may not be in politicians' interest, since they are not certain of being in office in the future when the returns on their investment are reaped. This creates a role for the IMF to tip the balance by signaling that it will not help to prop up shaky currency pegs and that it stands ready to assist countries that adopt policies of greater flexibility.

The recommendation that emerging markets abandoning their currency pegs consider inflation targeting is especially controversial. Inflation targeting has been attempted by only a handful of advanced-industrial countries, including Canada, the United Kingdom, Sweden and New Zealand. Moreover, the economic and political conditions that have supported its operation there are unlikely to be present in many emerging markets. In emerging markets, the pace of structural change introduces additional uncertainty into the link between the authorities' policy instruments and the inflation rate they are seeking to target. It being harder for them to articulate a model of those linkages, it is more difficult to convince the markets that a certain monetary stance today implies a certain inflation rate tomorrow. Perhaps most importantly, the authorities cannot credibly commit to targeting low inflation when the government budget deficit is out of control. This problem of "fiscal dominance" implies irresistible pressure for the central bank to help monetize budget deficits. Knowing this, inflation targeting will not be credible. Investors will not be reassured, and neither capital flows nor the exchange rate will be well behaved.

These are valid objections, but it is important to ask, as always, what are the alternatives? While emerging markets may find it difficult to make inflation targeting work, there is good reason to think that they will find alternatives like monetary targeting more difficult still. And the only thing that is worse than an imperfect monetary-policy operating strategy is no strategy at all. While excessive fiscal deficits are a problem for inflation targeting, they are an equally serious problem for any alternative monetary-policy strategy that the authorities might contemplate. Fiscal dominance is a critique of excessive deficits, not a critique of inflation targeting.

Brazil's recent experience lends credence to these arguments. It is the first case where an IMF program embraced inflation targeting as the framework for post-devaluation monetary policy. Although questions about the budget remained, the exchange rate stabilized and interest rates came down once the central bank adopted this operating strategy. This gives reason to hope that what worked in Brazil might also work in other emerging markets.

The IMF's principal shareholders, led by the United States, have signaled that Fund resources will no longer be used to prop up shaky currency pegs. If this commitment is credible, it will create strong incentives for emerging markets, no longer able to count on IMF support, to adopt policies of greater flexibility. But simply saying that the IMF will no longer prop up shaky currency pegs will not make it so. Once a currency is attacked, worries that its collapse will inflict a recession on the crisis country and that its distress might spread contagiously to other emerging markets may still impel the IMF to intervene, its reluctance to do so to the contrary, notwithstanding. And knowing that the Fund is likely to give in, the emerging markets in question will have no incentive to embrace greater currency flexibility as a precaution.

Lending credibility to this new IMF commitment not to prop up shaky currency pegs therefore requires institutional innovations to minimize the recessionary impact of devaluations and minimize the incidence and effects of contagion. The policy community's new emphasis on transparency and data dissemination is designed to address the contagion problem by making it easier for investors to distinguish weak and strong economies. As for recessions, devaluations are especially recessionary in emerging markets, because, as noted above, they inflate the cost of servicing short-term foreign-currency-denominated debts, potentially to unsustainable levels. The recessionary impact of devaluation can thus be minimized if countries limit their banks' and corporations' accumulation of short-term foreign-currency debts. The holding-period taxes used by Chile in the 1990s to lengthen the maturity structure of the external debt are the obvious means to this end.[14]

In addition, a credible commitment by the IMF not to run to the rescue of a country that would otherwise find it impossible to keep current on its obligations presupposes the existence of other mechanisms for dealing with problem debts. It is easy to *say* that the Fund should no longer bailout governments and their creditors, but it is hard not to *do* so as long as there do not exist other ways of addressing financial problems when they arise. The shortcoming of existing arrangements is that they make debt restructuring excessively difficult. Since many international bonds include provisions requiring the unanimous consent of bondholders to the terms of a restructuring agreement, there is an incentive for "vultures" to buy up the outstanding debt and hold the process hostage by threatening legal action. Unlike syndicated bank loans, most such bonds lack sharing clauses requiring individual creditors to share with other bondholders any amounts recovered from the borrower and thereby discouraging recourse to lawsuits.

Those who believe that countries may have to take occasional recourse to suspensions and subsequent restructurings argue that these provisions in bond covenants should be modified. Majority voting and sharing clauses would discourage maverick investors from resorting to lawsuits and other ways of obstructing settlements beneficial to the debtor and the creditor community alike. Collective-representation clauses, which specify who represents the bondholders and make provision for a bondholders committee or meeting, would allow orderly decisions to be reached.

This was suggested in 1996 by the G-10 and echoed by the G-22 and G-7 in a series of subsequent reports and declarations. In February 2000, the G-7 placed the issue on its work program for reforming the international financial system. But there has been little progress to date. And without progress on this front, the international community will lack credibility when it insists that it will not automatically run to the rescue of crisis-stricken countries, in which case the incentive for emerging markets to adopt policies of greater exchange rate flexibility will remain weak.

G-3 target zones

Authors like Bergsten and Henning (1996) and Volcker (1995) suggest that the advanced industrial countries have options not available to their developing brethren. Their banking systems and political systems are stronger, their economies more diversified. They possess the currency forward and futures markets (interbank markets in the first case, exchange-based markets in the second) needed for financial and nonfinancial firms to hedge their exposures and protect themselves from exchange rate volatility, and on which investors seeking to act as stabilizing speculators can take positions. Moreover, a durable system of target zones for the dollar, the euro and the yen with fluctuation bands of, say, ±15 percent would help to avoid the misalignments between major currencies that make life so difficult for developing countries (like the weak dollar–strong yen problem that helped to set the stage for the Asian crisis in 1996–97).

"Durable" is the key word here. For target zones for the dollar, yen and euro to solve problems and not create them, they must be credible and defensible. Unless the markets believe that the authorities are committed to their maintenance, they will speculate against them. Few observers would automatically believe that Alan Greenspan, Lawrence Summers and the US Congress to which they are accountable would be prepared to sacrifice domestic objectives like full employment and the control of inflation in order to defend an exchange rate target zone. Can we really imagine Alan Greenspan, seeing the dollar strengthen and inflation heating up as a result of fast US economic growth, *reducing* interest rates to keep the dollar in its band at the cost of additional inflation? Or some future Alan Greenspan, seeing the dollar weaken and the economy slow, *raising* interest rates to keep the dollar from falling despite rising unemployment?

A target zone bug would respond that if the credibility of the commitment to defend the band can be established, this tradeoff between domestic and international objectives will disappear. It will still be possible, they argue, for the authorities to direct monetary and fiscal policies at inflation and unemployment without driving the exchange rate beyond the edge of its band. This free lunch is the so-called "honeymoon effect" (Krugman and Miller, 1993) that arises when the commitment to defend the target zone is credible. It derives from the fact that, *assuming* sufficient credibility, speculation will be stabilizing – that is, it will tend to drive the exchange rate back toward the center of its band, or at least prevent it from diverging further as the limit of permissible fluctuations is reached. The argument goes as follows. Say that, absent the target zone, an increase in the money supply designed to stimulate growth and reduce unemployment would also weaken the exchange rate. But if the markets believe that the authorities are committed to preventing the exchange rate from continuing to weaken beyond a certain point, which they will do by reducing the money supply down the road, investors will buy the currency now in anticipation of its subsequent recovery, which will limit its current weakness. It is this credibility which creates an expectation of future policy adjustments that keeps the exchange rate from falling out of its band. The expectation that the central bank will lean against the wind to prevent the exchange rate from drifting outside its band in the future works to stabilize it in the present. The fact that the current exchange rate depends not just on the current money supply but on the entire expected future time path of money supplies relaxes the tradeoff between the exchange rate and other policy targets today. In technical terms, the elasticity of exchange rate with respect to the current money supply is less than in the absence of the target zone commitment.

Economists view free lunches with suspicion. In the present context, Clarida (1999) provides a catalogue of reasons for questioning whether the honeymoon effect will obtain.

- Even in the presence of the honeymoon effect (indeed, in order for the target-zone honeymoon to obtain), the central bank must attach priority to supporting the exchange rate and disregard all other goals of policy when the edge of the band is reached. The tradeoff between competing objectives may be attenuated when the level of the exchange rate is a nonissue, but it reemerges with a vengeance as pressure on the rate intensifies.
- If central banks instead follow Williamson (1993) by adopting "soft buffers" and allowing the currency to drop out of its band when pressures build, then the honeymoon effect will weaken or disappear, and the tradeoff between internal and external objectives will reemerge earlier.
- If they adopt another Williamson suggestion and never let the exchange rate bump against the edge of its band, instead adjusting the location of the band

to prevent the accumulation of speculative pressure, then the honeymoon effect will again be attenuated. Indeed, as the markets come to anticipate this behavior, the target-zone honeymoon may give way to a "separation" or "divorce" effect. If the markets expect the authorities to adjust the band downward when the exchange rate moves downward, then the elasticity of the exchange rate with respect to the money supply may rise rather than falling as it nears the edge of the band. Target zones with adjustable bands then create the possibility of "vicious spirals."

- When the dollar reaches the bottom of its band against the euro, the euro reaches the top of its band against the dollar. There is then the need for an assignment of responsibilities between the Fed and the ECB for keeping the rate within its band. If the country with the weak currency has sole responsibility, then exchange rate tensions will always be resolved by reductions in money supplies, which will be deflationary. It is not plausible that the markets will believe that the authorities are really prepared to countenance the indefinite pursuit of deflationary policies. If the country with the strong currency has sole responsibility, on the other hand, then exchange rate tensions will always be resolved by increases in money supplies, which will be inflationary. The markets will similarly disbelieve that the authorities are really prepared to tolerate the resulting inflationary bias. A credible target zone therefore requires a commitment for joint intervention by both countries whose bilateral rate the system is designed to stabilize. They will have to agree on what share of the intervention burden each of the two countries will shoulder. Thus, a credible system requires not just modest adaptations in domestic policies but systematic policy coordination between the partners. This sacrifice of autonomy is not something that central bankers are prepared to give lightly and therefore not something that the markets would be prepared to assume.

These are fundamental criticisms. They constitute serious grounds for questioning the feasibility of G-3 target zones.

How the international monetary system will look in twenty years

How then will the international monetary system look in 2020? My analysis discounts radical changes like a single world currency and three regional monetary unions centered on the dollar, the euro and the yen. It rules out pegged-but-adjustable exchange rates, crawling bands, target zones, and other intermediate arrangements in which governments try to have their cake and eat it too. But neither is a floating exchange rate likely to be attractive for small economies that are highly exposed to international trade and financial flows.

The three principal regions of the world economy, Europe, Asia and the Americas, are likely to square this circle in different ways. In Europe, where integration is a political as well as an economic and financial project, the euro and its associated institutions should provide the basis for an even larger zone of monetary stability. The countries of Eastern Europe want to join. Turkey wants to join. Others could follow in their train.

In the Americas, in contrast, the United States will not accede to the formation of an EU-style monetary union anytime soon. Dollarization is likely to be the solution for countries like Costa Rica and El Salvador with strong financial links to the United States who find it difficult to run an autonomous monetary policy. Other countries may adopt currency boards as a half-way house while they contemplate this final step. Meanwhile, larger, more diversified economies like Canada and Brazil may make a strategic decision to live with a floating exchange rate.

Asia's dilemma is particularly difficult. Its trade and financial flows are regionally diversified: neither the dollar nor the yen is an attractive currency-board anchor for most of the smaller countries of the region. Basket-based boards are conceivable, but they lack transparency and therefore credibility. Moreover, countries would have to agree on the composition of the basket in order for it to minimize intra-regional currency fluctuations. This requires a degree of political comity that does not exist. Moreover, basket-based boards with positive weights on the dollar, the yen and conceivably the euro do not promise a subsequent transition to monetary union. It is not clear, in other words, whether such a country would logically proceed to monetary unification with the United States, Europe or Japan. Hence, while Europe is likely to solve the currency conundrum through monetary unification and the Americas through dollarization, the plausible outcome in Asia, given the obstacles to the alternatives, is continued floating. One must hope that the countries of the region succeed in putting in place the institutional and political prerequisites necessary to effectively manage their managed float.

This vision of the international monetary architecture in the year 2020 suggests that the currency conundrum will not be solved by some grand design adopted at a new Bretton Woods Conference. It will be solved in an evolutionary fashion, with arrangements evolving in different ways in different parts of the world. Looking further down the road, it is possible to envisage more radical outcomes. But that is something for future generations to write papers about.

Notes

1 The locus classicus of this argument is Crockett (1994) and Eichengreen (1994).
2 In technical terms, the availability of reserves allows the authorities to engage in sterilized intervention, in which they attempt to support the exchange rate by selling foreign exchange without at the same time altering the domestic money supply. But when speculative sales of the currency are large relative to reserves, this strategy will not remain feasible. A credible defense will then require the authorities to buy the domestic currency that market participants sell, reducing the supply of domestic credit, raising interest rates, and tightening the screws on weak banks and corporates. The standard analysis of sterilized intervention, which suggests that it can be effective in the short run as a way of signaling the authorities' intentions, but only if it is backed up subsequently by unsterilized intervention (changes in the money supply) that indicates their willingness to put their money where their mouths are, is Dominguez and Frankel's (1993).

3 This is a simple illustration of how problems of multiple equilibria can arise in foreign exchange markets. Note that if the markets attack the currency peg collapses, but if they do not it can persist indefinitely. Thus, there are two equilibria, one in which the peg collapses and one in which it does not.

4 I choose this illustration because Williamson (1998) cites it as an example of the benefits of having a crawling band. For an account by an informed insider running parallel to mine, see Goeltom (1999).

5 See Hausmann *et al.* (1999) and Buiter (1999) for two discussions that question the value of monetary autonomy.

6 The operation of this factor is evident in the strikingly low correlation of savings and investment in particular regions of larger countries (within which a single currency circulates), compared to the much higher correlations for countries as a whole (Ingram, 1962; Eichengreen, 1990; Bayoumi and Rose, 1993; Bayoumi, 1997).

7 Calmfors (1998) obtains this result in a Barro-Gordon model of optimal monetary policy. He extends the Barro-Gordon framework to include in the government's loss function not just inflation and unemployment but also the amount of (costly) labor-market reform, where equilibrium unemployment is declining in the level of reform. In the standard one-shot game, there is an optimal amount of labor-market reform whose costs are just matched by the benefits in terms of the reduction in equilibrium unemployment (and hence expected unemployment) plus the benefits of the reduction in inflation (because lower equilibrium unemployment reduces inflationary bias). With dollarization, labor-market reform no longer results in a lower average rate of inflation. Hence, labor-market reform following dollarization is less, not more.

8 Dollarized economies tend to be special: historically, they have been very small and have had a highly unusual economic structure. This is why I focus on "near dollarizers," that is to say, countries that have adopted currency boards, like Argentina, and those which have formed monetary unions, as in Europe.

9 I present the evidence in Eichengreen (1999).

10 Dollarization will progress more rapidly if the United States supports it. So far, the attitude of the US Treasury has been, shall we say, ambivalent. Its worry is that placing the monetary fate of the entire Western Hemisphere in the hands of a small number of US citizens working in northwest Washington will create strains on the Federal Reserve. Dollarization by Panama is one thing, but dollarization by Argentina, Mexico and Brazil would be another. The larger the number of individuals outside US borders for whom the Fed makes monetary policy, the more intense the pressure will be for it to tailor its decisions to conditions beyond those prevailing in the fifty states. And the larger the number of such individuals, the greater the danger of a political backlash if the Open Market Committee neglects the impact of its policies south of the border. The Fed could be placed in the position of the Bundesbank in the 1980s and early 1990s, when the German central bank effectively set monetary conditions for the entire set of countries participating in the European Monetary System but was criticized for neglecting the impact of its decisions on its European partners. I return to these issues below.

11 I elaborate this argument in Eichengreen (1998), on which the remainder of this paragraph draws.

12 This is my favored interpretation of the political economy of EMU, as developed in Eichengreen and Ghironi (1996).

13 In other words, because the money-stock target may not produce a reasonable inflation outcome, the authorities will have an incentive to modify that target ex post, so it will not be credible ex ante.

14 There is an enormous debate over the effectiveness of these taxes. Some critics complain that evasion remains a problem. Others observe the lack of evidence that Chile's taxes limited the overall level of foreign borrowing. The second objection can be dismissed on the grounds that the goal was never to limit the overall level of foreign

borrowing but to alter its maturity structure, and on the maturity front the evidence is compelling. See Hernandez and Schmidt-Hebbel (1999) for the definitive analysis. More generally, Calvo and Reinhart (1999) find in a fifteen-country panel, including Chile, that the presence of capital controls is significantly associated with a lower share of portfolio plus short-term capital flows as a percentage of total flows. That they do not find the same when they look at portfolio flows alone suggests that the impact on short-term flows is doing most of the work. As for the first objection, it is important to recall that such a measure, to effectively lengthen the maturity structure of the debt, need not be evasion-free.

References

Bayoumi, Tamim (1997), *Financial Integration and Economic Activity*, Manchester: Manchester University Press.

Bayoumi, Tamim and Andrew Rose (1993), "Domestic Saving and Intra-National Capital Flows," *European Economic Review* 37, 1197–1202.

Bergsten, C. Fred and Randall Henning (1996), *Global Economic Leadership and the Group of Seven*, Washington, DC: Institute for International Economics.

Bronstein, Hugh (1999), "Argentina's Cavallo Calls for a Mercosur Currency," Reuters, 26 April.

Buiter, Willem (1999), "Optimum Currency Areas: Why Does the Exchange Rate Regime Matter? With an Application to UK Membership in EMU," unpublished manuscript, Bank of England and Cambridge University.

Calmfors, Lars (1998), "Unemployment, Labour-Market Reform, and Monetary Policy," unpublished manuscript, Institute for International Economic Studies, Stockholm University.

Calvo, Guillermo and Carmen Reinhart (1999), "Capital Flow Reversals, the Exchange Rate Debate, and Dollarization," unpublished manuscript, University of Maryland at College Park.

Clarida, Richard H. (1999), "G3 Exchange Rate Relationships: A Recap of the Record and a Review of Proposals for Change," unpublished manuscript, Columbia University.

Crockett, Andrew (1994), "Monetary Implications of Increased International Capital Flows," in Federal Reserve Bank of Kansas City, *Changing Capital Markets: Implications for Policy*, Kansas City: Federal Reserve Bank of Kansas City, pp. 331–364.

Dominguez, Kathryn and Jeffrey A. Frankel (1993), *Does Foreign Exchange Intervention Work?* Washington, DC: Institute for International Economics.

Eichengreen, Barry (1990), "One Money for Europe? Lessons from the U.S. Currency and Customs Union," *Economic Policy* 10, 188–187.

Eichengreen, Barry (1994), *International Monetary Arrangements for the 21st Century*, Washington, DC: The Brookings Institution.

Eichengreen, Barry (1998), "Does Mercosur Need a Single Currency?" NBER Working Paper No. 6821 (December).

Eichengreen, Barry (1999), "When to Dollarize," unpublished manuscript, University of California at Berkeley.

Eichengreen, Barry and Fabio Ghironi (1996), "European Monetary Unification: The Challenges Ahead," in Francisco Torres (ed.), *Monetary Reform in Europe*, Lisbon: Catholic University Press, pp. 83–120.

Eichengreen, Barry, Michael Mussa, Giovanni Dell-Ariccia, Enrica Detragiache, Gian Maria Milesi-Ferretti and Andrew Tweedie (1998), "Capital Account Liberalization: Theoretical and Practical Aspects," *Occasional Paper* no. 173, Washington, DC: IMF (August).

Frankel, Jeffrey A. (1999), "No Single Currency Regime is Right for All Countries or All Times," Graham Lecture, Princeton University (6 May).

Goeltom, Maranda (1999), "The Experience of Indonesia," in Jane Sneddon Little and Giovanni P. Olivei (eds), *Rethinking the International Monetary System*, Boston: Federal Reserve Bank of Boston, pp. 251–254.

Gordon, Robert (1999), "The Aftermath of the 1992 ERM Breakup: Was there a Macroeconomic Free Lunch?" NBER Working Paper No. 6964 (February).

Hausmann, Ricardo, M. Gavin, C. Pages-Serra and E. Stein (1999), "Financial Turmoil and the Choice of Exchange Rate Regime," unpublished manuscript, Inter-American Development Bank.

Hernandez, Leonardo and Klaus Schmidt-Hebel (1999), "Capital Controls in Chile: Effective? Efficient? Endurable?" unpublished manuscript, Central Bank of Chile.

Ingram, James C. (1962), *Regional Payments Mechanisms: The Case of Puerto Rico*, Chapel Hill: University of North Carolina Press.

Krugman, Paul and Marcus Miller (1993), "Why Have a Target Zone?" *Carnegie–Rochester Conference Series on Public Policy* (December), 279–314.

Masson, Paul (2000), "Exchange Rate Regime Transitions,' unpublished manuscript, Brookings Institution and Georgetown University.

Rubin, Robert (1999), "Remarks on Reform of the International Financial Architecture to the School of Advanced International Studies," *Treasury News* (21 April), RR-3093.

Tornell, Aaron and Andres Velasco (1995), "Fiscal Discipline and the Choice of Exchange Rate Regime," *European Economic Review* 39, 759–770.

Volcker, Paul A. (1995), "The Quest for Exchange Rate Stability: Realistic or Quixotic?" speech given at the Senate House, London University (29 November).

Williamson, John (1993), "Exchange-Rate Management," *Economic Journal* 103, 188–197.

Williamson, John (1996), *The Crawling Band as an Exchange Rate Regime: Lessons from Chile, Colombia, and Israel*, Washington, DC: Institute for International Economics.

Williamson (1998), "Crawing Bands or Monitoring Bands: How to Manage Exchange Rates in a World of Capital Mobility," *International Finance* 1, 59–80.

14 Pegging and stabilization policy in developing countries

Ramon Moreno

Introduction

The recent financial crises in emerging markets have renewed debate on the relative merits of pegged versus floating exchange rate arrangements and, in particular, have raised doubts about the long-run viability of pegged exchange rate regimes. Nonetheless, pegged regimes maintain their attraction. For example, Calvo and Reinhart (2000) find evidence that many countries actually intervene to smooth fluctuations in the exchange rate even though they claim to be floating. Some countries, such as Malaysia, have preferred to impose capital controls rather than give up exchange rate stability. The desire for exchange rate stability also is reflected in the ongoing interest in dollarization in Latin America and in common exchange rate arrangements in Southeast Asia. Other economies, such as Hong Kong and Argentina, have maintained currency board style arrangements that limit the freedom of monetary authorities to print money; and European nations formed the European Monetary Union in which they have given up their national currencies in favor of a common currency in order to promote trade.

Policymakers who peg the exchange rate are typically motivated by two arguments.

First, pegging to the currency of another successful monetary authority is believed to "import" that authority's policies and credibility and thereby lower inflation. These benefits of pegging are achieved through lower inflation expectations and through the monetary and fiscal restraint required by a peg. Second, pegging may contribute to faster output growth in the medium and long run by encouraging greater openness to international trade.

Pegging does entail costs, however. The monetary and fiscal restraint imposed by pegging reduces policymakers' ability to respond to shocks; as a result, the economy may experience increased output volatility or reduced welfare. Furthermore, it is not immediately obvious that pegging is a superior way of reducing inflation. In a neoclassical framework with optimizing agents, it can be shown that, given a path of output and fiscal policy, any inflation outcome achieved by an exchange rate peg can be achieved by an equivalent monetary target under a floating regime (Helpman, 1981). The case for pegging, therefore, relies on the existence of distortions that will be discussed later.

In this chapter, I attempt to shed further light on the implications of pegging for stabilization policy by selectively reviewing some of the recent theoretical literature and by comparing the behavior of certain macroeconomic indicators under both pegging and floating regimes in a sample of developing countries. Recent research addresses issues that could not be addressed by the traditional analysis of pegging and stabilization policy, which relies on a static open-economy IS–LM framework. In particular, recent research clarifies the dynamic incentives policymakers face under alternative monetary regimes, thus helping identify the conditions under which an exchange rate peg may lower inflation by enhancing credibility and the conditions under which pegging leads to greater macroeconomic policy restraint. The theoretical literature suggests that the effects of pegging could go either way. Pegging may enhance the transparency or controllability of monetary policy, so it may be more effective in lowering inflation expectations than other targets (such as money growth). However, under certain conditions a peg may be vulnerable to shifts in expectations that are arbitrary or caused by fiscal shocks. A peg may require greater fiscal restraint by limiting the availability of inflation tax revenue, but, given certain economic distortions, policymakers may find it less costly to adopt expansionary fiscal policies under a peg than under a float.

I also survey the implications of pegging for output growth and volatility. The recent empirical growth literature suggests that lower inflation and more openness stimulate growth. Pegging may therefore contribute to growth through these channels. Pegging may also affect the policymakers' ability to respond to shocks or to reduce the volatility of output, the latter being the traditional focus of the analysis of pegging and stabilization policy. Recent advances in the literature, which analyze the implications of pegging using general equilibrium models, permit comparisons of economic welfare under pegging and under alternative monetary regimes given a variety of shocks.

Because the predictions of the theoretical literature on the implications of pegging for macroeconomic performance are ambiguous. I also briefly compare the inflation and output outcomes under pegging to those under floating for a group of developing countries over the period 1975–99. The existing empirical evidence suggests that pegging is associated with lower inflation than floating and with about the same growth performance (Ghosh *et al.*, 1995; International Monetary Fund (IMF), 1997). However, the classification of exchange rate regimes used in these studies is based on what countries report to the IMF. These reports are thought to be inaccurate, as countries that peg often report they are floating (Edwards and Savastano, 1999; Calvo and Reinhart, 2000). My analysis classifies countries as pegging or floating based on observed exchange rate volatility rather than on reports to the IMF. I also attempt to control for the possibility that, during certain periods, macroeconomic performance under a floating regime either actually reflects policies adopted under pegging or may not be the result of the exchange rate regime. I confirm that inflation and inflation volatility are higher under floating than under pegging. However, output appears to grow faster under pegging than under floating.

The chapter is organized as follows. The next section discusses the choice of regime and the implications for inflation and monetary and fiscal policy. The section on "Pegging, output growth and volatility" examines their relationship. The section on "Stylized facts" briefly discusses the exchange rate classification method used in this chapter and then compares average performance under pegging and floating of: (i) inflation and output, (ii) indicators of macroeconomic policy and (iii) indicators of external sector behavior. The final section offers a summary and some discussion.

Pegging, credibility and macroeconomic policy

Until the second half of the 1970s, it was generally assumed that the interests of policymakers fully coincided with those of consumers and producers. However, more sophisticated analyses of the incentives of policymakers in a rational expectations setting, based on work by Kydland and Prescott (1977), revealed a fundamental source of conflict. Under certain conditions that are discussed below, policymakers have an incentive to introduce inflation surprises so as to maximize inflation tax revenue (Calvo, 1978) or increase output and employment (Barro and Gordon, 1983).

Inflation bias

To illustrate the policymakers' incentives, consider an economy producing a single good in which policymakers care about (squared) deviations of output and inflation from their respective target levels.[1] Labor market rigidities in this economy imply that the "natural" (zero inflation) level of output and employment are inefficiently low. Inflation is costly because, when anticipated, it reduces holdings of real money balances and the corresponding liquidity services money provides. Inflation also redistributes income, adversely affects the efficiency of resource allocation by introducing price volatility and adding noise to relative price signals and accentuates tax distortions.

In this economy, nominal wages are set for one period, based on an anticipated rate of inflation. At that wage rate, labor is supplied elastically to meet firms' demand. If inflation is higher than expected, real wages fall and firms' demand for labor rises, as do employment and output. The reverse is true when inflation is lower than expected.

Because output is below its efficient level, the central bank has an incentive first to announce a zero inflation target, but then, after wages are set, to surprise workers by increasing inflation above zero, thus lowering real wages and increasing output and employment in the short run. This "inflation bias" creates a credibility problem for the central bank, because rational workers will be aware of the bias. If they are, they will discount the central bank's promise of zero inflation and increase their nominal wage demands accordingly. The result is that, in equilibrium, inflation is higher while output and employment remain inefficiently low.

Economists have explored the credibility problem extensively, as well as various means of mitigating it. In the following, I discuss several papers that analyze the role of pegging as a means to enhance central banks' credibility.

Regime choice, transparency and credibility

One strand of the literature focuses on cases where the public is uncertain about whether the central bank is credible – that is, whether the central bank prefers low inflation or high inflation. Specifically, the public can learn about the central bank's preferences only by reviewing its behavior. Some observers have argued that, under these conditions, an exchange rate target is preferable to alternatives like a float with a monetary base target, because an exchange rate target is more "transparent."

Recent theoretical studies motivate the greater transparency of a peg by assuming either that a peg is more easily monitored or more "controllable" than the alternatives, such as a monetary base target. A peg is easier to monitor than monetary data, for example, because the peg is known immediately by market participants, whereas monetary data often are known only with a significant lag and may be subject to reporting errors.[2] A peg is more controllable in the sense that, under certain plausible assumptions, the inflation outcome that results from a peg is predictable. In contrast, the inflation outcome under a monetary base target is less predictable – actual inflation reflects not only planned inflation but also unpredictable shocks (to velocity or to the money multiplier).

Equilibrium inflation depends on the interaction between central bank actions and the public's perceptions of the central bank type, which influences expected inflation.[3] This interaction is modeled in a two-period setting by assuming that the public starts with a set of priors about the central bank's type. These priors are revised in the second period according to the central bank's actions in the first period.

The central bank must tradeoff the gain in output from increasing inflation today against the possible loss of reputation which precludes an inflation surprise tomorrow. The choice of regime has a bearing on this tradeoff. If a peg is adopted, the public can immediately observe the central bank's actions and tell that planned inflation is zero and may revise its expectations about the central bank's type accordingly. In contrast, under a float, the central bank's actions are harder to evaluate, either because the policy instrument cannot be easily observed or because lack of controllability implies that the central bank's inflation target is obscured by unobservable shocks (e.g. to velocity). Thus, a high-inflation type central bank may use a float to disguise its intentions under certain conditions.

Canavan and Tommasi (CT, 1997) explore how the public's ability to monitor the policy instrument affects inflation. To simplify the analysis, they first assume that the transparency of the instrument is given in a two-period setting. Then they examine the effects of the transparency of the signal and uncertainty about the central bank type on first-period inflation. The model reveals that a more transparent central bank signal (an exchange rate target) lowers equilibrium first-period inflation. Greater signal transparency encourages the public to place more weight on the signal, and less on its priors, in deciding whether the central bank is a low-inflation or a high-inflation type. (Higher signal transparency also lowers the dispersion of first-period inflation rates between low-inflation and high-inflation types.)

In addition, CT find that, independent of the signal, *less* (rather than more) public certainty about the central bank *type* also lowers first-period inflation. The reason is that both types want to build expectations for low inflation in the second period. The low-inflation type central bank wants expectations low because it will be easier to deliver low inflation in the second period. The high-inflation type central bank wants expectations low because the inflation "surprise" in the second period will be that much stronger.

CT also show that a high-inflation central bank would rather target the monetary base and allow the exchange rate to float, as the monetary base is a less transparent instrument. In contrast, a central bank that prefers low inflation will also prefer a more transparent instrument (a peg) to signal its type and differentiate itself more clearly from the high-inflation central bank. The alternative is to implement even lower inflation, which is costly.

Herrendorf (1999) develops a framework to analyze transparency issues that focus on "controllability." Much of his analysis is devoted to determining when reputation effects will be sufficiently strong to induce the high-inflation type central bank to adopt zero inflation in the first period. He shows that if the exchange rate is floating, this will occur under three conditions: (i) control over inflation is more precise; in this case, the public knows that velocity shocks are small, so if inflation is higher than zero, then the central bank is revealed as a high-inflation type, (ii) the central bank cares about the future (so reputation effects arising in the second period are given a higher weight) and (iii) the central bank starts out with a reputation for preferring low inflation.

If these conditions are not met, the high-inflation type central bank will plan "high" inflation (higher than zero). The inflationary bias is larger the less precisely inflation can be controlled, that is, the larger the shocks to money velocity. The reason is that these shocks give the high-inflation type central bank cover to disguise the fact that it is planning high inflation. This lowers the expected reputation cost of any given rate of planned inflation, making higher inflation more attractive. If velocity shocks are sufficiently large, reputation effects lose their force entirely.[4]

Herrendorf also shows when a peg imposes more discipline than a float, that is, when a high-inflation type central bank chooses zero inflation under a peg but plans positive inflation under a float. This occurs if: (i) the cost of exchange rate pegging is small, that is, imported inflation or real exchange rate volatility are low, (ii) policymakers attach a high value to the future, so reputation effects are assigned more weight, (iii) the central bank starts with a reputation for being "low-inflation type" and (iv) velocity shocks are large.

Assuming these conditions hold, the payoffs to central banks will vary according to the exchange rate regime in place (this is true even for the low-inflation type central bank, which always chooses zero inflation). The reason is that the public expects inflation to be lower under a peg, when both types of central banks choose zero inflation, and higher under a float, when high inflation will be chosen if a high-inflation type central bank is in office. It can be shown that the low-inflation type central bank will choose a peg if the credibility gains outweigh the costs from pegging associated with imported foreign inflation and shocks to the real exchange rate, which lead to suboptimal fluctuations in domestic output. It also can be shown that, under certain conditions, the high-inflation type central bank will choose an exchange rate peg if the low-inflation type central bank would do so; choosing a peg in the first period hides the fact that it is high-inflation type, thus lowering inflation expectations and maximizing the impact of the surprise when it abandons the peg in the second period.

Pegging, credibility and crises

Another strand of the literature emphasizes that the success of a pegged regime in curbing inflation expectations may be limited if (i) inflation expectations shift arbitrarily or (ii) the pegged regime is inconsistent with fiscal policy, possibly as a result of an unanticipated shock.

To illustrate the first case, suppose the central bank minimizes a loss function comprising squared deviations of output and inflation, as in the preceding discussion. As is well known, the inflation bias that tends to arise in this setting can be eliminated by setting the inflation rate to zero, which, in an open economy with purchasing power parity, can be accomplished by credibly pegging the exchange rate to a zero inflation currency forever. One way a country can do this is by surrendering its own currency, as argued by proponents of dollarization. However, the central bank then will be unable to adjust policy to respond to shocks, resulting in greater output volatility. A floating regime in which the central bank picks a rate of devaluation and inflation that minimizes its loss function is still preferable.[5]

The inflation bias may be reduced in a less costly manner if, apart from caring about deviations of output and inflation, the central bank also faces a fixed cost whenever the fixed exchange rate is realigned. This may be the political cost from breaking a commitment to peg or from strained relations with trading partners, particularly if the exchange rate peg reflects an international arrangement (like the Exchange Rate Mechanism of the European Monetary System in the 1980s). It is possible to show in this case that the central bank will adopt a fixed but adjustable exchange rate. It will keep the exchange rate pegged as long as shocks to the economy are small enough to ensure that the cost of maintaining a peg is lower than the cost of adjusting it. However, the policymakers will adjust the exchange rate whenever the shock is sufficiently large.

Lohmann (1992) argued that an institutional design that prompts the policymaker to pre-commit to low inflation with an escape clause is optimal, in the sense that it simultaneously minimizes inflation bias and output distortions.[6] However, it is possible to show that, in this framework, arbitrary changes in the inflation expectations of workers may trigger the escape clause. In particular, if for some reason workers fear that the central bank is going to devalue, they will increase their wage demands accordingly, reducing competitiveness and output, and, in effect, forcing the central bank to devalue. As a result, expectations of inflation (or currency devaluation) are self-fulfilling, and there are multiple equilibria consistent with differing ex ante inflation expectations (Obstfeld, 1996). Indeed, inflation expectations under the "escape clause" rule may be the same as under a floating regime, in which case the central bank incurs the cost associated with temporarily pegging and devaluing the currency without any reduction in inflation bias.

The vulnerability of monetary targets to shifts in expectations is highlighted by recent experience with efforts to stabilize the exchange rate through tighter monetary policy around episodes of currency crises. Recent empirical studies suggest that tighter monetary policy under crisis conditions either has no effect on the exchange rate (Kamien and Gould, 2002) or, if it does have any effect, the effect is very small (Dekle *et al.*, 2002).

To illustrate the second case, recall that, as emphasized by "first generation" currency crises models, a zero-inflation pegged regime must be consistent with an exogenously determined fiscal policy. Burnside, Eichenbaum and Rebelo (BER, 1998) develop an intertemporal equilibrium version of such a "first generation" model.[7] The central bank faces standard present value budget constraints, and it finances expenditures through lump sum taxes, seigniorage revenues and borrowing. (All agents, including the central bank, have access to international capital markets.) As is often assumed in this type of analysis, purchasing power parity holds, so that the rate of inflation equals the rate of devaluation of the currency.

BER first describe a sustainable peg in which the rate of expected and actual inflation is zero (no seigniorage revenues) so that the present discounted value of net future government revenues equals the value of today's net government debt. The present value of the deficit unexpectedly rises because of a rise in future transfer payments (in the context of the recent crises in emerging markets, the deficit could rise to subsidize a failing financial sector). It is possible to show that, under these conditions, the peg will be unsustainable.

BER assume that the central bank will finance the deficit by increasing the stock of money at a given time period, T, and then raise the growth of money supply permanently in a manner that satisfies the intertemporal budget constraint. They also assume that the pegged exchange rate will be abandoned when the net government debt reaches a certain threshold, and they highlight the various conditions that determine when that threshold will be reached. It is apparent in this setting that a pegged regime is associated with lower inflation, while a floating regime will be associated with higher inflation. However, this does not reflect any disciplining effect of the exchange rate on macroeconomic policy. Instead, the association occurs because of a fiscal shock that makes a peg unsustainable.

A model of the East Asian crisis by Corsetti, Pesenti and Roubini (CPR, 1998) has similar implications. However, CPR emphasize that the fiscal shock is a result of central bank guarantees to the financial sector that lead to an accumulation of contingent government liabilities to borrowers whose projects have had poor results. Once government liabilities reach a certain threshold relative to foreign reserves, the guarantee is no longer credible, so borrowers cash in, raising the measured government deficit. The expectation that at least part of this deficit will be monetized causes the peg to collapse.

Pegging and fiscal discipline

So far, we have focused on the relationship between the choice of exchange rate regime and monetary discipline or inflation. However, it is also sometimes claimed that the choice of exchange rate regime has implications for fiscal discipline. The models presented earlier cannot directly address this question, as they either ignore fiscal policy or assume it is not entirely under the control of policymakers.

The link between a peg and fiscal discipline is intuitive: pegging the exchange rate may reduce the revenue from money creation, so in some circumstances a decision to peg may require a fiscal adjustment to ensure sustainability. Chin and Miller (1998) provide an example of this in an overlapping generations model with optimizing agents who produce two goods – traded and nontraded – and are, respectively, borrowers and lenders. In their model, shocks may affect relative prices and interest rates, consequently affecting wealth, the distribution of income between lenders and borrowers and the government budget. In this setting, a peg may not be sustainable in some cases unless the government reduces its spending.

However, recent research reveals that pegging does not always imply a greater degree of fiscal discipline. Tornell and Velasco (2000) develop an intertemporal optimizing model of a small open economy with price flexibility and perfect capital mobility that describes how the choice of exchange rate regime may influence fiscal discipline, that is, the decision to limit government spending. In this setting, output is given. There is a representative (infinitely lived) agent who maximizes lifetime utility and dislikes inflation because real money balances (as well as consumption) are an argument in his utility function. The government includes a fiscal authority that has a given stream of revenue but that can spend (engage in fiscal transfers) as well as issue bonds. A monetary authority sets a rate of depreciation of the currency (which, assuming purchasing power parity, is equivalent to setting the rate of inflation) in a pegged regime, or sets the rate of growth of the money supply in a floating regime. The fiscal authority derives utility from the utility of the representative agent, which implies that the fiscal authority also dislikes inflation.

Three distortions ensure that the choice of exchange rate regime matters in this model. First, in addition to valuing the utility of the representative agent, the fiscal authority also values spending (fiscal transfers); that is, it likes to spend more than is socially optimal or than what a social planner who cares only about the welfare of the representative agent would spend. Second, the fiscal authority is impatient; it cares more about what happens up to a certain time horizon (T) than about what happens subsequently. This assumption may be motivated by the plausible idea that the government is run by politicians with limited tenure who, therefore, value the present more than does the general public. This assumption also yields a key feature of the model, namely that the decision to spend today is influenced by whether the inflation cost is borne today or tomorrow. Third, the monetary authority has limited independence; it can independently choose a monetary target (if floating) or a rate of depreciation (if pegging) up to time T, but after that it must adjust its policy (the revenue from money creation or the inflation tax) to satisfy the government budget constraint. (In what follows, I will call the period up to T "today" and the period after T "tomorrow.") This condition ensures that the monetary authority cannot simply set the entire path of monetary revenues, thus leaving the fiscal authority some leeway to determine the path of spending as well as to influence money growth and inflation outcomes after T.

How does the choice of regime influence the level of spending and the deficit and inflation behavior today or tomorrow? If a pegged regime is in place today (what Tornell and Velasco call a "predetermined exchange rate system") the rate of inflation will be determined by how much the central bank allows the exchange rate to depreciate. Any spending by the fiscal authority that cannot be fully financed by its revenues (including the inflation tax revenue) will have to be financed by borrowing. The intertemporal budget constraint of the government implies that inflation will have to rise in the future in order to service the additional debt. Thus, the inflationary cost of financing government spending under a pegged regime is borne tomorrow, not today.

This is in contrast to what happens if the central bank fixes the rate of nominal money growth today, allowing the exchange rate to float. If the fiscal authority runs a fiscal deficit, agents who know the government's intertemporal budget constraint will anticipate higher future inflation. This raises inflation today relative to the inflation that would have occurred under a peg (however, inflation tomorrow will be lower than the inflation that would have followed a pegged regime).

Will the fiscal authority spend more under pegging or under floating? For any given increase in spending, the timing of the inflation cost depends on the regime in place. Under pegging, the fiscal authority bears the inflation cost (arising from the disutility of the representative agent) tomorrow, while under floating the fiscal authority will bear some of the inflation cost immediately. For this reason, an impatient fiscal authority will tend to limit spending more under floating, when the penalty is imposed immediately. Tornell and Velasco's analysis also implies that if there is a sudden decline in fiscal revenues, a fiscal authority will respond with a sharper cutback on expenditures under a floating regime. They provide evidence from Africa indicating that following a reduction in revenues, CFA member countries that fixed their currencies to the French franc tended to adjust expenditures by less than neighboring countries that were floating. CFA is a common currency arrangement that stands for *Communaute Financiere Africaine* for its West African members and *Cooperation Financiere en Afrique Centrale* for its Central African members.[8]

Pegging, output growth and volatility

While I have focused on how the selection of an exchange rate regime may influence inflation outcomes, policymakers also typically are concerned with how such a choice affects output growth and volatility. Theory has little to say about the direct effects of the choice of exchange rate regime on growth; indeed, output is given in a number of the models discussed earlier. However, the choice of regime may affect output indirectly. If pegging reduces average inflation, it may encourage faster investment and growth by reducing uncertainty as well as the effects of the inflation tax. There is some empirical evidence that inflation is negatively related to growth (Fischer, 1993), although recent studies suggest that the relationship may be nonlinear. Ghosh and Phillips (1998) find (in their base specification) that inflation tends to be positively related to growth for inflation rates of about 3 percent or lower but is negatively related to growth at higher rates of inflation.

Pegging may also reduce real exchange rate volatility or limit real exchange rate appreciation, which may encourage greater openness. Greater openness, in turn, may stimulate growth by facilitating technology transfer and exposure to best international practices (Grossman and Helpman, 1991). Levine and Renelt (1992) show that openness is one of just two variables that are robust to specification changes in a standard growth regression, while Frankel and Romer (1999) find that openness affects growth even after correcting for endogeneity in the typical measures of openness.[9] However, as noted by Moreno (2000), the evidence that pegging encourages international trade (and therefore openness) is weak, with the exception of common currency areas. Neither is there a consensus on how pegging affects the real exchange rate, which, in turn, may influence openness. In Latin America, pegging generally is thought to be associated with real appreciation in the exchange rate, which may reduce openness and growth. In contrast, in East Asia, pegging is thought to be associated with real exchange rate stability or depreciation, which suggests the opposite.

Apart from influencing growth, the choice of regime may influence the business cycle through its impact on financing behavior and vulnerability to crises. Chang and Velasco (2000) argue that a pegged exchange rate makes an economy more vulnerable to currency collapses resulting from illiquidity. In addition, a pegged regime may amplify boom and bust cycles, in part by facilitating the external financing of risky projects made attractive by implicit government guarantees, as in Corsetti *et al.* (1998). In their model, implicit government guarantees, backed by foreign reserves, encourage borrowing from foreigners. As long as the guarantees and, consequently, the pegged regime are credible, borrowers experiencing adverse outcomes can cover any shortfalls through additional borrowing. During the pegged period, growth and investment expand past efficient levels, and the current account deficit rises. However, once reserves fall below a certain threshold, the peg is abandoned, the current account deficit experiences a reversal, and growth contracts to efficient levels.[10]

The analysis of the choice of exchange rate regime does not traditionally focus on the effects on output growth discussed above but, rather, on how regime choice affects the volatility of output in response to shocks from various sources. In an open-economy IS–LM setting, it can be shown that a pegged regime minimizes output volatility if there are shocks to money demand ("LM" shocks), while a floating regime minimizes such volatility if there are real shocks ("IS" shocks) or external shocks. If the sources of shocks are uncertain, a mixed response that reflects the relative volatility of the underlying shocks is called for (Boyer, 1978). A number of empirical studies suggest that external shocks are relatively important in explaining capital flows or currency crises (see Calvo *et al.*, 1993; Moreno and Trehan, 2000), suggesting that they also play an important role in business cycle fluctuations. If external shocks are more important than domestic shocks, the volatility of output will tend to be higher under pegged regimes than under floating regimes because the former would be less effective in insulating an economy from external shocks.

Unfortunately, the earlier theoretical literature on the choice of regime and economic shocks is not based on a general equilibrium framework, so it is impossible either to assess whether the conclusions are consistent with optimizing behavior or to perform welfare comparisons of alternative policies. Recent research addresses these concerns, providing new insights on the optimal choice of monetary regime.

Schmitt-Grohe and Uribe (2002) illustrate the costs of permanently pegging the exchange rate using Mexican data. They calibrate an equilibrium small open economy model with nontraded, exportable and importable goods sectors, with sticky prices. The economy faces three external shocks – terms of trade, world interest rate and import-price inflation – which account for 45 percent of the output error variance of Mexican output and the Mexican real exchange rate at 8-quarter to 16-quarter horizons. Schmitt-Grohe and Uribe compare the welfare costs of a permanent exchange rate peg (which they describe as dollarization) to a number of targets. These are the money growth rate, CPI inflation, nontraded goods inflation, an optimal devaluation rate rule (which responds to shocks to the terms of trade, import prices and the world interest rate), an *ad hoc* devaluation rate rule (dampening the response of the rate of devaluation to a global interest rate shock relative to the optimally derived rule in a way that the authors consider more plausible) and the crawling peg in place under the Mexican "*Pacto*" arrangement, in which the government negotiated its macroeconomic policies with the private sector and the labor unions.

Their estimates suggest that agents would rather give up between 0.1 and 0.3 percent of their nonstochastic steady-state consumption than adopt a permanent peg (dollarization). To illustrate the intuition, consider a rise in world interest rates, the most important influence on Mexican output. In response, aggregate demand falls, as does the equilibrium relative price of nontradables to tradables (because nontradables supply is less than perfectly elastic). Since prices are sticky, the nontradables price cannot fall if the exchange rate is pegged, so nontradables output falls instead. The best response would be a devaluation of the domestic currency, which would lower the price of nontradable goods and mimic the adjustment in a flexible-price economy.

Due to the complexity of their setup, Schmitt-Grohe and Uribe rely on simulations to assess the implications of their model. Obstfeld and Rogoff (2000) instead develop a one-period model which allows them to derive analytic solutions and discuss in more detail the implications of the choice of exchange rate regime on welfare, expected output and the expected terms of trade in a general equi-librium framework. The setting is a world economy consisting of two countries of equal size, each producing an array of differentiated tradable goods indexed over distinct intervals. Workers are monopolistic suppliers of a distinctive variety of labor services to the two sectors in the economy, tradables and nontradables. In this framework, the choice of regime matters because wages (but not prices) are sticky. Workers set their nominal wages before production and consumption, sup-plying labor elastically at that wage according to what firms demand in response to shocks to the economy. This demand, in turn, can be influenced by monetary policy. However, inflation surprises are ruled out. Obstfeld and Rogoff assume monetary authorities commit to a monetary *rule* and do not have the leeway to vary the rule each period. For this reason, the credibility issues discussed earlier do not arise.

An advantage of the Obstfeld and Rogoff approach is that it clarifies how eco-nomic uncertainty affects decisionmaking in an optimizing framework. For exam-ple, economic uncertainty is shown to influence ex ante wage setting, in turn affecting expected levels of consumption, output, and the terms of trade.[11] To assess the implications of alternative monetary rules, Obstfeld and Rogoff ana-lyze the case in which there is a shock to productivity that calls for an increase in output. If wages and prices are fully flexible, wages will adjust in response to the shock, and output will expand accordingly. If wages are sticky, however, this first best equilibrium is not automatically attained and must be accomplished through policy. It can be shown that if monetary authorities follow a particular procycli-cal monetary policy (set in response to both domestic and foreign productivity shocks) the optimal flexible price equilibrium can be replicated. The optimal rule expands the money supply in order to increase demand in response to the pro-ductivity shock. This monetary arrangement will typically imply floating, rather than fixed, exchange rates unless productivity shocks are perfectly correlated in the two countries.

The research cited in this section suggests that real GDP growth may be higher under pegging than under floating, if pegging stimulates investment spending or openness. However, a finding that growth is faster under pegging may be mis-leading. In some cases it may reflect the fact that a peg stimulates a boom that cul-minates in a bust. In this case, collapsing pegs that are classified as floating will typically be associated with slower output growth or contractions even if they reflect policies in place at the time of a peg.

The implications of a peg for output volatility, and the corresponding welfare implications of such volatility, are unclear. For example, pegging imposes higher welfare costs than alternative policy regimes by *increasing* output volatility in the face of external shocks. However, if there are shocks to productivity and wages are sticky, a peg may limit output adjustment by delaying adjustment in real wages and labor supply. Under these conditions, welfare may be enhanced by a pro-cyclical monetary policy under floating that may be associated with greater out-put volatility than is possible under a pegged regime. More broadly, the research cited suggests caution in attributing output performance to the choice of regime as well as in making normative statements.

Stylized facts

Classifying exchange rate regimes

As there is some ambiguity in how a decision to peg may be related to inflation or output, I attempt to describe some of the stylized facts of this relationship. For this purpose, I collected monthly exchange rate data to classify the exchange rate regimes and to identify currency crises (discussed briefly below). However, I use annual frequencies to describe the CPI inflation and real GDP from the International Financial Statistics CD-ROM of the IMF.

One popular approach (e.g. Ghosh *et al.*, 1995) to determining the kind of exchange rate regime uses the regimes reported by the countries themselves to the IMF, which appear in the annual publication *Exchange Rate Arrangements and Restrictions*. However, as noted by Edwards and Savastano (1999), Reinhart (2000) and Calvo and Reinhart (2000), the main disadvantage of this source is that the reporting often appears to be imprecise. Calvo and Reinhart (2000) study the empirical properties of exchange rates and of indicators of efforts to stabilize the exchange rate (foreign reserves, interest rates) and find that many countries that report to the IMF they are floating appear to be pegging. Fluctuations in the exchange rate of many self-proclaimed floaters are just as likely to fall within a narrow band (2.5 percent in either direction for monthly data). Calvo and Reinhart find that self-reported floaters actually experience more foreign reserve volatility, suggesting heavy intervention.

Table 14.1 illustrates the problems with classifying exchange rate regimes based on country's self-reporting. It lists the officially declared exchange rate regime in a small group of East Asian and Latin American economies as well as in Germany and Japan, and it compares the mean monthly percentage change (annualized by multiplying by 1,200) and the standard deviation of the currency against the US dollar. South Korea's "other managed float," for example, exhibits volatility that is similar to Argentina's US dollar peg. In addition, except for Brazil, the currencies of the self-described floaters among the emerging economies were much less volatile than the deutsche mark or the yen (note that the DM–$ volatility of about 10.5 is broadly representative of that currency's volatility since the 1970s (Moreno, 2000)).

In the last column of the Table 14.1, I draw on ongoing research and use a method to classify the exchange rate regime based on observed monthly exchange rate behavior.[12] The classification method of the exchange rate regime proceeds in four steps.[13] First, for each country, I identify the major currency against which it has the lowest lagging twelve-month volatility. Second, I check whether the lowest volatility, σ_{ij}, of currency i against major currency j falls below a threshold $\bar{\sigma}$. If so, I tentatively classify the regime in place in country i in that month as a peg against currency j. Otherwise, I classify the regime as floating. I use an (arbitrary) "intermediate" threshold volatility that is one-third the volatility of the DM–$ in the first half of 1993.[14]

Third, I define a new regime only if it is sufficiently *persistent*; for the purposes of this study, the minimum period is six months. This requirement addresses the

Table 14.1 Declared exchange rate regime and indicators of exchange rate behavior against the US dollar

Country	Officially declared exchange rate regime	Annualized mean monthly percentage change[a]	Standard deviation against US dollar	Estimated regime
East Asia				
Thailand	Peg to composite of currencies[b]	0.1	1.4	US dollar peg
Hong Kong	US dollar peg[c]	−0.2	0.4	US dollar peg
South Korea	Other managed float	2.5	0.9	US dollar peg
Latin America				
Argentina	US dollar peg	0.8	0.9	US dollar peg
Brazil	Independently floating	376.7	14.3	Float peg
Mexico	Other managed float[d]	−0.3	1.1	US dollar peg
Panama	US dollar peg (dollarized)	0.0	0.0	US dollar peg
Major currencies				
Germany	Independently floating	7.3	10.5	
Japan	Independently floating	10.5	9.4	

Notes

Data used in estimates are for first half of 1993.

a Mean is annualized by multiplying by 1,200.

b Australian dollar, deutsche mark, Indian rupee, Italian lira, South African rand or Russian ruble.

c According to the Hong Kong page of the report; the regime at the back of the report is misreported as "Other managed float."

d This is actually a crawling peg, with a daily limit of Mex. $0.00004 per US dollar on the depreciation of the maximum selling rate.

problem arising when the currency with the lowest volatility changes briefly (e.g. during the collapse of an exchange rate peg) but then reverts.

Fourth, in order to time regime switches more precisely, I add a percentage change criterion. If a switch in regime to fixed or floating is reported according to the lowest volatility criterion, the absolute percentage changes in the exchange rate from $t-1$ to $t-n$ ($n = 12$, and the check begins at $t-1$) are checked. A change in regime is said to begin in the first month in which the change in exchange rate is less than or equal to the change at t or less than 5 percent annualized (whichever threshold is higher will bind). Hong Kong's experience illustrates the usefulness of this criterion: Hong Kong switched from floating to a dollar peg in late 1983, but a simple volatility rule identifies the switch much later, in October 1984. This fourth step ensures that the switch is recorded in 1983.

Regime switches (from a peg to floating) also are identified for the Mexican peso in 1994 and for the Thai baht in July 1997.

To sum up, these four steps allow me to classify currencies as either floating or as pegged to one of the five major currencies (US dollar, yen, deutsche mark, French franc and sterling).

Exchange rate regimes, inflation and output

I use this classification scheme to examine the stylized facts of the relationship between exchange rate regimes, inflation and output, focusing on a sample of ninety-eight developing countries. I exclude developed countries because differences in their institutional characteristics may influence the interpretation of results. For example, inspection of the results for the full sample of countries suggests that wealthier nations tend to float, while poorer economies tend to peg. As wealthier countries also have greater macroeconomic stability that may be attributable to the quality of their institutions, including them complicates the interpretation.

Table 14.2 reports average percentage changes of inflation, real GDP and volatility (as measured by standard deviations) in pegged and floating regimes. The Z-test statistics of the significance of the difference of the means of inflation and output growth under pegged and floating regimes are also reported. The results reported in the first two rows suggest that inflation is lower and real GDP

Table 14.2 Inflation and real GDP growth (1974–98)

	Peg	*Float*	*Z-test*
Inflation (CPI)	16.6	147.6	−3.42***
	(95.4)	(1,099.9)	
Real GDP growth	4.3	3.2	4.37**
	(5.6)	(5.6)	
Excluding episodes of currency depreciation preceded by a peg and two periods after			
Inflation	14.1	142.5	−2.80**
	(98.8)	(1,141.6)	
Real GDP growth	4.6	3.6	3.43***
	(5.6)	(5.3)	
Excluding top 1% high-inflation episodes			
Inflation	12.7	36.7	−8.6***
	(25.6)	(76.6)	
Real GDP growth	4.4	3.3	3.86***
	(5.6)	(5.5)	

Notes
Figures reported are mean (standard deviation). Real GDP growth data exclude one extreme outlier observation.
*** Significant at 1 percent.
 ** Significant at 5 percent.

growth higher under pegging than under floating regimes. Also, in floating regimes, the inflation volatility is much higher while the output volatility is about the same.[15] These results may be compared to those of Ghosh *et al.* (1995) or IMF (1997). They find that while inflation is higher, real GDP growth per capita is about the same across pegged and floating regimes.[16] The results reported here rely on the estimates of the mean of the data series without controlling for other factors.

The theoretical literature allows for alternative interpretations of these results. For example, they fit conventional preconceptions of the pros and cons of fixed versus flexible regimes, namely that inflation is lower under pegging, perhaps stimulating more rapid growth. The table also suggests that the loss of policy flexibility under a pegged regime does not lead to higher output volatility. However, this last result should be interpreted with caution; the lower output volatility under a pegged regime may reflect the impact of factors our comparison does not account for, such as capital controls.

The theory reviewed above also cautions us that regimes are connected over time by the government's intertemporal budget constraint. Thus, inflation may be lower under pegging because of fiscal policies or other shocks that make the peg untenable rather than because of any disciplining effect of a pegged regime. Indeed, as emphasized in Tornell and Velasco (2000), the government can defer inflation to the future under a pegged regime by borrowing; the effect would be higher inflation under floating. Regardless of the interpretation, the results do give an idea of the variation in average inflation and growth across exchange rate regimes.

The remainder of Table 14.2 reexamines the data by accounting for the possibility of "survivor bias." Specifically, the results may reflect the impact of outliers. Inspection of median inflation rates (not reported) reveals that they are much lower than mean inflation rates. (However, the median under pegging is still lower than under floating, 8.5 percent versus 13.6 percent, respectively.) It can be argued that these outliers, which have a particularly strong effect on average inflation under floating, are misleading, in part because they may be associated with survivor bias – for example, high inflation often is associated with floating rates in the aftermath of currency crises, but such episodes need not be attributable to a floating regime.[17]

I account for the possible effects of survivor bias in two ways. First, assuming that the aftermath of a currency crisis is the result of the policies that preceded the crisis, I eliminate observations in the year of a currency crisis and the two years that follow, as long as the crisis is preceded by a peg. The definition of a crisis is broadly consistent with the exchange rate regime classification: a crisis is an event in which the percentage change depreciation at T exceeds the lagging twelve-month mean percentage change plus three standard deviations and is also larger than 25 percent. The criterion of three standard deviations accounts for greater volatility that may occur during periods of high inflation; the criterion of 25 percent rules out changes that may be proportionally large but are quantitatively small (e.g. a change of ten percentage points in the tightly pegged Argentinean exchange rate that involves fractions of the peso).

The results of this adjustment are in rows three and four of Table 14.2, which show average inflation and GDP performance excluding years in which there is a currency crisis and the two years that follow. Average inflation falls in both pegged and floating exchange rate regimes, but not by much. Inflation under a float continues to be considerably higher than under a peg, and the volatility of inflation rises rather than falls. However, the point estimate of the growth rate rises under floating, bringing it closer to the average under a pegged regime. Output volatility remains comparable across the two regimes.

Next, I eliminate episodes of very high inflation from the sample, presuming that the exchange rate regime is endogenous to such high inflation, and not vice versa. It is hard to think of any fixed exchange rate regime that can survive extreme episodes of high inflation. Even countries with capital controls face strong pressure to devalue when very high inflation reduces competitiveness. As a cutoff, I eliminate observations in which inflation is in the upper 1 percent for the full sample. These results are in the final two rows of Table 14.2 and show that average inflation and its volatility are reduced across all regimes even more sharply, although inflation and inflation volatility remain higher under floating than under pegging. Real GDP growth rates are similar to those observed in the full sample.

To sum up the stylized facts, inflation and the volatility of inflation tend to be higher and real GDP growth lower under floating than under pegging. The volatility in real GDP growth is roughly the same across exchange rate regimes.

Summary and discussion

In this chapter we discussed how a decision to peg might influence inflation and output. The theoretical survey reviewed the conditions under which pegging may be associated with different inflation and output outcomes as well as the factors that account for such an association. In particular, I reviewed the conditions under which a peg may or may not lower inflation expectations or encourage macroeconomic discipline. We also described the channels through which a peg might stimulate faster output growth, produce boom and bust cycles, or influence output volatility.

We have reviewed the stylized facts associated with pegged and floating exchange rate regimes, using an exchange rate classification based on the observed volatility of exchange rates. The comparison of mean values suggests that inflation and the volatility of inflation tend to be higher under floating than under pegging. The estimates suggest that episodes of pegging are associated with significantly faster (but no more volatile) real GDP growth than are episodes of floating.

The survey of the recent theoretical literature suggests that caution is needed in interpreting these stylized facts. For example, the lower inflation under pegging may indeed reflect greater macroeconomic discipline, as is often argued. Alternatively, a peg may be unsustainable, having no disciplining effect, but simply postponing inflation to some future date when the peg collapses. A similar ambiguity arises in interpreting more rapid growth under pegging, which may reflect the stimulus associated with reduced uncertainty, or unsustainable booms.

Appendix A1: data description and sources

From the International Financial Statistics (IMF) CD-ROM I obtained the following series: The end-of-period exchange rates (line ae), consumer prices (line 64), exports (line 70.d), real GDP (line 99b.r or 99b.p), population (line 99z. Due to lack of data, Brazil's CPI is substituted with wholesale prices (line 63). The end-of-period exchange rates (line ae) are used to calculate monthly percentage changes in the exchange rate.

The data range from 1974 to 1998, collected at an annual frequency except for CPI and end-of-period exchange rates, which were collected at a monthly frequency and then annualized when appropriate. A number of macroeconomic series contained missing values or did not contain values for the entire time span. Estimates then were constructed using the available data for each country from alternative sources, including FAME.

Full country set of ninety-eight developing or emerging market economies: Algeria, Argentina, Bahrain, Bangladesh, Barbados, Belize, Benin, Bhutan, Bolivia, Botswana, Brazil, Burkina Faso, Burundi, Cameroon, Central African Republic, Chad, Chile, Colombia, Democratic Republic of Congo, Republic of Congo, Costa Rica, Cote d'Ivoire, Cyprus, Dominican Republic, Ecuador, Egypt, El Salvador, Equatorial Guinea, Ethiopia, Fiji, Gabon, Gambia, Ghana, Grenada, Guatemala, Guinea-Bissau, Guyana, Haiti, Honduras, Hong Kong, Hungary, India, Indonesia, Islamic Republic of Iran, Jamaica, Jordan, Kenya, Korea, Kuwait, Lao People's Democratic Republic, Lesotho, Luxembourg, Madagascar, Malawi, Malaysia, Mali, Malta, Mauritania, Mauritius, Mexico, Morocco, Mozambique, Myanmar, Nepal, Nicaragua, Niger, Nigeria, Oman, Pakistan, Panama, Papua New Guinea, Paraguay, People's Republic of China, Peru, Philippines, Poland, Romania, Rwanda, Saudi Arabia, Senegal, Seychelles, Sierra Leone, Singapore, South Africa, Sri Lanka, Sudan, Swaziland, Syrian Arab Republic, Thailand, Togo, Trinidad and Tobago, Tunisia, Uganda, Uruguay, Vanuatu, Venezuela, Republic of Yemen, Zambia and Zimbabwe.

Notes

1 More precisely, the policymakers' objective function is:

$$L = (y_t - \bar{y})^2 + w\pi_t^2$$

where L is the loss function of policymakers, y_t is real output, $\bar{y}$ is the output targeted by policymakers, π is the rate of inflation, and w is the relative weight policymakers assign to high inflation. The targeted level of output $\bar{y}$ is assumed to be greater than the "natural" level consistent with zero inflation.

2 For example, data on the monetary base published by the IMF at the time of the Mexican peso crisis of December 1994 were about six months old. More timely data on Mexico or other emerging markets are available now on their respective central bank websites.

3 The analysis is extended to an open economy setting by assuming purchasing power parity, so that inflation and an exchange rate depreciation are the same thing. A depreciation (inflation) is costly, but, as in the preceding analysis, it can be beneficial if it is higher than anticipated by the public.

4 The conditions under which a "high-inflation type" policymaker will decide to maintain zero inflation under a peg are similar, although there are differences because the transparency of the peg unambiguously reveals the planned inflation rate of zero.

5 For further discussion of the implications of alternative arrangements see Lohmann (1992) and Obstfeld and Rogoff (1995, ch 9). On the other hand, Mendoza (2003) discusses in a general equilibrium model applied to Mexico how the credibility costs of not fixing given credit constraints may be so high as to warrant dollarization. Note that in Herrendorf's (1999) model, the "low-inflation type" central bank always chooses zero inflation, regardless of the size of the shock to the economy or the exchange rate regime chosen.

6 See also Flood and Isard (1989).

7 The model is a continuous time, perfect foresight endowment economy populated by an infinitely lived representative agent and a government. The original "first generation" models of Krugman (1979) and Flood and Garber (1984) are not intertemporal optimizing models but instead are motivated by the model of resource depletion of Salant and Henderson (1978). These models emphasize that a fiscal deficit is incompatible with a pegged regime because it will ultimately lead to the exhaustion of foreign reserves. Anticipating this, agents will attack the peg and suddenly deplete reserves at a well-specified point in time in which no capital gains or losses from the abandonment of the peg are possible.

8 A decision to peg does not always reflect a desire to limit inflation and may instead be the outcome of a political process, in which the number gaining from a peg exceeds the number losing from it. Chin and Miller's (1998) two-sector (traded and nontraded goods) model has this feature. In their model, shocks create distribution effects between producers in traded (debtors) and nontraded (creditors) goods via relative price and interest rate changes, influencing the choice of regime. In this case, while the decision to peg may have implications for fiscal discipline, such discipline is not necessarily the underlying motivation for policy.

9 Some recent research does cast doubt on the robustness of the relationship between inflation or openness and growth. Sala-i-Martin (1997) runs nearly two million regressions to compute the distribution of coefficients for various explanatory variables used in growth regressions and finds that inflation and openness are significant only in a small proportion of the cases. However, these regressions do not account for nonlinearities or simultaneity.

10 Output is given in the BER (1998) model, but the choice of regime affects the cyclical behavior of consumption. In their framework, the collapse of a peg may be associated with a contraction in consumption and corresponding reduction in money demand.

11 It also can be shown that expected utility rises with expected log expenditure, measured in tradables, and the expected log real exchange rate, but falls with greater volatility in expected spending or in productivity. This sets the stage for assessing alternative monetary regimes based on how they affect these variables.

12 Ghosh *et al.* (1995, p. 3), argue that focusing on observed volatility of the exchange rate provides no indication of the degree of commitment to a peg. However, it is unclear from the data or the theoretical discussion that a declared exchange rate regime provides any information on commitment, either.

13 As noted earlier, we use monthly data to classify exchange rate regimes, but the discussion later in this chapter will involve annual frequencies. To switch to annual frequency, we classify a country as pegging to the dollar in a given year if it was pegged to the dollar in most of the months. If there is a tie, the classification is based on the regime in place at the beginning of the year.

14 An alternative is to adopt a "strict" threshold volatility similar to the volatility of the Thai baht in the first half of 1993 as reported in Table 14.1. However, this threshold appears to be too strict to capture the many cases in which countries attempt to peg their currencies.

15 This estimate eliminates one extreme outlier observation for real GDP growth. If the outlier is not eliminated, the volatility under pegging is much higher.

16 Applying similar methods to a more recent sample to test the impact of currency boards, Ghosh *et al.* (1998) find that inflation is lower, and per capita real GDP growth higher, under currency boards than under alternative exchange rate regimes – whether pegged rates or floating. Their study relies on regression analysis, which provides a more systematic comparison than the stylized facts offered in this chapter. However, although the authors attempt to control for simultaneity, the results of such regression analysis are still difficult to interpret due to the theoretical issues raised above.

17 Edwards (1993) attempts to deal with survivor bias by assessing whether, for a given ten-year period, countries with a fixed regime had lower inflation in the first year. However, this approach leaves open the question of what happened in the succeeding nine years that may have influenced observed inflation rates.

References

Barro, Robert J. and David B. Gordon. 1983. "Rules, Discretion, and Reputation in a Model of Monetary Policy." *Journal of Monetary Economics* 12 (July) 101–121.

Boyer, Russell. 1978. "Optimal Foreign Exchange Market Interventions." *Journal of Political Economy* 86, 1045–1055.

Burnside, Craig, Martin Eichenbaum and Sergio Rebelo. 1998. "Prospective Deficits and the Asian Currency Crisis." *NBER Working Paper* No. 6758 (October).

Calvo, Guillermo. 1978. "On the Time Inconsistency of Optimal Policy in a Monetary Economy." *Econometrica* 46 (November) 1411–1428.

Calvo, Guillermo and Carmen Reinhart. 2000. "Fear of Floating." Unpublished manuscript. University of Maryland.

Calvo, Guillermo, Leonardo Leiderman and Carmen Reinhart. 1993. "Capital Inflows and Real Exchange Rate Appreciation in Latin America." *IMF Staff Papers* 40(1) 108–151.

Canavan, Chris and Mariano Tommasi. 1997. "On the Credibility of Alternative Exchange Rate Regimes." *Journal of Development Economics* 54, 101–122.

Chang Roberto and Andres Velasco. 2000. "Financial Fragility and the Exchange Rate Regime." *Journal of Economic Theory* 92, 1–34.

Chin, Daniel M. and Preston J. Miller. 1998. "Fixed vs. Floating Exchange Rates: A Dynamic General Equilibrium Analysis." *European Economic Review* 42, 1221–1249.

Corsetti, Giancarlo, Paolo Pesenti and Nouriel Roubini. 1998. "Paper Tigers? A Model of the Asian Crisis." *European Economic Review* 43 (June) 1211–1236.

Dekle, Robert, Cheng Hsiao and Siyan Wang. 2002. "Interest Rate Stabilization of Exchange Rates and Contagion in Asian Crisis Countries." In *Financial Crises in Emerging Markets*, eds, R. Glick, R. Moreno and M. Spiegel. Cambridge: Cambridge University Press, pp. 140–176.

Edwards, Sebastian. 1993. "Exchange Rates as Nominal Anchors." *Weltwirtschaftliches Archiv* 129, 1–32.

Edwards, Sebastian and Miguel A. Savastano. 1999. "Exchange Rates in Emerging Economies: What Do We Know? What Do We Need to Know?" *NBER Working Paper* No. 7228 (July).

Fischer, Stanley. 1993. "The Role of Macroeconomic Factors in Growth." *Journal of Monetary Economics* 32, 485–512.

Flood, Robert and Peter Garber. 1984. "Collapsing Exchange Rate Regimes: Some Linear Examples." *Journal of International Economics* 17 (August) 1–13.

Flood, Robert P. and Peter Isard. 1989. "Monetary Policy Strategies." *International Monetary Fund Staff Papers* 36 (September) 612–632.

Frankel, Jeffrey A. and David Romer. 1999. "Does Trade Cause Growth?" *American Economic Review* 89, 379–399.

Ghosh, Atish R. and Steven Phillips. 1998. "Inflation, Disinflation, and Growth." *IMF Working Paper* WP/98/68.

Ghosh, Atish R., Anne-Marie Gulde, Jonathan D. Ostry and Holger C. Wolf. 1995. "Does the Nominal Exchange Rate Regime Matter?" *IMF Working Paper* WP/95/121 (November).

Ghosh, Atish R., Anne-Marie Gulde and Holger C. Wolf. 1998. "Currency Boards: The Ultimate Fix?" *IMF Working Paper* WP/98/8.

Grossman, Gene M. and Elhanan Helpman. 1991. *Innovation and Growth in the Global Economy.* Cambridge, MA: MIT Press.

Helpman, Elhanan. 1981. "An Exploration in the Theory of Exchange-Rate Regimes." *Journal of Political Economy* 89, 865–890.

Herrendorf, B. 1999. "Transparency, Reputation, and Credibility under Floating and Pegged Exchange Rates." *Journal of International Economics* 49, 31–50.

International Monetary Fund. 1997. "Exchange Rate Arrangements and Performance in Developing Countries." Chapter 4 in *World Economic Outlook.*

Kamien, Steven and David Gould. 2002. "The Impact of Monetary Policy on Exchange Rates during Financial Crises." In *Financial Crises in Emerging Markets*, eds, R. Glick, R. Moreno and M. Spiegel. Cambridge: Cambridge University Press, pp. 121–139.

Krugman, Paul. 1979. "A Model of Balance of Payments Crises." *Journal of Money, Credit, and Banking* 11, 311–325.

Kydland, Finn E. and Edward C. Prescott. 1977. "Rules Rather than Discretion: The Inconsistency of Optimal Plans." *Journal of Political Economy* 85, 473–492.

Levine, Ross and David Renelt. 1992. "A Sensitivity Analysis of Cross-Country Growth Regressions." *American Economic Review* 82, 942–963.

Lohmann, Susanne. 1992. "Optimal Commitment in Monetary Policy: Credibility versus Flexibility." *American Economic Review* 82, 273–286.

Mendoza, Enrique. 2003. "The Benefits of Dollarization when Financial Markets Are Imperfect and Monetary Policy Lacks Credibility." *Journal of Money, Credit, and Banking* 43(5), 926–943.

Moreno, Ramon. 2000. "Does Pegging Increase International Trade?" *FRBSF Economic Letter* 2000–29 (September 29).

Moreno, Ramon, and Bharat Trehan. 2000. "Common Shocks and Currency Crises." *FRBSF Working Paper* 2000–05.

Obstfeld, Maurice. 1996. "Models of Currency Crises with Self-Fulfilling Features." *European Economic Review* 40 (April) 1037–1048.

Obstfeld, Maurice and Kenneth Rogoff. 1995. *Foundations of International Macroeconomics.* Cambridge, MA: MIT Press.

Obstfeld, Maurice and Kenneth Rogoff. 2000. "New Directions for Stochastic Open Economy Models." *Journal of International Economics* 50, 117–153.

Reinhart, Carmen. 2000. "The Mirage of Floating Exchange Rates." *American Economic Review* 90(2) 65–70.

Rogoff, Kenneth. 1985. "The Optimal Degree of Commitment to an Intermediate Monetary Target." *Quarterly Journal of Economics* 100 (November) 1169–1189.

Sala-i-Martin, Xavier. 1997. "I Just Ran Two Million Regressions." *American Economic Review* 87 (May) 178–183.

Salant, Stephen W. and Dale W. Henderson. 1978. "Market Anticipations of Government Policies and the Price of Gold." *Journal of Political Economy* 66 (December), 467–482.

Schmitt-Grohe, Stephanie and Marin Uribe. 2002 "Stabilization Policy and the Cost of Dollarization." *Journal of Money, Credit, and Banking* 56(2) 447–472.

Tornell, Aaron and Andres Velasco. 2000. "Fixed versus Flexible Exchange Rates: Which Provides More Fiscal Discipline?" *Journal of Monetary Economics* 45, 399–436.

15 EMU, the euro and the European policy mix*

The nascent stage

Jonathan Coppel, Martine Durand and Ignazio Visco

This chapter was written at the end of 1999 and presented at the AEA-ACAES Joint Session, 'EU and Euro Challenges for Asia-Pacific Co-operation', January 7–9, 2000, Boston, Massachusetts. Updated remarks are contained in the Appendix explicitly written for this volume in October 2002. Jonathan Coppel and Ignazio Visco have since left the OECD and are currently at the Reserve Bank of Australia and Banca d'Italia respectively.

Introduction

The euro has now been in existence for over a year with the conduct of monetary policy framed in the context of economic developments for the area as a whole. Initial fears, raised in some quarters, about problems concerning the transition and implementation of a single monetary policy did not materialise. Indeed, monetary policy and the stance adopted by the European Central Bank (ECB) have been broadly judged as appropriate. Inflation has stayed below 2 per cent, inflation expectations are low and recently output growth across the euro area started to increase. This was accompanied by substantial employment gains and a decline in the rate of unemployment to below 10 per cent for the first time in seven years. The Organisation for Economic Co-operation and Development (OECD) expects the recovery to continue over the next couple of years and without substantial inflationary pressures. In short, the first year of the euro has coincided with broadly positive economic outcomes and favourable prospects.

Against the background of an improving economic conjuncture, together with a current account surplus and expectations of narrowing interest rate differentials *vis-à-vis* the United States, several pundits predicted a little more than a year ago that the value of the euro would appreciate against the dollar and other currencies. But the opposite has occurred. Since the launch of the euro, its value has steadily declined by about 14 per cent against the dollar to reach a level close to parity and has also fallen, albeit in most cases by smaller magnitudes, against other major currencies. The ECB openly acknowledges that it closely monitors the exchange rate in order to assess the impact of currency movements on inflation, but has refused to express a view on what it considers the euro's 'fundamental' or medium-term equilibrium value. This, no doubt, partly reflects the difficulty of calculating reliable estimates of the directly unobservable concept of equilibrium exchange rates. On the other hand, since the depreciation of the euro has rekindled a debate on how well foreign exchange markets reflect fundamental determinants and led to calls for greater exchange rate stability, possibly through the introduction of formal exchange rate target zones, some notion of the equilibrium exchange rate is necessary, if only, in order to help assess such proposals.

This chapter focuses on these issues. Specifically, it attempts to assess whether the depreciation of the euro over the past year can be explained by economic fundamentals. But first, to give a better sense of perspective, this chapter compares recent exchange rate movements and measures of volatility with longer term trends. Against this background, the issue of exchange rate target zones and central bank interventions as devices to limit currency volatility are considered in the next section. The section also looks at the euro's prospects as an international currency. The section on the 'Prospective policies and economic developments in the euro area' is forward looking. It tries to gauge the future direction of the euro-area economy based on its structural characteristics and the known macroeconomic policy stance in the three main economic regions (the United States, Japan and the euro area itself). The potential implications for future exchange rate developments are then discussed. For illustrative purposes, the OECD's Interlink model is used to simulate the impact of significant exchange rate changes and of structural adjustment in the European labour and product markets on output, inflation and the external positions of the euro area itself and the other major regions.

Movements and volatility of the euro

Exchange rate movements reflect multifarious factors and hence it is difficult, if not impossible, to attribute changes in the value of a currency to specific events or developments. Exchange rates respond to divergent cyclical positions and monetary policies, differences in productivity growth and terms of trade developments, and are part of the necessary process to correct for external position imbalances. Views vary widely, however, on how well foreign exchange markets reflect fundamental determinants and how well they serve as an equilibrating force, and underlie policy prescriptions on the desirability, practicality and nature of government intervention in exchange rate markets. The main concerns with foreign exchange markets are twofold. First, some argue that if exchange markets are left alone, they may not always reflect fundamentals and can lead to large and possibly protracted deviations in the value of a currency from its long-run equilibrium level, and second they give rise to excessive exchange rate volatility. Such outcomes bear on policy, since they could result in significant and persistent effects on bilateral trade flows and generate protectionist trade pressures. These could indirectly lead to pressures for inappropriate policy choices, exacerbate output fluctuations and, in the context of the euro, risk undermining confidence in the new currency and thus damage its prospects as an international currency. Such concerns have led some commentators to advocate central bank interventions in currency markets in order to attempt to limit fluctuations in the euro, whereas others have gone further, calling for the introduction of target zones for the value of the euro *vis-à-vis* the dollar and the yen.[1] Evaluating the appropriate policy response to such concerns depends on a number of issues. First, do market exchange rates deviate from their 'fundamental' levels and if so, to what extent, for how long, and does it matter? Second, how volatile are exchange rates and has volatility changed over time, and does exchange rate volatility harm economic performance? And third, is it reasonable to expect the dollar/euro and yen/euro exchange rate to be stable in the current conjunctural context and how practical and effective would a dollar/euro and yen/euro exchange rate target zone be in terms of limiting exchange rate volatility?

What has happened to the euro?

Debate over appropriate exchange rate policy was quick to surface, following the launch of the euro and was no doubt prompted by the subsequent falls in its value against the dollar and the yen. At the beginning of 1999, when the euro was launched it was worth $1.18 against the US dollar whereas the yen traded at 134 yen to the euro. Since then it has depreciated by about 14 per cent *vis-à-vis* the US dollar, 22 per cent against the Japanese yen and 12 per cent against the pound sterling (Table 15.1). However, in effective terms, the depreciation of the euro has been less marked at about 10 per cent since the beginning of the year. This is because the combined weight of the yen, the dollar and the pound in the OECD euro effective exchange rate is around 50 per cent (Table 15.2) and other currencies have tended either to depreciate or to appreciate less against the euro.

Table 15.1 Euro exchange rates, period averages

		US$/euro	Yen/euro	Pound/euro	Nominal effective rate[a]	Real effective rate[a]
1995		1.32	124.3	0.84	100.0	100.0
1996		1.29	140.4	0.83	102.0	99.1
1997		1.13	137.0	0.69	95.5	90.4
1998		1.11	145.6	0.67	101.3	92.8
1999	Q1	1.12	130.8	0.69	103.8	93.2
	Q2	1.06	127.8	0.66	100.0	89.4
	Q3	1.05	119.1	0.65	98.9	88.2
	Q4	1.04	108.6	0.64	97.3	—
1999	July	1.04	124.1	0.66	98.5	88.1
	August	1.06	120.3	0.66	99.7	88.9
	September	1.05	112.9	0.65	98.4	87.5
	October	1.07	113.5	0.65	99.5	88.1
	November	1.03	108.5	0.64	97.2	—
	December	1.01	103.8	0.63	95.3	—
Memo item: per cent change since the launch of the euro (4/1/99)						
		−14.2	−22.4	−11.9	−9.6[b]	−7.0[c]

Source: OECD.

Notes
a Based on the OECD measure of the nominal and real effective exchange rates, 1995 = 100.
b Per cent change between January 1999 and December 1999.
c Per cent change between January 1999 and October 1999.

Table 15.2 Weights underlying the calculation of effective exchange rates[a]

	Euro area	United States	Japan
Euro area	—	16.02	15.34
United States	18.08	—	26.85
Japan	9.91	16.55	—
United Kingdom	21.48	4.58	3.59
Canada	1.13	18.90	1.35
Australia	0.41	0.52	1.20
Czech Republic	2.20	0.10	0.05
Denmark	2.45	0.26	0.36
Greece	0.72	0.06	0.03
Hungary	2.04	0.11	0.09
Iceland	0.04	0.01	0.01
Korea	2.38	3.37	6.16
Mexico	0.52	10.73	0.39
New Zealand	0.07	0.12	0.44
Norway	1.18	0.23	0.28
Poland	2.44	0.12	0.05
Sweden	5.17	0.95	1.17
Switzerland	7.25	1.18	1.61
Turkey	1.80	0.26	0.08
Russia	2.04	0.58	0.90
Chinese Taipei	2.70	4.52	5.96
Hong Kong	2.58	3.47	3.66
Singapore	2.23	2.99	3.55
China	4.58	6.26	14.27
Indonesia	0.92	0.87	2.44
Malaysia	1.44	2.20	3.55
Philippines	0.58	1.22	1.92
Thailand	1.14	1.44	3.25
India	1.25	0.89	0.57
Argentina	0.25	0.23	0.10
Brazil	1.00	1.27	0.79

Source: OECD.

Note

a Weights shown here are 1997 weights. These are based on bilateral exports and imports of manufactured goods. They capture competition faced by the three major OECD areas in their own market as well as in foreign markets from both domestic producers and exporters from third countries. In the calculation of effective rates the OECD uses weights from 1970 to 1997. For more details see Durand *et al.* (1998).

Measures of effective exchange rates are clearly sensitive to the choice of the set of countries and the weighting system underlying the calculations.[2] However, since January 1999, most indicators have pointed to similar effective depreciations (Figure 15.1). Indeed, according to the ECB measure, which includes only thirteen trading countries, the effective depreciation of the euro since its launch amounts to 12 per cent, whereas the International Monetary Fund (IMF) measure (which covers countries with trade weights greater than 1 per cent) points to an 11 per cent depreciation. On the other hand, the extent of euro appreciation[3]

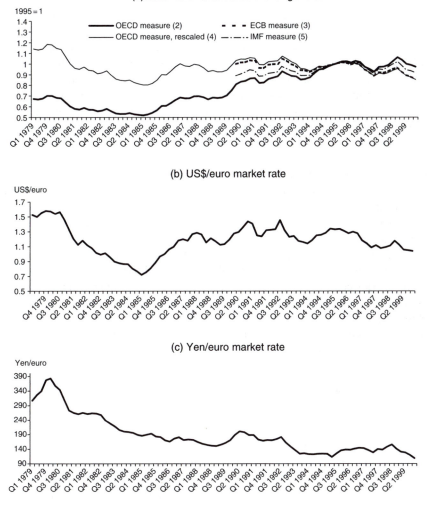

Figure 15.1 Euro exchange rates.[1]

Source: OECD.

Notes

1 Rates are quarterly averages.
2 Calculated with moving weights and thirty partner countries.
3 Calculated with fixed weights and thirteen partner countries.
4 Calculated as the OECD measure, rescaled to use fixed weights and thirteen partner countries.
5 Calculated with fixed weights and partner countries with trade weights greater than 1 per cent.

in the year and a half preceding its introduction differs quite markedly according to the country coverage of the various indicators. Given the large swings in some emerging market currencies over the past two years, their exclusion tends to understate movements in effective exchange rates. In particular, the euro is estimated to have appreciated by about 15 per cent between the third quarter of 1997 and the fourth quarter of 1998 according to the OECD measure. Rescaling this measure to include the same thirteen trading partners as the ECB, or using the ECB measure, would lead to an appreciation of about 8 per cent. The IMF measure for its part indicates a 13 per cent appreciation over that period.

Judging the present value of the euro also depends on the time-frame considered. Viewed over a longer perspective, in nominal terms the effective level of the euro has reached a level close to its past five-year average level. It is currently slightly above where it was in the middle of 1997 before the Asian crisis, and considerably higher than it was in the mid-1980s. When emerging market economies are excluded, especially Latin America, which registered hyper inflation and large depreciations in the 1980s, the present level of the euro nominal effective rate appears to be at its lowest point of the 1990s, but still above its mid-1980s level. Furthermore, the range between minimum and maximum per cent changes in exchange rate indices observed over the past five years is narrower for the euro compared with the yen or dollar. To illustrate, the maximum nominal effective exchange rate change for the yen and the dollar over the past five years was about 30 per cent. In contrast, the maximum variation for the euro over this period was closer to 15 per cent. Viewed over a longer perspective, therefore, the movements of the euro over the past year appear less dramatic than bilateral changes *vis-à-vis* the dollar would suggest.

The 'fundamental' value of the euro

Short-term considerations

Many economists and market participants, however, have been surprised by the decline of the euro. Prior to the launch of the new currency, most forecasts were confident that the euro would appreciate. Such predictions were based on an assessment of 'fundamentals', which a priori appeared in line with an appreciating currency; a positive economic outlook for the euro area, a continued current account surplus and expectations of narrowing differentials in euro short- and long-term interest rates *vis-à-vis* those in the United States. Changes in real interest rate differentials and cumulated current account balances as a share of Gross Domestic Product (GDP) have indeed in the past been correlated with major movements in the real bilateral euro/dollar exchange rate, although for Japan the sign of the correlation coefficient switches, which may reflect other offsetting factors (Table 15.3).

However, a significant force underlying the depreciation of the euro over much of 1999 seems to have been the improvement in US economic prospects relative to those in the euro area (see Corsetti and Pesenti, 1999). Indeed, the conjuncture

Table 15.3 Correlation coefficients between the real euro exchange rate and real interest rate differentials[a]

	1971Q1 to 1980Q3	1980Q3 to 1985Q1	1985Q1 to 1990Q4	1990Q4 to 1999Q3
Euro/$ vs. euro–US real short-term interest rate differential	−0.44	−0.40	−0.82	−0.65
Euro/yen vs. euro–Japan real short-term interest rate differential	0.39	−0.26	−0.52	0.17
Euro/$ vs. euro–US real long-term interest rate differential	−0.55	−0.73	−0.93	−0.79
Euro/yen vs. euro–Japan real long-term interest rate differential	0.55	−0.03	−0.38	0.20
Memorandum item				
Euro/$ vs. euro area net foreign asset position[b]	—	−0.43	−0.83	0.71
Euro/yen vs. euro area net foreign asset position[b]	—	0.56	−0.66	−0.34
DM/$ vs. German–US real short-term interest rate differential	−0.44	−0.69	−0.68	−0.24
DM/yen vs. German–Japan real short-term interest rate differential	−0.08	0.34	−0.01	−0.09
DM/$ vs. German–US real long-term interest rate differential	−0.61	−0.71	−0.89	−0.34
DM/yen vs. German–Japan real long-term interest rate differential	0.02	0.14	0.21	−0.21
Memorandum item				
DM/$ vs. German net foreign asset position[b]	−0.83	0.76	−0.78	−0.21
DM/yen vs. German net foreign asset position[b]	0.86	−0.63	−0.12	0.81

Source: OECD.

Notes

a The four periods correspond to periods of either major real appreciation or depreciation of the bilateral euro exchange rate *vis-à-vis* the US dollar and Japanese yen. Real exchange rates are based on CPI.

b Calculated as cumulated current account balances over the full period examined, as a percentage of GDP.

changed very quickly over the first few months of 1999. Output for the euro area as a whole suffered in response to the series of financial crises in emerging market economies, as well as political uncertainties in some member countries, which particularly hit industrial production. Measures of business confidence weakened and concerns were raised in some quarters over the prospect of deflation. On the other hand, the economic situation in the United States remained relatively buoyant and the near-term outlook was positive. The prospective divergence in relative cyclical positions correlated closely with the decline of the euro *vis-à-vis* the US dollar, and since mid-1999, *vis-à-vis* the yen (Figure 15.2). More recently, expectations of a relatively weak cyclical position in the euro area have been

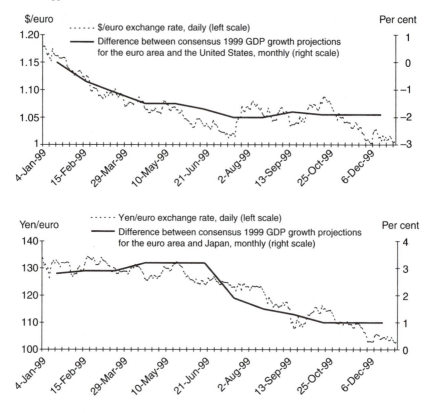

Figure 15.2 Cyclical divergence and euro market exchange rates.

Sources: OECD, ECB, *The Economist* monthly poll (various issues).

gradually replaced by a more positive outlook. The most recent OECD projections, finalised in November 1999 and which for the euro area are close to the consensus view, expect for the first time in several years that output levels in all major OECD regions will move towards their respective potential over the projection period, albeit marginally so in Japan. For the euro area, output could rise by 2.75 per cent in both 2000 and 2001 to virtually close the output gap, which is consistent with further and substantial reductions in unemployment and broadly steady inflation (Table 15.4).

Longer term considerations

The improved and more balanced economic outlook, however, does not appear to have provided much positive support for the euro. The apparent indifference of currency markets to shifts in short-term developments and prospects has rekindled a debate on the behaviour of market exchange rates *vis-à-vis* their longer

Table 15.4 Short-term projections for the euro area, percentage changes from the previous year[a]

	1980–85	1986–91	1992–97	1998	1999	2000	2001
Private consumption	1.2	4.1	1.0	2.9	2.4	2.6	2.7
Government consumption	2.1	3.1	1.0	1.3	1.6	1.1	1.0
Gross fixed investment	−1.3	6.2	0.3	4.3	4.6	4.3	4.4
Public	0.7	4.8	−3.0	3.5	3.8	2.8	2.7
Private residential	−2.7	3.4	1.8	−0.2	1.9	3.3	3.0
Private non-residential	−1.0	7.8	0.3	6.6	5.9	5.1	5.3
Final domestic demand	0.9	4.3	0.8	2.9	2.7	2.7	2.7
Stock building[b]	−0.1	0.0	0.1	0.5	−0.1	0.0	0.0
Total domestic demand	0.8	4.3	0.9	3.3	2.6	2.6	2.7
Exports	5.6	2.8	9.6	4.3	0.9	6.5	6.3
Imports	0.9	7.3	6.1	8.3	4.0	5.9	6.2
Foreign balance[b]	0.6	−0.5	0.6	−0.5	−0.5	0.2	0.2
GDP	1.4	3.8	1.5	2.8	2.1	2.8	2.8
Industrial production	0.3	2.7	1.5	4.0	0.5	3.3	3.1
Private consumption deflator	8.5	3.9	2.9	1.4	1.3	1.7	1.7
GDP deflator	7.9	4.1	2.5	1.6	1.3	1.5	1.6
Current account balance[c]	−0.4	0.7	0.6	1.3	0.8	0.7	0.8
Employment	−0.4	2.9	−0.2	1.5	1.5	1.2	1.1
Labour force	0.6	2.4	0.3	0.6	0.5	0.5	0.5
Unemployment rate[d]	8.6	9.6	11.2	11.1	10.2	9.6	9.1
Personal savings ratio (per cent)	14.7	12.9	13.8	11.5	11.4	11.3	11.2

Source: OECD (1999c).

Notes
a The 1999 figures are OECD estimates.
b Growth as a per cent of GDP in the previous year.
c Actual balance as a per cent of GDP. Intra euro area trade in goods and services exluded, but no adjustment has been possible for investment income and transfers due to the lack of required information.
d Level as a per cent of labour force.

term determinants. But while it is relatively straightforward to observe currency movements in exchange rate markets, the long-term or equilibrium value of an exchange rate is not observed. There are a number of empirical approaches for estimating the equilibrium exchange rate. The two most prominent examples are fundamental equilibrium exchange rates (FEERs) and purchasing power parities (PPP).[4] The PPP approach involves calculating international competitiveness ratios using aggregate price or cost indices (such as consumer prices, GDP deflators, export prices or unit labour costs) and conceptually is based on the 'law of one price'. The FEER (or macroeconomic balance) approach focuses on the real exchange rate needed to achieve medium-term internal and external equilibrium. These approaches, however, give a wide range of estimates, reflecting large uncertainty. For example, FEERs of the dollar *vis-à-vis* the Deutsche Mark calculated by

Williamson (1994), based on a range of macro models and underlying assumptions, vary by as much as 26 per cent. A more recent report (CAE, 1999) calculated a range of $1.07–$1.43 against the euro, while in a recent IMF paper, the equilibrium parity of the euro is estimated at about $1.26 per euro (Alberola *et al.*, 1999). Such numerical estimates are very fragile and are often derived from past behavioural relationships, which may no longer be appropriate. They differ considerably depending on the selected base period, are sensitive to the price measure used, to hypotheses made for price expectations, and to the choice of the basket of countries used for comparison and are subject to substantial variation over time. For example, in the case of Finland, Feyzioglu (1997) estimates that Finland's FEER has fluctuated by as much as 20–30 per cent during periods of 2–3 years.

The OECD publishes estimates of PPPs for its member countries and calculates from these estimates a euro PPP exchange rate. Both the PPP and spot exchange rate vary over time, but are rarely equal to each other (Figure 15.3). The euro/dollar exchange rate was about 30 per cent 'overvalued' in the mid-1980s, whereas over the 1990s the deviation of the market exchange rate from its PPP level averaged about 15 per cent. The mid-1980s corresponded to a period in

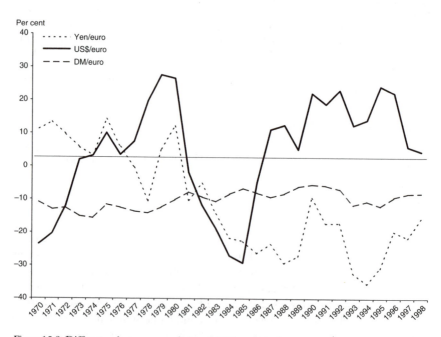

Figure 15.3 Difference between market and PPP euro exchange rate.[1]

Source: OECD.

Note

1 Difference between the market exchange rate and the PPP exchange rate, expressed as a percentage of the PPP exchange rate. A negative value implies an undervalued market rate compared with the PPP rate.

which the United States was pursuing a loose fiscal policy and a tight monetary policy, which put upward pressure on domestic interest rates, attracted large inflows of foreign capital and led to the currency appreciation, which in time corresponded to the widening of the US current account deficit to almost 3 per cent of GDP in 1987. By contrast, the 1990s were characterised by a growing imbalance between private saving and investment, and while in the 1980s the United States held a positive net foreign position, the more recent period saw a substantial accumulation of net foreign debt.

For the euro *vis-à-vis* the Japanese yen, fluctuations from the estimated PPP level have been equally large, although in the opposite direction since the mid-1980s (an 'undervalued' dollar and an 'overvalued' yen). The large and persistent deviations of the market exchange rate from its PPP level suggest that the series do not revert to their mean, or that if they do, the speed of adjustment is very slow. Indeed, statistical tests either fail to reject the hypothesis of a unit root in the case of the euro/dollar and the euro/yen – although for the latter the unit root test is rejected when a deterministic trend is included – or indicate that on average the half-time adjustment speed is about 3–4 years.[5]

PPPs as measured by the OECD are, however, imperfect for assessing equilibrium levels of exchange rates. Indeed, they are based on a comparison of prices of goods and services, not all of which are necessarily traded. Moreover, since they reflect prices of final expenditures, they include producers' mark-ups as well as indirect taxes. For all these reasons it would be better to compare prices of traded goods at the factory gate. Such comparisons are however difficult to conduct. Nevertheless, in order to address these types of issues, the OECD has over the years developed a number of indicators of competitiveness, that capture countries' ability to sell products in world markets. Such indicators include levels of unit labour costs in the manufacturing sector and indices of relative unit manufacturing labour costs, of manufactured export prices and of consumer prices. Because of data limitations, absolute cost comparisons can only be made for a limited number of countries and periods. Recent developments in relative costs and prices show that the recent real depreciation has fully unwound the real appreciation registered during the 1997–98 financial crises – which towards the end of 1998 also reflected some euro euphoria. Trends since the early 1970s indicate, however, that euro-area real effective exchange rates are still well above their low points reached in the mid-1980s – corresponding to the high values of the dollar real effective rate. Indicators of real effective exchange rates calculated by either the ECB or the IMF point to similar trends.[6] Worth noting, however, is the fact that variations in relative costs or prices are much less pronounced for the euro area than for either the United States or Japan (Figure 15.4).

Could exchange rate volatility be reduced?

The debate over whether an exchange rate should be an issue of direct policy concern often tends to focus on the degree of exchange rate volatility. At the launch of the euro, fears were expressed that the euro-area economy could suffer

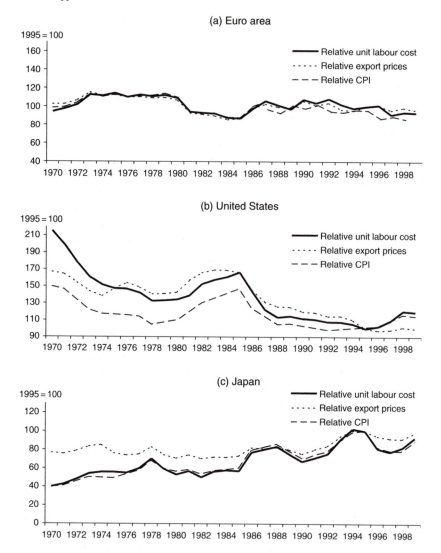

Figure 15.4 Trends in competitiveness indicators.
Source: OECD (1999c).

from excessive exchange rate volatility and that the advent of a new, potentially important international currency was a proper time to introduce mechanisms to reduce volatility in exchange markets. Volatility can be measured in many different ways. Table 15.5 reports one such measure: the standard deviation of quarterly changes in bilateral exchange rates for the major European currencies, the Japanese yen and the synthetic euro against the US dollar between 1979 and 1999. Over the twenty-year period, this measure of volatility is broadly the same for all the currencies shown, at about 5.5 per cent. The same calculation for the nominal effective and real effective exchange rates reveals a generally lower

Table 15.5 Volatility of bilateral and effective exchange rates, standard deviation of quarterly changes[a]

	Bilateral vs US$[b]	*Nominal effective exchange rates*[c]	*Real effective exchange rates*[c]
Germany	5.6	2.1	2.0
France	5.3	2.0	1.9
Italy	5.7	2.9	2.8
The Netherlands	5.5	1.6	1.7
Austria	5.5	1.1	1.1
Euro area	4.6	2.9	2.8
United States	—	2.8	2.9
Japan	5.3	4.6	4.5
United Kingdom	5.9	4.0	4.4

Source: OECD.

Notes

a Volatility is measured by the standard deviation of the quarterly growth rate, defined as the difference of the natural logarithm of the series multiplied by 100 over the period 1970Q2 to 1999Q3.

b Bilateral exchange rates are national currencies per US dollar.

c Based on the OECD measures of the nominal and real effective exchange rates, where the real effective exchange rates are based on CPI.

degree of volatility, but more variation across currencies. Among the currencies of countries shown and which were part of the European Exchange Rate Mechanism (ERM) the volatility of the nominal and real effective exchange rate was relatively low (except for Italy and the United Kingdom) at between 1 and 2 per cent. In part, this reflects these countries' exchange rate arrangements, which aimed to keep bilateral exchange rate movements within narrow bands. Since the majority of these countries' trade is with each other, their currencies have an important weight in their respective nominal and real effective exchange rate indices. For the euro area, on the other hand, historical volatility of the effective euro exchange rate is approximately 50 per cent higher (about 3 per cent on average), which reflects the fact that the constituent currencies are mostly from non-ERM countries. Euro-area effective exchange rate volatility, however, is broadly the same as for the US dollar and considerably lower than for the Japanese yen.

As one would expect, studies find that exchange rate volatility during the Bretton Woods era of fixed exchange rate regimes (1945–71) was low (Bordo and Eichengreen, 1993; Obstfeld, 1998). Indeed, fluctuations of quarterly changes in bilateral and effective nominal exchange rates were close to zero. But the Bretton Woods era was a period of low and widely restricted capital mobility, which made it relatively easy to maintain fixed parities. Of more practical relevance is whether exchange rate volatility has changed over the period spanning flexible exchange rate regimes. From this perspective there is only limited evidence that there has been an increase in volatility for the major currency areas. Figure 15.5 shows moving averages of month-to-month changes in bilateral exchange rates from 1973 up until late 1999. On this measure, the volatility of the Deutsche Mark against the dollar in the last decade is not particularly high by historical standards

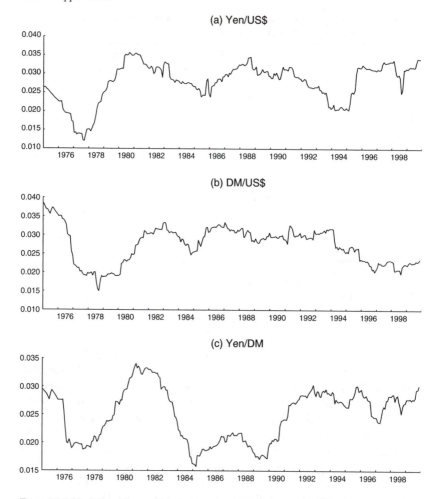

Figure 15.5 Variance of monthly changes in nominal exchange rates,[1] three-year moving window.

Source: OECD.

Note

1 Any month *t* in the graph shows the standard deviation of monthly changes in the logarithms of bilateral nominal exchange rates during the period from *t*-36 months to *t*, that is, during the last three years.

and considerably lower than during the 1980s. On the other hand, bilateral exchange rate volatility against the yen has been relatively high over the 1990s and seems to have increased since the beginning of 1999. However, such volatility appears to be more linked to moves in the yen than in the euro since the degree of yen/dollar volatility has also risen over this period. In addition, the incidence of large daily changes (more than 1 per cent) seems to have also risen, but again only for the yen (Figure 15.6).

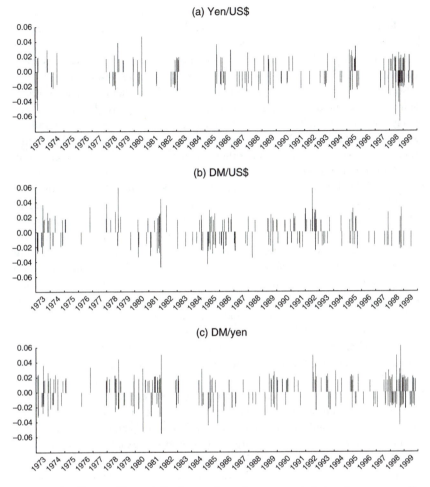

Figure 15.6 Incidence of large daily changes in exchange rates (relative changes exceeding 1.5 percentage points).

Source: OECD.

Even though exchange rate volatility does not appear to have increased and exchange rate fluctuations are now probably less important than before because the euro area is a relatively closed economy compared with the constituent member countries, the issue of whether to introduce target zones for the value of the euro *vis-à-vis* the dollar and the yen resurfaced in late 1998.[7] Advocates of target zones argue that excessive nominal exchange rate volatility has an adverse effect on trade and investment via increased uncertainty. Moreover, market exchange rates can diverge – and over protracted periods of time – from their fundamental level and thereby result in a loss of competitiveness and impact on bilateral trade flows. Empirical as well as theoretical studies, however, are less sanguine about the possible deleterious effects of exchange rate volatility on trade and investment (Bacchetta and van Wincoop, 1998). This may be because instruments are available that allow those engaged in trade to insure against short-term fluctuations (Viaene and de Vries, 1992). The availability of such instruments for major currencies and at a reasonable cost has increased considerably over the past few decades.

Even if target zones were agreed on among the three major currencies, it is not clear that wide fluctuations in their effective rates could be avoided. Given the relatively low weight that any of these currencies has in each other's effective exchange rate (Table 15.2), large fluctuations could still be associated with bilateral movements between them and other currencies. In addition, there are a number of problems related to the implementation of target zones. For instance, it would be difficult to convince participants to agree on the choice of central parity and the bands around it since there is no generally accepted method for calculating equilibrium exchange rates. In addition, the bands may not be credible and could require large swings in interest rates, which would effectively shift some volatility from the exchange market to money and bond markets. Interest sensitive sectors of the euro economy would face heightened risks, while those producing tradeable goods would benefit. Moreover, interest rate moves to keep exchange rates within bands may not necessarily be consistent with price stability and thus there is a risk that the credibility of monetary policy may be lost, raising risk premiums and undoing part of the benefits of monetary union.[8]

Large exchange rate fluctuations have also sometimes raised calls for more frequent central bank interventions in exchange markets. In the past, central banks of major countries have frequently intervened in exchange markets. For example, the US Federal Reserve has intervened 125 times in the dollar/yen market between 1985 and 1995. These interventions were generally carried out in collaboration with other central banks. Since then, interventions have been less frequent, but the amounts involved may have been larger. Most central bank interventions have generally been sterilised. In this case, the impact on exchange rates works through signal effects and expectations. In practice, the success of interventions has been rather limited, and only a few interventions seem to have had an impact over a short period of time. Ultimately, the success of interventions depends on the accompanying evolution in macroeconomic policies and conditions. Given the size and power of global capital markets, recent interventions have rarely led to long-lasting changes in expectations, unless they were accompanied by expected changes in more fundamental determinants of exchange rates.[9]

The euro as an international currency

While the euro officially came into existence at the beginning of 1999, it will not completely replace domestic currencies in circulation and be used to denominate all financial and other business transactions in member countries until the start of 2002.[10] The euro, however, is already emerging as a major international currency, which has implications for other countries as well as for monetary policy in the euro area. Before the launch of the euro, the Deutsche Mark was the only European currency that was used in a significant way as an international currency but its importance was nonetheless still minor compared with the dollar, which has dominated as the international currency since the First World War.

The use of a currency as an international money depends on a number of factors. These include the following:

- a large domestic market;
- a high exposure to trade, a large weight in global trade and exporter and importer preferences favouring the currency as a unit of account;
- the existence of a large and competitive financial market in which the currency denominated assets are actively traded;
- economic and political stability of the currency area, thereby favouring it as a 'safe haven' currency; and
- high quality and competitive pricing of cross-border payment systems.

The relative importance of these factors is difficult to isolate, not in the least because it is the combination of these traits that is critical. This is no doubt partly the reason for the limited use of the Japanese yen as an international currency despite its size and share of world trade. It is still too early to assess whether the euro will become a relevant international currency and a major competitor to the US dollar, but it has already gained considerable importance in the bond and money markets and as a reserve currency. Euro denominated bond issues by residents and non-residents in the first nine months of 1999 accounted for about 45 per cent of the bonds issued in the international market, which is approximately the same share as for US dollar denominated bonds and well exceeds the traditional aggregate share of bonds denominated in the member country currencies of the euro area (Table 15.6). And in the third quarter of 1999, new issues of euro denominated international bonds were larger than new issues in US dollars. Corporate debenture issues denominated in euros have soared, in part reflecting the hectic pace of European merger and acquisition activity. In addition, a number of sovereign issuers, such as Argentina, Brazil, Canada and South Africa, have launched sizeable euro-denominated issues so as to increase the weight of the euro in the currency distribution of their foreign debt.[11] And an increasing number of central banks have decided to hold a share, or increase their share, of official reserves in euros. At the end of 1998, about 14 per cent of official exchange reserves were denominated in euro area national currencies or European Currency Units (ECUs), against 57 per cent in dollars. This share is likely to rise because the euro is used as an anchor currency in over fifty countries, mostly in Europe and Africa. The euro is also likely to become a more important reserve currency in Asia and Latin America, as countries in these regions reassess their reserve management positions in the light of the new diversification opportunities offered by the euro. The Hong Kong monetary authority, for instance, recently announced its decision to increase the share of the euro in its official reserve portfolio from 10 to 15 per cent.

The fact that the euro is starting to play a significantly larger role as an international currency than individual country currencies previously combined has implications for monetary policy. For instance, if the international demand for the

Table 15.6 The euro as an international currency

	Amounts outstanding, year end			Net issues		
	1996	*1997*	*1998*	*1999Q1*	*1999Q2*	*1999Q3*
International bonds and notes						
Total issues in billion US$	2,975	3,332	4,100	231	332	286
Selected currencies	*Shares of total*			*Levels in billion US$*		
US dollar	38.1	43.8	45.2	56.9	46.4	40.0
Japanese yen	15.9	13.7	11.7	−4.9	−1.1	2.3
Euro-area currencies	25.5	23.7	23.9	38.2	43.0	50.4
Pound sterling	7.6	8.1	8.0	7.6	8.0	7.2
International money market instruments						
Total issues in billion US$	172	184	194	35	−8	23
Selected currencies	*Shares of total*			*Levels in billion US$*		
US dollar	56.9	57.3	57.3	6.9	−2.8	−0.5
Japanese yen	3.7	3.6	2.4	−1.2	0.1	0.1
Euro-area currencies	15.7	16.1	15.7	28.5	−6.5	18.0
Pound sterling	5.1	7.1	8.0	0.8	2.4	1.8
Official holdings of foreign exchange						
Total, in billion US$	1,553	1,599	1,635			
Selected currencies	*Shares of total*					
US dollar	53.7	54.2	56.9			
Japanese yen	5.2	4.5	4.9			
ECU	5.6	4.8	0.7			
Euro-area currencies[a]	13.8	13.2	13.0			
Pound sterling	3.0	3.2	3.7			
Others plus unspecified	18.7	20.1	20.8			

Sources: BIS, *Quarterly Review: International Banking and Financial Market Developments*, various issues; IMF, *Annual Report*, 1999.

Note
a Deutsche Mark, French franc and Dutch guilder only.

euro were erratic and accounted for a relatively large component of total demand for the currency, then the currency component of euro-area monetary aggregates would be volatile. This would render the monetary aggregates less useful as a guide to inflationary pressures in the domestic economy. The resistance by the Bundesbank to see the Deutsche Mark becoming an international currency was to a large extent explained by this type of argument, given that monetary aggregates were an important element in its strategy. Such considerations do not seem to prevail in the ECB monetary policy framework.

Prospective policies and economic developments in the euro area

There is a Dutch proverb that states *if one would know everything in advance, one could travel the world on twopence.*[12] This is perhaps no more true than when it comes to predicting the future value of an exchange rate. The objective of this section, however, is not to attempt to forecast the value of the euro *vis-à-vis* other currencies, but to shed some light on the implications that possible future developments in financial markets and policies may have on the macroeconomic performance of the euro area. Particular attention is also given to the implications for external positions in the main world economic regions. Even this goal, while considerably less ambitious, is subject to a wide range of uncertainty and prone to large errors. Part of the difficulty is that very few predictions of key economic variables, including the exchange rate, are truly unconditional. Indeed, in practice, macroeconomic projections usually either include normative elements or are based on a series of assumptions.

Nevertheless, for illustrative purposes, the OECD's Interlink model has been used to simulate a different path for exchange rates than the one embodied in the OECD short-term projections and the medium-term baseline[13] and to examine its effects on the main macroeconomic variables, also taking into account different policy responses. The underlying structure of the OECD's Interlink model is that of a short-run dynamic type model with properties in line with the Mundell–Flemming framework for evaluating the relative effectiveness of fiscal and monetary impulses and with neo-classical steady state characteristics.[14] The simulations undertaken here are described in more detail in the section 'Simulating a different path for exchange rates', but we first present an overview of structural conditions in the euro area and the expected stance of macroeconomic policy in the three main OECD economic regions, since these bear on the baseline against which the simulations are evaluated.

Euro-area structural characteristics and the implications for macroeconomic policy

The setting of macroeconomic policy by the EMU needs to be cognisant of structural characteristics in euro-area economies as well as at the aggregate level. Greater structural rigidities imply, *inter alia*, slower adjustment of real wages and other relative prices to excess demand or supply conditions in product and labour markets and consequently result in larger fluctuations in quantities in response to economic shocks. Structural rigidities are also generally associated with higher persistence in output and employment movements, implying longer cycles in response to shocks. This in turn puts limits on the speed at which macroeconomic policies can be used to reduce unemployment towards its long-run equilibrium and increases the risk of temporary shocks eventually affecting structural unemployment and potential output (hysteresis effects). In addition, structural features can influence the size, speed and symmetry of the monetary policy transmission mechanism and can contribute to worsen the trade-off between the volatility of inflation and output.

Structural rigidities manifest themselves through a number of channels, including a high degree of real wage resistance, slow mark-up adjustment and high persistence in employment and unemployment. A number of factors suggest that structural rigidities are more significant in the euro area than in other large and relatively closed economies such as the United States. These comprise the high dispersion of structural unemployment rates across the euro area,[15] more segmented capital, labour and product markets and the heterogeneity of wage determination institutions across the euro area.[16]

The expected macroeconomic policy stance in the euro area and the other major regions over the short and medium term

In principle, the adverse consequences of structural rigidities for the output infla-tion variance trade-off could be compensated for by an increase in the credibility of monetary policy. Higher credibility can help reinforce monetary policy actions by, for example, modifying the behaviour underlying wage and price strategies. Credibility is largely determined by how well a central bank performs in terms of fulfilling its inflation objective. But the process of gaining credibility and contain-ing inflation expectations can also be influenced by the institutional design of the monetary policy framework. For the euro area, a careful attempt has been made to gain credibility from the outset for the ECB by enshrining its price stability objective in the Maastricht Treaty (Article 105) and its independence (Article 7 of the European System of Central Banks (ESCB) statute). The ECB has quantified its price stability objective as keeping inflation (as measured by the Harmonised Index of Consumer Price (HICP)), below 2 per cent, while avoiding sustained declines in the general consumer price level.

Given the low level of inflation and inflation expectations in the euro area and the persistence of under-utilised resources, at least in a large part of the area, the monetary policy stance pursued by the ECB has been fairly relaxed (Table 15.7). Both short- and long-term interest rates are low in historical perspective. Long rates have dropped sharply since 1993, initially in response to fiscal consolidation and lower inflation, and in some countries also helped by some 'convergence play'. More recently, with volatile financial conditions in emerging market economies, government bond rates fell further in 1998, because of a shift in desired portfolio composition towards relatively less risky assets – the 'flight to quality'. However, with the improved economic situation in emerging markets, the flight to quality has partially reversed, and long rates over the past year have edged up by over 100 basis points (Figure 15.7). As a result, the slope of the yield curve is now largely positive and has steepened considerably compared with twelve months earlier. While nominal short-term interest rates are historically low, in real terms they are in line with their five-year historical average. The euro area short-term interest rate differential with the United States narrowed in 1998, but it has widened since. By the end of 1999, it amounted to some 150 basis points, and about 40 basis points in real terms, close to pre-European Monetary Union (EMU) levels. Given the persistently low levels of short-term interest rates in Japan, euro-area differentials *vis-à-vis* Japan have remained substantial since 1998.

Table 15.7 Monetary conditions in the major OECD regions, period average data

	Q1-98	Q2-98	Q3-98	Q4-98	Q1-99	Q2-99	Q3-99	Sep-99	Oct-99	Nov-99	Dec-99
Euro area											
Nominal short-term interest rates	4.0	3.9	3.8	3.4	3.1	2.6	2.7	2.7	3.4	3.5	3.5
Real short-term interest rates[a]	2.5	2.2	2.5	2.4	2.2	1.6	1.5	1.4	2.0	1.9	1.8
Nominal long-term interest rates	5.1	5.0	4.6	4.1	4.0	4.3	5.1	5.2	5.5	5.2	—
Real long-term interest rates[a]	3.7	3.4	3.3	3.1	3.1	3.2	3.8	3.9	4.1	3.6	—
Interest rate spread[b]	1.2	1.1	0.8	0.7	0.9	1.6	2.4	2.5	2.1	1.7	—
Nominal M3 growth	4.7	5.1	4.5	4.5	5.5	5.7	6.3	6.6	6.6	—	—
Differential between euro area and the United States											
Nominal short-term interest rates	−1.1	−1.1	−1.0	−0.8	−1.3	−1.8	−1.9	−1.9	−1.5	−1.6	−1.7
Real short-term interest rates[a]	−1.1	−1.1	−0.7	−0.3	−0.6	−0.8	−0.8	−0.6	−0.3	−0.4	−0.3
Nominal long-term interest rates	−0.5	−0.6	−0.6	−0.5	−1.0	−1.3	−0.8	−0.7	−0.6	−0.8	—
Real long-term interest rates[a]	−0.5	−0.6	−0.3	0.0	−0.2	−0.2	0.3	0.7	0.5	0.4	—
Interest rate spread[b]	0.6	0.5	0.4	0.3	0.3	0.5	1.1	1.3	0.9	0.8	—
United States											
Nominal short-term interest rates	5.1	5.0	4.8	4.3	4.4	4.5	4.6	4.7	4.9	5.1	5.2
Real short-term interest rates[a]	3.6	3.4	3.2	2.7	2.7	2.3	2.3	2.0	2.3	2.3	2.1
Nominal long-term interest rates	5.6	5.6	5.2	4.7	5.0	5.5	5.9	5.9	6.1	6.0	6.2
Real long-term interest rates[a]	4.1	4.0	3.6	3.1	3.3	3.4	3.5	3.3	3.5	3.3	3.1
Interest rate spread[b]	0.5	0.6	0.4	0.4	0.6	1.1	1.2	1.2	1.2	1.0	1.0
Nominal M2 growth	9.5	10.1	9.9	10.8	10.1	9.0	8.2	7.5	7.3	—	—
Japan											
Nominal short-term interest rates	1.0	0.7	0.7	0.6	0.5	0.1	0.1	0.1	0.3	0.4	0.3
Real short-term interest rates[a]	−1.0	0.3	0.9	0.1	0.6	0.3	0.1	0.3	1.2	1.2	0.7
Nominal long-term interest rates	1.9	1.6	1.4	1.1	1.9	1.5	1.8	1.8	1.8	1.8	1.8
Real long-term interest rates[a]	−0.1	1.3	1.6	0.6	2.0	1.8	1.8	1.9	2.7	2.6	2.2
Interest rate spread[b]	0.9	1.0	0.6	0.4	1.5	1.5	1.7	1.7	1.5	1.4	1.5
Nominal M2+CDs growth	4.6	4.2	4.3	4.6	4.2	4.1	3.4	2.4	—	—	—

Sources: OECD, Bloomberg, ECB.

Notes
a Short-term (three-month interbank rate) and long-term (ten-year government bonds) interest rates less the twelve month change in CPI.
b The difference between long- and short-term rates.

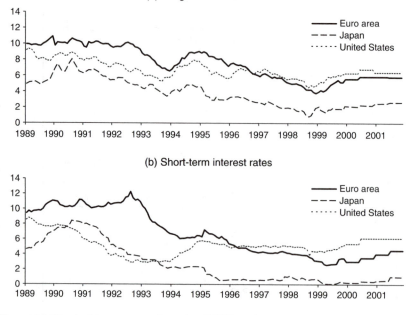

Figure 15.7 Nominal interest rates in major OECD regions.
Sources: ECB, Bloomberg; OECD (1999c).

    In the OECD's latest set of projections published in the December 1999 issue of the *Economic Outlook*, policy-controlled interest rates are assumed to rise to about 6.5 per cent by the end of 2000 in the United States as the economy, though slowing, is projected to continue to grow above potential and inflation picks up. In the euro area, with inflation pressures starting to build up, it is also assumed that the ECB will raise key rates, with three months market rates reaching about 4.5 per cent by the end of 2001. In Japan, market rates should remain very low, though slowly rising during the course of 2000 as the recovery takes hold. Over the medium term, assuming that gaps between actual and potential output are broadly eliminated in the United States and the euro area – a feature of the OECD medium-term scenario – would yield a further narrowing of both short- and long-term interest rate differentials between the euro and the United States. Despite a further rise in Japanese interest rates, differentials between the euro area and Japan should remain substantial, on the order of 150 basis points in 2005.
    The fiscal policy of countries in the euro area remains largely under the responsibility of national authorities according to the principle of subsidiarity – a presumption in favour of national sovereignty. Nonetheless, policy is formulated in the context of the provisions of the Stability and Growth Pact (SGP) which, given the current budgetary positions of most euro-area countries, imposes

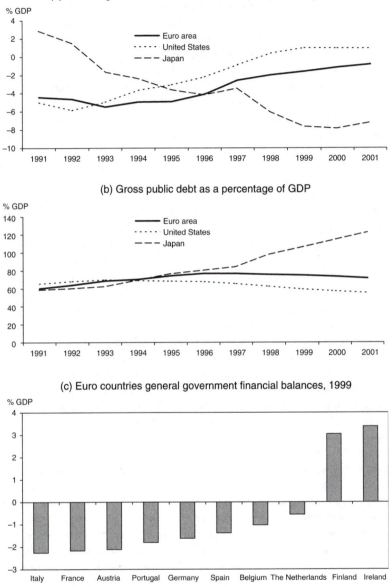

Figure 15.8 Fiscal indicators in the major OECD regions.

Source: OECD (1999c).

relatively tight constraints on fiscal policy, especially in large euro-area countries. Despite significant progress in budget consolidation in the run-up to EMU, establishing the full ability to pursue counter-cyclical policies will require measures beyond those required to achieve the completion of budget improvements needed to achieve the goals set out in EU countries' Stability and Convergence programmes in 2002 (Figure 15.8).[17] Indeed, the target budget balance – a necessary condition also given the prospective demographic pressures on the budgets of member states – would leave countries with little scope for discretionary actions to meet adverse shocks. In the United States, public finances have already moved into surplus and, provided pressures to cut taxes or to increase spending continue to be resisted, this trend is likely to continue over the medium term. In Japan, measures will have to be taken to arrest the explosive growth in public debt resulting from successive fiscal stimulus packages as soon as this can be done without compromising the current recovery.

Thus, except perhaps in Japan, fiscal policies are fairly predictable in the five years to come. Given that monetary policy is expected to continue to be geared towards price stability in all major regions, this implies that the constellation of policy mixes is not foreseen to yield major changes in the values of exchange rates over the short to medium run. This feature characterises the OECD medium-term reference scenario, which embodies paths for monetary and fiscal policies in the three major areas along the lines described above. As regards monetary policy, levels of interest rates are such that inflation is kept low, in line with medium-term objectives. Fiscal policies for their part imply reductions in gross public debt of about twelve percentage point of GDP in the United States and the euro area between 1999 and 2005, while in Japan, the ratio of gross public debt to GDP rises by more than 40 points. As a result of these policies, along with the assumption that commodity prices and exchange rates remain broadly unchanged in real terms, real output growth could average 2.5 per cent in the euro area compared with about 3 per cent in the United States and 2 per cent in Japan over the period 2002–05. Reflecting slow progress in the elimination of structural rigidities, unemployment should remain relatively high in the euro area, at about 8 per cent in 2005 (Table 15.8).

As a result, a major feature of this reference scenario is that the closure of output gaps in most areas and the narrowing of interest rate differentials take place at the same time real effective exchange rates are assumed to remain unchanged from their present levels. Given projected inflation developments, this also suggests that convergence in cyclical conditions and levels of interest rates are expected to yield little movement in nominal exchange rates over the medium term.

However, another important feature of the scenario is that the present level of current account imbalances between major OECD regions are likely to persist over the medium term. This implies that the United States could see a deterioration in its negative net foreign asset position by more than fifteen percentage points of GDP between 1999 and 2005, reaching about 35 per cent (Figure 15.9). The main counterpart would be a substantial rise in Japan's positive net asset

Table 15.8 The OECD medium-term reference scenario, percentage change from previous period

	1999	2000	2001	2002	2003	2004	2005
United States							
Real GDP growth	3.8	3.1	2.3	2.0	3.0	3.4	3.4
Inflation	1.6	2.3	2.4	2.3	2.2	2.2	2.1
Short-term nominal interest rate	4.6	5.7	6.1	5.5	4.8	4.8	4.8
Current account (% GDP)	−3.7	−4.3	−4.2	−4.0	−3.9	−3.8	−3.7
Japan							
Real GDP growth	1.4	1.4	1.2	2.1	2.2	1.7	1.8
Inflation	−0.3	−0.3	−0.3	0.2	0.5	0.5	0.5
Short-term nominal interest rate	0.3	0.3	0.8	1.8	2.3	2.8	3.0
Current account (% GDP)	2.7	2.8	3.0	3.0	2.9	2.9	2.9
Euro area							
Real GDP growth	2.1	2.8	2.8	2.6	2.5	2.4	2.3
Inflation	1.3	1.7	1.7	1.7	1.7	1.6	1.6
Short-term nominal interest rate	2.9	3.3	4.3	4.3	4.3	4.3	4.3
Current account (% GDP)	0.8	0.7	0.8	0.9	0.9	1.0	1.1
Total OECD							
Real GDP growth	2.9	2.9	2.6	2.5	2.9	2.9	2.9
Inflation[a]	1.8	2.1	2.1	2.0	2.0	1.9	1.9

Source: OECD (1999c).

Note
a Excluding Turkey.

position, and to a much lesser extent in the euro area's as well. Under the assumption of imperfect asset substitution, such a worsening in the US external position might still take some time before raising investors' concerns about its sustainability. Eventually, however, with no signs of stabilisation, these concerns could trigger a major change in expectations about the future paths of exchange rates, yielding in particular a sharp decline in the US dollar, which could propagate to other markets, in particular equity markets. This reversal of confidence in dollar denominated assets could have important consequences not only for the United States but for Japan and the euro area as well.

Simulating a different path for exchange rates

In theory, with perfect capital mobility and forward looking expectations, net foreign asset positions implicitly affect the exchange rate to the extent that they are built into the forward looking path of expected exchange rates as a terminal or equilibrium condition. Given this expected path, exchange rates then adjust to

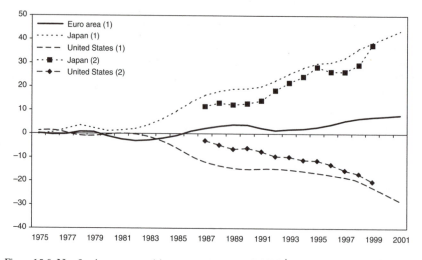

Figure 15.9 Net foreign asset positions as a per cent of GDP.[1]

Source: OECD.

Notes
1 Calculated as the cumulated current account balances, starting in 1975.
2 Actual net foreign assets.

clear the goods markets after a shock. In other words, this implies that net foreign assets or liabilities cannot accumulate over time much beyond a level that can be sustained in the long run. This equilibrium level may of course vary across countries reflecting differences in demographics, trends in productivity, savings and rates of time preferences. However, stabilising net foreign asset positions at their equilibrium levels requires adjustments in the trade balance that are most likely achieved through exchange rate changes. General equilibrium models of the type developed by the OECD in the context of its work on ageing (Turner *et al.*, 1998) or models with model-consistent expectations such as the IMF Multimod model[18] are consistent with this type of approach.

Based on this approach, however, the build-up in external imbalances witnessed since the mid-1990s suggests either that present and foreseen net foreign asset positions are compatible with equilibrium levels, or if these positions are judged unsustainable, that a correction in exchange rates should have already taken place to re-equilibrate saving and investment balances. The fact that this correction has not yet occurred is not necessarily inconsistent with the approach described above, but certainly points to a rather peculiar equilibrium path. Several reasons, such as imperfect capital markets can be advanced to explain the slow adjustment process towards equilibrium. If markets are truly rational, however, net foreign asset positions should at some point be part of the arbitrage condition and one should expect exchange rates to adjust in the future in response to the accumulation of foreign debt or assets. Alternatively, one could argue that markets have so far been myopic, but this cannot be expected to last forever, and in this case too, one might expect a change in behaviour leading to a correction in exchange rates.

Whatever the underlying behaviour, no attempt has been made here to model it. What has been done instead is to assume that a correction will take place in the near term and to look at the implications it might have on output, inflation and current account balances under different monetary policy responses. For this purpose, the OECD Interlink model, which embodies the following exchange rate determination, has been used:

$$e - e_{-1} = f(i - i^*, e^e - e_{-1})$$
$$e^e \quad = f(e_{-1}, p - p^*, p_{-1} - p^*_{-1}, p_{-2} - p^*_{-2})$$

where e and e^e are the actual and expected effective exchange rates expressed in logarithms, i and i^* are the domestic and (weighted) foreign short-term interest rates, and p and p^* are the domestic and (weighted) foreign GDP deflators (also in logarithms).

In the simulations, these conditions have been implicitly modified to take account of the net foreign asset positions. Given the current policy debate about the large and increasing US current account deficit and the risks it poses for the value of the dollar, this has been done by shocking the expected US effective exchange rate equation so as to generate a trade surplus sufficient to stabilise US net foreign liabilities at about 24 per cent of GDP over the medium term (compared with 35 per cent in 2005 in the baseline).[19] This has been achieved by implementing a sustained appreciation of about 30 per cent of all currencies against the US dollar. This implies no change in the bilateral exchange rates of the other countries – in particular the euro–yen exchange rate – although this is not so in effective terms, as the weight of the US dollar varies across countries.

The outcome of a dollar crisis scenario is reported in Figure 15.10. As mentioned earlier, the 30 per cent reduction in the effective dollar exchange rate relative to baseline from 2000 onwards is driven by concerns about the worsening US external position. The decline in the dollar is assumed to translate into a 25 per cent fall in US stock markets, reflecting the same loss of investor confidence. In turn, the correction in US equity markets is assumed to be accompanied by drops of about half as much in markets in major economies outside the United States.

The impact depreciation of the dollar has an immediate stimulatory effect on US net exports. This is to a large extent offset by the impact on private demand of the fall in financial wealth, resulting in changes in real GDP growth in the first two years of the simulation compared with baseline. However, in the absence of a timely and appropriate monetary policy response, the dollar weakening adds about 1.5 per cent to annual inflation over a fairly prolonged period (reflecting both higher import prices and a larger positive output gap). Consequences for areas outside the United States are substantial. In the euro area the currency

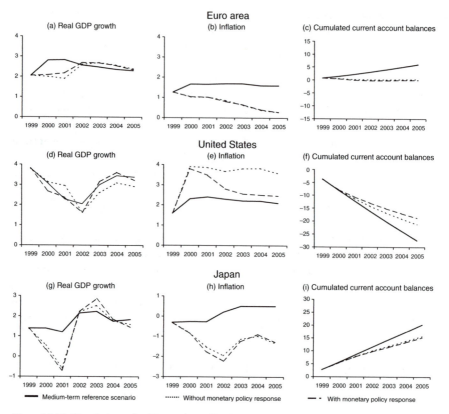

Figure 15.10 Simulation of a 30 per cent effective depreciation of the US dollar.

Source: OECD.

Note
Real GDP growth and inflation measured as the annual percent change and the cumulated current account deficit as a percent of GDP.

appreciation combined with the negative wealth effect subtracts about 0.75 per cent from both real output growth and inflation in each of the first two years of the simulation. In Japan, the impact is substantially larger, with real growth almost 1 per cent lower and inflation 1 per cent lower in these years.

A pick up in inflation to above 3.75 per cent in the near term in the United States and an inflation decline in the range of 1 per cent in the euro area would most likely induce responses from monetary authorities in both regions. In Japan, notwithstanding lower rates of growth and inflation pointing in practice to a period of deflation, monetary authorities are faced with the impossibility of adjusting short-term interest rates downwards given that these are already at their zero nominal floor at the beginning of the shock. In the United States and the euro area where monetary policy adjustments are possible, a feedback rule from inflation and output to short-term real interest rates has been built into the simulation.[20]

Indeed, maintaining short-term interest rates constant in real terms (the line shown as 'without monetary policy response' in Figure 15.10) – implying an increase in nominal rates of about 200 basis points in the United States and a decline of about 100 basis points in the euro area in 2000 – would be insufficient for inflation and GDP to return quickly to their baseline levels. Hence, interest rates are assumed to adjust further to ensure that this does take place.

In the euro area, this leads to a further lowering of interest rates (of about 200 basis points) in order to offset the disinflationary effects of appreciation of the euro and the negative wealth effect and their adverse impact on GDP (line shown as 'with monetary policy response' in Figure 15.10). Similarly, but in the opposite way, monetary tightening in the United States (equivalent to a further increase of about 150 basis points) and the weakening stock market play an important role in moderating inflation and also in stabilising real GDP growth at or near the baseline. Given monetary authorities' absence of room for manoeuvring, Japan suffers most significantly from the fall in net exports and real GDP because of appreciation of the yen, while deflation remains throughout (Figure 15.10).

The above policy response leads to a substantial widening of interest differentials between the United States and the euro area and Japan. It is nonetheless assumed that this opening in the differential has little or no impact on exchange rates over five years, as net external positions continue to play a dominant role in exchange rate expectations, since it is only over this time horizon that US net external assets stabilise at about 24 per cent of GDP, that is, about ten percentage points lower than in the baseline. As a counterpart, the cumulated Japanese current account surplus is about five percentage points lower than the baseline, while that of the euro area also declines by about the same amount.

Assuming that monetary policy credibility effects result in lower inflation expectations, one might expect a much faster decline in interest rates towards baseline levels in the United States with a parallel return of inflation towards these levels. In the same vein, euro area interest rates would not need to remain below baseline for such a prolonged period. If such a path for price expectations were then fed back into the expected exchange rate equation, this would ultimately lead to some renewed effective appreciation of the dollar, while the real effective exchange rate might remain at its baseline level. Altogether, this would permit a less costly adjustment in terms of the impact on net exports and real GDP in all areas.

The above scenario illustrates, however, that even a sharp correction in the dollar exchange rate, consistent with a substantial reduction in the external imbalances, would have, with an appropriate response from monetary policy, limited effects on the euro-area economy. Real GDP growth, in particular, would remain close to the baseline, as the easier monetary policy stance would balance the effects of the appreciation of the euro. The possibility that this stance, and perhaps the competitive pressure of a weaker dollar, might lead to an increase in investment and productive capacity beyond that resulting from the parameters of the Interlink model (where technical progress is exogenous) cannot be excluded.

This might produce a higher growth path for the euro area and possibly open a further channel for the reduction of external imbalances. As the evidence about this possibility is extremely limited, it is not explicitly considered here. However, the possibility that faster progress in the reform of product and labour markets might lead to a reduction in the structural unemployment rate in the euro area is examined in the next section

Assuming faster progress in structural reform in the euro area

As mentioned earlier, the simulations discussed in the previous section are based on the assumption that euro-area structural characteristics will not undergo major changes over the next five years. In particular the pace of labour and product market reform will not yield a significant reduction in the euro area NAIRU or, to put it differently, a significant up-tick in the level of potential output. The relatively slow pace of implementation of structural reform has sometimes been cited as one factor underlying the recent weakness in the euro exchange rate. The argument advanced is that foreign investors remain uncertain about the future potential rate of growth of the euro-area economy, given the persistence of structural rigidities, and thus prefer to invest in countries where expected rates of return are higher. If structural reforms were accelerated in the euro area so as to ultimately translate into a drop in the estimated value of the NAIRU of about two percentage points (i.e. a decline from 8.5 to 6.5 per cent), this would provide scope for the euro area to grow faster over the medium term without generating inflationary pressure. An alternative scenario incorporating such a decline in the euro-area NAIRU has been constructed using the same set of assumptions as for the

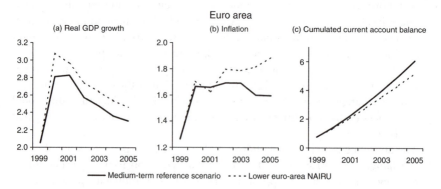

Figure 15.11 Simulation of a lower euro-area NAIRU.

Source: OECD.

Note
Real GDP growth and inflation measured as the annual percent change and the cumulated current account deficit as a percent of GDP.

original baseline (i.e. closing of the output gap and achievement of stated monetary and fiscal objectives). A lower NAIRU would allow the euro area to grow (substantially faster over the medium term than currently embodied in the reference baseline), at a pace only marginally lower than that of the United States (Figure 15.11). This rebalancing in growth prospects would work towards some limited appreciation of the euro *vis-à-vis* the dollar and the yen, which would also contribute to some correction in external imbalances.

Compared with the dollar depreciation scenario, the lower NAIRU scenario has somewhat more positive implications for prospects in Japan. Faster euro-area growth and euro appreciation against the yen contribute to raising Japan's net exports and real GDP growth. Implications for the United States are also positive as real GDP growth remains close to baseline but with a lower current account deficit. However, these positive effects on the major OECD areas remain limited, indicating that even substantial changes in the euro area's structural policy should not be seen as a major factor in redressing present world external imbalances.

Conclusions

One year ago, most economic observers predicted that fundamentals were such that the euro was set to appreciate. In fact the euro has depreciated against most major currencies. Numerous factors can influence exchange rates developments, both over the short and the longer term. Identifying determinants that drive short-term movements as well as those that impinge on the equilibrium value of the euro is a notoriously difficult task and empirical estimates tend to vary widely. Several forces appear to have been behind the depreciation of the euro since early 1999, but the difference in cyclical conditions in the United States and the euro area seems to have been a dominant factor. Considered over a long-term perspective, recent movements in the euro do not appear as dramatic as recent bilateral changes would tend to suggest: the euro is presently at about its past five-year average level expressed in nominal effective terms, while in real terms, it is above the low levels reached in the 1980s.

Predicting the future value of the euro with any precision is impossible and this chapter has made no attempt to do so. Rather it has tried to gauge the future direction of the euro-area economy given the known macroeconomic policy stance in the three major OECD regions and the euro area's structural characteristics. In this context, the OECD Interlink model has been used to analyse the implications of potentially large changes in exchange rates and of accelerated structural reforms in the euro area.

The results of this analysis show that even a sharp correction in the dollar exchange rate driven by concerns about the worsening US external position, would have, with an appropriate monetary policy response, only limited effects on the euro-area economy over the medium run. Furthermore, there is scope for the euro area to grow faster, without inflationary pressures, if a more rapid implementation of structural reforms translates quickly into a lower NAIRU. Such higher rates of growth in the euro area are, however, likely to yield only limited spillovers in the United States and Japan, and will in no way be sufficient to significantly reduce external imbalances.

Appendix

This chapter was originally written at the end of 1999. A number of the perspectives discussed in the chapter have evolved rather differently. This is perhaps most evident with respect to currency value movements. For instance, the chapter argued that the fundamental determinants of exchange rates augured in favour of an appreciating euro over the medium term. In the event, the euro further depreciated, reaching a low of 84 US cents in October 2000, equivalent to almost a 30 per cent depreciation since the euro's official debut in January 1999. Against a basket of currencies the subsequent further depreciation has been less pronounced, reflecting offsetting gains in value mostly against currencies of emerging market economies, which have a combined weight of almost one-third in the OECD measure of the euro effective exchange rate. Since the trough reached in October 2000, the euro has risen by about 15 per cent against both the US dollar and *vis-à-vis* a basket of currencies, to reach levels, in the second half of 2002, similar to when the chapter was finalised (Figure 15.A1).

The large depreciation in the euro through to October 2000, particularly against the US dollar is difficult to explain. The main factor appears to have been the strength in the dollar, rather than weakness in the euro *per se*, the former driven by a growing body of evidence through 1999 and 2000 indicating a structural improvement in potential growth in the United States and thus expected rates of return on assets. This attracted substantial capital inflows to the United States, as global portfolios were rebalanced, and acted as a source of US dollar currency strength. To be sure, there was also evidence to suggest

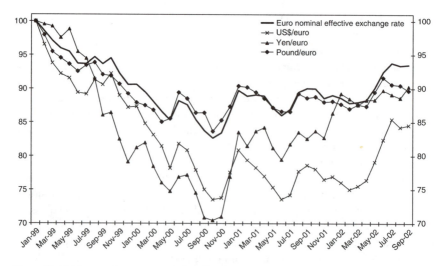

Figure 15.A1 Euro exchange rates index, Jan 1999 = 100.

a productivity improvement in the euro area. But this was largely confined to a few smaller countries, such as Finland and Ireland.[21] Elsewhere within the euro area the rise in output growth was largely cyclical. Indeed, while economic growth on average in the euro area accelerated through 1999 and averaged 3.5 per cent in 2000, its highest pace in a decade, output growth in the United States grew at an even faster rate, while inflation levels were broadly similar in both areas. It is fair to say, however, that these factors – growth differential *vis-à-vis* the United States and portfolio diversification away from euro-denominated securities – or other possible factors usually put forward – for example, differences in interest rates and returns on equity as well as rising oil prices – are not fully convincing to explain movements in the euro–dollar exchange rate. Indeed, as it became clear, at the end of 2000, that the US economy was moving into recession, the euro started to recover, reducing by half in the course of 2002 the loss that occurred after its launch, but it still remains weaker than what most analysts would consider an equilibrium level consistent with economic fundamentals.

It is conceivable that the steady depreciation of the euro following its launch crimped the speed with which the euro was adopted as an international currency. Official holdings of foreign exchange over the past three years have been broadly constant at some 13 per cent. In contrast, the euro has become an important international payments currency. The stock of international bonds and notes denominated in euros has risen some five percentage points, to reach a market share of almost one-third by the end of 2001, with a share of net issues not much short of 50 per cent. In the same period, the share of international money market instruments denominated in euros has increased by about 14 per cent, and is now more than double the 1997 level obtained by adding together all the instruments denominated in the currencies that have given rise to the euro. As expected, with individuals and businesses embracing the euro as an international currency, the task of measuring monetary aggregates has become more complicated. While the European Central Bank (ECB) has thus far modified frequently the compilation of M3 data, the poor relationship between M3 growth and inflation continues to limit the usefulness of monetary aggregates as an indicator of the stance of monetary policy, as recently acknowledged by the ECB.

Leading up to, and in the first three years since the euro was launched, many challenges have been successfully addressed, despite numerous predictions to the contrary. For example, the massive logistical task of replacing national currencies with the euro was implemented with no major problems, and the conduct of monetary policy itself has been widely considered appropriate, although the communication of policy decisions has not always been optimal. Looking ahead, a number of new policy challenges face the euro area. For instance, European Union enlargement will bring, in time, over ten additional national economies to the area. Current ECB monetary policy governance arrangements are unlikely to operate as efficiently if current practices are extended unmodified to embrace all these new members.

More immediately, fiscal positions in a number of countries are close to breaching the constraints of the Growth and Stability Pact. To consolidate budgetary positions in late 2002 and 2003 would represent a pro-cyclical fiscal stance, but to delay the task could equally engender a loss of confidence, weakening consumer and investment spending. The original paper identified this undesirable situation and argued in favour of budget consolidation – although giving more weight to cyclically adjusted fiscal positions – to establish the full ability to pursue counter-cyclical policies. In the event, fiscal policy was perhaps maintained for too long excessively loose in an attempt to bolster output. This worked for a while, but fiscal policy has limited scope to improve the productive potential of the euro area. This requires structural reforms. In this regard many of the points raised in the final section of the chapter still remain apposite. Some progress has been made, notably in sharpening the incentive to seek and retain work by better designs of tax and benefit systems and through education programs. But labour markets remain slow to adjust to shocks and in some product markets the lack of competition is an obstacle retarding the potential to achieve better economic outcomes, while financial integration is far from complete. Addressing these structural barriers remains one of the major challenges facing the euro area in the years ahead.

Acknowledgements

We thank our colleagues Claude Giorno and Alain DeSerres for comments and suggestions on previous article versions of this Chapter. We also thank Debra Bloch and Marie-Christine Bonnefous for statistical support, and Susan Gascard and Brenda Livsey-Coates for secretarial assistance. Views are ours and do not necessarily reflect those of the OECD or the authors' current affiliations.

Notes

1 See *inter alia* Bergsten (1998) and Coeuré and Pisani-Ferry (1999).
2 The OECD measure is based on a basket of thirty countries, compared with thirteen in the ECB series and uses moving rather than fixed weights. The IMF measure includes countries with trade weights greater than 1 per cent and uses weights averaged over the 1980–98 period. For more details on the OECD methodology, see Durand *et al.* (1998).
3 Pre-1999 series are compiled using the synthetic value of the euro based on its eleven constituent currencies, that is, eleven countries have been included in the indicator, even though they joined the European Monetary System at different points in time. More precisely, the synthetic euro–dollar exchange rate is calculated as a chain-linked index based on weighted changes in euro-area countries' bilateral dollar exchange rate. Weights applied are based on shares of euro-wide GDP at current dollar exchange rates in the previous period (moving weights). The value of the euro–dollar exchange rate of 4 January 1999 is used as the starting point to retropolate the series historically.
4 See Isard and Faruquee (1998) for more details.
5 See Nadal-De Simone and Razzak (1999), MacDonald (1999) and Rogoff (1999).
6 While, as seen earlier, these indicators may differ in nominal terms, reflecting whether emerging market economies are included in the calculations, this is no longer the case for indicators expressed in real terms since large depreciations in these economies have generally been accompanied by equally large price increases relative to their trading partners.

7 The formal stipulations concerning the choice of exchange rate regimes between the euro and other currencies require a considerable degree of consensus. The Maastricht Treaty specifies that the Council – made up of representatives of the Member States – acting unanimously and after consulting the ECB as well as without prejudice to the objective of price stability could 'conclude formal agreements on an exchange rate system for the euro in relation to non-euro currencies' (Article 109.1). Furthermore, in the absence of such an exchange rate system, the Council could 'formulate general orientations for exchange rate policy in relation to these currencies' (Article 109.2), possibly consisting of a unilateral policy of intervening whenever the euro is deemed too weak or too strong. On the other hand, according to a resolution of the European Council in December 1997, 'it is understood that general exchange policy guidelines *vis-à-vis* one or more non-Community currencies will be formulated only in exceptional circumstances' (Paragraph 45 of the Presidency Conclusions of the European Council meeting in Luxembourg on 12 and 13 December 1997). Thus, it is most likely that any formalised arrangement would require a consensus to be reached between the Council and the ECB. To date, however, proposals for target zones have met with criticism from the ECB. The ECB President has warned that target zones would pose a potential conflict with the ECB's mandate to achieve price stability and the ECB's Chief Economist has remarked that the benefits of monetary union could be in part lost if the ECB were not able to concentrate on European price stability, but had to take into account monetary developments in the United States. Thus, while the ECB does have the right to be consulted, it is difficult to conceive of any type of formal arrangement on which a consensus would be found.

8 For arguments against target zones see Hills *et al.* (1999), which also contains a dissenting view in favour of target zones by Bergsten and others, pp. 125–129.

9 For an analysis of the effectiveness of central bank interventions, see Catte *et al.* (1994), and comments therein, and Bénassy-Quéré (1999).

10 At the same time as the launch of the euro the payments systems gave users the opportunity to use cheques and credit cards debited from euro denominated accounts, but these payments represent a very small proportion of total transactions.

11 Part of these proceeds, however, have subsequently been converted to dollars to repay dollar denominated debt, which some commentators have cited as a factor contributing to the weakness of the euro, although given the magnitudes involved the overall impact would at best be marginal.

12 This quotation comes from Don (1999).

13 The OECD's bi-annual short-term projections assume a constant nominal exchange rate, along with a given path for commodity prices, a fiscal policy stance based on measures and stated policy intentions, where these are embodied in well-defined programmes, and a monetary policy stance in line with the official objectives of the relevant monetary authorities. At times, a constant nominal exchange rate assumption may be at odds with other assumptions about policy developments and some aspects of the projections. In that case, it highlights possible inconsistencies or tensions and thus provides a basis for policy recommendations to correct them. Similarly, in the OECD medium-term baseline, which extends the short-term projections over three additional years and is used mainly to provide a basis for comparisons with simulations and scenarios based on alternative assumptions, exchange rates are assumed to remain constant in real terms beyond the short-term horizon.

14 See Dalsgaard *et al.* (2001).

15 In 1998, these rates ranged between 5 and 5.50 per cent in the Netherlands, Portugal and Austria, around 8 per cent in Belgium, Germany and Ireland, and over 10 per cent in Finland, France, Italy and Spain (OECD, 1999b).

16 An approximate summary measure of the degree of real wage flexibility and the degree of real wage resistance can be broadly captured by estimating standard structural wage equations. An OECD survey (OECD, 2000) of EMU developments after one year reports the results of a wage equation, estimated for individual euro-area

countries and across the euro area as a whole, as well as for the United States. The results indicate a high sensitivity of real wages to unemployment in the long run, but point to a relatively high degree of short-run rigidity as indicated by the difficulty to find a negative and significant short-term effect. The results also suggest that the speed of adjustment of real wages towards their long-run equilibrium level is much slower in the euro area than in the United States. Half of the adjustment is complete in less than one-and-a half years in the United States, whereas in the euro area it takes about four-and-a-half years. Other empirical studies generally support both the finding that structural rigidities are more prevalent in the euro area than in the United States and that in the long run real wages in the euro area tend to be as sensitive to unemployment as in the United States (Scarpetta, 1996; Viñals and Jimeno, 1996; Balakrishnan and Michelacci, 1998; Nickell and Layard, 1998; Obstfeld and Peri, 1998). However, this clearly is not so over short horizons – reflecting slow adjustment – and is corroborated by the fact that unemployment has proved to be more persistent in the euro area than in the United States (Blanchard and Katz, 1997; OECD, 1999a).

17 See, in particular, Chapter IV of OECD (1999c) on the size and role of automatic fiscal stabilizers. See also, on economic policy co-ordination within the EMU, Visco (1999) and Durand (2000).

18 See Laxton *et al.* (1998).

19 Alternatively, in view of the large Japanese net foreign asset position, a similar exercise could have been conducted by simulating an appreciation of the yen *vis-à-vis* all other currencies. However, in view of the present conjuncture in Japan and the expected path of the recovery in the years to come, a substantial real appreciation of the yen – of the sort likely to be needed to substantially reduce net foreign assets – would induce a major recession with virtually no possibility for monetary policy to respond given the very low levels of short-term interest rates. Such a scenario is therefore highly unlikely to be achieved through a nominal appreciation. A more plausible scenario would be that of higher inflation induced by monetary policy, so as to engineer a real appreciation. The scenario presented here is a variant of one considered in OECD (1999c), where the effects of other possible market shocks and policy measures on the world economy have also been examined.

20 Such rules, an example of which is the Taylor (1993) rule, can shed light on the current and prospective level of interest rate developments, and they have become widely used to assess the level of policy-controlled interest rates (Bank for International Settlements, 1998 and International Monetary Fund, 1998).

21 For a detailed analysis see OECD (2001), *The New Economy Beyond the Hype*, Paris.

Bibliography

Alberola, E., S. Cervero, H. Lopez and A. Ubide (1999), 'Global equilibrium exchange rates: euro, dollar, "ins," and "outs," and other major currencies in a panel cointegration framework', *IMF Working Paper* No. 175.

Bacchetta, P. and E. van Wincoop (1998), 'Does exchange rate stability increase trade and capital flows?', *CEPR Discussion Paper* No. 1962.

Balakrishnan, R. and C. Michelacci (1998), 'Unemployment dynamics across OECD countries', *Working Paper* No. 9806, CEMFI, December.

Bank for International Settlements (1998), *Annual Report*.

Bénassy-Quéré, A. (1999), 'La BCE et l'Euro', *La Lettre du CEPII*, No. 182.

Bergsten, F. (1998), 'How to target exchange rates', *Financial Times*, 20 November 1998.

Blanchard, O. and L. Katz (1997), 'What we know and do not know about the natural rate of unemployment', *Journal of Economic Perspectives*, 11(1), 51–72.

Bordo, M. and B. Eichengreen (eds) (1993), *A retrospective on the Bretton Woods system: lessons for international monetary reform*, National Bureau of Economic Research Project Report, University of Chicago Press.

CAE (1999), *Architecture financiere internationale*, Conseil d'Analyse Economique, Paris, Rapport No. 18.

Catte, P., G. Galli and S. Rebecchini (1994), 'Concerted intervention and the dollar: an analysis of daily data' In: P. Kennen, F. Papadia and F. Saccomanni (eds), *The International Monetary System*, Cambridge University Press, Cambridge, UK.

Coeuré, B. and J. Pisani-Ferry (1999), 'The case against benign neglect of exchange rate stability', *Finance and Development*, 36(3), 5–9.

Corsetti, G. and P. Pesenti (1999), 'Stability, asymmetry and discontinuity: the outset of European Monetary Union', *Brookings Papers on Economic Activity*, December.

Dalsgaard *et al.* (2001), 'Standard shocks in the OECD Interlink model', OECD *Economics Department, Working Paper* No. 306.

Don, F.J.H. (1999), 'Forecasting in macroeconomics: a practitioner view', *CPB Netherlands Bureau for Economic Policy Analysis Working Paper*.

Durand, M. (2000), 'Challenges for economic policy co-ordination within EMU', *Empirica*.

Durand, M., C. Madaschi and F. Terribile (1998), 'Trends in OECD countries' international competitiveness: The influence of emerging market economies', *OECD Economics Department Working Paper*, No. 195.

Feyzioglu, T. (1997), 'Estimating the equilibrium real exchange rate: an application to Finland', *IMF Working Paper*, No. 109.

Hills, C., P. Peterson and M. Goldstein (1999), *Safeguarding prosperity in a global financial system – the future international financial architecture*, Report of an independent task force sponsored by the Council on Foreign Relations, Institute for International Economics, New York.

International Monetary Fund (1998), *World Economic Outlook*, September.

Isard, P. and H. Faruqee (eds) (1998), 'Exchange rate assessment: extensions of the macroeconomic balance approach', *IMF Occasional Paper*, No. 167.

Italianer, A. (1999), 'The euro and internal economic policy co-ordination', *Empirica* 26, 201–216.

Laxton, D., P. Isard, H. Faruquee, E. Prasad and B. Turtelboom (1998) 'MULTIMOD Mark III – the core dynamic and steady-state models', *International Monetary Fund Occasional Paper*, No. 164.

MacDonald, R. (1999), 'Exchange rate behaviour: are fundamentals important?', *Economic Journal*, 109, 673–691.

Masson, P. and T. Krueger (eds) (1997), *EMU and the International Monetary System*, IMF, Washington, DC.

Nadal-de Simone, F. and W. Razzak (1999), 'Nominal exchange rates and nominal interest rate differentials', *IMF Working Paper*, No. 141.

Nickell, S. and R. Layard (1998), 'Labour market institutions and economic performance', *Centre for Economic Performance Discussion Paper*, No. 407.

Obstfeld, M. (1998), 'Open-economy macroeconomics: developments in theory and policy', *Scandinavian Journal of Economics*, 100(1), 247–275.

Obstfeld, M. and G. Peri (1998), 'Regional non-adjustment and fiscal policy', In: D. Begg *et al.* (ed.) *EMU: Prospects and Challenges for the Euro*, Blackwell Publishers, Oxford.

OECD (1999a), *EMU: Facts, Challenges and Policies*, Paris.

OECD (1999b), *Implementing the OECD Jobs Strategy: Assessing Performance and Policy*, Paris.

OECD (1999c), *Economic Outlook*, No. 66, Paris.

OECD (2000), *EMU, One Year On*, Paris.

Rogoff, K. (1999), 'Monetary models of dollar/yen/euro nominal exchange rates: dead or undead?', *Economic Journal*, 109(459), 655–695.

Scarpetta, S. (1996), 'Assessing the role of labour market policies and institutional settings on unemployment: a cross country study', *OECD Economic Studies*, No. 26, 1996/I.

Taylor, J. B. (1993), 'Discretion versus policy rules in practice', *Carnegie Rochester Conference Series on Public Policy*, No. 39.

Turner, D., C. Giorno, A. de Serres, A. Vourc'h and P. Richardson (1998), 'The macro-economic implications of ageing in a global context', *OECD Economics Department Working Paper*, No. 193.

Viaene, J. and C. de Vries (1992), 'International trade and exchange rate volatility', *European Economic Review*, 36, 1311–1321.

Viñals, J. and J. Jimeno (1996), 'Monetary Union and European Unemployment', Banco de España, *Working Paper*, No. 9624.

Visco, I. (1999), 'Should economic policies be co-ordinated for EMU?', *OECD Observer*, January.

Williamson, J. (1994), 'Estimates of FEERs', In: J. Williamson (ed.) *Estimating equilibrium exchange rates*, Institute for International Economics, Washington, DC.

Questions for Part IV

1 What do the crises of the 1990s teach us about the role of exchange rate mechanism?
2 How does one choose the exchange rate regime? Can there be a consensus exchange rate regime? If not, why not?
3 Does pegging of the exchange rate help in lowering inflation expectations?
4 What were the dominant factors driving the euro down?
5 Would a correction in the exchange rate of the dollar have a large effect over the euro and euro-area economies?
6 What policy measures should the European Central Bank (ECB) recommend to contain the volatility of the euro?

Areas for further research

1 The locus classicus of an exchange rate regime.
2 The long-term viability of the pegged exchange rate.
3 The stability of the exchange rate as a policy target.
4 The prospects of the euro as an international currency.

Part V

Capital flows to emerging market economies

16 Capital flows to the emerging market economies

Stimulants and depressants

Dilip K. Das

(In the global financial system) capital is free to go where it is best rewarded, which in turn has led to the rapid growth of global financial markets. The result is a gigantic circulatory system, sucking up capital into the financial markets and institutions at the center and then pumping it out to the periphery either directly in the form of credits and portfolio investments, or indirectly through multinational corporations.

(George Soros, in *The Crisis of Global Capitalism*, 1998)

What are emerging market economies?

Although the term "emerging market" is of recent vintage, the phenomenon itself is centuries old. Weren't all the industrial economies of today emerging markets in one period or the other? Countries like Argentina, Britain, Japan and the United States were all emerging market economies at one point in time. Each one of these countries was also among the richest, in terms of per capita income. In the emerging market sense, the United States emerged around two centuries ago. After that it did take some backward steps and suffered reversals, yet the United States stood as economic history's premier example of a successful emerging market economy. Argentina is a diametrically opposite case. Around a century ago, when Argentina and Japan were both emerging market economies, Argentina was the richer of the two by a good measure. Argentina failed to complete its emergence, while Japan did so in the twentieth century to emerge the second largest global economy.

As barriers to trade and financial flows are coming down, a good number of developing economies have "emerged" and joined the ranks of emerging market economies. Over the last quarter century, financial globalization has expanded to the emerging market economies. This set of economies are somewhat imprecisely defined as the newly industrialized economies[1] (NIEs) and middle-income developing countries in which governments and corporations have access to private international capital markets, or can attract institutional portfolio investment, or both. Different international institutions include slightly different sets of countries in this category. For example, the Institute of International Finance (IIF) includes twenty-nine countries from Asia, Africa, Europe, Latin America and the

Middle East. The International Monetary Fund (IMF) includes all the NIEs and the middle-income developing countries in its definition of the emerging market economies. *The Economist* classifies twenty-five developing and transitional economies as emerging market economies. (Refer to Chapter 2, the section title "Globalization.")[2]

Sylla (1999) identified human and property rights as the basic requisite of becoming an emerging market economy. The national government should offer protection to human and property rights to both the citizens of the country and the nonresidents alike. The *sine qua non* of an emerging market economy is its sustained ability to attract global investment. Only an assurance of protection of property rights will attract global investors to the potential emerging market economy. Thus property rights is a fundamental, nonnegotiable condition, which an economy needs to establish before embarking on its road to becoming an emerging market economy. When an economy has the required human and natural resources, and lacks the third vital ingredient for growth, namely capital, it can wait until capital is domestically accumulated with advancing growth. The alternative course is that it convinces global investors of its latent economic potential. If it succeeds in doing so, the global capital infusion helps realize the economic potential of the country in a shorter time span to the mutual benefit of the global investor and the recipient economy. Thus the concept of emerging market is basically tied up with "arbitraging the difference between a country's current economic reality and its future economic potential."

To achieve the above-mentioned precondition, a country needs to have political stability, credible legal institutions that protect property rights and a liberal economic system. Statist economic systems are an anathema to emerging market economies. Second, a stable currency and a credible public finance system are indispensable. Together they provide a trustworthy means of servicing public debt and make them attractive to domestic and global investors. Third, the government should assist its private sector to develop attractive financial assets – securities and bond markets – and secondary markets where public and private securities can be traded on market value. In the initial phases, assistance in development of banking and financial institutions may also be required. Fourth, initiatives by the central banks would be needed in developing a system of supervision and regulation of the emerging financial system. Once these economic, legal and financial objectives are achieved and basic infrastructure established, governments should leave the arena for the private sector to get on with the development of the economy. Markets should be allowed to play their own role, although on specific occasions governments may play a corrective role. However, governments must not pursue their own objectives that are incompatible with economic growth. If the market perception of the role of the government is that of an unwarranted intervention, it would be highly detrimental to the cause of developing an emerging market economy.

Being able to attract global capital and becoming an emerging economy can be a great advantage to an economy.[3] Although there are some limitations and dangers, on balance becoming an emerging market economy is far more advantageous than not becoming one. Its advantages can be maximized by laying down a solid foundation of domestic financial institutions before making overtures to integrate with the global financial markets. This is an important lesson for the emerging market economies of the present era.

This chapter begins with the definitional issues and focuses on the domestic and global economic and financial environment affecting the emergence of an economy in the section "Environmental determinants." In some of the recent crises, particularly in the Latin American crisis of 1994–95 and the Asian crisis of 1997–98, large and steady capital inflows were partly responsible for instability in the currency and financial markets, therefore, this chapter begins with an examination of capital inflows into the emerging market economies. It focuses on the stimulants to capital inflows during the 1990s in the section "Stimulants to capital inflows." The section "Macroeconomics of financial flows" focuses on the macroeconomic factors in the emerging market and industrial economies which shaped the financial scenario of the late 1990s, particularly the events after July 1997.[4] The next two sections deal with the steady increase in private capital flows to emerging market economies and the sharp decline in them respectively. After a steady rise, they were reduced to a trickle in 2001. The section on "Emerging market financial crises," briefly elaborates on the two current emerging market crises, namely those afflicting Turkey and Argentina. In a globalizing financial market, speculators play an active role. The section "Institutional investors and emerging markets" analyses the modus operandi of speculators and the extent and intensity of the speculative attacks in the emerging markets. In the next section we examine whether some defensive measures can be taken by the central banking authorities against probable speculative runs. A summary of conclusions is provided in the last section.

Environmental determinants

Domestic and external economic and financial environment are among the two most important determinants of private financial inflows to, or outflows from, the emerging market economies. Until financial crisis struck the five Asian economies[5] in mid-1997, private capital flow to emerging market economies had gone on rising in a monotonic manner. In the rising volume of financial flows lay a valuable lesson for the emerging market economies, that markets reward strong fundamentals, sound financial and macroeconomic policies and commitment to reforms by the emerging market policy mandarins. Incongruous macroeconomic and financial policies destabilize economies and financial markets are sensitive to policy inconsistencies and their outcome. Market disapproval is forthwith reflected in the direction of financial flows. Furthermore, crisis-free and upbeat financial and economic external environment also stimulates capital flows to the emerging market economies. Conversely, a depressed external environment retards, even reverses, capital market flows to the emerging market economies.

External environment implies both regional and global environment. The contemporary period of financial globalization has witnessed several instances of national, regional and global economic turbulences. Between 1992 and 1998, three major regional currency crises and a major country default, took place. They were the European monetary crisis of 1992–93,[6] the Latin American crisis of 1994–95, the Asian crisis of 1997–98 and the 1998 default by the Russian Federation. Two of the three crises jolted the emerging market economies and affected global economic performance. So did the default by the Russian Federation. The litany of problems did not end. Serious financial problems followed in Brazil (1998–99) and Turkey[7] (2000–01). Argentinean economy not only suffered a crisis (2001–02) but also a sovereign default. It was caused by persisting with the fixed and overvalued exchange rate arrangement, proving that fixed exchange rate regimes are vulnerable to asymmetric shocks. In the section "Stimulants to capital flows," we shall see that together they worked as a depressant on the capital flows to emerging market economies.

The principal objective of this chapter is to delve into the "hows" and "whys" of the private capital flows into and out of the emerging market economies and to analyze what stimulated or depressed them. July 1997 turned out to be a turning point in the capital flows. Until this point they soared steadily and after reaching a peak, went into a steady decline. As the capital flows began to rise, speculators began to play an increasing role in the emerging market economies. They have frequently been accused of precipitating crises in these economies. This chapter analyzes their role and proposes what, if anything, can be done to defend the economy from their destabilizing effects.

Macroeconomics of financial flows

Several factors were responsible for improvement in the global economic performance during the 1990s, up until mid-1997. One of the principal factors was general improvement in the emerging market and industrial economies. These two subgroups performed markedly better than that in the 1980s. Institution of the Brady Plan in 1989 helped those emerging market economies that were struggling with debt-servicing problems. According to the statistics compiled by the IMF (1997) fiscal deficits for the emerging market economies fell from an average of 6 percent of the GDP in 1983–89 to 3 percent of GDP in 1990–96. Likewise, the average rate of inflation for this country group fell slowly first and sharply later. The rate of real GDP growth which had come down to 2.2 percent during the 1979–89 period, soared to 6 percent during the 1990–96 period. The rate of export growth was down to 6 percent for the former period, it rose to 11 percent for the latter period. The export surge facilitated debt-servicing, therefore, the ratio of external debt service payment to exports fell sharply between 1990 and 1996. Also, the ratio of external public debt to GDP fell from 54 percent in 1990 to 37 percent in 1966. A marked improvement in the macroeconomic performance was one of the fundamental reasons behind the improved access of this country group to international financial markets. The number of emerging market countries with Moody's credit rating rose from eleven in 1989 to fifty-two in 1997. Extensive privatization took place in these economies during the 1990s. These measures further opened these economies for external finance.

Likewise, evidence of macroeconomic improvement in the industrial economies abounds. For instance, average inflation rate fell from a little above 4 percent to less than 2 percent during this period. This resulted in a fall in nominal interest rates, both short- and long-term. The former declined from an average of 7.3 percent during 1987–90 to 4.3 percent during 1994–96. The long-term interest rates, likewise, fell from an average of 8 to 6.3 percent during the same periods. Declining interest rate in one set of economies and stronger fundamentals in the other have been alluded to while discussing the so-called push and pull factors. There was a well-publicized earlier view that it was only the downward interest rate movement in the industrial economies that was sufficient to trigger greater capital movement toward emerging market economies. It does not seem to be correct because it was the FDI flows that increased more during the 1990s as compared to the other private capital flows. These flows are largely unresponsive to small interest rate changes. Therefore, a pull factor was as important as the push factor.

This optimistic view cannot possibly be of the Pollyanna variety because industrial economies are known to go through cycles. As demonstrated in the section "Depressans to capital inflows" when the cycle takes a downward turn, the favorable capital market environment changes and so does the investor sentiment and market liquidity. The other possibility is that economic conditions in emerging market economies may deteriorate, which may cost them their access to the international financial markets. Under both these circumstances, the financial flows may be reversed. Therefore, sustainability must not be taken for granted. An important development in this regard was that the composition of the financial flows underwent a discernible transformation in the 1990s. Short-term flows in the form of bonds, equities and short-term instruments like certificates of deposit and commercial paper became popular instruments and accounted for a substantial proportion of total financial flows to emerging market economies. Due to their short maturities these flows are inherently unsustainable and the "hot money" argument became popular. It should, however, be noted that the composition of inflows varied considerably among economies. High relative volatility is one of the notions that have been associated with hot money. That is, hot money is likely to disappear or reverse itself, as soon as the perception of investors, or market sentiment regarding the emerging market concerned changes or the economy receives an external shock. However, on the basis of statistical time series for ten countries, Claessens *et al.* (1995) established that this distinction between hot and cold money is spurious. Long-term flows are as volatile as the short-term flows. The time it takes for an unexpected shock to a flow to die out is similar across flows. There was also little evidence that information about the composition of flows is useful in forecasting the overall level of flows, and this suggests that the overall capital account is independent of the type of flow. Thus, sustainability is neutral to the temperature of the flow, hot or cold. The evidence is consistent with the view that capital flows are fungible and endogenous with respect to external shocks.

The sustainability of financial flows is influenced by the exchange rate regime also. A flexible and pragmatic management of the exchange rate regime directly contributes to sustainability. During the post Bretton Woods period, most countries adopted one kind of floating exchange rate system or another. Not all the regimes were prudent, carefully contrived and successful. Some emerging market economies mismanaged them and allowed their flexible exchange rate regimes to become de facto fixed exchange rate systems. When the financial markets perceive such inconsistencies or policy weaknesses, speculative attacks are the result. Speculators perceive those economies as most vulnerable that have exchange rate flexibility. The Asian emerging market economies fell into this category during 1997–98. They made their currencies vulnerable to speculative runs by inadvertently making their currency regimes inflexible. When the trend became obvious, they took much too long to correct the policy error, and in the process opened their currency markets to speculative runs and depleted their foreign exchange reserves.

Stimulants to capital inflows

After the oil shock of 1973, money center banks found themselves with excess liquidity to invest. Initially a good deal of this capital was utilized for financing public debt in the form of syndicated loans. However, with the break up of fixed exchange rate regime, better performing developing economies were able to open up to greater capital mobility while keeping autonomy over their monetary policy. As discussed in Chapter 1, capital flows increased sharply during the latter half of the 1970s and early 1980s, leading to the debt crisis of 1982, which started with Mexico declaring a moratorium in July 1982 on its external liability. Brady Bonds were invented toward the late 1980s to resolve the debt crisis of the developing countries. This development subsequently helped in the development of bond markets for the emerging market economies. Investors in the industrial countries found that deregulation, privatization, merger and acquisitions (M&As) and advances in the information technology (IT) was making foreign direct investment (FDI) and equity investment in the emerging market more attractive than before and easy. The result was an FDI and equity investment spike in the emerging market economies in the 1990s (Mundell, 2000).

Advances in IT and computer technology are cited as one of the most important factors driving and supporting financial globalization, flow of financial resources to the emerging market economies and integrating them with the global economy. They have reduced the cost of communications, increased power of computers, shrunk the globe and made national boundaries less significant. New developments in IT facilitated collection and processing of information for the market participants as well as for monetary and banking authorities and banks. They made it possible to measure, monitor and manage financial risk for the market participants. Without computers pricing and trading of complex new financial instruments was not feasible. Managing large and rapid transactions, and then managing books for these transactions, which are widely spread across continents, and countries, could not be accomplished without the support of IT and computers.

As alluded to in Chapter 1, transnational corporations (TNCs) played a proactive role in the flow of capital to the emerging market economies. They expanded their networks by merging with or acquiring other national and international firms. They managed to "slice the value chain" and created production and distribution networks spanning the globe. As noted above, many emerging market economies began liberalizing their domestic economies in a methodical manner, lowering barriers to trade and financial flows, consequently increasing global trade in both goods and services. These developments resulted in heightened demand for trans-border financial flows. Therefore, an internationally mobile pool of capital and liquidity was created, which allowed financial globalization and flow of capital to emerging market economies.

Liberalized domestic economic strategies, advances in IT, and globalizing emerging market economies coalesced to catalyze financial innovation. Responding to the demand for trans-border financial flows, financial intermediation activity globalized. It was further buttressed by declining barriers to trade in financial services as well as deregulation and removal of entry restrictions on foreign financial institutions into domestic markets in a large number of emerging market economies. Consequently, trans-border flows increased at a rapid clip.

The regulatory authorities in the emerging market economies modernized their structure and role. Their new set of regulations facilitated a broader range of institutions to provide financial services. Also, new categories of nonbank institutions and institutional investors were launched. Gradually, investment banks, securities firms, asset managers, mutual funds, insurance companies, specialty and trade finance companies, hedge funds, and even telecommunications, software, and food companies began providing services similar to those traditionally provided by banks.

Economic and political developments during the first half of the 1990s led to an increase in financial flows from private capital markets to the emerging market economies. These developments included sweeping structural adjustments in the developing economies during the 1980s and 1990s, unpopularity of statist and protectionist policies, and adoption of market-friendly strategies. Intellectual zeitgeist changed during this period and the "Washington consensus" came to be widely accepted.[8] Unlike the late 1990s, the acceptance and popularity of the Washington consensus among the policy-making community was on the rise. Free markets and sound money were accepted as keys to economic development. Some analysts believe that the rise of the Washington consensus was a turning point in the world economic affairs (Krugman, 1995). During this period, in the industrial economies savings were becoming increasingly institutionalized. Assets of pension funds, insurance companies and mutual funds in the twenty-nine OECD (Organization for Economic Co-operation and Development) economies reached $29 trillion in 1995. Such has been the scale of saving accumulation that by the end of 1998, the total assets of mutual funds in the United States were esti-mated have overtaken those of banks, which have been the dominant financial intermediary for the past two centuries (*The Economist*, 1998). The same trend existed in Japan and the larger economies of Europe, namely, Germany, France and the United Kingdom. Financial institutions in these economies became large reservoirs of savings.

Due to the implementation of structural adjustment programs and several, and sound macroeconomic and financial policies, emerging market economies were far healthier in the 1990s – as reflected in their leading economic indicators – than before. As alluded to above, international capital is attracted by improve-ments in economic fundamentals. They work as a strong stimulant to private capital market inflows. In addition, institutional investors needed to diversify their portfolios and in their quest for global diversification could not overlook the promise of the emerging market economies. Thus, rising capital flows to emerging market economies provided large institutional investors risk-mitigation benefits that are associated with globally diversified portfolios. Slack GDP growth in the European Union and Japan had reduced investment opportunities in these economies during the first half of the 1990s, again stimu-lating a surge in capital flows into the emerging markets. This growing integra-tion of emerging markets into the international financial system is viewed by a number of observers as reestablishing the type of relationships between capital-importing and capital-exporting countries that existed in the earlier two periods of high capital mobility, that is, 1880–14 and the 1920s (Das, 1996a; Obstfeld and Taylor, 1997).

To put this analysis in perspective, a brief look at the financial scenario of the 1980s is essential. After the Latin American debt crisis of 1982–83, there was a sharp deterioration in the macroeconomic performance of many emerging mar-ket economies, therefore, net private capital inflows had declined to a trickle.[9] Several emerging market economies, particularly those in Latin America, experi-enced severe debt-servicing difficulties and their rate of inflation had accelerated. In addition, the most heavily indebted ones had the ratio of external debt to exports close to 375 percent in the latter half of the 1980s. Some market observers, therefore, argued that it could take several years before access was restored, despite several years of adjustment efforts (USS, 1990). Despite the pes-simism at the start of the decade of the 1990s, total net private capital flows to emerging markets in the 1990–96 period soared to $1,055 billion, more than seven times the amount they received over the 1973–81 period. These flows were also over nine times as large as net borrowings from official creditors during the same period.

Table 16.1 shows that total net capital inflows soared from $45.7 billion in 1990 to $213.8 billion in 1996 and net FDI from $18.8 billion to $113.5 billion over the same period. These are more than fivefold increases in net-terms. The trend in portfolio investment (particularly bonds) was not so smooth. They rose from $17 billion to $104.9 billion between 1990 and 1994, but declined in 1995. The financial crisis in Mexico had begun in late 1994. The net flows picked up again

Table 16.1 Private capital flows to emerging markets (1990–2001) (in billions of $)

	1990	1991	1992	1993	1994	1995	1996	1997	1998	1999	2000	2001
Total net flows	45.7	118.1	120.6	176.3	143.4	192.9	213.8	148.8	65.4	69.4	7.7	3.3
Foreign direct investment	18.8	31.5	35.3	57.9	84.7	93.0	113.5	142.6	154.7	163.8	153.4	175.5
Net portfolio investment	17.0	24.7	55.6	98.7	104.9	38.3	74.0	66.7	−4.6	33.9	−4.3	−30.2
Others	9.9	62.0	29.7	19.6	−46.3	61.7	26.4	−60.5	−84.7	−128.2	−141.4	−114.0
Asia	21.4	24.8	29.0	31.8	36.1	60.6	62.9	−22.1	−31.6	−13.9	−15.7	−16.2
Middle East and Europe	7.0	65.7	38.8	29.1	16.1	8.0	6.4	17.0	9.5	0.6	−24.0	−27.1
Western Hemisphere	10.3	24.1	55.7	61.4	44.1	46.7	79.7	86.1	71.3	43.9	42.5	27.1
Economies in transition	4.2	−9.9	3.1	19.7	15.9	44.8	16.3	23.1	19.8	13.9	0.8	4.2

Sources: International Monetary Fund, *World Economic Outlook*. Washington, DC, October 1999, table 2.2, page 52; International Monetary Fund, *World Economic Outlook*. Washington, DC, April 2002, table 1.4, page 30.

in 1996 reaching $74 billion, which was almost half the 1994 level. Likewise, other net investment, which includes mostly bank lendings, after rising sharply during the early 1990s, became negative in 1994, that is, withdrawals or repayments were larger than fresh investments. However, 1995 again saw steep increases in net flows. They reached $61.7 billion in 1996 (IMF, 1997a). It is worth pointing out that official capital flows during this period remained flat.

Private capital flows to the emerging markets were also stimulated by the trend toward globalization of markets for emerging market securities as well as toward broadening of investor base. Latin American securities were increasingly being sold in European and Asian markets. Similarly, with the growing involvement of mainstream institutional investors, the range of investors became more diverse. The pricing of emerging market securities was working reasonably well, consequently new investors were attracted toward them.

Geographical distribution of these financial flows was, and continues to be, uneven. In 1990, Asia received the largest proportion, 46.8 percent, followed by Latin America, 22.5 percent (Table 16.1). The emerging economies of the Middle East and Europe accounted for 15.3 percent of the total flows, while the economies in transition received 9.3 percent. In 1996, Asia's share of total private capital declined to 29.4 percent of the total. During the early 1990s, the bulk of the flows continued to be concentrated in a few Asian and European countries that had avoided debt-servicing difficulties in the 1980s and Latin American countries which were able to normalize their relations with private creditors. For a number of market re-entrants, the surge in capital flows complicated macroeconomic management. Either they had to face excessive monetary growth or upward pressure on exchange rate which implied loss of external competitiveness. By 1996, flows to the Latin American economies increased substantially to 37.3 percent of the total. This increase took place at the cost of other emerging market economies, particularly those in the Middle East and Europe whose proportion declined to 10.5 percent.

Over the last two decades, the composition of the net flows has undergone a considerable transformation (Table 16.1). The syndicated bank loans were a dominant instrument during the 1978–82 period, whereas portfolio investment, particularly bonds, and FDI became the most important instruments during the 1990s. The share of FDI reached 40 percent of total net private capital flows during the 1990–96 period. During the 1990s, bonds, equities and short-term portfolio investments such as certificates of deposit and commercial paper became popular. During the 1990–96 period, portfolio investment accounted for 39 percent of the total capital flows into the emerging markets. Perhaps the most significant change has been in portfolio equity flows, which rose from $17 billion in 1990 to $74 billion in 1996. In all, inflows of private capital rose from the equivalent of 3 percent of domestic investment in emerging market countries in 1990 to 13 percent in 1996. The financial institutions from the emerging markets participated increasingly in the international capital markets during the 1990s. This was the outcome of large foreign exchange reserves held by many, particularly China, Taiwan and other East Asian economies.

Although firm statistical data are still not available, there is evidence of capital flows among the emerging market economies. Precise statistics in this regard are not available because the capital account reporting systems of the emerging market economies provide relatively limited information about the country of origin of most capital flows. Asia has come to have a tradition of intra-regional flows since the mid-1980s (Das, 1996b). Outside of Japan, China, Republic of Korea, Hong Kong and Taiwan are substantial capital exporters in Asia. Taiwan has come to acquire the sobriquet of "the banker" for the region. However, Hong Kong SAR is the single largest outward investor among the emerging markets. Firms in Hong Kong SAR invested a total of $78 billion overseas in 1996, a major proportion (65 percent) of which went to China. While China remains a net importer of capital, its firms are beginning to invest abroad, with the financial services sector in the recipient countries attracting the largest share of these foreign investments. Chinese firms make large investments in Hong Kong, Indonesia, Malaysia, Singapore and Thailand. In Latin America, Chilean firms are known to make large intra-regional investments and acquisitions. Foreign acquisitions by them were worth $2.3 billion in 1996 (IMF, 1998). Most of these were the state-owned assets of Argentina, Brazil, Colombia and Peru. These assets could not be accumulated with the assistance of international financial markets. To finance these purchases, Chilean firms had floated bonds in the international financial markets.

Interest rates declined during the 1990s and there was a sharp fall in emerging market spreads. Since the financial markets in the industrial economies were highly liquid, it is often wondered whether compression in the emerging market spreads was excessive, to the point where credit risk was being underpriced. Some market analysts believe that abundant global liquidity and the quest for higher returns in the emerging markets did work together to produce a sharp decline in the emerging market spreads. Several empirical studies have analyzed the key pull and push factors behind the large-scale capital flows to the emerging market economies during the 1990s (Calvo *et al.*, 1996; Fernandez-Arias, 1996; Das, 1996a). The pull factors refer to the history of structural adjustment measures taken by the emerging market economies, their macroeconomic management and the political and noneconomic factors that have made them more creditworthy than before. The push factors include both structural and cyclical developments in international financial markets that have led investors to globally diversify their portfolios and turn to emerging markets in search of higher yields.

The structural adjustments and liberalization measures that were implemented in international financial markets during the 1990s, affected the scale, composition and direction of the capital flows. Two of the most important developments were the liberalization of domestic financial markets and capital account transactions. These two changes took place in both industrial and emerging market economies. One characteristic of these developments was that they were progressive and self-reinforcing and, therefore, once they were launched they continued to grow on their own. Bartolini and Drazen (1997) prepared an index of capital controls in emerging markets and demonstrated how capital controls were relaxed since the mid-1980s. Their index conclusively established that the decline in capital account restrictions facilitated the recent boom in capital flows to emerging markets. The correlation between the index and capital inflows for the 1982–96 period was −0.3. It provided a simple corroboration for the assumption that liberalization of external transactions is instrumental in attracting foreign capital. Another index developed by the World Bank (WB, 1997) shows that while more and more emerging markets are now better integrated into the international financial system, the process is still at an early stage. Two recent empirical studies also provided support to the premise that there is a growing degree of de facto integration of domestic and international financial markets. Also, it is becoming increasingly difficult to keep domestic financial market conditions isolated from developments in international markets (Dooley *et al.*, 1996)

The other two important developments were growing roles of institutional investors and securitization, which also resulted in increased flow of finance into portfolio investment (alluded to above), both bonds and equity, in emerging market economies during the 1990s. Emerging market securities are increasingly bought by institutional investors like mutual funds, insurance companies, pension funds and of late hedge funds. Seeking higher returns and greater diversification, these institutional investors sent only a small part of their capital to emerging markets, but since their portfolios were mammoth in size, even a small part of these portfolios created a rising tide of capital flowing to emerging markets. Growing securitization became more or less a global trend which in turn led to greater use of direct debt and equity markets. In the direct debt market lenders or investors hold a tradeable direct claim on the borrowers or borrowing firms. This works differently from indirect finance where an intermediary holds a nontraded loan asset and the saver holds a liability. This liability may be tradeable on the intermediary. Recent advances in IT proved to be a facilitating factor. They improved the capability of both investors and creditors to manage their portfolios and undertake better risk analysis of credit and market risks (Das, 1996a).

Depressants to capital inflows

If financial markets reward sound fundamentals, they punish the opposite. Crises and other turbulences in the global economy, no matter what the causal factors, have an adverse impact on the volume of capital market flows to the emerging market economies. They particularly affect the middle-income emerging markets badly. In 1997, the economic climate, and with that the financial market scenario, underwent a dramatic transformation. The financial turmoil that started in July 1997 in Thailand rolled on to other emerging market economies within and outside Asia in 1998. Capital flows to emerging market economies fell from $213.8 billion to $148.8 billion in 1997 – a 30.4 percent fall, steep by any measure. After the substantial market disturbances in late 1997, the outlook for emerging markets appeared to have improved in 1998, creating an impression that the Asian crisis was coming to an end. However, these expectations were belied and the turmoil continued unabated. It was reflected in a slowing down of capital flows to the emerging markets to $65.4 billion in 1998, which was a precipitous fall from their 1996 level (Table 16.1).

Depressed external economic environment was also reflected in a rise in bond yield spreads and a fall in equity prices. The devaluation and unilateral domestic debt restructuring by the Russian Federation worsened an already bad situation and a general apprehension of an all round emerging market financial crisis began to raise its head. After Brazil devalued its currency, there was a small recovery in the emerging markets in the first half of 1999 and by mid-1999 market access for the higher-rated or investment grade emerging market borrowers had improved.

However, yield spreads remained high and international capital markets remained closed to many emerging market corporations. Anemic flows during 1998 and 1999 *inter alia* reflected persistence of a higher degree of aversion to risks associated with lending to emerging markets on the part of commercial banks and stock analysts. In addition, there was a weaker demand for credit in several emerging markets, where borrowing firms were endeavoring to reduce indebtedness following recent crises. Many of these firms had taken on substantial short-term external debts, which they belatedly realized was a crisis prone strategy. Net private capital flows to Asia recovered temporarily in the last quarter of 1999 as portfolio equity flows increased and repayment obligations reduced significantly (IIF, 1999). However, on the whole this was a year of negative inflows for the Asian emerging market economies.

Although global economy picked up momentum in 2000, during 2001 it slipped into a mild recession. Emerging market economies saw their growth rate plunge. Growth in global trade underwent one of the most severe decelerations in modern times – from over 13 percent in 2000 to 1 percent in 2001 (WB, 2002a). Deteriorating growth prospects for the emerging market economies, the collapse in prices of technology stocks, the continuing crises in Turkey and Argentina, and increased concern over risk reduced demand for capital from the emerging market economies. Speculative grade borrowers saw a sharp fall in market access, faced much higher spreads, and sharply reduced capital flows. Majority of the emerging market borrowers from the private capital markets are speculative grade borrowers. In contrast, investment grade borrowers enjoyed improved terms. A further fall in capital flows was recorded in 2000 and in 2001 net emerging market flows were reduced to a trickle, $3.3 billion (Table 16.1).

External factors played a predominant role in reducing the flow of external finances to a trickle in 2001. The slowdown in industrial economies led to a decline in export revenues of the emerging market economies, the impact of which was only in part mitigated by the drop in international interest rates. Slower growth and the collapse of technology stock prices increased uncertainty and sharply reduced the wealth of investors in high-risk assets, and thus reduced their appetite for risk. Net portfolio investment in emerging market economies had risen to $33.9 billion in 1999, but after that they turned into net outflows and shrank to −$4.3 billion in 2000 and further to −$30.2 billion in 2001.

Portfolio investment flows are extremely sensitive to external economic environment. Although crises in Argentina and Turkey did not set in any contagion, the external economic environment was far from encouraging. Therefore, global investors lost confidence in the emerging market economies. Asian and Middle Eastern emerging market economies were found to record the largest outflows.

Estimates for 2002 were not encouraging. During the second quarter of 2002, the US GDP grew by only 1.1 percent.[10] Infectious greed took hold of corporate America and led to a series of accounting scandals. Although a moderate to a weak recovery in the United States was on track during the first half of 2002, corporate malpractices and accounting fiddles had a devastating impact over the United States and global bourses. Global economic and financial environment was severely undermined by volatility in the stock markets, which in turn had created an extremely high degree of uncertainty in the investment climate. In the first two weeks of July 2002, the Dow Jones Industrial Average and the S&P 500 index had lost 14.5 percent of their respective values. The FTSE 100 index in London was down by more than 40 percent in mid-July from its peak (*The Economist*, 2002). The Dow Jones lost four years of bull-market gains by the third week of July 2002.

European stock markets suffered more than those in the United States and stock market indexes lost eight years of bull-market gains. In addition, the European economies were not as quick as the United States and had not started recovering from the 2001 recession and Japanese economy was still in the doldrums. Other important bourses around the globe, particularly those in Asia, were also volatile and sunk in gloom. Three Latin American economies, namely, Argentina, Brazil and Uruguay, were facing serious economic disruption. The problems facing the three countries were different and require different solutions. The one thing they had in common was that outside help was needed to resolve them. Therefore, probability of acceleration in financial flows to emerging market economies in the short term did not exist. Gloom was expected to persist in the immediate future.[11]

Emerging market financial crises during 2000–02

The financial crises of the 1990s have been enumerated in the section "Environmental determinants." They afflicted major middle-income emerging market economies and spilled over into the 2002–02 period (WB, 2002b). Contagion effect of the crisis of the 1990s spread both regionally and in some cases globally. Few generalizations can be made regarding the causes of each one of these crises and economic instability in countries that were the sources of crises. They differed in several important respects. Common elements in all these instances of economic instability were shortcomings in external financial management and defects in corporate and financial sector governance. Turkey and Argentina both had serious problems in these areas, so did the earlier crises of the 1990s.

The Argentinean crisis was born out of the build up of vulnerabilities after the highly successful exchange rate based stabilization program of the early 1990s.

Argentina had adopted a dollar-based currency board in 1991, which had served the economy well by curing it of the high and long-standing inflation problem. The Turkish crisis was rooted in its high public sector deficit. It reached 12 percent of the GNP in 2000. This was compounded by high levels of public sector debt, reaching 90 percent of GNP and the following difficulties in rolling over short-term debts. These debts were as large as the foreign exchange reserves of Turkey. Adoption of a crawling peg did not work out for Turkey. Its objective was to reduce the high inflation rate but it encouraged large capital inflows, resulting in a substantial build up of foreign exchange liabilities for the banking system. In February 2001, it had to be abandoned.

A conspicuous difference between these two crises and the ones in the 1990s was regarding the contagion effect to other emerging market economies and other debt markets. While the crises of the 1990s had a quick and decisive effect, in the cases of Turkey and Argentina, this effect was close to none. Evidence of investors retreating from other emerging markets due to crisis in these two economies was infinitesimal. Even Brazil was not seriously affected by crisis in its neighbor to the south. The correlation between secondary market bond spreads in different emerging market economies is a measure of the spread of contagion. Between Argentina and fifteen other emerging market economies correlation of spreads on bonds rose from 0.27 before the exacerbation of the crisis to 0.47 after the crisis became full-blown in October 2000. Similarly, correlations of spreads on Turkish bonds increased from 0.12 before the crisis to 0.39 after the crisis (WB, 2002b). It cannot be ignored that this was the period of global slowdown when there is a general rise in spreads and also in volatility of spreads. Therefore, measured correlations tended to rise with increases in volatility. The Argentinean crisis not setting in a serious contagion was noteworthy because it was a crisis of large dimensions, eventually leading to a sovereign default. It was comparable to the August 1998 default by the Russian Federation, which spawned serious dislocation across global financial markets.

Another evidence of weak impact of crises in these two economies over the other emerging markets is provided by the index of emerging market spreads, which had remained almost stationary until September 2001. Again, there is no evidence from the stock market prices showing that the Argentine or Turkish crises affected other emerging market economies, except for the impact on Brazil. One reason for the weak contagion effect was the missing element of surprise. Investors were aware of the problems and what could be the possible outcome. Besides, most investors were less leveraged this time than during the earlier crises. Therefore, they did not need to liquidate assets across-the-board to meet margin calls.[12]

Contagions need not go through the regional or global economy like an avalanche. Experience with so many crises now shows that they can be contained. Most emerging market economies that are well integrated with the global capital markets have strengthened their ability to withstand shocks by adopting flexible exchange rate regimes, disciplined domestic monetary policies, and most importantly, limited short-term external liabilities and limited near-term refinancing needs. These measures help in stalling the spread of problems.

Institutional investors and emerging markets

There is a downside of emerging markets being well integrated into global financial markets. Presence of large institutional investors in the global financial markets works as a stimulant for the emerging markets as well as exposes them to some vulnerability. As they were large absorbers of emerging market securities, the emerging markets became vulnerable to their capability of intense speculative attacks. These institutional investors can take substantial short positions in a weak currency through spot, forward and currency options markets. According to one estimate the total assets of hedge funds, traders and speculative-type mutual funds have grown to well over $100 billion (F&D, 1997). These institutions are known to create large leveraged positions. At times they leverage their capital by ten times, or more.[13] Thus, the magnitude of financial resources controlled by speculative-type mutual funds is large. Therefore, compared to the past, more international reserves and more complex intervention strategies are needed to off-set their speculative attacks. The emerging markets having inflexible or less flexible exchange rate regimes are most vulnerable to speculative attacks. It needs to be clarified that when we say "speculators" we do not have any negative connotations attached with this group of people. It is not used in a pejorative sense. Besides, in the financial markets any economic agent, be it a large domestic or foreign firm, an investment bank, a hedge fund, a domestic or foreign mutual fund, a clairvoyant individual who keeps a discerning eye on the movements of the financial market and the economy, can turn to speculation at an opportune moment.

When financial sector weaknesses become apparent in an economy and its fundamentals begin to deteriorate it will necessarily attract the attention of the institutional investors and currency speculators. A currency crisis becomes predictable. It has, however, been noticed that a currency crisis precipitates well before the deteriorating fundamentals have reached a point at which the exchange rate would collapse. The crisis precipitates as soon as a speculative run begins. To the uninformed onlooker, this gives an impression that the currency crisis has been sparked by the speculative attack and that weakness in fundamentals or financial sector were not the basic causal factors. Once a currency crisis-like situation develops, "herding" behavior or "bandwagon effect" soon aggravates it. There is evidence that foreign exchange markets are inefficient (Krugman, 1997) and that they do not make the best use of available information, which leads to herd behavior.[14] The waves of market participants taking short positions, whatever the initial motivation, is magnified through sheer imitation. This develops almost into a stampede, causing a sharp depreciation in the value of the currency. This is what happened to the Czech koruna, the Thai baht, the Philippine peso, the Malaysian ringgit, the Indonesian rupiah and the Korean won during their 1997–98 crises. The bandwagon effect is also precipitated by awareness that other investors have "special information." Kehoe and Chari (1996) have argued that such bandwagon effects in markets with private information create a sort of "hot money effect," alluded to earlier, that at least sometimes causes foreign exchange markets to overreact to news about national economic prospects.

The currency markets also over-react because agents manage foreign investments in crisis-prone economies, not by principals. These traders or money managers, be they from a mutual fund or a hedge fund, have a lot to lose from staying in a currency which is being considered by their profession as "ripe for depreciation." They have little motivation to stay in that currency and prove their peers wrong. Since traders and money managers are compensated on the basis of comparison with other money managers, they have strong incentives to act alike even if their personal instincts suggest that the judgment of the market is wrong. The trader's or money manager's thought line is as follows, "It'll be worse to lose money on the won depreciation when others do not than losing the same amount in a general currency rout."

In the recent past, a strong tendency toward contagion has been observed in speculative runs on currencies. Empirical proof of this tendency was provided by Eichengreen *et al.* (1996). Their estimates, based on data from twenty countries spanning three decades, revealed that attacks on foreign currencies raise the probability of an attack on domestic currency by 8 percent. Contagion in foreign exchange markets essentially uses two channels of international transmission. The first channel is trade links, that is, the speculative runs spill over contagiously to other countries with which the subject country trades. The second channel is macroeconomic similarities, where the speculative runs spread to other countries having similar economic conditions and policies. The effect of a contagion operating through trade was found to be stronger than that of contagion spreading as a result of macroeconomic similarities.

Inflexible or pegged exchange rate regimes *vide ut supra* always attract speculators.[15] A speculative attack requires establishment of a net short position in the domestic currency. To attack a currency, say the peso, a speculator takes a short position in the peso. He sells it to a bank through relatively long-dated (at least a month) forward contracts. To balance this short position the bank will immediately take a long position. That is, the bank will sell the peso on the spot market for, say, dollars for the conventional two-day settlement. In this process, the bank has balanced its currency mismatch. So far, this is only one half of the balancing act because it continues to face a maturity mismatch. In order to close this maturity mismatch this bank will transact a foreign exchange swap. That is, it will deliver dollars for pesos in two days and deliver pesos for dollars thirty days forward. This is a standard wholesale transaction in normal periods.

When a speculator takes a short position, the domestic central bank plays the role of a customer in the forward currency market. Or the central bank is the counter party for the speculating entity. It sells the required amount in hard currency (generally the dollar) to the speculator. The central bank's domestic currency receipt from the forward contract becomes a one-month loan to the speculator who is taking a short position. If the central bank does not provide the credit directly, it must come through its money market operations. From the above mechanics it is clear that if the central bank plans to dissuade the speculators, it should raise the cost of short positions. Short-term interest rates are allowed to rise, tightening conditions in financial markets and making it more costly for speculators to obtain a net short position by borrowing domestic currency.

Defending against a speculative run

The first defensive strategy that a central bank adopts against a speculative run is sterilized intervention, which may occur in both the foreign exchange markets, that is, spot and forward markets. When it is done in spot market, the direct consequence is depletion of foreign exchange reserves. This also implies a reduction in the monetary base resulting from the sale of foreign exchange by the central banking authority. Thus, the size of foreign exchange reserves work as a limiting factor although borrowing from the international markets or multilateral financial institutions can augment them. Intervention in the forward market is a different ball game because it does not result in an immediate reduction in the foreign exchange reserves and the monetary base does not shrink. This is the reason why some central banks prefer the latter to the former. For instance, when the Korean won first came under a speculative attack in the months of October and November 1997, the government immediately responded by sterilizing intervention in the forward market because it wanted to preserve its foreign exchange reserves.

A speculative attack requires the establishment of a net short position in the domestic currency. Therefore, if speculators are to be dissuaded from making speculative runs, short-term interest rates should be allowed to rise, tightening conditions in financial markets which in turn makes it more costly for speculators to obtain a net short position by borrowing domestic currency. However, this defensive strategy cannot be sustained for an extended period because high short-term interest rates are detrimental for the real economy. If the economy is slowing down, high interest rates work in a pro-cyclical manner causing a deeper downturn in the economy. To ward off such a situation countries do create a two-tier system or interest rate. The two-tier system prevents speculators from getting domestic credit but the nonspeculative, productive, capital needs are met at the normal rates of interest.

Market manipulating capability of hedge funds has plagued the policy makers for sometime. It bears repeating that hedge funds are not large relative to financial markets as a whole, although they may be large relative to a particular emerging market. To reduce the volatility-creating activities of hedge funds, policy makers can consider margin and collateral requirements for all financial market participants. Such measures would affect – and discourage – hedge funds more than other investors because they are heavy users of credit. Governments can also undertake more fundamental reforms to deal with market volatility. Reduction in information asymmetry will discourage herd behavior in the currency and financial markets. If investors run with the herd, they do so to emulate the actions of other investors, assuming that the other investors know something they do not know themselves. Therefore, providing better information regarding market conditions would help discourage herd behavior.

Markets are well aware that inflexible regimes are fragile in the face of adverse external or domestic shocks. Therefore, market participants are likely to speculate against pegged rates in the face of such shocks. Either the defense of pegged rates proves to be costly in the face of speculation (as in Argentina in 1995) or the market pressure leads to the abandonment of the pegged rate (as in several ERM countries in 1992, or Mexico in 1994 and several Asian economies in 1997). Thus, to keep a crisis at bay central banks should not – or rarely – adopt inflexible pegs (Sachs, 1997). Perhaps less obviously self-fulfilling panics are also much easier to handle by floating exchange rate regimes compared with pegged rate regimes. A pegged exchange rate regime can only be justified under special circumstances. For instance, it could be considered appropriate under an optimal currency union with one or more countries. In such a case, a common central bank can act as lender of last resort for the whole union. A second case for justifiable pegging could be an extremely open and diversified economy with an extremely flexible labor market. Such an economy can adjust to external shocks through internal deflation *if necessary*, rather than depreciation. Also, by virtue of diversification, such an economy may be less likely to be hit by serious external shocks than an economy which is highly concentrated in a few export goods. Hong Kong and Estonia, both have currency boards, because they more or less meet the second condition.

The strongest defense against a speculative run on a currency is to have such a macroeconomic environment which is sound, functional, pragmatic, a currency peg which is realistic and flexible and a financial sector having a sound framework of prudential norms. To attain these objectives the macroeconomic policy must avoid inconstancies and the currency peg must be supportable. Adverse effects of inflation, large budget deficits or unsustainable exchange rates on the macroeconomy and the financial sector can be compounded by capital inflows – particularly the short-term ones. If the policy inconsistencies are not avoided, and the economic and currency value scenarios are perceived as weak and inflexible, the currency becomes a target for one-way bets for speculators.

Most, if not all, emerging market economies have liberalized and deregulated their financial markets in the recent past. Many a crisis was related to financial market liberalization, especially the elimination of controls on international financial movements. Cautious, gradual, calculated and, therefore, prudent liberalization works as a defensive measure. This is a significant lesson from the crises of the 1990s. Several of these crises distinctively exhibited a boom–bust cycle, that is, a large but ephemeral wave of capital inflows accompanied a pegged exchange rate. When the inflows stabilized, the exchange rate needed to be devalued and the subsequent devaluation was delayed until a serious macroeconomic crisis had developed.

The Asian crises and those before them in Argentina, Mexico, Venezuela, Israel, Sweden and Norway have proved that it is dangerous to liberalize capital restrictions without a number of safety valves. These safety valves control the large and sudden inflows and outflows of capital which have become a common feature of global financial markets. Two entities can potentially work as safety valves: (a) the degree of exchange rate flexibility and (b) strengthened domestic financial institutions which would be less vulnerable to fluctuations in the value of their assets. Other than these two safety valves, it might be pragmatic to have some prudential restrictions on short-term capital inflows as well. For instance, central banks can make commercial banks sterilize a stipulated part of their short-term capital inflows by keeping them in noninterest bearing deposits, or at least low-interest bearing deposits. This measure will defend the emerging market economies from the herd instinct of speculators which drives them to seek safety in numbers.

Gradual liberalization is another way out. If the financial markets are liberalized gradually, as in Chile, domestic financial institutions are not able to take on foreign debt of large dimensions. Their borrowing limits are reached only gradually, which in turn dampens the boom–bust cycle. Also, gradual liberalization keeps the real exchange rate from appreciating fast. Therefore, the subsequent devaluation needed after the stabilization of the capital inflows is less dramatic. An optimal sequencing of the liberalization process may have to work through the following stages: free inflow of foreign direct investment, followed in sequence by liberalization of portfolio equity investment, long-term borrowing by nonfinancial institutions, short-term borrowings by non-financial institutions and finally short-term borrowings by commercial banks. This sequence, operating gradually will go a long way in eliminating the boom–bust cycle.

An amber signal is warranted here. Foregoing statements must not be seen as a stand against liberalization of financial sector. What I am saying is that rapid liberalization, in the absence of sound macroeconomic policies, adequate regulatory and prudential norms, and supervision and monitoring can create problems in the financial sector. Liberalization reduces the ability of institutions to survive poor performance, as rising competition reduces the rents and profitability of the financial sector. If on top of that there is government intervention, the crisis situation develops earlier. The economy becomes an attractive proposition for speculators. While I am casting a vote against globalization of financial markets, I am stressing the need for not allowing globalization to race ahead of national and/or international supervisory regimes.

The financial crises of the 1990s, particularly those in the Asian economies have called into question the ability of the global financial system to manage transnational financial flows of such large dimension as prevalent at present. The foundation of the current international financial system was laid in 1946 when the dimension of transnational capital flows (a) was tiny, (b) limited among the industrial economies and (c) there were little short-term financial flows involved. The systemic needs of the present period vary widely from those of the past. It is well recognized in most quarters and there are calls for "a new financial architecture." Various proposals were floated at the time of the spring meetings of the IMF and the World Bank in the third week of April 1998, when the world's economic rule makers converged on Washington. Although a consensus on the contours of the new financial architecture was far away, a great deal of thought was given to the birth of the new financial architecture. If the new architecture is so devised that whenever a financial crisis breaks out due to short-term fund movements the losses are shared by those who made mistakes, the emerging market economies will benefit. This will ensure that investors in short-term instruments will also be held responsible and, therefore, will share part of the post-crisis cost with the recipient emerging market economy.

Capital controls in the form of quantitative restrictions and taxes are frequently resorted to as defensive measures and some scholars (like Rudigar Dornbusch) support their utility for short periods. However, the experiences of the 1960s and early 1970s reveal that expectations of controls increase the probability and the frequency of speculative runs and balance of payments crises. It was also observed that transitory controls increased the volatility of exchange rates. Thus, controls prove to be counterproductive. A noteworthy characteristic of this period (known as the Bretton Wood period) was the high frequency as well as severity of speculative runs and balance of payments crises both in developing and industrial economies. Of these, the sterling crises of 1964–67, and the dollar and French franc crises of 1967–69 are rather well known. These experiences also vouch for the fact that capital controls create self-fulfilling expectations of currency depreciation.

The experience of the 1990s shows that financial crises are stirred up by – and feed on – undercapitalized banks. They are more vulnerable self-fulfilling panics and more prone to excessively risky borrowings. Since most emerging market economies lack effective and efficacious supervising and monitoring institutions, the book value of their capital overstates the amount of shareholder equity. Bad assets are generally not written down expeditiously. Therefore, regulatory regime for these economies should be stricter than that for the industrial economies. Minimum capital-to-asset ratio of 8 percent, the so-called BIS[16] norm, may be grossly inadequate for the emerging market economies. Therefore, BIS-plus prudential norms are recommended as a defensive strategy. Having a sound capital base and adopting higher prudential standards will make the banking sector less vulnerable at the time of market panics.

Summing-up

Private capital flow to emerging market economies are determined by economic fundamentals of the recipient economy and the external economic environment, which includes both regional and global environment. Financial markets reward sound financial and macroeconomic policies and commitment to reforms by the emerging market policy mandarins. Incongruous macroeconomic and financial policies destabilize economies and financial markets are sensitive to policy inconsistencies and their outcome. Market disapproval is forthwith reflected in the direction of financial flows.

Global economic policy milieu during the first half of the 1990s had worked strongly toward stimulating private capital flows to the emerging market economies. Some of its principal strands were wide ranging structural adjustments in this group of economies, adoption of market-friendly strategies, acceptance of the Washington consensus, and increasing institutionalization of savings in the industrial economies. Improved fundamentals in the emerging market economies, trend toward globalization and a stable global economic environment also worked as strong stimulants to capital inflows in these economies. Private capital flows into the emerging market economies went on increasing in a monotonic manner and peaked in 1996. The global economic environment was transformed by the crisis is Thailand in July 1997. Financial flows to emerging market economies went on a decline until net flows were reduced to a trickle in 2001. Although crises in Turkey and Argentina did not have a contagion effect, external factors had a lot of question marks in 2000 and 2001. Consequently net portfolio investment turned negative. This was a case of serious loss of investor confidence in the emerging market economies. After the debacle at Enron and Andersen at the Wall Street, WorldCom disaster followed. Revelations of one accounting scandal after another drove the Wall Street and with that other important stock markets around the globe to the edge of a precipice. Estimates for 2002 were, therefore, of continuance of poor financial flows to emerging market economies.

The presence of institutional investors in the global financial markets exposed the emerging market economies to some vulnerabilities. They could potentially take substantial short positions in a weak currency. When financial sector weaknesses became apparent, institutional investors and currency speculators were attracted toward them, making a currency crisis imminent. The well-known "herding" behavior of investors immediately made this situation worse. The currency markets overreact because it is the agents who manage investment, not the principals. Economies having inflexible exchange rate regimes are considered more vulnerable by speculators. History has demonstrated that speculative currency runs have occurred in periods of high capital mobility and fixed exchange rates.

However, the blame that is heaped on speculators for a currency crisis is perhaps excessive. They determine the timing of the eruption of a crisis; it would have occurred without their endeavors anyway. Hedge funds have also drawn a lot of ire. Although they are market players, a level-headed analysis shows that they cannot precipitate a currency crisis on their own, when there are no price bubbles.

Normally central banks resort to adopting sterilized intervention as the first defensive strategy against a speculative run. Raising short-term interest rates to dissuade speculators from taking short positions in the domestic currencies is another method, although this defensive strategy cannot be sustained for a long time. To reduce the volatility-creating activities of hedge funds, policy makers can consider raising margin and collateral requirements for all financial market participants. Such measures would discourage hedge funds more than other investors because they are heavy users of credit. Central banks should not adopt inflexible exchange rate pegs. Not adhering to unsustainable pegs can work as a helpful defensive strategy. The strongest defense against a speculative run is to have such a macroeconomic environment which is sound, functional, pragmatic, a currency peg which is realistic and flexible, and a financial sector having a well-laid out framework of prudential norms. In addition, excessively rapid liberalization of capital account does more harm than good to the financial sector of an economy. Liberalization of capital account should be cautious and sequential. That is, liberalization of short-term flows should gradually follow that for long-term flows.

Notes

1 Chile, Hong Kong SAR, Korea (Republic of), Singapore and Taiwan. Hong Kong is a special administrative region (SAR) of the People's Republic of China.
2 *The Economist*. 2003. "Emerging Market Indicators." January 25, p. 102.
3 The three case studies by Sylla (1999) convincingly establish this fact.
4 Financial crisis in Thailand began on July 2, 1997.
5 In the latter half of 1997 financial crisis struck Indonesia, Korea, Malaysia, the Philippines and Thailand. Other Asian economies, including Hong Kong SAR and Singapore were also adversely affected by the crisis.
6 In the international finance literature they are also known as the ERM crises of 1992–93. It needs to be clarified that the ERM crises had little to do with capital flows, although speculators had an active role in these crises.
7 In mid 2002, Turkey was the largest borrower from the IMF and its financial crisis had not yet ended.
8 John Williamson's original definition of the Washington consensus involved ten different aspects of economic policy. One may, however, roughly summarize this consensus, at least as it influenced the beliefs of markets and governments, more simply. Liberalize trade, privatize state-owned enterprises, balance the budget, peg the exchange rate, and one will have laid the foundations of an economic take-off. Find a country that has done these things, and one may confidently expect to realize high returns on investments.
9 The annual average for the 1983–89 period was $11.6 billion. We are only considering net private capital flows.
10 Revised statistics issued by the US government on July 31, 2002 showed that the US economy grew much more slowly than expected in the second quarter of 2002 – by only 1.1 percent at an annualized rate. The revised statistics also indicated that the 2001 recession was significantly worse than previously estimated, and growth in the first quarter of 2002 a bit less impressive than earlier statistics had indicated. The backward changes implied a necessary downward revision to America's spectacular productivity figures and cast doubt on the "miracle" of the new economy.
11 This chapter was completed in August 2002, when Dow Jones Industrial Average, and the FTSE 100 index, after slipping for months, came close to a mini-crash and created volatility in all the important stock markets around the globe. The WorldCom accounting scandal and bankruptcy followed the Enron and Andersen debacle. Andersen, the legendary accounting and consulting colossus, was convicted of obstruction of justice during the biggest accounting scandals in the US corporate history. By August 2002, the debacle had cost investors more than $300 billion and put tens of thousands out of work. Insular and inbred, Andersen was unable to respond swiftly to crises. Its collapse represented an unimaginable failure of leadership and governance (BW, 2002). WorldCom sought Chapter 11 protection on July 22, 2002. With more than $107 in assets, this was the largest US insolvency ever. It was twice as large as Enron's record bankruptcy filing a few weeks before. Revelations of one major accounting scandal after another in the United States drove the global stock markets to the edge of a precipice.
12 This section draws on WB 2002b. Refer to Chapter 2, pp. 43–5.

13 What is stated here is a generalization and, therefore, as correct as a generalization. After the near collapse of the Long Term Capital Management (LTCM), New York, in the last quarter of 1998, it became known that while the base funds of LTCM were $5 billion, the leveraged funds were of the order of $1,000 billion.

14 One of the best studies of herding behavior is to be found in Shiller (1989), where he analyzed the herding behavior of investors during the 1987 stock market crash. The only reason consistently given by those selling stocks for their actions was the fact that prices were plummeting.

15 This statement has been made in the current context. A polemist may question it by stating that the Bretton Woods period was not known for speculative attacks on currencies.

16 The Bank for International Settlements, Basle, Switzerland.

References

Bartolini, L. and A. Drazen. 1997. "When Liberal Policies Reflect External Shocks, What Do We Learn?" *Journal of International Economics*, Vol. 42. May. pp. 249–73.

Business Week (BW). 2002. "Fall from Grace." August 2. pp. 45–6.

Calvo, G.A., L. Leiderman and C.M. Reinhart. 1996. "Inflows of Capital to Developing Countries in the 1990s," *Journal of Economic Perspective*, Vol. 10 (Spring), pp. 123–39.

Claessens, S., M.P. Dooley and A. Warner. 1995. "Portfolio Capital Flows: Hot or Cold?" *The World Bank Economic Review*, Vol. 9. No. 1. pp. 153–74.

Das, Dilip K. 1996a. "Emerging Markets and Macroeconomic Stabilization," *Journal of the Asia Pacific Economy*, Vol. 1, No. 3.pp. 319–46.

Das, Dilip K. 1996b. *The Asia-Pacific Economy*, London, The Macmillan Press Ltd.

Dooley, M.P., D.J. Mathieson and L. Rojas-Suarez. 1996. "Capital Mobility and Exchange Market Intervention in Developing Countries," WP/96/131, Washington, DC, International Monetary Fund.

Eichengreen, B., A. Rose and C. Wyplosz. 1996. "Speculative Attacks on Pegged Exchange Rates," in M. Canzoneri, P. Masson and V. Grilli (eds) *Transatlantic Economic Issues*, Cambridge, UK, Cambridge University Press.

Fernandez-Arias, E. 1996. "The New Wave of Private Capital Flows: Push or Pull?" *Journal of Development Economics*, Vol. 48. March. pp. 389–418.

Finance and Development (F&D). 1997. "Capital Flow Sustainability and Speculative Currency Attacks." December. pp. 8–11.

Institute of International Finance (IIF). 1999. *Capital Flows to Emerging Market Economies*, Washington, DC. September 25.

International Monetary Fund (IMF). 1997. *International Capital Markets: Developments and Prospects.* Washington, DC.

International Monetary Fund (IMF). 1998. *World Economic Outlook.* April. Washington, DC.

International Monetary Fund (IMF). 1999. *World Economic Outlook.* October. Washington, DC.

International Monetary Fund (IMF). 2002. *World Economic Outlook.* April. Washington, DC.

Kehoe, P. and S. Chari. 1996. "Contagious Currency Crises," (mimeo).

Krugman, P. 1995. "Dutch Tulips and Emerging Markets," *Foreign Affairs*, July/August. pp. 25–44.

Krugman, P. 1997. "Currency Crises." Paper presented at the NBER Conference on 17 October 1997, in Chicago, Illinois (mimeo).

Mundell, R. 2000. "A Reconsideration of the Twentieth Century," *American Economic Review*, Vol. 90. No. 3. pp. 327–40.

Obstfeld, M. and A.M. Taylor. 1997. "The Great Depression as a Watershed: International Capital Mobility over the Long Run." NBER Working Paper No. 5960. Cambridge, MA, National Bureau of Economic Research.

Sachs, J. 1997. "Alternative Approaches to Financial Crises in Emerging Markets," Discussion Paper No. 568. Harvard Institute for International Development. Cambridge, Massachusetts. January.

Shiller, R. 1989. *Market Volatility*, The MIT Press, and Cambridge, MA.

Sylla, R. 1999. "Emerging Markets in History: United States, Japan and Argentina," in R. Sato (ed.) *Global Competition and Integration*, Boston, Kluwer Academic Publishers. pp. 427–44.

The Economist. 1998. "Scared of Heights?" March 28. pp. 16–18.

The Economist. 2002. "In the Balance." July 22. p. 19.

The Economist. 2003. "Emerging Market Indicators." January 25. p. 102.

United States Senate (USS). 1990. "Implementation of the Brady Plan." Hearing Before the Subcommittee on International Debt of the Committee on Finance, March 2.

The World Bank (WB). 1997. *Private Capital Flows to Developing Countries: The Road to Financial Integration*, New York, Oxford University Press.

The World Bank (WB). 2002a. *Global Economic Prospects*, Washington, DC.

The World Bank (WB). 2002b. *Global Development Finance*, Washington, DC.

17 Coping with crises in emerging markets*

Adjustment versus financing

Jeffrey A. Frankel

Response to crises in the emerging market economies

In the early 1990s, an unprecedented number of developing countries joined world financial markets, as a step in the processes of liberalization, globalization, and industrialization. The preceding chapter provides a great deal of details regarding this issue. The post-1990s witnessed a wave of emerging market crises, which began in Mexico in December 1994, exploded in East Asia in 1997, and over the subsequent four years hit the Russian Federation, Brazil, Turkey, and Argentina, among other countries. Sovereign default by the Russian Federation had a serious impact over the global financial markets, albeit not the same can be said about the more recent sovereign default by Argentina. These crises and sovereign defaults and their severe real effects pose a challenge to those who manage emerging market economies as well as to those who advise them.

This chapter delves into how the emerging market economies respond to sudden adverse developments in their balance of payments. It falls into four parts: (i) the general framework of financing-versus-adjustment as we have hitherto understood it, (ii) what instruments are to be employed to attain the adjustment targets, (iii) the actual pattern of adjustment that we have seen in recent crises, and, finally (iv) the question as to whether and how the financing-versus-adjustment framework can still be viewed as relevant today after what we have learned.

Financing-versus-adjustment

The classic question regarding financing-versus-adjustment is: in the aftermath of an adverse real shock, for example, a movement in terms of trade, how much of the impact on the trade balance should be financed by borrowing from abroad, from capital inflows, and how much of the impact should be offset by adjustments to macroeconomic policies? The standard answer from economic theory is that if

* This is a revised version of a comment in *Issues in Reform of the International Monetary System*, edited by Peter Kenen and Alexander Swoboda (International Monetary Fund: Washington, DC), 2001. At the time the original comment was presented, the author had recently departed from the position of Member, US Council of Economic Advisers, under President Bill Clinton.

the shock is largely transitory, then it should be mostly financed. Given the growth and globalization of financial markets over the preceding quarter century, most of this financing should be from the private sector; but if sufficient private capital flows are not available, then official finance, particularly from the International Monetary Fund (IMF), should supply the rest. Indeed, it should be conditional on the country following sound policies.

However, in practice, we have seen from the international debt and financial crises of the 1980s and 1990s that private capital flows tend to exacerbate shocks rather than offset them, to be pro-cyclical rather than countercyclical as they should be in theory. In the early 1980s, for example, a contraction in markets for many of the commodities produced by developing countries was followed by reduction in capital flows, not an increase. Thus the "share of the shock that is financed" has turned out to be, not just small, but negative – perhaps worse than negative 100 percent. In some cases, it appears that the entire shock *was* the withdrawal of capital.

Sometimes it is possible to identify an initial real shock. In the case of the 1997–98 Asian crisis it would be the steep downturn in the world market for semi-conductors and other manufactures in 1996. But even in these cases, the loss in capital inflows is clearly the dominant change in the balance of payments, more than doubling any plausible measure of the initial loss in the trade balance. These are the "sudden stops."[1] The recent reversal in capital inflows to Thailand – from 18 percent of GDP in 1996, to an outflow of 8 percent of GDP in 1997 – is apparently the record-holder. Even in more common cases, the swing is large. As a result the affected countries have been forced to convert large trade deficits quickly into large trade surpluses.

Decidedly the balance has indeed shifted away from financing, and perforce toward adjustment. Given the countercyclical nature of the capital flows, is the financing-versus-adjustment framework even relevant? Should we perhaps dispense with it altogether? We could interpret the initial shock as trade balance *plus private capital account*, and interpret the financing response as solely official finance. Then the question would be: to what extent should the IMF and other public institutions step in to fill the gap? This is an extremely important question, involving key issues of moral hazard, of greater private sector involvement as a component in public rescue packages ("bailing in" as opposed to "bailing out"), and of political willingness in G-7 countries to provide resources on the unprecedented scale that would seem to be required. Although these issues are important, they generally are discussed under rubrics other than financing-versus-adjustment. Therefore, we shall emphasize on private sector financing. But before we offer an interpretation of where the financing-adjustment framework can still be useful, we would like to consider how adjustment is carried out, both in the traditional framework and in reality in recent episodes of crises.

Adjustment by expenditure-reduction versus expenditure-switching

In the traditional framework there are two categories of policy instruments: expenditure-reducing policies such as monetary contraction and expenditure-switching policies such as devaluation. The pair matches up nicely with the existence of two policy targets, namely, internal balance and external balance. Consider a graphical representation with the interest rate and exchange rate (price of foreign currency) on the two axes. To satisfy external balance, there is an inverse trade-off between the two instruments. A devaluation and an increase in the interest rate are each ways of improving the trade balance – the latter by reducing expenditure – and so the more you have of one the less you need of the other.

If external balance is defined as equilibrium in the overall balance of payments, including the capital account along with the trade balance, the relationship is still downward-sloping, since a devaluation and an increase in the interest rate are both ways of making domestic assets more attractive to global investors. To satisfy internal balance, the trade-off is traditionally considered to be upward-sloping. An increase in the interest rate reduces the domestic demand for domestic goods, while a devaluation increases the net foreign demand for domestic goods. If you have more of one, you also need more of the other to prevent excess supply or excess demand. The existence of two independent instruments implies the possibility of attaining both targets simultaneously, at the intersection of the internal and external balance schedule. In the aftermath of an adverse shock in the foreign sector, for example, the right combination of devaluation and monetary contraction will restore balance of payments equilibrium while maintaining real economic growth. It is illustrated in Figure 17.1.

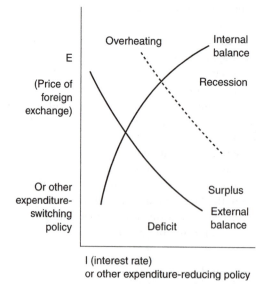

Figure 17.1 Attaining internal and external balance: traditional version.

How does it work in reality?

This is not the way things actually work.[2] By now we have had enough experience with crises in emerging markets that the traditional framework needs to be modified. The simple generalization seems to be that all developing countries that are hit by financial crises go into recession. The reduction in income is the only way of quickly generating the improvement in the trade balance that is the necessary counterpart to the increased reluctance of international investors to lend. External balance is a jealous mistress that can only be satisfied if internal balance is left to go wanting.

Some critics of the IMF say that the recessions are the result of Fund policies, specifically the insistence on monetary contraction. They claim that the mix of a lower interest rate combined with devaluation would successfully maintain internal balance. They often make the point that high interest rates are not in practice especially attractive to foreign investors when they carry increased probability of default (and associated recession). This is true. But in my view it is not the most important correction in the traditional framework. Even if interest rates do not have as big a positive effect on the capital account as our earlier models of high financial integration suggested, so that the graphical relationship may be flatter, I believe that the sign of the effect is still the same. One cannot normally attract many investors by *lowering* interest rates. Therefore, the external balance line still slopes downward. Claims that high rates are damaging to the real economy willfully ignore the lack of an alternative, if the external balance constraint is to be met.

Where the traditional framework needs most to be modified is the relationship giving internal balance, not that giving external balance. By now the evidence seems strong that devaluation is contractionary, at least in the first year, and perhaps in the second as well. We have long been aware of various potential contractionary effects of devaluation in developing countries. A total of ten such effects are identified in standard textbooks,[3] of which the difficulty of servicing dollar debts has turned out to be by far the most important in recent crises. But a mainstream view has been that any negative effect from a devaluation was eventually offset by the positive effect of stimulus to net exports, so that by the second year, when the latter had gathered strength, the overall effect on output had turned positive.[4]

However, one must judge the negative effects stronger than we thought, and the positive effects weaker. Calvo and Reinhart (2001) calculate that exports do not increase at all after a devaluation, but rather are down for the first eight months. The export side, at least, was supposed to be unambiguously positive. Apparently production is derailed by corporate financial distress, absence of trade credit, and increased costs of imported inputs, even when the production is for the purpose of export. Imports fall sharply; indeed crisis-impacted countries have for this reason experienced sharp increases in their trade balances beginning as soon as two or three months after the crisis.[5] But this is clearly a response to the unavailability of finance and collapse of income and spending, and not to relative prices. In other words, it is expenditure-reduction, not expenditure-switching.

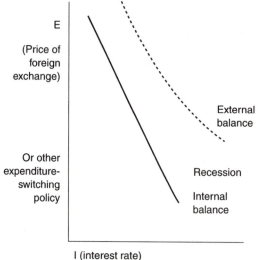

Figure 17.2 Attaining internal and external balance: when devaluation is contractionary.

If devaluation is contractionary, then the internal balance line slopes down, not up (as illustrated in Figure 17.2). Moreover, the slope is disturbingly similar to the slope of the external balance line. It is hard to see where the two intersect, if they intersect at all. This means that it is hard to see what combination of policy instruments, if any, can simultaneously satisfy both internal and external balance, after an adverse shock has shifted the latter outward. The depressing conclusion is that there is no escape from recession. All policy instruments work via reduction in income in the short run – devaluation, fiscal contraction, and monetary contraction. Even structural policy reform, such as insisting that bad banks go under, is likely to have a negative effect on economic activity in the short run. Notwithstanding that, I support the IMF's new emphasis on the latter sort of conditionality packages prepared for the East Asian emerging market economies during the 1997–98 crises.

Could, therefore, one conclude that the financing-versus-adjustment framework is no longer useful? I think that the framework may still be relevant during the (relatively brief) period after a terms-of-trade or other real shock arises, but before the financial or currency crisis hits. It is hard to identify and date the former, even with the benefit of hindsight. But I have in mind the interval of about one year preceding December 2001 in Argentina, July 1997 in East Asia, and December 1994 in Mexico (where the shock was political instability earlier in the year and increases in US interest rates), and July 1982 in Latin America. In each case, policy-makers responded to deterioration in their trade or capital accounts by running down foreign exchange reserves or shifting to short-term borrowing.[6] They succeeded in this way in postponing macroeconomic adjustment and in postponing crisis. But when the crisis came it was that much worse, requiring at that point the unfortunate pattern we have discussed – turning all dials to contractionary settings – as the only way of satisfying the constraints imposed by finicky international investors.

Hindsight is said to be 20/20. It would have been better in these cases if the countries had spent these short intervals adjusting rather than financing, at a time when there was still a meaningful trade-off between the two and the choice set had not yet been narrowed in such an unattractively constrained manner. These considerations suggest that the G-7 and IMF have been on the right track recently in emphasizing surveillance and in conditioning supra-normal post-crisis finance on countries having followed appropriate policies immediately pre-crisis – whether it is adjusting interest rates or exchange rates. The trick is thus having the economic acumen and political will to recognize that an adverse shock has occurred and to enact prompt adjustment. This element is even more crucial than calculating the right amount of adjustment or choosing among the available instruments to carry it out.

Notes

1 See Calvo and Reinhart (2001).
2 See Krugman (1998).
3 For instance, refer to Caves *et al.* (2002). For an exposition, see Cordon (1993).
4 See Edwards (1986) and Kamin (1988).
5 The pattern of adjustment in Thailand and Korea in 1998 looks very similar to Mexico in 1995.
6 Or shifting to floating rate borrowing. Studies of leading indicators of currency crises, even before the East Asia episodes, showed that the magnitude of current account deficits was less important than the composition of the financing, with heavy reliance on short-term (and floating-rate) bank flows or the running down of foreign exchange reserves strongly raising the probability of crisis. See Frankel and Rose (1996) and Kaminsky *et al.* (1998).

References

Calvo, G. and C. Reinhart. 2001. "When Capital Flows Come to a Sudden Stop: Consequences and Policy Options," in P. Kenen and A. Swoboda (eds) *Key Issues in Reform of the International Monetary System*, Washington, DC, International Monetary Fund.

Caves, R., J. Frankel, and R. Jones. 2002. *World Trade and Payments*. 9th edition. pp. 520–6. Boston, MA, Addison Wesley Longman.

Cordon, M.W. 1993. "Absorption, the Budget, and Debt: The Wonderland of Possibilities," in H. Herberg and N.V. Long (eds) *Trade, Welfare and Economic Policies: Essays in Honor of Murray C. Camp*, Ann Arbor, University of Michigan Press.

Edwards, S. 1986. "Are Devaluations Contractionary?" *Review of Economics and Statistics*, Vol. 68, No. 3, pp. 501–8.

Frankel, J.A. and A. Rose. 1996. "Currency Crashes in Emerging Markets: An Empirical Treatment," *Journal of International Economics*, Vol. 41, No. (3/4), pp. 351–66.

Kamin, S. 1988. "Devaluation, External Balance and Macroeconomic Performance: A Look at the Numbers," *Studies in International Finance*, No. 62. Princeton, NJ, Princeton University Press.

Kaminsky, G., S. Lizondo, and C. Reinhart. 1998. "Leading Indicators of Currency Crises," *IMF Staff Papers*, Vol. 45, No. 2, pp. 1–48.

Krugman, P. "Latin America's Swan Song," September 1998. http://web.mit.edu/krugman/www/swansong.html

18 Patterns of capital flows to emerging markets

A theoretical perspective*

Zhaohui Chen and Mohsin S. Khan

Introduction

Private capital flows to developing countries and transition economies grew rapidly in the early 1990s, reaching $216 billion in net terms in 1996.[1] They then fell sharply in the wake of the Asian financial crisis in 1997–98 so that by 2000 private net capital flows to these two country groups only amounted to $23 billion – almost a tenfold decline from the peak in 1996. The magnitude and volatility of capital flows over the decade of the nineties have presented both opportunities and challenges to the recipient countries, and much has been written about the causes, consequences, and policy implications of capital flows.[2]

Aside from their size, there were two particularly interesting features about capital flows to the developing world. First, the surge in capital inflows during the 1990s was not uniform across all developing-country regions. Indeed, five countries – Brazil, China, Korea, Mexico, and Thailand – alone accounted for over half of total inflows, and about a dozen countries accounted for nearly 80 percent of all flows to developing countries. Most of the capital went to Asia and Latin America, and other developing regions such as Africa and the Middle East benefited relatively little. Furthermore, financial markets in Latin America developed earlier than those in the Asian emerging markets, and the region has witnessed more portfolio flows, and the associated portfolio-flow volatilities, than emerging markets in Asia.

Second, the composition of capital flows changed substantially in the 1990s compared to the flows during earlier periods. In the late 1970s and in the 1980s, debt flows, in particular syndicated bank loans, were the largest component of capital flows going to developing countries. In the 1990s there has been a significant increase in portfolio investments and foreign direct investment (FDI) in developing countries. During the period 1990–97, the share of FDI in total private flows was nearly 70 percent in developing countries' capital inflows as a whole, while the rest was mainly portfolio investments. It is interesting to note that the

* We are grateful to Eduardo Borensztein, Ricardo Caballero, and Michael Dooley for the helpful discussions and comments on this paper. The views expressed are the sole responsibility of the authors, and do not necessarily reflect the opinions of the institutions with which they are affiliated.

sharp reversal in capital flows to developing countries that occurred in the wake of the Asian financial crisis was mainly in portfolio investments and bank loans (in Asia). In contrast, FDI flows remained strong and in fact even rose in the late 1990s.[3] Generally, it is argued that FDI is the most desirable form of foreign capital as it brings along positive externalities, such as increased access to foreign markets, management expertise, and the opportunity to acquire modern technology. Moreover, it is widely acknowledged that portfolio flows exhibit greater volatility, as they are less costly to reverse than FDI. This phenomenon was certainly evident in the post-1997 era. All in all, it is true that in the 1990s Asia, and particularly East Asia, received the largest share of private foreign capital, and also the stable kind of capital flows in the form of FDI, as compared to the more volatile portfolio flows going into Latin America. While FDI is generally considered desirable, there are certain costs associated in attracting it, such as tax concessions, provision of infrastructure, etc. Portfolio flows, however, often come without such concessions, and even in the face of certain taxes or costs.

The pattern of capital flows to emerging market economies leads to the following questions that this chapter addresses:

- Why are there different forms of capital flows, that is, FDI, portfolio equity flows, and bank lending?
- Why are some forms of these flows more dominant than others in certain geographical groups of countries?
- Under what conditions are portfolio flows better than FDI?

It is well known that capital flows are affected by many different factors, such as political risk, macroeconomic factors, external factors, regulatory controls, tax incentives, investors' business strategies, and so on. While the effects of these factors have been discussed extensively in the literature, the results of such discussions do not as yet offer a clear consensus as to why the volume, and particularly the composition, of capital flows vary across emerging markets. Basically, to explain the patterns of capital flows, careful theoretical analyses need to be undertaken.

In this chapter, we focus on the *financial aspect* of capital flows to emerging markets. In other words, we take all other nonfinancial factors as given, and study how the *cost of financing* to the recipient countries affects the pattern of capital inflows or, alternatively, how the expected excess returns of investing in an emerging market affects foreign investors' decisions. Of course, in a frictionless world, the cost of financing does not arise, and the composition of capital flows does not matter.[4] However, in a world with imperfect financial markets – such as those observed in developing countries or in emerging markets – such costs may be quite high. This chapter will show how inefficient financial markets, when combined with the countries' growth profiles, can lead to different patterns of capital flows.

The approach taken here is similar in spirit to that of Razin *et al.* (1996), who use the cost-of-financing argument to explain different forms of capital flows. They assume asymmetric information between foreign and domestic investors and derive the costs of financing for various forms of capital flows. Specifically, they find "green field" FDI to be the least costly, followed by debt flows and then by portfolio equity flows. The reason why "green field" FDI is less costly is that the participation of foreign partners in the management of the firm circumvents the costly asymmetric information problem.

Unlike Razin *et al.* (1996), however, we derive our results from the inefficiency of the domestic financial market itself. Specifically, we model financial market inefficiency as a result of asymmetric information between outside investors who rely on information in the domestic financial market and insiders of the firms. Such information asymmetry is typical in an underdeveloped financial market where information is not properly disclosed and processed due to weak, or even nonexistent, accounting and disclosure rules and primitive market infrastructure. A novel feature of the analysis is that private agents are assumed to minimize the impact of asymmetric information through optimal contracts and renegotiation designs, in line with the recent literature on contract and regulation. Even when such private market efforts have been allowed for, areas of market failure still remain. We then derive the cost of financing based on the foreign investor's required rate of return, which is the expected return conditional on the host country's investment opportunity distribution and the severity of the host country's financial market failure. Our analysis allows us to make several predictions of the patterns of capital flows based essentially on a host country's growth and financial market parameters.

Our model can also explain the large reversals of portfolio flows commonly seen in emerging markets during financial crises, such as the Mexican crisis of 1995, and the contraction of portfolio flows throughout the emerging market world during the Asian financial crisis of 1997. Such reversals of portfolio flows are a result of a semi-developed equity market in the context of moderate economic growth. This finding complements the more recent studies by Chan-Lau and Chen (1998, 2001, 2002), where they build a financial crisis model inspired by the Asian financial crisis, in which debt flow reversals are explained in the framework of an a imperfect banking system.

Theoretical explanations

Explanations of the patterns of capital flows proposed in this chapter are based on a theoretical model of the *cost of financing* in a country's equity market. The basic building blocks of our model are the theories of *investment trap* and *emerging market premium* of Chen and Huang (1995, 1996).

For simplicity, we consider a representative firm with an ongoing investment project and a new investment opportunity. Given that the market is inefficient, we derive the expected return to foreign investment on the new investment project. To quantify the degree of market inefficiency, it is necessary to make some assumptions without loss of generality. Here we assume a specific form of inefficiency resulting from information asymmetry between corporate insiders and outsiders in the financial market. As we said earlier, such information asymmetry is typical in developing countries or emerging markets where the financial market is not well developed. The insiders of the firm, that is, the existing shareholders or the management, know the true value of the firm and the value of any new project the firm can undertake. However, the outsiders, that is, potential new share-holders relying on the information provided by the financial market, may not know the true value of the firm and of its new projects. If the firm's shares are over-priced in the financial market, then the insiders will have an incentive to issue new shares to finance certain new projects, even though the projects are known by the insiders to yield negative returns. Similarly, if the firm's shares are undervalued in the market, then the insiders will drop certain new investment projects, even though the returns of these projects are known by the insiders to be positive.

While these inefficient investment problems have been well known since the original work of Myers and Majluf (1984), it was only recently that researchers began to look at ways to resolve the problem using optimal contracts between the managers and the existing shareholders (Dybvig and Zender, 1991). Such con-tracts usually index the manager's compensation to the changes in market prices of the firm's shares, so that the manager will automatically make the efficient investment decisions. Chen and Huang (1995) find that such optimal contracts work only to a certain extent. As long as there is asymmetric information between the firm's insiders and the financial market, there will be an "investment trap" in which over-investment and under-investment occur. Furthermore, the size of the trap is proportional to the degree of asymmetric information. One way to meas-ure the degree of asymmetric information is to take the absolute value of the actual deviation of the market valuation from the true value of the firm, divided by the market price. Another way to measure it is the expected value of such deviation (similar to a standard deviation). In principle, the less developed is the market infrastructure, for example, the greater the problems with accounting standards, and information disclosure and transmission, the larger the investment trap.

Figure 18.1 provides a visual presentation of the investment trap. The two shaded intervals (investment trap) are where inefficient investment decisions are made. In the interval $(\underline{r}^*, 0)$, the returns on investment are negative but the proj-ects are still taken by the firm. In the interval $(0, \bar{r}^*)$, the investment projects have positive returns but are not pursued by the firm. The upper and lower limits of the investment trap, $\underline{r}^*$ and $\bar{r}^*$, are related to the degree of asymmetric information.

Chen and Huang (1995) give exact formulas for the upper and lower limits of the investment trap. For our purpose, we can assume that $\underline{r}^* = -\bar{r}^*$ holds approxi-mately, as they differ by a fixed incentive parameter which, theoretically, can be arbitrarily small.[5] For convenience, we use the symbol $r^*(=\underline{r}^*)$ as a measure of the degree of market inefficiency.[6]

Consider the investment problem from the foreign portfolio equity investor's standpoint. Assume that the foreign investment is small relative to the host coun-try's equity market, so that any investment action does not affect the market price. Consider two simple economies, A and B, with identical distributions of invest-ment opportunities – the returns on new investment projects in each country can be defined as i.i.d. $\mathcal{N}(\mu, \sigma^2)$.[7] Here, μ is the mean return when all investment proj-ects are pursued indiscriminately. Of course, indiscriminate investment is unlikely

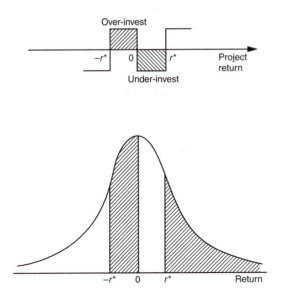

Figure 18.1 Investment trap and return distribution.

in reality if the market and corporate governance are at work. For example, in the ideal case of efficient capital market and optimal corporate governance, projects with negative returns are not pursued by the firms. Nevertheless, the notion μ is useful as it represents the average natural rate of return to investments in the economy. Since returns in an economy are related to the future growth, as a conceptual matter, we shall interpret μ as the economy's *growth potential*.

Now take Economy A as the reference economy, with a perfect financial market and an optimal market-indexed corporate governance mechanism, so that perfect investment decisions can be made (i.e. the trap size $r_A^*=0$). In this economy, all projects with negative returns are dropped, and all positive return projects are undertaken. So, the expected return conditional on perfect financial market and corporate governance is

$$E[r|r_A^*] = \frac{\phi(-\mu/\sigma)}{1 - \Phi(-\mu/\sigma)} \qquad (1)$$

where $\phi(\cdot)$ and $\Phi(\cdot)$ are, respectively, the probability density function and the cumulative density function of the standard normal distribution. The calculation above involves the moments of truncated distributions.[8] For simplicity the country subscript has been omitted on the right-hand side of the equation. When μ is high, the model economy resembles a high growth economy with a developed financial market. When μ is set to a low level (say, a normalized level of zero), the model economy captures the feature of the low growth, developed economies, to which we shall refer as the "west."

Next, assume that Economy B has an investment trap of size r_B^* (>0). The expected return is therefore defined over the two shaded areas in Figure 18.1. Algebraically, this is represented by:

$$E[r|r_B^*] = \frac{\phi((r^*-\mu)/\sigma)+\phi((-r^*-\mu)/\sigma)-\phi(-\mu/\sigma)}{1+\Phi(-\mu/\sigma)-\Phi((r^*-\mu)/\sigma)-\Phi((-r^*-\mu)/\sigma)} \tag{2}$$

As a typical emerging market is, by definition, less efficient than the financial market in a developed economy, Economy B in our analysis can be defined as an emerging market economy. Chen and Huang (1996) define the *emerging market premium* (*discount*) as the difference between the expected returns in the two economies, that is, $E[r|r_B^*]-E[r|r_A^*]$.

Now, consider the case where the two economies have the same growth potential, μ, then:[9]

$$E[r|r_B^*]-E[r|r_A^*] = \frac{\phi((r^*-\mu)/\sigma)+\phi((-r^*-\mu)/\sigma)-\phi(-\mu/\sigma)}{1+\Phi(-\mu/\sigma)-\Phi((r^*-\mu)/\sigma)-\Phi((-r^*-\mu)/\sigma)}$$

$$-\frac{\Phi(\mu/\sigma)}{1-\Phi(-\mu/\sigma)} \tag{3}$$

Equation (3) above depicts the excess (or shortfall) of the expected return in the emerging market economy as compared to the expected return in an otherwise identical economy with a developed capital market. When the return differential on the left-hand side of the above equation is negative, portfolio equity investors from Economy A will buy into Economy B only at a discount. When the return differential is positive, however, the same investors from Economy A are willing to pay a premium to invest in Economy B.

Because of the nonlinearity of the probability distribution functions, the relationship between the premium and the size of the investment trap is not monotonic in general, and is also affected by other parameters such as μ and σ. Figure 18.2 shows a numerical example of the ups and downs of investment returns in emerging markets. The vertical axis is the emerging market premium (or discount, when negative), calculated using equation (3) for the following parameter ranges: $0 \leq r^* \leq 1$, $0 \leq \mu \leq 3.5$, and $\sigma = 1$. As we can see, there is a discount for countries with a large r^* (i.e. a highly inefficient financial market) and a small μ (i.e. a low growth potential). However, as we can expect from the nonlinear function, there is a twist in the relationship as the two parameters increase to certain levels – there the excess return becomes positive. In other words, foreign investors (from Economy A) will *pay* a premium for investing in the emerging market. When the two parameters further increase, however, the premium (discount) diminishes, as can be seen from the flat surface toward the rear of the graph. This is because the main portion of the density mass of the investment opportunity distribution either falls into the large trap (when r^* is very large) or is excluded from the investment trap (when μ is strictly greater than r^*). In the former case, the expected return in the emerging market is small as in the case of

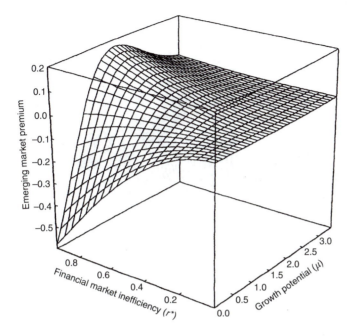

Figure 18.2 Emerging market premium over the economy with identical growth potential and an efficient financial market.

the perfect market with a large μ. In the latter case, the effect of the trap is small so the difference between the expected returns in the two markets is small.

From the above exercise we can infer the following propositions:

Proposition 1 (Intraregional flows) *With high enough growth potential, countries with less developed equity markets may be able to attract foreign portfolio equity investments from countries with similarly high investment potentials but more efficient financial markets. However, when the growth potential is too low, such intraregional flows will not occur.*

Figure 18.3 plots, for extended parameter ranges, the excess returns in the emerging market economy over a reference economy (Economy A) with zero potential return and a perfect financial market, that is, $\mu A=0$, $r_A^* = 0$ This reference economy can be viewed as a proxy for a typical low-growth "western" economy with a highly developed financial market. The figure therefore captures the attractiveness of different economies from the viewpoint of the investors of a typical "western" country. Only those economies with positive return premia can attract western investment. Graphically, these economies are the ones situated in the "high ground" area toward the left, rear part of Figure 18.3. These economies exhibit special configurations of market efficiency and investment potential. Both parameters tend to be high, with the growth effect outweighing the effect of inefficiencies in the financial market.

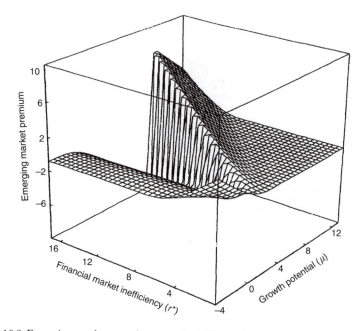

Figure 18.3 Emerging market premium over the "Western" economy.

Proposition 2 (Distribution of capital flows)   *The economies that are able to attract portfolio equity flows from "Western" countries exhibit a suitable configuration of growth potential and financial market inefficiency. Both parameters should be high enough, with the positive effect of growth outweighing the effect of the inefficient financial market. Further, the attractiveness of these economies to "Western" equity portfolio investors tends to diminish if the dominance of the growth parameter becomes too extreme.*

So far we have not considered the effect of the world interest rate.[10] If this interest rate is used for the "west" as the reference return, we can imagine it acting as a horizontal hyperplane in Figure 18.3. Only the economies above the plane are able to attract portfolio equity flows from the "west," and again they tend to be the ones described in Proposition 2. However, a lowering of the interest rate plane will help more economies emerge above the plane, and such economies tend to be the ones with high growth potentials and relatively developed financial markets (e.g. the East Asian economies), and the ones with poor financial markets but very high growth potentials. The increasing number of economies eligible for "western" funds leads to the competition for funds. On the supply side, the number of economies exporting capital (the right, front corner) will also increase as the interest rate falls. Hence, the following proposition:

Proposition 3 (Competition effect of low interest rate)   *An interest rate cut in the "West" increases the supply of capital to the rest of the world, and leads to more* *developing economies competing for funds from the "West." The newly emerging competitors include countries with high growth potentials and relatively efficient financial markets, and countries with very high growth potentials and relatively inefficient financial markets.*

This proposition differs from the general statement about the role of the interest rate in the literature. It applies only to the selected economies from both the demand side and the supply side. In particular, it sheds light on the diversion of capital to Asian and Latin American economies following cuts in the world interest rate.

We now discuss the possibility of sudden reversals of capital flows. From Figure 18.3, we can see a deep "valley" in which economies have extreme difficulties attracting foreign portfolio investment due to high financing costs. Economies at the bottom of the "valley" typically have their growth potentials (even large ones) dominated by financial market inefficiencies. These economies are unable to attract equity portfolio flows due to the high costs of financing. Economies on the upper hills of the "valley," however, can attract large capital flows at times. Being situated on a steep slope, however, they are especially vulnerable to changes in their growth potential and their financial market integrity as perceived by foreign investors – a small change in either can throw these economies into the "valley." This leads to the following proposition:

Proposition 4 (Fatal attraction)   *A catastrophic change in financing costs, and therefore a sudden capital flow reversal, may occur for certain economies experiencing (perceived) changes in their return potentials and/or financial market integrity. Such economies tend to be the ones with a moderate growth/market efficiency configuration where the two parameters are not extreme relative to each other.*

Practically speaking, economies that are prone to "fatal attractions" are those that have a mediocre growth potential and a semi-developed financial market. Note also that while a slight change in the market perception about the economy and its financial market may lead to catastrophic changes, changes in the interest rate only lead to moderate changes in a country's financing cost. This helps distinguish "fatal attractions" from real attractions.

So far, we have focused only on a specific form of capital flows, namely portfolio equity flows. Bonds and bank lending can be discussed in a similar manner, as there also exists inefficiencies such as the insider–outsider information asymmetry in debt financing. The inefficiencies can be attributed to an underdeveloped bond market or a weak banking sector. A modification will have to be made, however, to capture the default risk. The exact formulas for foreign debt investment premiums can be different, but the qualitative results should remain the same. Inefficiencies in the domestic debt market and banking sector may lead to inefficient investment decisions by the borrowing firms, raising the cost of financing in international borrowing. In view of the large body of literature on debt contracts, we do not pursue the analysis further in this chapter. Instead, we focus our discussions on the interactions between different forms of capital flows.

Depending on the degree and nature of the various forms of financing, the cost of financing the different forms of capital flows may be different. As discussed in Razin *et al.* (1996), direct managerial involvement by "green field" FDI partners can circumvent the financial market inefficiencies, and therefore may offer a cheaper alternative to portfolio financing. Of course, "green field" FDI also entails its own costs, such as cultural barriers and project specificity requirements. To the extent that such costs are smaller than the cost of portfolio financing, FDI can be the preferred form of capital flow. In light of our analysis above, FDI can be an especially useful substitute to portfolio equity flows when the cost of the latter is high. From Figure 18.3, we know that this is the case for countries that exhibit both high growth potential and a high level of financial market inefficiency, but with growth not high enough to compensate the negative effect of the inefficient financial market (i.e. the countries inside the "valley").

Proposition 5 (Composition of capital flows)   *The choice of the preferred form of capital flow, other things equal, depends on the relative financing costs of capital flows. When the premium on portfolio equity flow is high, portfolio equity flow may be the dominant form of capital flow. When the premium is strongly negative, as in the case of relatively high growth but extremely inefficient equity market, other forms of capital flows, such as FDI and debt, may be preferred.*

A word about official flows is in order. As we can see, a country's growth potential and its financial market structure play an important role in attracting private capital flows. But, for countries with virtually no growth potential and no financial market, official grants and assistance become the default option. Furthermore, as long as the country has some growth potential and some financial market structure, official flows can be very useful in better allocating the private resources.

Different forms of capital flows may also present positive externalities to each other. Debt, for example, has been long recognized to provide an extra control on corporate governance, while FDI can increase the country's external collateral value, and help the transmission of information to foreign investors, thereby reducing the financing costs of debt and portfolio equity flows.

So far we have assumed that the foreign investor is small relative to the domestic market, so that his action does not affect the domestic asset prices. If foreign investors act as a large player, as in the case of US mutual funds and hedge funds in some emerging markets, then the liquidity of the domestic market also comes into play. When large foreign investors act together in a concerted way, they may not invest much in an illiquid market to begin with. This is because a large inflow of foreign capital into an illiquid market may exacerbate the investment trap effect by creating further deviations of the market prices from the underlying values of the firms. Therefore inefficient investment would be encouraged, which may reduce the expected returns to foreign investments. In the case where foreign investors act sequentially, they may create a short-run spiral of the equity price in the market, as each investor's action creates a further deviation of the market price from the true value of the underlying firm.

Concluding remarks

There are many factors affecting international capital flows to emerging market economies, and understanding these can help to explain the observed patterns of capital flows. In this chapter, we have focused on the cost-of-financing aspect of capital flows. We have shown how the level of financial market development in the host country can affect the amount as well as the composition of capital inflows. More interestingly, we have demonstrated that a rich variety of capital flow patterns can be generated by the interaction of the degree of financial market development in the recipient country and the country's growth potential. Further, we have shown how to conduct a comparative static analysis for different levels of the world interest rate. The model opens a door to broader macroeconomic analyses, as the effects of various macroeconomic factors such as fiscal and monetary variables can be channeled through either the growth or the financial market parameters in our model.

The analysis in this chapter has a number of policy implications. While the absolute levels of growth potential and financial market development are relevant to capital flows, the relative magnitude of the two is also important. For example, contrary to popular belief, better financial market infrastructure does not always help attract foreign portfolio flows. So, structural reforms should aim at the appropriate level of financial development that is consistent with the country's growth potential. Sometimes, a country can take advantage of its high growth potential and relatively underdeveloped financial market to attract portfolio capital easily. However, if the financial market is extremely inefficient relative to its growth potential, then the cost of attracting portfolio capital can be prohibitively high. In the latter case, it pays for the country to improve its financial market. However, such improvement should be fast and reasonably complete in order to avoid the dangerous middle stage where the growth and market parameters are moderately relative to each other – economies in such a middle stage are vulnerable to significant volatility of capital flows. The short-term policy priority for countries in such a stage should be to ensure macroeconomic stability and the integrity of the financial market and of the banking sector, as a slight change in market perception of the two indicators can trigger a reversal of capital flows.

In policy discussions, it is commonly maintained that FDI is a better form of financing than portfolio flows. Controlling for the nonfinancial externalities of the two kinds of flows, our analysis shows that the difference between the two mainly lies in the financing costs. The policy implication can then be very different. For example, for a fast-growing country that experiences a high level of FDI but a very small amount of portfolio flows, conventional judgment tends to say that the quality of the capital flow is "good." From our cost-of-financing perspective, however, it may indicate that, other things being equal, the country's financial market is too backward for the country to reap the full benefit of its high growth potential. In other words, due to the high cost of portfolio financing, the country cannot attract portfolio flows and instead has to rely on FDI as a (sometimes financially more costly) substitute. Similar arguments can be extended to bank financing.

In conclusion, there is as yet no widely accepted explanation as to why the volume and composition of capital flows differs among the various emerging market countries. The model proposed in this chapter is an attempt to provide a simple unifying framework within which such a question can be examined. But it is obviously not the last word, and there are many areas in which it could be explained. These extensions are necessary if we are to have a better understanding of how developing countries can attract the preferred size and kind of capital flows from abroad.

Notes

1 Based on the IMF World Economic Outlook data base.
2 The period of the surge in capital inflows is well covered in papers by Claessens, Dooley, and Warner (1995), Khan and Mathieson (1996), Calvo, Leiderman, and Reinhart (1996), and in the recent comprehensive survey by Lopez-Mejia (1999). For an analysis of the post-Asian crisis period, see Calvo and Reinhart (2000), Razin and Sadka (2001), and Calvo, Izquierdo, and Talvi (2000).
3 In 1997 FDI in developing countries was $128 billion. It stayed at about this level during 1998–2000, and then rose to $149 billion in 2001.
4 This is a straightforward extension of the irrelevance principle of Modigliani and Miller (1958).
5 See Chen and Huang (1995) for details.
6 This is, in fact, half the size of the investment trap.
7 Of course, the single distribution case is only for illustrative purposes. An economy may have different types of investment projects with different mean returns and variances, typically associated with different industries. This possibility can be discussed in our framework by focusing on capital flows to specific classes of investment projects. The normal distribution is used as a reasonable approximation of the actual distribution of investment opportunities.
8 See Maddala (1983) for the technical details.
9 Note that, for simplicity, country subscripts have been omitted on the right-hand side of the above equations.
10 The interest rate is normalized to zero in the original model of Chen and Huang (1995).

References

Calvo, G., L. Leiderman, and C. Reinhart (1996): "Inflows of Capital to Developing Countries in the 1990s." *Journal of Economic Perspectives* 10, 123–39.

Calvo, G., L. Leiderman, and C. Reinhart (2000): "When Capital Flows Come to a Sudden Stop: Consequences and Policy." In: P.K. Kenen and A.K. Swoboda (eds), *Reforming the International Monetary and Financial System*. Washington, DC: International Monetary Fund.

Calvo, G., A. Izquierdo, and E. Talvi (2002): "Sudden Stops, the Real Exchange Rate and Fiscal Sustainability: Lessons from Argentina." Inter-American Development Bank Working Paper # 469. Washington, DC: Inter-American Development Bank.

Chan-Lau, Jorge and Zhaohui Chen (1998): "Financial Crisis and Credit Crunch as a Result of Inefficient Financial Intermediation – With Reference to the Asian Financial Crisis." IMF Working Paper 98/127. Washington, DC: International Monetary Fund.

Chan-Lau, Jorge and Zhaohui Chen (2001): "Crash-Free Sequencing Strategies for Financial Development and Liberalization." IMF Staff Papers 48, 179–98.

Chan-Lau, Jorge and Zhaohui Chen (2002): "A Theoretical Model of Financial Crisis." *Review of International Economics*, 10(1), 1.

Chen, Z. and H. Huang (1995): "Investment Trap." Financial Markets Group Working Paper No. 227, London: London School of Economics.

Chen, Z. and H. Huang (1996): "Emerging Market Premium." Unpublished, International Monetary Fund.

Claessens, S., M.P. Dooley, and A. Warner (1995): "Portfolio Capital Flows: Hot or Cold?" *The World Bank Economic Review* 9, 153–74.

Dybvig, P.H. and J.F. Zender (1991): "Capital Structure and Dividend Irrelevance with Asymmetric Information." *Review of Economic Studies* 4, 201–19.

Khan, M.S. and D. Mathieson (1996): "The Implications of International Capital Flows for Macroeconomic and Financial Policies." *International Journal of Finance and Economics* 1, 155–60.

Lopez-Mejia, A. (1999): "Large Capital Flows: Causes, Consequences, and Policy Responses." IMF Working Paper WP/99/17. Washington, DC: International Monetary Fund.

Maddala, G.S. (1983): *Limited Dependent and Qualitative Variables in Econometrics*, Cambridge, UK: Cambridge University Press.

Modigliani, F. and M. H. Miller (1958): "The Cost of Capital, Corporate Finance and the Theory of Investment." *American Economic Review* 48, 261–97.

Myers, S.C. and N.S. Majluf (1984): "Corporate Finance and Investment Decisions When Firms Have Information That Investors Do Not Have." *Journal of Financial Economics* 13, 187–221.

Razin, A., E. Sadka, and C.-W. Yuen (1996): "A Pecking Order Theory of Capital Inflows and International Tax Principles." IMF Working Paper WP/96/26. Washington, DC: International Monetary Fund.

Razin, A. and E. Sadka (2001): "Country Risk and Capital Flow Reversals." NBER Working Paper 8171. Cambridge MA: NBER.

Questions for Part V

1 Enumerate the factors responsible for stimulating capital flows to the emerging market economies.
2 What was the role of the institutional investors in integrating the emerging market economies with the global economy?
3 What are the optimal responses to sudden adverse real shocks in the balance-of-payments of the emerging market economies?
4 How do the level of development and potential of growth of the recipient economy influence the patterns of capital flows to the emerging market economies?
5 In an emerging market context, do capital market flows exacerbate shocks rather than offset them?
6 Are portfolio flows to the emerging market economies, despite the possibility of sharp reversals, better than foreign direct investment?

Areas for further research

1 Is the distinction between hot and cold money spurious?
2 Sovereign defaults and responses to them.
3 IMF policies in the crisis-ridden emerging market economies cause recession. Opine.
4 Trends in portfolio investment in the emerging market economies.

Part VI
Financial and currency crises

19 On crises, contagion and confusion*

Graciela L. Kaminsky and Carmen M. Reinhart

In 1998, *so many families living in the fashionable suburb of San Pedro Garza Garcia invested in Russian bonds that it became known as San Pedrosburgo. Now this wealthy enclave feels more like Stalingrad...*

(*The Wall Street Journal*, November 18, 1998. On explaining why the Mexican stock market plummeted in August and September of 1998 as leveraged investors faced margin calls.)

Introduction

No doubt, historians will remember the early 1980s as a period of systemic crisis in the emerging market economies. The Latin American countries, with their high debt burdens, fell like dominoes into an abyss of successive devaluations, banking crises, and deep and protracted recessions. Several countries in Asia, after three successful economic decades, were also deeply shaken. Yet, possibly, because much of the blame was placed on poor domestic policies and high real interest rates in the United States, little attention was given at the time to the possibility that financial crises could be contagious. After the *Tequila* crisis of 1994–95, the Asian flu of 1997–98 and the Russian virus of 1998, not to mention the Exchange Rate Mechanism (ERM) crisis of 1992 and 1993 in Europe, economists are now producing a growing volume of research on the "new" subject of contagion.

Yet, contagion has been understood to be different things across different studies. Crises could be synchronous across countries because of a common adverse shock (i.e. a rise in world interest rates). But symmetric shocks are usually not included in most definitions of contagion. In an early study on the subject, Calvo and Reinhart (1996) distinguish between fundamentals-based contagion, which arises when the infected country is linked to others via trade or finance, and "true" contagion which is the kind that arises when common shocks and all channels of potential interconnection are either not present or have been controlled for. Most often, true contagion is associated with herding behavior on the part of investors – be it rational, as in Calvo and Mendoza (1998), or not.

Few studies have attempted to examine empirically the channels through which the disturbances are transmitted. In this chapter, we attempt to fill this gap by analyzing how fundamentals-based contagion could arise due to both trade links and the largely ignored financial sector links. We examine the role of various creditors, including international banks and mutual funds, traders' potential cross-market hedging, and bilateral and third-party trade in the propagation of crises. Some of the conclusions that emerge from our analysis are:

First, as other studies have suggested, we find evidence that contagion is more regional than global.[1] But evidence on the channels of transmission, suggest there are dangers in extrapolating from history. While inter-regional trade in goods and services has not increased markedly in the past few years (a notable exception is Chile's rising trade with Asia), inter-regional trade in assets has skyrocketed. This makes it more likely that if Korean asset prices fall, so too will Brazilian asset prices.

Second, susceptibility to contagion is highly nonlinear. A single country falling victim to a crisis is not a particularly good predictor of crisis elsewhere, be it in the same region or in another part of the globe. However, if several countries fall prey, then it is a different story. That is, the probability of a domestic crisis rises sharply if a core group of countries are already infected.

Third, observational equivalence is a serious obstacle in understanding the channels of transmission. Is the regional complexion of contagion due to trade links, as some studies have suggested, or is it due to financial links – particularly through the role played by banks? Our results suggest that it is difficult to distinguish among the two, because most countries that are linked in trade are also linked in finance. In the Asian crises of 1997, Japanese banks played a similar role in propagating disturbances to that played by US banks in the debt crisis of the early 1980s. Indeed, when we group countries in accordance with their exposure to a common creditor, knowing that there is a crisis in that core group has a higher predictive power than knowing that a country in the same bilateral or third-party trade clusters. The improvement obtained in forecasting performance of controlling for financial sector links in our sample is greater than the improvement to be gained by controlling for trade links.

Fourth, an analysis of two potential victims of contagion, Argentina after Mexico and Indonesia after Thailand indicates that financial linkages were the more likely culprits, given that both bilateral and third-party trade links with the infected country were weak. In the case of Indonesia, it was also part of the same Japanese commercial bank borrowing cluster as Thailand.

The chapter is organized as follows. The next section briefly reviews the theories of contagion and takes stock of the existing empirical evidence on these issues. The section on "The incidence of contagion" assesses the incidence of contagion across regions and time, while the section "On channels of transmission" attempts to discriminate across the various channels of transmission. The final section discusses some of the recent contagious episodes and concludes.

Theory and evidence: a review

Models of contagion have attempted to provide a framework that explains why a shock in one country may be transmitted elsewhere. Our review of this literature emphasizes the empirical implications of these models.

Defining contagion

As noted, the definition of contagion has varied considerably across papers. Eichengreen *et al.* (1996) focused on contagion as a case where knowing that there is a crisis elsewhere increases the probability of a crisis at home. This is the definition of contagion that we will explore in the remainder of this chapter. Specifically, we control for a broad range of country-idiosyncratic fundamentals (i.e. real exchange rate, reserves, etc.) and for fundamentals, which are common across countries (i.e. international interest rates). What we are really interested in are the possible links, be it through trade or finance, that give rise to "fundamentals-based" spillovers. Hence, our analysis does not directly speak to the issue of "animal spirits" or herding behavior.

Theories of contagion and their empirical implications

To explain why crises tend to be bunched, some recent models have revived Nurkse's story of competitive devaluations, which emphasized trade, be it bilateral or with a third party.[2] Once one country has devalued, it makes it costly (in terms of a loss of competitiveness and output) for other countries to maintain their parity. Hence, an empirical implication of this type of model is that we should observe a high volume of trade among the "synchronized" devaluers.[3]

Another family of models has stressed the role of trade in financial assets, particularly in the presence of information asymmetries. Calvo and Mendoza (1998) present a model where the fixed costs of gathering and processing country-specific information give rise to herding behavior, even when investors are rational. Kodres and Pritsker (1998) focus on the role played by investors who engage in cross-market hedging of macroeconomic risks. In either case, these models suggest that the channels of transmission come from the global diversification of financial portfolios. As such, they have the empirical implication that countries that have more internationally traded financial assets and more liquid markets are likely to be more vulnerable to contagion. Cross-market hedging usually requires a moderately high correlation of asset returns. The implication is that countries whose asset returns exhibit a high degree of comovement with the infected country (such as Argentina with Mexico or Malaysia with Thailand) will be more vulnerable to contagion via cross-market hedges.

Calvo (1998) has emphasized the role of liquidity. A leveraged investor facing margin calls needs to sell (to an uninformed counterpart) his or her asset holdings. Because of the information asymmetries, a "lemons problem" arises and the asset can only be sold at a firesale price. A variant of this story can be told about an open-end fund portfolio manager who needs to raise liquidity in anticipation of future redemptions. In either case, the strategy will be not to sell the asset whose price has already collapsed but other assets in the portfolio. In doing so, however, other asset prices are depressed and the original disturbance spreads across markets.

One potential channel of transmission that has been largely ignored in the contagion literature but that is stressed in this chapter is the role of common lenders, in particular commercial banks. US banks had an extensive exposure to Latin America in the early 1980s, much in the way that Japanese banks did during the Asian crisis of 1997.[4] The behavior of foreign banks can both exacerbate the original crisis, by calling loans and drying up credit lines, but can also propagate crises by calling loans elsewhere. The need to re-balance the overall risk of the bank's asset portfolio and to recapitalize and provision following the initial losses can lead to a marked reversal in bank credit across markets where the bank has exposure.

The bulk of the empirical literature suggests that there is evidence of contagion, be it of the fundamentals-based spillovers or of the animal spirit, sunspot variety. Very few studies, however, have aimed at examining the possible underlying causes. Eichengreen *et al.* (1996) attempted to discriminate among a bilateral trade link channel and a "wake-up call hypothesis," where similarities to the crisis country in fundamentals lead investors to reassess the risk of the other countries. Glick and Rose (1998) studied these issues further in a broader country context, while Wolf (1997) sought to explain the pairwise correlations in stock returns by bilateral trade and other common macroeconomic fundamentals. All studies conclude that trade linkages play an important role in the propagation of shocks. Because trade tends to be more intra- than inter-regional in nature, some of these studies conclude that this helps explain why contagion tends to be regional rather than global. With a couple of exceptions, financial sector linkages have been largely ignored (see Frankel and Schmukler, 1998; Kaminsky and Schmukler, 1999).[5]

The incidence of contagion

In this section we examine the links among currency crises both globally and regionally. To proceed, we need to identify the dates of currency crises, gauge the odds of a crisis in a country when other countries are in turmoil, and control for the relevant economic fundamentals. Our sample is based on monthly data for 1970–98 and it includes eighty currency crises episodes for a number of industrial and developing countries. The former include: Denmark, Finland, Norway, Spain and Sweden. The latter focus on: Argentina, Bolivia, Brazil, Chile, Colombia, Indonesia, Israel, Malaysia, Mexico, Peru, the Philippines, Thailand, Turkey, Uruguay and Venezuela. An analysis of transition economies in the aftermath of Russia would have provided useful insights on contagion channels, but our methodology requires sufficiently long time series so as to allow us to distinguish between what is the "normal" behavior of an indicator during "tranquil" periods and "anomalous" behavior during crises periods. The transition economies offer little capacity to assess what is normal.[6]

Definition of crisis

Most often, speculative attacks have been resolved through a devaluation of the currency or its flotation. But central banks can and do use contractionary monetary policies and sell their foreign exchange reserves to defend the currency. High interest rate defenses were not uncommon in the wake of the Asian and Russian crises, while Argentina lost 20 percent of its foreign exchange reserves in a few weeks following the Mexican peso crisis of 1994. Thus, an index of currency crises should capture these different manifestations of speculative attacks, be they successful or otherwise. However, in the 1970s and early 1980s many of the countries in our sample had regulated financial markets with no market-determined interest rates. For this reason, our crisis index only incorporates reserve losses and depreciation. The index is a weighted average of these two indicators with weights such that the two components have equal sample volatility. This weighting scheme prevents the much greater volatility in the exchange rate (owing to several episodes of mega-devaluations) to dominate the crisis measure.[7] Because changes in the exchange rate enter with a positive weight and reserves enter with a negative weight, large positive readings of this index indicate speculative attacks. Readings that are three standard deviations above its mean are classified as crises. Less extreme readings (say two standard deviations from the mean), which we do not examine here, would identify periods of turbulence. The crises readings from this index do map well onto the chronology of events (i.e. devaluations, suspension of convertibility, etc.) for these countries.

Contagion: preliminary assessment

To examine whether the likelihood of crises is higher when there are crises in other countries, we begin by calculating the unconditional probability of a crisis. The unconditional probability that a crisis will occur in the next twenty-four months over the entire sample is simply the number of currency crises in the sample times twenty-four divided by the number of observations. As shown in Table 19.1, under the heading $P(C)$, these calculations yield an unconditional probability of 29 percent. We next calculate a family of conditional probabilities. If knowing that there is a currency crisis elsewhere helps predict a currency crisis at home, then, the probability of a currency crisis, conditional on that information, denoted by $P(C|CE)$, should be higher than the unconditional one. Table 19.1 also reports the adjusted noise-to-signal ratio for the various groupings.[8] The lower the noise-to-signal ratio, the more reliable is the indicator.

First, as regards the results presented in Table 19.1, at least at the global level, knowing that there is a single crisis elsewhere is not a particularly helpful piece of information for predicting a future crisis. This contrasts with the results presented in Eichengreen *et al.* (1996), who find stronger evidence of the predictive capacity of a crisis elsewhere variable. We suspect, however, that their results are influenced by the heavy representation of European countries in their sample. As we will discuss below, the pattern of contagion seems to be more regional than global in scope and the predictive ability of knowing that there is a crisis elsewhere depends importantly on where elsewhere happens to be. However, if one-half or more of the countries in the sample are having currency crises, this increases the likelihood of a crisis to 55 percent, or almost double the

Table 19.1 The incidence of global contagion: currency crises, 1970–98

Proportion of other sample countries with crises (%)	Adjusted noise-to-signal ratio, N/S	Unconditional probability of a crisis	Probability of a crisis conditioned on crises elsewhere, P(C|CE)	Difference between conditional and unconditional probability of a crisis, P(C|CE) − P(C)
0–25	1.23	29.0	20.0	−9.0
25–50	0.64	29.0	33.0	4.0
50 and above	0.26	29.0	54.7	25.7
Memorandum items				
Real exchange rate[a]	0.10	29.0	67.0	38.0
Imports	1.10	29.0	26.0	−3.0

Note

a The real exchange rate is used as a comparison as it provides the best performance among the univariate indicators considered in Kaminsky and Reinhart (1996) and Kaminsky (1998). By contrast, imports were among the indicators which fared among the worst.

unconditional probability of crisis of 29 percent. Indeed, this result is similar to those found in some of the empirical papers on bank contagion. When the problem becomes that systemic, the chances of escaping unscathed are slim. Thus, it appears that the relationship between the probability of a crisis at home and the number of crises elsewhere is highly nonlinear.

We also examined these probabilities at the regional level (Table 19.2). There are three groups: Asia, which includes Indonesia, Malaysia, the Philippines and Thailand; Europe, which encompasses the four Nordic countries in our sample plus Israel, Turkey and Spain: and Latin America, which consists of Argentina, Bolivia, Brazil, Colombia, Chile, Mexico, Peru, Uruguay and Venezuela. In all three regions the probability of a crisis conditioned on crisis elsewhere increases sharply as the number of casualties rise. When the proportion of infected countries increases over the 50 percent hurdle, the conditional probability of crisis increases from about 27 to 67 percent in Asia; in Latin America it increases from 29 to 69 percent if half or more of the countries are in crisis.

Macroeconomic fundamentals

Naturally, an epidemic may arise when multiple individuals are exposed to a common virus. The global analogy to the common virus can be found in international interest rate fluctuations, which have had much to do in explaining the cycles in capital flows to emerging markets.[9] Since, in turn, abrupt swings in capital flows have done much to trigger currency crises we need to control for such common fundamentals as well as those that are country-specific. The approach taken here follows the "signals" approach described in detail in Kaminsky and Reinhart (1999) and the construction of a composite leading indicator of currency crises

Table 19.2 The incidence and evolution of regional contagion: Asia, Europe and Latin
America

Proportion of other sample countries in the region with crises (%)	Asia			Europe			Latin America		
	N/S	*P(C)*	*P(C|CE)*	*N/S*	*P(C)*	*P(C|CE)*	*N/S*	*P(C)*	*P(C|CE)*
0–25	1.37	26.8	19.8	1.37	28.6	14.7	1.29	29.4	18.3
25–50	1.30	26.8	15.3	0.58	28.6	32.3	0.77	29.4	30.8
50 and above	0.03	26.8	67.4	0.51	28.6	35.0	0.16	29.4	68.6

Note
Full sample: 1970–98.

outlined in Kaminsky (1998). A brief sketch of this methodology follows and the
interested reader is referred to those papers for greater detail.

We begin by constructing a composite index that captures the fragility of the
economy on the eve of crises. The index summarizes the behavior of eighteen
individual financial and macroeconomic time series. Each indicator may issue one
or more signals or warnings in the twenty-four months preceding the crisis.[10] For
example, there may be an unusually sharp decline in foreign exchange reserves or
in stock prices. If a signal is issued, it is assigned a value of 1. Hence, if all
eighteen indicators issued a signal on a given month the value of the composite
indicator would be 18 if all signals were weighted equally. However, as shown in
earlier papers, the quality of the indicators is highly heterogenous.[11] For this reason, we weigh each signal by the inverse of the noise-to-signal ratio of the particular indicator that is issuing the signal. We can then construct a sample-based
vector of conditional probabilities for currency crises. One set of probabilities will
control for the macroeconomic fundamentals, denoted by $P(C|F)_t$, another set of
probabilities will control for both the fundamentals and information about crises
elsewhere, $P(C|F, CE)_t$, and a third, which we call the "naive" forecast controls for
neither – hence, it is the simple unconditional probability of crisis. To assess the
marginal contribution of knowing whether and how many crises are elsewhere we
conduct a horse race between the naive forecasts, those that take into account the
fundamentals, and those that also add information on crises elsewhere. To evaluate the average closeness of the predicted probabilities of crises and the actual
realizations, as measured by a 0–1 dummy variable, we

$$QPS^k = 1/T \sum_{t=1}^{T} 2(P_t^{kt} - R_t)^2$$

calculate the quadratic probability score (QPS), where $k = 1, 2, 3$ refers to the
indicator, P_t^k, refers to the probability associated with that indicator and R_t are the
0–1 realizations. The QPS ranges from 0 to 2, with a score of zero corresponding
to perfect accuracy. Table 19.3 reports the scores, for the naive forecasts, the

Table 19.3 Contagion and the fundamentals: the QPS 1970–98

	Naive (1)	Contagion (2)	Fundamentals (3)	Fundamentals and contagion (4)	Percent improvement in forecasts
Full sample	0.386	0.350	0.313	0.308	1.6
Asia	0.285	0.239	0.301	0.213	29.2
Europe	0.378	0.325	0.316	0.297	6.0
Latin America	0.380	0.334	0.304	0.289	4.9

forecasts on the basis of the macroeconomic fundamentals and the forecasts that also take into account information about crises elsewhere. The scores are given for the entire sample, as well as the regional groups. The main result that arises from this exercise is that adding information about crisis elsewhere reduces the prediction error, even after the fundamentals have been accounted for. The gains from incorporating information on crises elsewhere are highest for Asia (a 29 percent improvement in forecasting accuracy, shown in the last column). For Latin America and Europe, the gains are more modest and in the 5–6 percent range.

On the channels of transmission

We next turn our attention toward investigating what some of the international propagation mechanisms may be. Specifically, we consider four channels through which shocks can be transmitted across borders; two channels deal with the linkages among financial markets, be it through foreign bank lending or globally diversified portfolios, and two deal with trade in goods and services.

Common bank creditor

As discussed in the section on "Theory and evidence: a review," the studies that have attempted to analyze the channels through which contagion arises have found a prominent role for linkages on the basis of trade in goods and services. However, this line of enquiry does not speak to the fact that countries that engage in trade in goods and services typically also have strong connections through financial arrangements that facilitate trade – particularly through commercial banks. Just as there appears to be natural regional trade blocs, so there appear to be regional blocs that depend on a single common creditor country. This may help explain cross-border spillovers, since if a bank is confronted with a marked rise in nonperforming loans in one country, it is likely to be called upon to reduce the overall risk of its assets by pulling out of other high risk projects elsewhere – possibly in other emerging markets. Furthermore, it will lend less (if at all), as it is forced to recapitalize, provision and adjust to its lower level of wealth.

Tables 19.4 and 19.5 present evidence on the incidence of regional borrowing arrangements from both the perspective of the borrower as well as the perspective of the lender for Asia and Latin America. On the eve of the Thai crisis, 54 percent of Thai liabilities were to Japanese banks. Most of the other countries in the region, with the exception of the Philippines, which has fared well by comparison, also depended heavily on Japanese commercial bank lending. From the perspective of the Japanese banks, Thai exposure was also not trivial. It accounted for the highest share of claims on emerging markets (22 percent) and more than twice that of China. As the Thai crisis unraveled, taking advantage of the short-term nature of their credits, Japanese banks began to call loans – not just in Thailand but all over the region. Commercial bank credit to the five affected countries (Indonesia, Korea, Malaysia, the Philippines and Thailand) shifted from an inflow of over $50 billion in 1996 to an outflow of $21 billion in the following year. A regional liquidity crunch got under way.

While it is tempting to conclude that such transmission mechanisms are new to the global economy, they have been with us for some time. Mexico's share of US claims on total claims on emerging markets was also the highest among emerging markets in 1982 and, like its Thai counterparts, it was also 22 percent (Table 19.5). Also like the Asian cluster, Latin American countries obtain their lion's share of

Table 19.4 Banks: liabilities as a percent of borrower's total liabilities on the eve of the Tequila and Asian flu crises

Borrower	Liabilities to Japan		Liabilities to the United States	
	As of June 1994	As of December 1996	As of June 1994	As of December 1996
Asia average	37.2	30.1	12.8	12.2
China	39.5	32.3	1.9	4.9
Indonesia	54.0	39.7	7.7	9.5
Korea	29.4	24.3	10.0	9.4
Malaysia	40.2	36.9	11.3	10.5
Philippines	17.2	11.7	39.4	29.4
Thailand	56.8	53.5	7.1	7.2
Latin America average	7.1	5.2	28.8	26.3
Argentina	5.3	4.0	31.2	29.5
Brazil	10.6	7.6	22.7	27.1
Chile	8.8	5.2	31.2	27.9
Colombia	13.0	7.8	26.6	24.6
Mexico	7.3	8.7	34.2	28.4
Peru	7.5	2.9	15.9	17.4
Uruguay	0.7	0.8	35.2	30.2
Venezuela	3.7	4.2	33.3	25.6

Sources: Bank of International Settlements, *The Maturity, Sectoral, and Nationality Distribution of International Bank Lending* and United States Treasury, *Treasury Bulletin*.

Table 19.5 Banks: liabilities as a percent of lender's total liabilities on the eve of the debt, Tequila and Asian flu crises

Borrower	Liabilities to Japan		Liabilities to the United States		
	As of June 1994	As of December 1996	As of June 1982	As of June 1994	As of December 1996
Asia sub-total	53.6	67.3	10.1	18.1	24.4
China	9.7	10.3	0.1	0.7	2.1
Indonesia	11.7	13.0	0.2	2.6	4.1
Korea	9.9	14.3	5.4	5.2	7.2
Malaysia	3.9	4.8	0.2	1.7	1.8
Philippines	0.7	0.9	2.0	2.6	3.0
Thailand	14.6	22.1	0.4	2.8	3.9
Latin America sub-total	7.1	5.8	61.5	58.8	48.6
Argentina	1.2	1.1	8.4	10.6	10.2
Brazil	3.9	3.0	16.1	13.0	14.2
Chile	0.6	0.5	4.0	3.6	3.3
Colombia	0.8	0.8	1.9	2.5	3.2
Mexico	3.0	3.2	22.2	21.8	13.4
Peru	0.2	0.1	1.6	0.5	1.1
Uruguay	0.0	0.0	0.3	1.3	1.0
Venezuela	0.4	0.3	7.0	5.5	2.2

Sources: Bank of International Settlements, *The Maturity, Sectoral, and Nationality Distribution of International Bank Lending* and United States Treasury, *Treasury Bulletin*.

Note
Lender's total claims represent the total claims on developing countries, excluding other BIS countries and offshore banking centers.

their commercial bank credit from US banks and like in the Asian crises, US banks pulled out from Latin America at the time of the debt crisis.

To step beyond the anecdotal evidence and systematically investigate whether common creditors (banks) are a possible channel of contagion, we clustered a sub-set of the countries in our sample into two groups – that group which borrows mostly from US banks and that group which relies heavily on Japanese commercial bank lending. We could not identify a common European bank cluster in our sample. The first group encompasses most (but not all) of the Latin American countries in our sample and includes: Argentina, Brazil, Chile, Colombia, Mexico, Uruguay and Venezuela. Bolivia and Peru were excluded as they have more heterogeneous sources of international bank credit. The Philippines, which has an exposure to US banks that is about three times the average for Asia and comparable to many of the Latin American countries, is also included in this cluster. The Japanese bank cluster thus comprises of Indonesia, Malaysia and Thailand. Had China and Korea been part of our sample, these would have been included in the Japanese bank cluster, as these countries relied on Japanese bank credit (Table 19.4).

Table 19.6 Contagion and banking clusters

Proportion of other sample countries in the region with crises (%)	Bank clusters				
	N/S	P(C)	P(C|CE)	P(C|CE) − P(C)	[P(C|CE) − P(C)]/P(C)
0–25	1.507	31.5	19.2	−12.3	−39.0
25–50	0.903	31.5	28.4	−3.1	−0.9
50 and above	0.071	31.5	83.5	52.0	165.0

QPS

	Naive (1)	Contagion (2)	Fundamentals (3)	Fundamentals and contagion (4)	Difference between columns (4) and (3) and standard error[a] (5)
Score	0.394	0.291	0.304	0.245	−0.059* (0.017)

Notes
* Denotes significance at standard confidence levels. The Japanese bank cluster includes Indonesia, Malaysia and Thailand. United States bank cluster includes Argentina, Brazil, Chile, Colombia, Mexico, the Philippines, Uruguay and Venezuela.
a The standard error was estimated with robust methods.

Table 19.6 reports the results for the joint estimation of conditional and unconditional probabilities for the two banks clusters. We estimate these jointly as disaggregation among the two clusters can be subject to small sample problems, in that the number of crises in the subsample are relatively small. The marginal contribution of knowing that a country in that cohort has a crisis does not add much information when there are few crises. However, once several countries in the cohort become infected, the conditional probability of a crisis jumps to 83.5 percent, well above the comparable conditional probability of 54.7 percent for a crisis elsewhere reported in Table 19.1 and the unconditional probability of 31.5 percent for the bank clusters.[12] These results suggest, that perhaps much of what has been attributed to trade has to do with financial sector linkages. Furthermore, the QPS scores for forecasts that include information on both fundamentals and crises elsewhere in the bank cluster are significantly lower at all standard confidence levels than those that do not control for crises in the cluster (Table 19.6, column 5).

Liquidity channels, mutual funds and cross-market hedging

While banks are important common lenders, they are not the only lenders to the emerging world. Portfolio flows to emerging markets surged in the early-to-mid-1990s. Hence, just as a commercial bank may call its loans to Malaysia after Thailand has a crisis, so can a diversified investor choose (or be forced by margin calls) to sell his or her Argentinean bond and equity holdings after Mexico devalues. Some of the models that stress this form of contagion were discussed in

the section on "Theory and evidence: a review." In order to be of any consequence, however, this channel of transmission requires that there be sufficient
asset market liquidity. If bond and equity markets are so underdeveloped that
portfolio flows are trivial, then clearly this channel of transmission is not likely to
be quantitatively important. In other words, if country's equity or bonds are not
internationally traded to begin with, such liquidations are not a problem.

Table 19.7 provides a profile of emerging market mutual fund holdings on the
eve of the Asian crisis. It is clear that there is a wide diversity of representation
across markets, with Hong Kong, Brazil and Mexico (in that order) being among
the most highly represented (and also the most liquid) markets. It is noteworthy
that two Latin American countries that did not even experience as much as a mild
hiccup in their equity markets around the Mexican crisis are Colombia and
Venezuela (see Calvo and Reinhart, 1996), which are barely represented in the
mutual fund portfolios.

Table 19.7 Emerging market mutual fund holdings

Country	Major country holdings June 30, 1997	
	US$ billions	*Percent*
Total Asia	85.04	55.55
Bangladesh	0.03	0.02
China	3.74	2.44
Hong Kong	23.46	15.33
India	8.98	5.87
Indonesia	6.66	4.35
Korea	9.43	6.16
Malaysia	9.01	5.88
Pakistan	0.71	0.46
Philippines	3.68	2.40
Singapore	5.03	3.29
Sri Lanka	0.21	0.14
Taiwan	10.00	6.53
Thailand	4.11	2.68
Total Latin America	44.02	28.75
Argentina	4.56	2.98
Brazil	20.01	13.07
Chile	4.36	2.85
Colombia	0.81	0.53
Mexico	11.76	7.68
Peru	1.33	0.87
Venezuela	1.19	0.78

Notes
The figures cover all dedicated emerging market funds – both
regional and single country – that are registered or listed in a developed market (excluding the emerging market funds that are registered
and traded in the emerging markets themselves).

Table 19.8 Daily stock price index correlations: December 1991 to December 1996 (US dollars)

Country	Arg.	Bra.	Chi.	Col.	Ind.	Kor.	Mal.	Mex.	Per.	Phi.	Rus.	Tha.	Tur.	Ven.
Argentina	1.00													
Brazil	0.37	1.00												
Chile	0.38	0.24	1.00											
Colombia	−0.01	0.15	0.02	1.00										
Indonesia	0.38	0.28	0.39	0.20	1.00									
Korea	0.09	0.00	0.20	0.13	0.10	1.00								
Malaysia	0.17	−0.09	0.12	0.02	0.50	0.20	1.00							
Mexico	0.56	0.36	0.34	−0.10	0.32	0.29	0.28	1.00						
Peru	0.44	0.40	0.45	0.21	0.22	0.32	0.14	0.53	1.00					
Philippines	0.35	0.05	0.25	0.24	0.63	0.09	0.61	0.30	0.29	1.00				
Russia	0.15	0.10	0.49	−0.14	−0.19	−0.19	−0.14	0.10	0.30	0.26	1.00			
Thailand	0.25	0.01	0.37	0.05	0.54	0.24	0.60	0.30	0.24	0.68	0.02	1.00		
Turkey	0.02	0.11	−0.07	−0.05	0.27	0.11	0.18	−0.04	−0.04	0.18	−0.39	0.14	1.00	
Venezuela	0.24	0.16	0.01	0.24	0.18	0.16	0.12	−0.06	0.012	0.32	0.22	0.09	−0.08	1.00

Source: International Finance Corporation, *Emerging Stock Markets Factbook 1997*.

While there is broad variation across markets in the extent to which they are represented in global investor's portfolios, there is also quite a degree of diversity in the extent that asset price returns correlate across countries. Table 19.8, which shows the pairwise correlations of stock returns (in US dollars) across selected markets, provides evidence in this regard. For the sake of simplicity, we will classify a pairwise correlation of 0–0.20 as low, 0.21–0.40 as moderate, and above 0.40 as high. Using these three grids it is easy to see that the highest correlations among returns occur among the Southeast Asian economies now mired in crises, Indonesia, Malaysia, the Philippines and Thailand. It is also evident that high intra-regional pairwise correlations are rare and that the highest correlation in Latin America is between Argentine and Mexican stock returns.

Hence, on the basis of liquidity and correlation considerations, one would expect a higher degree of cross-market hedging across the four Southeast Asian countries (although they are only moderately liquid) and among Argentina, Brazil, Peru and Mexico (two of which are comparatively liquid) and all four are correlated. Yet, formally investigating this possible channel of interconnectedness is fraught with difficulty. First, unlike the prevalence of bank lending, these transmission channels are relatively recent, as emerging market funds and portfolio flows to these countries, were virtually nonexistent prior to the 1990s. Second, there may be marked swings in the liquidity of these markets, as sovereign debt can cease to be considered a liquid asset overnight.

With these shortcomings in mind, and taking the results as tentative, we formed two clusters of countries that exhibited a high degree of comovement in their asset returns. The first cluster includes the four Southeast Asian economies in our sample. South Korea, had it been part of our sample, would have been excluded from this cluster on the basis of its low historical correlations with the East Asia four. For Latin America the high correlation cluster includes Argentina, Mexico and Peru. Needless to say, a shortcoming of these clusters is that they are based entirely on recent correlations and give no weight to the role of market liquidity. The joint conditional and unconditional probabilities for the high-correlation groupings are reported in Table 19.9. In terms of the comparison between conditional and unconditional probabilities, the conditional probability of this cluster at 80.4 percent (for the 50 percent and above category) is well above the unconditional probability, although the improvement is not as substantial as that obtained from the bank cluster. However, the QPS scores paint a very compelling picture – the QPS scores that control for crises elsewhere in the cluster are significantly higher than those that just control for fundamentals. Furthermore, the improvement in forecasting accuracy is bigger than that obtained with the bank clusters. However, it is important to be cautious about over-interpreting these results as the incidence of portfolio flows and the widespread use of cross-market hedges has a much shorter history than bank lending in this sample and it is a phenomenon of the 1990s.

Trade links

Perhaps because trade in goods and services has a longer history in the post Second World War period than trade in financial assets, or because of far better

Table 19.9 Contagion and high correlation clusters

Proportion of other sample countries in the region with crises (%)	Bank clusters				
	N/S	*P(C)*	*P(C|CE)*	*P(C|CE) − P(C)*	*[P(C|CE) − P(C)]/P(C)*
0–25	5.100	33.3	5.5	−27.8	−83.5
25–50	0.577	33.3	54.1	20.8	62.5
50 and above	0.389	33.3	80.4	47.1	141.4

QPS

	Naive (1)	*Contagion* (2)	*Fundamentals* (3)	*Fundamentals and contagion* (4)	*Difference between columns (4) and (3) and standard error*[a] *(5)*
Score	0.381	0.186	0.343	0.158	−0.185[*] (0.014)

Notes

[*] Denotes significance at standard confidence levels. The Asian high correlation cluster includes Indonesia, Malaysia, the Philippines and Thailand. The Latin American cluster includes Argentina, Brazil and Peru.

[a] The standard error was estimated with robust methods.

data availability, trade links have received the most attention in the literature on contagion. In this section we examine two types of trade links. The most obvious is bilateral trade among other countries and the infected country(ies). The second type of link is more difficult to quantify, which involves competition in a common third market. For the countries in Asia and Latin America in our sample, identifying a common third party is not a difficult task. The United States figures prominently in trade with Latin America (not unlike the bank credit clusters) and Japan figures prominently in Asian trade. However, all five crises countries in Asia in 1997 also export extensively to Hong Kong and Singapore. While sharing a third party is a necessary condition for the competitive devaluation story it is clearly not a sufficient one. If a country that exports bananas to the United States devalues it is not obvious why this would have any detrimental effect on a country that exports semiconductors to the United States. Hence, clearly the composition of trade will play a key role in determining whether the third-party trade links carry any weight. Previous studies that have examined the trade links have not addressed this issue altogether.

Tables 19.10 and 19.11 convey information about the extent of bilateral trade and third-party trade on the eve of three crises episodes, the debt crisis, the Mexican peso crisis of 1994 and the Asian crisis of 1997. There are several features worth noting. As regards the most recent crises, it is hard to see bilateral trade as the force behind contagion. The share of exports that is destined to other Asian crises countries (including Korea) is not very large. For instance, Malaysia's exports to Indonesia, Korea, the Philippines and Thailand combined only amount to 9 percent of its exports. For this reason we do not identify an Asian bilateral trade cluster. Understanding why Brazil and Mexico have been so

Table 19.10 Asia and Latin America inter- and intra-regional trade: exports to Asia

Country	Exports to the rest of emerging Asia [a]			Exports to the rest of emerging Asia and China, Hong Kong, Japan and Singapore		
	1982	*1995*	*1997*	*1982*	*1995*	*1997*
Asia average	6.8	9.0	9.6	48.8	54.7	54.7
Indonesia	4.4	12.2	12.8	69.7	56.6	55.7
Korea	4.1	7.8	9.7	30.0	48.7	49.6
Malaysia	8.1	9.0	9.9	61.1	56.8	59.3
Philippines	8.0	9.8	7.7	40.2	41.7	40.9
Thailand	9.4	6.3	8.0	41.9	52.6	52.7
	Exports to emerging Asia			Exports to emerging Asia and China, Hong Kong, Japan and Singapore		
	1982	*1995*	*1997*	*1982*	*1995*	*1997*
Latin America average	1.2	2.3	2.0	9.0	10.5	8.7
Argentina	0.6	2.8	3.3	7.4	13.4	13.2
Brazil	1.8	4.6	3.8	10.7	17.5	14.4
Chile	1.4	8.3	9.9	16.1	33.7	37.5
Colombia	0.2	0.6	0.3	4.6	6.0	3.6
Mexico	1.4	0.2	0.1	8.8	2.4	2.0
Peru	3.2	5.8	4.1	21.1	26.0	23.6
Uruguay	0.2	1.4	1.4	3.4	11.7	10.1
Venezuela	0.3	0.1	0.1	5.1	2.7	1.9

Source: International Monetary Fund, *Direction of Trade Statistics.*

Note

a Other emerging Asia includes those countries listed in the table.

adversely affected in the aftermath of the Asian flu is even harder as, on average only 2.3 percent of Latin American exports go to the Asian five. The most compelling case for bilateral trade links between the Asian crises countries and Latin America is clearly Chile, whose exports to Asia have been rising over time. Similarly, on the eve of the Tequila crisis only 1.7 percent of Argentine exports were destined for Mexico.[13] Yet clearly, important bilateral trade links are revealed in Tables 19.10 and 19.11. Most noticeable is the high level of bilateral trade among the Mercosur members (Argentina, Brazil and Uruguay) and also Chile. Hence, a devaluation of the real would be expected to have important consequences for Argentina and Uruguay by way of trade – although it is important to remember that Argentina and Brazil are still relatively closed economies, with ratios of trade as a percent of GDP far below those recorded in the Asian and European countries in our sample.

Table 19.11 Asia and Latin America inter- and intra-regional trade: exports to Asia

Country	Exports to the Latin America			Exports to the rest of Latin America and the United States		
	1982	1995	1997	1982	1995	1997
Asia average	2.4	2.4	2.5	20.7	21.8	21.7
Indonesia	4.2	1.4	1.1	20.0	18.1	17.5
Korea	3.1	4.7	4.7	31.9	24.0	21.0
Malaysia	0.3	1.6	1.5	12.0	22.3	19.8
Philippines	0.9	1.0	2.4	32.5	36.9	37.1
Thailand	0.2	1.0	0.9	12.9	18.7	20.6
	Exports to the rest of Latin America			Exports to the rest of Latin America and the United States		
	1982	1995	1997	1982	1995	1997
Latin America average	19.8	18.9	20.4	50.2	66.1	71.3
Argentina	20.4	40.9	49.3	33.8	49.9	57.1
Brazil	15.6	23.0	27.7	36.1	41.9	45.4
Chile	19.4	19.2	16.8	41.0	33.1	32.5
Colombia	21.7	29.7	28.4	45.0	63.8	66.6
Mexico	8.8	5.6	6.0	61.2	89.9	91.6
Peru	11.0	17.1	18.2	42.0	34.4	44.4
Uruguay	30.5	53.3	56.0	38.3	59.3	62.0
Venezuela	39.5	33.6	33.8	66.3	82.8	85.4

Source: International Monetary Fund, *Direction of Trade Statistics.*

The case for third-party trade links is much more compelling for some of the Asian countries. Table 19.12 shows that Malaysia and Korea, in particular, export many of the same goods to the same third parties. This leaves Indonesia largely unexplained. Third-party trade also does not appear to account for the Tequila effects on Argentina and Brazil, whose exports have little in common with Mexican exports (See Table 19.13).

To examine these issues more formally, we constructed three trade clusters, a Latin American bilateral trade cluster, which consists of the Mercosur members and Chile; a third-party Asian group, which does not include Indonesia as its structure of exports is very distinct from the others and; a third-party Latin group, which includes Brazil, Colombia, Mexico and Venezuela. These four countries have the largest share of bilateral trade with the United States and some similarities in the structure of their exports. For instance coffee plays a prominent role in both Colombian and Brazilian exports while oil plays a similar role for Mexico and Venezuela and, to a lesser extent, Colombia. As with the bank and correlation clusters, we jointly estimate the conditional and unconditional probabilities

Table 19.12 Contagion and trade clusters

Proportion of other sample countries in the region with crises (%)	Third-party trade clusters					Latin America high bilateral trade cluster				
	N/S	$P(C)$	$P(C\|CE)$	$P(C\|CE) - P(C)$	$[P(C\|CE) - P(C)]/P(C)$	N/S	$P(C)$	$P(C\|CE)$	$P(C\|CE) - P(C)$	$[P(C\|CE) - P(C)]/P(C)$
0–25	1.51	27.6	21.8	−5.8	−21.0	0.53	37.4	29.3	−8.1	−21.4
25–50	1.54	27.6	21.3	−6.3	−22.8	2.34	37.4	15.6	−21.8	−58.3
50 and above	0.57	27.6	58.3	30.7	111.2	0.08	37.4	84.7	47.3	126.0

QPS

	Naive (1)	Contagion (2)	Fundamentals (3)	Fundamentals and contagion (4)	Difference between columns (4) and (3) and standard error[a] (5)
Score Third-party trade	0.375	0.354	0.312	0.283	−0.029 (0.018)
Score Latin America bilateral trade	0.433	0.377	0.345	0.314	−0.031 (0.017)

Notes

The Asian third-party cluster includes Malaysia, the Philippines and Thailand. The Latin American third party includes Brazil, Colombia, Mexico and Venezuela; the bilateral trade cluster includes the Mercosur countries plus Chile. Since there is little bilateral trade among the five affected countries no bilateral cluster is reported.

a The standard error was estimated with robust methods.

Table 19.13 The composition of exports: Argentinean and Brazilian exports of Mexico's top exports (percent of total exports, 1994)

Description	Mexico	Argentina	Brazil
Oil	10.8	7.1	0.0
Automobiles	8.6	1.2	1.2
Insulated electric wire	4.8	0.1	0.1
Televisions	4.3	0.1	0.0
Engine parts	3.8	0.9	2.0
Automobile parts	3.4	2.6	2.9
Radio/amplifier parts	3.2	0.1	0.1
Electric switches, relays, etc.	3.2	1.3	0.3
Other electric machinery	2.7	0.0	0.1
Computers	2.0	0.3	0.2
Transportation vehicles	1.6	1.7	2.0
Semi conductors	1.5	0.0	0.2
Radios	1.5	0.1	0.7
Furniture	1.4	0.1	0.7
Electric power machinery	1.3	0.0	0.3
Total	54.1	15.6	10.9

Source: Statistics Canada, World Trade Database.

for the third-party trade Asian and Latin American clusters. For bilateral trade, only the results for Latin America are reported, given that no Asian bilateral trade cluster was identified.

The results are reported in Table 19.13. The strongest results are those for the Latin American bilateral trade cluster, where the difference between the conditional and unconditional probability is 47.3 percent, which compares favorably with the results reported in Table 19.1, which are on the basis of crisis elsewhere and do not control for how elsewhere is defined. However, the third-party (and the bilateral) trade clusters do not compare favorably to the two financial linkages clusters results reported in Tables 19.6 and 19.9. Also, while the QPS scores decline when we control for crises elsewhere in the trade cluster, these improvements are not statistically significant when compared to the scores of the forecasts that control only for fundamentals. Hence, by these criteria, both types of trade clusters underperform the financial sector links previously discussed.

Recent episodes and conclusions

To sum up, our analysis suggests that financial sector links via common bank lenders are a powerful channel of fundamentals-based contagion; the difference between the conditional and unconditional probability, $P(C|CE) - P(C)$, for the bank cluster is the highest at 52 percent (a 165 percent increase). This perform-ance is followed by the high-correlation cluster $[P(C|CE) - P(C) = 47.1$, which represents a 141 percent increase], bilateral links $[P(C|CE) - P(C) = 47.3$, which is a 126 percent increase], and a less impressive performance by the third-party trade cluster $[P(C|CE) - P(C) = 30.7]$, which is only somewhat higher than the global crisis elsewhere results [P(C│CE) − P(C) = 25.7]. Besides these ordinal rankings, the QPS scores indicate an improvement in forecasting accuracy for all clusters; however, only in the case of the bank cluster and the high-correlation cluster are these improvements statistically significant at standard confidence levels. In the remainder of this final section we next turn our attention to two recent "contagious" episodes, the aftermath of the Mexican peso crisis and the floatation of the Thai baht. The aim is to assess through which channels these crises spread. We discuss both trade and financial links.

As regards the potential role of bilateral and third-party trade linkages in these recent episodes, Malaysia would be the most closely linked with Thailand, with Korea and the Philippines having more moderate exposure (Table 19.14). Trade can certainly not help explain Argentina and Brazil following the Mexican devaluation nor Indonesia following the Thai crisis. Exposure to Japanese banks, which pulled out rapidly across the region was common to all the affected countries except Hong Kong. While both Brazil and Argentina are in the same US bank cluster as Mexico, banks were not at the heart of the problem in 1994 as they were in the early 1980s.

Most of the affected Asian countries, except Korea had high asset return correlations with Thailand, although none except Hong Kong had particularly liquid markets. The same is true of stock returns in Argentina, which have the highest correlation with Mexico of any country in the region. Here it is hard to separate cause and effect. A high correlation may reflect past contagion, but to the extent that current cross-hedging strategies use such historical correlations as a guide, it could be the vehicle for future contagion. In sum, it would appear that financial sector linkages, be it through banks on through international capital markets have much to say in how shocks are propagated in recent crises episodes, particularly for Argentina, Brazil and Indonesia.

Table 19.14 Composition of exports: Asian exports of top Thai exports (percent of exports, 1996)

Description	Thailand	Korea	Indonesia	Malaysia	Philippines
Radio/amplifier parts	4.8	3.8	2.0	7.3	2.5
Semiconductors	5.3	15.4	0.3	18.0	9.1
Footwear	3.7	1.0	4.3	0.1	0.9
Calculation machines	4.6	0.7	0.5	6.6	1.0
Electric switches, relays, etc.	1.7	1.1	0.4	1.9	0.8
Computers and accessories	5.1	3.2	0.4	2.9	1.5
Jewelry	1.7	0.3	0.7	0.6	0.2
Televisions	1.7	1.5	0.1	3.0	0.4
Refrigerators	1.5	0.4	0.1	1.4	0.0
Shellfish	4.3	0.3	2.3	0.2	1.7
Rubber	4.4	0.0	4.2	2.2	0.2
Fish	1.4	0.2	0.2	0.1	0.7
Rice	3.4	0.0	0.0	0.0	0.0
Total	44.3	27.9	15.4	44.4	18.8

Source: Statistics Canada, World Trade Database.

We have examined the incidence of contagion and some of the channels through which fundamentals-based contagion can arise. Some of the arrangements that have linked countries together are quite old – trade in goods and services and strong ties through a common bank lender and can help shed light on earlier crises clusters, like the debt crisis of the early 1980s. Indeed, trade links and exposure to a common creditor appear to help explain the observed historical pattern of contagion. Yet, one should be cautious about extrapolation, as some of the channels through which shocks are transmitted are relatively new to emerging markets. After all, less than a decade ago there were only a handful of mutual funds that had any exposure to emerging markets to begin with. Cross-market hedges have become commonplace in emerging market trades. Clearly, these financial market channels need to be better understood and quantified if policymakers around the globe hope to develop a "financial architecture" that makes countries less crisis-prone and susceptible to contagion.

Notes

* This paper was prepared for the Duke University conference "Globalization, Capital Market Crises and Economic Reform." The authors wish to thank Patrick Conway, Alan Drazen, Aart Kray, Gian Maria Milesi-Ferretti, Vincent Reinhart, Roberto Rigobon, Jorge Roldos, Andres Velasco, two anonymous referees and conference participants at Arizona State University; the Bank of England, University of California, San Diego, and the World Bank for useful comments and discussion; Sergio Schmukler for kindly providing the data on mutual funds and Ian Anderson, Mark Giancola and Ioannis Tokatlidis for superb research assistance.
1 Eichengreen *et al.* (1996), Glick and Rose (1998) and Wolf (1997) all examined the scope for trade links and links through common macroeconomic fundamentals that may lead investors to classify countries similarly.
2 See Gerlach and Smets (1995) and Corsetti *et al.* (1998).
3 As a story of fundamentals-based contagion, of course, this explanation does not speak of the fact that central banks often go to great lengths to avoid the devaluation in the first place.
4 European banks had also increased their exposure to Asia in recent years.
5 See Frankel and Schmukler (1998) and Baig and Goldfajn (1998).
6 Problems with limited data availability, particularly for financial indicators, precluded us from including countries in Sub-Saharan Africa. A full description of the data set is presented in Kaminsky and Reinhart (1999).
7 See Kaminsky and Reinhart (1999) for details.
8 For a detailed discussion of the construction of the adjusted noise-to-signal ratio see Kaminsky and Reinhart (1999).
9 See Calvo and Reinhart (1996).
10 Hence, we have the following two by two matrix,

	Crisis occurs in the following 24 months	*No crisis occurs in the following 24 months*
A signal is issued	A	B
No signal is issued	C	D

A "perfect" indicator would only have entries in cells A and D and a noise-to-signal ratio (calculated as [B/(B + D)/A(A + C)]) of zero.

11 The noise-to-signals ratios for the indicators are given in Kaminsky and Reinhart (1999).

12 The crisis-elsewhere criteria does not distinguish between being in a particular cohort or outside it.

13 These bilateral trade statistics are not reported in the tables but are available from the authors.

References

Baig, T. and I. Goldfajn, 1998, *Financial Market Contagion in the Asian Crisis* (Washington, DC, International Monetary Fund).

Calvo, G.A.,1998, *Capital Market Contagion and Recession: An Explanation of the Russian Virus* (College Park, Maryland, University of Maryland).

Calvo, G.A. and E. Mendoza, 1998, *Rational Herd Behavior and the Globalization of Securities Markets* (College Park, Maryland, University of Maryland).

Calvo, S. and C.M. Reinhart, 1996, "Capital Flows to Latin America: Is There Evidence of Contagion Effects?" In: G.A. Calvo, M. Goldstein and E. Hochreitter, eds, *Private Capital Flows to Emerging Markets* (Washington, DC: Institute for International Economics).

Corsetti, G., P. Pesenti, N. Roubini and C. Tille, 1998, *Structural Links and Contagion Effects in the Asian Crisis: A Welfare Based Approach* (New York, New York University).

Eichengreen, B., A. Rose and C. Wyplosz, 1996, Contagious Currency Crises, National Bureau of Economic Research Working Paper No. 5681.

Frankel, J.A. and S. Schmukler, 1998, "Crisis Contagion, and Country Funds: Effects on East Asia and Latin America," Center for Pacific Basin Monetary and Economic Studies WP No. PB96-04, Federal Reserve Bank of San Francisco, September 1996." In: R. Glick, ed., *Managing Capital Flows and Exchange Rates: Lessons from the Pacific Rim*, (Cambridge, Cambridge University Press).

Gerlach, S. and S. Frank, 1995, "Contagious Speculative Attacks," *European Journal of Political Economy*, 11, 5–63.

Glick, R. and A. Rose, 1998, *Contagion and Trade: Why are Currency Crises Regional?* (Berkeley, University of California).

Kaminsky, G.L., 1998, Currency and Banking Crises: The Early Warnings of Distress, International Finance Discussion Paper No. 629, October, Board of Governors of the Federal Reserve System.

Kaminsky, G.L. and C.M. Reinhart, 1999, "The Twin Crises: The Causes of Banking and Balance-of-Payments Problems," *American Economic Review* 89(3), 473–500.

Kaminsky, G.L. and S. Schmukler, 1999, What Triggers Market Jitters? A Chronicle of the Asian Crisis, International Finance Discussion Paper No. 634, April, Board of Governors of the Federal Reserve System.

Kodres, L. and M. Pritsker, 1998, A Rational Expectations Model of Financial Contagion, Board of Governors of the Federal Reserve System, mimeo, October.

Wolf, H.C., 1997, Regional Contagion Effects in Emerging Markets, Working Papers in International Economics, G-97-03, Princeton University.

20 What caused the Asian crisis?*

Peter G. Warr

Introduction

Over the decade or so ending in the mid-1990s, the East Asian region was the fastest growing in the world. Metaphors like 'miracle economies', 'dragons', 'tigers' and so forth were widely used to characterise the extraordinary success of these economies. By 1998, these earlier descriptions seemed irrelevant, even somewhat embarrassing. Countries previously lauded as superstars of economic performance had suffered unprecedented financial and banking crises and now languished under severe recessions, in some cases requiring international assistance, including extensive International Monetary Fund (IMF) programmes, to assist their recovery. But despite the intense interest in the Asian 'miracle' economies, the crises of 1997 and the depth of the recessions that resulted astonished almost all observers (Bhagwati, 2001; Stiglitz, 2001).

This chapter focuses on the three most prominent cases: Thailand, Indonesia and Korea. Each of these countries was an outstanding economic performer prior to the financial crises of 1997. By 1998, each was in deep recession, having abandoned its fixed, or almost fixed exchange rate policy prior to the crises in favour of a floating exchange rate after it, but with a very much depreciated currency. Moreover, having previously been considered examples of macroeconomic management that other developing countries might emulate, all three were now subject to stringent and humiliating IMF supervision.[1] What caused the dramatic change?

The Asian crisis had three components:

(i) a *currency crisis*, a rapid outflow of financial capital in anticipation of a possible currency depreciation, inducing depletion of reserves, and forcing a radical change of policy – in this case abandonment of fixed exchange rates in favour of floating rates during a period of loss of confidence;

* Helpful discussions with Prema-chandra Athukorala, Bhanupong Nidhiprabha and David Vines are gratefully acknowledged. The author is responsible for all defects.

(ii)   a *financial crisis*, a collapse of domestic financial institutions induced by the currency depreciations and high domestic interest rates, which resulted from the currency floats; and

(iii) an *economic crisis*, a contraction of output causing a loss of government revenue, loss of employment and consequent loss of household incomes, producing serious hardship for large numbers of people.

The currency crisis occurred first. The financial crisis resulted directly from it and the economic crisis arose from the combined effects of both. In the absence of the currency crisis, the other two would not have occurred. Accordingly, explaining the currency crisis is the focus of this chapter.

The literature provides two rival depictions of the causes of the currency crisis. The most common is the *contagion* theory. According to this description, Thailand experienced a financial panic, due to such factors as corrupt government and corporate practices, inadequately supervised banks and venal currency speculators. Confidence in the currency and banking system collapsed, capital flight resulted, provoking a float of the Thai currency and a drastic decline in its market value. Investors who had not gotten out in time were ruined. These events led to a loss of confidence in the prospects of other East Asian countries. International investors and fund managers lumped all of the various East Asian countries into a common conceptual category, such that neighbouring countries, with otherwise perfectly healthy economies, suffered the same loss of confidence that had just devastated Thailand, with similar results.

The 'contagion' theory draws on the analogy with a viral infection, which spreads through the air unpredictably. There is no defence, except through defensive measures like capital controls. The implication is that unless the Thai crisis could have been anticipated, there was no way to predict the crises that other countries would suffer. It was only the contagion that came from elsewhere, in this case Thailand, which caused their problems. That is, the crises in countries other than Thailand were not predicted because they were inherently non-predictable in terms of the economic fundamentals of these countries, with the possible exception of capital controls (see for instance, Das, 2000).

Many leading economists hold views close to this. For instance, Bhagwati (1998) writes that 'none of the Asian economies that were hit [by the crisis] had any serious fundamental problems that justified the panic that set in to reverse the entire huge capital inflows [and] ... [T]he only explanation that accounts for the massive net [capital] outflows is panic and herd behaviour'. Similarly, according to Tobin (1998, p. 353), the recent Asian example shows that 'countries can suffer liquidity crises through no fault of their own'. Radelet and Sachs (1998) infer that 'the crisis was triggered by dramatic swings in creditors' expectations about the behavior of other creditors, thereby creating a self-fulfilling – although possibly individually rational – financial panic' (p. 43). Economists belonging to the 'statist' school of thought on East Asian development have also been attracted to the panic theory in their attempts to justify state-engineered 'guided lending' in some countries (particularly in Korea) during the period leading up to the crisis (see for instance, Chang *et al.*, 1998; Wade, 1998).

A defect in this theory is that it attempts to explain how Thailand's crisis was exported to others – through 'contagion' – but it does not provide a coherent explanation of why Thailand's crisis occurred. Such factors as corruption, poor bank supervision and so forth, have been features of the Thai economy for decades (Pasuk and Baker, 2002). Why they should produce a crisis in 1997 and not earlier is left unexplained by the 'contagion' account. In any case, the implication is that Thailand's crisis was caused by Thai-specific factors quite different from the 'contagion', which transmitted it to neighbouring countries.

A second defect is that it is not apparent why investors would be so ignorant as to assume that *all* countries of a particular region were similar. In fact, not all East Asian economies suffered crises, and the presence or absence of capital controls did not seem a complete explanation for the differences. Taiwan, China, Singapore and India, while very different, did not experience the same financial panics as Thailand, Indonesia, Korea, Malaysia and the Philippines? If the contagion theory was correct, why did some of Thailand's neighbours succumb to the contagion while others did not? At best, the 'contagion' theory seems incomplete.

An alternative is the *vulnerability* theory. According to this account, some economies were vulnerable to a crisis because of fundamental economic features, which predisposed them to severe crises *if* they were subject to shocks, which initiated the expectation of an exchange rate devaluation. The concept of vulnerability does not mean that a crisis *will* occur, only that if something happens to undermine confidence the result may be severe. The analogy with a tightrope walker may be helpful. If the rope is a few inches above the ground, then a slight loss of balance due, say, to an unexpectedly strong gust of wind, is easily accommodated. But if the rope is high above the ground – a state of vulnerability – then any loss of balance could be disastrous.

There is a large difference between the two extreme forms of the contagion and vulnerability interpretations. The vulnerability account implies that observable features of economies may leave them more or less susceptible to crises. The most extreme versions would say that if high levels of vulnerability develop then a crisis is inevitable and any random event could actually provoke it. Extreme forms of the contagion theory deny, or at least dismiss, the importance of observable signs of vulnerability. But intermediate variants are possible and in general these seem more reasonable than either extreme.

Most of the literature dealing specifically with East Asia has taken an intermediate position of one kind or another, but very little evidence for vulnerability has generally been identified. For example, Hill (1999) writes that 'it needs to be emphasised that the majority of pre-crisis economic and financial indicators in the crisis economies looked quite healthy' and mentions levels of saving, fiscal balances, inflation, current account deficits, debt/GDP ratios and levels of international reserves, adding that 'in explaining the crisis it is important to distinguish between the trigger and the subsequent contagion effects' (p. 8).

Similarly, in the case of Indonesia, McLeod (1998) emphasises that in macroeconomic terms the Indonesian economy was seemingly performing well prior to the crisis. He reviews various macroeconomic outcomes such as declining levels of inflation, declining budget deficits, rising levels of exports and imports and levels of total capital inflow exceeding current account deficits, leading to increasing foreign exchange reserves. McLeod (1998) concludes that 'at the macroeconomic level, then, there was little or no sign of the turmoil that was to emerge' (p. 32).

These descriptions of the crisis, and many like them, are not necessarily averse to the notion that the country concerned was vulnerable to a currency crisis, but they typically fail to identify any specific indication of vulnerability in the pre-crisis period. The macroeconomic variables which are cited seem to have been selected from an endless possible list and it is generally unclear what principles have guided the selection. The problem is analytical. In the absence of a conceptual framework within which vulnerability has a clear meaning, it is hardly surprising that none is found.

Intermediate explanations for the crisis, which are closest to the contagion end of the spectrum generally place principal emphasis on international speculators, irrational behaviour of hedge fund managers, unstable international capital markets and so forth. The intermediate variants closest to the vulnerability end of the spectrum relegate the contagion story to the role of one possible form of trigger, but only one possible form. While a trigger may be required to provoke a crisis, the vulnerability perspective focuses primary attention on the economic conditions that may turn such a trigger into a crisis in one type of economy but not in another.

But what if all crises were different, with vulnerability taking different and unpredictable forms each time? If so, the 'vulnerability' account may not be particularly useful; there may be no way to know in advance which forms of vulnerability to look for. The sources of vulnerability could only be discovered ex post. It is therefore important to determine whether the sources of vulnerability to a currency crisis are relatively stable over time.

The degree to which the vulnerability argument can be sustained has considerable policy relevance. If clear evidence can be established of increasing vulnerability prior to the crisis itself, using information that was in principle available at the time, this will mean that the signs of growing danger were available but insufficiently noticed. This will in turn mean that had these signs been properly heeded, policy actions, which may have averted the worst effects of the crisis could have been taken but were not. To the extent that this is true, the immense social cost of the crisis is in part attributable to an analytical failure, a failure on the part of government officials, international institutions and independent researchers, to draw proper attention to the signs of growing vulnerability and the danger that they indicated.

The intermediate forms which are closest to the pure 'contagion' end of the spectrum place principle emphasis on international speculators, irrational behaviour of hedge fund managers, unstable international capital markets and so forth. The intermediate variants closest to the pure 'vulnerability' end or the spectrum relegate the 'contagion' story to the role of one possible form of 'trigger', but only one possible form. While a trigger may be required to provoke a crisis, the vulnerability perspective focuses primary attention on the economic conditions that may turn such a trigger into a crisis in one type of economy but not in another. But what are these conditions that make an economy more or less vulnerable to a crisis?

The degree to which the vulnerability argument can be sustained has considerable policy relevance. If clear evidence can be established of increasing vulnerability prior to the crisis itself, using information that was in principle available at the time, this will mean that the signs of growing danger were available but insufficiently noticed. This will in turn mean that had these signs been properly heeded, policy actions, which may have averted the worse effects of the crisis could have been taken but were not. To the extent that this is true, the immense social cost of the crisis is in part attributable to an analytical failure, a failure on the part of government officials, international institutions and independent researchers like academics, to draw proper attention to the signs of growing vulnerability and the danger that they represented. That is what this chapter will argue.

The next section of the chapter addresses this question and identifies three conditions of vulnerability. The 'Implementation' section asks whether the vulnerability account fits with the experience of Thailand, Indonesia and Korea.[2] In particular, it asks whether it might have been possible to identify the conditions of vulnerability in these three economies *prior* to the crisis itself. The 'Evidence' section explains the empirical procedures adopted in the chapter and the final section concludes.

Theory

A currency crisis occurs when market participants lose confidence in the currency of a particular country and seek to escape assets denominated in that currency. Because investors try to avoid short-term capital losses, they exit from countries where they expect that a large nominal exchange rate depreciation will soon take place. Thus, the fundamental concerns governing their action are the likelihood that the currency would depreciate should capital inflows reverse, and the possible magnitude of that depreciation. Under what conditions might asset owners make a radical upward revision in their assessment of the probability of a large currency depreciation?[3]

Vulnerability versus trigger

Vulnerability means susceptibility to a currency crisis. The concept must be understood in relation to the concept of a *trigger*. As Dornbusch (1997, p. 21) notes, '[V]ulnerability means that *if* something goes wrong, then suddenly a lot goes wrong' (emphasis added). A state of vulnerability by itself does not give rise to a currency crisis. There needs to be a certain disturbance (a trigger) that will push a vulnerable situation into an actual collapse. Some likely disturbances are policy errors such as a minor devaluation in the context of a significant and persistent overvaluation of the real exchange rate, failure to implement a promised crucial policy reform, or simply a contagion – investor panic spreading from events in a neighbouring crisis country. Since an actual currency crisis requires both vulnerability and a trigger, analysis of vulnerability alone could not be expected to enable one to predict the timing of a currency crisis.

Determinants of vulnerability

The central focus of the concept of vulnerability is that owners of assets wish, on the one hand, to obtain high returns from these assets and, on the other, to avoid the risk of capital losses. A central danger in terms of possible capital loss is a large exchange rate depreciation in the country where the assets are located, when the assets are priced in terms of the local currency. Owners of internationally mobile assets are constantly revising their assessments of the probabilities of large exchange rate movements, which may affect the capital values of their assets. Vulnerability to capital flight arises when there is an increase in the probability that owners of internationally mobile assets will form the expectation of a large nominal depreciation. Under what conditions might relatively small external shocks cause asset owners to make a radical upward revision in their assessment of the probability of a large devaluation?

We identify three such determinants of a possible large revision of expectations. The analysis builds on the discussion of the Mexican crisis of 1994 and its aftermath provided in Sachs *et al.* (1996). These authors point out that some Latin American economies, notably Brazil and Argentina, apparently suffered from significant contagion effects resulting from Mexico's crisis whereas others, notably Colombia and Chile did not. Drawing in part on the work of Krugman (1996), Sachs *et al.* identify three variables which, according to them, help explain the differences in these country experiences.

Suppose that a country is maintaining a pegged exchange rate and that a substantial and unexpected outflow of capital suddenly occurs – due to some trigger causing a loss of confidence in the capacity of the central bank to maintain the exchange rate. Can the peg be defended? First, we note the accounting identity:

$$\Delta R = K - C \tag{1}$$

the change in the level of reserves (a flow) is equal to the net balance on capital account, K, plus C, the net balance on current account (both flows). Suppose, for simplicity, that the current account was initially in deficit, the capital account was initially in surplus and that the two magnitudes were approximately equal, implying that the net change in the level of reserves was zero. Starting from this position, a capital outflow now implies a lower level of the net balance on capital account. If nothing else changes, the level of reserves must fall.

Three policy responses are now possible. First, the authorities could defend the currency and permit the level of reserves to decline until confidence is restored. Whether this is possible depends on the adequacy of the level of reserves in relation to the possible size of the capital outflow. In particular, the smaller the level of reserves (a stock) relative to the volume of short-term foreign liabilities (also a stock), the lower is the credibility of this policy response. If reserves are inadequate to meet a sudden outflow caused by an investor panic and the government still wishes to maintain the exchange rate peg, then it is necessary to ameliorate the loss of reserves by containing the right-hand side of the above identity – the negative value of the net balance on capital account plus the net balance on current account.

The second possible response is an increase in the interest rate. This may be expected to ameliorate the downward pressure on the level of reserves in two ways. First, it helps maintain relative expected returns to investment in the given country by compensating for the potential loss of return due to (the expected) exchange rate depreciation. This reduces, and possibly reverses, the net deficit on capital account, which resulted from the investor panic. Second, it may bring about a reduction in domestic absorption (private consumption and investment), which in turn reduces the negative value of the net balance on current account.

But the feasibility of using interest rate policy in the event of a speculative outflow depends on the health of the domestic financial institutions. If these institutions have been operating with unsound (fragile) asset portfolios characterised by high non-performing loans, low levels of capital adequacy and other related weaknesses, an interest rate increase is likely to engineer a domestic credit squeeze, bank failure and business bankruptcies leading to economic collapse. Therefore, the more fragile the banking system, the less scope exists for the government to use interest rate policy to defend the currency and the less credible is the policy option of raising interest rates to defend the currency.

If the solution of increasing interest rates cannot be adopted, then the required adjustment has to come through the third possible response – a depreciation of the real exchange rate, by which we mean an increase in the domestic prices of tradables relative to non-tradables. Real exchange rate depreciation facilitates a domestic expenditure switch against tradables and towards non-tradables, and thus accommodates a reduction in the current account deficit. Maintaining the existing exchange rate peg means that the nominal prices of tradables will remain roughly constant. A real depreciation therefore requires a decline in the nominal prices of non-tradables and this will require a monetary and/or fiscal contraction, and presumably a recession, depending on the downward flexibility of non-tradables' prices. The required degree of real depreciation and thus the required magnitude of this recession will be greater the more appreciated is the real exchange rate relative to the level compatible with lower capital inflows.

It is important to emphasise that a steady, systematic appreciation of the real exchange rate that occurs in line with changes in underlying economic circumstances is not problematic. If a country borrows to invest and/or attracts significant foreign direct investment, the resulting capital inflow naturally strengthens the real exchange rate – which is the expected effect of an inward transfer. An appreciation can also be a reflection of deep reforms that open up large and lasting opportunities for economic expansion. The 'Balassa–Samuelson' effect – long-term improvement in productivity that normally has a greater price lowering effect on tradables than on non-tradables – can be another factor. Provided these events are permanent rather than temporary, real appreciation arising from them should not cause concern about the macroeconomic health of the economy.

A persistent, excessive appreciation (exchange rate misalignment), that is, an appreciation caused by temporary, reversible events, is what bothers investors and may induce a run on the currency. Such an appreciation implies that the authorities may be unable to defend the currency successfully in the event of a speculative capital outflow because the required real depreciation consistent with lower capital inflows may be too large. In sum, the relevant question is not the actual *level* of the real exchange rate, but its *sustainability*. There is no unique benchmark against which to judge the current level of the real exchange rate. On the other hand, a real exchange that is far higher than ever before and which continues to appreciate is suspicious even when past major reforms and access to capital markets have justified some real appreciation.

The discussion so far points to three key indicators that may help in assessing a country's vulnerability to a currency crisis:

- adequacy of reserves relative to the stock of volatile (mobile) capital,
- financial sector fragility, and
- real exchange rate misalignment.

A state of *vulnerability* – a situation where there is reason to doubt the ability of the country to defend the currency in the event of a sudden loss of confidence on the part of the holders of internationally mobile financial assets – can be created by one or a combination of these factors. Does this way of looking at things help explain the crises in Thailand, Indonesia and Korea? Yes.

Implementation

There is no unique way of implementing the above concepts empirically. Further discussion is thus needed on the empirical procedures adopted in this study.

Adequacy of reserves

What surprised observers of the Asian crisis, as well as most of its participants, was the rate at which very large volumes of funds could be presented at central banks for conversion into foreign exchange and thereby the rapidity with which seemingly adequate reserves could be placed upon unexpected pressure. The standard measures of 'reserve adequacy', which focus on the capacity of reserves to finance imports has nothing to do with this concept. What presumably requires attention is the stock of funds, which can be presented at short notice against reserves, that is, the volume of volatile capital.

Returning to the balance of payments identity given by equation (1) above, the capital account balance reflects the following components: foreign direct investment (F); equity, consisting of stock market purchases (S); debt instruments (D), such as bonds; bank credit – long term (B_L) and short term (B_S); non-resident bank accounts (N) other, unrecorded items (U).

As normally conceived, the elements of the above list which are 'non-volatile' in the short run consist of F, B_L and possibly some components of U. The other components are considered more volatile, but these assignments are ultimately empirical matters. Suppose we divide K in equation (1) into two components: volatile and non-volatile. For reasons, which will become apparent we use the notation

$$K = \Delta K^* + \Delta K^0 \qquad (2)$$

where ΔK^* and ΔK^0 denote the changes in the *stocks* of volatile and non-volatile foreign capital, respectively. Rearranging equation (1),

$$C + \Delta K^0 = \Delta R - \Delta K^* \qquad (3)$$

The right side of this equation may be conceived as the change in the vulnerability of reserves to capital flight. It is apparent that the right side may be negative even though reserves are rising. For example, let there be a current account deficit of 80 ($C = -80$) and a capital inflow of 100. Then $\Delta R = 20$. Now suppose this capital inflow is equally divided between volatile and non-volatile components. Then $\Delta R - \Delta K^* = -30$ and reserves have become more vulnerable to attack motivated by capital flight.

Large current account deficits are not necessarily required for vulnerability to increase. Focusing on the left-hand side of equation (3), the point is the size of the current account deficit compared with the volume of non-volatile capital inflow. When the former exceeds the latter, vulnerability increases. If this situation continues for long enough, the accumulated *stock* of volatile capital may become large relative to the stock of international reserves, making reserves vulnerable to capital outflow. To obtain measures of vulnerability based on this line of reasoning what is required is calculations of the accumulated *stock* of volatile capital, which may then be compared with the volume of reserves.

Except for reserves, where data on stocks is published, the stocks described above must be assembled by the researcher. Balance of payments data for each country are used for this purpose. The exercise is commenced a decade before the first data point shown. The magnitude of capital stocks in this initial year is assumed to be zero and net flow data are used to assemble the stocks shown, using the inventory method. Figures 20.1 through 20.3 show the results of applying these concepts to the balance of payments data of Thailand, Indonesia and Korea.

Financial sector fragility

Building upon the theoretical discussion of vulnerability in the previous section, two measures of financial sector fragility are used in this study. First, the ratio of total loans outstanding from the banking system to GDP is used as a measure of exposure of the banking system to increased interest rates. As the loan/GDP ratio rises, the average quality of loans may be expected to fall. An increase in interest

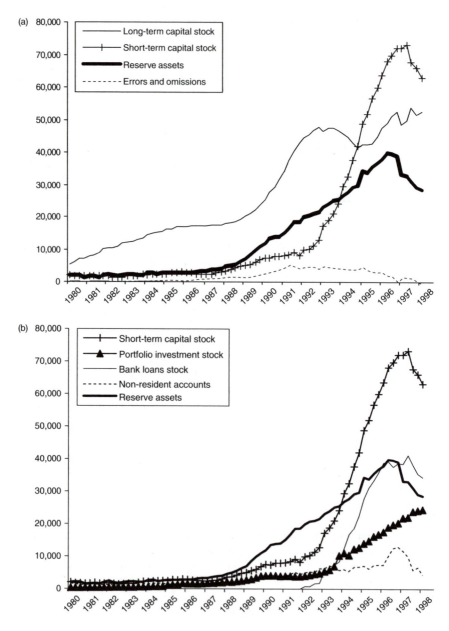

Figure 20.1 (a) Thailand: stocks of long- and short-term capital and international reserves, 1980–97. (b) Thailand: components of short-term capital stocks and international reserves, 1980–97.

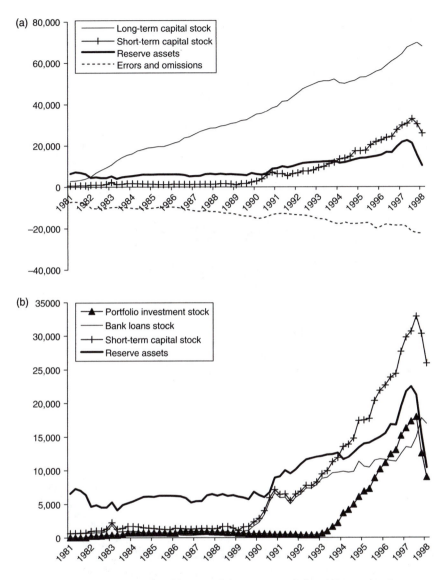

Figure 20.2 (a) Indonesia: stocks of long- and short-term capital and international reserves, 1981–97. (b) Indonesia: components of short-term capital stocks and international reserves, 1981–97.

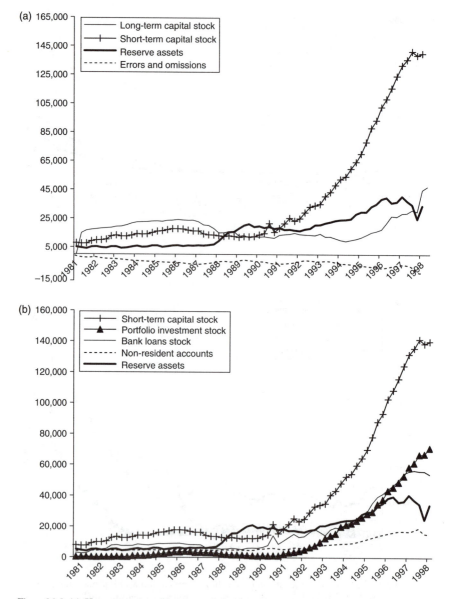

Figure 20.3 (a) Korea: stocks of long- and short-term capital and international reserves, 1981–97. (b) Korea: components of short-term capital stocks and international reserves, 1981–97.

rates will bankrupt weaker borrowers leaving them unable to service their loans. If the average quality of loans has deteriorated, as through a prolonged credit boom, this will leave the banking system exposed to higher interest rates because large numbers of bankrupt borrowers may make the banks themselves insolvent. Second, the ratio of foreign liabilities to total loans is used as a measure of exchange rate exposure of the banking system. As this ratio increases, so does the exposure of the banking system to an exchange rate depreciation because such a depreciation will raise the costs of servicing foreign loans relative to bank revenues. All data come from central bank sources for the respective countries.

Real exchange rates

The literature talks about two types of measures of the real exchange rate: (i) measures of the relative prices of traded to non-traded goods within the country; and (ii) measures of the prices at which that country's traded goods can exchange internationally compared with the traded goods of other countries. They are not the same. These two measures relate to two different concepts of 'competitiveness'. Measure (i) relates to the capacity of industries producing (internationally) traded commodities within Thailand to compete for resources with Thai industries, which produce goods that are non-traded. It is therefore about *domestic competitiveness*, the capacity of one type of Thai industry to compete for *resources* against other types of Thai industries. Measure (ii) is about the capacity of traded goods produced within Thailand to compete for *sales* against imperfect substitutes for them, which are produced by traded goods producers within other countries. It is therefore about *international competitiveness*.

Traded/non-traded goods relative prices

The Australian model of the balance of payments rests upon the distinction between traded and non-traded goods and services and on the different manner in which their prices are determined. Exponents of the model have demonstrated its analytical value, but empirical applications are rare. The problems are, first, that assembling indices of the prices of actual traded and non-traded goods and services is laborious and costly, and second, that the concepts of traded and non-traded goods and services – also referred to as tradables and non-tradables, respectively – are abstractions.

For an index of 'tradables' prices we turn to wholesale price data using commodities which correspond approximately to the analytical category of traded commodities – ones which enter into international trade and whose domestic prices are determined by exchange rates, international prices and any domestic taxes, which may apply to them. The index is formed by using the weights applying to these commodities in the construction of the wholesale price index. 'Non-tradables' prices are assembled similarly using consumer price series and aggregating the resulting price data using the weights applying to these

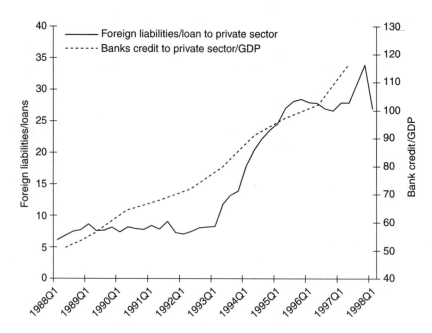

Figure 20.4 Thailand: bank exposure, 1988–97.

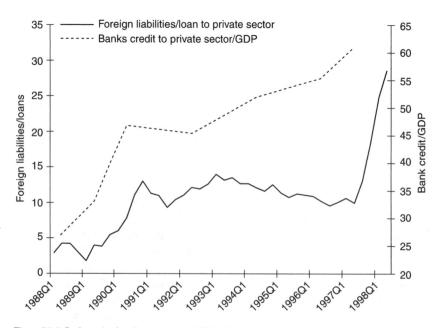

Figure 20.5 Indonesia: bank exposure, 1988–97.

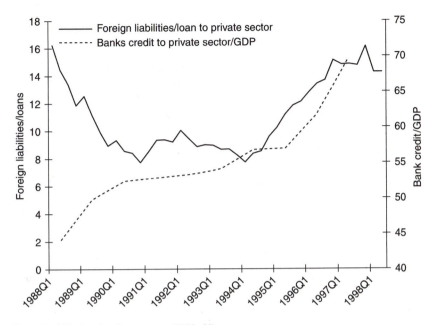

Figure 20.6 Korea: bank exposure, 1988–97.

commodities in the construction of the consumer price index. It must be recognized that assigning actual commodities to each of these categories always involves a degree of arbitrariness. The results are presented in the series labelled 'relative price' in Figures 20.4 through 20.6.

Competitiveness indices

We shall also present data on other measures of real exchange rates, also commonly called measures of 'competitiveness'. All three are based not on domestic relative prices but on nominal exchange rates adjusted by foreign and domestic price levels. The general form of these measures is

$$E^R = EP^*/P \tag{4}$$

where E denotes the nominal exchange rate, measured in units of domestic currency per unit of foreign currency, P^* is a measure of foreign prices, measured in foreign currency, and P is a measure of domestic prices, measured in domestic currency. The measures chosen for P^* vary. Some studies use foreign wholesale prices while others use foreign consumer prices and the foreign country weights used to aggregate them also vary, including domestic export shares to these countries, import shares and even 'trade' shares, the sum of exports and imports. The measures used for *P* also vary, some measures using consumer prices, others wholesale prices.

The two most commonly used in the literature are labelled the 'IMF/World Bank Index', the export share weighted sum of trading partner consumer price indices, each multiplied by the bilateral exchange rate, divided by the domestic consumer price index; the 'Morgan–Guaranty Index', where the two consumer price indices described above are replaced by foreign and domestic wholesale price indices, respectively).

Finally, the series labelled 'Preferred Index' replaces foreign consumer prices in the numerator of the 'IMF/World Bank RER Index' with foreign wholesale prices, but it retains the domestic wholesale price index in the numerator. This index is preferable to either of the other two as a proxy for traded goods prices relative to non-traded goods prices. The reason is that the share of traded goods in wholesale price indices is thought to be higher than its share in consumer price indices. Thus, the numerator of this index, the export share weighted sum of foreign wholesale price indices, each multiplied by the bilateral exchange rate, may be taken as a (very rough) proxy for domestic traded goods prices and the denominator, the domestic consumer price index, may be taken as a (very rough) index of domestic non-traded goods prices. For the reasons demonstrated in Warr (1986), all three of these exchange rate-based measures, but especially the first two, may be expected to understate the magnitude of a real appreciation, compared with changes in the domestic relative prices of traded goods to non-traded goods.

Evidence

Adequacy of reserves

The data for Thailand show that the short-term capital increased relative to reserves throughout the boom decade preceding the crisis but especially after 1993.[4] By 1994, the total stock exceeded the volume of Thailand's international reserves and by 1997 was roughly double the level of reserves. These facts are by now relatively uncontroversial. Figures 20.2 and 20.3 show that virtually the same circumstances applied to Indonesia and Korea. The crisis was preceded by a large increase in the volume of short-term capital relative to reserves. The adequacy of reserves declined markedly in the years preceding the crisis in each of these countries.

Financial sector fragility

Figures 20.5–20.7 show that the crisis in each of the crisis-affected countries was preceded by a domestic credit boom. In all but Indonesia there was a large increase in foreign liabilities relative to total loans. The vulnerability of the banking sectors to interest rate increases had risen markedly.

Real exchange rates

In each of the crisis-affected countries the real exchange rate, properly measured, appreciated significantly over the boom period preceding the crisis.[5] Do external exchange rate changes explain this outcome? The question arises because it is now well understood that the depreciation since 1995 of the Japanese yen and other currencies relative to the US dollar meant that any currency pegged to the dollar would suffer a real appreciation and each of the crisis-affected countries was indeed pegging to the dollar. But the answer is no.

The real appreciations within Thailand, Indonesia and Korea demonstrated in Figures 20.7–20.9 were not confined to the period since 1995, when the US dollar was appreciating. A large real appreciation within Thailand can also be seen in the first five years of the 1990s when the dollar was *depreciating* relative to the yen and other currencies. Much of the real appreciation from 1990 to mid-1997 was already evident by mid-1994, well before the appreciation of the US dollar began. External exchange rate changes were clearly relevant, but they were not the main causal factor.

The principal cause of the real appreciations indicated resided in forces operating *within* the Thai, Indonesian and Korean economies – not external exchange rate adjustments. A principal source was the demand effects of very large foreign capital inflows, only partially sterilised. The effect of the real appreciations was that it undermined the competitiveness of traded goods industries in these

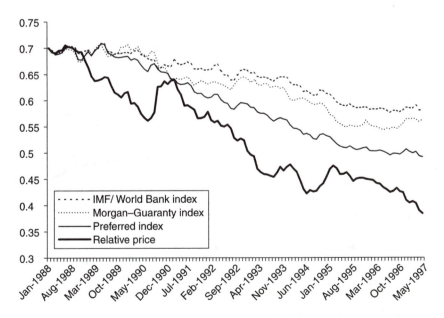

Figure 20.7 Real exchange rate indices: Thailand, 1988–97.

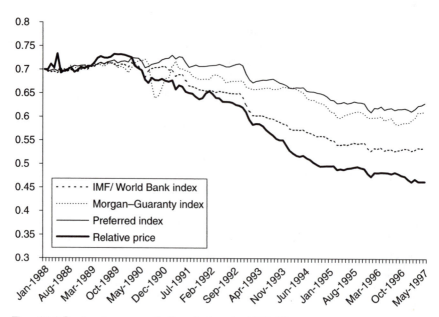

Figure 20.8 Real exchange rate indices: Indonesia, 1988–97.

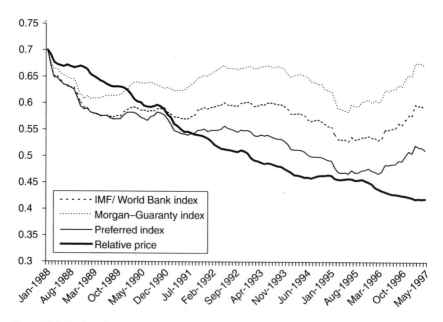

Figure 20.9 Real exchange rate indices: Korea, 1988–97.

countries, meaning their capacity to attract resources within the domestic economy in competition with non-traded goods sectors.

Conclusions

In an earlier paper (Warr, 1999) it was argued that Thailand was vulnerable to a currency crisis by the mid-1990s. This vulnerability took the form of: (a) build-up of a large stock of mobile capital relative to reserves; (b) development of a highly exposed banking sector; and (c) a large real exchange rate appreciation since the late 1980s. The key concept of vulnerability builds on earlier work by Dornbusch and others. The present chapter focuses on the three IMF bailout countries – Thailand, Indonesia and Korea – and shows that by 1996 exactly these three conditions applied to *all three*.

The significance of this finding is that a focus on 'contagion' as the cause of the Asian crisis is unsatisfactory because it misses two basic facts: (1) some Asian countries suffered crises while others did not; and (2) those which did exhibited the very same vulnerability that characterised Thailand in 1997. The policy lesson is to avoid vulnerability. A first step in avoiding vulnerability is to monitor it appropriately. The analysis of this chapter provides guidance as to which variables should be included in such monitoring efforts.

Notes

1 Another East Asian country, the Philippines, was also under IMF supervision in 1998 but its experience is significantly different from the three countries discussed in this chapter. The Philippines had been a poor economic performer and under a continuous close relationship with the IMF for many years prior to 1997.
2 See also Athukorala and Warr (2002) for a further discussion of the ideas presented in this chapter and an extension of the empirical analysis to non-crisis countries.
3 Throughout the discussion we assume that the country under consideration is in an adjustable (quasi) peg exchange rate regime – a characterisation that is valid, during the period leading up to the crisis, for all countries covered in this study.
4 Warr (1999) provides an explanation for the rapid increase from 1993 onwards.
5 For a further discussion of the Korean case, see Warr (2000).

References

Athukorala, P. and P.G. Warr (2002), 'Vulnerability to a Currency Crisis: Lessons from the Asian Experience', *The World Economy*, 25, 23–57.

Bhagwati, J. (1998), 'Asian Financial Crisis Debate: Why? How Severe?', paper presented at the international conference *Managing the Asian Financial Crisis: Lessons and Challenges*, Asian Strategic leadership Institute and rating Agency Malaysia, 2–3 November 1998 Kuala Lumpur.

Bhagwati, J. (2001), 'The Asian Economic Crisis: What Do We Know Now?', chapter 5 in his *The Winds of the Hundred Days: How Washington Mismanaged Globalization* (Cambridge, MA: MIT Press), pp. 51–60.

Chang, H.-J., H.J. Park and C.G. Yoo (1998), 'Interpreting the Korean Crisis: Financial Liberalisation, Industrial Policy and Corporate Governance', *Cambridge Journal of Economics*, 22(4), 735–746.

Das, Dilip K. (2000), *Asian Crisis: Distilling Critical Lessons*, United Nations Conference on Trade and Development (UNCTAD), Geneva. Discussion Paper No. 152. December 2000. 33 pp.

Dornbusch, R. (1997), 'A Thai–Mexico Primer: Lessons for Outmaneuvering a Financial Meltdown', *The International Economy*, September/October, 20–23 and 55.

Hill, H. (1999), 'An Overview of the Issues' in H.W. Arndt and Hal Hill (eds), *Southeast Asia's Economic Crisis: Origins, Lessons, and the Way Forward*, Institute of Southeast Asian Studies, Singapore, pp. 1–15.

Krugman, P. (1996), 'Are Currency Crises Self-fulfilling', in B.S. Bernanke, and J. Rotenberg (eds), *NBER Macroeconomics Annual*, MIT Press, Cambridge and London, pp. 345–378.

McLeod, R. (1998), 'Indonesia', in Ross H. McLeod and Ross Garnaut (eds), *East Asia in Crisis*, Routledge, London, pp. 31–48.

Pasuk P. and C. Baker (2002), *Thailand: Economy and Politics*, 2nd edn, Oxford University Press, Kuala Lumpur.

Radelet, S. and J. Sachs (1998), 'The East Asian Financial Crisis: Diagnosis, Remedies, Prospects', *Brookings Papers on Economic Activity*, 2, 1–89.

Sachs, J.D., A. Tornell and A. Velasco (1996), 'Financial Crises in Emerging Markets: The Lessons from 1995', *Brookings Papers on Economic Activity*, 1, 147–215.

Stiglitz, J. (2001). 'From Miracle to Crisis to Recovery: Lessons from Four Decades of East Asian Experience', in J.E. Stiglitz and S. Yusuf (eds), *Rethinking the East Asian Miracle*, Oxford University Press, New York, pp. 509–526.

Tobin, J. (1998), 'Asian Financial Crisis', *Japan and the World Economy*, 10, 351–353.

Wade, R. (1998), 'From "Miracle" to Cronyism: Explaining the Great Asian Slump', *Cambridge Journal of Economics*, 22(4), 693–706.

Warr, P.G. (1986), 'Indonesia's other Dutch Disease: Economic Effects of the Petroleum Boom', in J.P. Neary and S. van Wijnbergen (eds), *Natural Resources and the Macroeconomy*, Basil Blackwell, Oxford, pp. 288–320.

Warr, P.G. (1999), 'What Happened to Thailand?', *The World Economy*, 22(7), 631–650.

Warr, P.G. (2000), 'Macroeconomic Origins of the Korean Crisis', in H. Smith (ed.), *Looking Forward: Korea' After the Economic Crisis*, Asia Pacific Press, Canberra, pp. 23–40.

21 The crisis of 1998 and the role of the central bank

David A. Marshall

Introduction and summary

A key mission of the US Federal Reserve System is to safeguard the economy against systemic financial crises. This concern with financial crises stems from a long-held belief that they are associated with declines in economic activity. In the US, there is clear evidence that financial panics and recessions are somehow related (Mishkin, 1991). In the case of the Great Depression, Bernanke (1983) argues that the disruption in financial intermediation transformed a severe down-turn into a "protracted depression." More recently, the Asian financial crisis in 1997 was followed by sharp declines in economic activity. (Indonesia, Korea, Thailand, and Malaysia all experienced two-quarter decline in gross domestic product (GDP) of over 12 percent.) This historical record has led to a pervasive belief that systemic crises in the financial sector have consequences that are far more than sectoral. Rather, they appear to affect the entire economy, perhaps through the unique role played by financial intermediation.

The most recent financial crisis in the US occurred in late summer and fall of 1998. On August 17, the Russian government devalued the ruble, defaulted on its ruble-denominated debt, and imposed a moratorium on payments to foreign creditors of Russian financial institutions. Following these actions, asset values fell precipitously in all Group of Seven (G-7) countries, and there is evidence of widespread withdrawal of liquidity from financial markets. Particularly dramatic was the near collapse and eleventh-hour recapitalization in late September of Long-Term Capital Management (LTCM), a large hedge fund.

From a US perspective, these events might be described as an "incipient" crisis, because there is little evidence of damage to Western economies. Arguably, this is because of the decisive action by the Federal Reserve (Fed) in cutting the target federal funds rate in three successive 25 basis-point moves. The second of these moves, on October 15, was particularly noteworthy, since it occurred between regularly scheduled meetings of the Federal Open Market Committee (FOMC). Intermeeting rate cuts of this type are rare; the October 15 action was the first such action since April 1994. In the next section, I provide evidence that the end of this incipient crisis coincided almost exactly with the October 15 rate cut. In particular, credit spreads abruptly narrowed on October 16 (one day after the Fed move), and stock markets in all G-7 countries started to recover a week to ten days prior to the October 15 move. (That stock markets anticipated the rate cut is no surprise. For at least a week prior to the move the financial press reported rumors of a possible intermeeting rate cut.)

The way this incipient crisis ended is somewhat puzzling. The crisis had a clear trigger: the Russian default and devaluation in mid-August. Western financial institutions were directly affected by the default if they held Russian liabilities. Furthermore, the Russian default may have signaled higher default risk for sovereign debt from other emerging or transition economies. So it is not surprising that uncertainty grew about institutions' solvency (with attendant increases in asset price volatility and credit spreads). What is puzzling is the way the crisis appears to have abated with the Fed's second rate cut. Why would the problems (both direct and informational) associated with the Russian default be reduced by a mere 50 basis-point cumulative cut in the overnight interest rate? If the crisis was associated with higher default risk of emerging-economy debt, why would the Fed's rate cut have dramatically reduced this default risk? Similarly, if the crisis was associated with an increased informational asymmetry among financial institutions, why would the 50 basis-point cut in the federal funds rate have reduced this asymmetry?

In this chapter, I argue that the crisis can be characterized as an episode of potential *coordination failure*, triggered by – but ultimately distinct from – the events in Russia. I propose a simple model of financial crises as coordination failure. The model qualitatively matches the following features typically associated with financial crises:

1   Abrupt shifts between a state of adequate liquidity provision and a state of aggregate illiquidity (the latter being a case where institutions with liquidity refuse to lend to those needing liquidity).
2   A "flight to quality," whereby institutions with funds to invest preferentially choose a low-risk, low-return asset.
3   Fear among lenders that credit quality among potential borrowers has deteriorated.
4   Real costs in economic output.
5   Sudden declines in asset values.
6   A role for the central bank's open market operations in containing the crisis.

In particular, the model provides one potential explanation for why the Fed's action on October 15, 1998, eliminated the danger of a full-blown crisis. This model contributes to the growing literature developing formal models of financial crises and financial fragility. Notable examples of these include Chang and Velasco (1998), Lagunoff and Schreft (1998), DenHaan *et al.* (1999), and Chari and Kehoe (1998, 2000).

Coordination failure can emerge in any economy where the profitability of a given agent's investment depends on the decisions of the other agents in the economy. In the model of this chapter, the possibility of coordination failure arises from the essential function of financial markets: to match potential users of capital (borrowers) with potential providers of capital (lenders) in an environment of asymmetric information. Borrowers and lenders match via a search procedure. In this model, multiple equilibria are possible. A *high-coordination equilibrium* can occur in which all lenders and all borrowers enter the match, maximizing the expected output of the economy. However, there are times when a *low-coordination equilibrium* is possible in which all good-quality (i.e. highly creditworthy) borrowers refrain from entering the match. Knowing that only poor-quality borrowers seek loans, potential lenders refuse to lend. I identify this low-coordination equilibrium with a financial crisis.

In the model, the low-coordination equilibrium cannot exist if the risk-free real interest rate is sufficiently low. This suggests a potential role for the central bank. If monetary policy can affect real interest rates, the central bank can extinguish the low-coordination equilibrium if it reduces the real interest rate sufficiently via an aggressive monetary expansion. That the Fed has the power to do so is suggested by the events of 1991–93. As I discuss in a section "Examples of central bank action: the events of 1991–93," there is evidence that banks cut back on lending activity in the early 1990s. Following a shift to a more expansionary monetary policy in mid-1991, in which the real federal funds rate fell from 2.5 percent to 0.5 percent, lending activity moved back to normal levels.

Unlike the Fed's action of 1991–93, the monetary expansion in fall 1998 was too small, and the consequent effect on real interest rates too marginal, to have a substantial direct effect on lender incentives. Rather, I interpret the intermeeting rate cut of October 15 as a signal that the Fed's *policy rule* had changed. Before the intermeeting move, market participants were uncertain whether the Fed would compromise its focus on price stability (and the associated tight money policy) even in the face of severe financial market strains. I argue that the intermeeting move was interpreted by market participants as signaling a shift to a *state-contingent* policy: focus on price stability *unless* a financial crisis becomes imminent; temporarily abandon that focus if the threat of financial crisis becomes severe. In this chapter, I formally model such a policy, and I show that, in principle, such a policy can extinguish the low-coordination equilibrium. Furthermore, if this policy is credible, it never has to be implemented: The policy itself removes the possibility of coordination failure. That is, monetary expansion is an "off-equilibrium path" that enforces the high-coordination equilibrium.

Below, I review the facts of the crisis of fall 1998, highlighting key features that I will seek to replicate in the theoretical model. Then, I describe the basic coordination failure model. Finally, I show how the central bank can avert coordination failure by implementing an appropriate and credible state-contingent monetary policy.

Brief review of the events of fall 1998

Here, I review the crisis and provide evidence for the following assertions:

1   The crisis was associated with large declines in equity values, increased volatility in financial markets, widening credit spreads, and an increased demand for US Treasury securities.

2   During the crisis, there was a reduction in available liquidity, as institutions with loanable funds reduced the volume of funds available to the market.
3   The crisis rapidly abated following the Fed's intermeeting cut in the federal funds rate on October 15, 1998.

Financial markets showed evidence of potential problems starting around mid-July 1998. However, the onset of the crisis is usually associated with the Russian devaluation and default in August 1998. This denouement was in large part forced by declining hard currency inflows over the preceding several months as oil prices fell. On August 17, Russia defaulted on its ruble-denominated public debt. At that time, this stock of debt represented $61 billion, 17 percent of Russian GDP. At the same time, Russia declared a ninety-day moratorium on all foreign obligations of Russian financial institutions. Finally, the ruble exchange rate zone was substantially widened, amounting to a de facto devaluation of 25 percent. The exchange rate zone was completely abandoned ten days later.[1] As I discuss below, Western financial markets reacted negatively to these developments. In response, the FOMC cut the federal funds rate by 25 basis points at its next regular meeting on September 29. This move by the Fed did not calm the financial markets.[2] On October 15, in an unusual intermeeting move, the FOMC made an additional 25 basis-point rate cut. Observers point to this intermeeting move as marking the end of the crisis.

The data in Figure 21.1 characterize more fully the impact of these events on Western financial markets. As shown in Figure 21.1, panel A, the US S&P 500 index peaks in mid-July 1998, with a small local peak in mid-August 1998 (vertical dashed line) following the Russian default. Thereafter, there is a sharp decline in stock values, amounting to more than 18 percent over the three months from peak to trough. The S&P 500 index bottomed out on October 8, one week before the FOMC's intermeeting rate cut on October 15 (vertical solid line). The biggest close-to-close rise of this period was from October 14 to 15. It is no surprise that the market trough occurred one week before the Fed intermeeting action, since there was speculation prior to the Fed's action that an intermeeting rate cut was likely.[3] The behavior of the federal funds futures market supports this interpretation. Through October 7, futures prices implied an expected federal funds rate through the end of October of 5.22–5.24 percent, implying little probability of a rate cut. On October 8, this expected federal funds rate dropped to 5.18 percent, which is consistent with a 50 percent probability of a quarter-point rate cut around mid-October.[4]

The behavior of stock indexes for the other six countries in the G-7 is roughly comparable to that of the US indexes. In all cases, the market peaks in mid-July, falls steeply, and starts to turn up about one week before the October 15 rate cut. The total market declines over this three-month period were quite pronounced, ranging from 18 percent in Japan to over 28 percent in Canada, Italy, and France.[5]

Figure 21.1, panel B displays the value of the Chicago Board Options Exchange (CBOE) volatility index (a measure computed by the CBOE from implied

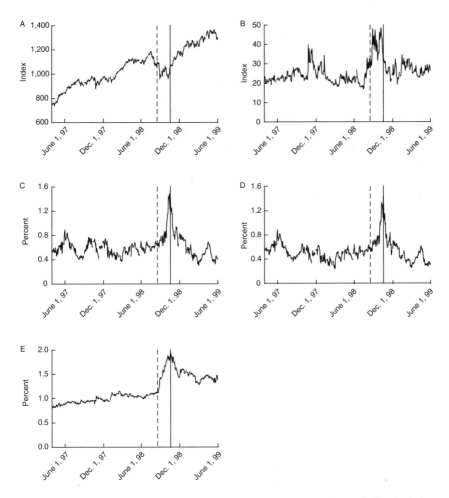

Figure 21.1 US financial market indicators, March 1997–June 1999. A. S&P 500 index. B. CBOE volatility index. C. 3-month interbank spread. D. 3-month default spread. E. 10-year default spread.

Sources: Board of Governors of the Federal Reserve System (panels A, C, D, E); Chicago Board Options Exchange (panel B).

Notes

The vertical dashed lines indicate August 17, 1997, the date of the Russian default. The vertical solid lines indicate October 15, 1997, the date of the Federal Reserve's Intermeeting cut in the federal funds rate. Panels C, D, and E display three US credit spreads: the interbank spread (panel C) is the three-month interbank yield minus three-months Treasury bill yield. The three-month default spread (panel D) is the three-month commercial paper yield minus three-month Treasury bill yield. The ten-year default spread is the ten-year AAA corporate bond yield minus ten-year Treasury bond yield.

volatilities on a number of option contracts).[6] These data show that uncertainty (and associated risk) in financial markets rose steeply in mid-August 1998. The date of the first pronounced jump was actually August 27, when the closing value of this index rose to 39.16 (compared with the previous day's close of 30.66). This date corresponded to the Russian government's announcement that it was abandoning its trading band for the ruble. In trading on August 27, the ruble fell 40 percent against the deutschemark. In addition, on that date Deutsche Bank lost its AAA rating from Standard and Poor's when it revealed that it had unsecured Russian credit risk amounting to almost $750 million. For the next seven weeks the volatility index stayed at a level that was unprecedented, except for the period around the 1987 stock market crash. The index remained at or near 40 until October 15 (the date of the intermeeting rate cut),[7] when it fell to 35.95 (compared with the previous day's close of 41.31). Within two trading days the index had fallen to around 30, remaining between 20 and 30 through the end of 1999.

Figure 21.1, panels C, D, and E display three US credit spreads: the interbank spread (three-month interbank yield minus three-month T-bill yield), the short credit spread (three-month commercial paper yield minus three-month T-bill yield), and the long credit spread (ten-year AAA corporate bond yield minus ten-year T-bond yield). These credit spreads confirm the inference from Figure 21.1, panel B that there was an abrupt increase in perceived credit risk from mid-August to mid-October. In particular, they show a pronounced spike starting in late September 1998 (around the time of the LTCM rescue) and continuing until October 16, one day after the FOMC's intermeeting rate cut. The peak in the long credit spread during this period is the highest in the 1990s, and the peak in the other two credit spreads is only exceeded during this decade by that observed during the 1990–91 recession.[8]

There is evidence that the increase in perceived credit risk was associated with a substantial drying-up of liquidity. That is, institutions with loanable funds became more reluctant to extend unsecured loans. The Federal Reserve Board of Governors' Senior Loan Officers Survey in September[9] revealed a marked increase over the August survey in the number of banks tightening loan standards and raising loan rates. (See Figure 21.2, panels A and B.) A principal reason reported by banks for these actions was "a reduced tolerance for risk." Interestingly, there was a substantial increase in the number of banks reporting *decreased* loan demand. The respondents generally attributed this reduced demand to reductions in both merger and acquisition activity and fixed investment. This suggests that the reduction in loan activity was due to both a reduced willingness of lenders to bear default risk *and* a reduced interest of borrowers in expanding economic activity. While reports of tightened loan standards continue through the November survey, the reduction in loan demand appears to have reversed by November.

The Bank for International Settlements (BIS, 1999) surveyed a number of market participants about the events of fall 1998. The survey results confirm the perception that risk levels were elevated and liquidity provision diminished in

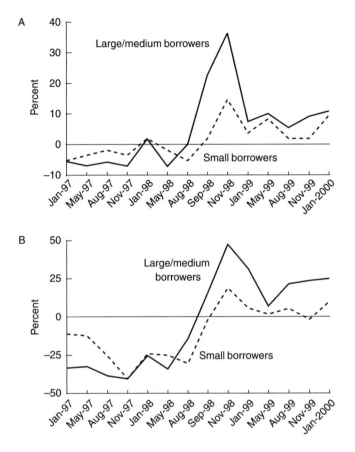

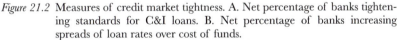

Figure 21.2 Measures of credit market tightness. A. Net percentage of banks tightening standards for C&I loans. B. Net percentage of banks increasing
spreads of loan rates over cost of funds.

Source: Board of Governors of the Federal Reserve System, Senior Loan Officers Survey.

Note
This figure plots data from the Federal Reserve Board's Senior Loan Officers Surveys from
January 1997 through January 2000. Responses to the January, March, August, and November
surveys report bank credit policies over the preceding three months. The September 1998 survey reports bank credit policies over the preceding month only.

the period from mid-August through mid-October 1998. They point to an
"unprecedented" widening in bid/ask spreads and even to "one-sided markets,"
where sellers of risky securities could not find a buyer at any price. On numerous
occasions, market makers in government securities simply withdrew from trading
and refrained from posting quotes.[10] The BIS interviewees report a flight to
the most liquid, "on-the-run" (i.e. most recently issued) Treasury securities.

For example, by early October, the yield spread between 28-year and 30-year Treasury bonds had widened to 29 basis points from just 7 basis points in mid-August (although the 28-year issues are just as free from default risk as the 30-year on-the-run bonds). Salomon Smith Barney reported that this spread was the widest it had ever recorded.[11] Continued ability to trade Treasury securities in any desired quantity was assured only for the on-the-run issues. The flight to quality even devolved, "for a brutal but short-lived period"[12] to a flight to cash. A number of participants reported reductions in credit lines to other financial institutions. This drying-up of liquidity exacerbated price volatility and increased credit risk associated with institutions that relied on market funding. Interestingly, the infusion of funds to LTCM, facilitated by the Federal Reserve Bank of New York in late September 1998,[13] seemed to *exacerbate* the liquidity crisis. Participants in the BIS survey interpreted the Fed's role as a signal that the Fed believed that the crisis was far worse than previously thought. Finally, the BIS interviewees perceived the October 15 rate cut as the turning point of the crisis. In its summary of interviews with market participants, the BIS states, "The second monetary easing by the Fed (October 15) signaled the beginning of the abatement of financial strains. At that time, traders clearly understood the commitment of the Federal Reserve to fix the problems."

To summarize, the period from mid-August to mid-October 1998 was characterized by rapid declines in stock values, rapid increases in uncertainty, and a reluctance of institutions with loanable funds to provide loans. The crisis appears to have abated in US financial markets with the Fed's intermeeting rate cut of October 15. In particular, the stock market recovery, the narrowing of credit spreads in fixed income markets, and the decline in the CBOE volatility index all commenced around October 15. Other more qualitative measures of the crisis, such as the Board of Governor's Senior Loan Officers Survey, the BIS interviews with market participants, and reports in the financial press, are also consistent with this interpretation.

What generated the crisis?

It is perhaps no surprise that the Russian default and devaluation triggered turmoil in Western financial markets. There was a good deal of uncertainty about the direct exposure of Western financial institutions to the Russian default. Furthermore, Western investors may have interpreted the Russian default as evidence against the creditworthiness of other emerging economies. Investors were particularly concerned about Argentina, Brazil, and Mexico, which are far more important than Russia for US trade.[14] (In fact, Brazil devalued its currency in mid-January 1999.) Figure 21.3, which plots Brady bond yields,[15] shows how the Russian default triggered an increase in perceived credit risk for these three Latin American countries that eclipsed the increase following the 1997 Asian crisis. In all three countries, the yields more than doubled following the Russian default in mid-August 1998. (The yield spike for Brazil was particularly pronounced.) However, this explanation for the crisis does not fully account for the way it

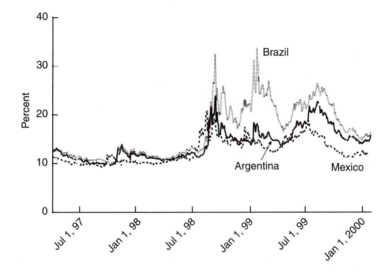

Figure 21.3 Brady bond yields for Argentina, Brazil, and Mexico (April 1997–January 2000).

Source: Bloomberg.

Note
This figure plots yields from dollar-denominated sovereign debt ("Brady bonds") issued by Argentina, Brazil, and Mexico.

ended. It is hard to imagine that the exposure of Western institutions to emerging and transitional economies or the informational asymmetry about these exposures would have been reduced by a 50 basis-point reduction in the federal funds rate. Similarly, the creditworthiness of borrowers in these economies would not have been affected substantially by the Fed's action. Thus, while the Russian default clearly triggered the financial crisis, the crisis appears to have taken on a self-fulfilling aspect over and above the damage attributable to the actions of the Russian government.

Other financial crises have also involved sudden shifts between crisis and non-crisis states without a commensurate change in fundamentals. The Asian crisis of 1997 provides an example, although in that case the sudden shift occurred at the beginning of the crisis. The Asian crisis was completely unforeseen by financial markets. In particular, in none of the Asian crisis countries do interest rates or forward exchange rates move prior to the speculative attacks leading to the initial Thai devaluation.[16] Furthermore, the Asian crisis was not triggered by any shock to fundamentals commensurate with the magnitude of the subsequent debacle. While there were clear problems with market fundamentals in these countries (in particular, the poor state of their banking sectors), these problems were well known months or even years prior to the crisis.[17] It appears that any theory of systemic financial crisis must incorporate the possibility of sudden, untriggered shifts between crisis and noncrisis states.

Modeling financial crisis as coordination failure[18]

As described earlier, the financial crisis of fall 1998 had a number of characteristics that have been associated with crises more generally. There was a sudden shift between crisis and noncrisis states without a commensurate change in fundamentals. The crisis state was characterized by a sharp reduction in liquidity provision with a corresponding flight to quality. The crisis was associated with a decline in asset values, as reflected in stock market indexes.[19] In addition, the crisis of 1998 shows clear evidence of an increase in perceived default risk. Finally, the end of the 1998 crisis was associated with an unusual action by the central bank (a change in the target federal funds rate between regularly scheduled FOMC meetings).

In this section, I propose a simple model of financial crisis that, in principle, can accommodate these patterns. My approach focuses on the possibility of coordination failure. In coordination models, an investor benefits if he chooses the same strategy as other investors. Thus, investors will tend to "coordinate" on a particular strategy. A multiplicity of equilibria can emerge, each associated with a different pattern of coordination. Suboptimal equilibria are then associated with coordination failure: the failure to coordinate on the socially optimal choices. In a familiar example, known as *external increasing returns to scale*, the productivity of a particular firm's capital investment is high only if there is a high level of aggregate economic activity. Therefore, a firm may only want to choose a high level of investment if enough *other* firms also choose a high level of investment (thereby assuring a high level of aggregate activity). If other firms choose low investment, aggregate activity will be low, and an individual firm's investment productivity may be too low to justify a high investment level. In this example, there are two equilibria: one where all firms "coordinate" on high investment, the other where all firms have low investment.[20]

In the model I present here, the possibility of coordination failure arises from the essential nature of financial relationships – the need to match potential borrowers with potential lenders in an environment of asymmetric information. In particular, lenders must search for borrowers and vice versa. As the total number of borrowers and lenders rises, this search process becomes more productive. That is, the rate at which borrowers and lenders match goes up. In other words, the matching process exhibits a *thick markets externality*: everyone benefits as the number of participants in the market rises.[21]

This thick markets externality gives rise to the possibility of a coordination failure equilibrium: if lenders believe that there are few high-quality borrowers searching for loans, and simultaneously the high-quality borrowers believe that there are few lenders willing to extend credit, an equilibrium can emerge where both lenders and borrowers forsake the loan market in favor of alternative investments. In effect, all parties have "coordinated" on nonparticipation, so the optimal strategy for any individual agent is not to participate.

Basic structure of the model

The basic model is completely static. There are two types of risk-neutral agents: borrowers (N_{borr} in number), who are endowed with a project but no liquidity; and lenders (N_{lend} in number), who are endowed with one unit of liquidity but no project. A borrower can operate his project in two mutually exclusive ways: *autarkically*, without any liquidity inflow from outside; or *with investment*, which requires borrowing one unit of liquidity from a lender. A borrower must decide at the beginning of the period whether to operate the project autarkically or whether to seek a loan. In other words, once the borrower has decided to seek a loan, the possibility of autarkic production is precluded.

Borrowers are randomly assigned one of two types of projects, *bad* (assigned with probability p^b), and *good* (assigned with probability $(1 - p^b)$). The quality of the project is private information to the borrower. Good projects pay $R^{autarky}$ with certainty if operated autarkically; they pay R with certainty if operated with investment, *provided* the borrower has found a lender willing to lend. Bad projects pay 0 if operated autarkically; if operated with investment, bad projects pay R with probability θ and $R^{salvage}$ with probability $(1 - \theta)$, again provided borrower has found a lender willing to lend. Informally, a bad borrower defaults on his loan with probability $(1 - \theta)$; $R^{salvage}$ represents the salvage value of the project that is available to satisfy the lender's claim. Finally, if a borrower seeks a loan but fails to match with a lender, he receives zero.

An interpretation[22] of these two types of borrowers is that bad borrowers are in severe financial distress. If they do not get an immediate liquidity infusion, they will be forced into bankruptcy. Even if they do receive liquidity, financial distress may impair their productivity with probability $(1 - \theta)$. In contrast, good borrowers can stay in operation without liquidity, albeit at a lower output. However, there is an up-front cost to structuring the project to utilize liquidity. My assumption that a good borrower who tries to obtain a loan and fails receives zero is equivalent to a specification where the up-front cost equals $R^{autarky}$ and the output with liquidity (before the up-front cost is paid) equals $R + R^{autarky}$.

Lenders have one unit of liquidity, which they can use in two mutually exclusive ways. First, they can invest it at a gross risk-free rate R^f. Second, they can attempt to find a borrower to whom to lend. If a borrower and a lender match, the loan contract takes the following exogenous specification:[23] if R is produced, the lender receives R_{lend} (where R_{lend} is an exogenous parameter satisfying $R_{lend} \geq R^{salvage}$) and the borrower receives $R_{borr} \equiv R - R_{lend}$; if $R^{salvage}$ is produced, the borrower is in default, so the lender receives the full salvage value $R^{salvage}$ and the borrower receives nothing. Finally, if a lender does not find a borrower, she simply ends up with her unit of liquidity.[24] To summarize, the payoffs are as follows:

$$
\text{Payoff to good borrower} = \begin{cases} R_{borr} & \text{if borrower matches with lender} \\ 0 & \text{if borrower attempts to match with} \\ & \text{lender and fails} \\ R^{autarky} & \text{if borrower operates project autarkically.} \end{cases} \tag{1}
$$

$$\text{Payoff to bad borrower} = \begin{cases} R_{\text{borr}} & \text{if borrower matches with lender and project} \\ & \text{produces } R \\ 0 & \text{if borrower attempts to match with lender} \\ & \text{and fails or} \\ & \text{if borrower matches with lender and project produces} \\ & R^{\text{salvage}} \text{ or if borrower operates project autarkically.} \quad (2) \end{cases}$$

$$\text{Payoff to lender} = \begin{cases} R_{\text{lend}} & \text{if lender matches with borrower and project} \\ & \text{produces } R \\ R^{\text{salvage}} & \text{if lender matches with borrower and project} \\ & \text{produces } R^{\text{salvage}} \\ 1 & \text{if lender attempts to match with a borrower and} \\ & \text{fails} \\ R^{\text{f}} & \text{if lender uses the risk-free investment and does not} \\ & \text{attempt to match with a borrower.} \quad (3) \end{cases}$$

The matching procedure

According to equations (1)–(3), the expected payoff to an agent who attempts to match depends on the probability of consummating the match. Suppose that there are a total of B borrowers seeking loans and L lenders seeking to match with borrowers. I denote the probability that a given borrower matches with a lender by $\text{prob}_{\text{borr}}(B, L)$. Similarly, the probability that a given lender matches with a borrower is denoted $\text{prob}_{\text{lend}}(B, L)$. (In equilibrium, the expected number of matches equals $B \times \text{prob}_{\text{borr}}(B, L) = L \times \text{prob}_{\text{lend}}(B, L)$.)

If either B or L equals zero, both $\text{prob}_{\text{borr}}$ and $\text{prob}_{\text{lend}} = 0$ (i.e., if there are no borrowers or lenders, there can be no matches). It is also natural to assume, in the language of Mortensen and Pissarides (1998), that borrowers and lenders are *complements*. That is, it is easier for a borrower to find a match if there are more lenders, and vice versa. (Formally, $\partial \text{prob}_{\text{borr}} / \partial L > 0$ and $\partial \text{prob}_{\text{lend}} / \partial B > 0$.) In addition, following Mortensen and Pissarides (1998), I assume that there is a *congestion effect*. An increase in the number of borrowers decreases the probability that a given borrower will match, and vice versa. (Formally, $\partial \text{prob}_{\text{borr}} / \partial B < 0$ and $\partial \text{prob}_{\text{lend}} / \partial L < 0$.)

Finally, I assume that the expected number of matches displays *increasing returns to scale*. This is equivalent to the condition that as the number of borrowers and lenders increases equiproportionally, both $\text{prob}_{\text{lend}}$ and $\text{prob}_{\text{borr}}$ increase. This is a natural assumption to make for many types of matching problems. Consider the problem of finding a taxi cab in a medium-sized city. If there were only one rider looking for a cab and one cab looking for a fare (as might be the case at 2:00 a.m.), the probability of a match would be very low. If there were 10,000 riders and 10,000 cabs, the probability that a given rider would find a cab would be much higher (this intuition is formalized in the model developed in Appendix A).[25] During rush hour, there are many riders competing for cabs and there are many cabs searching for riders. At 2:00 a.m., there are few riders searching for cabs, but there are also few cabs. Needless to say, it is easier to find a cab during rush hour, in spite of the greater competition from other riders.

Increasing returns is implied by a number of search models that have been proposed in the literature. In Appendix A, I discuss a number of these and I develop one model in detail. Diamond (1982) and others note that increasing returns in the matching technology can give rise to multiple search equilibria. I exploit this feature in the next section.[26]

High-coordination and low-coordination equilibria

The matching technology implies that the decision of borrowers whether to enter the match affects the probability that a given lender will match and, therefore, affects the expected payoff to the lender from entering the match. Similarly, the decisions of lenders affect the expected payoff of the borrower. This implies the possibility of coordination failure between borrowers and lenders and, thus, the possibility of multiple equilibria. We define a *high-coordination equilibrium* as one in which all lenders enter the match and all borrowers enter the match. Of course, a lender will enter the match if and only if her expected payoff from entering the match equals or exceeds R^f. Using the payoffs given in equation (3), in a conjectured high-coordination equilibrium this condition can be written as

$$\text{prob}_{\text{lend}}(\mathcal{N}_{\text{borr}}, \mathcal{N}_{\text{lend}})((p^b\theta + 1 - p^b)R_{\text{lend}} + p^b(1 - \theta)R^{\text{salvage}})$$
$$+ (1 - \text{prob}_{\text{lend}}(\mathcal{N}_{\text{borr}}, \mathcal{N}_{\text{lend}})) \geq R^f. \tag{4}$$

Similarly, a good borrower will enter the match if and only if his expected payoff from entering the match equals or exceeds R^{autarky}. In a conjectured high-coordination equilibrium, this condition is

$$\text{prob}_{\text{borr}}(\mathcal{N}_{\text{borr}}, \mathcal{N}_{\text{lend}})R_{\text{borr}} \geq R^{\text{autarky}}. \tag{5}$$

Note from equation (2) that the bad borrowers always enter the match, since the payoff from entering the match dominates the autarkic payoff to the bad borrower of zero. Therefore, equations (4) and (5) are sufficient for the existence of a high-coordination equilibrium.

I define a *low-coordination equilibrium* as one where no lenders enter the match and only bad borrowers enter the match. The payoff to lenders in the low-coordination equilibrium is R^f. The payoff to good borrowers is R^{autarky}, and the payoff to bad borrowers is zero. If there are no lenders in the match, there is clearly no incentive for good borrowers to defect from the equilibrium strategy of autarky (since $\text{prob}_{\text{borr}}(1, 0) = 0$). However, there may be an alternative strategy for a lender that could break the low-coordination equilibrium. Let the total number of bad borrowers be denoted $\mathcal{N}_{\text{bad}}$. (The expected value of $\mathcal{N}_{\text{bad}}$ is simply $p^b N_{borr}$.) If, starting in a low-coordination equilibrium, a lender decides to defect from the equilibrium strategy by entering the match, her probability of matching with a borrower is $prob_{lend}(N_{bad}, 1)$ (since only bad borrowers are in the match in a low equilibrium). Her expected payoff conditional on a successful match is $\theta R_{lend} + (1 - \theta)R^{salvage}$. Therefore, a low-coordination equilibrium can only be sustained if the expected payoff to this alternative strategy is less than the payoff to a lender in the low-coordination equilibrium:

$$prob_{lend}(N_{bad}, 1)(\theta R_{lend} + (1 - \theta)R^{salvage}) + (1 - prob_{lend}(N_{bad}, 1)) \leq R^f. \qquad (6)$$

The left-hand sides of equations (4) and (6) give the value to a lender of entering the match in the high-coordination and low-coordination equilibria, respectively. Similarly, the left-hand side of equation (5) gives the value to a good borrower of entering the match in the high-coordination equilibrium. For a particular base line parameterization,[27] Figure 21.4 displays how these values are affected by changes in the model parameters. Specifically, the left-hand column of plots in Figure 21.4 shows how the left-hand sides of equations (4) (solid lines) and (6) (dashed lines) change as a particular model parameter is varied; the right-hand column does the same for the left-hand side of equation (5) (dot-dashed lines). The five parameters that are varied in Figure 21.4 are: number of lenders, as fraction of total population (first row of plots); R^{lend}, as a fraction of R (second row); $R^{salvage}$, as a fraction of R (third row); θ (fourth row); and p^b (fifth row).

The behavior of these values is intuitive. The value to lenders of entering the match for both equilibria is strictly decreasing in the ratio of lenders to total population (reflecting the greater competition from other lenders); the corresponding value to good borrowers is strictly increasing in this ratio (reflecting the higher probability of matching with a lender). Not surprisingly, increasing R_{lend}/R, the fraction of output received by lenders, increases the value of the match to lenders, but decreases that value to borrowers. For both equilibria, the value of the match is increasing for lenders in $R^{salvage}$ and θ (the probability that a bad project produces R). Neither of these parameters affects the value of the match for good borrowers. Finally, an increase in p^b, the probability of bad projects, reduces the value of the match for lenders in the high-coordination equilibrium, but increases the value of the match for lenders in the low-coordination equilibrium. In the high-coordination equilibrium, increasing p^b simply increases the probability of borrower default. In the low-coordination equilibrium, however, an increase in p^b increases the number of borrowers seeking loans. (Recall that only bad borrowers seek loans in the low-coordination equilibrium.) This increases the probability of a match for a lender contemplating deviating from the equilibrium strategy.

Suppose the borrower condition for a high-coordination equilibrium (equation (5)) holds. That is, suppose $R^{autarky}$ lies below the dashed line in any of the plots in the right-hand column of Figure 21.4. Then the existence of the high- or low-coordination equilibrium depends on the level of the risk-free rate R^f relative to the solid and dashed lines in the plots in the left-hand column. If R^f is above both lines, then neither equilibrium exists for these parameter values. If R^f is below the solid line but above the dashed line, then both low-coordination and high-coordination

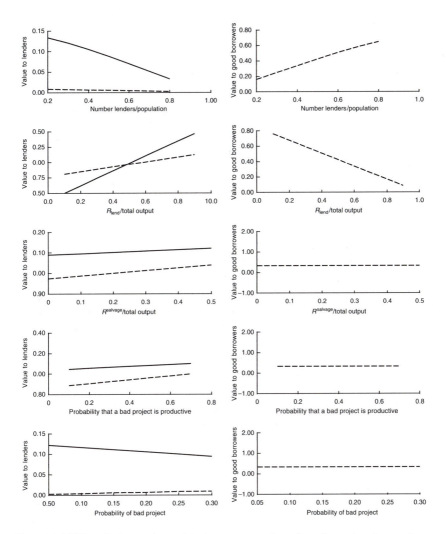

Figure 21.4 Effect of changes in model parameters on the value of entering the match.

Notes
For a particular set of baseline parameters, this figure illustrates how the value of entering the match implied by the model changes as five parameters of the model are varied. The left-hand column of figures plots the value of a lender entering the match in the high-coordination equilibrium (left-hand side of equation (4), represented by the solid lines) and the low-coordination equilibrium (left-hand side of equation (6), represented by the dashed lines) changes as the following five parameters change: number of lenders, as fraction of total population (first subplot); payoff to the lender R_{lend}, as a fraction of total output (second subplot); salvage value of a bad borrower's project R^{salvage}, as a fraction of total output (third subplot); probability that a bad project is productive θ (fourth subplot); and the probability that a given project is bad, p^{b} (fifth subplot). The right-hand column of figures plots the value of a good borrower entering the match in the high-coordination equilibrium (left-hand side of equation (5)), as the same five parameters are varied. The baseline parameters are as follows: $N_{\text{lend}} = 20$; $N_{\text{borr}} = 30$; $R = 2$; $R_{\text{lend}} = 1.2$ (so $R_{\text{borr}} = 0.8$); $R^{\text{salvage}} = 0.5$; $p^{\text{b}} = 0.2$; $\theta = 0.75$. Parameter N_{bad} is set equal to its expected value of 6. I use the model of $\text{prob}_{\text{lend}}$ and $\text{prob}_{\text{borr}}$ described in Appendix A, equations (19) and (20), with parameter $M = 10$.

equilibria exist. If R^f is below both the solid line and the dashed line, then a high-coordination equilibrium exists but no low-coordination equilibrium exists. Thus, if equation (5) holds, the high-coordination equilibrium can be enforced by setting R^f sufficiently low.

Finally, there may also be additional "mixed" equilibria where a fraction of lenders and/or good borrowers enter the match, while the remaining agents choose the alternative strategies (investing risk-free for lenders, operating the project autarkically for the borrowers.) I discuss the conditions for these mixed equilibria in Box 21.1. The possibility of mixed equilibria complicates the analysis of this model. For the purposes of this chapter, I assume that these mixed equilibria are never observed. In the next section, I focus only on the low- and high-coordination equilibria.

Interpreting the model as a theory of financial crises

I associate the low-coordination equilibrium in the model with a financial crisis. This equilibrium captures many characteristics associated with financial crises. In this simple model, asset values and output can both be measured by the expected payoff to a borrower's project; both are clearly lower in the low-coordination equilibrium than in the high-coordination equilibrium.[28] There is a clear flight to quality in the low-coordination equilibrium, coupled with a drying-up of liquidity: lenders invest in the risk-free asset instead of making loans, so the aggregate quantity of liquidity provided falls to zero. There is a perception of declining credit quality: if we were to ask a lender why she refrained from making loans, she would answer that the risk of default was too high (since all borrowers actually entering the match in the low-coordination equilibrium are bad borrowers). This is the sort of response given by lending institutions in the BIS interviews and the Board of Governors' Senior Loan Officers Survey, discussed earlier. It is also consistent with widening credit spreads. Furthermore, there is a reduction in demand for liquidity on the part of borrowers, a pattern that was also reported in the September Senior Loan Officers Survey.

This model is also consistent with sudden switches between normal and crisis states without any change in underlying fundamentals (as represented by the model's parameters). While I do not model dynamics explicitly, a multiple-equilibrium model of this type can be incorporated into a dynamic model in which switches between coordination states are driven solely by changing expectations. If enough lenders in the economy become pessimistic about the aggregate number of borrowers entering the match (or vice versa), then a low-coordination equilibrium will emerge, validating their pessimism ex post. Thus, all that would be needed to model the abrupt switches between crisis and noncrisis states would be to model switching between optimism and pessimism in the economy.[29]

Financial crises and the role of the central bank

Perhaps the most interesting feature of the model presented here is that it suggests a role for the central bank in dealing with financial crises. We can see from equation (6) that a liquidity crisis (i.e. a low-coordination equilibrium) is only possible if the real risk-free rate is sufficiently high. If the central bank can affect the real risk-free rate through open market operations, it can extinguish the possibility of a liquidity crisis by reducing the risk-free rate until the left-hand side of equation (6) exceeds the right-hand side. Intuitively, if the risk-free rate is so low that a lender expects a higher return by seeking to match with a borrower *even if all borrowers are believed to be of bad quality*, then the low-coordination equilibrium cannot be sustained.

Example of central bank action: the events of 1991–93

One interpretation of monetary policy in the early 1990s is that the Fed used open market operations in the manner suggested in the preceding section. The recovery from the 1990–91 recession appeared to be impeded by a so-called credit crunch. Responding perhaps to the introduction of risk-based capital requirements, banks reduced their volume of loan provision, investing instead in Treasury securities and other low-risk assets. One can see this process in Figure 21.5, panel A, which displays fixed income securities as a fraction of total banking assets. Note that fixed income securities as a percentage of total assets rose from just over 15 percent at the beginning of 1990 to over 20 percent in the beginning of 1993. While this is far less dramatic than the complete coordination failure in the low-coordination equilibrium of the model, this process can be interpreted as a slow shift away from full coordination.

In mid-1991, the FOMC started reducing the federal funds rate in an effort to encourage more lending. This policy shift is evident in Figure 21.5, panel B, which displays the real federal funds rate (defined here as the difference between the nominal federal funds rate and the ex post monthly CPI inflation rate) from 1989 through 1997. Note that the real funds rate declines to an extremely low level (between 0.5 and 0 percent) between late 1992 and February 1994. As in the simple model, the effect is to reduce the return on alternative assets, making even the relatively low risk-adjusted return on loans seem reasonably attractive.[30] As shown in Figure 21.5, panel A, banks did shift away from non-loan assets to loans following the implementation of this policy. It is possible that the increased loan growth was due to some change in the economic or regulatory environment other than the extremely low real interest rates. However, these patterns in the data are certainly consistent with the intuition that lenders are more willing to lend when the return to alternative investments is low, and that the central bank can influence this alternative return.

Particularly interesting is what happened after the FOMC reversed course starting in February 1994 and allowed the real interest rate to return to its level of early 1990. If banks' willingness to lend depended only on the return on alternative assets, the banks presumably would then have cut back on their loan provision. In fact, Figure 21.5, panel A shows that banks continued to increase their lending. This suggests that there may have been an element of coordination failure in the credit crunch. Once the economy had securely moved to a high-coordination state, it could remain there even after the FOMC raised real interest rates to a higher level.

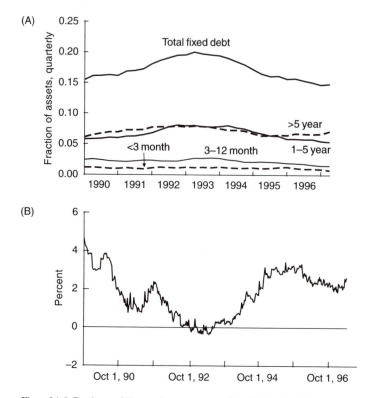

Figure 21.5 Bank portfolios and monetary policy, 1989–97. A. Fixed income securities as fraction of total assets 1989: Q1–97:Q1. B. Real federal funds rate, October 1989–March 1997.

Source: Call reports (panel A); author's calculations, using data from the Bord of Governors of the Federal Reserve System (panel B).

Note
Panel A displays fixed income securities as a fraction of total bank assets. The uppermost black line displays total fixed income securities. The other lines in the graph disaggregate the securities by maturity. Panel B displays the real federal funds rate, computed as the nominal federal funds rate minus the one-month CPI inflation rate.

Policy alternatives implied by the model

According to the model, a central bank can prevent financial crises by keeping interest rates extremely low all the time. However, this strategy conflicts with the central focus of monetary policy: to establish a reputation as a force for price stability. Even if the Fed could act against the possibility of a low-coordination equilibrium by decisively reducing Treasury yields, such an action would be costly, not only in its direct effect on future inflation, but also in eroding the credibility of the Fed's commitment to containing inflationary pressures.

In principle, a central bank could reconcile these two competing imperatives by establishing a credible *state-dependent* policy: enforce a low interest rate *only* when there is clear evidence that a financial crisis is imminent. The advantage of such a policy is that the low interest rate is rarely implemented, yet the possibility that it might be implemented moves the economy to a preferred equilibrium. In fact, when I incorporate such a state-dependent policy into the simple model developed earlier in the chapter, the low interest rate is *never* implemented. In the language of economic theory, it is an *off-equilibrium path* that enforces the high-coordination equilibrium.

As an example of such a state-dependent policy, consider the aftermath of the October 1987 stock market crash. There is considerable anecdotal evidence that many banks were reluctant to provide the liquidity needed to settle trades made during the day of the crash. This withdrawal of liquidity may have represented a low-coordination equilibrium: if a given bank is likely to be repaid only if the aggregate provision of liquidity is high, it may be individually rational for each bank to withhold liquidity. In response the Fed announced a state contingent policy: "The Federal Reserve ... affirmed today its readiness to serve as a source of liquidity to support the economic and financial system."[31] The operative word is "readiness." Knowing that the Fed stood ready to ensure adequate liquidity in the market, it became rational for individual banks to provide liquidity to their clients. In the event, no significant liquidity disruptions were observed,[32] yet the Fed itself did not actively provide the liquidity: discount window borrowing by member banks did not increase significantly, and the increase in nonborrowed reserves was small.

In September 1998, investors were uncertain whether a state-dependent policy was in place.[33] One can interpret the intermeeting rate cut on October 15, 1998, as a credible signal that the Fed had shifted to this sort of state-dependent policy. It seems more plausible to interpret the effect of this rate cut to its role as a signal than to any direct effects. Certainly, the interest rate cuts in fall of 1998 were much smaller than those in 1990–91, clearly not sufficient to substantially change investors' incentives directly. There is evidence that financial markets perceived the intermeeting rate cut as signaling a policy change. According to the *Wall Street Journal*, "the economic indicators that the Fed usually tracks – the unemployment rate, the pace of orders for factory goods and retail sales, among other things – don't explain the Fed's sudden action, since many of those indicators have suggested that the economy is relatively healthy. Rather, officials at the Fed ... have been focused on unusual signs of stress in the financial markets."[34] In the words of analysts at Morgan Stanley Dean Witter, the Fed's "unexpected easing" signaled a "new aggressiveness."[35] Market participants' perception of a change in Fed emphasis is consistent with the minutes of the FOMC's deliberations. In the minutes of the September 29 meeting,[36] the financial market turmoil is noted, but it is seen primarily as one factor among many affecting inflationary pressures through aggregate demand. In particular, "The members did not believe that the tightness in credit markets and strong demand for safety and liquidity were likely to lead to a 'credit crunch. ...'" A 50 basis-point cut is explicitly ruled out because "the risk of rising inflation ... was still present, especially in light of the persistence to date of very tight labor markets and relatively robust economic growth." In contrast, the minutes of the FOMC teleconference preceding the intermeeting rate cut of October 15 do not mention inflationary pressures at all. Rather, an additional rate cut is motivated "to help settle volatile financial markets and cushion the effects of more restrictive financial conditions on the ongoing expansion." Following the October 15 action, members of the FOMC describe the move as a (temporary) shift of focus from price stability to financial stability. For example, the *Wall Street Journal* cited Federal Reserve Bank of St Louis President William Poole as saying that "[the recent market instability] and the circumstances surrounding it are so unusual in the context of U.S. history that policy makers must concentrate on dealing with this situation for the time being."[37] According to the same article, Governor Roger Ferguson "indicated that the Fed would be willing to cut rates aggressively at any hint of a recession."

In the following section, I incorporate such a state-dependent policy into the simple model outlined earlier. I argue that such a policy, if credible, may have been sufficient to eliminate the possibility of coordination failure without requiring the central bank to actually implement any substantial interest rate reductions. To formalize this idea, I extend the model so that the central bank acts in real time. I then demonstrate that the low-coordination equilibrium can be eliminated if agents believe that the monetary authority will act in the future to eliminate coordination failure should coordination failure become likely.

Modeling a state-dependent central bank policy

To model a central bank interest rate policy that actively responds to a developing liquidity crisis, I need to modify the simple model to make precise the notion of "incipient crisis." I do so in the following (admittedly highly stylized) way. Suppose that there is a preliminary period before the matching of borrowers and lenders. At the beginning of this preliminary period, each lender is assigned at random a mood of *pessimism* or *optimism*. A pessimist believes that the low-coordination equilibrium will prevail *provided* a low-coordination equilibrium could exist (i.e. provided equation (6) could hold). An optimist believes that the high-coordination equilibrium will prevail, again provided this equilibrium could exist (i.e. equations (4) and (5) could hold). In addition, in the beginning of the preliminary period the N_{lend} lenders are assigned an index $i = 1, ..., N_{\text{lend}}$. They then must declare (irrevocably) in order of their index assignment whether they will enter the match or invest in the risk-free technology. After all N_{lend} lenders have declared, the match is held, projects are operated, and payoffs are made, as in the simple model.

Let Q_i denote the number of lenders who have declared that they are in the match through the ith lender, so $Q_{N_{\text{lend}}}$ denotes the total number of lenders committed to entering the match at the end of the preliminary period. As I show in proposition 1 below, if $Q_{N_{\text{lend}}}$ is sufficiently high (i.e. if $Q_{N_{\text{lend}}}$ is greater than or equal to a particular threshold N^*) a low-coordination equilibrium cannot exist. A pessimist with index i will assume that the low-coordination equilibrium will prevail *unless* Q_{i-1} (weakly) exceeds this threshold.

Now, I develop this idea more fully. For simplicity, I consider a case where the central bank can choose one of two interest rates: R^{high} and R^{low}, where R^{high} is consistent with both equilibria. That is, when $R^f = R^{high}$, equations (4)–(6) all hold. (I discuss conditions on R^{low} below.) If $R^f = R^{high}$, the equilibrium that emerges depends on the beliefs of the lenders about $Q_{N_{lend}}$. In particular, there exists an N^* such that, if it is believed that $Q_{N_{lend}} \geq N^*$, it is optimal for *all* good borrowers to enter the match. The smallest such value of N^* is given by

$$N^* = \min N \quad \text{s.t.} \quad \text{prob}_{borr}(N_{borr}, N) R_{borr} \geq R^{autarky}. \tag{7}$$

The existence of $N^* \leq N_{lend}$ follows from the assumption that a high-coordination equilibrium exists (i.e. equation (5) holds).

To proceed, I must make an additional assumption. Let V_{lend} denote the value to a lender of entering the match. V_{lend} depends on both the total number of lenders in the match and the number of good borrowers in the match. An explicit expression for V_{lend} is given in equation (12) in Box 21.1. I assume that

$$V_{lend} \text{ is strictly decreasing in the total number of lenders in the match.} \tag{8}$$

A sufficient condition for assumption (8) to hold is given in equation (17) in Box 21.1.

Proposition 1 *Suppose equations (4) and (8) hold. If all lenders believe that $Q_{N_{lend}}$ will be at least as big as N^*, then all lenders enter the match, so $Q_{N_{lend}} = N_{lend} \geq N^*$. This implies, first, that their beliefs are ratified ex post, and, second, that the high-coordination equilibrium prevails. (The proofs of all propositions are in Appendix B.)*

Proposition 1 tells us that the central bank can ensure that the high-coordination equilibrium will prevail if it can ensure that at least N^* lenders commit to entering the match. As in the previous model, it can do so by setting R^f sufficiently low. To formalize this possibility, let us assume that

$$(\theta R_{lend} + (1 - \theta) R^{salvage}) > 1 \tag{9}$$

and let R^{low} satisfy

$$\text{prob}_{lend}(N_{bad}, N^*)(\theta R_{lend} + (1 - \theta) R^{salvage}) + (1 - \text{prob}_{lend}(N_{bad}, N^*)) \geq R^{low}. \tag{10}$$

Equation (9) means that the expected payoff to a lender conditional on matching with a bad borrower exceeds the payoff from failing to match. It ensures that the left-hand side of equation (10) is increasing in prob_{lend}.

Proposition 2   *If the central bank sets $R^f = R^{low}$ and equations (9) and (10) hold, the high-coordination equilibrium is enforced.*

Proposition 2 tells us that the central bank can eliminate the low-coordination equilibrium by permanently setting the risk-free rate sufficiently low (in particular, low enough so equation (10) holds). In reality, however, this low interest rate policy is a very costly way to deal with the possibility of financial crisis. As I discussed above, the excessively expansionary monetary policy needed to keep interest rates at R^{low} may directly conflict with the central bank's primary mission of price stability. If so, a better central bank rule is to set $R^f = R^{high}$, but commit to switching to R^{low} if there is evidence of an incipient crisis. Informally, the central bank can measure the tone of the market by looking at the ratio Q_i/i. This ratio gives the fraction of the first i lenders who will enter the match, so this ratio measures the "skittishness" of the market. If the central bank observes a low value of Q_i/i (presumably because the random assignment of the first i indexes fell disproportionately on pessimists), it may be concerned that a financial crisis is brewing.

In the formalism of this model, let "incipient crisis" be defined as any point i^* in the declaration sequence such that

$$Q_{i*} + (N_{lend} - i^*) = N^*. \tag{11}$$

In other words, if such an i^* is reached, then *all* of the remaining lenders must declare themselves in the match to ensure that there are N^* lenders seeking to match with borrowers. Since the goal of the central bank is to ensure that at least N^* lenders enter the match, this is the "last chance" for the central bank to do so.

Central bank rule

The proposed central bank rule is as follows:

- Set $R^f = R^{high}$ as long as no $\{i^*, Q_{i*}\}$ satisfying equation (11) is reached.
- The first time $\{i^*, Q_{i*}\}$ satisfying equation (11) is reached, set $R^f = R^{low}$ from that point on.

Proposition 3   *If this rule is credible, the only equilibrium is high-coordination with $Q_i = i$, $\forall i$, and $R^f = R^{high}$.*

According to proposition 3, the second branch of the rule is an off-equilibrium path that is never observed in equilibrium. Thus, the best of all possible worlds is obtained: liquidity crises are ruled out without compromising the goal of price stability. Proposition 3 specifies that the rule must be credible. I do not attempt to formalize how "credibility" is to be established. Authors such as Chari *et al.* (1998) and Christiano and Gust (2000) stress the importance of the central bank establishing a credible commitment to price stability if expectations-driven inflationary episodes are to be avoided. Proposition 3 suggests that a credible commitment to financial stability may serve an analogous role in avoiding financial crises.

Box 21.1 Mixed equilibria

In a mixed equilibrium, some lenders and/or good borrowers enter the match, while the remaining agents choose the alternative strategies (investing risk-free for lenders, operating the project autarkically for the borrowers). If there were a continuum of agents, these mixed equilibria would require agents to be indifferent between entering the match and using the alternative strategies. If one takes seriously the constraint that the number of agents of each type be an integer, then the conditions for a mixed equilibrium must take into account the effect on the matching probabilities were an agent to deviate from the equilibrium.

To write down the conditions for a mixed equilibrium, it is convenient to define functions V_{lend} and V_{borr} that measure the value of entering the match for lenders and borrowers, respectively. Let B_{good} denote the number of good borrowers entering the match, and let L denote the number of lenders entering the match. Recall that all bad borrowers enter the match (since the value of autarky for bad borrowers is zero). Therefore, the fraction of bad borrowers in the match is $N_{\text{bad}}/(N_{\text{bad}} + B_{\text{good}})$, and (analogously with the left-hand side of equation (4)) the value to a lender of entering the match is

$$V_{\text{lend}}(B_{\text{good}}, L) \equiv \text{prob}_{\text{lend}}(N_{\text{bad}} + B_{\text{good}}, L)$$

$$\times \left(\left(\frac{\theta N_{\text{bad}}}{N_{\text{bad}} + B_{\text{good}}} + \frac{B_{\text{good}}}{N_{\text{bad}} + B_{\text{good}}} \right) R_{\text{lend}} + \frac{(1-\theta)N_{\text{bad}}}{N_{\text{bad}} + B_{\text{good}}} R^{\text{salvage}} \right)$$

$$+ \left(1 - \text{prob}_{\text{lend}}(N_{\text{bad}} + B_{\text{good}}, L) \right). \tag{12}$$

The value of entering the match for a good borrower is given by the analogue to the left-hand side of equation (5):

$$V_{\text{borr}}(B_{\text{good}}, L) \equiv \text{prob}_{\text{borr}}(N_{\text{bad}} + B_{\text{good}}, L) R_{\text{borr}}. \tag{13}$$

If there were a continuum of agents, so the defection of a single agent from the equilibrium strategy would not affect the matching probabilities, then a mixed equilibrium would be a pair $\{B_{\text{good}}, L\}$ satisfying

$$0 < B_{\text{good}} < N_{\text{borr}} - N_{\text{bad}}, \tag{14}$$

$$0 < L < N_{\text{lend}},$$

for which

$$V_{\text{lend}} (B_{\text{good}}, L) = R^{\text{f}} \tag{15}$$

$$V_{\text{borr}} (B_{\text{good}}, L) = R^{\text{autarky}}.$$

If (as I assume throughout this chapter) there are an integer number of agents of each type, then a conjectured defection from the equilibrium strategy changes $\text{prob}_{\text{lend}}$ or $\text{prob}_{\text{borr}}$ and, therefore, changes V_{lend} or V_{borr}. To take this explicitly into consideration, I must modify equation (15). Assume that

$$V_{\text{lend}} \text{ is decreasing in } L. \tag{16}$$

Since $\text{prob}_{\text{lend}} (B, L)$ is strictly decreasing in L, a sufficient condition for assumption (16) is

$$\left(\frac{\theta N_{\text{bad}}}{N_{\text{bad}} + B_{\text{good}}} + \frac{B_{\text{good}}}{N_{\text{bad}} + B_{\text{good}}} \right) R_{\text{lend}} + \frac{(1 - \theta) N_{\text{bad}}}{N_{\text{bad}} + B_{\text{good}}} R^{\text{salvage}} > 1 . \tag{17}$$

In other words, the expected payoff to a lender from a successful match exceeds the payoff from entering the match but failing to match. Note that V_{borr} is decreasing in B_{good}, because $\text{prob}_{\text{borr}} (B, L)$ is strictly decreasing in B. Under assumption (16), a mixed equilibrium is a pair $\{B_{\text{good}}, L\}$ satisfying equation (14) and

$$V_{\text{lend}} (B_{\text{good}}, L + 1) \le R^{\text{f}} \le V_{\text{lend}} (B_{\text{good}}, L)$$

$$\tag{18}$$

$$V_{\text{borr}} (B_{\text{good}} + 1, L) \le R^{\text{autarky}} \le V_{\text{borr}} (B_{\text{good}} + 1, L).$$

The logic behind equation (18) is straightforward. If the first set of inequalities in equation (18) holds, then a lender in the match has no incentive to switch to the risk-free asset (since the value of being in the match exceeds R^{f}), and a lender investing risk-free has no incentive to switch to entering the match (since, by entering the match, the total number of lenders in the match will equal $L + 1$, and the value to being a lender in the match when the total number of lenders equals $L + 1$ is dominated by the risk-free rate). A similar logic holds for borrowers if the second set of inequalities in equation (18) holds.

Discussion

Is this what happened in October 1998?

One interpretation of the FOMC's interest rate cut on October 15, 1998, is that it was an intentional signal that Fed had shifted from an unequivocal focus on price stability to a policy of "price stability unless there is a pressing need to deter a financial crisis." In the formalism of the model, the former policy sets $R^f = R^{high}$ always, while the latter policy is given by the policy rule described above.

There are clearly other possible explanations for the ending of the fall 1998 crisis. One such explanation is that the reduced interest rates increased the collateral value of firms' fixed income portfolios, thereby increasing their borrowing capacity. But the effect of a 50 basis-point interest rate cut on the value of debt holdings is small, especially for the short-term securities generally used as collateral. In any event, the turmoil in fall of 1998 was associated with a "flight to quality," which raised the value of the Treasury securities that typically collateralize liquidity loans. Another explanation is that the open market operations used to implement these interest rate cuts increased the total supply of reserves in the system, increasing the amount of liquidity available to be borrowed. Again, this explanation seems wanting. In contrast to the period from 1991 to 1993, when there was an extended and pronounced increase in the volume of liquidity in circulation, the volume of reserves in fall 1998 was relatively unchanged.

Perhaps a more straightforward explanation for the abrupt reversal of the 1998 crisis is that financial intermediaries believed that the Fed had implicitly agreed to provide all financial institutions with a guarantee. In particular, the role of the Federal Reserve Bank of New York in the recapitalization of LTCM may have been interpreted as a commitment to provide similar services to other intermediaries with similar problems. I do not believe that the facts support this explanation. Following the announcement of the LTCM rescue plan, *the crisis actually deepened*. Measures of credit spreads and market volatility deteriorated during the two weeks between the LTCM rescue and the Fed's intermeeting action on October 15. Furthermore, market participants reported that the Fed's role in the rescue served to exacerbate market fears, not ameliorate them. Thus, the data seem to contradict the hypothesis that the LTCM rescue was interpreted as an extension of the safety net.

Finally, the October 15 rate cut may have signaled a changed policy stance regarding International Monetary Fund (IMF) funding rather than monetary policy. The Russian fiscal crisis virtually assured that a good deal of IMF resources would flow to Russia. Without an increase in funding levels, the IMF's resources to deal with other countries' problems (most importantly, Latin America) would have been substantially reduced. The increase in Brady bond yields, documented in Figure 21.3, may have reflected concerns that less IMF funding would be available to deal with future Latin American problems following the Russian crisis. During 1998, the US Congress was considering an increase in America's IMF funding quota. However, there was considerable Congressional opposition to increased funding. Perhaps the October 15 rate cut was interpreted as a signal that the Fed would work with greater intensity to secure increased IMF funding.

This interpretation is certainly possible. However, it relies on a less direct mechanism than the monetary policy interpretation I put forth in this chapter. It places a good deal of weight on the Fed's influence with Congress. Furthermore, the Fed was already on record supporting the proposal to increase IMF funding (see Chairman Greenspan's testimony to Congress on May 21, 1998), so the October 15 rate cut would have represented at best a strengthening of this position, not a reversal of a previously held position. Finally, the data are not entirely consistent with this explanation. As shown in Figure 21.3, the peak in Latin American Brady bond yields during 1998 happened in mid-August (Mexico) or mid-September (Brazil and Argentina), not in mid-October when the presumed signal occurred.

Costs of a state-contingent policy for financial crises

In the theoretical model described here, the state-contingent policy rule is costless to implement, since the low interest rate is never actually imposed in equilibrium. Of course, the real world is not so simple. In reality, there would doubtless be crises that could not be extinguished by the belief that the central bank's rule specifies a particular off-equilibrium path. As a practical matter, this sort of policy rule would require aggressive monetary expansion from time to time. Actions of this type have costs. Each time such a monetary expansion is implemented, the central bank compromises its primary objective of price stability. Any time it injects liquidity into financial markets in an effort to counter potential crises it faces the difficult task of negotiating a "soft landing" – removing the liquidity after the crisis has abated without triggering a recession. Furthermore, if the state-contingent policy rule weakens the commitment to price stability, the resulting instability might even increase the possibility of financial crises. Finally, if private market participants believe that the central bank will always act to successfully counter financial turmoil, they may engage in less vigilant risk management than they would otherwise. This so-called "moral hazard" problem may actually increase the chances of an incipient crisis. Policymakers must take all of these issues into consideration before adopting a state-contingent rule as a practical policy doctrine.

Conclusion

In this chapter, I propose a precise characterization of financial crisis. I argue that coordination problems arise generically in financial markets. I associate financial crisis with a condition of coordination failure, in which low levels of financial intermediation become self-justifying. I also argue that the central bank, through its ability to affect real interest rates, may be able to extinguish the low-coordination trap. This argument supports a role for the central bank in countering systemic financial disruptions.

Having said this, there may be circumstances in which the central bank's power to affect real rates is insufficient to stave off a crisis. In particular, if potential lenders are sufficiently pessimistic about returns from lending, crisis aversion may require a real interest rate below that achievable by open market operations. In addition, the use of open market operations to counter financial crises is not without cost. Open market operations can only have a temporary effect on real rates. Prolonged use of this tool to reduce real interest rates would run directly counter to the central bank's primary goal of price stability. In principle, the central bank is better off establishing a credible contingent policy, whereby a liquidity injection is only made when there is evidence that a crisis is forthcoming. In the simple model presented here, a credible policy of this type never has to be implemented in equilibrium. In reality, of course, life is not so simple. There would doubtless be cases where the central bank would have to implement an expansionary monetary policy to counter an incipient crisis. Thus, this chapter's policy implications have benefits and costs that must be carefully weighed by policymakers when considering practical policy formulation. Nonetheless, this chapter does provide a formal justification for the central bank as an essential institution in dealing with financial crises.

Appendix A: increasing returns to scale in matching

Increasing returns to scale in matching can be derived from a number of more primitive search models. For example, Mortensen and Pissarides (1999) describe an environment in which each lender has a list of telephone numbers that includes the numbers of potential borrowers, and each borrower has a similar list that includes the numbers of potential lenders. If borrowers and lenders choose numbers at random, the probability of a match displays increasing returns. Kultti (1998) describes a somewhat more elaborate model.[38] In his approach, lenders are posted at fixed locations, and borrowers randomly choose a location. If there is a lender at the location and there are no other borrowers, a match is made with certainty. If there is a lender and more than one borrower at the location, a borrower is chosen at random to match with the lender. Finally, if there is no lender at the location, no match is made. One can think of these locations as bank branches, where some branches have exhausted their loan capacity. Kultti (1998) shows that if the number of locations does not change as the number of borrowers and lenders increases, the matching probabilities display increasing returns.[39]

Now, I consider in greater detail a micro model of matching, similar to Kultti's (1998), that implies increasing returns. Suppose there are M locations. To successfully match, a lender and a borrower must go to the same location. They cannot communicate before traveling to a location, so the event of a lender and a borrower being in the same location is purely random. Ex ante, all locations look the same to both lenders and borrowers. I assume that lenders and borrowers make their location decision at random, independently of the other lenders and borrowers. Therefore, the probability that a given borrower or a given lender arrives at any particular location is $1/M$.[40]

An interpretation of this set-up is that the "locations" are banks or other intermediaries. Lenders are agents with excess liquidity. To match with borrowers, the lenders must go through an intermediary. Lenders choose the intermediary at random. Similarly, borrowers visit intermediaries at random to apply for a loan.

The loan application process is sufficiently time-intensive that a borrower can only apply at one intermediary.

Suppose there are l lenders and b borrowers at a given location. If $l = 0$ or $b = 0$, no matches take place at that location. If $l = b$, all the lenders and borrowers at that location match with probability one. If $l > b$, the b borrowers are allocated randomly among the lenders, so the probability of a given lender obtaining a match is b/l, and all borrowers obtain a match with probability 1. Similarly if $b > l$, the probability of a given borrower obtaining a match is l/b, and all lenders obtain a match with probability 1. To summarize,

$$\text{prob \{lender matching} \,|\, b, l\} \min\left(\frac{b}{l}, 1\right),$$

$$\text{prob \{lender matching} \,|\, b, l\} \min\left(\frac{b}{l}, 1\right).$$

I now compute the unconditional probability that a lender will match. Let B denote the number of borrowers seeking loans, and let L denote the number of lenders seeking to match with borrowers. The probability that a given lender will be at a particular location is $1/M$. For $n = 0, 1, \ldots, L$, the probability that n lenders will arrive at a particular location is denoted by $p_l(n|L)$, as follows:

$$p_l(n|L) = \frac{L!}{n!(L-n)!}\left(\frac{1}{M}\right)^n\left(1 - \frac{1}{M}\right)^{L-n}.$$

Similarly, for $n = 0, 1, \ldots, B$, the probability that n borrowers will arrive at a particular location is denoted by $p_b(n|B)$, as follows:

$$p_b(n|B) = \frac{B!}{n!(B-n)!}\left(\frac{1}{M}\right)^n\left(1 - \frac{1}{M}\right)^{B-n}.$$

To determine $\text{prob}_{\text{borr}}(B, L)$, the probability that a given borrower matches, one must sum over all possible values of l and b:

$$\text{prob}_{\text{borr}}(B, L) = \sum_{l=0}^{L}\sum_{b=0}^{B-1}\min\left(\frac{l}{b+1}, 1\right)p_b(b|B-1)p_l(l|L). \tag{19}$$

In the second summation, I sum only to $B - 1$ because we are concerned with the number of *other* borrowers that show up at the same location as the given borrower. There are only $B - 1$ other borrowers. The expression for $\text{prob}_{\text{lend}}(B, L)$, the probability that a given lender matches with a borrower, is analogous:

$$\text{prob}_{\text{lend}}(B, L) = \sum_{b=0}^{B}\sum_{l=0}^{L-1}\min\left(\frac{b}{l+1}, 1\right)p_b(b|B)p_l(L-1). \tag{20}$$

The increasing returns property is illustrated in the first panel of Figure 21.A1. As both L and B rise, the probability of a match (given by equation (19) or (20)) increases. As illustrated in the last two panels of Figure 21.A1, equation (19) implies that the probability of a given borrower matching is increasing in the number of lenders, L, (holding B constant) and decreasing in the number of borrowers B (holding L constant). Similarly, the probability of a given lender matching is increasing in B and decreasing in L.

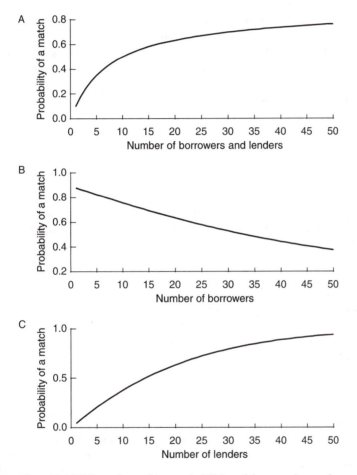

Figure 21.A1 Effect of matching probabilities of increase in numbers of borrowers or lenders. A. Probability of a match as number of borrowers and lenders increase. B. Probability that borrower matches as number of borrowers increases. C. Probability that borrower matches as number of lenders increases.

Note
The top panel gives the probability that a lender or borrower matces as both the number of lenders and the number of borrowers increase at the same rate. The middle panel gives the probability that a borrower matches as the number of borrowrs increases (holding lenders fixed). The bottom panel gives the probability that a borrower matches as the number of lenders increases (holding borrowers fixed).

Appendix B: proofs of propositions

Proposition 1   Let functions V_{borr} and V_{lend} be defined as in equations (12) and (13) of Box 21.1. $\text{Prob}_{\text{borr}}(B, L)$ is increasing in L and decreasing in B. Therefore, the condition

$$Q_{\mathcal{N}_{\text{lend}}} \geq \mathcal{N}^*$$

and equation (7) imply that $V_{\text{borr}}(B_{\text{good}}, Q_{\mathcal{N}_{\text{lend}}}) \geq R^{\text{autarky}}$ for all $B_{\text{good}} \leq \mathcal{N}_{\text{borr}} - \mathcal{N}_{\text{bad}}$. This implies that all good borrowers enter the match. However, if all good borrowers enter the match, then equations (4) and (8) imply that the value of entering the match to a lender exceeds R^f, regardless of the decisions of the other lenders.[41] Therefore, all lenders enter the match. This ends the proof.

Proposition 2   If $R^f = R^{\text{low}}$, equations (9) and (10) together imply that if $Q_{i-1} < \mathcal{N}^*$, it is optimal for the ith lender to enter the match, *even if no good borrowers enter the match*. This follows because equation 9 ensures that, for arbitrary $\mathcal{N}^\%$,

$$\text{prob}_{\text{lend}}(M^{\text{low}}, \mathcal{N}^\%)(\theta R_{\text{lend}} + (1 - \theta)R^{\text{salvage}}) + (1 - \text{prob}_{\text{lend}}(M^{\text{low}}, \mathcal{N}^\%))$$

is decreasing in $\mathcal{N}^\%$. (Recall that $\text{prob}_{\text{lend}}(M^{\text{low}}, \mathcal{N}^\%)$, is decreasing in $\mathcal{N}^\%$. As more lenders compete with a given lender, the probability that a lender matches goes down.) This in turn means that at least $\mathcal{N}^*$ lenders will enter the match, regardless of what any of the other lenders or good borrowers do, so $Q_{\mathcal{N}_{\text{lend}}} \geq \mathcal{N}^*$. According to proposition 1, this is sufficient for the high coordination equilibrium to prevail. This completes the proof.

Proposition 3   To prove proposition 3, note that the monetary policy rule ensures that there will always be at least $\mathcal{N}^*$ lenders committing to enter the match. By proposition 1, this is sufficient to ensure that the high-coordination equilibrium prevails. This completes the proof.

Notes

1 An account of the events surrounding the Russian default can be found in Perotti (2000).
2 Immediately following the announcement of the rate cut, the Dow Jones Industrial Average dropped. Press reports indicate that many investors expected a bigger rate cut. The US Chamber of Commerce described the move as "underwhelming in its modesty," (Schlessinger and Wessel, 1998b) and investors in bond futures "were treating a half-point cut by year's end as a certainty, and a half-point cut tomorrow as a reasonable possibility," (Schlessinger, 1998). The federal funds futures market supports this assertion. From September 25 through 28, the price of the October federal funds futures contract implied an expected fed funds rate of around 5.16 percent for the month of October (down from 5.5 percent before September 29). This implies that investors put substantial probability on a cut of 50 basis points or more at the September FOMC meeting.
3 "[M]arkets had been rife with rumors about the possibility of an intermeeting move for the past week or so. ... " in Greenlaw (1999).
4 The fed funds futures market gives a forecast of the thirty-day average federal funds rate over the month of October. The funds rate was already at 5.25 percent. A rate cut in

mid-October to 5.00 percent would move the thirty-day *average* of October rates to 5.125 percent. If investors only assigned a 50 percent probability to such a rate cut, the expected average rate would be approximately 5.18 percent.

5 The magnitudes of the declines were as follows: UK, 23 percent; Germany, 19 percent; Japan, 18 percent; Canada, 28 percent; Italy, 32 percent; and France, 29 percent.

6 I would like to thank Eileen Smith of the CBOE for providing me with these data.

7 The actual peak in the volatility index came on October 8, 1998, the date of the trough in the S&P500 index.

8 The behavior of default spreads for other G-7 countries gives a less clear picture of the start and end of the crisis. For Canada, France, Italy, and the UK, these spreads move roughly in line with the US data (although the interbank spread for France is so volatile that it is difficult to identify peaks and troughs with any degree of certainty). The German interbank spread peaks in November 1998, several weeks after the peak in US data. Finally, the behavior of default spreads in Japanese data is rather different from the other G-7 countries. In particular, the Japanese interbank spread shows little evidence of a liquidity crisis until a pronounced spike in mid-November 1998, well after the crisis abated in the US.

9 The Board of Governors' Senior Loan Officers Survey can be found on the Internet at www.federalreserve.gov/boarddocs/SnLoanSurvey. The surveys in August and November 1998 followed the Board's usual procedure of asking respondents about credit conditions over the preceding three months. Therefore, the November survey reflected most of the crisis period. In contrast, the September 1998 survey was a special survey that only asked about credit conditions over the previous month.

10 This characterization of markets during the crisis is confirmed by other sources. For example, Morgan Stanley Dean Witter reported a sharply reduced volume of activity across the corporate borrowing spectrum (Roach, 1998). Similarly, a strategist at Merrill Lynch asserted that "there were literally occasions when you could not get a bid of any kind for debt that was a reasonable risk" (*The Economist*, 1998, p. 75).

11 See Schlessinger and Wessel (1998a).

12 BIS (1999, p. 42).

13 The role of the Federal Reserve Bank of New York in the recapitalization of LTCM was limited to providing meeting facilities for the involved parties. The Fed provided no funds in the LTCM workout.

14 According to the US Department of Commerce, Bureau of the Census (1998), the US exports of goods and services to Argentina, Mexico and Brazil in 1997 exceeded $93 billion (13.5 percent of total US exports), while US imports from these countries totaled almost $98 billion (11.2 percent of US total). In contrast, US exports to Russia totaled $3.4 billion (0.49 percent of the US total) with imports from Russia totaling $4.3 billion (0.50 percent of the US total).

15 Brady bonds are US dollar-denominated obligations of various developing countries, mainly in Latin America.

16 For Indonesia and Malaysia, swap yields for maturities up to two years and forward exchange rates for up to one year closely track the spot exchange rates for these currencies. That is, these forward-looking markets did not anticipate the currency devaluations. Data on these particular markets are not available for Korea and the Philippines, but yields on government bonds (five-year maturity for Korea, one-year maturity for the Philippines) display the same patterns as the Indonesian and Malaysian swap yields: they do not budge until these countries devalued their currency. The only country where interest rates (as measured by swap yields) and forward exchange rates moved before the devaluation was Thailand. For that country, both rates started to increase six weeks before the devaluation of the baht. However, this coincided with the initial speculative attacks on the baht and the Thai government's initial attempts to defend its currency peg.

17 See Burnside *et al.* (2001).

18 In developing this model I benefited from extensive discussions with François Velde.

19 These second and third characteristics were also associated with the Asian Crisis of 1997. The reduction in liquidity provision took the form of a reversal of short-term capital flows from Western countries. Needless to say, stock markets fell precipitously in all five Asian crisis countries.

20 In this example, which is discussed in Cooper and John (1988), there can be more than two equilibria.

21 The classic demonstration of how a search model can give rise to a thick markets externality is Diamond (1982).

22 I'd like to thank Eric French for suggesting this interpretation.

23 It would be preferable to have the contract emerge as the equilibrium outcome of a bargaining game. This approach is not straightforward to implement. The Nash (1953) axiomatic approach to solving the two-person bargaining problem does not generalize to a game with asymmetric information. An alternative would be to specify a noncooperative bargaining game. For example, one could assume that either the borrower or lender is randomly given the right to make a single take-it-or-leave-it offer. (Mortensen and Pissarides, 1998, note that this game under full information implies the same solution as a particular version of the Nash bargaining problem.) It is beyond the scope of this chapter to explore the range of noncooperative game theoretic approaches to this problem. As a result, I adopt the simple expedient of an exogenous contract.

24 My assumption that a lender who fails to match gets a zero net return captures the idea that there is some opportunity cost to committing to provide loans, rather than investing exclusively in the risk-free investment. However, the analysis would not be changed substantially if a lender who fails to match received a small positive return.

25 Lagos (2000) develops a model of passenger-cab matching that implies constant returns to scale. The difference between this model and the model I develop in Appendix A is that Lagos (2000) assumes a continuum of passengers and cabs, whereas my model assumes that both passengers and cabs are discrete and finite in number.

26 More recently, DenHaan *et al.* (1999) and Burdette *et al.* (2000) propose search models that give rise to nontrivial multiple equilibriums even with constant returns to scale.

27 The baseline parameters used in Figure 21.4 are: $N_{lend} = 20$; $N_{borr} = 30$; $R = 2$; $R_{lend} = 1.2$ (so $R_{borr} = 0.8$); $R^{salvage} = 0.5$; $p^b = 0.2$; $\theta = 0.75$. Parameter N_{bad} is set equal to its expected value of 6. I use the model of $prob_{lend}$ and $prob_{borr}$ described in Appendix A, equations (19) and (20), with parameter $M = 10$.

28 Of course, this static model cannot address the question of why existing assets decline in value. If existing productive assets utilize a continued flow of credit to maintain high profitability, a reluctance of lenders to provide credit would presumably reduce asset values. However, it would require a dynamic extension of this model to analyze this effect formally.

29 In the literature on financial fragility, this is typically done by assuming an exogenous "sunspot process," whose realization determines the state of optimism in the economy. (See, e.g. Chang and Velasco (1998), Christiano and Harrison (1996) and Burnside *et al.* (2000).) I do not explicitly implement this approach for rendering the model dynamic, but to do so would be straightforward.

30 While Figure 21.5, panel B displays the real overnight interest rate, the relevant rate for bank incentives is the expected rate of return from holding longer term fixed income securities. Forecasting expected real holding period returns is a process fraught with difficulty, and I do not attempt to do so here. However, simple term structure models (such as the expectations hypothesis) imply that expected real holding period returns move with short-term real interest rates. Figure 21.5, panel B suggests that the expected returns relevant to bank decisions fell substantially as a result of the Fed's expansionary policy from 1991 to 1993.

31 Quoted in "After the crash," by Alan Murray, *Wall Street Journal*, October 21, 1987 (page unknown).

32 For an account of these events, see the Securities Exchange Commission report "The October 1987 market break," excerpted in Robert W. Kamphuis, Jr, Roger C. Kormendi,

and J.W. Henry Watson (eds), *Black Monday and the Future of Financial Markets*, Homewood, IL: Irwin, 1989.

33 For example, the Morgan Stanley Dean Witter *Global Economic Forum* of September 25, 1998, noted that a large rate cut at the FOMC meeting four days later "... may reflect a potentially profound transformation in the Fed's basic philosophy." The forum argued "... that the biggest risk of all is that the world's policy makers may not be up to the task at hand." Similarly, Jacob Schlesinger wrote in the *Wall Street Journal* of September 28, 1998, that "an easing of monetary policy would mark a swift and amazing turnaround in the central bank's fundamental economic outlook. For well over a year, the Fed's greatest concern has been inflation, not recession."

34 Schlesinger and Wessel (1998a), p. A3.

35 Morgan Stanley Dean Witter (1999).

36 Minutes of the FOMC can be obtained from the Fed website www.federalreserve.gov/fomc

37 Schelssinger and Ip (1998).

38 See also Hall (1999).

39 More generally, this result holds if the number of locations increases at a slower rate than the number of borrowers and lenders.

40 This explicitly rules out equilibria of the form, "All borrowers and all lenders choose to go to the kth location with probability 1."

41 This assertion uses the fact that equation (8) implies that $V_{\text{lend}}\,(B, L)$ is decreasing in L. Therefore, if $V_{\text{lend}}\,(N_{\text{borr}} - N_{\text{bad}}, N_{\text{lend}}) \geq R^{\text{f}}$, then $V_{\text{lend}}\,(N_{\text{borr}} - N_{\text{bad}}, L) \geq R^{\text{f}}, \forall L \leq N_{\text{lend}}$.

References

Bank for International Settlements (BIS) 1999, "A review of financial market events in Autumn 1998," Committee on the Global Financial System, Basel, Switzerland, October.

Bernanke, Ben S., 1983, "Nonmonetary effects of the financial crisis in the propagation of the Great Depression," *American Economic Review*, 73(3), 257–276.

Burdette, Kenneth, Ryoichi Imai, and Randall Wright, 2000, "Unstable relationships," University of Pennsylvania, manuscript.

Burnside, Craig, Martin Eichenbaum, and Sergio Rebelo, 2000, "On the fundamentals of self fulfilling currency attacks: The role of government guarantees to foreign bank creditors," Northwestern University, working paper.

Burnside, Craig, Martin Eichenbaum, and Sergio Rebelo, 2001, "Prospective deficits and the Asian currency crisis," *Journal of Political Economy*, 109(6), 1155–1197.

Chang, Roberto and Andres Velasco, 1998, "The Asian liquidity crisis," Federal Reserve Bank of Atlanta, working paper, No. 98–11.

Chari, V.V. and Patrick J. Kehoe, 2000, "Financial crises as herds," Federal Reserve Bank of Minneapolis, working paper, No. 600.

Chari, V.V., Lawrence J. Christiano, and Martin Eichenbaum, 1998, "Expectation traps and discretion," *Journal of Economic Theory*, 81(2), 462–492.

Chari, V.V., Lawrence J. Christiano, and Martin Eichenbaum, 1998, "Hot money," Federal Reserve Bank of Minneapolis, staff report.

Christiano, Lawrence J. and Christopher Gust, 2000, "The expectations trap hypothesis," *Economic Perspectives*, Federal Reserve Bank of Chicago, Second Quarter, pp. 21–39.

Christiano, Lawrence J. and Sharon G. Harrison, 1996, "Chaos, sunspots, and automatic stabilizers," Federal Reserve Bank of Chicago, working paper, No. WP-96-16.

Cooper, Russell and Andrew John, 1988, "Coordinating coordination failures in Keynesian models," *Quarterly Journal of Economics*, 103(3), 441–463.

DenHaan, Wouter J., Garey Ramey, and Joel Watson, 1999, "Liquidity flows and fragility of business enterprises," National Bureau of Economic Research, working paper, No. 7057.

Diamond, Peter A., 1982, "Aggregate demand management in search equilibrium," *Journal of Political Economy*, 90(5), 881–894.

Economist Newspaper Limited, The, 1998, "Alan Greenspan's miracle cure," *The Economist*, October 24, p. 75.

Greenlaw, David, 1999, "U.S.: a shocker!," *Global Economic Forum*, Morgan Stanley Dean Witter, October 16, available on the Internet at www.msdw.com/GEFdata

Hall, Robert, 1999, "Reorganization," National Bureau of Economic Research, working paper, No. 7181.

Kamphuis, Jr, Robert W., Roger C. Kormendi, and J.W. Henry Watson, (eds), 1989, "The October 1987 market break," in Securities Exchange Commission report, *Black Monday and the Future of Financial Markets*, Homewood, IL: Irwin.

Kultti, Klaus, 1998, "Scale returns of a random matching model," *Economics Letters*, 58, 277–280.

Lagos, Rigardo, 2000, "An alternative approach to search frictions," *Journal of Political Economy*, 108(51), 851–873.

Lagunoff, Roger and Stacey Schreft, L. 1998, "Financial fragility with rational and irrational exuberance," *Journal of Money, Credit, and Banking*, Part 2, August 1999, 31(3), 531–60.

Mishkin, Frederic, 1991, "Asymmetric information and financial crises: a historical perspective," in *Financial Markets and Financial Crises*, National Bureau of Economic Research, project report, London and Chicago: University of Chicago Press, pp. 69–108.

Morgan Stanley Dean Witter, 1999, *Global Economic Forum*, October 19, available on the Internet at www.msdw.com/GEFdata

Mortensen, Dale and Christopher Pissarides, A..1999, "New developments in models of search in the labor market," *Handbook of Labor Economics*. Volume 3B, 1999, pp. 2567–2627, Handbook in Economics, Vol. 5, Amsterdam, New York and Oxford: Elsevier Science, North-Holland.

Murray, Alan, 1987, "After the crash," *Wall Street Journal*, October 21.

Nash, John, 1953, "Two-person cooperative games," *Econometrica*, 21, 155–162.

Perotti, Enrico, 2000, "Banking regulation under extreme legal underdevelopment: lessons from the Russian meltdown," University of Amsterdam, manuscript.

Roach, Stephen, 1998, *Global Economic Forum*, Morgan Stanley Dean Witter, New York, October 16, available on the Internet at www.msdw.com/gef/

Schelssinger Jacob M., 1998, "Whys, wherefores of a possible rate cut," *Wall Street Journal*, September 28.

Schelssinger Jacob M. and Greg Ip, 1998, "Fed officials are upbeat on economy, signal further rate cuts if necessary," *Wall Street Journal*, October 23.

Schlesinger Jacob M. and David Wessel, 1998a, "Fed cuts interest rates a quarter point in a surprise move to shore up markets," *Wall Street Journal*, October 16.

Schlesinger Jacob M. and David Wessel, 1998b, "Fed cuts short-term rates by 0.25 point," *Wall Street Journal*, September 30, p. A3.

Sprague, O.M.W., 1910, *History of Crises under the National Banking System*, U.S. Senate, 61st Congress, Washington, DC, Government Printing Office, No. 538.

US Department of Commerce, Bureau of the Census, 1998, "U.S. international trade in goods and services – Annual revision for 1997," Washington, DC, No. FT 900, available on the Internet at www.census.gov/foreign-trade/Press-Release/97_press_releases/Final_Revisions_1997/

Questions for Part VI

1 Contagion is more of a regional phenomenon than a global one. Do you agree?
2 Are financial links responsible for creating a contagion? If so. What are the channels of transmission?
3 How did the highly successful Asian economies managed to fall to a crisis after decades of success?
4 Did exchange rates play a role in the Indonesian, Korean and Thai crises?
5 "Flight to quality" was an important market-related reason behind the crisis of the 1990s. Opine.
6 What antidotes can the central bank provide to an economy that is heading toward a crisis?

Areas for further research:

1 What does a "contagion" really mean?
2 Were the crises of the 1990s currency, financial or economic crises/or were they a combination of all three?
3 Financial crisis, financial fragility.
4 Central banking in a globalized financial market.

Part VII

Financial and macroeconomic issues

22 Financial restructuring in banking and corporate sector crises – what policies to pursue?

Stijn Claessens, Daniela Klingebiel and Luc Laeven

Introduction

Whether a cause or an effect, a systemic banking and corporate crisis is often part of a currency crisis.[1] Resolving a banking and corporate crisis involves many policy choices ranging from macroeconomic (including monetary and fiscal policy) to microeconomic (including capital adequacy rules and corporate governance requirements), with reforms varying in depth. These choices involve trade-offs, including the amount of government resources needed to resolve the crisis, the speed of recovery, and the recovery's sustainability. Despite considerable analysis, these trade-offs are not well known – an oversight that occasionally leads to conflicting policy advice and larger than necessary economic costs. Even less is known about the political economy factors that make governments choose certain policies.

This chapter reviews knowledge about the trade-offs involved in policies related to systemic financial and corporate restructuring. It finds that a consistent framework for bank and corporate restructuring is the key factor for success – and one that is often missing. Consistency is needed in many areas and involves, among other elements, ensuring that there are sufficient resources for absorbing losses and that private agents face appropriate sticks and carrots for restructuring. Moreover, sustainable restructuring requires deep structural reforms, which often require addressing political economy factors upfront.

The chapter complements the literature review with some new empirical analysis using data for 687 corporations from eight crisis countries. It investigates the quantitative importance of some specific government policies: liquidity support to financial institutions, the guaranteeing of the liabilities of the financial system during the early phase of the crisis, and the establishment of a public asset management company during the restructuring phase. It finds that a package of these measures can facilitate quicker recovery by the corporate sector from a crisis and assist in the sustainability of the recovery. The particular policies come with large fiscal costs, however, leading to trade-offs in terms of an equitable distribution of the benefits and cost of the government intervention and, possibly in terms of the ultimate growth impact.

The chapter proceeds as follows. The next section presents an overview of the general characteristics of banking system and corporate sector crises. The section

"Literature on banking and corporate sector crises," reviews the literature on such crises. Empirical evidence on the effects of crisis resolution policies using firm-level data from a set of crisis countries is provided by the section that follows the reviews. The last section concludes.

Characteristics of banking and corporate crises

A systemic banking and corporate crisis is a situation where an economy faces large-scale financial and corporate distress within a short period.[2] Recent examples include the crisis in Nordic countries in the early 1990s, in Mexico in 1994–95, in East Asian countries after 1997, and in transition economies in the 1990s (though for transition economies, financial distress and structural problems had been longer-term phenomena). Banking and corporate crises appear to have become more common since the early 1980s: Caprio and Klingebiel (2002) identify ninety-three countries that experienced a systemic financial crisis during the 1980s or 1990s (Figure 22.1). It also appears that crises became deeper in the 1990s relative to earlier periods (Bordo *et al.*, 2001).

In a systemic crisis, partly as a result of a general economic slowdown and large shocks to foreign exchange and interest rates, corporate and financial sectors experience a large number of defaults and difficulties repaying contracts on time. As a result nonperforming loans increase sharply. This situation is often accompanied by depressed asset prices (such as equity and real estate prices) on the heels of run-ups before the crisis, sharp increases in real interest rates, and a slowdown or reversal in capital flows (Table 22.1). In countries with longer-term financial distress and other large-scale structural problems – such as several transition economies – a systemic crisis may not be accompanied by such changes in asset prices and capital flows, partly because run-ups in prices and capital flows may not have occurred.

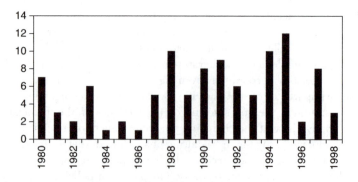

Figure 22.1 Frequency of systemic banking crises.

Sources: Caprio and Klingebiel (2002); authors' calculations.

Note
The frequency on the vertical axis indicates the number of countries that had a crisis starting in the year on the horizontal axis (total sample of crisis countries is ninety-three).

Table 22.1 Patterns of systemic banking crises

Country	Crisis year	Fiscal cost (% of GDP)	Peak NPL (% of loans)	Real GDP growth (%)	Change in exchange rate (%)	Peak in real interest rates (%)	Decline in real asset prices (%)
Finland	1992	11.0	13	−4.6	−5.5	14.3	−34.6
Indonesia	1998	50.0	65–75	−15.4	−57.5	3.3	−78.5
Korea	1998	37.0	30–40	−10.6	−28.8	21.6	−45.9
Malaysia	1998	16.4	25–35	−12.7	−13.9	5.3	−79.9
Mexico	1995	19.3	30	−6.2	−39.8	24.7	−53.3
Philippines	1998	0.5	20	−0.8	−13.0	6.3	−67.2
Sweden	1992	4.0	18	−3.3	+1.0	79.2	−6.8
Thailand	1998	32.8	33	−5.4	−13.7	17.2	−77.4

Sources: "Crisis year" is the peak crisis year, from Caprio and Klingebiel (2002, as reported in Klingebiel and Laeven, 2002). The "fiscal costs as % of GDP" variable is from Honohan and Klingebiel (2002). The "peak non-performing loans as % of total loans" variable is from Caprio and Klingebiel (2002) in the case of Indonesia, Korea, the Philippines, and Thailand; Lindgren *et al.* (1996) in the case of Finland and Sweden, and Krueger and Tornell (1999) in the case of Mexico. The "real GDP growth" variable equals the percentage change in real fourth-quarter GDP in the crisis year compared to real fourth-quarter GDP one year before the crisis year. CPI inflation is used to get the real growth in GDP, and the growth in GDP is in terms of local currency. GDP data are from IFS (IMF). The inflation rate equals the percentage change in the CPI during the crisis year and is from IFS. The "change in the exchange rate" equals the percentage change of the exchange rate versus the US dollar during the first quarter of the crisis year. An increase in the exchange rate indicates an appreciation. The exchange rate data are from IFS. The "real interest rate spike" equals the peak in the real money market rate during crisis year. For the Philippines, the real discount rate is reported instead of the money market rate, due to data unavailability. The interest rate data are from IFS. The "real growth in asset prices" variables is the largest drop on a monthly basis in the stock market index during the crisis year compared to the level of the stock market index in January of the year before the crisis year. The return is in local currency and corrected for inflation. We use the Datastream global market indices for Finland, Mexico and Sweden, and the IFC global market indices for the other countries.

Developments in crisis countries highlight the complicated coordination problems that arise between corporations, between the corporate and financial sectors, between the government and the rest of the economy, and with respect to domestic and foreign investors. In a systemic crisis the fate of an individual corporation and the best course of action for its owners and managers will depend on the actions of many other corporations and financial institutions as well as the general economic outlook. The financial and corporate sectors, always closely intertwined, both need restructuring in a systemic crisis, and the actions taken affect their liquidity and solvency. The government must set the rules of the game and be a prominent actor in restructuring. And investors, domestic and foreign, will await the actions of owners, the government, labor, and others – often implying a shortage of foreign and domestic capital when it is most needed.

A crisis and its coordination problems are typically aggravated by institutional weaknesses, many of which likely caused the crisis in the first place. Bankruptcy and restructuring frameworks are often deficient. Disclosure and accounting rules may be weak for financial institutions and corporations. Equity and creditor rights may be poorly defined. And the judiciary is often inefficient. There is usually also a shortage of qualified managers in the corporate and financial sectors, as well as a lack of qualified domestic restructuring and insolvency specialists – partly because there may be no history of corporate and financial sector restructuring. The government itself may face credibility problems because it may have been partly to blame for the crisis, and in general faces many time consistency problems – such as how to avoid large bailouts while also restarting the economy.

These complicated coordination problems suggest that systemic crises are difficult to resolve. Many observers have tried to develop best practices for resolving such crises. We next review that literature.

Literature on banking and corporate crises

Governments have used many approaches to try to resolve systemic bank and corporate distress. Resolving systemic financial distress is not easy, and opinions differ widely on what constitutes best practice. Many different and seemingly contradictory policy recommendations have been made to limit the fiscal costs of crises and speed recovery. Empirical research supporting particular views remains limited, and most research is limited to individual cases.

Sheng (1996) was the first attempt to distill lessons from several banking crises. Caprio and Klingebiel (1996) expanded on those lessons using additional crises. The main lesson from both efforts is that managing a financial crisis is much different in industrial countries than in emerging markets because emerging markets have weaker institutions, crises are often larger, and other initial circumstances differ. As a result best practices from industrial countries do not easily transfer to developing countries. Another key lesson is that there are many trade-offs between various policies.

In reviewing the literature on financial restructuring, especially in emerging markets, it is useful to differentiate between three phases of systemic restructuring. During the first phase, which can be called the containment phase, the financial crisis is still unfolding. During this phase governments tend to implement policies aimed at restoring public confidence to minimize the repercussions on the real sector of the loss of confidence by depositors and other investors in the financial system. The second phase involves the actual financial, and to a lesser extent operational, restructuring of financial institutions and corporations. The third phase involves structural reforms, including changes in laws and regulations, privatization of any nationalized financial institutions and corporations, and so on. Here we discuss the containment phase, the restructuring of financial institutions, and the restructuring of corporations.

Containment phase

Policymakers often fail to respond effectively to evidence of an impending banking crisis, hoping that banks and corporations will grow out of their problems.[3] But intervening early with a comprehensive and credible plan can avoid a systemic crisis, minimize adverse effects, and limit overall losses (Sheng, 1996). Early intervention appears to be especially important in stopping the flow of financing to loss-making financial institutions and corporations and in limiting moral hazard in financial institutions and corporations gambling for survival.

Experience also suggests that intervention and closing of weak financial institutions need to be properly managed. Uncertainty among depositors needs to be limited; otherwise the government may have to try to resolve a loss of confidence with an unlimited guarantee on the liabilities of banks and other financial institutions. But in practice, ad hoc closures are more the norm and often add to uncertainty, triggering a systemic crisis. For example, in late 1997 the closing of sixteen banks in Indonesia triggered a depositor run because depositors were aware that some politically connected banks known to be insolvent were kept open (Lindgren *et al.*, 2000). Similarly, the suspension of finance companies in Thailand increased uncertainty among depositors as well as borrowers.

Reviewing several cases, Baer and Klingebiel (1995) suggest that, to avoid uncertainty among depositors and limit their incentives to run, policymakers need to deal simultaneously with all insolvent and marginally solvent institutions. Intermittent regulatory intervention makes depositors more nervous and undermines regulatory credibility – especially if regulators had previously argued that the institutions involved were solvent.[4] Moreover, in emerging markets regulations are often weak, supervision is limited, and data on financial solvency are poor, so intervention tools need to be fairly simple.

For example, a rehabilitation program for undercapitalized financial institutions – which involves institutions indicating how they plan to meet capital adequacy requirements in the future – requires careful government oversight and good financial statements. But such features are often missing in developing countries. Instead of relying on rehabilitation that requires good oversight and data, regulators could apply a 100 percent (marginal) reserve requirement on deposit inflows and other new liabilities, limiting weak banks' ability to reallocate resources in a detrimental way.

There are two schools of thoughts on whether to use liquidity support and unlimited guarantees during the containment phase.[5] Some argue that crisis conditions make it almost impossible to distinguish between solvent and insolvent institutions, leaving the authorities with little choice but to extend liquidity support. Moreover, it is argued that an unlimited guarantee preserves the payments system and helps stabilize institutions' financial claims while restructuring is being organized and carried out (Lindgren *et al.*, 2000).

Others argue that open-ended liquidity support provides more time for insolvent institutions to gamble (unsuccessfully) on resurrection, facilitates continued financing of loss-making borrowers, and allows owners and managers to engage in looting. Supporters of this view also argue that a government guarantee on financial institutions' liabilities reduces large creditors' incentives to monitor financial institutions, allowing bank managers and shareholders to continue gambling on their insolvent banks and increasing fiscal costs. They further point out that extensive guarantees limit government maneuverability in allocating losses, often with the end result that government incurs most of the cost of the systemic crisis (Sheng, 1996).

In practice, there is a trade-off between restoring confidence and containing fiscal costs. Evidence on these trade-offs comes from Honohan and Klingebiel (2002), who show that much of the variation in the fiscal cost of forty crises in industrial and developing economies in 1980–97 can be explained by government approaches to resolving liquidity crises. The authors find that governments that provided open-ended liquidity support and blanket deposit guarantees incurred much higher costs in resolving financial crises. They also find that these costs are higher in countries with weak institutions.

Most important, Honohan and Klingebiel find no obvious trade-off between fiscal costs and subsequent economic growth (or overall output losses). Countries that used policies such as liquidity support, blanket guarantees, and particularly costly forbearance did not recover faster. Rather, liquidity support appears to make recovery from a crisis longer and output losses larger – a finding confirmed by Bordo *et al.* (2001). Thus it appears that the two most important policies during the containment phase are to limit liquidity support and not extend guarantees. And where institutions are weak, governments may need to use simple methods in dealing with weak banks and a loss of confidence to avoid higher fiscal contingencies and costs.

Restructuring financial institutions

Once financial markets have been stabilized, the second phase involves restructuring weak financial institutions and corporations. Restructuring is complex because policymakers need to take into account many issues. Financial restructuring will depend on the speed at which macroeconomic stability can be achieved because that determines the viability of corporations, banks, and other financial institutions, and more generally the reduction in overall uncertainty. But macroeconomic stability often requires progress on financial and corporate restructuring, and so cannot be viewed independently of the restructuring process (see Burnside *et al.*, this volume and Park and Lee, this volume).

Restructuring refers to several related processes: recognizing and allocating financial losses, restructuring the financial claims of financial institutions and corporations, and operational restructuring of financial institutions and corporations. Recognition involves the allocation of losses and associated redistribution of wealth and control. Losses – that is, differences between the market value of assets and the nominal value of liabilities held by financial institutions and corporations – can be allocated to shareholders (through dilution), to depositors and creditors (by reducing the present value of their claims), to employees (through reduced wages) and suppliers, and to the government or the public (through higher taxes, lower spending, or inflation). Here we discuss the restructuring of financial institutions; the next section discusses the restructuring of corporations.

To minimize moral hazard and strengthen financial discipline, governments can allocate losses not only to shareholders but also to creditors and large depositors who should have been monitoring the banks. Often, however, governments assume all losses through their guarantees. There are exceptions to the model of governments guaranteeing all liabilities in an effort to restore confidence. Baer and Klingebiel (1995) show that in some crises – notably in the United States (1933), Japan (1946), Argentina (1980–82), and Estonia (1992) – governments have imposed losses on depositors with little or no adverse macroeconomic consequences or flight to currency. In these cases economic recovery was rapid and financial intermediation, including household deposits, was soon restored. Thus allocating losses to creditors or depositors will not necessarily lead to runs on banks or end in contraction of aggregate money, credit, and output. In a related vein, Caprio and Klingebiel's (1996) review of country cases indicates that financial discipline is further strengthened when bank management – often part of the problem – is changed and banks are operationally restructured.

Besides loss allocation, financial and corporate restructuring crucially depend on the incentives under which banks and corporations operate. Successful corporate debt workouts require proper incentives for banks and borrowers to come to the negotiating table (Dado and Klingebiel, 2002). The incentive framework for banks includes accounting, classification, and provisioning rules – that is, financial institutions need to be asked to realistically mark their assets to market. The framework also includes laws and prudential regulations. Regulators should ensure that undercapitalized financial institutions are properly disciplined and closed. The insolvency system should enable financial institutions to enforce their claims on corporations, allow for speedy financial restructuring of viable corporations, and provide for the efficient liquidation of enterprises that cannot be rehabilitated. Proper incentives also mean limited ownership links between banks and corporations (since otherwise the same party could end up being both debtor and creditor).

Adequately capitalized financial institutions are a key component of a proper incentive framework, because financial institutions need to have sufficient loss absorption capacity to engage in sustainable corporate restructuring. In a systemic crisis, capital will often have to come from the government through recapitalization. But general experience – supported by recent events in East Asia – suggests that recapitalization of financial institutions needs to be structured and managed to limit moral hazard. In their analysis of forty bank crises, Honohan and Klingebiel (2002) find that repeated, incomplete recapitalizations tend to increase the fiscal costs of resolving a crisis. One possible explanation is that marginally capitalized banks tend to engage in cosmetic corporate restructuring – such as maturity extensions or interest rate reductions on loans to nonviable corporations – rather than writing off debts.

Besides adequate capitalization, preferably by private shareholders, banks' incentives to undertake corporate restructuring can be strengthened by linking government financing to the restructuring. For example, a capital support scheme in which additional fiscal resources are linked to corporate restructuring through loss sharing arrangements can induce banks to conduct deeper restructuring.

Regardless, especially in weak institutional settings, limits on the actions of marginally capitalized banks will typically be necessary.

In principle, governments should only capitalize or strengthen the capital base of financial institutions with charter and franchise value. But apart from political economy problems, it is often difficult for governments to distinguish good banks from bad. Risk sharing mechanisms with the private sector, such as cofinancing arrangements with government equity infusion (in the form of preferred shares) when the private sector provides capital, can help identify better banks. This setup still requires decent institutions to avoid misuse. Especially in a weak institutional environment with limited private capital, governments may want to rely more on hard budget constraints on weak banks (such as a 100 percent marginal reserve requirement on new deposits) to prevent a large leakage of fiscal resources, including through excessive guarantees on financial institutions' liabilities. And good banks may need to be actively coerced to receive support, because they may resist government interference. But without some support, good banks may not be able to provide financial intermediation to corporations, aggravating the crisis.

Restructuring corporations

Providing the right incentives. The nature of a systemic crisis, and the already close links between the solvency and performance of the corporate and financial sectors in normal times, make it clear that bank restructuring needs to be complemented by corporate restructuring. To start corporate restructuring, corporations should quickly be triaged into operationally viable and not financially distressed corporations, operationally viable but financially distressed corporations, and financially and operationally unviable corporations. In a normal restructuring of an individual case of financial distress, private agents will make these decisions and start the operational and financial restructuring.[6] But in a systemic crisis case-by-case restructuring will be difficult because the incentives under which agents operate are likely not conducive, private capital is typically limited, and coordination problems are large.[7]

Nevertheless, the starting point is providing proper incentives for private agents to allow and encourage market-based, sustainable corporate restructuring. Given that the crisis was likely partly induced by weaknesses in the environment in which the corporate sector operated, the first step for government will have to be creating an enabling environment. Depending on country circumstances, this can imply undertaking corporate governance reforms, improving bankruptcy and other restructuring frameworks, making the judicial system more efficient, liberalizing entry by foreign investors, changing the competitive framework for the real sector, or introducing other supportive structural measures. In general, the political economy of reform suggests that a crisis can often be a time to get difficult structural reforms accepted or at least initiated (Haggard, 2001).

Most crisis countries do reform the incentives for restructuring (see World Bank, 2000; Stone, 2000a,b; Claessens *et al.*, 2001; and Dado and Klingebiel, 2002 for different groups of crisis countries), though the strengths and depth of the reforms differ. For example, Indonesia adopted a new bankruptcy system to replace its pre-Second World War Dutch code in August 1998, twelve months after its crisis started. Similarly, Thailand's Senate approved the Act for the Establishment of and Procedure for Bankruptcy Court, intended to increase the efficiency of judicial procedures in bankruptcy cases, in February 1999, nineteen months after its crisis began. But despite the act's adoption, bankruptcies in Thailand remained few in number and fraught with difficulties (Foley, 2000).

Beyond fixing the environment, it can be necessary to provide extra incentives for private agents to engage in (quick) corporate restructuring. These incentives can involve tax, accounting, and other measures. Banks, for example, may be given more tax relief for provisioning or restructuring loans. Corporations may be given more favorable accounting relief for recognizing foreign exchange losses. In the wake of its crisis, the Republic of Korea adopted more favorable tax rules for corporate restructuring, though they ended up being misused through cosmetic rather than real restructuring. Some countries have offered guarantees on exchange rate behavior, such as Indonesia's INDRA scheme and Mexico's FICORCA scheme; see Stone (2000b). The efficiency of such measures should be evaluated from various perspectives, taking into account their benefits for restructuring and public finance as well as their possible redistributive effects. But while such measures may speed recovery, they often do not contribute to fundamental reforms. In any case, the general opinion is that such measures should be temporary (i.e. with sunset clauses).

Improving the framework for restructuring. Even when adequate for normal times, a revamped bankruptcy and restructuring framework might not be sufficient during a systemic crisis given the coordination problems and weaknesses in other aspects of the institutional framework. Thus governments have created special frameworks for corporate restructuring, such as the "London rules"[8] first used in Mexico and then in several East Asian countries (Indonesia, Korea, Malaysia, and Thailand). The London rules involve an out-of-court accord, under regular contract or commercial law, that all or most creditor institutions are coerced to sign. With such an accord, agreements reached among most creditors can often be enforced on other creditors without formal judicial procedures.

Arbitration with specific deadlines – and penalties for failing to meet the deadlines – can also be part of the accord, avoiding a formal judicial process to resolve disputes.[9] The degree of such enhancements to the London rules has varied among countries. In East Asia, the frameworks in Korea, Malaysia, and Thailand were the most conducive to out-of-court restructuring, while the framework in Indonesia was the least (Claessens *et al.*, 2001). These differences appear to partly explain the variations in the speed of restructuring in these four countries.

The most far-reaching proposal for enhancing the restructuring framework is "super-bankruptcy" (or "super Chapter 11"), a temporary tool that allows corporate management to stay in place and forces debt-to-equity conversions (Stiglitz, 2001). This tool can preserve firms' value as going concerns by preventing too many liquidations and keeping in place existing managers, who arguably most often know best how to run the firms. An important issue is when to call for a super Chapter 11 – that is, when is a crisis systemic, and who has the authority to call for such a suspension of payments? Political economy factors should be taken into account, because some debtors could gain disproportionately from a suspension of payments. To date no country has taken this approach.[10]

Even with a better enabling environment, agents will likely be unable to triage corporations quickly and proceed with restructuring. The resulting debt overhang or deadlock in claims can be especially risky when institutions are weak, and can greatly increase the final costs to the public sector of resolving the crisis. Weak banks may continue to lend to corporations that are "too big to fail," partly as a way of gambling for resurrection, and so delay sustainable corporate restructuring. Owners of defunct enterprises may strip assets, leaving only shells of liabilities for creditors. Even financially viable corporations may stop paying promptly if faced with an insolvent banking system.

In such cases it may be necessary in the short run to use hard budget constraints to limit the flow of resources to weak corporations from weak financial institutions or other sources. To increase credit to corporations that can actually repay and limit lending to weak corporations it may also be necessary to have temporary across-the-board mechanisms for certain types of borrowers (such as small and medium-size enterprises) or certain activities (such as trade financing). The need for such blunter tools will increase with a country's institutional weakness. Indonesia's market-based approach to corporate restructuring, for example, seems to have had little impact and probably only led to further asset stripping.

Choosing a lead agent. As a next step it is often necessary for government to more directly support corporate restructuring. As with support for the financial system, it is essential to restructure strong and viable corporations, and not weak ones. But all too often, unviable corporations (such as those considered too big to fail) receive support instead of deserving, operationally viable corporations. This was the case with Korea's large *chaebols* and with Indonesia and Thailand's large family-controlled conglomerates. These firms ended up receiving disproportionately large financing during the first phase of the crisis while smaller firms lacked even working capital (Domac and Ferri, 1999). Thus it is crucial to choose a lead agent that ensures proper analysis of corporations' prospects as well as durable operational and financial restructurings.

The main choice for the lead agent in restructuring is between the government and the private sector. Many approaches are possible. A centralized asset management corporation will put the government in charge. Recapitalization of private banks will put the banks in charge. Under other models investors and corporations can become the lead agent, with the government sharing the risks. Banks can work out nonperforming loans, for example, but with some stop-loss arrangements with the government. Or nonperforming loans can be transferred to a number of corporate restructuring vehicles that, though state-owned, can be privately run by asset managers with incentive stakes.

Most important is that the lead agent have the necessary capacity to absorb losses as well as the institutional capacity, incentives, and external enforcement mechanisms to effect restructuring. Undercapitalized banks, for example, will not be very effective restructuring agents. And without a working bankruptcy regime, private agents will not be able to force recalcitrant debtors to the negotiating table – as in Indonesia and in Thailand, where the restructuring of Thai Petrochemical Industry took three years.

Countries often choose a mix of these approaches when dealing with a systemic crisis. In 1995 Mexico tried both an asset management corporation and a more decentralized approach. The four East Asian crisis countries (Indonesia, Korea, Malaysia, and Thailand) all eventually used asset management corporations, all used out-of-court systems for corporate restructuring, and most used, after some initial period, fiscal stimulus and monetary policy to foster economic growth. In addition, all enhanced, to varying degrees, their basic frameworks for private sector operations, including bankruptcy and corporate governance frameworks, liberalization of foreign entry in the financial and corporate sectors, and so on. But success has varied with the intensity of these measures (Claessens *et al.*, 2001).

Empirical evidence on these mechanisms is limited but tends to favor the decentralized model. A study of seven centralized approaches using asset management companies found that most of the corporations did not achieve their stated objectives with corporate restructuring (Klingebiel, 2001). The study distinguishes corporate restructuring asset management corporations from bank rehabilitation asset management companies. Two of the three corporate restructuring companies did not achieve their narrow goal of expediting restructuring. Only Sweden's asset management company successfully managed its portfolio, acting in some instances as the lead agent in restructuring.

Rapid asset disposition vehicles fared somewhat better, with two of four – in Spain and the United States – achieving their objectives. These successes suggest that asset management corporations can be effective, but only for narrowly defined purposes of resolving insolvent and unviable financial institutions and selling their assets. But even achieving these objectives requires many ingredients: a type of asset that is easily liquefied (such as real estate), mostly professional management, political independence, a skilled human resource base, appropriate funding, adequate bankruptcy and foreclosure laws, good information and management systems, and transparent operations and processes.

The findings by Klingebiel (2001) on asset management companies are corroborated by a review of three East Asian countries (Dado, 2000). The centralized asset management companies in Indonesia and Korea did not appear likely to achieve their narrow goal of expediting bank or corporate restructuring, while Malaysia's was relatively successful, aided by that country's strong bankruptcy system. Success has also varied when a mix of approaches is tried. In Mexico neither the asset management company nor the enhanced restructuring framework was effective, possibly because fundamental reforms were lacking (Mexico's bankruptcy regime, e.g. was not revamped until four years after its crisis). Export-led growth appears to have led Mexico's recovery after 1995 (though growth did not resolve banking problems; see Krueger and Tornell, 1999).

Dado and Klingebiel (2002) analyze decentralized restructuring in seven countries – Argentina, Chile, Hungary, Japan, Norway, Poland, and Thailand. They find that the success of this approach depended on the quality of the institutional framework, including accounting and legal rules, and on initial conditions, including the capital positions of banks and ownership links. In Norway the government built on favorable initial conditions to attain a solid overall framework for the decentralized approach. The biggest improvement to the overall framework was made in Chile, with favorable results. Poland and Hungary ranked behind Chile, though Poland improved its framework much faster than Hungary. Thailand made little progress on strengthening its framework. In Japan, despite many reforms to the overall framework, efforts remained blocked by large ownership links. And Argentina relied solely on public debt relief programs and did not change its overall framework for restructuring.

Changing ownership structures. Just as a crisis can offer a window for structural reform, it can provide an opportunity to reform a country's ownership structures. As a direct party to the restructuring process, the state often becomes the owner of defunct financial institutions and corporations. This development severely complicates the resolution of the crisis, because government may not have the right incentives or capacity to effect the needed operational and financial restructuring. At the same time, large indirect ownership by the state of the financial and corporate sectors provides an opportunity to change ownership structures as part of restructuring. This move can have several benefits.

First, the changes can correct ownership structures that contributed to the crisis and so help prevent future crises. To the extent, for example, that ownership concentrated in the hands of a few families contributed to the crisis – as argued by some for East Asia – government could try to widen ownership structures.

Second, government can try to obtain political support for restructuring by reallocating ownership.[11] One option is to re-privatize financial institutions or corporations in a way that redistributes ownership among the general public or employees of the restructured institution. Another option is to use some of the state ownership to endow unfunded pension obligations from a pay-as-you-go system. In this way government can create ownership structures that over time will reinforce its reforms.

Third, changing ownership structures can introduce third parties who have better incentives and skills in restructuring individual corporations and determining financial relief. One option is to transfer nonperforming loans to a fund jointly owned by private and public shareholders, but with the private stake having lower seniority. Private shareholders in the fund would then have the right incentives when deciding on the financial viability of a corporation, but without having full formal ownership of the assets. Public resources would be provided only when all parties – creditor banks, other creditors, new private investors, the government, and the private shareholders in the fund – had reached agreement with the corporation.

Pursuing supportive macroeconomic policies. Another common theme in the literature is that corporate restructuring should occur in the context of supportive macroeconomic policies. The right macroeconomic policies (fiscal and monetary) can speed the recovery of overall activity and corporate output. The appropriate fiscal stance has been extensively reviewed, especially in the context of the East Asian crisis. A review by the International Monetary Fund suggests that East Asian countries' fiscal stance was too tight initially (Lane *et al.*, 1999). The appropriate monetary stance has been more controversial and is still being debated (see Drazen, 2003 and Cho and West, 2003), but mainly in terms of defending the exchange rate.

An important related aspect is the effect on the corporate sector through a possible credit crunch. Microeconomic-based empirical literature suggests evidence of a credit crunch early in the East Asian crisis (Claessens *et al.*, 2000; Colaco *et al.*, 2000; Dollar and Hallward-Driemeier, 2000). The crunch was likely the result of tighter capital adequacy requirements and the monetary policies being pursued. More generally, it has been found that while tighter capital adequacy rules have minimal effects on aggregate credit provision, borrowers from weak banks are affected by tighter regulation and supervision (BIS, 1999). Given the unbalanced financial systems in East Asia – where banks dominate and little alternative financing was available, and many banks were fragile even before the crisis (Claessens and Glaessner, 1997) – it is likely that, at least initially, banking weaknesses and tighter regulation and supervision led to a credit crunch for East Asian corporations (Domac and Ferri, 1999). Following this initial crunch, corporations may have ended up with a debt overhang, with a consequent need for financial restructuring.

Additional empirical evidence on the effects of crisis resolution policies

In this section, we shed more light on the costs and benefits of alternative crisis resolution policies. Specifically, we empirically investigate how policies affect the performance and financial structures of individual corporations. We focus on the corporate sector for several reasons. First, the final purpose of resolution policies, even if directed toward the financial sector only, is a revitalization of the real sector and overall economic growth. Using corporate sector indicators can thus provide a better measure of the final outcome. Second, the effects of policies can be more precisely measured by focusing on the corporate sector rather than the financial sector. The performance of banks, for example, will be highly affected by government financial actions, such as recapitalization, and therefore may not provide a good indication of the real outcomes achieved. Third, measuring the impact of resolution policies on a micro rather than a macro level (e.g. by GDP) allows us to better differentiate across policies. We can control, for example, for country characteristics, such as different corporate sector structures, when studying policies commonly adopted.

We collect company-specific data for a sample of crisis countries around the period of crisis in each respective country. Our sample selection proceeded as follows. We collected company data from WorldScope for all emerging markets and developed countries that were classified by Caprio and Klingebiel (2002) as having had a systemic financial crisis. We had to exclude all crises prior to 1989 since

WorldScope does not have sufficient data before 1989. We also had to exclude countries for which the crisis period is difficult to time, either because of multiple crises (such as in Argentina) or because the crisis stretches over a long period of time without clear peaks or ends (such as Japan). This left us with seventeen countries with a systemic crisis. We had to further exclude some countries for which we did not have a significant number of corporations with available data. This set of excluded countries includes nine transition countries (Bulgaria, Czech Republic, Estonia, Hungary, Latvia, Lithuania, Poland, and Slovenia) and Venezuela. For Venezuela, for example, we only had nine corporations for the whole sample period.

Given the data availability, we are left with eight crisis countries, namely Finland, Indonesia, South Korea, Malaysia, Mexico, Philippines, Sweden, and Thailand. For each country, we distinguish three periods. The crisis year is the year of the peak of the crisis as identified by Caprio and Klingebiel (2002). The pre-crisis year is defined as the average of the three years before the peak of the crisis and the post-crisis year as one year after the peak of the crisis. Table 22.2 reports the sample of crisis countries, and their respective crisis years.

In total, we have company-specific data from WorldScope for 687 firms. The data could suffer from a bias if many sampled firms entered bankruptcy during the crisis years. For most countries, however, the set of firms is quite similar between pre- and post-crisis period. In fact, the data set includes more firms during the crisis year than during the pre-crisis year.[12] This suggests that the data set does not suffer from a large survivorship or other reporting bias. The notable exception is the Republic of Korea for which the number of firms reporting in the post-crisis period is significantly less than those in the pre-crisis and crisis periods. The main reason is that at the date of data collection many Korean firms had not yet reported their financial statements for 1999.[13]

In estimating the impact of resolution policies on the performance of the corporate sectors, we distinguish between the depth of the crisis, the recovery after the crisis and the sustainability of the recovery. As a measure for the depth of the crisis, we use the difference in a corporation's operating income, defined as

Table 22.2 Sample crisis countries and crisis years

Country	Pre-crisis	Peak of crisis	Post-crisis
Finland	1989	1992	1993
Indonesia	1995	1998	1999
S. Korea	1995	1998	1999
Malaysia	1995	1998	1999
Mexico	1992	1995	1996
Philippines	1995	1998	1999
Sweden	1989	1992	1993
Thailand	1995	1998	1999

Sources: Caprio and Klingebiel (2002); authors' definitions.

earnings before interest and taxes with depreciation added, as a ratio of sales, that is, EBITDA-to-sales, between the pre-crisis and during-crisis period. Similarly, our measure for the degree of recovery of corporate performance is the difference in EBITDA-to-sales between the post-crisis and during-crisis period. And our measure for the sustainability of the recovery is the difference in EBITDA-to-sales between the post-crisis and pre-crisis periods.

Table 22.3 reports summary statistics of the company-specific data for EBITDA-to-sales, interest coverage, leverage, debt composition (share of short term) and share of payables (trade) relative to total assets, the main variables used in the empirical analysis, across all countries. It is worth noting that the interest coverage figure (measured as operating income to interest payments) reflects both firm profitability and debt structure. We find that, measured by EBITDA-to-sales, firms performed the worst during the crisis year. Firms had a worse interest coverage during the crisis year than before and were more leveraged at the peak of the crisis than before the crisis. Firms generally reduced the share of short-term debt over the crisis period, while the share of trade debt was mostly unaffected by the crisis. We also find that, although both the performance and capital structure of firms improved after the peak of the crisis, firms did not reach pre-crisis performance levels and financing structures within two years after the peak of the crisis.

These general trends are also reflected in Figures 22.2 and 22.3 that plot respectively the EBITDA-to-sales and interest coverage ratios for the three periods. The earnings and interest coverage distributions shift to the left between the pre-crisis and the crisis period, and then recover somewhat, but not to the distribution before the crisis. When measuring performance and sustainability using other measures, similar results are obtained. For example, the median operating return on assets falls from 5.5 percent in the pre-crisis period to 1.4 percent during the crisis period and then recovers to 2.8 percent in the post-crisis period. And the median ratio of the market to book value of equity moves from 1.8 before the crisis period to 0.7 during the crisis period, to recover to only 1.03 in the post-crisis period.

Table 22.3 also reports the summary statistics for individual countries for the same set of variables. The patterns for each country are generally the same as for the overall medians. Some exceptions are Finland, Indonesia, Mexico, and Sweden, where post-crisis corporate sector performance is on average better than pre-crisis performance. In these countries, some corporations may have benefited from the depreciation of the exchange rate, explaining the better performance. This is not the case for the other countries: in Thailand, for example, post-crisis performance is actually the worst of all three periods. Korea and Malaysia correspond to the pattern for the whole sample, with the recovery performance above the crisis level, but below the pre-crisis level. In terms of interest coverage, the picture is more uniform across the countries: some deterioration during the crisis generally followed by an improvement. The exceptions are Malaysia and Thailand where the average interest coverage ratios decline throughout.

Table 22.3 Descriptive statistics (means, with medians in brackets, and number of observations)

Country	EBITDA/sales			Interest coverage			Debt-to-assets			Short-term debt/total debt			Payables/total assets			No of obs.
	Pre-crisis	Crisis	Post-crisis	Pre-crisis	Crisis	Post-crisis	Pre-crisis	Crisis	Post-crisis	Pre-crisis	Crisis	Post-crisis	Pre-crisis	Crisis	Post-crisis	
All	0.216 [0.168]	0.120 [0.133]	0.167 [0.144]	8.333 [3.125]	2.499 [1.299]	4.863 [1.739]	0.314 [0.312]	0.427 [0.390]	0.424 [0.356]	0.536 [0.513]	0.547 [0.520]	0.504 [0.431]	0.087 [0.070]	0.080 [0.059]	0.084 [0.059]	687
Finland	0.129 [0.107]	0.136 [0.122]	0.157 [0.131]	2.272 [1.587]	1.697 [1.266]	3.184 [1.724]	0.370 [0.357]	0.432 [0.412]	0.409 [0.398]	0.253 [0.207]	0.259 [0.242]	0.281 [0.237]	0.092 [0.070]	0.086 [0.055]	0.092 [0.059]	67
Indonesia	0.256 [0.226]	0.089 [0.153]	0.292 [0.274]	9.813 [3.448]	2.942 [0.645]	9.785 [2.500]	0.323 [0.329]	0.595 [0.609]	0.503 [0.493]	0.652 [0.746]	0.710 [0.969]	0.552 [0.422]	0.097 [0.057]	0.079 [0.046]	0.076 [0.038]	54
Korea	0.162 [0.140]	−0.029 [0.119]	0.170 [0.141]	2.235 [1.515]	−0.274 [1.053]	2.125 [1.852]	0.481 [0.453]	0.566 [0.450]	0.668 [0.390]	0.505 [0.495]	0.569 [0.590]	0.463 [0.414]	0.110 [0.100]	0.092 [0.083]	0.110 [0.066]	50
Malaysia	0.226 [0.181]	0.008 [0.130]	0.122 [0.146]	16.848 [6.667]	4.061 [1.333]	5.187 [1.120]	0.212 [0.192]	0.386 [0.299]	0.390 [0.299]	0.667 [0.762]	0.630 [0.624]	0.647 [0.676]	0.075 [0.051]	0.066 [0.041]	0.067 [0.045]	180
Mexico	0.258 [0.207]	0.241 [0.225]	0.307 [0.272]	10.215 [3.280]	2.665 [1.835]	4.411 [3.125]	0.258 [0.287]	0.338 [0.319]	0.330 [0.303]	0.403 [0.336]	0.431 [0.362]	0.338 [0.252]	0.081 [0.050]	0.071 [0.050]	0.079 [0.059]	49
Philippines	0.337 [0.271]	0.186 [0.175]	0.215 [0.175]	7.661 [4.348]	−1.908 [0.799]	2.681 [1.282]	0.258 [0.272]	0.319 [0.296]	0.320 [0.335]	0.567 [0.495]	0.505 [0.466]	0.451 [0.321]	0.104 [0.090]	0.102 [0.074]	0.098 [0.072]	46
Sweden	0.144 [0.112]	0.109 [0.088]	0.162 [0.119]	3.621 [2.778]	0.448 [1.118]	3.832 [2.000]	0.299 [0.280]	0.323 [0.346]	0.307 [0.310]	0.380 [0.299]	0.346 [0.309]	0.318 [0.246]	0.099 [0.093]	0.087 [0.078]	0.099 [0.086]	94
Thailand	0.247 [0.200]	0.255 [0.200]	0.130 [0.130]	6.304 [3.226]	4.222 [2.222]	5.840 [0.952]	0.406 [0.411]	0.504 [0.532]	0.507 [0.509]	0.619 [0.651]	0.689 [0.777]	0.635 [0.693]	0.078 [0.059]	0.080 [0.053]	0.084 [0.059]	147

Source: WorldScope.

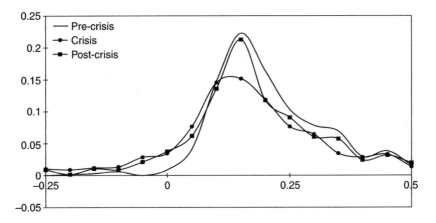

Figure 22.2 EBITDA-to-sales across periods (fraction of firms).

Source: WorldScope.

Note
The sample includes firms from eight countries: Finland, Indonesia, South Korea, Malaysia, Mexico, Philippines, Sweden, and Thailand. The figure presents the distribution of EBITDA-to-sales averaged across all firms in the eight countries. The figure is smoothed.

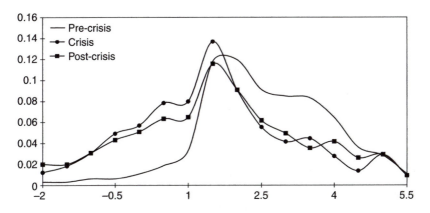

Figure 22.3 Interest coverage across periods (fraction of firms).

Source: WorldScope.

Note
The sample includes eight countries: Finland, Indonesia, South Korea, Malaysia, Mexico, Philippines, Sweden, and Thailand. The figure presents the fraction of firms with specific interest rate coverage across all firms in the eight countries. The figure is smoothed.

Apart from industry and other corporation specific factors, such as corporations' initial financial structures, differences in policies adopted may explain some of the differences. Our literature review, and in particular Honohan and Klingebiel (2002), motivate the specific policy measures we investigate. Honohan and Klingebiel identified for a large sample of countries those policy measures, which could be systematically linked to the fiscal costs of resolving a systemic crisis. The three specific policy variables we use from their analysis are: (1) whether the central bank has provided liquidity support to financial institutions during the crisis or not; (2) whether the government has guaranteed bank liabilities or not; and (3) whether the government has established a publicly owned, centralized asset management company or not. As noted in section "Literature on banking and corporate crises," Honohan and Klingebiel show that these three measures particularly increased the overall fiscal costs of resolving a crisis, controlling for a number of country-specific factors. Since we investigate whether these policies resulted in improved performance and financial sustainability of the corporate sector, we can shed some light on whether a trade-off might exist for certain policies between fiscal costs and corporate sector outcomes.

Table 22.4 presents the policy measures taken in the sampled countries. There are many similarities in policies across countries. Almost all countries' governments, for example, guaranteed the liabilities of the financial sector during the crisis, and only the Philippines did not. About half of the countries had extensive liquidity support to the financial sector and similarly about half did establish a public asset management corporation. The Philippines is the only country that did not undertake any of the three resolution measures. The correlation between the implementation of these policy measures is substantial,[14] suggesting that they tend to be implemented as a package.

Given the limited number of countries in our sample and the fact that the policy measures are correlated, it is difficult to assess the impact of the implementation of each of the three policy variables in isolation and regression results from using individual policy dummies could be unreliable. We therefore create a composite policy index in our empirical work. This policy index, called "Policy,"

Table 22.4 Resolution policies across sampled countries

	Yes	*No*
Guarantee	Finland, Indonesia, Korea, Malaysia, Mexico, Sweden, Thailand (7)	Philippines (1)
Liquidity support	Finland, Indonesia, Korea, Mexico, Thailand* (5)	Malaysia, Philippines, Sweden (3)
Public AMC	Indonesia, Korea, Malaysia, Mexico (4)	Finland, Philippines, Sweden, Thailand (4)

Source: Honohan and Klingebiel (2002).

Notes
No. of countries adopting each policy is indicated in parenthesis.
* Indicates that liquidity support is provided to nonbank financial institutions only, not to deposit and money banks as well.

Table 22.5 Policy index across crisis countries

Country	Policy index
Finland	2
Indonesia	3
South Korea	3
Malaysia	2
Mexico	3
Philippines	0
Sweden	1
Thailand	3

Source: Honohan and Klingebiel (2002); authors' calculations from Table 22.4.

Note
The policy index is defined as the sum of the number of resolution measures taken to restore financial stability in the country. The three resolution measures considered include the provision of guarantees, liquidity support and the set-up of a public asset management company.

is simply defined as the sum of the number of resolution measures taken to restore financial stability in the country. The three resolution measures considered include the provision of guarantees, liquidity support and the setup of a public asset management company. The "Policy" variable thus ranges from zero to three. Table 22.5 shows the value for the Policy variable for the eight crisis countries.

As company-specific control variables, we use each corporation's initial leverage ratio (measured as total debt-to-assets), initial debt composition (measured as short-term debt-to-total debt), size (measured as the natural logarithm of sales), and use of trade debt (measured as payables-to-assets). To control for any sectoral differences across firms, we use industry dummies (based upon two-digit SIC codes) in the regressions.

Using these variables, we aim to answer the following questions. What are the effects of the announcement of these policies during the containment phase on firm performance and sustainability? Does the implementation of the set of resolution measures during the resolution phase of a crisis affect the speed of firm recovery? In addition to the resolution policies themselves, we also want to assess how certain firm-specific factors influence both the speed and the sustainability of the recovery of the corporate sector.

We use the following specific model to explain the depth of the crisis, as measured by the deterioration of firm profitability, the EBITDA-to-sales ratio (Model 1).

$$\frac{EBITDA}{Sales}(\text{pre-crisis}) - \frac{EBITDA}{Sales}(\text{crisis})$$

$$= f \text{ (Policy index, Initial firm-specific variables (pre-crisis),}$$
$$\text{Industry dummies)} \tag{1}$$

We use first differences, rather than percentage changes, because EBITDA-to-sales ratio can take on non-positive values. Given that the model is specified in first differences, and since we also control already for many firm specifics, we can ignore any fixed firm effects. With the "policy index" variable being our main focus, we also ignore any other changes in the macro environment. We therefore assume that, conditional on a crisis taking place, the effect of the implementation of the crisis resolution measures dominate all other changes in country-specific effects. While we include industry dummies in all regressions, these are not reported. In terms of firm-specifics, we expect that larger firms and firms with sounder debt structures suffer less from a crisis. We further expect that trade debt may act as an important substitute for bank financing during a crisis. Given that the number of observations per country differ, we estimate Model 1 using both ordinary least squares (OLS) and weighted least squares (WLS) with weights related to the number of observations. All results are presented in Table 22.6.

High firm profitability at the onset of the crisis is found to be strongly correlated with the depth of the crisis. Our interpretation is that the profitability of these firms rose to abnormally high levels until the onset of the crisis, possibly as a result of a credit boom preceding the crisis, and shortly thereafter experiences a sharp decline during the credit crunch. Larger firms are found to be less affected by the crisis than smaller firms. This may be because larger firms were more diversified and could absorb the shocks better. It could also be that banks renewed credit more easily for larger firms and stopped rolling over credits for small and not well connected firms. We also find a sharper decline in corporate profitability for firms with larger shares of short-term debt, suggesting that such firms were affected by the increases in interest rates that occurred during the crisis period and were more exposed to the risks of banks not renewing credit lines. Furthermore, the regression results show that firms that depended more on trade debt were more affected. This suggests that firms themselves were also less willing to offer each other trade credit during a financial crisis. This could be because of a decreased ability of many debtors to repay the credit, or more generally, because of uncertainty on the financial health of firms. The finding on short-term and trade debt together suggest that firms which had healthier financing structures – lower debt-to-equity leverage and more long-term debt – managed the crisis better.

We do not find that the crisis resolution measures had any impact on reducing the drop in profitability in our sample of countries, as the coefficient on Policy is insignificant. One interpretation is that this set of crisis resolution measures are not sufficient or the right type of measures to stop the downfall in corporate profits. Another interpretation is that these measures can only be implemented past the peak of a crisis, making them ineffective to limit the decline. Either interpretation sheds doubt on the common policy advice to adopt these measures quickly.

We use the same type of regression model to explain the (relative) recovery of the profitability of firms (Model 2).

$$\frac{EBITDA}{Sales}(\text{pre-crisis}) - \frac{EBITDA}{Sales}(\text{crisis})$$

$$= f\left(\frac{EBITDA}{Sales}(\text{pre-crisis}) - \frac{EBITDA}{Sales}(\text{crisis}), \text{Policy index},\right.$$

$$\left. \text{Initial firm-specific variables (pre-crisis), Industry dummies} \right) \quad (2)$$

Table 22.6 Depth of crisis: EBITDA/sales

Variable	OLS (1)	WLS (2)
Constant	0.112	0.224
	(0.183)	(0.199)
EBITDA/sales pre-crisis	0.522**	0.531***
	(0.244)	(0.120)
Sales	−0.018*	−0.024**
	(0.042)	(0.010)
Payables	0.504**	0.492**
	(0.255)	(0.208)
Leverage	0.079	0.147
	(0.089)	(0.097)
Short-term debt	0.228***	0.171***
	(0.053)	(0.059)
Policy	0.010	0.007
	(0.109)	(0.015)
Adjusted R-squared	0.117	0.133
Durbin–Watson stat	1.99	2.06
No. of observations	603	603

Notes
Dependent variable is the difference between the EBITDA-to-sales ratio in the pre-crisis year and the EBITDA-to-sales ratio in the crisis year. "Pre-crisis EBITDA-to-sales pre-crisis" is the EBITDA-to-sales ratio in the pre-crisis year.

"Policy" is an index of policy measures directed toward restoring financial stability. It is the sum of three dummy variables. The first dummy variable takes value one if the government has issued an unlimited guarantee on bank liabilities, and zero otherwise. The second dummy variable takes value one if the government has provided open-ended liquidity support to financial institutions, and zero otherwise. The third dummy variable takes value one if the government has established a publicly owned, centrally managed asset management company, and zero otherwise. "Sales" is the natural logarithm of net sales in thousands of US dollars in the pre-crisis year. "Payables" is the payables-to-total assets ratio in the pre-crisis year. "Leverage" is the total debt-to-assets ratio in the pre-crisis year. "Short-term debt" is the short-term-to-total debt ratio in the pre-crisis year. We include industry dummies, but these are not reported. We report heteroskedasticity-corrected standard errors between brackets. Model (1) is estimated using ordinary least squares. Model (2) is estimated using weighted least squares with weights related to the number of country observations.
*** Indicates significance at a 1% level.
 ** Indicates significance at a 5% level.
  * Indicates significance at a 10% level.

We again use first differences because the EBITDA-to-sales ratio can take on non-positive values. Compared to Model 1, the main difference in the regression setup is that we use the drop in firm profitability (the dependent variable in Model 1) rather than the initial level of firm profitability as independent variable. This way we control for the possibility that profitability recovers more for firms that are hit more during the initial stage of the crisis. We estimate Model 2 again using both OLS and WLS, with the results presented in Table 22.7.

Table 22.7 Recovery from a crisis: EBITDA/sales

Variable	OLS (1)	WLS (2)
Constant	−0.394**	−0.293**
	(0.157)	(0.141)
EBITDA/sales drop	0.772***	0.738***
	(0.138)	(0.062)
Sales	0.025*	0.016**
	(0.014)	(0.008)
Payables	0.544***	0.154
	(0.171)	(0.151)
Leverage	0.044	0.054
	(0.095)	(0.064)
Short-term debt	0.050	0.035
	(0.058)	(0.038)
Policy	0.036***	0.041***
	(0.012)	(0.011)
Adjusted R-squared	0.459	0.541
Durbin–Watson stat	2.06	2.20
No. of observations	592	592

Notes
Dependent variable is the difference between the EBITDA-
to-sales ratio in the post-crisis year and the EBITDA-to-sales
ratio in the crisis year. "EBITDA-to-sales drop" is the difference between the EBITDA-to-sales ratio in the pre-crisis year
and the EBITDA-to-sales ratio in the crisis year.
   For additional notes see Table 22.6.

We find that the recovery of firm profitability is strongly correlated with the
decline in firm profitability during the initial stage of the crisis, suggesting a large
mean-reversion in firm profitability around the crisis period. However, firm profitability does not recover completely to its pre-crisis level, suggesting that it may
take more than one year to recover from a crisis or that there is a permanent loss.
The sharp recovery is in line with the results of Eichengreen and Rose (in this volume), Dooley and Verma (in this volume), and Lee and Park (in this volume) that
the V-shaped recovery is the norm in currency crises. We also find that the recovery of larger firms is slightly better than those of smaller firms, suggesting that
larger firms may be in a better position to absorb shocks as they are more diversified or because larger firms are politically better connected than smaller firms.
   The other firm specific variables are generally not statistically significant, possibly as we already included firm-specific decline in profitability in the regression
which has strong explanatory power. Surprisingly, however, firms' financing structures do not appear to affect recovery. This may reflect some offsetting effects. On
one hand, more risky financing structures should make it more difficult for firms
to obtain financing to resume their operations. On the other hand, there can be
incentive effects from tighter financing situations. It has been found, for example,
for a sample of US firms that perform poorly for a year that higher pre-distress

leverage increases the probability of operational restructuring, thus accelerating recovery (Ofek, 1993).

Interestingly, we find that the policy index is strongly correlated with the recovery in firm profitability. This suggests that the implementation of measures directed toward restoring the financial health of banks, such as removing non-performing loans from banks' balance sheets, have a positive spillover effect toward firms by increasing banks' ability to resume lending to more viable firms, thus accelerating the recovery of firms. The quantitative importance of the policy variable is significant. Firm profitability would have increased on average by around 10 percent if the country would implement all three crisis resolution measures considered.[15] Of course, these are simulated results for the average country and actual results will differ widely across countries. In Sweden, many loans were removed from banks' balance sheets and corporate sector performance recovered relatively quickly. This happened also in Indonesia, but the gains in corporate sector performance have been very limited, if any, so far, while the fiscal costs have been very large.

To assess the sustainability of the recovery, we investigate the factors influencing the difference in corporate performance after the crisis and before the crisis. We estimate the following model (Model 3).

$$\frac{\text{EBITDA}}{\text{Sales}}(\text{post-crisis}) - \frac{\text{EBITDA}}{\text{Sales}}(\text{pre-crisis}) = f(\text{Policy index},$$

$$\text{Initial firm-specific variables (pre-crisis), Industry dummies).} \quad (3)$$

Model 3 has the same explanatory variables as Model 1. The dependent variable tries to measure the lasting impact of the crisis on firm profitability. If the dependent variable is small, that is, the firm's profitability has recovered to the level from before the crisis, then the recovery from the crisis can be thought to be sustainable. The regression results are presented in Table 22.8.

We find that firms with high profitability at the onset of the crisis do not recover fully over the crisis period to pre-crisis levels or profitability. This suggests that these firms had either unsustainable levels of firm profitability, possibly associated with a pre-crisis credit boom, or that it takes more than one year for firms to recover fully from a systemic crisis. We also find some evidence that firms with relatively large amounts of short-term debt before the crisis have greater difficulties to recover to their pre-crisis levels of firm profitability, possibly reflecting difficulties in resolving their financial distress. The other, firm-specific variables are not statistically significant.

We find that post-crisis levels of firm profitability are closer to their pre-crisis levels for firms in those countries that took (more) crisis resolution measures. According to the regression results, the simultaneous implementation of all three policy measures under consideration would increase firm profitability by some 12 percentage points of sales.

The policy index being a composite index does not allow us to disentangle the different effects of the three policy measures on changes in firm profitability.[16]

Table 22.8 Sustainability: EBITDA/sales

Variable	OLS (1)	WLS (2)
Constant	0.095	−0.171
	(0.168)	(0.146)
EBITDA/sales pre-crisis	−0.840***	−0.565***
	(0.127)	(0.117)
Sales	0.006	0.019***
	(0.012)	(0.007)
Payables	−0.155	−0.233
	(0.151)	(0.159)
Leverage	−0.001	−0.007
	(0.076)	(0.063)
Short-term debt	−0.060*	−0.024
	(0.032)	(0.039)
Policy	0.040***	0.033***
	(0.013)	(0.012)
Adjusted R-squared	0.306	0.202
Durbin–Watson stat	1.96	2.06
No. of observations	598	598

Notes
Dependent variable is the difference between the EBITDA-to-sales
ratio in the post-crisis year and the EBITDA-to-sales ratio in the pre-
crisis year. "EBITDA-to-sales pre-crisis" is the EBITDA-to-sales ratio in
the pre-crisis year.
 For additional notes see Table 22.6.

Nevertheless we speculate that our findings are the results of two types of actions.
The provision of liquidity support and the extension of unlimited guarantees
both restore confidence in the financial system and indirectly help improve the
performance of corporations. And the establishment of public asset management
companies directly alleviates firms' financial conditions by removing nonperforming loans of corporations from banks and granting financial relief. Of
course, these measures come at (substantial) fiscal costs.

 The regression results may suffer from a potential endogeneity problem if the
implementation of the crisis resolution measures is more likely in countries with
a deeper financial crisis. In this case there would be reverse causality between the
dependent variable, "drop in EBITDA-to-sales," and the "policy" index variable.
We performed some tests for the existence of this problem and did not find evidence that would suggest a major endogeneity problem in the regression results.
Specifically, the policy index variable is not significantly correlated with the drop
in EBITDA-to-sales between the pre-crisis period and the crisis period (the
dependent variable in Model 1), nor with the firms' initial debt structures (as
measured by debt-to-total assets or short-term debt to total debt in the pre-crisis
period).[17] Also, an ordered probit or logit model with the policy index as dependent variable and the change in EBITDA-to-sales and debt structure indicators as
explanatory variables does not produce any significant results. This suggests that
reverse causality is not a major problem.

We also tested the robustness of our dating of the start of each crisis as we may have dated the crisis too late. We therefore ran the same regressions in Models 1 and 2 with a different crisis year, namely one year earlier than the crisis years reported in Table 22.2. We found results that are very similar to those reported in Tables 22.6 and 22.7. Again, we find that crisis resolution measures do not help to prevent the decline in firm profitability during the early stage of the crisis, but are effective (though costly) in terms of the recovery from a crisis. For ease of presentation we do not include these results.

Conclusions

The literature on systemic restructuring emphasizes the need for governments to actively intervene to overcome the many coordination problems in a systemic crisis and to relieve the shortage of financial capital, both of which impede progress with case-by-case restructuring. The core issue in dealing with a systemic crisis then becomes how to resolve coordination issues while preserving or enhancing incentives for normal, market-based restructuring and transactions. Achieving both goals requires consistent government policies, both among issues and sectors, and over time.

The literature also stresses that fiscal and monetary policies have to support the recovery process in a systemic crisis. Policies must strike the right balance between supporting the exchange rate and avoiding a serious credit crunch created by high interest rates. Supportive policies also cover other dimensions, such as the strictness of capital adequacy requirements and whether an allowance should be made for automatic rollover of payments by small and medium-size enterprises during the early phases of a crisis. As extensively debated in the context of the East Asian crisis and earlier (e.g. following Chile's 1982 crisis), these supportive policies have not always been in place during systemic crises.

Especially during the containment phase of a systemic crisis, but also afterward, governments have to balance achieving stability with aggravating moral hazard. One dimension is avoiding the extension of government guarantees of financial institutions' liabilities, which can create moral hazard and reduce freedom in future loss allocations. Another dimension is the closing or suspension of some financial institutions. Though it signals a certain supervisory stance and limits moral hazard, closing financial institutions can inhibit the restoration of depositors' confidence. In some systemic crises where the institutional framework for bank resolution was weak and there was much uncertainty among depositors and investors on the intrinsic value of the banking system, closing banks without addressing the large problems in the financial system aggravated the crises.

Consistent financial reform involves, among other things, changes in prudential regulation affecting financial institutions' profitability and the availability of private capital. Capital adequacy requirements, for example, need to be made consistent with current and future bank profitability and the availability of new private capital. Raising capital adequacy requirements during a systemic crisis is often not useful because capital is negative, bank earnings are low or negative, and little or no new capital is available.

Consistent reform is also needed for public recapitalizations. Any public recapitalization of banks must take into account the availability of fiscal resources. In several crisis countries the recapitalization of financial institutions with government bonds did not restore public confidence because limited fiscal resources were available to back the bonds. A related intertemporal consistency issue in any crisis is government credibility. We did not address this issue directly in this chapter, but ex ante consistency is a precondition for credibility.

Finally, approaches to restructuring must be consistent with a country's institutional capacity. Institutional deficiencies can rule out approaches in some countries that may be best practices in other countries. These best practices can include heavy reliance on a market-based approach to corporate restructuring – where banks are recapitalized and asked to work out debtors. But where corporate governance and financial regulation and supervision are weak, such an approach may be a recipe for asset stripping or looting rather than sustainable restructuring. Thus emerging markets and industrial countries will need different approaches to systemic restructuring.

While many of these lessons are often mentioned in the literature we reviewed, best practice policies are often not applied. Mistakes can be made in the middle of a crisis. Afterward, it is easy to point out these inconsistencies. But even before there have been many clear cases of inconsistent financial restructuring programs. These inconsistencies usually develop because policymakers are trying to overcome political constraints, and it is hard to judge whether they do so in the most efficient manner. But inconsistencies can also reflect genuine differences of opinion among policymakers and advisers on what constitutes best practice – as with the need to guarantee all liabilities during the early stages of a crisis. The end result is similar, in that consistency is often lacking.

Specific lessons from the empirical part of the chapter reinforce some of the general lessons, and add new evidence to some that may be more controversial. The analysis on data of corporate sector performance suggests that a package of government guarantees on bank liabilities, the provision of liquidity support and the setup of public asset management companies help both the recovery and sustainability, but that these policies do not mitigate the depth of the crisis. Although the empirical results suggest that measures such as asset management companies can help in the short run, they may not provide the right incentives for banks and firms to improve firm capital structures in the long run. And for all measures, there will be a trade-off, while they may speed up recovery, they also have been shown to increase fiscal cost.

More generally, government efforts to restructure need to take into account the political economy factors behind the causes of a crisis and its resolution. In this context there might be ways to change ownership structures in a systemic crisis so that recovery is expedited and a more sustainable outcome results. But while we lack complete understanding of systemic crises, we know even less about the political economy of systemic crises.

Notes

1 In this chapter *systemic* is used to refer to a crisis that is large relative to a national economy, not necessarily large relative to the global economy or a crisis that has other global spillovers.

2 We do not try to identify the exact causes of systemic distress or determine whether currency crises are caused by systemic financial distress in banks and corporations or vice versa. For such analysis, see Edwards and Frankel (2002).

3 There are many political economy reasons why policymakers may not wish to act – thereby giving rise to a crisis – but we do not discuss them here (see Haggard, 2001).

4 Baer and Klingebiel also point out that a comprehensive approach places less demand on supervisory resources. Under a piecemeal approach, insolvent and marginally solvent institutions would continue to exist while other insolvent institutions were being closed or restructured. Marginally solvent institutions would be subject to moral hazard and fraud while being unable and unwilling to raise additional capital. Especially in an environment with weak supervision, comprehensive approaches are thus more necessary.

5 A third school argues that the granting of government guarantees is the outcome of political economy circumstances, and so is often a foregone conclusion. See Dooley and Verma (this volume).

6 Financial restructuring for corporations can take many forms: reschedulings (extensions of maturities), lower interest rates, debt-for-equity swaps, debt forgiveness, indexing interest payments to earnings, and so on. Operational restructuring, an ongoing process, includes improvements in efficiency and management, reductions in staff and wages, asset sales (such as a reduction in subsidiaries), enhanced marketing efforts, and the like, with the expectation of increased profitability and cash flow.

7 For other papers on systemic corporate restructuring, including specific case studies, see Claessens *et al.* (2001).

8 The London rules are principles for corporate reorganization first proposed in the United Kingdom in the early 1990s. Because the rules were not designed for systemic corporate distress, countries have tightened them in various ways.

9 Out-of-court negotiations and bankruptcy or other legal resolution techniques are not the only ways of dealing with financial distress. Economists have been proposing alternative procedures for some time, centering on versions of an asset sale or cash auction. Cash auctions are easy to administer and do not rely on the judicial system (Hart *et al.*, 1997). While attractive from a theoretical perspective, these proposals have not had recent followers except Mexico in 1998.

10 While bankruptcy laws differ considerably even among industrial countries, there has been a general move from more creditor-friendly regimes that are liquidation-oriented, to more debtor-friendly regimes that are more restructuring-oriented (Westbrook, 2001).

11 Regardless of the changes in ownership and the relationships between debtors and creditors, the government may want to create a special social safety net for laid-off workers to help sustain political support for restructuring over time. See Levinsohn *et al.* (2003) for the case of Indonesia.

12 We have data on 990 firms for the pre-crisis years, 1,183 firms for the crisis years and 889 firms for the post-crisis years. In the regressions we use a balanced panel of 687 firms.

13 This reporting discrepancy may still result in a sample selection bias if, for example, late reporting is more common among unprofitable firms than among profitable firms. This would lead us to overestimate the recovery and the effects of any policies adopted on the speed of recovery.

14 The simple correlation between "liquidity support" and "guarantees" is 49 percent, between "liquidity support" and "public AMC" 47 percent and between "guarantees" and "public AMC" 49 percent.

15 The average increase of around 10 percent equals three times the regression coefficient of the policy index variable in Model 2.

16 We noted earlier that such an exercise would produce highly unreliable results because of the high correlation among the three policy measures and the limited number of countries in the sample. We therefore do not make this effort.

17 The correlation between the policy index variable and the difference in EBITDA-to-sales in the pre-crisis period and the crisis period is only 3 percent; between the policy index variable and the initial debt-to-assets ratio 14 percent (but not significantly different from zero); and between the policy index variable and the initial short-term debt-to-total debt ratio 11 percent (also not significantly different from zero).

References

Baer, Herbert and Daniela Klingebiel, 1995, "Systematic Risk When Depositors Bear Losses: Five Case Studies," *Research in Financial Services: Private and Public Policy*, Volume 7, pp. 195–302.

Bank for International Settlements (BIS), 1999, "Capital Requirement and Bank Behaviour: The Impact of the Basle Accord," Basle Committee on Banking Supervision Working Paper 1, BIS, Basle, Switzerland, April.

Bordo, Michael, Barry Eichengreen, Daniela Klingebiel, and Maria Soledad Martinez-Peria, 2001, "Is The Crisis Problem Growing More Severe?," *Economic Policy* 16, Issues 32 (April), 51–82.

Caprio, Gerard and Daniela Klingebiel, 1996, "Bank Insolvencies: Cross-country Experience," Policy Research Working Paper 1620, World Bank, Washington, DC.

Caprio, Gerard and Daniela Klingebiel, 2002, "Episodes of Systemic and Borderline Financial Crises," in *Managing the Real and Fiscal Effects of Banking Crises* (Daniela Klingebiel and Luc Laeven, eds), World Bank Discussion Paper 428, World Bank, Washington, DC, pp. 31–49.

Cho, Dongchul and Kenneth D. West, 2003, "Interest Rates and Exchange Rates in the Korean, Philippine, and Thai Exchange Rate Crises," in *Managing Currency Crises in Emerging Markets* (Dooley, Michael P. and Jeffrey A. Frankel, eds), pp. 11–30.

Claessens, Stijn and Thomas Glaessner, 1997, "Are Financial Sector Weaknesses Undermining the East Asian Miracle?," *Directions in Development*, World Bank, September. 1–39. (ISBN 0-8213-4406-9).

Claessens, Stijn, Simeon Djankov, and Lixin Colin Xu, 2000, "Corporate Performance in the East Asian Financial Crisis," *World Bank Research Observer* 15(1), 23–46.

Claessens, Stijn, Simeon Djankov, and Daniela Klingebiel, 2001, "Financial Restructuring in East Asia: Halfway There?" in *Resolution of Financial Distress* (Stijn Claessens, Simeon Djankov, and Ashoka Mody, eds), World Bank Institute, Washington, DC, pp. 229–59.

Claessens, Stijn, Simeon Djankov, and Ashoka Mody (eds), 2001, *Resolution of Financial Distress*, World Bank Institute, Washington, DC.

Colaco, Francis, Hallward-Driemeier, Mary, and Dominique Dwor-Frecaut, 2000, "Asian Manufacturing Recovery: A Firm-Level Analysis," in *Asian Corporate Recovery: Findings from Firm-Level Surveys in Five Countries* (Dominique Dwor-Frecaut, Francis Colaco, and Mary Hallward-Driemeier, eds), World Bank, Washington, DC, pp. 1–19.

Dado, Marinela, 2000, "Note on Centralized Asset Management Companies in Indonesia, Korea and Thailand," Mimeo, World Bank, Washington, DC.

Dado, Marinela and Daniela Klingebiel, 2002, "Decentralized, Creditor-Led Corporate Restructuring: Cross-Country Experience," Mimeo, February, World Bank, Washington, DC.

Dollar, David and Mary Hallward-Driemeier, 2000, "Crisis, Crisis, Adjustment, and Reform in Thailand's Industrial Firms," *World Bank Research Observer* 15(1), February, 1–22.

Domac, Ilker, and Giovanni Ferri, 1999, "The Credit Crunch in East Asia: Evidence from Field Findings on Bank Behavior," Mimeo, World Bank, Washington, DC.

Drazen, A. 2003, "Interest Rate Defense against Speculative Attack as a Signal: A Primer," in *Managing Currency Crises in Emerging Markets* (Dooley, Michael P. and Jeffrey A. Frankel, eds), National Bureau of Economic Research Conference Report 37-54, The University of Chicago Press, 408pp.

Edwards, Sebastian and Jeffrey A. Frankel (eds), 2002, *Preventing Currency Crises in Emerging Markets*, National Bureau of Economic Research Conference Report, The University of Chicago Press, 720pp.

Foley, Fritz, 2000, "Going Bust in Bangkok: Lessons from Bankruptcy Law Reform in Thailand," Harvard Business School, Business Economic Department, Mimeo, January, Cambridge.

Haggard, Stephen, 2001, "The Political Economy of Financial Restructuring in East Asia," in *Resolution of Financial Distress* (Stijn Claessens, Simeon Djankov, and Ashoka Mody, eds), World Bank Institute, Washington, DC, pp. 261–303.

Hart, Oliver, Rafael La Porta Drago, Florencio Lopez-de Silanes, and John Moore, 1997, "A New Bankruptcy Procedure that Uses Multiple Auctions," *European Economic Review*, 41, 461–73.

Honohan, Patrick and Daniela Klingebiel, 2002, "Controlling the Fiscal Costs of Banking Crises," in *Managing the Real and Fiscal Effects of Banking Crises* (Daniela Klingebiel and Luc Laeven, eds), World Bank Discussion Paper 428, World Bank, Washington, DC, pp. 15–29.

Klingebiel, Daniela, 2001, "The Role of Asset Management Companies in the Resolution of Banking Crises," in *Resolution of Financial Distress* (Stijn Claessens, Simeon Djankov, and Ashoka Mody, eds), World Bank Institute, Washington, DC, pp. 341–79.

Klingebiel, Daniela and Luc Laeven (eds), 2002, *Managing the Real and Fiscal Effects of Banking Crises*, World Bank Discussion Paper 428, World Bank, Washington, DC.

Krueger, Anne and Aaron Tornell, 1999, "The Role of Bank Restructuring in Recovering from Crises: Mexico 1995–98," NBER Working Paper 7042.

Lane, Timothy, Atish Ghosh, Javier Hamann, Steven Phillips, Marianne Schultze-Ghattas, and Tsidi Tsikata, 1999, "IMF-Supported Programs in Indonesia, Thailand and Korea," IMF Occasional Paper No. 178, June 30, Washington, DC.

Levinsohn, James, Steven Barry and Jed Friedman, 2003, "Impacts of the Indonesian Crises: Price Changes and the Poor," in *Managing Currency Crises in Emerging Markets* (Dooley, Michael P. and Jeffrey A. Frankel, eds), pp. 393–424.

Lindgren, Carl-Johan, Gillian Garcia, and Matthew I. Saal, 1996, *Bank Soundness and Macroeconomic Policy*, International Monetary Fund, Washington, DC.

Lindgren, Carl-Johan, Tomás J.T. Baliño, Charles Enoch, Anne-Marie Gulde, Marc Quintyn, and Leslie Teo, 2000, "Financial Sector Crisis and Restructuring: Lessons From Asia," Occasional Paper 188, International Monetary Fund, January 21, Washington, DC.

Ofek, E. 1993, "Capital Structure and Firm Response to Poor Performance: An Empirical Analysis," *Journal of Financial Economics* 34(1), 3–30, August.

Sheng, Andrew, ed., 1996, *Bank Restructuring: Lessons from the 1980s*. Washington, DC.: World Bank.

Stone, Mark, 2000a, "Large-Scale Post-Crisis Corporate Sector Restructuring," Policy Discussion Paper 00/7, International Monetary Fund, Washington, DC.

Stone, Mark, 2000b, "The Corporate Sector Dynamics of Systemic Financial Crises," Policy Discussion Paper 00/114, International Monetary Fund, Washington, DC.

Stiglitz, Joseph, 2001, "Bankruptcy Laws: Some Basic Economic Principles" in *Resolution of Financial Distress* (Stijn Claessens, Simeon Djankov, and Ashoka Mody, eds), World Bank Institute, Washington, DC, pp. 1–23.

Westbrook, Jay, 2001, "Systemic Corporate Distress: A Legal Perspective," in *Resolution of Financial Distress* (Stijn Claessens, Simeon Djankov, and Ashoka Mody, eds), World Bank Institute, Washington, DC, pp. 47–64.

World Bank, 2000, *East Asia: Recovery and Beyond*, Washington, DC.

23 Buoyant investment in OECD economies

How much can the fundamentals explain?[*]

Florian Pelgrin, Sebastian Schich and
Alain de Serres

Introduction

In several OECD countries, investment rates in the business sector grew strongly in the second half of the 1990s, reflecting mostly a rapid acceleration in the purchase of machinery and equipment, notably in volume terms. In some cases, the strength of private investment relative to output growth had raised concerns about the risk of a capital overhang and the prospect of a prolonged period of slow capital formation in order to bring investment levels back to more sustainable levels. While it is possible – even likely – that the stock market boom combined with the rapid decline in computer prices has fuelled investment demand to an excessive level, in particular in the United States, the size of the overhang and the required correction is more difficult to evaluate. The concern was that a large capital overhang could have limited the effectiveness of monetary policy and could thereby have influenced the timing and speed of recovery in the United States and elsewhere. While the recent numbers indicate that the worst fears are unlikely to materialise, investment may rebound less sharply than during previous recoveries. The purpose of this chapter is to assess the contribution of fundamental determinants to the change in investment in the second half of the 1990s, based on the estimation of a system of panel co-integration equations for gross business investment.

Besides the level of output, the determinants include a measure of the cost of capital and an indicator of financial market development. While the former is a key driver of investment in the neo-classical model pioneered by Jorgensen (1967), its role in both cross-country and time-series empirical work has often proved difficult to capture, owing in part to measurement and identification problems. In contrast, the inclusion of a variable intending to capture the influence of

* This chapter draws on Pelgrin *et al.* (2002a). The authors are grateful for helpful comments from Jorgen Elmeskov, Michael Feiner, Mike Kennedy, Michael Kiley, Mike Leahy, Alain Trognon and Ignazio Visco. They also thank Veronica Humi, Oona McAleese and Paula Simonin for excellent secretarial and editorial assistance.

financial market development is not derived directly from the basic neo-classical model. It follows instead from the contribution of recent studies suggesting that financial intermediation affects growth through various channels, including its effects on saving and investment rates as well as on the efficiency of capital allocation (Pagano, 1993; Levine, 1997; Leahy *et al.*, 2001). Following a methodology similar to that found in Benhabib and Spiegel (2000), the present chapter takes this simple neo-classical investment model as a base model for the empirical analysis and then adds indicators of financial development to examine whether they contain any further explanatory power.

In this chapter we use relatively recent panel co-integration techniques that exploit more fully the information available in the variation of the variables over time compared with methods used in other studies, generally based on a pure cross-section of long-run averages and thus ignoring the time-series dimension (Levine, 1997; Wachtel, 2001).[1] As shown by Arestis and Demetriades (1997) and Arestis *et al.* (2001), exploiting the time-series variations in financial development measures could be important and may yield noticeably different results from cross-section analysis. Using time-series analysis for five industrialised countries, Arestis *et al.* (2001) find a much smaller coefficient estimate for stock market capitalisation than previous (cross-section) studies and conclude that the role of stock market capitalisation is probably overestimated in cross-section studies. To exploit the time-series variation, we apply the panel co-integration tests suggested by Kao (1999) and Pedroni (1995), and use four different panel estimators (OLS, bias-corrected OLS, FMOLS and DOLS).

The section on 'Development in investment rates' briefly reviews the recent stylised facts on investment and presents the empirical model. The main results from the estimation of the investment equations corresponding to four-panel co-integration techniques are discussed in the section on 'Data and empirical results'. Overall, they largely conform to the prediction of the basic neo-classical model; while the long-run parameter on the level of real output is very close to unity, the cost of capital measure is found to have a significant negative long-term impact on investment, with a parameter size close to one in some cases. The results also confirm earlier evidence concerning the existence of a long-run relationship between financial development and investment. The relationship is stronger when financial development is measured by private credit issued by deposit money banks than stock market capitalisation or total value traded. The section on 'The investment boom' examines the contribution from the main determinants to the change in investment in the second half of the 1990s. Conclusions follow in the last section.

Development in investment rates

Several OECD countries experienced a robust increase in both total and private investment during the second half of the 1990s, the main exceptions being Japan and Norway. The rebound in gross fixed capital formation, following several years of weak growth, was mainly driven by business investment, with public investment remaining flat. In fact, over that period, real business investment has risen even more strongly relative to real Gross Domestic Product (GDP) than suggested by the ratio of nominal investment spending to nominal GDP, owing to the drop in the relative price of capital goods. After moving more or less in line with real output throughout the 1980s and early 1990s, real investment has pulled away in the following years, most notably in the United States, the United Kingdom, Canada, Sweden, Denmark and Greece, despite a particularly strong output performance (Figure 23.1). While investment is typically more volatile

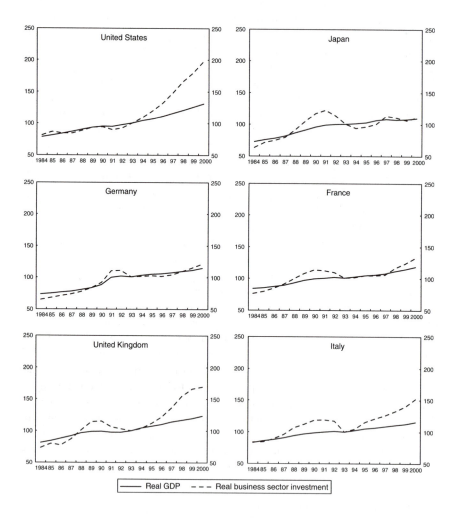

Figure 23.1 Real output and business investment, 1993 = 100.

Source: OECD.

Note
1 Including forecasts.

than output, such a large and persistent gap between the two series is difficult to explain by traditional multiplier effects alone. This has raised the issue of sustainability, lest other determinants can account for the buoyancy of investment in the late 1990s observed in many countries.

To examine this issue, a set of panel equations for gross business investment in volumes is estimated using a co-integration technique. The specification of the equations and the set of determinants are based on the neo-classical theory of investment (see Annexe). Based on this simple conceptual framework, gross investment can be determined in the long run by a small set of variables, which includes the level of output, the real interest rate, the relative price of capital goods and the depreciation rate. The limited set of determinants mostly reflects the large number of simplifying assumptions unlikely to be met in the real world. Relaxing some of these assumptions would lead to an extension of the set of determinants in several directions. For instance, properly taking into account the effect of taxation in the cash-flow relationship would lead to a specification of the user cost of capital, which would include terms reflecting the corporate tax rate, the rate of investment tax credit and the discounted value of tax depreciation allowances. Tax factors can vary substantially both over time and across countries and such changes can be important for investment but also complicated to capture empirically, especially in a cross-country set-up. For example, the boom/bust cycle in non-residential structure investment observed in the United States in the 1980s has been related to the Tax Reform Act of 1986. Furthermore, allowing for taxation and uncertainty implies that the financial cost of capital (or the rate used to discount future revenues) is unlikely to be independent from the choice of financial mix by the firm and should therefore be measured as some combination of the cost of debt and equity. In practice, such a measure would also be difficult to construct for a large pool of countries.

However, one empirical feature that the neo-classical model seems to share with alternative models of investment such as Tobin's Q or variants of the Euler-equation approach, is the difficulty of identifying significant and robust relative price effects on the rate of capital formation at the aggregate level, regardless of how much sophistication goes into the construction of the cost of capital (Chirinko, 1993; Hassett and Hubbard, 1997).[2] Stated differently, it has become almost a stylised fact in empirical work on investment that the latter is much more correlated with output than it is with the cost of capital, even though, as pointed out many years ago by Shapiro (1986), 'neo-classical theories of investment view output as the consequences of firms' choice of capital stock and other factors, not the cause'. This general finding has recently been confirmed even in the context of panel data (e.g. Velt, 2001; Schich and Pelgrin, 2002). Both studies found that quantity variables (output, profits) dominate empirically price variables (real interest rate, relative prices or taxes) as investment determinants on a macroeconomic level. In fact, empirical research over the past several years has increasingly turned to industry or firm-level data in order to find significant cost-of-capital effects on investment, especially at medium to high frequencies.[3]

One possible reason for the difficulty encountered in capturing a significant cost of capital effect relates to measurement problems, especially at the aggregate level. Such problems may even have worsened recently as a result of the shifting composition of capital towards information and communication technology (ICT) equipment – a trend not confined to the United States (Colecchia and Schreyer, 2001). The rapid increase in computer power and quality of telecommunication equipment have made the measured relative price of ICT equipment fall quite rapidly in the growing number of countries using hedonic price measurement. Given the difficulty of properly quantifying rapid quality improvements, measuring the price of ICT equipment has become particularly problematic and has called into question the assumption that different types of capital goods can be aggregated into one homogeneous capital good with a representative cost. Another explanation for the weak correlation between investment and the cost of capital effect is the classic identification problem that plagues the empirical results based on reduced-form estimates of a specification that include endogenous regressors. A third explanation is found in the literature on capital market imperfections. In a world of imperfect competition and asymmetric information, the nature of the access to credit may vary both across firms and time – with some firms being liquidity constrained – implying that investment decisions may not be independent from internal cash flow or profitability even in the long run. In such a case, the real interest rate and the cost of capital may not reflect the true cost of borrowing faced by firms, especially the smaller ones more likely to be dependent on specific sources of credit such as bank lending.

In this context, financial markets perform several functions that may help reduce the effect of such imperfections. They facilitate the trading, hedging, diversifying and pooling of risk, the efficient allocation of resources, the monitoring of the allocation of funds of managers and the mobilising of savings. Measures of financial system developments can thus have an independent impact on investment. While constructing measures of the user cost of capital that take into account the main features of corporate taxation in a large set of countries is beyond the scope of this chapter, the set of long-run determinants of investment is extended to include proxies for financial system developments.

Building on previous empirical work showing that the extent of financial market development can provide a significant contribution to output growth via its impact on investment, four alternative proxies for financial market developments have been introduced to capture these influences. First, *liquid liabilities*, which consist of currency and interest-bearing liabilities of bank and non-bank financial intermediaries, are used as a proxy for the overall size of the financial intermediary system. Second, the *private credit* provided to the private sector by deposit money banks, which consists of the total claims of deposit money banks on the private sector is intended to measure the degree of financial intermediation. Third, the ratio of *stock market capitalisation to GDP*, which consists of the value of shares listed, aims at capturing the ease with which funds can be raised in the equity market. Fourth, the *value traded* corresponds to the value of domestic shares traded on domestic exchanges divided by GDP. Each of these proxies has shortcomings. Since they include deposits by one financial intermediary in another, liquid liabilities suffer from a double-counting problem. Private credit only captures the financing intermediated banks and thus ignores the growing importance of the financing through other institutions or the securities market. More generally, these two variables better represent the size of the banking system than financial system development *per se*. This limitation applies particularly to liquid liabilities that could be high even in places where financial assets are not widely available. As for the two stock market variables, they suffer from the fact that by measuring values rather than volumes they are affected by equity price movements, rising indeed strongly in the 1990s. As a result, they may also capture the effect of the cost of equity on investment, which is not taken into account in the measure of the cost of capital. Indeed, the link between investment decisions and stock market valuation is at the heart of the Tobin's Q model according to which investment increases when firms' market value is higher than their replacement cost.

So far empirical evidence on the finance–investment link for the sample of developed countries has been mixed with several studies failing to identify a significant role of finance for economic development. King and Levine (1993) found that excluding OECD countries from their full sample of developed and developing countries did not affect the significance of the relationship between financial development and investment. This is consistent with the view that the links are significant for non-OECD, but not for OECD countries. Fernandez and Galetovic (1994) confirmed the weak relationship of financial development and investment in a direct test of this relationship for OECD countries. More recently, however, Schich and Pelgrin (2002) and Beck and Levine (2001) both identified a significant link for OECD countries, on the basis of different methodologies.

In order to assess the possible influence of financial market development on investment levels across countries or over time, the basic neo-classical specification (see Annexe) is augmented to incorporate one of the suggested proxies:

$$i_{i,t} = \beta_{1,i} y_{i,t} + \beta_{2,i}(c_{i,t} - p_{i,t}) + \beta_{3,i} f_{i,t} + u_{i,t} \tag{1}$$

where $f_{i,t}$ is a proxy of financial development and $u_{i,t} = \alpha_i' + \varepsilon_{i,t}$, α_i' is an individual fixed effect and $\varepsilon_{i,t}$ is a random error term.

Data and empirical results

Data

The empirical analysis uses data on investment, output, a crude measure of the cost of capital and four measures of financial development for a panel of nineteen OECD countries from 1970 to 1999.[4] Gross investment is measured by the log level of real private business sector fixed capital formation. The output variable is the real private GDP. The cost of capital is measured as $\log(1 + r\, P_I/P)$, where r is a real long-term interest rate (derived from government securities) and

P_I/P is the ratio of a deflator of private non-residential fixed capital formation to an output price deflator (to adjust for relative price changes between capital goods and output). There was a decline trend in the relative price of capital goods throughout the 1980s and 1990s, which has contributed to put downward pressures on the cost of capital. As mentioned above, a set of four financial development indicators – liquid liabilities, private credit of deposit money banks, stock market capitalisation and total value traded as a share of GDP – is used. The data source for these four indicators' variables is the World Bank's financial development database, where the data are only available until 1996 or 1997, in the case of OECD countries. For the purpose of the current study, the base has been updated to 1999 using the same methodology and data sources as in Beck *et al.* (1999).

Estimation results

Four different homogeneous panel co-integration approaches are used, after having rejected the hypotheses of no co-integration for the variables in equation (1). The approaches are the standard Ordinary Least Squares (OLS), BCOLS (bias-corrected OLS), FMOLS (fully modified OLS) and DOLS (dynamic OLS) estimators described in Kao and Chiang (2000). Selected results are reported in Table 23.1; more details are available in Pelgrin *et al.* (2002b) and in Pelgrin and Schich (2002). The main findings are the following:

- In most cases, the coefficient on real GDP is significant and very close to unity, in conformity with theoretical priors. Exceptions are found in the case of the OLS estimator and in one instance when the BCOLS estimator is used.
- Second, the measure of the cost of capital (adjusted real interest rate) is almost always negative as predicted. Moreover, it is almost always significant when private credit, stock market capitalisation or value traded are added to the basic specification. In the latter two cases, the coefficient on the cost of capital is close to unity when the DOLS method is used, consistent with the Cobb–Douglas production function specification.
- Third, the alternative proxies for financial market development are systematically significant, irrespective of the specific indicator and estimator chosen.

Given the traditional difficulties in identifying any significant cost of capital effect in empirical aggregate investment equations, the finding of relatively high coefficients on the adjusted real interest rate is an important result especially as, in the case of the FMOLS and DOLS methods, this is obtained jointly with the finding of a unit coefficient on output. The higher parameter values for the cost of capital obtained under the FOMLS and DOLS are consistent with earlier findings by Caballero (1994) for US data. Applying the Stock and Watson (1993) procedure similar to the DOLS approach used in this chapter, the author found a coefficient on the cost of capital close to -1 in a regression for US capital equipment, where

Table 23.1 Panel estimates of investment equations, 1970–99

	Benchmark model without financial development	Inclusion of financial development variables			
		Liquid liabilities	Private credit	Stock market capitalisation[a]	Total value traded[a]
OLS estimates					
Financial development[b]		0.162	0.115	0.045	0.019
		(0.037)**	(0.022)**	(0.013)**	(0.008)**
GDP	1.230	1.158	1.158	1.423	1.396
	(0.031)**	(0.034)**	(0.036)**	(0.049)**	(0.045)**
Adjusted real interest rate	−0.290	−0.291	−0.445	−0.376	−0.409
	(0.191)	(0.187)	(0.187)**	(0.169)**	(0.137)**
Memorandum item: R^2	0.78	0.78	0.79	0.88	0.88
Bias-corrected OLS estimates					
Financial development[b]		0.219	0.145	0.045	0.016
		(0.071)**	(0.045)**	(0.015)**	(0.008)**
GDP	1.181	1.083	1.048	1.352	1.393
	(0.076)**	(0.078)**	(0.082)**	(0.078)**	(0.080)**
Adjusted real interest rate	−0.300	−0.299	−0.508	−0.305	−0.313
	(0.256)	(0.247)	(0.246)**	(0.202)	(0.204)**
Memorandum item: R^2	0.78	0.78	0.79	0.88	0.88
FMOLS estimates					
Financial development[b]		0.387	0.257	0.045	0.036
		(0.074)**	(0.046)**	(0.016)**	(0.008)**
GDP	0.926	0.931	0.933	0.931	0.933
	(0.079)**	(0.081)**	(0.085)**	(0.081)**	(0.084)**
Adjusted real interest rate	−0.259	−0.183	−1.071	−1.704	−1.810
	(0.266)	(0.256)	(0.254)**	(0.211)**	(0.213)**
Memorandum item: R^2	0.73	0.77	0.77	0.74	0.79
DOLS estimates[c]					
Financial development[1]		0.180	0.166	0.064	0.041
		(0.076)**	(0.050)**	(0.018)**	(0.009)**
Gross domestic product	1.004	0.995	0.998	1.006	1.005
	(0.082)**	(0.084)**	(0.092)**	(0.090)**	(0.093)**
Adjusted real interest rate	0.105	0.090	−0.505	−1.227	−0.969
	(0.275)	(0.266)	(0.274)*	(0.232)**	(0.235)**
Memorandum item: R^2	0.54	0.62	0.68	0.72	0.76

Notes

Standard deviation shown in brackets.

  * Significant at 10 per cent level.

** Significant at 5 per cent level.

a When measuring financial development by stock market and total value traded, data availability required reducing the sample size to sixteen countries. Excluding stock market capitalisation from the sample leads to a coefficient estimate for GDP of a similar magnitude.

b Financial development is alternatively proxied by liquid liabilities, private credit, stock market capitalisation and total value traded.

c The results shown here are those for our preferred lead–lag combination. They are one lead and no lag (1, 0) for the model without financial development, (1, 0) for liquid liabilities, (2, 0) for private credit and (0, 2) for stock market capitalisation and total value traded.

the unit coefficient on output is imposed. In this regard, the smaller coefficients obtained on output and the cost of capital in the cases of OLS and, to a lesser extent, BCOLS are not surprising given that, as pointed out by Chen *et al.* (1999) and Caballero (1994), both approaches have a non-negligible bias in small samples. On that account the FMOLS and DOLS are preferable and should be given more weight.

The significance of proxies for financial development provides support to the hypothesis that the latter is conducive to investment even in high-income countries, confirming earlier results reported in Leahy *et al.* (2001). It also expands on past work that has failed to identify a significant role for financial development in investment and capital accumulation in OECD countries, based on methods that do not fully exploit both the cross-sections and time dimensions. In this regard, however, the evidence captured by the time series dimension could well reflect factors other than financial development. In particular, the stock market variables may capture elements of the user cost of capital, which are missing in the measure used in the specification. Such an omission may in fact bias the results in finding extra effects from financial developments, especially along the time-series dimension.

To test for the sensitivity of the results to the developments of the late 1990s, characterised by strong stock market gains and substantial declines in the relative price of capital goods, the equations have been re-estimated over the sample 1970–95. The results shown in Table 23.2 are generally similar to the ones obtained over the full sample. While private credit, stock market capitalisation and total value traded are always significantly positive, the estimated coefficients suggest a much stronger role for private credit than for stock market indicators (stock market capitalisation and total value traded). This may reflect the importance of the so-called *bank-lending channel* of transmission of financial shocks to the real economy. In countries where private banks still represent the main source of capital funding for a large number of firms (such as in continental Europe), investment can be quite sensitive to changes in banks' deposits, in particular if the latter cannot easily substitute between deposits and other sources of funds such as bonds or equities (Kashyap and Stein, 1994). In such a case, an adverse shock on banks' liabilities, following for instance a tightening of monetary policy can generate a credit crunch and an abrupt retrenchment in investment, over and above the effect from the rise in the cost of capital. The results would thus suggest that despite the growing trends towards securitisation, bank lending remains a predominant source of capital funding in the majority of countries in the sample.

To shed further light on this, a 'horse-race' exercise was conducted where private credit was included jointly with either stock market capitalisation or total value traded in. In both cases estimates support a much stronger effect of private credit on business investment than the two measures of stock market developments, though both variables remain significant, at least at the 10 per cent margin. This differs from several previous empirical studies, but confirms specifically the hypothesis by Arestis *et al.* (2001) that standard cross-section analysis tends to overestimate the role of stock market capitalisation. On the other hand, a comparison

Table 23.2 Panel estimates of investment equations, 1970–95

	Benchmark model without financial development	Inclusion of financial development variables			
		Liquid liabilities	Private credit	Stock market capitalisation[a]	Total value traded[a]
OLS estimates					
Financial development[b]		0.117	0.087	0.039	0.020
		(0.042)**	(0.024)**	(0.015)**	(0.006)**
GDP	1.174	1.122	1.094	1.476	1.416
	(0.037)**	(0.041)**	(0.043)**	(0.060)*	(0.055)**
Adjusted real interest rate	−0.174	−0.164	−0.267	−0.408	−0.468
	(0.189)	(0.189)	(0.190)	(0.189)**	(0.184)**
Memorandum item: R^2	0.74	0.74	0.75	0.84	0.84
Bias-corrected OLS estimates					
Financial development[b]		0.168	0.120	0.037	0.012
		(0.072)**	(0.046)**	(0.017)**	(0.008)
GDP	1.125	1.048	1.013	1.416	1.391
	(0.078)**	(0.082)**	(0.087)**	(0.086)**	(0.092)*
Adjusted real interest rate	−0.187	−0.169	−0.315	−0.410	−0.515
	(0.251)**	(0.247)	(0.246)	(0.220)*	(0.232)**
Memorandum item: R^2	0.74	0.74	0.75	0.84	0.84
FMOLS estimates					
Financial development[b]		0.398	0.273	0.036	0.030
		(0.075)**	(0.048)**	(0.018)**	(0.009)**
GDP	0.925	0.931	0.932	0.932	0.931
	(0.081)**	(0.085)**	(0.090)**	(0.090)**	(0.097)**
Adjusted real interest rate	−0.180	−0.107	−0.980	−1.441	−1.513
	(0.262)	(0.257)	(0.256)**	(0.233)**	(0.245)**
Memorandum item: R^2	0.71	0.72	0.71	0.67	0.71
DOLS estimates[c]					
Financial development[b]		0.169	0.178	0.058	0.037
		(0.078)**	(0.051)**	(0.020)**	(0.010)**
GDP	1.005	0.995	0.996	1.004	1.004
	(0.085)**	(0.090)**	(0.099)**	(0.103)**	(0.106)**
Adjusted real interest rate	0.126	0.107	−0.446	−0.975	−0.709
	(0.273)	(0.268)	(0.271)*	(0.262)**	(0.271)**
Memorandum item: R^2	0.51	0.59	0.68	0.71	0.73

Notes
Standard deviation shown in brackets.
 * Significant at 10 per cent level.
** Significant at 5 per cent level.
a When measuring financial development by stock market and total value traded, data availability required reducing the sample size to sixteen countries. Excluding stock market capitalisation from the sample leads to a coefficient estimate for GDP of a similar magnitude.
b Financial development is alternatively proxied by liquid liabilities, private credit, stock market capitalisation and total value traded.
c The results shown here are those for our preferred lead–lag combination. They are one lead and no lag (1, 0) for the model without financial development, (1, 0) for liquid liabilities, (2, 0) for private credit and (0, 2) for stock market capitalisation and total value traded.

of the full and shorter sample also shows that the size and significance of the coefficient on private credit has diminished since 1995 relative to that of stock market capitalisation, a factor consistent with the growing importance of sources of financing other than bank loans.

The investment boom of the late 1990s: how much can be explained?

In order to see whether the general rise in investment rates in the second half of the 1990s in OECD countries could be largely explained by the set of determinants, the contributions of the variables to the change in the level of investment has been calculated. The results, which are based on the estimates from the specification using stock market capitalisation and on the DOLS method, are presented in Table 23.3. They show that the change in business investment between 1995 and 1999 can be largely explained by the determinants in the cases of Germany, France, Italy, Belgium and Spain. In contrast, only between about one-third and one-half of the increase in business investment over the same period in the United States, Japan, United Kingdom, Canada, Denmark and Austria can be accounted for by changes in real GDP, the cost of capital and stock market capitalisation. To a lesser, albeit significant, extent increases in investment in Australia, Greece, the Netherlands and Sweden cannot be fully explained either. Considering that the approach focuses on the contribution of the long-run coefficients, it may be that some of the unexplained rise might be captured by short-run dynamic factors. In fact, a rise in the long-run desired capital stock typically leads to an overshooting in investment without implying an overshooting in the capital stock, as is well known from the accelerator mechanism. However, assuming a reasonable speed of adjustment, short-run dynamic factors could only play a limited role over a five-year period. Hence, the results from the empirical analysis would still support the view that investment has exceeded its long-run equilibrium level in a number of countries.

The difficulties in explaining the rise in investment in some cases may also reflect the absence of factors, which cannot be easily incorporated in the context of regression analysis based on information that is pooled across a relatively large set of countries and that focuses on the flow equilibrium. Starting from the simple capital accumulation identity $K_{t+1} = (1 - \delta)K_t + I_t$, that is equation (A1.3) in the Annexe, and after expressing capital and investment as a ratio of output, one can find that in steady-state equilibrium, the investment *rate* is a function of the capital–output ratio, the depreciation rate and the trend growth rate of output:

$$i = \frac{k(g + \delta)}{(1 + g)} \tag{2}$$

where i is the ratio of real gross business investment to real GDP and k is the capital–output ratio. The contributions of a change either in trend output growth (g) or the depreciation rate (δ) to the long-run stock equilibrium are not really

Table 23.3 Contributions to the changes in real business investment between 1995 and 1999

	United States	Japan	Germany	France	Italy	United Kingdom	Canada	Australia	Austria	Belgium	Denmark	Greece	The Netherlands	Spain	Sweden
Percentage changes in investment	50.3	10.5	12.1	18.2	21.3	48.9	44.3	34.8	23.1	24.5	42.3	52.1	36.2	32.9	29.9
Contribution from															
Real GDP	17.5	5.0	6.1	9.8	6.7	11.5	15.7	18.8	9.8	10.2	10.9	12.9	15.9	15.9	11.4
Adjusted real interest rate	0.5	1.3	0.8	1.8	5.5	3.9	1.9	3.7	0.8	2.0	4.7	3.3	2.5	5.3	4.1
Stock market capitalisation	3.6	0.1	5.2	4.2	5.7	1.8	2.7	1.6	1.8	10.3	2.2	21.4	6.5	8.4	6.0
Total explained[a]	21.5	6.4	12.0	15.9	17.9	17.2	20.3	24.2	12.3	22.5	17.8	37.6	24.9	29.6	21.5

Note
a May not exactly add up due to rounding.

captured in the regressions reported above, even though they could have played a significant role in some countries, in particular the United States. For instance, investment can be expected to rise faster than output for several years when an economy is adjusting to a higher trend output growth rate, which requires a higher investment rate to be maintained in the long run. Although it has become clearer recently that part of the sharp acceleration in US output in the 1990s was cyclical, a higher trend growth rate nevertheless looks likely to be sustained in the medium run.

Likewise, the possible change in the rate of depreciation has not been taken into account in the measurement of the cost of capital and therefore in the empirical estimates. And, while the shifting composition of capital towards computers and software, which tend to depreciate faster, may have increased the cost of capital and thereby reduced the desired capital–output ratio (k in equation (2)), it would also have raised gross investment requirements. Estimates for the United States based on data for net capital stock and gross investment suggest an increase in the depreciation rate from around 4 per cent in the late 1980s to nearly 9 per cent the late 1990s.[5] Given that part of this implicit increase reflects market depreciation (i.e. capital losses due to the faster decline in capital goods' relative price) it probably overstates the extent of physical depreciation (i.e. the loss of value due to the ageing of the asset). Nevertheless, even a more modest increase to around 6 per cent would, if sustained, have a huge impact on the longer run equilibrium gross investment rate in the United States.

Table 23.4 Estimates of underlying 'steady-state' business investment rates (as a per cent of total GDP)

	Capital output ratio[a]	Potential growth[a]	Depreciation rate[a]	Steady-state investment rate[b]	Current investment rate[c]
United States	2–3	3–3.5	5–7	13–25	15
Japan	2–3	1.25–1.75	3–5	7–17	16
Germany	2–3	2–2.5	2.2–4.5	7–17	13
France	2–3	2.25–2.75	2.5–4.5	7–15	12
Italy	2–3	2–2.5	2–4	6–15	14
United Kingdom	2–3	2.25–2.75	3–5	10–18	14
Canada	2–3	2.75–3.25	3–5	8–17	13

Notes

a Given the pitfalls in properly measuring capital output ratios and depreciation rates at the aggregate levels, and fact that these could be changing, a range of plausible assumptions is used. A range is also used for trend growth based on the OECD's latest estimates.

b Under the steady-state assumption of a constant capital–output ratio (K/Y), this is calculated by $[(g + \delta)/Y(1 + g)]$, where g is the potential GDP growth rate and δ is the rate of depreciation. The result from this calculation is then multiplied by the ratio of real business sector GDP to real total GDP (average 1996–2000) so as to make it comparable to the current business investment rate (last column), which is expressed as a per cent of total.

c Real business investment as a share of real GDP in the year 2000. This ratio of real terms is reported for with the steady-state rate; in countries using chain-weighting aggregation methods, it represents only approximation of the true underlying real investment.

To illustrate the potential influence of these two factors, equation (2) can be used to compute rough estimates of steady-state investment rates for G-7 countries on the basis of assumptions regarding the trend growth rate of GDP, the capital–output ratio and the depreciation rate (Table 23.4). Looking at the results, it stands out that despite the capital spending boom of the late 1990s, the US business investment rate, at around 15 per cent, would still be at the low end of the range of estimated steady-state rates if it were assumed that the rise in trend output growth and the depreciation rate were permanent. Taken at face value, these simple calculations would suggest that if some excess investment took place during the 1990s, the recent retrenchment might have already brought the investment rate to a more sustainable level. A similar conclusion is reached by Tevlin and Whelan (2000) who argue that the US investment boom of the late 1990s can be attributed to the rise in capital depreciation and the higher sensitivity of investment to the cost of capital. Our results for other G-7 countries show current business investment rates within the 'sustainable' range, albeit generally closer to the upper end.

Conclusions

In this chapter, a set of business investment equations for OECD countries has been estimated using panel co-integration techniques over the period 1970–99. In addition to the level of output and the cost of capital, the set of determinants included alternative measures of financial market development. The estimation was performed based on OLS as well as on three alternative procedures correcting for parameter biases in finite samples. In most cases, the results were consistent with the predictions of the basic neo-classical model. First, the coefficient on output is close to one, consistent with a constant capital–output ratio in the steady state. Previous papers often have either identified coefficients significantly different from one or had to impose a unit coefficient a priori. Second, the user cost of capital measure is negative and significant, as expected. The finding of a strong cost of capital effect has always been difficult to obtain in the case of aggregate data.

The alternative proxies for financial market development – liquid liabilities, private credit, the ratio of stock market capitalisation to GDP and the value of domestic share traded – are systematically significant, irrespective of the specific indicator and estimator chosen. While this can be seen as providing some support for the hypothesis that financial development contributes to growth through its effect on the level of investment, these variables could also capture elements of the user cost of capital, which are missing from the measure of relative price used in the estimates. Among the proxies for financial development, the estimated coefficients suggest a stronger role for private credit, than for stock market indicators. However, the relative significance of the latter has grown during the second half of the 1990s.

Based on these estimation results, the rise in the volume of business investment observed in a number of countries during the second half of the 1990s can only be partly explained by output growth, the steady decline in the relative price of capital goods and, until mid-2000, the relatively low cost of equity financing. This is particularly the case for most countries where real business investment has been buoyant, but also for Japan where investment has grown very modestly. On that basis, the empirical analysis would tend to support the view that investment has exceeded its steady-state level, not least in the United States. In the latter case, however, increases in depreciation rates associated with the changes in the composition of capital, may have boosted gross investment sufficiently to make the current investment rate look sustainable.

Annexe: conceptual framework

In the neo-classical theory of investment (Jorgensen, 1967), the long-run desired capital stock can be derived from the solution of a multi-period profit maximisation problem by a representative firm. In a simple version of the framework that ignores tax considerations and uncertainty, the profit or cash-flow relationship of the firm can be simply expressed as:

$$R_t = P_t Y_t - (W_t L_t \lambda_t) - q_t I_t \tag{A.1}$$

where P_t is the output price, Y_t is real output, W_t is the efficiency wage, L_t is the number of hours worked, λ_t is an index of labour-augmenting technical progress, q_t is the price of investment good (under the assumption of no adjustment costs) and I_t is gross investment. The production technology can be characterised by a two-factor Cobb–Douglas production function with Harrod-neutral technical progress and constant returns to scale:

$$Y_t = A \cdot K_t^\alpha \cdot (L_t \lambda_t)^{1-\alpha} \tag{A.2}$$

where K is the aggregate capital stock and α represents the share of capital in total income. Assuming that capital depreciates at the rate δ, capital accumulates according to the following identity:

$$K_{t+1} = (1-\delta)K_t + I_t \tag{A.3}$$

The standard objective of the firm is to maximise the present value of the future path of revenues (A.1) under the constraints of technology (A.2) and the capital accumulation process (A.3).

$$V_t = \sum_{i=1}^{T} \frac{R_{t+i}}{\prod_{j=1}^{i} (1 + r_{t+j})} \tag{A.4}$$

where r_t is the nominal discount rate. The firm's problem consists of choosing K_t and L_t to maximise the present value V_t. Under the simplifying assumption of no adjustment costs, the multi-period dimension is reduced to a two-period optimisation problem. Substituting (A.1) to (A.3) into (A.4) and taking the derivatives with respect to K_t gives the familiar first-order condition linking capital to real output and the relative price of capital.

$$K_t = \alpha Y_t \Bigg/ \left[\frac{q_t}{p_t} \left(\frac{(1 + r_t)}{(1 + \pi_t)} - 1 + \delta \right) \right] \tag{A.5}$$

where $(1 + \pi_t) = q_t / q_{t-1}$, the rate of change of the price of the capital good, also referred to as the rate of market depreciation, which is distinct from the rate of physical depreciation δ that measures the loss of value due to the ageing of the asset. Following Jorgensen's approach and ignoring time indices, the cost of capital can be defined as

$$c = q \left(\frac{(1 + r)}{(1 + \pi)} - 1 + \delta \right) \tag{A.6}$$

and re-write the equilibrium condition as:

$$K = \frac{\alpha Y}{(c/P)} \tag{A.7}$$

Equation (A.7), which represents a long-run equilibrium condition, can be estimated as a co-integration relationship between capital, the level of real output and the real user cost of capital. Note that although the endogenous variable in (A.7) should be the capital stock, there are certain conditions under which it can be replaced by gross investment while keeping the rest of the specification unchanged. The equivalence stems from the fact that according to the capital accumulation identity (A.3), and assuming a constant growth rate of the capital stock in the steady state, gross investment can be expressed as a constant fraction of the capital stock:

$$I_t = (g + \delta) K_{t-1} \tag{A.8}$$

where g is the (constant) growth rate of real output and the capital stock. In the steady state, K_{t-1} can be replaced by its long-run equilibrium value as given by (A.7). Under these conditions, a long-run relationship between gross investment, output and the cost of capital can be written in log–linear form:

$$i = \alpha + y - (c - p) \tag{A.9}$$

where $\alpha = \log(g + \delta) + \log(\alpha)$ and $c - p$ stands for the real user cost of capital. Except for the difference in the constant terms, this long-run equilibrium expression for gross investment is equivalent to that for the capital stock. The main advantage of this specification is that compared to gross investment, the reliability of aggregate capital stock data has in many countries been increasingly called into question, reflecting serious measurement difficulties.

Notes

1 Another traditional approach in the literature is to aggregate data over a time period of five years or ten years in a panel framework. The temporal aggregation may bias the results and induce an apparent relationship even if no relationship is present. Instrumental variables and GMM estimators do not necessarily solve this problem.
2 Evidently, exceptions to this general finding exist. For example, Ashworth and Davis (2001), using time series analysis on G-7 country data, identify a significant role for the user cost only in the case of Germany. See also Caballero (1999) for a number of other exceptions. They are found especially in the case of studies focusing on machinery and equipment as well as on low frequency correlations between the key variables.
3 For example, Mojon *et al.* (2001) use disaggregated data over fifty-one 'representative' industries to investigate the investment behaviour and find significant negative effects from industry-specific user cost measures in Germany, France, Italy and Spain, with a long-run coefficient which is not significantly different from one. This confirms earlier findings reported in Hassett and Hubbard (1997) that the consensus emerging from studies based on US micro data suggested an elasticity of investment to the user cost of capital of between -0.5 and -1.0.
4 The sample includes: Australia, Austria, Belgium, Canada, Denmark, Finland, France, Germany, Greece, Italy, Japan, Netherlands, New Zealand, Norway, Spain, Sweden, Switzerland, United Kingdom and United States. In cases where less than twenty observations were available for a country, it was eliminated from the regression specification. For example, in the specifications where financial development is measured by data on stock market capitalisation, Finland, New Zealand and Norway (with 15, 13 and 17 observations, respectively) were excluded.
5 This is obtained from rearranging the capital accumulation identity to solve for the depreciation rate. Tevlin and Whelan (2000) show that as a result of the shift in the compositional mix, the aggregate depreciation rate for *equipment* in the United States has risen from 0.13 in 1990 to 0.16 in 1997.

References

Arestis, P. and P.O. Demetriades (1997), 'Financial development and economic growth: assessing the evidence', *The Economic Journal*, 107, 783–99.

Arestis, P., P.O. Demetriades and K.B. Luintel (2001), 'Financial development and economic growth: the role of stock markets', *Journal of Money, Credit and Banking*, 33 (1), 16–41.

Ashworth, P. and E.P. Davis (2001), 'Some evidence on financial factors in the determination of aggregate business investment in the G-7 countries', *National Institute of Economic and Social Research (NIESR) Discussion Paper* No. 187, October.

Beck, T. and R. Levine (2001), 'Stock market, banks and growth: correlation or casualty?', *Policy Research Working Paper* No. 2670, The World Bank Research Group Finance, September.

Beck, T., A. Demirgüç-Kunt and R. Levine (1999), 'A new database on financial development and structure', World Bank, *mimeo*, June.

Benhabib, J. and M.M. Spiegel (2000), 'The role of financial development in growth and investment', *Journal of Economic Growth*, 5, 341–60.

Caballero, R.J. (1994), 'Small sample bias and adjustment costs', *Review of Economics and Statistics*, 76(1), 52–58.

Caballero, R.J. (1999), 'Aggregate investment', in J.B. Taylor and M. Woodford (eds): *Handbook of Macroeconomics*, Vol. 1, Elsevier Science, Amsterdam.

Chen, B., S. McCoskey and C. Kao (1999), 'Estimation and inference of a cointegrated regression in panel data: a Monte Carlo study', *American Journal of Mathematical and Management Sciences*, 10, 75–114.

Chirinko, R.S. (1993), 'Business fixed investment spending modelling strategies, empirical results, and policy implications', *Journal of Economic Literature*, XXXI, December, 1875–911.

Cho, D. and Kenneth D. west (2003), 'Interest rates and exchange rates in the Korean, Philippine, and Thai exchange rate crisis', in M.P. Dooley and J.A. Frankel (eds), *Managing Currency Crises in Emerging Markets*, National Bureau of Economic Research Conference Report, The University of Chicago Press.

Colecchia, A. and P. Schreyer (2001), 'ICT investment and economic growth in the 1990s: is the United States a unique case? A comparative study of nine OECD countries', *OECD STI Working Paper* No. 2001/4.

Drazen, A. (2003), 'Interest rate defense against speculative attack as a signal: A primer,' in M.P. Dooley and J.A. Frankel (eds), *Managing Currency Crises in Emerging Markets*, National Bureau of Economic Research Conference Report, The University of Chicago Press.

Fernandez, D.G. and A. Galetovic (1994), 'Shumpeter might be right – but why? Explaining the relation between finance, development and growth', from School of Advanced International Studies, the Johns Hopkins University and *Departamento de Ingeniería Industrial, Universidad de Chile*, respectively, 14 August.

Hassett, K. and R. Hubbard (1997), 'Tax policy and investment', in A. Auerbach (ed.), *Fiscal Policy: Lessons From Economic Research* MIT Press, Cambridge.

Jorgensen, D.W. (1967), 'The theory of investment behavior', in *Determinants of Investment Behavior, Universities National Bureau Conference Series*, No. 18, R. Ferber (ed.), Columbia University Press, New York, pp. 129–55.

Kao, C. (1999), 'Spurious regression and residual-based tests for cointegration in panel data', *Journal of Econometrics*, 90, 1–44.

Kao, C. and M.H. Chiang (2000), 'On the estimation and inference of a cointegrated regression in panel data', *Advances in Econometrics*, 15, 179–222.

Kashyap, A.K. and J.C. Stein (1994), 'Monetary policy and bank lending', in Gregory Mankiw (ed.), *Monetary Policy*, Ch. 7, NBER studies in business cycles, Vol. 29, The University of Chicago Press, pp. 221–61.

King, R.G. and R. Levine (1993), 'Finance and growth: Schumpeter might be right', *The Quarterly Journal of Economics*, August.

Leahy, M., S. Schich, G. Wehinger, F. Pelgrin and T. Thorgeirsson (2001), 'Contributions of financial systems to growth in OECD countries', *OECD Economics Department Working Papers* No. 280, January.

Levine, R. (1997), 'Financial development and economic growth: views and agenda', *Journal of Economic Literature*, XXXV, 688–726, June.

Levinson, J., S. Berry and J. Friedman (2003), 'Impacts of the Indonesian economic crises: price changes and the poor,' in M.P. Dooley and J.A. Frankel (eds), *Managing Currency Crises in Emerging Markets*, National Bureau of Economic Research Conference Report, The University of Chicago Press.

McCarthy, J. (2001), 'Equipment expenditures since 1995: the boom and the bust', *Current Issues in Economics and Finance*, Vol. 7, No. 9, Federal Reserve Bank of New York.

McCoskey, S. and C. Kao (2001), 'Comparing panel data cointegration tests with an application to the 'Twin Deficit Problem,'' *Jounary of Propogation in Probability and Statistics*, 1, 165–198.

Mojon, B., F. Smets and P. Vermulen (2001), 'Investment and Monetary Policy in the Euro area', *European Central Bank Working Paper* No. 78.

Pagano, M. (1993), 'Financial markets and growth: an overview', *European Economic Review*, 37, 613–22.

Pedroni, P. (1995), 'Panel cointegration: asymptotic and finite sample properties of pooled time series tests with an application to the PPP hypothesis', *Working Paper in Economics*, Indiana University.

Pelgrin, F. and S. Schich (2002), 'Panel cointegration analysis of the finance–investment link in OECD countries', *OFCE Working Paper* No. 2002(2), January.

Pelgrin, F., S. Schich and A. DeSerres (2002a), 'Increases in investment in the 1990s: the role of output, cost of capital and finance', *OECD Financial Market Trend* No. 83, November.

Pelgrin, F., S. Schich and A. DeSerres (2002b), 'Increases in business investment rates in OECD countries in the 1990s: how much can be explained by fundamentals?', *OECD Economics Department Working Paper* No. 327, April.

Schich, S. and F. Pelgrin (2002), 'Financial development and investment: panel data evidence for OECD countries from 1970 to 1997', *Applied Economics Letters*, January, pp. 1–7.

Shapiro, M.D. (1986), 'Investment, output and the cost of capital', *Brookings Paper on Economic Activity*, I.

Stock, J. and M. Watson (1993), 'A simple estimator of cointegrating vectors in higher order integrated systems', *Econometrica*, 61, 783–820.

Tevlin, S. and K. Whelan (2000), 'Explaining the investment boom of the 1990s' Federal Reserve Board, Washington, *mimeo*.

Velt, I.J. (2001), 'The determinants of investment: an overview', *Technical Note*, European Commission.

Wachtel, P. (2001), 'Growth and finance – what do we know and how do we know it?', presented at the conference 'Financial Markets, the New Economy and Growth', University of Rome 'Tor Vergata'.

Questions for Part VII

1 Enumerate the policy measures that affect the depth of the crisis and ease the recovery.
2 'Sticks and carrots are the key to successful bank and corporate restructuring.' What are your views?
3 What are the principal factors behind sustainable reforms and restructuring?
4 What were the principal reasons behind the investment boom of the 1990s in the European Union economies?

Areas for further research

1 Corporate governance and corporate crisis. The case of Asian financial crisis.
2 Systemic corporate and financial restructuring.
3 Liquidity support to financial institutions in a crisis situation.
4 The finance and growth nexus.
5 Investment and monetary policies in the Euro area.

Index